Confronting War
FOURTH EDITION

D0162172

Confronting War

An Examination of
Humanity's Most Pressing Problem

FOURTH EDITION

by Ronald J. Glossop

McFarland & Company, Inc., Publishers
Jefferson, North Carolina, and London

ALSO BY RONALD J. GLOSSOP
AND FROM MCFARLAND

*World Federation? A Critical Analysis of
Federal World Government* (1993)

Frontispiece: A view of the statue "Let Us Beat Our
Swords into Ploughshares," a gift of the Soviet Union
to the United Nations, installed in 1959 (photograph
courtesy of the United Nations).

LIBRARY OF CONGRESS CATALOGUING-IN-PUBLICATION DATA

Glossop, Ronald J., 1933–
     Confronting war : an examination of humanity's most pressing
problem / by Ronald J. Glossop. — 4th ed.
          p.   cm.
     Includes bibliographical references and index.

     ISBN 0-7864-1121-X (softcover : 50# alkaline paper) ∞

     1. War.   2. International relations.   3. Conflict management.
4. International organization.   5. World politics — 21st century.
I. Title.
U21.2 .G66   2001   2001018216
355.02 — dc21

British Library cataloguing data are available

Cover images ©2001 PhotoSpin

Manufactured in the United States of America

McFarland & Company, Inc., Publishers
     Box 611, Jefferson, North Carolina 28640
          www.mcfarlandpub.com

For Bobby and Ryan and the other
young people of planet Earth

Seed Corn Must Not Be Ground—*Käthe Kollwitz lithograph used with permission of Artists Rights Society, New York, N.Y.*

War, and the preparation for war,
is one of the greatest obstacles to human progress,
fostering a vicious cycle of arms buildups, violence, and poverty.
— *Oscar Arias*

Table of Contents

Part Three. The Contemporary Situation

Part Four. Proposals for Solving the War Problem

List of Illustrations, Maps, and Charts

Preface

There was a time when slavery was considered to be a natural and necessary part of human affairs. Then some sensitive and thoughtful persons began thinking of slavery as a social problem. Eventually outright slavery was virtually eliminated from human society.

The same type of evolution may be taking place with regard to the problem of war. For most of human history the only perceived problem related to war was how to conquer the enemy. It is only within the past hundred years that more than a few philosophers and statesmen have regarded war as a social disease, as a sickness of society which needs to be abolished. As the weapons of war and terrorism have become ever more devastating and as the proportion of people affected has increased, civilians even more than military personnel, it has become clear that war is more than just one of many social problems. The war problem is the most urgent problem facing humanity, especially because of the way that it consumes the natural resources and human ingenuity very much needed to address other problems. The increasing availability of not only nuclear weapons and long-range missiles but also biologically engineered weapons and other technologically advanced products has created a situation where either the war problem gets solved or humanity risks extinction.

Various efforts have been made to alert us to the problem of war and to indicate how the problem might be solved. But just as some people argued that slavery should not and could not be eliminated because it was a necessary part of human society grounded in human nature, so it has also been argued that war should not and cannot be eliminated because it is a necessary part of human society grounded in human nature. On the other hand, just as some persons put forth arguments about why slavery must be ended, so some persons have put forth arguments about

why war must be ended. They have also made proposals concerning how to do it.

The purpose of this book is to familiarize the reader with some of the facts, ideas, and arguments related to the war problem and its solution. It is my hope that it will be useful especially to high school and college students and that it will stimulate their teachers to offer formal courses on the subject of war and peace.

Our global situation changes with the passage of time. In 1982 when the first edition of *Confronting War* was written, a main concern of most of humanity was the danger of a nuclear holocaust growing out of the struggle between the United States of America and the Soviet Union. In 1987 when the second edition was written, it seemed that the Cold War might be ending because of the great changes occurring in the Soviet Union under Mikhail Gorbachev. At the time of the third edition in 1994, the Soviet Empire, and even the Soviet Union itself, had been dismantled. The perceived threat of a nuclear holocaust seemed much more remote as the number of nuclear warheads diminished. Mention of "war" no longer gave rise immediately to the image of a nuclear confrontation between the big powers. Instead that word called to mind a multitude of "ethnic" and "religious" conflicts, more often within countries than between them.

A fourth edition of this book has become necessary not because the general principles put forth in the earlier editions have proved to be mistaken but because new events are occurring which need to be chronicled and discussed. The historical parts of many different chapters have required updating to include the occurrences of the past six years. I have made some slight changes in the manner of presentation and in the organization of the material. A couple of new maps have been added, but occasionally material has been omitted due to length of this new edition.

In connection with this fourth edition I want to express my special thanks to William Feeney of the Department of Political Science of Southern Illinois University at Edwardsville (SIUE). I have learned much from him during our 27 years of team-teaching our interdisciplinary course on "The Problem of War and Peace." Equally important is the fact that he has carefully reviewed and commented on the whole manuscript of this fourth edition, making suggestions about how to improve the wording as well as noting items that require more attention. I am especially grateful to Professor Feeney for his comments because our leanings on controversial issues are often in opposite directions. At the same time, that very fact makes it imperative that I make it clear that although I have benefited greatly from his recommendations there are also many of his suggestions which I have not followed.

Let me again express my thanks also to James Geier for permission to use without cost his "Nuclear Weapons Chart" on page 164 and to the Arms Control and Foreign Policy Caucus for permission to use without cost the map of the former Yugoslavia on page 46.

As with previous editions, I wish to thank my wife Audrey for her patient support and encouragement and especially for her help with proofreading of both the manuscript and the page proofs.

Ronald J. Glossop
December 2000

Part One.
Introduction to the War Problem

1.   The Nature of the War Problem

War is about power and the use of physical violence to determine which party in a conflict will prevail. Imagine a situation where someone puts a gun to your head and orders you to do something which you very much don't want to do. War is like that except that war involves a whole group of people coercing another group. It is about domination and submission. War is what happens when the leaders of opposing groups of people say to one another, "The only way you will get what you want is over our dead bodies." The result is many dead bodies.

War is about physical force being used to resolve a conflict of wills. As Simone Weil so unforgettably expresses it in her comments on war as portrayed in Homer's *Iliad*, force

> is that *x* that turns anybody who is subjected to it into a *thing*. Exercised to the limit, it turns man into a thing in the most literal sense: It makes a corpse out of him. Somebody was here, and the next minute there is nobody here at all.[1]

In war living persons are turned into mere things. Their wills are either coerced into submission or eliminated. Gwynne Dyer in the introduction to his monumental volume *War* adds the necessary social and political dimension to this characterization of war.

> [T]he essence of war is killing other people in order to force the community they represent to do our bidding.[2]

The crucial factor in war is not which of the opposing groups has "righteousness" on its side (both groups are sure that it is on their side) but which group has the power to force the other group to capitulate. From a historical point of view, war is about groups developing new weapons of increasing destructiveness in order to force the other side to accept what they would otherwise reject. As the decades pass, with the exception of guerrilla warfare, the winner is more and more likely to be determined by which side has the most destructive and most technologically advanced weapons rather than which side has the fiercest and largest number of fighters. As the weapons become ever more destructive, it also becomes ever more questionable whether anything which might be "won" by war is worth the destruction which occurs. War, which in the past may have been a somewhat tolerable way of dealing with conflicts between groups, is now likely to be a disaster even for the "winner," as well as many others not at all involved.

This book is about war and about alternative ways of resolving conflicts of interest. It is about why such group-against-group conflicts occur and about why they sometimes result in the violent struggles we call "war" while on other occasions such conflicts get resolved without large-scale violence. It is an inquiry about how war in human society might be reduced or even eliminated.

Many people are beginning to think about war as a disease of society that needs to be diagnosed and then prevented rather than as a necessary and unavoidable part of existence such as eclipses and earthquakes that will occur no matter what we do. This book is based on the assumption that war is a problem which humans must address. The view adopted is that we are reasonable and humane enough to want

3

to abolish war, that we are capable of understanding the factors which cause wars, and that we can take action to shape our attitudes and institutions so that war is eliminated. We should be able to replace war with nonviolent ways of resolving conflicts of interest between groups. Undoubtedly one big obstacle to be overcome is the force of habit and traditional thinking which tends to focus on the issue of how to make the enemy submit to our demands. To see war as a social problem which needs to be solved by means of a cooperative effort requires a major shift in our thinking.

In humanity's earliest days our most urgent problems involved the struggle to survive against the forces of nature — against wild animals and exposure to freezing temperatures, against floods and droughts, insects and disease. These dangers from nature are by no means completely behind us, as the AIDS epidemic has made clear. In addition, we must now also be more careful not to misuse our power over nature in such a way that we ourselves become threats to our own future existence. Nevertheless the past progress of humankind in dealing with threats from the natural world provides a basis for optimism about our capacity to deal with similar problems in the future. We can become aware of danger and take appropriate preventive action. The situation is not so promising with regard to the danger of death and destruction from the activities of our own species; here it seems that some fundamental rethinking is in order.

The Importance of the War Problem

Of the many problems facing humanity as we make the transition to the twenty-first century, which one is most important? Certainly the great increase in the numbers of people on the earth, largely as the result of the benefits of modern sanitation techniques, new pesticides, and scientifically based medicine, constitutes a problem of the first magnitude. How can all these people be fed? How can the debris from so many people living at ever higher levels of consumption be absorbed by nature? How can there possibly be enough

nonrenewable resources to meet the demands of larger and larger numbers of persons each of whom uses more and more resources and discards more and more wastes?

But there is an even more urgent problem for humanity, our continued readiness to use violence as a way of working out our disagreements. Perhaps the point can best be made with a story. Suppose that a crew of astronauts has just been launched toward the moon in a space vehicle. At first there are some minor difficulties in getting the spaceship on exactly the right course, but with the aid of ground control the proper maneuvering is accomplished. After a while, as the burden of taking care of the various tasks abates, the members of the crew fall into discussing religion and politics. There are various opposing opinions among the crew, and as the discussion continues it becomes more and more heated. The crew members become increasingly absorbed in their dispute. A red warning light begins to glow in the spaceship, but because of their involvement in the religious and political debate the crew members pay no heed. Another light comes on, and then another. There is trouble with the oxygen-supply system. There is trouble with the water-supply system. There is trouble with some of the waste-removal systems. But the astronauts are so involved in their dispute that they pay no attention to these difficulties. Ground control calls to them in desperation: "Please stop arguing with each other and give full attention to the problems which threaten your survival. Those of you who still have plenty of air and water must divert some to those others who will soon become disabled if they don't get any." But there is no cessation of the arguing, nor is there much sharing of the air and water. In fact the various members of the crew are now vehemently shouting at each other and even trying deliberately to harm one another.

We who are observing this scene from our secure places on the earth would undoubtedly be appalled. We all could see clearly that the priorities of these astronauts have been subverted by their emotional involvement in their dispute. Although these astronauts were having various problems with regard to their spaceship, it would be evident to us who are witnessing this event that their main problem is an overinvolvement in their quarreling with each other. To be sure there are several problems requiring attention such as oxygen supply and water supply and waste removal, but these problems could readily be solved by cooperative action. Their most urgent need is to control their disputations so they can tend to these other problems. They don't necessarily need to come to an agreement on the religious and political issues they are debating. All that is required is that they control their conflicts so that the disputing does not interfere with the fundamental mutual problem of survival. And they don't need to share all resources equally. All that is required is that those who are in desperate need get enough not to die or to be otherwise prevented from making their contributions to the common effort.

In a similar manner, an outside visitor to the earth would be appalled by the stupidity of the people on this planet. We are pouring huge amounts of our scarce resources and problem-solving talent into a struggle to control or do away with each other while problems crucial to our mutual survival receive only the most marginal attention.[3] Rather than sharing resources, those who have more than others spend large amounts for ever more sophisticated weapons so that they can continue to be richer in a relative sense, even though they actually end up having less than they would have if they produced more non-military goods, shared some of their wealth with those less fortunate, and forgot about the weapons. The people on this planet and their national leaders tend to be as short-sighted as the astronauts on the spaceship in our story.

The end of the Cold War in 1989 may have led some people to believe that war is no longer a significant problem for us who live on this planet. It is true that the short-term danger of a nuclear holocaust is much less today than it was in 1985, but the long-term danger is not less. In fact, we can be relatively sure that if we do not find a different way of running our world the danger of disaster will be even greater than in the past. Nuclear weapons

and the knowledge of how to make them will not be eliminated but will spread to more and more countries. Also, scientists and engineers have been continuously developing chemical, biological, bacteriological, and laser weapons. Furthermore, new devices for war such as organisms developed by genetic engineering or computer viruses to sabotage the enemy's computer systems will surely be invented. The current situation was summed up very perceptively by Michael Renner when he observed that "the cold war may be dead, but the war system is alive and well: the war-making institutions remain in place, the permanent war economy continues to command large-scale resources, and perhaps most important, the view that military rivalry among states is both rational and inevitable — known in political science as the 'realism' school — still enjoys wide allegiance."[4]

Those who think that environmental problems are more important than the war problem should not forget that ecological leader Barry Commoner has told us that "peace among men must precede the peace with nature"[5] and that marine biologist Jacques Cousteau has cogently asked, "Why protect fish if the planet is going to be destroyed?"[6] We do in fact have some significant environmental problems requiring our attention, but as the story about the astronauts above suggests, we should be able to deal with them successfully if we just stop fighting so much among ourselves.

The Four Aspects of the War Problem

There are several aspects to the war problem. So far we have mentioned only the first, the huge expenditure of scarce public funds and research talent getting ready for war. We should also call attention to the need to pay the costs of veterans from past wars and their survivors. In the United States required payments to veterans and their dependents now amounts to $1 billion per month, and the total over the next 70 years is predicted to be $1.9 trillion.[7] The huge expenditure of limited public resources for past wars and preparation for possible wars in the future is a great impediment to our quest for a better life even if no more actual war ever comes. In 1988 at the peak of the Cold War worldwide military expenditures amounted to $923 billion a year, that is, over $2.5 billion each day![8] That military spending represented five percent of the world's gross product or one out of every twenty dollars spent for all goods and services in the world.[9] And that is how much was being spent even when no major wars were being fought by the larger, richer countries. During World War II the nations fighting the war spent 40 percent of their gross national product for military purposes,[10] but even now some nations spend huge amounts just getting ready for war. For example, in 1998 Afghanistan was spending 14.5 percent of its gross domestic product on the military while for Saudi Arabia the figure was 15.7 percent.[11] This military spending consumes goods and services that might have been used to meet other human needs. Joshua Goldstein, author of *Long Cycles: Prosperity and War in the Modern Age,* notes that "as a rough rule of thumb, for every 1 percent of gross national product devoted to military spending, overall economic growth is reduced by about one-half a percent."[12] Economist Kenneth Boulding observed that from 1945 to 1978 "the world war industry has probably averaged something like 6 to 10 percent or perhaps even more of the total world product. Summing this over thirty years means that the human race lost at least two full years, perhaps more, of its total product, which might have been devoted to making everybody richer."[13] That figure is especially tragic when we think of how desperately the poorer countries of the world need financial resources for capital investment, education, and social infrastructure. At the same time, we should note that the end of the Cold War has made a big difference. Annual world military spending in 1998 had dropped to $785.269 billion, and military spending as a percentage of the gross world product had dropped from 5.2 percent in 1985 to 2.6 percent in 1998.[14] Nevertheless, a return to something like the tensions of the Cold War could rapidly reverse that downward trend.

The second aspect of the problem of war, the one that came to mind most immediately for most people between 1955 and 1990, is the danger of a nuclear holocaust in which the big powers would unleash on each other the many thousands of nuclear warheads they had ready to launch.[15] With the end of the Cold War this aspect of the war problem has receded from public awareness. The tense moments of the Cuban missile crisis of October 1962[16] seem far removed from the present situation. Nevertheless at the beginning of the year 2000 the acknowledged nuclear powers (the United States, Russia, Britain, France, and China) still have over 31,500 nuclear warheads, 10,500 for the United States and 20,000 for Russia.[17] These figures do not include the nuclear warheads of Israel, India, and Pakistan. Although some warheads are being deactivated or dismantled, new types of nuclear warheads are still being designed, and new long-range missiles to carry nuclear warheads are still being produced.[18] These missiles can go one-third of the way around the world in just a half-hour, and the nuclear warheads on them are at least 20 times more powerful than the bombs dropped on Hiroshima and Nagasaki.

During the last years of the Cold War (1981–89), it was noted that a nuclear exchange between the Soviet Union and the U.S. would not only produce an incredible amount of damage to the immediate targets but also would produce so much smoke and soot from the resulting fires that the whole world would experience a "nuclear winter"[19] where plants would no longer grow. This "nuclear winter" would be followed by an "ultraviolet spring" where the ozone layer would no longer be dense enough to protect life from damaging ultraviolet radiation from the sun. Nuclear explosions would destroy that protective ozone layer much more rapidly and thoroughly than do chloroflurocarbons (CFCs) in the atmosphere. It is possible that all higher forms of life would die from these effects of a nuclear exchange plus the high levels of radioactivity, which would last at least for decades.

We don't like to think about the disastrous consequences of nuclear war, so we are only too glad to suppose that the danger is completely behind us. The danger is certainly less now than it was in the early 1980s, but nuclear weapons have not disappeared, and more and more countries can be expected to acquire them in the years ahead. The danger of a nuclear holocaust would suddenly reappear if tensions again developed among nations which have a substantial number of nuclear weapons. Two different 1997 studies for the U.S. military "both assert that nuclear deterrence as we know it is essential and that robust nuclear forces are required."[20] It seems that the end of nuclear weapons is not near at hand.

But the war problem confronting us is not limited to the possibility of a nuclear disaster. The third aspect of the war problem is the occurrence of "conventional" (nonnuclear) wars. It is worth remembering that during the ninety-five years from 1900 to 1995, the number of human deaths from war amounted to 109,745,500 (more than a million people a year!),[21] but less than 200,000 of these deaths were due to nuclear weapons. Wars without nuclear weapons have been rampant since the end of World War II, and all of them which occurred between 1970 and 1990 were fought in the less developed countries.[22] Examples of such "conventional" wars include Israel versus her Arab neighbors, Iran versus Iraq, India versus Pakistan (wars which occurred before 1998 when both countries demonstrated their capability to explode nuclear weapons), China versus Vietnam, and Iraq against Kuwait as well as the more recent fighting among the newly independent republics which formerly were constituent parts of Yugoslavia. The scale of the destruction in these conventional wars demonstrates that our aim must be the elimination of war, not just nuclear weapons.

Nevertheless nuclear weapons do pose a special problem. Forming a bridge between the danger of nuclear war (the second aspect of the war problem) and the danger of conventional international war (the third aspect of the war problem just discussed) is the issue of the proliferation of nuclear weapons to other countries. Although not officially acknowledged as a nuclear state, it is generally believed that Israel has at least 200 nuclear warheads.[23]

South Africa, which once built nuclear weapons, dismantled them and converted its nuclear facilities to the building of nonnuclear high-explosive technological devices.[24] India detonated a nuclear device in 1974, but did not openly pursue a nuclear testing program to develop weapons until May of 1998, when five underground tests (one being a thermonuclear device) were conducted.[25] Just over two weeks later Pakistan conducted its first nuclear tests.[26] Other countries which have seemed to be seeking the capability to build nuclear weapons include Iraq and North Korea.[27] Nations such as Canada, Japan, Germany, Sweden, Italy, South Korea, the Chinese on Taiwan, Argentina, and Brazil undoubtedly could develop the capability of making nuclear weapons rather quickly should they choose to do so.

Beyond knowing how to build nuclear weapons, a nation which wants to construct such weapons must have either enriched uranium or plutonium. The supply of these two crucial difficult-to-acquire materials has so far been fairly well controlled by the present nuclear powers plus Canada and Germany, but the control is not perfect as the cases of Israel, India, Pakistan, and North Korea show. Furthermore, the capability of enriching uranium or producing plutonium can make a country independent of the need for an external supply. The facilities needed to conduct such operations are not easy to hide, but during the 1980s Iraq succeeded in conducting a program to separate plutonium from other radioactive wastes without being detected by the International Atomic Energy Agency.[28]

The fourth aspect of the war problem which needs to be addressed is the occurrence of fighting between groups within one country. These *intranational* wars are still wars, and in fact it is this aspect of the war problem that first comes to mind in this post–Cold War period. As Michael Renner notes: "Most wars since 1945 have been internal conflicts. Between 1989 and 1997, only 6 out of 103 armed conflicts were international."[29] Taking account of such facts, Michael Klare comments:

In the past, "war" meant a series of armed encounters between the armed forces of established states, usually for the purpose of territorial conquest or some other clearly defined strategic objective. But the conflicts of the current era bear little resemblance to this model: most take place within the borders of a single state and entail attacks by paramilitary and irregular forces on unarmed civilians for the purpose of pillage, rape, or ethnic slaughter — or some combination of all three.

Ethnic and internal warfare is the most common form of armed violence in the late twentieth century, and it is likely to remain the dominant form for some time to come.[30]

Sometimes this internal fighting is joined by national military forces from outside the country as has occurred in places such as Vietnam, Bangladesh, Afghanistan, Cyprus, and Cambodia. More and more often, however, the fighting within a country has led to the intervention of international peace-keeping forces under the auspices of the United Nations or the North Atlantic Treaty Organization (NATO) or some other international organization as has happened in Somalia, Haiti, Cambodia, Angola, Rwanda, Yugoslavia, East Timor, Liberia, and Sierra Leone. Such intervention by the international community into disputes within countries raises some difficult and significant issues regarding national sovereignty. On the other hand, if the U.N. or other international organizations do not intervene to resolve these disputes, won't they just become more and more violent? Discussions of the war problem which deal only with war between different countries are incomplete. Any satisfactory solution to the war problem cannot ignore this issue of how to deal with these armed conflicts within national boundaries.

We see, then, that there are four aspects of the war problem which must be addressed:

(1) large expenditures of public funds needed for other things,

(2) danger of nuclear war and resultant nuclear holocaust,

(3) international war with conventional/non-nuclear weapons, and

(4) intranational war, often between ethnic groups.

In fact, acceptable solutions to the war problem must encompass all four aspects of it. Any proposed solution that does not, for example, eliminate arms races and drastically cut expenditures for military forces and weapons is not a complete one. Views about how to deal with the war problem must also consider conventional wars and wars within countries as well as the danger of nuclear war.

War is undoubtedly a great calamity for humanity, but focusing on the horrible dilemmas and consequences of war as is often done in art and literature only reminds us of the magnitude of the problem. That approach can generate an emotional reaction against the horrors of war and maybe even a greater appreciation of the need to do something to deal with the war problem, but such a focus does not by itself help us to eliminate, or even reduce, warfare. Even further removed from our present purpose are those discussions about war that take place in a military context and that focus on how to fight more effectively or how best to develop and use new weapons. The purpose there is not how to prevent war but how better to win wars when they occur. The viewpoint taken here is that war is a problem to be solved, a social disease whose causes need to be diagnosed and then the proper medicine prescribed and applied.

The material in this book about the war problem is organized in accord with the steps to be followed in trying to solve any problem. *First,* we need to *clarify* exactly what *the problem* before us is. We do this for the war problem by examining the meaning of the key terms "war," "peace," and "justice" in Chapter 2. *Second,* we begin *gathering information* about our problem, which in the case of the war problem means looking at history; we try to learn what we can about war from that source in Chapter 3. *Third,* we do our *diagnosis*; we consider and evaluate hypotheses about what causes war (*Why do wars occur? Does war serve some purpose?*) in Chapters 4 through 7. *Fourth,* in Chapters 8 through 12 we *observe* the contemporary situation *in more detail,* being guided to what sorts of things are worth closer observation by our theories about what causes war. *Fifth,* in Chapters 13 through 16 we classify and survey various *prescriptions* for dealing with the war problem and analyze their strengths and weaknesses; that is, we consider whether particular proposals would be likely to help solve the problem and whether they might even have some unintended harmful consequences. The final step in solving any problem is *taking action* guided by the deliberation which has taken place in the previous steps; this concluding phase of the process of dealing with the war problem is addressed in the final "A Note to the Reader."

2.   The Conceptual Framework

In order to deal with the problem of war, it will be helpful to begin by considering exactly what is meant by the terms "war" and "peace." We also need to think about the meaning of another term which is crucial to the war problem, namely, the word "justice." After making clear what these key terms mean, we can turn our attention to some observations about the important relations between peace on the one hand and justice on the other.

The Meaning of the Term "War"

The first step in problem-solving is to develop a very clear idea of exactly what the problem is. We need to define in a careful way precisely what we mean by the term "war."[1] A good definition of "war" will help us to focus on the central problem to be addressed, how to eliminate, or at least diminish, the amount of war in the world. Having a good definition of "war" will also keep us from getting side-tracked into questions which are not directly relevant to the issue before us. We need to find a definition of "war" broad enough to include both civil wars and international wars but narrow enough to exclude feuds (such as that between the Hatfields and the McCoys), riots (such as that which destroyed the Watts area of Los Angeles in 1965) and intense political action (such as the effort of some persons in Quebec to separate that province from the rest of Canada), things which we would not ordinarily call "wars."

Here is the definition of "war" to be used in this book: *War is large-scale violent conflict between organized groups which already are governments or which seek to establish their own government over some territory.* It is impossible

---

War is:
(1) large-scale violent conflict
(2) between organized groups
(3) which are or aim to be governments
(4) over some territory.

---

to overemphasize the importance of this definition of "war" as a basis for understanding our discussion of this topic.

In primitive societies there is no formal government, and therefore there cannot be any war as we have defined it. Certain tribes may have lived in certain areas and may have tried to keep others out, but the rules to be followed were often not very precise (there was not yet any writing), and it was not always clear exactly who had the power to make them or enforce them. Furthermore, the borders or limits of where these rules applied were not always clearly or carefully determined. Sometimes violent conflicts between groups occurred at the edges of their hunting and fishing areas, but it was not what we would call "war" as we understand that term today. Such skirmishes between not-very-well-organized groups which lack a government (an acknowledged political authority which makes and enforces laws) as well as a carefully delineated territory is usually called "primitive warfare." Such violent conflicts are not very different from the clashes that have been observed to occur between groups of chimpanzees.[2] Despite the use of the word "warfare," so-called "primitive warfare" does not conform to our contemporary understanding of the word "war." As Gwynne Dyer observes, primitive warfare "is an important ritual, an exciting and dangerous game, and perhaps even an opportunity for self-expression, but it is not about power in any recognizable modern sense of the word, and it most certainly is not about slaughter."[3]

In civilized societies, however, the crucial elements mentioned in our definition of "war" are present. The small group of leaders that has the authority to make and enforce the rules for the whole society has come to be formally differentiated as "the government." The government has the acknowledged responsibility to determine what policies the group as a whole will pursue. (Note the relation between the words "policy" and "political" as in "political power." Note also that for most of the agrarian period of human society the policies adopted are usually for the benefit of the small group of rulers who are making the rules and not necessarily for the good of the whole society.) The rules that the government makes to implement its policies are called "laws," and the persons who have the responsibility for enforcing these laws are called "the police" or "the authorities." The laws typically incorporate a requirement to pay some kind of taxes to support the activities of the government. The limits or borders of each city-state or nation-state or empire come to be clearly marked. Outsiders may be required to get special permission to come within the borders. The government makes it clear that it is in control of this territory.

Consequently, after the beginning of civilization and the establishment of formal governments our definition of war becomes applicable: *War is large-scale violent conflict between organized groups which already are governments or which seek to establish their own government over some territory.* War occurs when some organized group other than the government uses large-scale violence to challenge the right of this group of leaders to rule over this territory. The challenging group may be the government of some other land which is seeking to add this territory to what it already controls. Or the challengers to the government may be a group living within this territory that seeks to throw off the rule of the existing government and establish its own. That is, (A) war may be between two or more different governments for control of some territory, or (B) war may be between a government and one or more organized groups of rebels within its own territory who desire to establish their own government. These two possible kinds of war will be discussed at greater length later.

A crucial point to be noted about the implications of our definition of "war" is that *not all conflict* is war but only *large-scale violent* conflict. Those who maintain that war can never be eliminated often back up their view with the claim that we will never be able to eliminate all conflict. A close look at the first part of our definition makes it clear that it is not necessary to get rid of all conflict in order to get rid of war. We need only to manage or control the conflict so that it does not become *violent on a large scale.* In some situations conflict may even be a very desirable thing. Conflict may stimulate needed social changes. It is worth noting that on this important issue of the relation between conflict and war, paying attention to our precise definition of "war" has already saved us from making the common but nevertheless mistaken assumption that we must eliminate all conflict before we can eliminate war.

Of course we sometimes do speak figuratively of "war" between the sexes or of a "cold war" between countries, but when pushed we are inclined to say that these conflicts are not really wars, but only *like* wars because they are so intense. Consider, for example, how strange it would be to talk about a "hot war." Wars are necessarily "hot." They necessarily involve violence on a large scale. In a "cold war," on the other hand, there is only a great readiness to use violence, though some scattered cases of violence may actually occur. There may be crises when it seems that the conflict will break into real war, but in a cold war no actual large-scale violence between the antagonists themselves occurs. A "cold war" is not really a war at all. It is only a conflict which has the obvious potential to become an actual war.

As we try to apply our definition of war to actual situations, there may be a problem of indicating exactly when a conflict has become sufficiently violent to qualify as a war. What if much property is destroyed but no lives are lost? Should such a conflict be called a "war"? What if only a few people are killed? Must some minimum number of deaths occur before we say that a war is occurring? There are certainly borderline cases in which it is difficult to decide whether there is enough violence to classify them as wars. Social scientists interested in comparing the amount of warfare in different historical periods or in different geographical regions will need to decide somewhat arbitrarily that they are going to regard a violent conflict as a war only if a certain minimal number of deaths have occurred or if a certain number of soldiers have been committed to battle.[4] Fortunately, our general discussion of the war problem does not require such a level of precision. There are some situations with so much large-scale violence that we can unhesitatingly describe them as "wars." We can focus our attention on these unambiguous situations and view ourselves as having made considerable headway in solving the war problem if we can figure out how to deal successfully with these unquestionable cases of warfare.

The second crucial idea in our definition of war is that the participants must be members of *organized groups*. Even the most violent conflict between one person and another individual person is not a war. We might be inclined to make an exception in the case where these two persons are functioning as official representatives of their respective groups and where their one-on-one battle will determine which group is victorious, as was the case in the biblical meeting of David and Goliath; but even then we would want to say that this one-on-one confrontation between selected warriors is a substitute for a battle between the two opposing armies; that is, it is a substitute for a real war between opposing groups. Moreover, if two groups just happen to fall into fighting with each other (as might possibly happen if two groups of different races or nationalities were in the same locale) we would not be inclined to call it a war unless the groups were organized with leaders who give orders and followers who carry them out.

War involves the notion of coordinated group action, and thus it cannot take place without some organization within the groups which confront each other. It should be noted, too, that although the actual fighting is typically done by military forces, the war is not merely between army and army.[5] Especially in modern warfare the military forces typically need to be supported by the rest of the society, which provides weapons, food and medical supplies, new recruits, financial resources, and psychological support. If the military forces could fight wars by themselves, govern-

ments would not find it necessary to address propaganda to get support from the whole population as they have done for over a century.

It is partly due to the fact that war is fought between organized groups that it seems so utterly immoral to the individuals who are actually doing the fighting. In war two young persons who know nothing of each other as individuals may be trying to kill each other on the battlefield. They have nothing against each other as individuals. In fact, in other circumstances they might have become the very best of friends. But during wartime these individuals are trying to kill each other simply because they are members of groups which have entered into war against each other. Furthermore, usually they have just been born into one group or the other and had nothing to do with the fact that these groups are now at war with each other. Yet they are out there on the battlefield trying to do away with one another. As the French philosopher Blaise Pascal observed:

> Can anything be more ridiculous than that a man should have the right to kill me because he lives on the other side of the water, and because his ruler has a quarrel with mine, though I have none with him?[6]

The third crucial idea in our definition of warfare which becomes applicable in the civilized period is the notion that war involves *government*.[7] A government is part of a system for group control in which a certain individual or relatively small group of individuals is recognized not only by those in that society but also by governments of other societies as having the authority to decide policy for its whole society and thus to make laws which are binding on that whole group. This power of the government to set policy and to make and enforce laws in accord with that policy is what we mean by "political power." A large-scale violent conflict is called a "war" in the modern sense only if the goal is to determine which group of individuals is going to rule a particular territory, that is, to determine who is going to have recognized political power over that area. For example, violent conflict between opposing groups of hoodlums or drug-peddlers (sometimes called "gang war"), even if it becomes rather large-scale and involves rather well-defined "territories," still falls outside of our definition of "war" in the civilized period. Why? Because these groups aim to gain control of illegal activities rather than to acquire the kind of acknowledged law-making and law-enforcing authority which belongs to governments. Nevertheless, especially when these outlaw groups mark off particular territories where they control various illegal activities, we can see some similarity between gang warfare and primitive warfare.

One of the disconcerting things about many contemporary popular accounts and discussions of particular wars is that they totally neglect the political dimension of the conflict. They may focus on particular acts of bravery or cruelty, on the brutality and violence of the fighting, on the weaponry, on the strategies being pursued by the opposing sides, on the character of the leaders, on the historical background of the conflict, and so on. Still if these discussions do not take account of the political aspects of the situation, that is, of the policies that the opposing sides intend to implement if they win, they are missing the whole point of the war. They are ignoring the fact that the aim of warfare is to be able to determine the policies that will be adopted in the society that inhabits that territory. Undoubtedly, ruling groups will generally want to adopt policies which to some extent favor only themselves, but the degree to which they intend to do this can vary. Furthermore, focusing on what policies are to be pursued after the war is over instead of which group of persons is going to be in control may even make the war unnecessary. It may be that compromise policies can be worked out that all groups can accept and agree to jointly implement.

The fourth crucial idea in our definition of warfare is the notion of some marked-off *territory* or geographical area in which the government has authority. For most of human history this territory over which control is exercised has been on land where the limits or borders could be rather readily marked, often by some natural boundary such as a river or a lake. Even then, however, difficult questions

could arise about the exact location of the boundary such as "How far out into the river or lake does one's territory go?" As human capabilities have expanded, the question of territorial limits for a government have become more complicated to set and to enforce. For example, "How far out into the ocean does a national government's authority reach?" or "How far up into space does a government's authority reach?" Furthermore, "What is the situation in those areas out beyond any government's control?" The problem becomes even more complex with the Internet and the widespread use of electronic signals where the notion of a spatial boundary makes no sense. With regard to something like electronic signals, can the concept of a spatial boundary for the limits of a government's authority have any applicability? Will technological advancements eventually require some modification or elimination of the very concept "government over some territory" which is part of our definition of "war"? Are we perhaps moving into a new post-civilized state of human society in which the institutions and practices of our 10,000-year-old civilized state of human society (like war) are no longer understandable or applicable?[8]

When we consider the implications of our definition of war in the current civilized period (*"large-scale violent conflict between organized groups which already are governments or which seek to establish their own government over some territory"*), we see that in a world composed of over 200 nation-states two main kinds of wars are possible. The first kind occurs when one governed society (or a group of them) fights another governed society (or a group of them). This type of violent conflict between national governments is *inter*-national war (literally, war *between* nations). The second kind of war occurs when there is a struggle between groups for control of the government within a governed territory. This is *intra*-national war (literally, war *within* a nation). Further distinctions can be made within these two basic types. For example, international wars may be between countries (or groups of countries) which are nearly equal technologically and militarily, or they may occur between a technologically advanced nation and a not-so-advanced one. In the latter case the war would be called an *imperialistic* or *colonial* war when the more advanced nation is seeking to establish its control over the territory of the less advanced nation, and it would be called a *war of national liberation* when the less advanced nation is seeking to reestablish its control over its own territory. Within the class of intranational wars we can distinguish between a *secessionist (or separatist) war,* in which some region tries to secede or separate itself from the nation of which it is a part; a *territorial civil war,* in which the opposing groups occupy fairly well-defined geographical areas within the country and seek to expand the area which they control (possibly eventually totally conquering the other side and taking over the whole land); and a *revolutionary war,* in which an organized group seeks to overthrow the present government and establish itself as the decision-maker for the whole nation.

Kinds of Modern Warfare

International war (between nations)
  a) war between nearly equal groups
  b) imperialistic or colonial war
  c) war of national liberation

Intranational war (within a nation)
  a) secessionist (or separatist) war
  b) territorial civil war
  c) revolutionary war

It should be noted that a particular war may exemplify more than one type. For example, there may be a struggle for control of the government between two groups within a nation-state where one or both of these groups gets assistance from other nation-states. In that case the war is both intranational and international. The wars in Korea, Vietnam, Afghanistan, and Angola were of this type. In fact, this kind of war which is both intranational and international was very common during the period of the Cold War between the United States and the Soviet Union (1947–1989).

It should also be noted that there can be various policy goals and ways of implementing

them within a leadership group. The government is a smaller group than the society as a whole, but that does not mean that everyone in the government or everyone in the leadership of a revolutionary group agrees on all issues. A common situation is that some more moderate members of a government or of an opposition leadership group are much more ready to work out compromises with the opposition than are the more doctrinaire leaders. Thus we often find the leaders of a government or a revolutionary group trying to work out compromise agreements while some members of their own leadership group are trying to keep these compromises from being implemented. It is generally more difficult to generate support for the compromises than to appeal to feelings of group loyalty in opposition to them. It also takes only one or two violent incidents to stop an agreement from being implemented. All this taken together means that it is much easier to keep a war going than to work out an agreement between the opposing sides.

How are acts of terrorism related to war? Terrorism, the carrying out of unexpected acts of violence designed to intimidate or coerce, may be used by various kinds of groups. It has even been, and still is, used by governments to intimidate their own citizens. *Political terrorism* as the term is usually used today refers to "low-intensity" or "sporadic" warfare carried out by groups so small and weak that they would have no chance of winning a more traditional kind of war.[9] Political terrorists may in particular circumstances be seeking some specific goal such as money for their organization or the release of some of their members who have been imprisoned. Sometimes they are just seeking to harass their enemies. Often their aim is to gain public attention and some support for their cause, which might otherwise be totally ignored. As in the case of military attacks in war, people tend to evaluate terrorist activities on the basis of their sympathy or antipathy to the aims of the terrorists. In the Middle East, for example, Israelis have condemned the Palestine Liberation Organization (PLO) for activities very similar to what they themselves did before Israel became a nation. Although there may be an inclination to think of terrorism as in some sense "illegal," in fact terrorism *for political purposes* is generally regarded in international law as a kind of warfare in which the terrorists are soldiers for one side.[10] The intermittent violence of terrorists is thus viewed as a scaled-down version of ordinary warfare. Many of the proposals for dealing with the war problem discussed later in this book could be applied to conflicts involving terrorism. Also, since terrorists are usually seeking attention for their cause, it seems that a system might be devised whereby small groups seeking political change in opposition to those in power would be allowed a continuing opportunity to publicize their views, but only so long as they do *not* engage in violence.

Since we have defined "war" as *"large-scale violent conflict between organized groups which already are governments or which seek to establish their own government over some territory,"* it is evident that the goal of warfare is the acquisition of recognized political power over some territory. Each of the groups engaged in a war wants to be acknowledged as having the authority to set policies in the same territory. Not being able to arrive by bargaining or negotiation at some mutually acceptable policies to be implemented, one group seeks by violence to compel the other group to accept its unconditional governance over the territory in question.

An Alternative to War?

Having defined what the term "war" means, it may be useful, even at this very early stage of our investigation of the war problem, to ask, "Is there *an alternative to war* for determining who will have the political power over some territory?" Well-known anthropologist Margaret Mead argued that warfare is a social invention and that it could be eliminated if we had a new social invention to deal more adequately with the problem of social conflict. She claims that:

warfare, by which I mean recognized conflict between two groups *as groups*, in which each group puts an army ... into the field to fight and kill, if possible, some of the members of the army of the other group — that warfare of this sort is an invention like any other of the inventions in terms of

which we order our lives, such as writing, marriage, cooking our food instead of eating it raw, trial by jury, or burial of the dead, and so on.

...I think that we might turn to the history of other social inventions, and inventions which must once have seemed as firmly entrenched as warfare. Take the methods of trial which preceded the jury system: ordeal and trial by combat.... The invention of trial by jury gradually replaced these methods until only witches, and finally not even witches, had to resort to the ordeal.... [T]he old method was replaced by a new social invention. The ordeal ... went out because a method more congruent with the institutions and feelings of the period was invented. And, if we despair over the way in which war seems such an ingrained habit of most of the human race, we can take comfort from the fact that a poor invention will usually give place to a better invention.

For this, two conditions, at least, are necessary. The people must recognize the defects of the old invention, and someone must make a new one.[11]

Let us consider the possibility of an alternative to war by slightly modifying our definition of that term. Suppose that we take our definition of "war" and change the one word "*violent*" to "*nonviolent*." We then would have this definition of *something* other than war: "large-scale *nonviolent* conflict between organized groups which are seeking political control over some territory."

> **Something [what is it?] is:**
> "large-scale NONVIOLENT conflict between organized groups which are governments or aim to be governments over some territory."

The question is, What is the "invention" that we are defining when we say that this something-or-other is "large-scale *NONVIOLENT* conflict between organized groups which are seeking to become the government over some territory?" This definition seems to be a fairly good definition of *the political process within a democratic society*. For example, in the United States we have the Republican Party and the Democratic Party and other smaller parties. These political parties are "organized groups" with their different platforms of policies which they would like to make into law for the whole state or the whole country. Instead of having a violent battle with weapons to determine which party gets to take control, debating takes place and an election is conducted. Those candidates with the most votes become "the government" until the next election. The rulers are determined by ballots rather than bullets. Furthermore, unlike a conflict which has been decided by war, the losers in the balloting can look ahead to the next election as an opportunity to reverse the results.

To apply the same principle to a particular issue, a very emotional one, let us look at the situation with regard to policy on abortion. Should abortions be legally permitted (in the various states and in the country as a whole) or should they be partially or totally outlawed? The Pro-Choice group wants them to be permitted while the Pro-Life group wants them to be outlawed.[12] Some compromises are possible in terms of permitting abortions under certain circumstances but forbidding them otherwise, but even the acceptability of the compromises are disputed. Here we have intense conflict between at least two organized groups each seeking to become the government so that they can implement policies which reflect their own views. There has been some violence at abortion clinics and even some killings of physicians who perform abortions. Still for the most part the battle takes place within the democratic political and judicial institutions established to resolve such conflicts nonviolently.

Those who resort to violence in this democratic context are condemned even by those on the same side of the issue, partly on grounds that using violence will cost that side votes in the next election. In this battle within the democratic political framework, the winner is determined by which side gets the most votes. This use of voting to resolve policy conflicts nonviolently seems to provide an attractive alternative to war. Since war consists of using violence to become the government, it seems that the implementation of democratic political procedures to determine which group will gain how much political power should make war unnecessary and thus obsolete. Casting ballots seems to be a far better way of resolving the conflict than shooting bullets and rockets and nuclear weapons at each other.

The adoption of democracy is also important to peace within a society in another way, namely in the role to be played by that smaller group of people who make up the government. Throughout most of civilized history, the government was composed of rulers who held that dominant position because of their superior military capability or economic position (which elite position then could be passed on to their children by special educational advantages such as learning how to use weapons or how to read and write). Rulers were expected to use their control of the government to enhance the status of themselves and their family and friends. With the advent of the election of rulers, a new kind of expectation develops. The people who are voting (usually only a very small proportion of the whole population, at least at first) want to have rulers who will serve them and their interests. The rulers undoubtedly continue to expect to be well-off themselves, but they now know that in order to get elected they must also be perceived as looking out for the interest of those who can vote. As the voting franchise is gradually widened to include more people, a larger number need to be persuaded that they will be better served by this candidate than that one. Using personal wealth to try to influence voters to support those candidates perceived to be more friendly to those who have economic power becomes more common. As more and more people become voters and become better informed about what is in their own interest, the welfare of the rulers in the government very gradually becomes less separable from what is good for the whole society. The government is expected to be the servant of the people with little opportunity of separate gain for the rulers themselves.[13] After that has occurred, the readiness to battle with armaments to take control of the government fades. Why fight just to become a servant of the public? Perhaps one could be seeking honor or fame but not riches.

Margaret Mead argued that in order to replace the social invention of war with something else, we must find a better social invention which deals with the same problem. It seems that in fact we already have this social invention, namely, political struggle and voting within a democratic society. We see that it works rather well within many countries. Maybe eliminating *intranational* war means spreading democratic political procedures to more and more countries. Maybe eliminating *international* war means spreading democratic political procedures to the global level in the framework of some kind of democratic world government. These are ideas to be examined at greater length as our discussion of the war problem continues.

Let us pause at this point to compare our definition of war with the view put forth by Carl von Clausewitz in his classic book *On War.* Clausewitz writes, "War is a mere continuation of policy by other means....War is not merely a political act, but also a real political instrument,... a carrying out of the same by other means."[14] He says that wars are "only the expressions or manifestations of policy itself."[15] That is, the aim of warfare is to advance the political power of the governments of the states engaged in the fighting. Military matters are necessarily subordinate to the political aims being pursued. When groups are engaged in warfare against one another, it is the future political power of those groups which is at stake. Which group will end up in control of the territory about which there is a dispute? Which group will get to be the government over that territory and then institute its policies by means of specific laws? For Clausewitz the fighting of a war is merely the ultimate means for settling the issue of whose policies will be enacted and whose laws will be enforced in the disputed territory. Our definition of war is completely consistent with his observations.

The crucial difference between Clausewitz's concept of war and ours is that Clausewitz assumes that warfare is a totally natural and legitimate way of working out conflicts between countries when a national government cannot get what it wants by other means such as diplomacy or threats of force. The governments of the nation-states are viewed by him as separate selfish entities, and he assumes that they are justified in using violence when necessary to coerce other states into accepting their will. On the other hand, our definition of war allows us to view the resort to violence in order to resolve conflicts as a kind of *failure* for human society. War is a social *sickness* that breaks out when better, less violent ways of resolving conflict within the wider community are not used, are tried and do not succeed, or are not available. Conflict between groups is indeed a natural situation, but when the conflict degenerates into large-scale violence, something has gone wrong. We can view groups which resort to the violence of war as parts of the larger society of humanity which should be provided with some means of working out their conflicts in nonviolent ways. There should be some world-wide democratic political institutions by means of which the conflicts can be worked out without resorting to violence. It seems that the sickness of war at all levels (that is, both *within* countries and *between* countries) should be curable by the same kinds of democratic political and judicial institutions which keep conflict under control within most democratic national communities.

This section on "An Alternative to War?" can be brought to a close by making an observation about the framework in which we should search for a solution to the problem of war. Many philosophers and religious thinkers as well as members of the general public think that the solution to the problem of war is to be sought in the way that *individuals* think and act. The problem of war has generally been viewed as an *ethical* problem which individuals must deal with on their own by being kind to other individuals or even adopting a nonviolent life-style. Obviously, the thinking and actions of individuals can have an impact on whether war gets abolished, but our definition of war as well as this discussion of an alternative to war should make it evident that any solution to the problem of war in the end must involve influencing our *social* practices and modifying our *social* and *political* institutions. The problem of war is a problem to be dealt with in *social philosophy* and by the *social sciences* such as sociology, economics, and political science. Individual action is going to be useful largely to the extent that it is addressed to social issues and social attitudes and so-cially-oriented organizations. Working for peace ultimately must involve some kind of concern about and participation (direct or in-direct) in politics.

The Meaning of the Term "Peace"

The term "peace" may be taken to mean simply "the absence of war." That is the way that most people understand the word "peace." Nevertheless many writers on this topic dis-tinguish between what they call *"negative peace"* (the mere absence of war) and what they call *"positive* peace" (a peace in which there is no exploitation of some individuals or groups by others, that is, where there is no injustice). This distinction is parallel to that which might be made between *"negative* healthiness" (the mere absence of sickness) and *"positive* health-iness" (not only the absence of sickness but also physical fitness, good muscle tone, and so on). For those who make this kind of distinction with regard to "peace," positive peace is nec-essarily a good thing (because it contains the notion of justice) while negative peace is not (because justice is not part of the concept). Consequently, it is suggested that the term "peace" should be used only in the sense of positive peace.[16]

Alternative meanings of the word "peace":

Negative peace is the mere absence of war.

Positive peace is no large-scale violence and ALSO no readiness to use violence because there is little if any injustice or exploitation within the community.

The motivation for using the term "peace" to refer only to positive peace is ad-mirable, but nevertheless this suggestion should be rejected. The aim of expanding the meaning of "peace" in this way is to ensure that the discussion of how to solve the prob-lem of war does not focus only on eliminat-ing violence while ignoring the issue of social justice. But the effort to define "peace" in this more morally positive way seems not to be faithful to our normal use of that word. Also,

if the word "peace" is to be restricted only to positive peace, what term should we use to describe negative peace? Furthermore, and most importantly, it seems that restricting the term "peace" to positive peace actually would *interfere* with our thinking clearly about the is-sues of peace and justice and their interrela-tions. Peace and justice are both desirable things to have in a society, but they are not be-cause of that the same thing. If we were to use the word "peace" to mean only a just peace, we would be forced to overlook certain distinc-tions which must be made if we are to under-stand the problems involved in creating an ideal society. It is important to realize that in concrete everyday social situations "peace" and "justice" often refer to *opposing* ideals; those who are well off and want to preserve the *sta-tus quo* focus on preserving "peace" while those who feel left out and want change call for "jus-tice." This point should become clearer after the discussion of "justice" that comes later.

The tension between "peace" and "justice":

"Peace" usually means keeping things as they are, so those who are doing well tend to emphasize "peace" more than "justice."

"Justice" often means changing things to make them fairer, so those who aren't doing well emphasize "justice" more than "peace."

Let us therefore use the word "peace" in the negative sense to mean simply the absence of war. Is peace in this negative sense of mere absence of war necessarily a good thing? At first glance negative peace certainly seems to be a better state of affairs than war. In peace-time there may or may not be injustice, but in a war there is bound to be a lot of injustice. People are killed or maimed and their prop-erty is destroyed simply because they are on the other side, or sometimes simply because they are in the way. Bombs and machine-gun fire do not always hit the objects at which they were aimed, and they almost always hit other things besides. Also, even the enemy soldiers at which they are aimed may have had little or no choice about participating in the war. Fur-thermore, peace promotes positive attitudes. It tends to make people more humane and sympathetic toward those in other groups, while war tends to make them more suspicious and spiteful toward all persons even remotely related to the enemy group.

Still it is possible for peace in this negative sense to be a very bad thing. A society in which a ruthless dictator rules with an iron hand in an arbitrary and oppressive way may strictly speaking be peaceful in the sense that there is no overt war. There may be an abundance of killing and torturing which results in resentment and hatred, but still there is peace in the sense of tranquillity because no one even dares to begin resisting the commands of the dictator. Thus it is quite possible to conceive of a peaceful situation in which there is so much injustice and killing that even war would be better. In the 20th century even more people died at the hands of their own oppressive governments than have died in wars.[17] It can be argued that under some conditions the injustice becomes so gross that even violence and war are justified. This situation leads to the notion of a "just war," a concept to be explored more fully after our discussion of "justice."

Nevertheless since even a negative unjust peace is still peace, the role of government in maintaining peace and order within a society is evident. Government serves many other purposes, such as defending the society against other societies, maintaining communication and transportation facilities, educating the young, providing clean water and other essential services, regulating trade, and so on, but one of the main purposes of government is the preservation of public order, that is, the preservation of peace within the society. In order to do this, a government must have some device for managing conflict among its own members. Thus governments have police forces and jails in order to physically subdue those who try to disturb the peace. Usually there are laws so that people will know in advance what types of behavior will be punished by the government. In a republic these laws are made by representatives elected by the people. On the other hand, in other societies the laws may be made by a king or dictator or by some group with absolute authority. The kinds of behavior which get punished may not be based on "laws" at all but only on the whims and dictates of the ruler at that moment. Nevertheless even under these authoritarian types of government, the art of governing develops. This art consists of adjudicating the conflicting interests of different groups so that peace is preserved within the society. It is especially imperative for the rulers that injustices severe enough to cause general rebellion be avoided.

Even though governments function as peace-makers within their own society, they tend to function as war-makers in relation to each other. Each government pursues its own interests and, theoretically at least, the welfare of its own people. Thus there is competition between governments for the goods of the earth. Strong governments (in the military sense) will tend to take land and resources from societies with weak governments. As a result, governments tend to build up their military might so that they can take from others rather than having things taken from them. In situations where it is not obvious which government is stronger or where the weaker government will not merely yield to the stronger, war may occur as a way of settling the issue. Thus governments tend to be war-makers in relation to other governments even while being peace-makers within their own territorial boundaries.

**The role of government
in "war" and "peace":**
Within its territory governments seek to keep conflict nonviolent and to promote *peace*. With regard to other societies governments tend to make *war* to protect themselves.

It should be noted that it is possible to have peace in a society even if there were no government to adjudicate conflicts between groups and the individuals of which they are composed. Conflicting groups and individuals are often able to work out their differences among themselves. In the same way national governments are often able to use diplomacy to work out differences among themselves and thus to remain at peace with each other. But the fact is that over a period of time there are almost always some intense conflicts which cannot be resolved by the parties involved. Within a government these conflicts get resolved in the political process and by the courts, with the enforcement assistance, if necessary, of the police. But when there is no government with law-making and enforcement powers for resolving conflicts, which is presently the case among nations (that is, there is no world government), then violence or threats of violence may be used to decide which group gets its way. Since this possibility is a very real one, most national governments maintain a powerful military force so that they will not need to give in when a conflict reaches the stage where it gets resolved by a contest of force.

Even within nations there may be large-scale violent conflicts in the form of civil wars. One of the main purposes of governments is to maintain peace, but they don't always succeed. Nevertheless for the most part within a governed society organized group violence seldom breaks out and peace is the usual situation. On the other hand, in the absence of a recognized and trusted government to adjudicate conflicts, opposing groups are more likely to arm themselves in order to protect their interests by violence when necessary.

The Meaning of the Term "Justice"

In the present context the term "justice" is being used to refer to an ideal social situation where the goods of a society are distributed among the population as they *ought* to be. But how ought things to be distributed? What kinds of laws should be enacted to get a fair distribution? It cannot merely be assumed that things should be distributed as in fact they are, nor can it always be assumed that the laws should be as they are. If that were the case, it would never make sense to ask whether *any* society or *any* law is unjust. To say that the present distribution of goods is unfair or unjust or that the existing laws are unfair or unjust is to indicate that there is some ideal or standard of justice which is not being implemented in this society.

The view that justice is a matter of accepting the existing distribution of goods and obeying the existing laws, whatever the laws say, is not completely senseless, however. We have noted in our discussion of "peace" that one function of government is to adjudicate in a nonviolent way the conflicts between its members as they individually and collectively pursue their interests. When the government serves as a truly neutral arbitrator in these disputes, each party to the conflict has the obligation to restrain itself in accord with the judgments of the government in order to preserve the peace. If the government really is impartial, each party to the dispute is faced with a choice between (1) living in a society where conflicts about who gets what are peacefully resolved by the government or (2) living in a society where conflicts are resolved by resort to force. Thomas Hobbes, a prominent seventeenth-century English political philosopher, called this latter situation, where there is no government to resolve disputes, a state of war of every individual against every other. Where all conflicts are resolved by the use of force, there is no security of person or possessions for anyone. As Hobbes noted, in such a situation life would be "poor, nasty, brutish, and short."[18] There would be neither peace nor justice. The institution of a truly neutral arbitrator, on the other hand, with the force to subdue those who will not voluntarily obey the laws and judgments of the government, would bring both peace and justice. If such an ideal situation existed where the government is completely unbiased, then justice might well be defined as having goods distributed just as they presently are and abiding by whatever the laws require.

The trouble is that in actual situations the government is usually not a neutral arbitrator either when making laws or when enforcing them. For example, in a Western-style democracy groups and individuals with large amounts of money are usually able to influence the law-making process much more than people with little in the way of financial resources. Thus the laws are more likely to protect and promote the interests of the very rich than of the very poor. On the other hand, after a Communist revolution has occurred, a government is instituted with the explicit purpose of making laws which favor the poorer "working class" at the expense of the more affluent members of the society, whose property may simply be confiscated by the government. The same kind of bias exists also in the enforcement of the law. In most courtrooms in the West the well-dressed and well-educated are often dealt with less harshly than the poorly dressed and poorly educated. Richer persons will also probably have better lawyers representing them. On the other hand, under a newly instituted Communist government persons from a previously wealthy family can expect harsher treatment than poor persons. So where is justice? Governments are often biased toward some and prejudiced against others.

As already noted, whenever we speak of the decisions of a government as *unjust*, it is implied that we have some independent standard of justice by which we are able to make this judgment. What is this standard of justice? Plato quoted the poet Simonides as offering the suggestion that justice is done when all persons get what is due them.[19] One can hardly quarrel with this definition, but it still leaves open the question of how we should distribute the goods of society so that all persons do in fact have the amount that they *ought* to have.

This issue of deciding how much different people in a society *ought* to get is one of the most controversial issues in social philosophy, so it should not be supposed that a short discussion of "justice" or "fairness" can be completely adequate. Still, some basic points can be made. There are two central but opposing principles that must be balanced when this question of justice is being considered.

On the one hand there is the principle that *everyone should be equal.* The basic belief here is that all people are members of the same human family. Any differences among them are due to factors over which they ultimately have no control. People do not choose to be male or female. They do not choose to be black or white or yellow or brown or red. They do not choose where they are to be born, what talents or disabilities they inherit, or what kind

of environment they have when they are children. People do not choose to be handicapped or slow in learning or lacking in energy or to be born in a poor undeveloped country rather than a rich developed one. As people grow older, they will make choices, but even then the choices they make will have been determined to a great extent by these other earlier factors over which they had no control. This *principle of equality* displays itself in the claim that workers should be paid on the basis of how many hours they work rather than some getting paid more and others less on the basis of the kind of work they happen to be able to do. It is the basis of the feeling that the more fortunate members of a family should help those in the family who are less fortunate. The principle of equality is also the basis of the feeling that it is grossly unfair for some people to be extremely rich while others who work just as hard are extremely poor. What is fair about a world where some people need to constantly worry about dieting so they don't get too fat while others need to worry about how to get enough food for their babies that they do not suffer mental retardation the rest of their lives?

On the other hand there is also another principle of justice, the *principle of merit*, namely, the principle that *those who are able to accomplish more by virtue of their talents and hard work should reap greater individual rewards and should be able to keep what they have acquired rather than being forced to share what they have with others who do less and have less.* The basic belief here is that it is unfair to just take things away from those who have acquired them through hard work or ingenuity and give these things to others who have not earned them. People need to be given an incentive to exert themselves by allowing them to accumulate more than others who do not contribute as much. Supporters of this principle of merit claim that people will work harder over a longer period of time for personal gain than they will when the only motive is the welfare of the whole society. If people who do work hard and acquire goods are always forced to share with people who just loaf and do nothing, won't everyone eventually

just do nothing? The validity of this principle
of merit is supported by the actions of pur-
chasers of goods and services who generally
display a readiness to pay more for better quality. Consumers generally are not ready to pay
others on the basis of how long it takes to do
or produce something. Their concern rather is
with the quality of the goods or services being
purchased.

Justice requires balancing two somewhat opposite principles.

The principle of equality: Everyone in the
community should be treated the same and
should have about the same amount of
goods.

The principle of merit: Some persons in
the community deserve to have more than
others because they work harder and
contribute more.

Arguments can be given to support both
of these principles. Defenders of the *principle
of equality* argue that those who are well off are
not necessarily more talented or harder working than those who have less. The social system, including the government, has usually
been designed to make sure that those persons
and groups who have wealth and privileged
positions maintain them for themselves and
their children. Those who contribute more to
society are able to do so only because society
or some part of it has first contributed more
to them. Cooperation is more essential than
competition for promoting the welfare of the
society as a whole. Excessive competition
tends to destroy human relations and compassion for others. On the other hand, defenders of the *principle of merit* argue that if
talent and hard work are not rewarded then
the society as a whole will soon have a lower
standard of living. People who have accumulated property must be allowed to keep it. Talented persons won't use their talents, and people will not exert themselves much if they will
be just as well off when they loaf. Competition is required to get people to develop their
capabilities. Without rewards for excellence
there will be little or no concern to keep the
quality of goods and services high.

It might seem that the ideal way of reconciling these two principles of equality and
merit is to emphasize *equality of opportunity*
for everyone while having actual personal rewards based on the use made of one's opportunities. But even equality of opportunity
would not be sufficient to produce justice because some people happen to inherit more talent while others are born with disabilities
which they did not choose to have. Also, people do not exist as isolated individuals but live
in families and have children. If a husband
and wife own things in common, how is it
possible to reward one and not the other? And
the situation gets even more intricate when we
consider children, since one of the things parents most want is a good future for their own
children. They usually want their children to
have *better* educational opportunities and *better* social opportunities than other children.
They want their children to be *more* affluent
and *more* influential than other people's children. They are more concerned that *their* children not be threatened by starvation and sickness than that other people's children be
preserved from these dangers. It is not that
they don't care about other children; they
merely care more about their own.

Furthermore, people want this concern
about their own children reflected in the policies of their government. For example, think
of the outcry from Americans if it were suggested that the United States government
make contributions on the order of $50 billion
a year to UNICEF or some other agency concerned with the welfare of children in poorer
countries in order to modify just slightly the
difference in opportunity between American
children and the children who live in these
other countries. Or consider the outcry which
would occur even if the expenditure per pupil
had to be equalized throughout all the schools,
public and private, in the United States. Or
consider how much opposition there would
be to a law that would prohibit the inheritance of more than $100,000 by any individ-
ual on the grounds that such gifts destroy
equality of opportunity for everyone. People
in positions of privilege do not want equality
of opportunity for all children; they feel that

one of the important things they have earned by virtue of their talents and hard work is the privilege of sending their children to better-than-average schools and giving them advantages which other children don't have. Yet where is the justice when some children have so much greater opportunities than others? So goes the struggle between the principle of equality and the principle of merit.

It does not take much imagination to see that persons who are not so well off, either within a particular society or in relation to the human race as a whole, will see great wisdom in the principle of equality. They believe that their inferior position is due to the poverty of their parents, to poor health which is debilitating no matter how hard they would like to work, and to historical developments completely outside their control which have put them in a disadvantaged position. They have much less than others, but they do not believe that it is because their efforts are in any way inferior. In fact it seems to them that they work even harder than the more privileged persons but end up with less. On the other hand, persons who are well off, either within a particular society or in relation to the human race as a whole, will see great wisdom in the principle of merit. They believe that their privileged position is due to their superior intelligence, their greater industriousness, their generally superior genetic make-up, or the better economic and political institutions of their society. They have much more than others, but they believe this situation is fair because they deserve to have more.

These differing viewpoints about what principle of justice should be emphasized produce a new basis for the perception of social situations and consequently for social conflict. We will return to these ideas when we consider the ideological aspects of the contemporary world scene in Chapter 8. For the moment we can say that different opinions about what is just arise from the fact that people and nations, whether rich or poor, find it difficult to maintain a disinterested point of view. Their own interests always seem much more important than other people's. Furthermore, they do not see how much their own viewpoint is influenced by their present position. The poor believe that if they were rich, they would be much more generous in helping the poor than the present rich are. The rich believe that if they were poor, they would be much less resentful than the present poor are. It is doubtful if either of these beliefs is generally true, either within national societies or within the global society of nations.

Meanwhile, what can be said about justice? It seems that justice involves some kind of delicate balance between the principle of equality on the one hand and the principle of merit on the other. The fact that people in positions of privilege usually make and enforce the laws would suggest that most governments tend to underemphasize the principle of equality and overemphasize the principle of merit. They tend to be less concerned about having equality of opportunity for everyone than about maintaining "law and order" and preserving "peace." On the other hand, those who are protesting against the injustice of governments may be inclined to overlook the value of merit entirely and to view "justice" as nothing but equality. They tend to be more interested in getting equality, sometimes even by violent means, than in preserving a peace which they perceive as designed to maintain an unjust society.

Surely it is not easy to establish just governments, that is, governments which properly balance these two principles of equality and merit, even for national societies. The challenge of the future is to establish a governance system on a global basis that will provide a just peace for the whole world. That project will be even more difficult.

The "Just War" Concept

A venerable tradition in dealing with the problem of war is the concern with the question of when it is "just" or "right" to get involved in the violence of war (in Latin *"jus ad bellum"*) and what kinds of use of violence are justifiable once war is going on (in Latin *"jus in bello"*). It should be noted that these questions are only tangential to our central concern of how to eliminate war. In fact, they are addressed to an entirely different issue, namely, what is the morally correct way to behave as long as wars are going to occur? This whole long and widely debated "just war" tradition is built on the assumption that there always will be wars; the problem then becomes how to constrain behavior so that wars are not fought when there is no morally good reason for them and so that wars are not more vicious than they need to be. Even though the "just war" tradition is not directly relevant to the issue of how to eliminate war, it has been an important part of thinking morally about war. Furthermore, as long as wars are still being fought and a great deal of international law has been formulated to address the issue of what kind of behavior is acceptable during war, a brief discussion of the "just war" viewpoint is in order.[20]

The two parts of the "just war" issue:
"*jus ad bellum*": When is it O.K. to resort to war?
"*jus in bello*": What kinds of behavior are appropriate or inappropriate during a war?

Historically, the beginning of the just war tradition is traceable back to the Greeks during the Peloponnesian Wars of the fifth century B.C.E. and then to Cicero in the first century B.C.E.[21] The source for much modern thinking on this issue is St. Augustine (C.E. 354–430), Christian Bishop of Hippo. The early Church had been totally pacifist, but Augustine argued that sometimes it was morally necessary to use force (violence) in order to combat evil. For example, it would not be right for a Christian to stand by refusing to use force while a criminal was mistreating an innocent defenseless person. The Christian was to be motivated by concern for both the victim and the offender and was not to use more violence than necessary to prevent the evil. Nevertheless, moral duty requires that the offender be stopped from injuring the innocent person, by force if necessary. Extending this pattern of thinking to the arena of international relations, one country can justly go to war against a second country which is unjustly attacking a third country if there is no other way of stopping the evil and if the use of force is only as great as is necessary to stop the wrong.

Although Augustine was an important person in the development of the "just war" tradition, later Christian thinkers such as Thomas Aquinas (1225–1274) were instrumental in transmitting it to later generations. Other non-Christian sources of this "just war" viewpoint were the chivalric tradition of Medieval Europe, concepts used in old Roman law, and the developing European political order where the use of force was connected to the preservation of public order.[22] Some important issues for this tradition in modern warfare are determining when "humanitarian intervention" is justified, figuring out how to direct military action against combatants without harming non-combatants, especially in intranational wars, and deciding whether some weapons such as nuclear devices or lasers which blind enemy soldiers are just too indiscriminate and too inhumane to be allowed in any kind of warfare.

The seven basic principles of the "just war" theory were summarized by the 17th century legal philosopher Hugo Grotius as follows: First, there must be a just cause for resorting to force; some evil is to be prevented or rectified. Second, there must be a legitimate recognized authority to authorize the initiation of the war. Third, the use of force must be done with the right intent; the motive must be to stop evil with no expectation of personal glory or other gain. Fourth, the amount of force must be proportional, that is, no more than what is needed to prevent or rectify the wrong. Fifth, force is justified only as a last resort when there is no other way of dealing with the evil. Sixth, war must be undertaken with the aim of getting peace and not for some other gain or purpose. Seventh, there must be a reasonable expectation that the act of intervention taken as a whole will produce more good than evil, which would include the idea that those trying to stop the evil really have a good chance of accomplishing that goal without inadvertently leading to even more evil happening in the long run.[23] These principles enunciated by Grotius are now generally amplified by reference to statements in the Charter of the United Nations to the effect that the threat or the use of force in international relations is not to be used except in cases of individual or collective self-defense.[24]

The second issue addressed by "just war" theory concerns how war is to be conducted. The first point here is that innocent bystanders (noncombatants, civilians) are not to be harmed ("the principle of discrimination"). The second point is that the particular actions being used during war need to be constrained so that they do not exceed what is needed to accomplish the end and do not result in more evil than good. This second point is an extension of "the principle of proportionality" except that now it is being applied to the problem of how to fight a war rather than trying to decide whether to engage in war at all. In this new context it is called "the principle of double effect," the notion that *each action* performed during a just war has some good effects in stopping injustice but also some bad effects in harming others, and the good must exceed the evil or that action is unjust.

The "just war" tradition offers a middle way between pure pacifism (which shuns any use of violence for any reason) and unrestrained realism (which advocates unrestrained use of violence in order to prevail over one's enemy). It is based on the notion that there is a "natural law" or moral order about what is right and what is wrong and that it is legitimate to use force in order to stop violations of the natural law. If those who care about justice are not allowed to use force to stop injustices (to maintain "law and order"), then those who use unrestrained force to advance their own interests will not be held in check. That absence of any kind of check on injustice would lead to even more violence since everyone would be required to use force to protect their own interests.

But there are some difficulties for "just war" theory. First, exactly what does the "natural law" prescribe? Not everyone is in agreement on exactly when injustice is being done. For example, suppose one very small group of people gains possession of almost all the land available in a given area (considerably more than they can actually make use of) and then institutes a government with laws that prevent others from ever owning or using any of that

land. Would it be unjust for other people who have been excluded from that land to use force to try to break up or change that system of government so that the land could be more evenly distributed? Does the "natural law" dictate that people should be able to keep whatever they already possess? Or does the "natural law" say that there are other principles of justice which require equality of opportunity and a certain degree of sharing? And of course what makes this kind of situation even more troubling is that those who own the land are going to have one view of what is just while those who are being excluded will have a different view of what is just. We could have a very violent war with both sides quite convinced that they are engaged in a "just war." Such a situation is not uncommon in modern warfare. Usually both sides are confident that their cause is just and that they must use force to overcome injustice because there is no other way of correcting the existing unjust situation. In this connection, another criticism that can be advanced against the "just war" approach is that it tends to keep the parties to a conflict focused on what has happened in the past (who did what to whom?) rather than on what could be done by the two sides working together in the future to resolve the conflict.

Second, there are special difficulties for the "just war" theory in connection with modern society and modern warfare. Can these principles of "just war" be applied in any meaningful way? For example, how can one engage in modern warfare and not kill substantial numbers of "innocent civilians" who just happen to be in the way when explosives detonate or fires spread? Also, are there many "innocent civilians" in a modern war? Aren't the farmers who are providing food for the military forces just as much a part of the war effort as the military forces themselves? What about the engineers who are designing new weapons? Are they innocent civilians, or are they perhaps even more important to the war effort than most of the soldiers? What about the educators who are teaching future engineers and soldiers how to read and do mathematical calculations? What about the factory workers who are manufacturing the weapons and the uniforms the military forces will use? What about the young people, many of whom after less than a year of training will take their place in the military forces? In modern "total war" it seems that most of the society is involved in the war effort. Trying to discriminate between combatants and noncombatants seems futile.[25] Besides, people generally do not have much of a choice as to whether they are going to be part of the military forces or not. Why assume that the person in the enemy society who wears a uniform is a more legitimate target than others who are not wearing uniforms? And finally, are not the leaders of the enemy society more likely to be responsible for the war than the soldier on the battlefield? Yet there is a tradition that leaders of the other side are not to be assassinated.

There are also difficulties about how "just war" theory can be applied to the use of modern weapons, especially nuclear weapons.[26] Isn't the destruction caused always going to far exceed any good that could come from their use, especially when one considers the long-lasting radioactivity, the possibility of "nuclear winter," and the enduring effects on the environment — including possibly the end of all life? Is there any way that one can "justly" use nuclear weapons? That issue was referred to the World Court (that is, the International Court of Justice or ICJ) by the U.N. General Assembly in December, 1994 for an advisory legal opinion.[27] On July 8, 1996 the World Court issued the advisory judgment that

> threat or use of nuclear weapons would generally be contrary to the rules of international law applicable in armed conflict, and in particular the principles and rules of humanitarian law;
> However, in view of the current state of international law, and of the elements of fact at its disposal, the Court cannot conclude definitively whether the threat or use of nuclear weapons would be lawful or unlawful in an extreme circumstance of self-defense, in which the very survival of a State would be at stake.[28]

But this was only an advisory opinion about the legality of nuclear weapons according to existing international law. Note that it says that the use of nuclear weapons is acceptable when necessary to insure the survival of a State. It should also be noted that the Court was very divided on the issue, being tied 7 to 7 until President Mohammed Bedjaoui of Algeria cast the deciding vote in favor of this statement.[29]

Furthermore, even if the statement of the ICJ is taken to be the definitive moral conclusion about the use of nuclear weapons, other questions still remain. Can a strategy of nuclear deterrence through the threat of massive retaliation be "just" even though the actual use of nuclear weapons is almost always contrary to international law? That is, can one justly threaten to use the weapons if it would be illegal to actually use them? On the other hand, if one's enemy has nuclear weapons, isn't it necessary to be prepared to use them in order to deter the enemy from using theirs? In that case, how many nuclear weapons are "enough"? Other kinds of weapons are also becoming ever more cruel and destructive — napalm, chemical and biological weapons, lasers to cause blindness, and so on. Can modern warfare be "just" under any circumstances?

There are so many philosophical and moral dilemmas related to "just war" theory in the modern world that the only sensible course of action appears to be to work as intelligently and energetically as possible to abolish war as a way of resolving social conflict. That is, instead of focusing on *when* it is just to fight wars and *how* it is just to fight wars as "just war" theory does, it seems that our thought and action concerning the war problem should be focused more on the problem of how to eliminate war altogether.

Further Reflections on Peace and Justice

As already noted, the question of justice concerns the proper distribution of the goods and benefits of a society among its members. We have also noted that the general tendency of governments is to be conservative, to preserve the present social order with its greater opportunities for the children of privilege rather than to institute changes which would create more equal opportunities for the less privileged children. Thus tension exists between the quest for peace (often viewed as simply preserving the status quo) and the quest for justice (where violence may seem to be the only way of changing an unjust existing situation). Three additional observations on the relations between peace and justice are in order.

The first issue is *whether governments instituted to promote peace can also be expected to promote justice.* In light of what has been said above, it might be assumed that once a government is established there will be less justice with regard to the distribution of goods and benefits than if there were no government at all because the government will probably be controlled by the powerful to maintain their positions of privilege. But what would the situation be without a government to keep peace? Ruthlessness and violence would be rewarded by gains in possessions and power. Consequently there would be a tendency of the powerful to use their power in an unrestrained way to become even more powerful. Once a government is established, the powerful may use it as an instrument to maintain their power, but in the absence of government the powerful will have other instruments (paid bodyguards and warriors, specially designed weapons, and so on) to maintain their power. The point could be put this way: Government does not necessarily produce justice, but the lack of government probably will allow, and even reward, a great deal of injustice. Whether the injustice with government will be greater or less than the injustice without government depends on the particular situation and the particular kind of government to be instituted.

If a world government were instituted over the national governments, would the distribution of the goods of the earth among the various nations be more or less just than it is at present? It can be supposed that such a world government would be dominated by the more powerful nations, at least at first.[30] Otherwise, those nations would not even allow it to be formed. Once a government was established, the more powerful nations would undoubtedly try to use it to maintain their po-

sitions of privilege. Would the less powerful, poorer nations be better off with such a government or without it? Without it, they are virtually at the mercy of the more powerful nations, which can use their superior economic and military power to impose whatever terms they desire. With it, they are still in a situation dominated by the more powerful nations. Which situation would be more just would depend on specific things such as the acquisition of nuclear weapons and long-range delivery systems by the poorer nations (which would make them less at the mercy of the more powerful nations) and the precise voting arrangements and structure that would exist in the world government (which might be arranged so that the poorer nations were less at the mercy of the richer ones). Only after examining details would it be possible to say whether a fairer distribution of goods among the nations would be more likely with such a government or without it. A critical feature for promoting justice in the long run would be having the kind of government which permits peaceful change to eliminate injustice.

The second point to be considered with regard to the relation between peace and justice concerns *the desirability of conducting war to eliminate what are considered to be unjust inequalities in wealth.* To understand this point we must begin by noting that there are two different viewpoints that can be taken with regard to the measurement of wealth. People may evaluate their wealth *relatively* in terms of what they have compared to others, or they may evaluate their wealth in *absolute* terms, that is, in terms of what goods and services and burdens they actually have regardless of what others have. In a peaceful situation there may be a great disparity between what the rich have and what the poor have, but the poor may still be better off in absolute terms than they would be if they were to conduct a war against the rich. That is, the poor within a society may unite in a war against the rich in order to end what is perceived as an unjust situation. The probable result is that everyone in the society would end up worse off than before. War can destroy the wealth of the rich, but it cannot by itself make the poor as a whole richer. War does not produce goods but only destroys them. Of course, some of the leaders of the poor may confiscate some of the leftover goods of the rich for themselves, but then all that has happened is that one group of rich persons has been replaced by another group of slightly poorer persons. And that is the situation if the poor *win* the war! If they try to rebel but *lose,* it is likely that they will be even more oppressed than before.

It could be argued that a violent revolution by the poor against the rich might change an oppressive system and thus would be worthwhile in the long run even if it were a failure from the short-term point of view. Conceivably such a change for the better is possible. The crucial issue is whether the new leaders will prove to be different from the ones they replaced and whether the new system will put more restraints on the power of the leaders than the old system did. The first one or two generations of leaders after the revolution might well be vividly aware of what they fought to change and might be particularly on guard against special privileges for leaders and their families and friends, but at least by the third generation the leaders are much less likely to be concerned about such issues. Also it is very unlikely that the new leaders will be more restricted in their powers than the old leaders had been because the new rulers will claim that they must be unrestrained in order to make all the changes they feel are so necessary. Nevertheless, it is conceivable that a violent revolution may result in a society which is more just.

Suppose the poorer nations of the world eventually acquired enough nuclear weapons to be able to cause considerable damage to the richer nations. Suppose they then threatened the richer nations saying that wealth must be shared more equitably or they will use the weapons. The richer nations would probably not yield to such a threat and might even issue a counter-threat. The poor nations could argue, "You have more to lose than we do" (which is true), but the richer nations could argue, "You will be even worse off after a war with us than you are now" (which is also true). Consider the situation if the poor nations were

able to launch a surprise nuclear attack destroying a great deal of the wealth of the richer nations and eventually developing a new international system to modify the distribution of goods among nations so that there is more equality. Even if things worked out as the poor nations had planned, from an absolute point of view all nations would be worse off than before the war. Moreover, it is not certain over the long run that the new system would be more just than the old one. Furthermore, it is really much more probable that in a war the rich nations would prevail over the poor ones. They also might well be provoked by such an attack to be even more oppressive toward the poorer nations than they had been before. A world government which would allow for peaceful change would be a much better alternative for the poorer nations.

The third point to be noted with regard to the relation between peace and justice is that *justice in a society produces both peace and prosperity.* In a society where there is a general consensus that opportunities are approximately equal, that the goods and burdens of the society are fairly distributed, and that the laws of the society are equitable and impartially enforced there is little likelihood of group violence. Even if a few individuals have some personal gripes, they will be unable to get any substantial following if they try to organize a violent rebellion. Also, when the poorer people who are in greater need of more goods have the money to buy them, the industries of the society are stimulated. Unemployment is reduced, and consequently crime is reduced. As more people work, production is increased and the demand for goods is further increased. Prosperity is promoted by having some wealth in the hands of poorer people.

Let us consider how this principle would work at the international level. Suppose that all tariffs and restraints on international trade now erected by the richer countries were eliminated so that these markets would be opened to the poorer countries. Suppose also that some system were in place to guarantee that a small portion of the income of the richer nations were regularly transferred to the poorer ones.[31] The present resentment felt by the governments of the poorer nations toward the richer nations would be greatly reduced. Although there might be some concern in some of the richer nations as patterns of employment shifted to accord with the new situation, the long-term reaction would be one of satisfaction as the prices for many consumer goods are reduced and the market for exports expands. Unemployment in the less developed countries would decline, and demand for goods from the developed countries would increase. Threats of violence against the investments of those living in richer nations would be virtually eliminated. The gap between poor and rich nations would be reduced, every nation would be better off in absolute terms, and the likelihood of any kind of violence would be greatly reduced. This hypothetical program of peace and prosperity through greater justice can be contrasted with the present world system in which the more powerful nations maintain their positions of superiority through military might, control of the rules of international trade, and restrictions on immigration. This present system focuses on preserving the relative superiority of the richer nations, but all nations are poorer in absolute terms than they could be under an international system with greater equality of opportunity.

On the basis of this observation that a just social system produces peace and prosperity, it has been argued by many writers that the best way to produce peace is to promote justice.[32] But there are problems here, too. One person's view of what is just is not the same as another's. Also, for some persons the use of violence can be justified if it promotes justice. Care must be exercised by those who adopt such a view since the quest for justice may itself be the cause of war. On the other hand, leaders concerned about peace but insensitive to issues of justice are not blameless when their maintenance of a grossly unjust social system results in war. As former U.S. President John F. Kennedy said, "Those who make peaceful revolution impossible will make violent revolution inevitable."[33]

3.   The Historical Framework

The history of warfare cannot be separated from the history of humanity in general. One of the most significant changes in the way humans live, what Kenneth Boulding in *The Meaning of the Twentieth Century* has called "the first great transition," is the shift from precivilized to civilized society which began about 10,000 years ago.[1] That agricultural revolution marked the transition from the old nomadic life-style of hunting, fishing, and gathering whatever nature might provide to the new way of cultivating crops and relying on domesticated animals to provide a reliable source of meat, milk, and eggs as well as materials for clothing. This change in life-style at the end of "the New Stone Age" also later brought with it the development of cities and of writing, two developments which are still used to determine if a group of people are "civilized" or not.

Civilization meant a radical change in the way our ancestors lived, bringing with it not only more organized control over nature in the form of agriculture and domesticated animals but also more organized control over the people living within the society in the form of government. It also brought warfare in the sense of an organized violent struggle for power between one society and another. As Gwynne Dyer observed in *War*: "Civilization, first and foremost, was the discovery of how to achieve power over both nature and people, and it cannot be denied that it went to our heads: on the one hand, pyramids and irrigation canals; on the other hand, wars of extermination."[2] There is overwhelming evidence that government and the problem of war emerged together along with civilization.[3] In fact, both organized ("civilized") warfare and formal coercive government seem to have come into existence either (1) as a result of comparatively peaceful agricultural peoples being conquered by invading nomadic war bands or (2) as a result of competition for resources among groups where there was no opportunity for the losing group

to just leave and live elsewhere. The prevailing group then organized the resultant society in such a way that its power could be used not only to maintain control over the defeated group within that society but also to wage war against other societies.[4]

So when did "civilized warfare" begin? To quote Dyer again, "It can never be proved, but it is a safe assumption that the first time five thousand male human beings were ever gathered together in one place, they belonged to an army. That event probably occurred about 7000 B.C.—give or take a thousand years—and it is an equally safe bet that the first truly large-scale slaughter of people in human history happened very soon afterward."[5] In the next two or three thousand years the kind of serious warfare in which such slaughter was common spread to more and more of the newly civilized societies.

The striving for power by the rulers of the most ancient city-states of Mesopotamia is not essentially different from the struggles for power among the leaders of modern nation-states.[6] Nevertheless there is a change in war, a steady increase in the size of the communities involved and a never-ending evolution of the weapons used in fighting these struggles. The continuing occurrence of war in human society, even while the ways in which wars are fought are changing, leads naturally to the question, "How has warfare evolved over the centuries?" and then to the question, "Is there any reason to believe that a solution to the war problem is more imperative now than it was in past ages?" But first, let us review the history of warfare and empires in the Western world up to 1900 and then in the whole world during the 20th century.

The History of Warfare Between Sovereign States

Among the earliest known city-states are those which flourished about 5000 B.C.E.

(Before the Common Era) in the Tigris-Euphrates Valley. The rulers of city-states such as Eridu, Nippur, Ur, Uruk, Assur, Umma, Sumer, Lagash, and Kish engaged in the same kind of struggles for wealth and power that we find among modern nations. Evidence of this exists in the form of peace treaties inscribed in clay about 3000 B.C.E.[7] Thus the pattern of struggles for power among sovereign states is at least 5,000 years old. At times the struggle is interrupted when one sovereign state establishes an empire by conquering all the others close enough to contend for land and other advantages, but the peace is always temporary. When the leader who has created the empire dies, it may disintegrate as a struggle for power takes place among his previous subjects. Or the newly created empire may come into conflict with other empires built of previously competing states.

One of the earliest recorded empires was created in the Tigris-Euphrates Valley about 2500 B.C.E. by Lugal-zaggasi of Uruk. This Sumerian empire was then conquered and incorporated into the much larger empire of Sargon of Akkad, which continued until the 20th century B.C.E. In the 18th century B.C.E. Hammurabi established a Babylonian empire which lasted 200 years. In the 15th century B.C.E. the Mitanni established an empire which reached from the Mediterranean to western Iran. The Assyrians freed themselves from Mitanni control in the 14th century B.C.E. and then established an empire of their own.

Starting as a separate political entity first unified about 3000 B.C.E., the Egyptian state eventually spread its influence northward into Syria, where it came into conflict with the Hittites from Asia Minor and the Mitanni living along the eastern shores of the Mediterranean. About 1400 B.C.E. these three nations entered into a nonaggression pact, and a century later the Hittites and Egyptians formed an alliance against the expanding Assyrian empire. Nevertheless the Assyrians established control over Palestine in the 8th century B.C.E. and took control of Egypt in 675 B.C.E. But the Egyptians and Babylonians revolted and with the help of the Medes destroyed the Assyrian capital of Nineveh in 612 B.C.E.

The rise and fall of one power after another continued as the Persians conquered Lydia in western Asia Minor and then Babylon (538 B.C.E.). Under Darius I in the 5th century B.C.E. the Persian empire reached from the Danube River to the Indus River and from what is now southern Russia to southern Egypt. The city-states of Greece had managed to fight off the Persians even while fighting among themselves but fell in 338 B.C.E. to the Macedonians under Philip. Philip's son Alexander the Great then led the Greeks in the conquest of Egypt and the rest of the territory previously held by the Persians (331 B.C.E.).

To the west the Romans began their expansion in the 3rd century B.C.E. by defeating the Carthaginians. Then they conquered Macedonia, Greece, and their Numidian rivals in northern Africa. Despite class struggles in Rome itself, Roman power had spread to western Europe, Asia Minor, Egypt, and the east coast of the Mediterranean before the beginning of the Christian era. Although confronted by the Germanic "barbarians" on the north, the Roman government succeeded in maintaining the famous *Pax Romana (Roman Peace)* in the Mediterranean for 500 years. Nevertheless, as a result of invasions by the Visigoths, Huns, Vandals, and others the western part of the Roman Empire ceased to exist as a political unit after 476. In the 7th century the eastern part of the Empire came under attack as the Muslim Saracens conquered Palestine, Egypt, the rest of north Africa, and Spain. The Muslim advance into western Europe was stopped at Poitiers in 732 by the Franks under Charles Martel. In 800 Martel's grandson, Charlemagne, was crowned Emperor of the new western Roman Empire by the Pope. In the 10th century the Vikings, Varangians, and Norsemen from the north, the Magyars and Bulgarians from the east, and the Turks from the southeast made new incursions into what had been the Roman Empire. The result was a Christian Europe composed of many separate political entities plus the remains of the Byzantine Empire in southeastern Europe.

The largest land empire ever known was

then carved out of Asia and eastern Europe by the Mongols under Genghis Khan (1162–1227). But as often happens, the victors were conquered by the culture of the vanquished both in China and in Muslim western Asia. The Ottoman Turks put an end to the eastern Roman Empire, conquering Constantinople in 1453. The separate Christian kingdoms of Europe banded together to stop the Turkish expansion and won a naval victory at Lepanto in 1571, but when the threat was gone they again went their separate ways.

In western Europe the period 1350–1650 was marked by violence and more violence as peasants fought feudal nobles, townspeople fought feudal nobles, kings fought Emperor and Pope, Protestants fought Catholics, and one nationality fought another. The fighting came to a climax in the Thirty Years' War (1618–1648), a war which started mainly as a conflict between Catholics and Protestants but ended with more emphasis on loyalty to king and country. The Treaty of Westphalia at the end of that war is usually taken to mark the beginning of the European state system. Competition among many of these European nations escalated with regard to control of territory in the Americas, Asia, and the coasts of Africa. From this point on, the history of these non-European areas, which has not been discussed although it generally reveals the same kind of struggles for power found in Western history,[8] becomes woven into the history of the competition and warfare of the European state system.

The late 17th and early 18th centuries saw the British successfully checking the expansion of Spanish and French power. The Seven Years' War ended in 1763 with the British in control of all of Canada and most of what is now the eastern part of the United States as well as the east coast of India.

The last half of the 18th century saw the beginning of one very important technological/cultural revolution and two political revolutions. The Industrial Revolution involved using machines, made possible by new scientific knowledge, rather than relying on animals or human labor to get work done. It led to great increases in productivity first in England and then in northern Europe and North America. (By the 20th century this industrialization, which Kenneth Boulding in *The Meaning of the Twentieth Century* calls "the second great transition,"[9] had spread to the whole world.) In the political arena the United States of America came into existence as some of the colonists in North America successfully revolted against British rule (1775-1781). The other political revolution started in France in 1789 when the middle classes rebelled against the king and the landed aristocracy. The victorious French revolutionaries under the leadership of Napoleon Bonaparte then became a threat to the nobility in all the other nations of Europe.

French rule was extended over much of the European continent, but eventually the combined forces of Russia, Sweden, Prussia, Austria, and England, aided by nationalistic uprisings against the French in Spain and Austria, put an end to the Napoleonic effort. The Congress of Vienna (1814–1815) redrew the map of Europe with territorial gains for the victors. In America, the Louisiana Purchase of land from France (1803) had greatly expanded the size of the United States while the just-mentioned Napoleonic Wars in Europe gave many Latin American countries the chance to win their independence from Spain and Portugal. In Europe nationalism became an important factor in the unification of Italy and Germany in the middle of the 19th century. Nationalism was also a factor in the 19th century westward expansion of the United States even though that movement was briefly interrupted by the very bloody Civil War (1861-1865).

In the last part of the 19th century and early part of the 20th century the industrialized European powers, led by Britain and France, completed the extension of their control over the not-yet-industrialized peoples of Africa and Asia. Only Japan, which had adopted Western industrialism as the result of American prodding, was immune from conquest. In fact, a newly-industrialized Japan embarked on expanding its own influence by taking some territory not only from China (1894-1895) but even from big-power Russia

(1904–1905). For the most part, however, the industrialized countries negotiated their conflicts with each other while using their superior military power to subdue the nonindustrialized societies. While the European powers focused their expansionary efforts on Africa and Asia, the United States expanded its territory and influence in North America at the expense of native Americans, Mexicans and other Latin Americans, and a declining Spain. In Europe itself from 1815 to 1914 Britain acted as a "balancer" in the struggles for power among the various continental countries and thus managed to preserve the "Pax Britannica" for a hundred years. Nevertheless there were some minor wars such as in the Crimea (1853–1856) and three wars between Prussia and its neighbors climaxing with the Franco-Prussian War (1870–1871).

Antagonisms developed in the early 20th century as the industrialized countries competed ever more intensely for colonies and military superiority. The Italians, irked by France's takeover of Tunis, joined Germany and Austria-Hungary in the Triple Alliance in 1882. The French, still smarting from defeat in the Franco-Prussian War, formed an anti-German alliance with Russia. The British, concerned about the growing economic and military power of Germany, entered into agreements with Japan and then with France and Russia. Competition for influence in the Balkans between Austria-Hungary and Russia provided the fuel for war, and the assassination of the heir to the throne in Austria-Hungary by a group of Serbian terrorists called "the Black Hand" provided the spark that started World War I in 1914. Austria-Hungary, having received assurance of assistance (the so-called "blank check") from Germany against Russia if needed, attacked Serbia. The German strategy for fighting an anticipated two-front war against Russia and France (the von Schlieffen plan) called for focusing the main military effort at first against France on the assumption that it would take the less industrialized Russians more time to get their forces mobilized. When the Russians decided to mobilize to possibly help the Serbs against Austria-Hungary, the Germans demanded that

they stop, but the Russians refused. Germany then declared war on both Russia and its ally France. The Germans attacked France through neutral Belgium (another part of the von Schlieffen plan), but that crass violation of a treaty signed by Germany guaranteeing Belgium neutrality led Britain to join France and Russia against the Germans.

As the war continued Turkey and Bulgaria joined Germany and Austria-Hungary while Italy (despite its previous defensive alliance with Germany and Austria), Romania, Japan, the United States, and some smaller nations joined France and Britain. The Russians withdrew from the war in December of 1917 after the Bolshevik Revolution, yielding a great deal of territory to Germany and allowing the Germans to throw all of their forces into the fight on their western front. Nevertheless the battle lines across France changed little as large numbers of troops from both sides lost their lives in futile attacks on the entrenched opposing forces. Finally, fresh American soldiers arrived and enabled the Allies to drive the Germans back and bring an end to the fighting in November 1918.

The Treaty of Versailles (1919) provided that Germany should lose all of its overseas possessions, some of its territory in Europe, and most of its military power. Germany was forced to pay reparations to the victors, particularly to France, on whose soil most of the fighting had taken place. The territory which the Russians had previously yielded to the Germans became the independent nations of Estonia, Latvia, Lithuania, and Poland. Czechoslovakia was created, and Austria and Hungary were separated. Several smaller Balkan nations were combined to form Yugoslavia. (See maps on page 34.) At U.S. President Woodrow Wilson's insistence the Treaty of Versailles also provided for the establishment of the League of Nations to preserve the peace, but Wilson was unable to persuade the U.S. Senate to ratify the treaty. Consequently and ironically, the United States never became a member of the organization that he had fathered.

Unfortunately, the peace was not preserved. The struggle for power among the

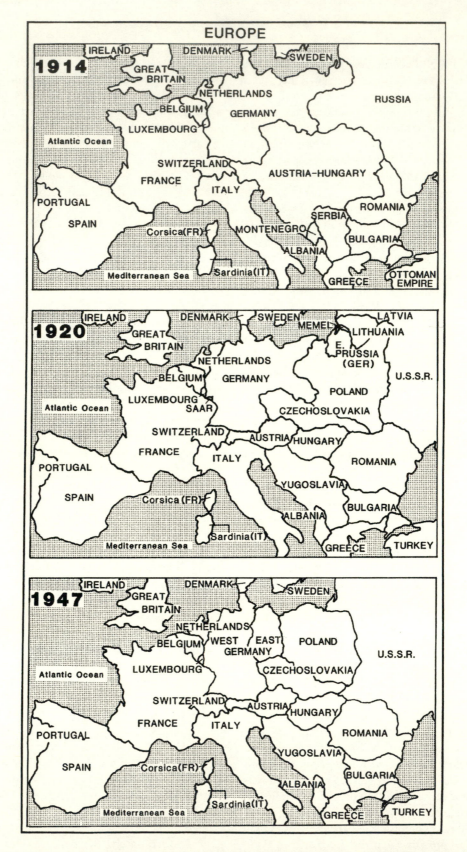

Political boundaries of Europe before World War I, between the wars, and after World War II.

nations went on as usual. In 1931–1933, Japan took Manchuria by force from China. In 1935–1936 Italy conquered Ethiopia, which had been one of the few non-colonized nations in Africa. The worldwide depression of the early 1930s led to the widespread raising of national tariffs in an effort to protect domestic industries, but the end result was a catastrophic drop in international trade which made the depression even worse. The poor economic situation also permitted the rise to power of Hitler and the Nazis in Germany. The failure of France and Britain to act decisively against Japan, Italy, or the first militaristic and expansionist efforts of Germany only resulted in further aggressive moves by the fascist nations. In the Spanish Civil War (1936–1939) the fascist Franco, with help from Mussolini in Italy and Hitler in Germany, won control of Spain from the newly elected combined democratic-socialist-Communist forces, who got only token support from Britain, France, and the Soviet Union.

The democratic capitalists in Britain and France and the Communists in Russia each tried to direct Hitler's growing military might against the other. At Munich in 1938 the British and French, in a vain effort to appease Hitler, gave him permission to move eastward and take over the western part of Czechoslovakia (the Sudetenland where many German-speaking people lived), but he responded by soon taking the whole country. The Soviets made their countermove in the summer of 1939, signing a nonaggression pact with Hitler and agreeing to divide Poland between themselves and the Germans. This pact assured Hitler that he would not need to worry about a two-front war if he attacked France and the other democracies to the west.

The German invasion of Poland in September of 1939 is usually regarded as the beginning of World War II, even though the Japanese invasion of China marked the start of the war in Asia in 1937. The attack on Poland finally triggered a military response from France and Britain. Nevertheless, the fast-moving German forces quickly took Denmark, Norway, Luxembourg, Belgium, the Netherlands, and France while the Soviets

took not only their part of Poland but also Estonia, Latvia, Lithuania, part of Finland, and part of Romania. The Japanese captured French Indo-China. The Germans continued their expansion into Yugoslavia, Greece, and North Africa. In June of 1941 Hitler launched a surprise attack against the Soviet Union, his supposed ally. In December of that same year the Japanese attacked Pearl Harbor, Hawaii, in a forceful threat intended to get the United States out of the western Pacific. At first the Soviets in Europe and the Americans in Asia suffered huge losses to the well-armed and well-trained German and Japanese forces, but gradually the Allies turned the tide of battle. Soviet forces began pushing the Germans back in eastern Europe while American, Canadian, and British forces crossed the English Channel into France in June 1944. Allied forces led by the United States drove the Japanese back island by island in the western Pacific. Germany surrendered on May 8, 1945. Japan officially surrendered on September 2 of that same year after the Americans had dropped newly developed atomic bombs on Hiroshima and Nagasaki. U.S. President Franklin Roosevelt, aware of the U.S. Senate's rejection of Wilson's League of Nations after World War I, led the effort to bring the United Nations into existence and the United States into its membership even before World War II came to an end. The nations which had united to defeat the fascists were now to unite to preserve the peace.

Wars Since 1946

Within three years after the end of World War II, the Cold War broke out between the Communist Soviet Union and the democratic capitalist Western powers. In March 1947 U.S. President Harry Truman announced a new U.S. policy of assistance to governments threatened by Communist-led military action. This Truman Doctrine indicating a new strategy of actively "containing" Communism marked a major departure from the previous isolationist stance of the United States. In June 1947 the United States launched a giant relief program, the Marshall Plan, to help a devastated Europe recover from the war and prevent the people there from turning to Communism. The Soviet Union kept its military forces in eastern Europe in order to establish a buffer zone on its western front. Quarrels developed over the terms of peace ending World War II. In eastern Europe Stalin did not permit the free elections to which Americans thought he had agreed. Germany was divided into an eastern part controlled by the Soviet Communists and a western part controlled by Britain, France, and the United States. In 1948 the Communists staged a coup d'état in Czechoslovakia. They then tried to keep the Western powers from moving into or out of West Berlin, which was completely surrounded by Communist-held east Germany. The Western powers responded by developing an airlift to transport supplies into West Berlin, in effect daring the Communists to try to stop the planes. In 1949 the Western countries formed a new tightly organized anti-Soviet military alliance, the North Atlantic Treaty Organization (NATO). When a newly independent West Germany was allowed to join NATO in 1955, the Communists countered by forming their own alliance of the Soviet-controlled eastern European countries called the Warsaw Treaty Organization (WTO) or Warsaw Pact.

In China the Nationalists and the Communists continued their civil war which had begun even before the Japanese attack on China in 1937. The Communist forces under Mao Zedong took over all of mainland China and drove the Nationalist forces to the island of Taiwan in 1949. In 1950 in a divided Korea Communist forces in the northern part of the country attacked the non–Communists in the southern part. South Koreans resisted this attack with the help of American troops as well as that of several other nations after the U.N. Security Council declared the North Koreans guilty of aggression. After early losses to the Communists, the U.N. forces eventually fought their way back into North Korea and then pushed northward toward the Korean border with China. Chinese Communist "volunteers" entered the war and drove the U.N. forces back south. A truce finally set the border between North and South Korea close to

where it had been when the war started. A demilitarized zone was established, but no peace treaty was ever signed, so Korea remained a divided country with the north controlled by Communists and the south by non-Communists. Developments such as the accession to North Korean leadership of Kim Jong Il in October 1997 after the death of his father Kim Il Sung (July 1994) and the election of conciliatory Kim Dae Jung in February 1998 to the presidency of South Korea have led to the possibility that this long-lasting Cold War conflict may gradually be coming to an end.

In what had been French Indo-China the battle between Communism and capitalism was concentrated in Vietnam. During World War II Japan had taken control of this region. Vietnamese Communists under the leadership of Ho Chi Minh conducted guerrilla warfare against the Japanese, sometimes getting help from American special forces. When the Japanese surrendered in 1945, Ho, who viewed himself as the George Washington of Vietnam, assumed that his country would now be able to gain its independence. The French, however, wanted to reestablish their control over this resource-rich area. Consequently, Ho's guerrillas now turned their efforts to battling the French military forces. The decisive Communist victory over the French occurred at Dienbienphu in 1954. The peace agreement provided for a temporarily divided Vietnam with Ho's Communist forces in charge of the North and the non-Communists in charge of the south. Elections were to be held within two years to establish a government over a unified country. Some Americans had been sympathetic with Ho's fight for independence, but others were more concerned about his Communist ideology, especially in view of the Communist takeover of China in 1949 and the battle against Communist forces in Korea in 1950–1953. It was widely anticipated that if an election were to occur Ho would win and become leader of a unified Vietnam. Leaders in the United States decided to try to prevent this on grounds that a Communist victory in Vietnam would lead to Communists taking over in Cambodia, Laos, and even other Asian countries (the "domino theory").

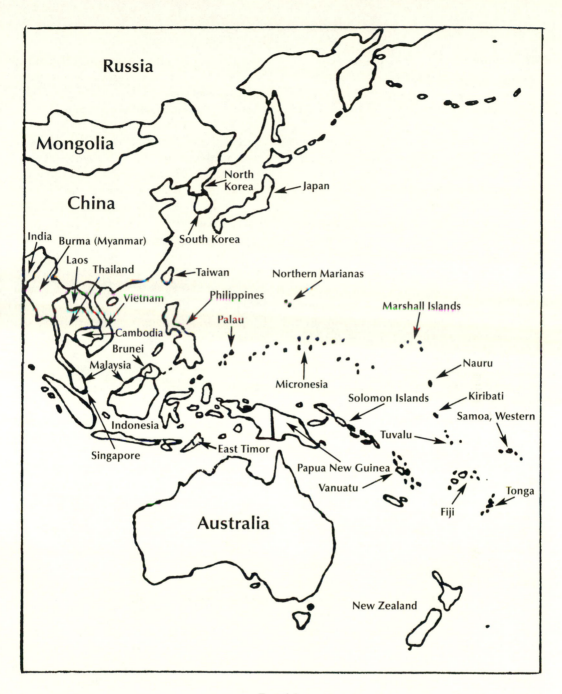

East Asia

This viewpoint led the Americans to decide to intervene and help the non-Communist south Vietnamese to maintain control in that part of the country. Just providing military advisors proved insufficient, however, so gradually more and more American forces were sent to Vietnam to halt "the spread of Communism." A major problem was that these American forces were perceived by many Vietnamese as preventing their country from escaping foreign domination. Vietnamese persistence along with protests within the United States finally led to American withdrawal in 1973. Less than two years after American personnel left, the non-Communist south Vietnamese forces surrendered. Cambodia and Laos were both taken over by the Communists just as the domino theorists had predicted.

What those theorists had not anticipated, however, was a 1979 invasion of Communist Vietnam by Communist Chinese forces, a territorial battle which flared briefly again in 1987.

A prime feature of the period after World War II was the gaining of independence by Asian and African colonies of western European nations, a change which both the Soviet Union and the United States favored, but for very different reasons. The Soviets wanted the opportunity to introduce socialism into the former colonies of the capitalist countries while the United States, having been a colony itself, wanted these colonies to become politically independent countries as it had done 175 years earlier. One result of this situation is that often in these former colonies there was an internal struggle between those who wanted a very militant socialist revolution and those who wanted a less radical change to an independent capitalistic country. In this struggle the Soviets tried to help those who favored a socialist grass-roots revolution while the United States and its allies tried to help the groups, usually the upper classes, who favored capitalism. This outside assistance usually included arms and other kinds of military assistance. The result was militaristic struggles rather than non-violent conflicts between these groups with opposing ideologies.

In some cases, as with Vietnam, independence came for these former colonies only after a long military struggle against the old colonial power.[10] In Algeria, Kenya, Indonesia, and Angola, for example, the former French, British, Dutch, and Portuguese rulers were driven out after long battles. In other cases colonies became independent nations with little or no military action against the former colonial power. For example, in 1946 the United States granted the Philippines the independence promised 45 years earlier during the Spanish-American War. Most African countries were able to make a rather peaceful transition from colony to independent nation-state, though many of them subsequently experienced internal strife.

On the Indian subcontinent the British left in 1947, nudged by the nonviolent resistance led by Gandhi. Unfortunately, enmity between Hindus and Muslims led to fierce fighting that continued even after predominantly Hindu India and predominantly Muslim Pakistan became separate independent countries. The first war between them lasted from independence in 1947 until 1949. As a result of a 1962 border war between India and China, Pakistan and China became friends against their common enemy India. In the India-Pakistan War of 1965-1966 much of the fighting again focused on who would control the strategic state of Kashmir lying between them. In 1971 an internal conflict within Pakistan led to East Pakistan, with assistance from India, becoming the separate country of Bangladesh. The tension between India and Pakistan remains high and has become even more dangerous as both countries displayed their capability to explode nuclear weapons in May 1998. The Kashmir dispute continues unresolved.

As the example of India and Pakistan just discussed illustrates, one feature of the post–World War II period has been wars between newly created or newly independent nations. Another example is Palestine where an ongoing conflict between the newly created state of Israel and the Arabs in that region has led to a series of wars. The conflict started with the adoption of a 1947 U.N. General Assembly resolution calling for the creation of a Jewish state and an Arab state in this area which had been placed under British control by the League of Nations. The Jews claimed they needed a homeland as a haven from persecution while the non-Jewish Arabs already living there protested against being required to become part of a newly created Jewish state. Fighting between Arabs and Jews broke out even before British forces left. In May 1948 the Jews proclaimed the existence of Israel and militarily defended it against the Arabs who wanted to destroy it. In fact, the 1949 truce left Israel in control of a bit more land than authorized by the 1947 resolution.

In 1956 the fighting resumed when the Israelis joined British and French forces trying to punish Egypt for nationalizing the Suez Canal owned by their citizens. U.S. President

ISRAEL

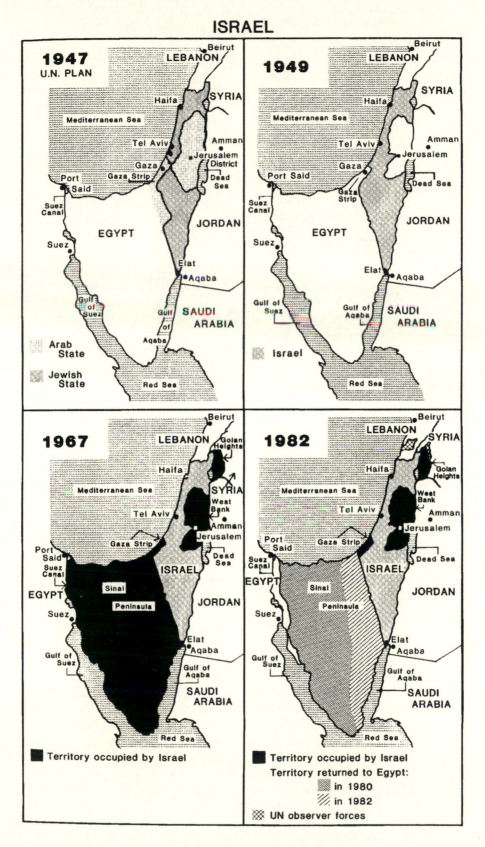

Israel and its neighbors.

Eisenhower, eager to keep the Soviets from sending troops into the region, worked with the Russians in the United Nations to stop the fighting. But in 1967 a third war erupted as Israel, unable to get help in overcoming an Egyptian blockade, launched a lightning attack on Egypt, Syria, and Jordan. In six days the Israelis gained control of the whole Sinai Peninsula, the Gaza Strip, the West Bank, all of Jerusalem, and the Golan Heights. The U.N. Security Council passed Resolution 242, calling for Israel to return the land it had just taken in exchange for recognition of its right to exist. In October 1973 a fourth war broke out, initiated this time by Arabs who had become impatient with the lack of progress in getting land back from the Israelis. The Israelis were pushed back at first but they soon regained all the territory they had lost and more. Again U.N. forces were stationed along the border to stop further fighting. The Camp David accords of September 1978 led to the Egyptian-Israeli peace agreement of March 1979 wherein Israel returned occupied territory in the Sinai Peninsula to Egypt in exchange for Egypt's recognition of Israel's existence as a nation. A "land for peace" agreement had been worked out with the Egyptians, which meant that the existence of the state of Israel was much less precarious.

But the warring did not cease. In June 1982 Israel invaded an internally chaotic Lebanon in an effort to eliminate the harassing military activities of the Palestine Liberation Organization (PLO) located in that country, but after three years of continuous fighting Israel pulled its forces back to a narrow strip of land just north of the Israel-Lebanon border. In 1988 the Palestinians living within the territory controlled by Israel launched a massive civil-resistance movement (the Intifadeh) demanding complete self-determination and freedom from military oppression. This protest presented Israel with a difficult choice. One possibility would be to try to continue indefinitely the subjugation of the large non-Jewish population living within the boundaries of Israel. Otherwise this large number of Palestinians would become full-fledged voting citizens, which would threaten the Jew-

ishness of the state of Israel. The other option was to allow the Palestinians to become citizens of their own separate state. The problem with this alternative, however, was that such a Palestinian state might become an instrument for the destruction of Israel.

In November 1988 the Palestinian National Council proclaimed the existence of an independent Palestinian state. At the same time PLO leader Yassir Arafat, in deference to the concerns of other countries such as the United States, renounced the use of terrorism and recognized the right of Israel to exist. The U.N. General Assembly, meeting in Geneva in December 1988, acknowledged the existence of an independent state of Palestine by a larger vote than the 1947 vote which had legitimized the existence of Israel.[11] After much negotiation supported by the United States and other nations, in September 1993 Israeli leader Yitzak Rabin and Palestinian leader Yassir Arafat signed a "Declaration of Principles" setting down the general terms of an agreement that would establish a Palestinian state alongside Israel. Negotiations continue on the many details still to be worked out such as exactly where the boundaries between the two states will be, the status of the Palestinian refugees whose ancestors had lived in the territory which is now part of the state of Israel, what will happen to Jewish settlements in territory claimed by the Palestinians, and — most difficult of all — the status of Jerusalem, which both groups want to be their capital city.

In many parts of the less-developed world independence has been followed by violent internal struggles for control of the new national governments. In Africa such disputes have occurred in Algeria, Angola, Burundi, Chad, Congo, the Democratic Republic of the Congo, Ethiopia, Ghana, Kenya, Liberia, Morocco/West Sahara, Mozambique, Nigeria, Rwanda, Sierra Leone, Somalia, South Africa, Sudan, Uganda, Zambia, and Zimbabwe.[12] Eritrea gained its independence from Ethiopia in 1993 after 19 years of fighting, and then had another border war against Ethiopia in 1998–2000. In Sri Lanka there has been ethnic violence between Tamils and Sinhalese since 1984. On the Mediterranean island nation

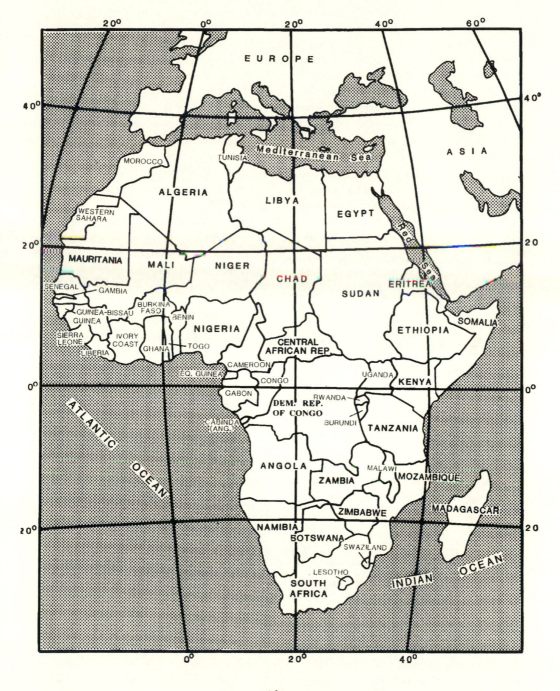

Africa

of Cyprus fighting began between the Greek and Turkish inhabitants shortly after independence in 1960, and in 1974 there was an invasion from Turkey in support of the Turkish Cypriots. In Indonesia after years of struggle East Timor got its independence in 1999.

In the Philippines there has been recurring civil strife, and in May 2000 ethnic conflict led to political violence in the island nation of Fiji in the Pacific.

But post–World War II warring has not been restricted to the newly independent countries. The conflict between Catholics and Protestants in Northern Island about the proper political status for that region waxes and wanes but a peaceful resolution has still not been implemented. Latin America has witnessed violent internal struggles in Bolivia, Argentina, Colombia, Cuba, the Dominican Republic, Guatemala, Chile, Nicaragua, El Salvador, Jamaica, Peru, and Haiti. El Salvador and Honduras fought each other in the "Soccer War" in 1969. In 1982 Argentina and Britain fought over control of the sparsely populated Falkland Islands–Malvinas in the South Atlantic. United States military forces invaded Grenada in 1983 and Panama in 1989. Internal struggle in Afghanistan starting in 1978 led to intervention by the Soviet Union from 1979 to 1989. In Iran in 1978 the Ayatollah Khomeini led an Islamic fundamentalist revolution ousting the Shah, and two years later Iraq attacked Iran in a war that lasted until 1988.

Despite all these "local wars" in various places, the critical struggle in the world from 1947 until 1989 was the Cold War between the Communist Soviet Union on the one hand and the democratic capitalist United States on the other. These two super-powers were engaged in an intense arms race which included nuclear arsenals with tens of thousands of nuclear warheads. Their military power, including their supply of nuclear weapons, greatly exceeded that of all other countries, and they were involved in most of the other conflicts just discussed. They were unquestionably engaged in an ideological struggle for world domination.

The pinnacle of the Cold War was the Cuban missile crisis of October 1962. Communist Fidel Castro had just led a revolution to take over Cuba at the beginning of 1959. In May 1961 an American-assisted attempted invasion of Cuba at the Bay of Pigs failed. The Russians apparently decided that they could not only deter future American counter-revolutionary efforts against Cuba but also improve their strategic nuclear position relative to the United States by putting nuclear-tipped missiles into Cuba (just as the United States had done in Turkey). U.S. President John Kennedy ordered American ships to try to keep the Russians from shipping in the materials needed to complete their project. The world held its breath as the Russian freighters approached the American ships which were to stop them. American planes with nuclear bombs were in the air headed toward Russia. On both sides missiles with nuclear warheads were poised to be launched. At the last moment Russian leader Nikita Khrushchev ordered the Russian ships not to try to run the blockade. An all-out nuclear war had been avoided.

This Cuban missile crisis suggested to both sides that it was time to consider ways to avoid having the same thing happen again. In 1963 the Partial Nuclear Test Ban was signed to stop putting ever more radioactive materials into the atmosphere. Nuclear tests were still needed to develop new weapons, but now they would be conducted underground. In fact, the nuclear arms race became even more intense as the Russians were determined not to have to back down again while the United States was determined not to permit the Russians to get nuclear superiority.

In order to have some kind of restraint in the nuclear arms race, treaties were adopted to limit the quantity of launchers each side could have. The most important was the Strategic Arms Limitation Treaty (SALT I) of 1972. It tried create a situation in which each side would be reluctant to launch a nuclear attack because of fear of retaliation by the other side. The principle was called "Mutual Assured Destruction" (MAD). That MAD strategic equilibrium required that one limit not only the number of offensive launchers but also the number of defensive missiles available to knock down incoming missiles. Thus part of SALT I was the Anti-Ballistic Missile Treaty (ABM Treaty) designed to limit defensive weapons.

Ronald Reagan, who became U.S. President in 1981, did not like the MAD strategy. He was not comfortable with the notion that if the Soviets launched a nuclear attack his only option as President would be to launch a retaliatory attack having no aim but revenge. He wanted some kind of defense to

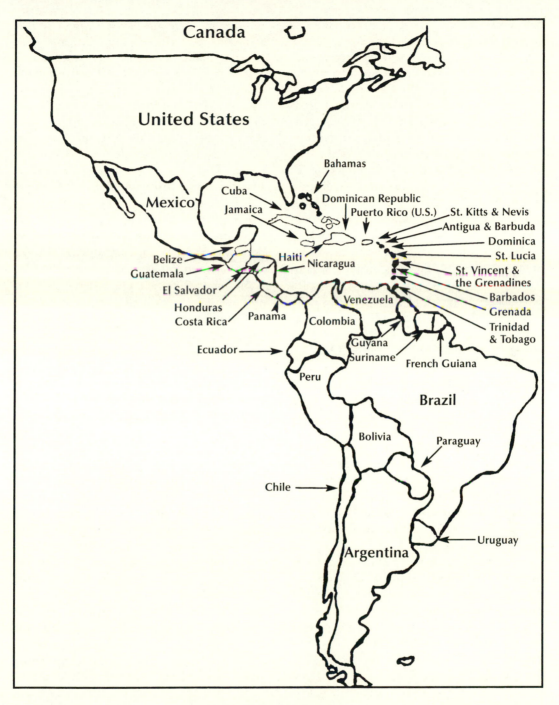

Latin America

stop incoming missiles. The proposed solution was a Strategic Defense Initiative (SDI) or "Star Wars Defense" based on satellites in space that could destroy an enemy missile just after it was launched. The problem with such a missile defense system is that it undermines the stabilizing equilibrium of MAD. The side with a defense system has an overwhelming strategic superiority. In fact, whoever has such a defense system actually gains an *offensive* advantage because a first strike could be launched and then the defense system used to wipe out whatever retaliatory strike the other side could still muster.

If the Americans were to try to build such an expensive defense system, in order to preserve equilibrium the Russians would need to do the same, but could they afford it? President Reagan was confident that the U.S. economy could support such military expenditures but that the Russian economy could not. Mikhail Gorbachev, who became leader of the Soviet Union in 1985, realized that Reagan was right. In fact, the Soviet economy was already faltering. Thus, Gorbachev, who was well educated about Western ways of thinking and doing things, tried to reform the Soviet system so that it would be more open and productive. He was also eager to enter into arms agreements that would slow the arms race. The beginning of the end of the Cold War came when Reagan and Gorbachev met in Reykjavik, Iceland in October 1986. One subsequent result was the signing of the Intermediate-Range Nuclear Forces (INF) agreement in December 1987. Gorbachev was indicating that he wanted to end the arms race. He also made other conciliatory moves such as withdrawing Soviet forces from Afghanistan in April 1988 and stopping the use of Russian forces to silence expressions of pro-independence views in the Soviet-controlled eastern European satellite countries such as Poland. In November 1989 he even allowed the Berlin wall to be torn down.

Gorbachev apparently did not realize the impact his reforms of openness, democratization, and restructuring would have. The last thing he wanted was the break-up of the Soviet Union. But those who had been oppressed for so many years realized that now was their chance to get out of the old system. As a result the satellite countries began declaring their independence from Russian rule. Then in March 1990 Lithuania, one of the 15 republics making up the Soviet Union, declared its independence. Gorbachev was not willing to use Russian military force to stop it if that was what the people wanted. In August 1991 some Soviet leaders tried to carry out a coup to remove Gorbachev from power before he could sign a treaty allowing any of the re-

publics to leave the Soviet Union if they wanted to do so. The coup failed, but it resulted in public and military support for Boris Yeltsin to take the very large Russian Republic and its resources out of the Soviet Union. The Soviet Union itself came to an end, and in December of 1991 Gorbachev resigned as its last president. The Cold War was over. The United States was the sole remaining superpower. During the four years from 1987 to 1991 the world had witnessed a transformation similar to what typically happens at the end of a war.

Simultaneous with the end of the conflict between the Soviet Union and the United States was another historic event, the Persian Gulf War of 1990-1991. On 2 August 1990 the military forces of oil-rich Iraq invaded the smaller oil-rich country of Kuwait. The U.N. Security Council, unable to act during the Cold War because of the veto power of the two superpowers, was now able to condemn Iraqi aggression. At first economic sanctions against Iraq were adopted, but they were ineffective. Consequently, on 29 November 1990 the U.N. Security Council authorized anyone who could do so to use whatever power necessary to get the Iraqis out of Kuwait. The United States took the lead in organizing a coalition to take military action against Iraq. The first phase of the action was massive air attacks which began in January 1991 after a deadline for Iraqi withdrawal had passed. Just over a month later a 100-hour very successful ground attack began. The Iraqis had no choice but to surrender. The responsibility for inspecting to eliminate all weapons of mass destruction from Iraq was turned over to the United Nations. The Iraqi aggression had been repelled. U.S. President George Bush, who had once served as U.S. Ambassador to the United Nations, spoke of a "New World Order" made possible by the end of the Cold War. Now the United Nations, under the leadership of the United States with its overwhelming military might and no longer encumbered by Soviet vetoes in the Security Council, could ensure that "the rule of law" would be enforced throughout the world. The concern of other countries was that the United

States was somewhat unilaterally deciding what is lawful and what is not regardless of what the rest of the world thinks.

The end of the Cold War allowed for the authorization of many new U.N. peacekeeping operations throughout the world. This happened not only because Russia (which had taken the place of the Soviet Union on the Security Council) was no longer vetoing such efforts but also because the United States was more ready to allow the United Nations to send in observer missions and monitor elections even in Latin America, but U.S. support for U.N. missions was changed to opposition in October 1993 by an incident in Somalia where 18 Americans were killed. U.S. President Bill Clinton blamed the United Nations for these deaths even though those killed were under U.S. command and were acting without the knowledge or support of U.N. officials.[13] This unfortunate incident became an excuse to stop U.S. support for any kind of new U.N. mission of any kind.

Nevertheless there was another conflict occurring during this period and shortly afterward where both the United Nations and the United States were involved, namely, the conflict in the former Yugoslavia. It had two phases, the Bosnia phase and the Kosovo phase. In June 1992, just two months after Bosnia and Herzegovina[14] had been recognized as a separate country no longer part of Yugoslavia, some U.N. forces were moved into that new country from their previous assignment in Croatia as part of the U.N. Protection Force. Its task was to protect civilians, mainly those dispensing humanitarian assistance.[15] Bosnia, and especially its capital Sarajevo, was ethnically diverse — Muslims, Serbs (mainly Eastern Orthodox Christians), and Croats (mainly Roman Catholic Christians). Radovan Karadzic used military force to try to create an ethnically pure Serbian section of Bosnia which then could be joined with the province of Serbia, still part of Yugoslavia, into a Greater Serbia. The U.N. Protection Force, not being given any orders from U.N. headquarters to fight back, was reduced to merely helping Bosnian Muslims to flee from death at the hands of the Serbs. By the summer of 1995, due to military support coming into Bosnia from Croatia as well as Muslims in Iran, Serbs in both Croatia and Bosnia were in retreat. On 12 October 1995 the United States intervened diplomatically in an effort to maintain a multiethnic Bosnia rather than having it geographically divided with the western part becoming integrated into Croatia and the eastern part joined to Serbia and possibly no contiguous geographical area at all for the Muslims. This American goal was achieved to some extent on paper at least by the Dayton Peace Accords signed on 21 November 1995. Elections were held in September 1996 to determine government leaders of the three groups, and all three winners were hardline nationalists. Peace is being maintained by a NATO-led Stabilizational Force (SFOR).

The conflict in Kosovo (the southern part of Serbia) became violent in the last part of 1998 as the ethnic Albanian Kosovo Liberation Army (KLA) began attacking Yugoslav police trying to protect Serbs living in Kosovo where ethnic Albanians are a 90 percent majority. The United States intervened diplomatically at the Rambouillet Conference in France with a demand that Yugoslav security forces in Kosovo be replaced by NATO forces. When Serbian leader Slobodan Milosevic refused, NATO began air strikes in Kosovo and Serbia on 24 March 1999. On 3 June 1999 Milosevic agreed to outside forces to monitor the situation in Kosovo. On 25 September 2000 an election was held for President of Serbia. The groups opposed to Milosevic finally worked together to elect Vojislav Kostunica though it was only the crowds in the street and the refusal of the police and military to fire on them that finally led Milosevic to acknowledge his defeat.

One of the outcomes of the strife in the former Yugoslavia was the creation by the U.N. Security Council on 22 February 1993 of a special War Crimes Tribunal to investigate the crimes committed during these ethnic battles. An effort has been made to focus attention on those commanding that such crimes be committed as well as on the individuals who actually did the killing, raping,

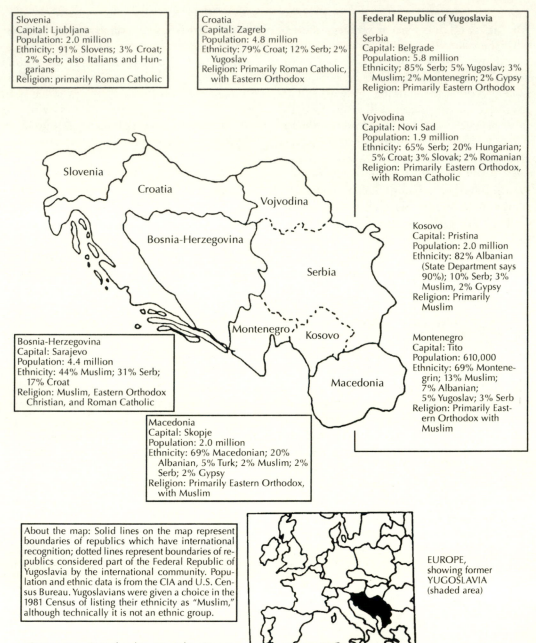

Slovenia
Capital: Ljubljana
Population: 2.0 million
Ethnicity: 91% Slovens; 3% Croat; 2% Serb; also Italians and Hungarians
Religion: primarily Roman Catholic

Croatia
Capital: Zagreb
Population: 4.8 million
Ethnicity: 79% Croat; 12% Serb; 2% Yugoslav
Religion: Primarily Roman Catholic, with Eastern Orthodox

Federal Republic of Yugoslavia

Serbia
Capital: Belgrade
Population: 5.8 million
Ethnicity; 85% Serb; 5% Yugoslav; 3% Muslim; 2% Montenegrin; 2% Gypsy
Religion: Primarily Eastern Orthodox

Vojvodina
Capital: Novi Sad
Population: 1.9 million
Ethnicity: 65% Serb; 20% Hungarian; 5% Croat; 3% Slovak; 2% Romanian
Religion: Primarily Eastern Orthodox, with Roman Catholic

Kosovo
Capital: Pristina
Population: 2.0 million
Ethnicity: 82% Albanian (State Department says 90%); 10% Serb; 3% Muslim, 2% Gypsy
Religion: Primarily Muslim

Bosnia-Herzegovina
Capital: Sarajevo
Population: 4.4 million
Ethnicity: 44% Muslim; 31% Serb; 17% Croat
Religion: Muslim, Eastern Orthodox Christian, and Roman Catholic

Montenegro
Capital: Tito
Population: 610,000
Ethnicity: 69% Montenegrin; 13% Muslim; 7% Albanian; 5% Yugoslav; 3% Serb
Religion: Primarily Eastern Orthodox with Muslim

Macedonia
Capital: Skopje
Population: 2.0 million
Ethnicity: 69% Macedonian; 20% Albanian, 5% Turk; 2% Muslim; 2% Serb; 2% Gypsy
Religion: Primarily Eastern Orthodox, with Muslim

About the map: Solid lines on the map represent boundaries of republics which have international recognition; dotted lines represent boundaries of republics considered part of the Federal Republic of Yugoslavia by the international community. Population and ethnic data is from the CIA and U.S. Census Bureau. Yugoslavians were given a choice in the 1981 Census of listing their ethnicity as "Muslim," although technically it is not an ethnic group.

EUROPE, showing former YUGOSLAVIA (shaded area)

Source: Arms Control and Foreign Policy Caucus

Parts of the former Yugoslavia.

and torturing. For example, the tribunal has indicted Serb leaders Radovan Karadzic, Ratko Mladic, and Slobodan Milosevic. The tribunal has also indicted Croats and Muslims in its efforts to prosecute all guilty parties regardless of ethnicity. One of the biggest problems has been getting custody of the indicted parties so that they can be sent to the court in The Hague for trial, but arrests have been made and monetary rewards have been offered to those who help bring indicted persons to the tribunal for trial.

Following the precedent set by the establishment of this special tribunal, another was established 8 November 1994 for genocide and other crimes committed in Rwanda where a group of Hutus massacred a large number of Tutsis in April and May 1994. Trials and convictions of some high-ranking leaders have been carried out.

As a result of the creation of these two *ad hoc* tribunals and the realization that similar atrocities are being committed at other places, at a conference in Rome in July 1998 a treaty was adopted to create a permanent International Criminal Court.[16] This treaty will go into effect when it is ratified by 60 countries. The effort to establish such an international tribunal to try *individuals* rather than national governments for violating certain international laws represents a giant step forward in the protection of human rights. It is an alternative to allowing government leaders to do whatever they want, especially to their own citizens, without being held accountable. The implementation and functioning of such a tribunal should help to decrease the number of wars in the world as national leaders come to realize that their power is not unlimited and that they are not immune to prosecution for their deeds.

The end of the Cold War has produced a very fluid situation in international affairs. For the moment the threat of a major war between nuclear powers seems to have receded. It is not clear exactly what kind of "world system" will result, though it seems that it will be a world with the United States very much in charge and probably sharing global decision-making to some extent with the other industrialized democracies in western Europe, Japan, and Canada. The United Nations apparently will be used as an instrument for policy but will be kept financially weak and dependent upon these rich nation-states. The same dependence on the more powerful national governments will probably also be the situation for other international organizations. If past history is an indication of what will happen in the future, we can expect that eventually some other country (maybe China) or group of countries (maybe a united Europe or a Western Pacific alliance with Japan as leader) will challenge the U.S. militarily for world

leadership. But perhaps the long war-filled period of a "civilized" world based on agriculture and state sovereignty and coercion by physical force is coming to an end. It may be that we are entering a new "post-civilized" world based on industrialization and technology, on a system of non-coercive global governance, and on the peaceful exchange of goods and services in order to get what we want.[17] The implementation of the International Criminal Court to hold individual government leaders accountable for their actions should also help to minimize the kind of behavior which causes wars. It is exciting to be alive during this period of human history which could conceivably see the end of the war problem for human society.

The Changing Nature of War

As already noted, warfare is as old as civilization. Yet wars fought in the 20th century are very different from wars fought four or five thousand years ago. For example, the global scope of the two world wars of the 1900s was much wider than that of the purely regional wars of earlier periods. Even more evident is the difference in the weapons used. The changing nature of war depends on the evolution of weapons,[18] but it depends at least as much on changes with regard to who has or is able to contend for political power and what their viewpoints are. As our definition of war indicates, the aim of warfare is the maintenance or acquisition of political power; weapons are merely the means used to accomplish that goal.

We can distinguish six periods in the evolution of war in the Western world.[19] (1) The "Ancient War Period" starts at the very beginning of civilization and in Europe comes to an end at the close of the Middle Ages with the introduction of gunpowder about 1350. (2) Then begins the "Post-Feudal Gunpowder Period" which concludes with the Thirty Years' War (1618-1648). (3) The "Limited War Period" lasts from 1650 to the beginnings of the industrial revolution and democratic political thinking about 1775. (4) The "Modern War Period" goes from the American and French

Revolutions through the Napoleonic Wars and the American Civil War to the beginning of World War I in 1914. (5) The "Total War Period"[20] includes World War I (1914-1918), World War II (1937-1945), and the first few years after that when nuclear weapons and the virtually unstoppable intercontinental missiles to deliver them were first being tested. (6) The "Nuclear Stalemate Period" starts about 1960 after the Soviet Union developed missiles that could deliver nuclear warheads onto the United States, and it continues to the present.

> ### Six historical periods in the history of warfare:
> Ancient War Period (7000 B.C.E.–A.D. 1350);
> Post-Feudal Gunpowder Period (1350–1650);
> Limited War Period (1650–1775);
> Modern War Period (1775–1914);
> Total War Period (1914–1960);
> Nuclear Stalemate Period (1960–present).

During the "Ancient War Period" from the very beginning of civilized warfare and organized armies about 7000 B.C.E. until the middle of the 15th century C.E. only minor changes occurred in the manner in which wars were fought.[21] The chief weapons were swords, spears, shields, and bows and arrows. The chief defensive strategy was to build a high wall around one's home city while the chief offensive strategy was to conduct a siege of the enemy's home city. The aim of a siege was to get the other side to surrender by preventing those inside the city walls from getting any food or other supplies or to so weaken them that they could no longer resist an attack. Those attacking a walled city might use various devices such as battering rams or catapulted stones to damage the gates or the walls, while those inside would use devices such as arrows and hot tar or boiling water to keep the attackers away from the walls. In order to protect itself from a siege, each city would equip an army with shields, swords, and spears in order to try to maintain a supply of food from the surrounding land.

All the fighting was done on foot at first, but after 2500-2000 B.C.E. horses gradually came into use. Armor was worn both by the foot soldiers and those mounted on horseback. Various special skills were developed — javelin

throwing, throwing stones with a sling, shooting a bow while mounted on horseback, fighting from a horse-drawn chariot, and operating a catapult to throw large stones. Field fortifications (walls and trenches) were built. Ships transported troops and supplies. Eventually other ships were designed to ram the transport ships, either sinking them or disabling them, leaving them at the mercy of the attackers. In the 9th and 10th centuries the Vikings capitalized on using ships as vehicles for surprise raids on settlements along rivers and sea coasts. Inventions before the 14th century such as saddles and stirrups for those on horseback, the crossbow, and the long bow expanded the size of the battlefield but did little to change the overall conduct of war.

During the 300-year "Post-Feudal Gunpowder Period" starting about 1350 when gunpowder was first introduced to Europe from China, several major changes in the way war was fought took place. Catapults were replaced by cannons while bows and arrows were replaced by guns and bullets. The first guns were not nearly as effective as bows, but the cannons quickly proved to be superior to catapults as devices for bombardment. A crucial victory for gunpowder occurred in 1453 when the Turks used cannons to break openings in the walls of Constantinople, proving to all that a stone wall no longer provided a secure defense against attack.[22]

One major impact of the introduction of guns was the end of armored knights on horseback. In fact, one of the general consequences of the introduction of guns was a reduction in the gap between the military and coercive power of the nobility relative to the ordinary person. One could learn to shoot a gun rather quickly, but learning how to use a spear and shield while wearing armor and riding a horse took a great deal of training, something only the rich could afford. This switch to guns also meant that kings could recruit armies of paid soldiers, thus decreasing their reliance on the nobles under them. Firearms were gradually improved and became even more widely used during the 16th and early 17th centuries. Nevertheless the musketeers in the military were still accompanied by pikemen armed with spears who could protect them in close combat. Not until bayonets were mounted on muskets at the end of the 17th century did the pikemen become obsolete.[23]

During the "Limited War Period"[24] from the middle of the 17th century to the last part of the 18th century, war almost took on the character of a game between opposing commanders, usually drawn from the old nobility and now employed by kings. The other soldiers were landed peasants and others from the lower classes, but at the same time they were also thoroughly trained (actually "conditioned" might be a more appropriate word) professionals who were too valuable to lose in battles where rows of men armed with muskets fired volleys at each other from a distance of 50 paces. The spirit of the Enlightenment also suggested that the conduct of war should be rational and restrained. Consequently, armies tried to maneuver for advantageous positions, and the outmaneuvered commander of a unit might simply surrender before much fighting took place. The rest of the population, a vast majority, had little to gain or lose as the result of the war games being played between the armies of one king and those of another.

As already noted in our historical account of war between sovereign states, in the "Modern War Period" which began in the last part of the 18th century a new style of war-fighting developed, partly as the result of the beginnings of the industrial revolution and partly because of changes in viewpoint about who should have political power. An important improvement in weaponry was the development of the rifle so that it could shoot a spiraling, elongated bullet. As a result, the rifle, often used to shoot game, had a much longer range and was much more accurate than a musket. It was aimed at a very specific target, not simply pointed in the general direction of the enemy as was the case with muskets. Rifles were used with devastating effectiveness against the British by the Yankee hunter frontiersmen in the American Revolutionary War. The principle that a spiraling projectile has a greater range and more accuracy was also applied to larger weapons, so old-style cannons were replaced by rifled artillery. The superiority of the rifle

and rifled artillery was not lost on the weapons makers, and the industrial revolution meant that a very adequate supply of these more accurate weapons would be available for subsequent wars.

New thinking about who should have political power was at the very core of the American Revolutionary War (1775–1781) and the French Revolution (1789–1799). The change came as the result of the rebirth of the old Greek idea of the equality of all citizens and the notion that a state should be controlled by the citizens rather than by the nobles and a king. The greater equality among persons in military capability brought about by the use of guns was probably also a factor in this change. The thinking of the participants in these revolutionary wars was different too. They were citizens-become-soldiers who were motivated by loyalty to their community rather than to a king. In the American Revolution colonial legislatures had called on citizens to join in the battle for independence from Britain and King George III. On the British side, however, the soldiers were often paid mercenaries more interested in getting their pay from the king than larger political issues. In the French Revolution the nonprofessional but highly-motivated ordinary French citizens took up arms against the king's paid professional soldiers in order to defend the ideals of "liberty, equality, and fraternity."

In the Napoleonic Wars (1803-1815) nationalism became the new motivator. French citizen-soldiers now fought for the glory of France while the rest of the citizenry identified with the successes and defeats of that national army. The royal leaders of other European countries, fearful of what the success of the French forces would mean, eventually tried to motivate their own soldiers by appeals to nationalistic loyalty rather than just the fact that they were being paid by the king. Limited war fought by paid soldiers for the king was being replaced by unlimited war fought on the basis of loyalty to one's nation. This kind of nationalistic motivation continued after Napoleon's defeat in 1815 and provided support for the European governments as they conquered foreign lands and then defended these colonial empires. The industrial revolution provided the superior arms the Europeans (including the Europeans in the United States) needed to subdue the non-industrialized native peoples of Africa, Asia, and the Americas while nationalistic fervor provided the motivation for the armed forces to gain and maintain control of these colonies.

In the "Total War Period" which includes the two World Wars the industrialized countries began turning this mix of machine-produced weaponry and nationalistic motivation against one another. There were no more readily accessible areas inhabited by "savages" to be conquered so the industrialized countries began fighting each other for control of the areas to be exploited. The industrial revolution also played a key role in promoting the desire to control new areas, because industry needed an increasing supply of cheap raw materials and colonies could provide them. Colonies also provided a place to sell the manufactured goods being produced. And if the native populations couldn't or wouldn't buy what was being produced in the homeland, then those colonized areas would also be populated by Europeans who would buy the products from the factories back home. Of course, by the 20th century it was not only the Europeans who were in the colony game but also the Americans and the Japanese.

The new weaponry made available by industry and new technology in the 20th century included not only improvements in rifles and artillery but also the development of landmines, wire entanglements, grenades, torpedoes, machine guns, tanks, submarines, and bombs dropped from airplanes. Inventions originally intended for civilian uses — railroads, steam-powered ships, trucks, the telegraph and then the radio, airplanes, helicopters — were adapted to military uses. Military needs dictated other inventions — tanks and other armored vehicles, poison gas, antiaircraft guns, aircraft carriers, radar, jet-propelled aircraft, rocket-powered missiles, nuclear bombs, thermonuclear (hydrogen) bombs, nuclear-powered submarines, napalm, chemical and biological weapons, artificial satellites for information gathering and navigational assistance, precision-guided munitions, armor-penetrating shells, laser weapons, and so on. Modern scientific knowledge was and still is making available an ever wider range of destructive possibilities, and modern industry guaranteed that once new destructive weapons were invented they would soon be produced in substantial quantities.

All these new weapons also produced another aspect of "Total War," namely, the end of much concern about killing "innocent civilians." This change in viewpoint about civilians had at least two sources. One source was the extreme ethno-centric view that all persons in the enemy group were less-than-truly-human, so why make any effort to avoid hurting those who were civilians? This kind of immoral disregard for the lives of humans not of one's own ethnic group was probably facilitated to some extent by the attitude of Europeans in the 16th through the first years of the 20th century that the "savages" of America, Africa, and Asia were less than human. The other source was the view that winning the war by whatever means was more important than saving the lives of a few people who just happen to be in the way. The view on the part of many of those making the decisions was that it was too bad that some innocent bystanders got killed but that what was important was winning the war. Some critics of the indifference to civilian casualties have emphasized the dropping of the atomic bombs on Hiroshima and Nagasaki, but very large numbers of civilians were killed, sometimes deliberately, in raids using large conventional bombs or incendiary bombs such as occurred in Shanghai (1932), Guernica (1937), Warsaw (1939), Rotterdam (1940), London (1940–41), Hamburg (1943), Dresden (1945), and Tokyo (1945).

Another side of "Total War" was displayed during World War II and also afterward. Military needs came to occupy ever more people and consume ever more money during World War II,[25] but even during the Cold War (1947-1989) a substantial proportion of the population and the national budget in the Soviet Union and the United States as well as in other countries, was committed to getting ready for war. The national defense effort included the building of weapons, the designing of new weapons, and the development of any new technologies that might have military uses. The education of young people so they would be able to invent new weapons and otherwise contribute to being ready for war was also a part of the national defense program. Not only during war but also during peacetime, the distinction between military personnel who are essential to the war effort and civilian personnel who have nothing to do with war, a distinction that was so obvious in the middle of the eighteenth century, no longer seemed applicable. Even though the Cold War is no longer with us, it provided a glimpse of the degree to which all aspects of a society can be subordinated to military concerns not only when war is occurring but also when war is only a possibility. And in an anarchic international system, there is always some possibility of war. Consequently in the "Total War Period" an important issue for national governments even during peacetime was how to provide for national security. What needs to be done in order to be prepared to fight a war?

The development of nuclear weapons in 1945 at the end of World War II was the first step toward the "Nuclear Stalemate Period," but it didn't begin until about 1960 when the Soviet Union developed the missiles which gave it the capability to make a retaliatory nuclear attack on the United States. It must be remembered, of course, that only eight countries (the United States, Russia, Britain, France, China, India, Pakistan, and Israel) now actually have nuclear weapons and the missiles to deliver them, so not all countries have moved into the "Nuclear Stalemate Period." The notion of a stalemate strictly applies only when there is a conflict between two states or groups of states both of which have nuclear weapons at their disposal, either themselves or by virtue of having an ally who is ready to use them on their behalf. Consequently, even during this period of nuclear stalemate many smaller wars still occur between and within countries that lack such weapons. Furthermore, the "Total War Pe-

riod" could quickly return even for nuclear powers if international tensions increase because it is not yet certain that we have really entered a "Nuclear Stalemate Period" even for countries with nuclear weapons.

The long Cold War illustrates the start of the "Nuclear Stalemate Period."[26] By 1960 both the United States and the Soviet Union had large numbers of nuclear weapons, and the means of delivering them. Both were deterred from using them because of fear of a retaliatory nuclear attack. A specific example of where the possibility of nuclear war seems to have led to restrained behavior is the Cuban missile crisis in 1962. The risk of a nuclear attack led Soviet leader Khrushchev to decide not to try to go through the American naval blockade. If there had been no nuclear weapons at that time, it seems very likely that a war would have occurred. Despite extreme tensions and intense feelings and even some hot wars in some regions of the world, the United States and the Soviet Union managed not to use these weapons for 40 years.

We have already noted how the introduction of guns into Europe destroyed the superiority of the armored knights on horseback and led to greater equality in the status of individuals. It now seems that nuclear weapons plus missiles to deliver them may do something similar with regard to the equality of nations. (Although our focus is on the international stalemate resulting from nuclear weapons, other new technological developments such as chemical and biological weapons and the possibility of sabotaging computers also have devastating capabilities which discourage resort to warfare.) Weapons which use nuclear energy are so much more powerful than all previous weapons that they have introduced a totally new dimension into war. Consider the fact that one U.S. Trident submarine can deliver 24 megatons of destructive power. (See chart on page 164). That is eight times as much firepower as both sides delivered in the whole six years of World War II. A country which has a few nuclear weapons (or some biological and chemical weapons) can threaten to use these weapons against even a large country. Even the leaders of large and powerful countries must take such a threat seriously.

The notion that the "Nuclear Stalemate Period" has arrived will be tested in the conflict between India and Pakistan. Those two countries have had several wars against each other. What will happen now that both countries have nuclear weapons and the long-range missiles to deliver them? Will they now be more circumspect about getting into a war with each other? Could they afford such a war? When a cost-benefit analysis of a possible nuclear war is conducted, how many inhabited cities can be sacrificed in order to gain control over a little more land in Kashmir? The tremendous destructive capability of nuclear weapons plus the possession of virtually unstoppable missiles to deliver them means that the inclination to go to war to decide some issue should be checked.

Another aspect of the "Nuclear Stalemate Period" is the question of whether nuclear weapons are useful as weapons of war even if they are somewhat useful in intimidating others. What if the Russians had not backed down during the Cuban missile crisis? Suppose that the United States had delivered a large number of nuclear warheads onto the various cities and military installations of the Soviet Union with almost no response from the Soviets. A factor that must be considered with regard to using nuclear weapons is the likelihood that use of these weapons will have a long-term devastating effect on the attacking country and its population even if there is no counter-attack by the other side. The atmospheric radioactivity and the depletion of the protective ozone layer will have negative effects on everyone, not just those against whom the nuclear weapons were launched. Also, who would have the responsibility of taking care of all the helpless victims who happen to survive? Wouldn't that task fall to the attackers? Still another issue to be considered is, Would the government of the United States which launched such an attack have increased its political power (which is the aim of warfare), or would many survivors in the United States as well as the rest of the world just refuse to give any further support to a government which had launched such a monstrous attack?

And what is the situation if there is a retaliatory response so that we have a full-scale nuclear exchange between two nuclear powers? Such an exchange might well annihilate all life on Earth, if not immediately then gradually as the radioactivity is spread everywhere and the protective ozone layer is destroyed. It is ironic that people can be so concerned about a moderate release of radioactive material from the nuclear power plant at Chernobyl in 1986 and not realize that the negative consequences of that event are nothing compared with what will happen in an exchange of nuclear weapons. People are rightly concerned also about the release of ozone-layer-destroying CFCs into the atmosphere but seem less aware that damage to the ozone layer would be incomparably greater from an exchange of nuclear weapons. War with nuclear weapons has been rightly described as a "war without winners."

Another way in which nuclear weapons have an impact on war is related to the decision to begin a war. In the days before nuclear weapons and long-range missiles to deliver them, leaders could decide to launch a war and be relatively confident that they themselves would not personally suffer as a result for at least a couple of years. With nuclear weapons and long-range missiles it is quite possible that they would be killed within hours. When leaders themselves are at this level of risk, it can be supposed that they will be much more reluctant to start a war.

The existence of nuclear weapons obviously has not put an end to war, especially for countries which do not have nuclear weapons. But among the big powers likely to be engaged in a big war, the availability of nuclear weapons does make a great difference.[27] The long Cold War between the United States and the Soviet Union would undoubtedly have become a hot war if they had not had nuclear weapons. The fact that there was such a long and intense conflict but no outbreak of war between them has led some writers to begin to use the expression "Pax Atomica,"[28] the nuclear peace. We cannot be sure that it will last. After all, the past development of "horrible weapons" has not prevented wars from continuing and getting even more horrible.[29] Still, we seem to have entered a new period in the history of warfare where the weaponry has become so destructive that the best option seems to be to develop an alternative to war for resolving international conflicts.

This period of stalemate among the big powers has also been accompanied by the increase of wars within countries in the less industrialized, less politically mature parts of the world. These "wars of the third kind" have become the predominant kind of war since the beginning of the nuclear age at the end of World War II in 1945.[30] It is these wars within states-in-the-making that will require special attention in the first part of the 21st century. Nevertheless we need to remember that peace between the established states may require more than just nuclear deterrence. The current hegemonic influence of the United States could get challenged by other nations with a devastating war as the result, just as a challenge to the hegemonic influence of the British Empire in the early 20th century resulted in World War I.

The Present Urgency of the War Problem

Is the solution of the war problem of any particular urgency at the present time? Has the availability of weapons of mass destruction created a stalemate in which no nation will dare to attack another? Is there any danger that scientists will develop new nonnuclear weapons which will make "conventional" wars more devastating than they have been in the past? Does the end of the Cold War present us with some opportunities for developing a more satisfactory world order which will eventually be lost if not used? Will the cost of preparing for future wars be a drag on the economy of richer countries and a hindrance to economic development for poor countries?

In dealing with the urgency of solving the war problem we need to recall the various aspects of the war problem outlined in the first chapter. The first aspect is the huge outlay of money and effort which presently goes into getting ready for war. Current worldwide expenditure for military purposes is over $785 billion a year.[31] Over 33.8 percent of this world-wide total ($265.89 billion) is spent by the United States,[32] even though its proportion of the world's population is only 5 percent. In fact, the 1999 U.S. military budget is greater than the next ten countries combined,[33] though in comparing these figures one must remember that all kinds of military expenses (for salaries for military personnel, for researching and purchasing new weapons, and for developing new weapons systems) tend to be higher in the United States than in most other countries.[34] As the weapons of war become ever more sophisticated, it can be expected that the weapons themselves will cost more and the military personnel who use them and maintain them will need to be paid more. It may be necessary to raise pay levels considerably in order to recruit enough soldiers with the needed capability as well as to induce them to stay in the military. The most important financial factor will be the high purchase price of more sophisticated weapons because of the great cost of developing ever more sophisticated weapons systems, such as the missile defense system currently being developed by the United States. The need to keep technologically ahead of all other countries, not only potential enemies, generates a virtually open-ended demand for more money for new weapons research and development. Even if actual war never comes, if the war problem is not solved the cost of getting ready for war is likely to be an increasing burden. There will also be the continuing cost of storing or getting rid of nuclear waste from the making and recycling of nuclear warheads. The huge military budgets of the U.S. and Russia in the tense periods of the Cold War provide a glimpse of what may lie ahead if new rivalries develop, not only between major powers but also between smaller and poorer countries.

We can also look at this issue of how much it costs to fight or prepare for war in terms of the percentage of the Gross Domestic Product (GDP) which is devoted to military spending by countries which are in a war or faced with a likelihood of war. Here are figures for 1998 for some of them:

Eritrea	35.8 percent of GDP
Saudi Arabia	15.7 percent of GDP
Afghanistan	14.5 percent of GDP
North Korea	14.3 percent of GDP
Oman	13.6 percent of GDP
Kuwait	12.9 percent of GDP
Qatar	12.0 percent of GDP
Angola	11.7 percent of GDP
Israel	11.6 percent of GDP[35]

Such a large rate of expenditure for "defense" demonstrates the high cost of being in a war or preparing for war for both rich and poor countries. Note too that these figures reflect only that part of the cost which is being recorded as expenditures for "defense." They don't show the cost of lost lives or of replacing property destroyed in war.

The second aspect of the war problem is the danger of nuclear war and its possible disastrous consequences. The destructiveness of nuclear weapons makes it obvious that such a war would be vastly more devastating than anything humankind has previously experienced. As previously noted, one U.S. nuclear-powered submarine carries more destructive power than was unleashed by both sides during all of World War II. The number of nuclear weapons has been declining since the end of the Cold War because of reductions by the Americans and the Russians, but the five long-established acknowledged nuclear powers together still have more than 30,000 nuclear warheads (10,500 for the United States, 20,000 for Russia, 185 for Britain, 450 for France, and 400 for China).[36] Only the United States and Russia have committed themselves to reducing their stockpiles of nuclear weapons. At the end of 1998 13,000 of their warheads were on strategic (long-range) weapons, 5,972 for the Russians[37] and 7,200 for the United States.[38] Even if the goals set by the START II agreement are reached in a few years, the U.S. and Russia would still together have about 7,000 nuclear warheads on strategic weapons.[39] Even as the United States dismantles some nuclear weapons, it is nevertheless simultaneously building new ones.[40] Israel, India, and Pakistan also have nuclear weapons, and other countries such as North Korea and Iraq have been trying very hard to develop them along with the missiles to deliver them.

With the U.S. and the former Soviet Union dismantling many nuclear warheads, a substantial amount of the crucial enriched uranium and plutonium needed to build nuclear weapons could conceivably end up in the wrong hands. There is also the danger that unemployed Soviet nuclear scientists might sell their knowledge and skills to the highest bidder. It is very possible that several other countries will have nuclear weapons by the year 2020. If protecting one's national interests in the international arena means having more military power than anyone else, how can we suppose that countries which do not yet have nuclear weapons won't try to get them or some other kind of new and even deadlier weapons? Unless the way the world system works is changed, we can expect that there will eventually be new nuclear arms races, possibly between India and Pakistan, possibly between Israel and some Arab countries, possibly between the United States and China, possibly between Japan and China.

If nuclear weapons were ever used in very large numbers, even the nations not directly attacked would be adversely affected by the radiation, the atmospheric dust and smoke from nuclear explosions and the resulting fires, and the depletion of the ozone layer. Historically the increasing destructiveness of weapons was much more gradual than is the case with nuclear weapons. The introduction of nuclear weapons and intercontinental ballistic missiles represents a shift in destructiveness and the range at which it can be employed unlike any change in earlier history. It is a vastly greater break from the past than that which occurred when gunpowder was introduced or when airplanes were put to military uses. We are faced with "a qualitatively new situation in relation to war — the possibility and probability of annihilating the human race and all other forms of life on the planet earth."[41]

The notion that big powers possessing substantial numbers of nuclear weapons might get involved in a war but not use their nuclear weapons overlooks the logic of war and the tremendous advantage which comes from using nuclear weapons first rather than second. The aim of war is to use military power to prevail, to impose one's will on the other side. In such a situation if either side were facing defeat, it would want to use nuclear weapons rather than surrender. At the same time the side which was winning the war would want to use its nuclear weapons before sustaining such an attack from a desperate opponent. The side facing defeat would know that the prevailing side would be making that kind of calculation, so it would be led to use its nuclear weapons before the other side expected it. But the same logic would also lead the prevailing side to want to use its nuclear weapons before the losing side tried to launch an unexpected attack. Following this logic through to its end, each side would want to use its nuclear weapons as soon as the situation had deteriorated to one in which the conflict was to be resolved by force. Those who argue for nuclear surgical strikes in a limited nuclear war assume a detachment on the part of the leaders of both sides which, if it existed, would not allow any kind of war to develop in the first place. It seems that the only alternative to a nuclear disaster is to prevent *any* war between major nuclear powers from breaking out in the first place.

Our good fortune in making it through the Cuban missile crisis plus the other high points of tension in the Cold War may have engendered a false sense of security. But if there has already been one arms race with each side being ready to launch over 20,000 nuclear warheads, a similar thing could happen again. Having played Russian roulette and been lucky enough to have found an empty chamber, we cannot afford to blithely suppose that things would turn out so well the next time. It would be best to find a way of avoiding that dangerous game.

The third aspect of the war problem is the possibility of conventional war between nonnuclear powers. There is always the danger that the big nuclear powers would get dragged into such a war just as big powers got dragged into World War I as the result of disputes between smaller nations. Also it must be remembered that conventional weapons themselves are becoming more and more destructive. Missiles can be used for the long-distance targeting not only of nuclear warheads but also of conventional and chemical warheads, and the increasing precision of smart bombs and precision-guided missiles means that it is not necessary to have a nuclear explosion to destroy the target. It has been noted that new devices such as cluster bombs and fuel air explosives mean that "both in lethality and in area covered, so-called conventional weapons today approach small nuclear weapons in destructive power."[42] The development of technology is such that more and more countries will obtain these very destructive nonnuclear weapons and will be ready to use them in war if that is what it takes to prevail. It should be obvious that these "little" conventional wars are small only by comparison with what might be expected in a war using nuclear weapons.

The fourth aspect of the war problem is the occurrence and the threat of the occurrence of civil wars. Indeed, these "wars of the third kind" are becoming the most prevalent kinds of war at the present time.[43] Many of these intranational wars are the result of intense ethnic rivalries which we don't yet know how to handle. The ready availability of weapons with substantial firepower plus the development of techniques of guerrilla warfare plus the existence of devices for duplicating printed materials and tape cassettes and videocassettes at low cost has given those dissatisfied with a government and its policies a much greater opportunity to mobilize a revolt. Another important factor relevant to civil war is the widespread belief that the government has the responsibility to promote the general welfare of the society. If important problems go unsolved, the government is blamed — even if the matter is outside of its power. Also, the upper classes no longer have a monopoly on knowing how to use weapons or how to read, write, think, and speak out about social issues. Since the poor are now more aware of what will promote their interest and since those interests are usually not the same as the interests of those who hold political power, civil war between these groups with opposing interests is much more likely than in the past.

There is still another way in which a solution to the war problem is more urgent today than in the past, at least from the perspective of ordinary citizens. There was a time, as late as the 18th century, when anyone who didn't want to participate in a war could simply ignore it. Armies employed by kings fought against each other and did little to disturb ordinary citizens, who for the most part were completely indifferent concerning whether they were to be subjects of King A or King B. But, as we have noted, that is no longer the case. Now even civilian jobs have military significance, and during a war any citizen is likely to be the subject of an enemy attack. As we have already pointed out, in modern warfare the number of civilians getting killed greatly exceeds the number of military personnel getting killed. World War II meant a gigantic upheaval in the lives of millions of people, but there were some places (part of Latin America and Africa) where the war made little difference, at least directly, to the lives of the people there. If there is a World War III with nuclear weapons, however, no one will escape. Even people in nations which have no involvement in the war will be affected by radioactive fallout, by large amounts of dust and smoke in the atmosphere, and by the alteration of the ozone layer which protects them from excessive amounts of ultraviolet radiation from the sun.

Smaller wars now have a wider impact, too. Americans learned in 1973-74 that war in the Middle East made a great deal of difference in the availability and price of oil. The same was true with regard to the civil war in Iran in 1978-79 when the price of gasoline again rapidly increased. Civil wars in Central America may have an impact on the prices Americans pay for coffee or fresh fruits and vegetables. On the other hand, such wars may eventually open up new opportunities for people in some less developed countries — education, medical care, and better housing.

Solving the problem of war is more urgent now than in the past also because the higher cost of war preparations must be borne by the general public. For example, in the United States, even though the Cold War is over, in 1998 military expenditures averaged over $80 per month per person ($320 per month for a family of four),[44] and that does not even count the huge amount needed to pay off the national debt, a large proportion of which is due to past military spending. This cost of preparing for war even in peacetime means less goods and services for everyone both directly and in terms of less productivity in the long run. In less developed countries as well as more advanced ones, military spending means less much-needed government money for schools, medical care, police and fire protection, roads and public transportation, and other social services.

Today no persons anywhere on earth can truthfully say that solving the war problem makes no difference to their own lives.

Part Two.
Causes of War

4.   The Cause of War:
General Considerations

Our basic assumption is that war is a disease of society. It is a sickness that we would like to eliminate. This analogy leads to the expectation that perhaps wars could be prevented if we learned more about what causes them. As a result of this pattern of thinking, a great deal has been written and said about what causes wars.[1] In dealing with this issue it is worth pausing to consider exactly what is involved in saying that one kind of event causes some other kind of event. Then we need to look at the phenomenon of individual human aggressiveness and consider what relationship, if any, it has to those violent conflicts we know as wars.

Investigating the Cause of War

There are at least four senses in which the word "cause" can be used: (1) a necessary condition, (2) a sufficient condition, (3) a necessary and sufficient condition, and (4) a contributory factor.

(1) A "cause" in the sense of a *necessary condition* means that the effect cannot occur if the cause (whatever it is) is absent (that is, not present). If the necessary condition of something is known, one will then know how to prevent that event from occurring. For example, the presence of oxygen is a necessary condition for materials such as wood and paper to burn and keep on burning. It follows that one can extinguish such a fire by using a gas such as carbon dioxide, which is much heavier than oxygen, to prevent oxygen (the necessary condition) from getting to the burning wood or paper. The carbon dioxide smothers the fire by keeping oxygen from getting to it.

(2) A "cause" in the sense of a *sufficient condition* means that the effect must occur whenever the cause (whatever it is) is present. If the sufficient condition of something is known, one will know how to make it occur. For example, the flow of electricity through a wire made of a metal such as aluminum or copper is a sufficient condition to produce heat. It follows that one can make heat (for a toaster or an electric blanket, for example) by producing a flow of electricity through a metal wire (the sufficient condition).

(3) A "cause" in the sense of a *necessary and sufficient* condition means *both* that the effect cannot occur if the cause (whatever it is) is absent *and* that whenever the cause (whatever it is) is present the effect must occur. If the necessary and sufficient condition of something is known, one will know both how to prevent it and how to produce it. For example, the flow of electricity through the filament of an incandescent light bulb is the necessary and sufficient condition of the bulb giving off light. One can stop the bulb from glowing by cutting off the supply of electricity (the necessary condition), and one can make the bulb glow by letting electricity flow through the filament (the sufficient condition).

(4) A "cause" in the sense of a *contributory factor* means that the effect is *more likely*

57

to occur because of the presence of something, but the relationship is *not* a *necessary* one. It is possible for the cause to be present and the effect not to occur, and it is also possible for the cause to be absent and the effect to occur anyway. If a contributory factor of something is known, one will be able to make it more probable or less probable but will not be able to guarantee any results. For example, smoking cigarettes is a contributory factor to developing lung cancer. That means that smoking cigarettes makes it *more likely* than one will develop lung cancer. Nevertheless some people smoke cigarettes and don't get lung cancer, and others don't smoke but still get lung cancer. There is no *necessary connection* between smoking cigarettes and developing lung cancer, but there is a *probabilistic* connection.[2] Those who smoke cigarettes are *increasing the probability* that they will get lung cancer, and those who don't smoke cigarettes are *decreasing the probability* that they will get lung cancer.

How do these four different senses of "cause" apply to the problem of the cause of war? It seems that if our goal is to prevent wars, we should search for some *necessary conditions* of war. We could then eliminate war by eliminating any one of these necessary conditions. The problem is to discover some necessary condition that we could and would want to eliminate.[3]

Our definition of "war" mentions several things that must be present in order to have a war. These things are necessary conditions. Consider, for example, that the existence of war as we have defined it requires the existence of groups of people. If we eliminated all people or somehow made it impossible for people to form groups, we would eliminate war. But these proposed cures are worse than the disease. We need to find something less drastic.

According to our definition war is large-scale violent conflict between organized groups. It seems that if we eliminated all conflicts between groups, we would then also have eliminated war, that is, *violent* conflicts between groups. Trying to eliminate all conflicts between groups is certainly less dras-tic than eliminating all groups. But the problem with this approach is that eliminating *all* conflict between groups is even more difficult than simply eliminating the large-scale violent conflicts which constitute war. Those who think that the only way of eliminating war is to eliminate *all* conflicts of interest between groups are focusing on an even more difficult problem than they had to begin with. Furthermore, as we have previously noted, in some situations conflict may even be desirable.

What is to be said about the view that since individual human aggression is a necessary condition for the carrying on of war, the way to eliminate war is to eliminate *all* individual human aggression? Once again, it seems that eliminating all human aggression is a more difficult task than eliminating war. We need not achieve that virtually impossible goal in order to rid the world of war.

Since it seems that we cannot find any necessary condition for war except those whose elimination would either be undesirable or even more difficult than the elimination of war itself, we need to look elsewhere for ideas on how to prevent wars.

Let us consider this problem of preventing war in terms of the "cause" of war in the sense of a *sufficient condition*. It seems that what we need to find is not the sufficient condition to produce *war* but rather the sufficient condition for producing *peace*. Is there anything which when present always produces peace? Theodore Lentz, the father of peace research, observed that just as medical researchers interested in preventing disease sometimes focus their attention on unusually healthy groups of people to learn what produces such good health, so peace researchers should focus their attention on peaceful societies to learn what produces them.[4] Efforts to find peaceful societies have reached the conclusion that most of these peaceful societies are pre-industrial.[5] The search has just begun, however, and there are some nations such as Switzerland and Sweden which seem to have very good records in avoiding wars with other countries during the past 200 years. Investigators are also turning their attention to the cause of peace *within* countries. There are many nations which have been relatively free from internal strife for long periods of time (including Switzerland and Sweden). We need to examine these societies and their institutions to try to discover the cause of peace within these communities. In the second chapter we tried to find something which is "an alternative to war" on the basis of changing the word "violent" to "nonviolent" in our definition of "war" (see Chapter 2, page 15). If that discussion is on the right track, it seems that a properly functioning democratic society where leaders are chosen by a vote of the people might be a sufficient condition of peace.[6]

Since the concept of "cause" as "necessary and sufficient condition" does not involve any issues not already discussed in connection with the separate concepts of necessary condition and sufficient condition, only the concept of *contributory factor* remains to be considered in our quest for understanding the cause of war. The use of the word "cause" to mean "contributory factor" is most likely to be relevant when one is considering the causes of some very complex phenomena, and there can be little doubt that war is a very complex phenomenon. When people say that *nationalism* is a cause of war or that *individuals who make profits from selling arms* are a cause of war, they are most likely using the word "cause" in this sense of *contributory factor* rather than in the stronger sense of necessary condition. They are claiming merely that if nationalism were reduced, or if the profits from selling arms were reduced, the likelihood of war would be reduced. They are *not* claiming that one cannot have a war unless nationalism is present or that one cannot have a war unless some people are making profits from selling arms. Nationalism and profiting from arms sales are things that may make war *more likely* but they are not causes in the sense of necessary conditions for war.

One must remember, however, that being a cause of something in the sense of being a contributory factor is not just a matter of being correlated with that thing. For example, suppose that for many different na-tions over some period of time one finds a positive correlation between (1) military spending and (2) the number of casualties suffered in war. That is, (1) spending more on the military and (2) having more war casualties are things that seem generally to go together. Does this prove that high military spending *causes* a nation to get involved in war and suffer many casualties as a result?[7] Saying that it is *more likely* that a nation with high military spending will be engaged in war and suffer casualties is not the same as saying that high military spending *causes* (is a contributory factor to) involvement in war and casualties. For example, there may be tension between two nations which leads them to increase their military spending. A war accompanied by high casualty counts may follow. But such a war might have occurred even sooner and been even bloodier if one of the nations had not increased its military spending in the face of tension. The positive correlation between a country's military spending and its casualties from war might be the reflection of some common cause for both (increased tension) rather than a causal connection between military spending on the one hand and the occurrence of war on the other.

There is still another point related to the issue of causation which needs to be considered in seeking to discover the cause of war. We have previously noted the analogy which can be drawn between war and disease. Suppose that some physicians were to address themselves to the cause of disease. They would probably begin by noting that there is no cause of disease *in general* but only particular diseases with particular causes. They would probably note that some particular diseases can be put into classes on the basis of their various causes — diseases caused by bacteria, diseases caused by viruses, diseases caused by genetic factors, diseases caused by toxic chemicals in the environment, and so on. They would then note that any attempt to make statements about *the cause* of all these various kinds of diseases is bound to fail.

Couldn't a similar point be made with regard to the subject of the cause of war? Perhaps it is inappropriate to try to make any judgments about *the cause* of war *in general.* Perhaps one should begin by examining particular wars and the particular causes of those wars. Then one could try to classify these cases of wars on the basis of their different kinds of causes. World War I and World War II may be superficially similar in that they are the only two world wars in history, but in terms of their causes they may in fact be very different. Trying to discover some cause of war which is operative in both World War I and World War II (as well as all other wars) may be an exercise in futility. Furthermore, even in particular wars there seem to be several contributory factors with little expectation of deciding in a particular war which ones were most decisive.[8]

Once particular wars had been classified on the basis of their causes (if indeed that could ever be done with any kind of consensus), the next step would be to identify symptoms that appear before each kind of war actually breaks out. Then the knowledge about the various kinds of wars could be used to try to prevent particular wars. The situation would be similar to that of a physician who is familiar with different kinds of diseases and their symptoms and who can thus diagnose any developing particular illness and prescribe the right medicine for it. Ideally one could learn what type of "medicine" to use when symptoms of a particular kind of war appear so that the threatened war could be avoided. Even if such knowledge ever became available, however, it is questionable whether a knowledgeable "physician" of society would be consulted by political leaders or that anyone would pay much attention to taking the "medicine" which the "physician" of society prescribed.[9] In any case, it is evident that we are far from being able to deal with the problem of war in this manner. Previous efforts to classify wars have usually focused on their size rather than their cause, a situation comparable to classifying diseases in accord with the number of persons who suffer from them. Focusing on the *effects* of war or of disease is not likely to help us to discover the *causes.*

Before we leave this analogy between war and disease, we should note that there are some particular diseases such as some kinds of cancer where there are no known necessary and/or sufficient conditions. The only kinds of causes that are known are some contributory factors. Here we have a closer analogy with the situation of finding the causes of various kinds of wars. The best that can be done is to compile a list of the factors which make war more likely and then try to minimize each of them.[10]

What has been said in this section on the various meanings of the word "cause" is directly relevant to the examination of various theories concerning the cause of war to be undertaken in Chapters 5 and 6. All these theories must be viewed as being about *contributory factors* which are purported to be operative in some wars but not necessarily in all wars. We will be aiming to make true statements about the causes of war in the sense of some things which seem to be contributory factors in some wars. It is somewhat regrettable that our discussion of the cause of war will be carried on in such an imprecise way, but the present state of our ignorance permits no other approach.[11]

Individual Human Aggression

Aggression can be defined as "*any form of behavior that is intended to injure someone, physically or psychologically.*"[12] It is important to realize that when we use the term in this sense being "aggressive" is quite a different thing from being "*assertive.*" One can be assertive without intending to injure others. Our meaning of aggression is also different from "breaking the rules." There are often rules about not injuring others, but it is the injuring of others which is crucial to the behavior being classified as "aggression," not the breaking of rules. Note also that when the aggression is carried out *in order to accomplish some other goal* such as coercing other persons to do something they don't want to do or gaining the approval of others or punishing a child, it will be classified as "*instrumental aggression,*" but it is still aggression. It also is worth noting that it is quite possible to commit aggression, especially instrumental aggression, without being angry. If the intent of an act is to harm someone, the act is aggression even though no feeling of anger has occurred. The term "violence" refers to a particular kind of aggression. *Violence* is an "extreme form of aggression, *a deliberate attempt to do serious physical injury.*"[13] Thus violence can include actually killing the other individual.

Although the definition of "aggression" we are using focuses on doing harm to and possibly even killing another person, we don't want to overlook the relation between aggression and seeking status or dominance over others. One way for an individual to establish dominance is through the use of physical force or even violence against others, but it is not the only way, especially among humans. An individual can achieve higher status or dominance over others by being very clever or by being good at some highly-regarded skill such as peace-making or by being able to persuade others.[14] In many species of animals, including primates, there is competition for status or dominance, especially but not exclusively among males. This dominance can be mainly physical, but there are cases where a super-aggressive physically dominant individual is simply forcibly driven out from the group by collective action.

One can see parallels here between the role of aggression among individuals and the role of war among groups. *Individuals* within a group may use physical force or even violence to compete for status or dominance, and in war it is the *groups* which use physical force and even violence to compete against one another for status or dominance. Just as cleverness and other abilities, not just pure physical force, can be used by individuals to gain status and establish their dominance, so technological knowledge, sophisticated intelligence gathering, and other capabilities, not just pure physical superiority, can be used by groups such as nation-states to gain status and establish their dominance. And just as with individuals, if one dominant group becomes too aggressive, the others can join together to subdue it.

In chapter two we defined "war" as "large-scale violent conflict between organized groups which already are governments or groups which seek to establish their own government over some territory." Even though war consists of group fighting against group, ultimately the fighting must be done by individuals. These individuals will be using violence against the individuals in the opposing group. In war that extreme form of aggression is instrumental since its goal is to get the other side to capitulate. It is important, however, to distinguish between the aggressive behavior of *individuals as individuals* on the one hand and the aggressive behavior of *individuals as representatives of groups* which are at war with each other on the other. The explanation of the former type of behavior may have very little to do with understanding the latter type of behavior. The motives for the aggressive behavior in the two cases may be very different. Giving causes for the aggressive behavior of individuals as individuals is definitely not the same as giving causes for war.[15]

Although there is a question about how relevant the study of *individual* human aggression is to the war problem, it is appropriate to discuss the topic simply because many persons addressing the war problem have thought that it is relevant.[16] Furthermore, even if the relationship between individual aggression and warfare is not as direct as some writers have assumed, whatever relationship does exist can be better understood once the basis of individual aggression is understood.

Three main groups of theories have been advanced to account for individual aggressive behavior. The first group sees aggression as rooted in the biological nature of human beings. The second group sees aggressive behavior as instigated by the unpleasant feelings that accompany frustration. The third group of theories sees aggression as the result of one's social conditioning. These three approaches to the issue of why individuals are aggressive[17] are sometimes considered to be mutually exclusive, but they aren't. In fact, often proponents of one view note the need to incorporate the insights of the other approaches. For example, one supporter of Konrad Lorenz and the biological approach pointed out that it is a "fallacious idea that what is inborn cannot be affected by education."[18] The issue is rather how much emphasis to put on each kind of theory when one tries to understand aggression or control it.

According to the biological-instinctual theories, humans, like other animals, are born with a propensity or drive to be aggressive. Such behavior may be triggered by specific kinds of situations, such as defense of one's territory, but it may also, according to Konrad Lorenz and others, just "explode"[19] with no external stimulation. Sigmund Freud wrote of an instinct of destruction.[20] Robert Ardrey links aggressive behavior with what he calls "the territorial imperative"[21] and writes of the "weapons instinct"[22] which he believes developed in the killer apes from which humans are descended. Another proponent of this ethological approach is Desmond Morris.[23] A quite different version of the biological-instinctual approach has been put forth by Peter Corning. He emphasizes the evolutionary adaptiveness of the various inborn aggressive responses to specific kinds of situations.[24]

Biological-instinctual theorists rely to some extent on ethology, that is, on studies of animals in their natural environment. They find that aggressive behavior is exhibited primarily in three kinds of situations. First, there is aggressive behavior, primarily but not exclusively among males, for status or dominance in the "pecking order" within the group. Second, there is aggressive behavior among males of territorial species for individual territory within the group's overall territory. Third, there is collective aggressive behavior by males to defend the group and its territory from other groups. Defense of the young, primarily by females, may be mentioned as a fourth specific situation where aggressive behavior occurs, but among the theorists mentioned above only Corning seems interested in this particular manifestation of aggression.

Strong evidence that there is at least some biological, hormonal basis for aggression comes from the different levels of aggressive behavior between males and females, both in humans and non-human animals.[25] This sex difference is apparent even in young children. Although various hormones may be involved, the most important one for aggression seems to be the male sex hormone testosterone.[26] It affects both the development of the brain and the activation of the physiological mechanisms for certain behavior patterns. Even pre-natal females exposed to testosterone while in the uterus will display a greater tendency to aggressive behavior. There also seems to be a definite positive correlation between levels of testosterone in the blood and the degree of aggressive behavior in males, although this correlation is not as great in better educated, higher income males. Most criminal behavior in virtually all societies, especially that which involves physical attacks on other people, is committed by males after puberty and before old age, that is, when levels of testosterone are highest. Nevertheless some research is raising questions about whether the presence of more testosterone in the blood is something which produces aggression, something which merely exaggerates aggression, or possibly something that is the result of successful aggression.[27] The higher testosterone levels of dominant males may be the effect of achieving high status rather than something that causes it, and levels of aggressive behavior seem to reflect what is socially approved or disapproved as much as levels of testosterone. Nevertheless there is a strong correlation between levels of testosterone and amount of aggressiveness suggesting that there is at least some relation between that hormone and aggressive behavior.

Advocates of the biological-instinctual approach also appeal to careful observations of behavior by anthropologists and others which show striking parallels between what animals do and the behavior of humans, especially children and primitive peoples.[28] These many instances, it is claimed, show beyond doubt that there are genetic factors greatly influencing human aggressive behavior, including not only individual aggression but also intergroup warfare. That does not mean that the behavior cannot be modified by experience, but it does mean that those who want to make such modifications should know about the biological base on which they must build.[29] For example, we should realize that humans do have natural inhibitions against killing our own kind but these have been undermined by at least three developments: (1) the cultural development of viewing other ethnic groups as if they were not humans but members of another species, (2) the technological development of weapons that allow us to kill at a distance without perceiving our individual victims, and (3) the development of knowledge which allows the psychological manipulation of soldiers to nullify their natural inhibitions not to kill other humans.

A second group of theories about the cause of individual human aggression are those which view aggressive behavior as the result of hostility brought about by frustration. According to this approach, human beings are viewed as goal-oriented organisms. As long as they are making adequate headway in achieving their ends they do not become frustrated and aggressive, but when they are blocked from reaching their goals they become more irritable. This theory developed by John Dollard and his colleagues at Yale claimed that any kind of frustration leads to aggressive behavior.[30] Leonard Berkowitz has developed a revised version of the theory which emphasizes that frustrations generate aggressive tendencies only to the extent that they are unpleasant and that the unpleasantness depends on our expectations for satisfaction.[31] He also notes that people learn how to react to such frustrations on the basis of what kind of behavior pays off. If behaving aggressively gets us what we want, then we will learn to be aggressive while if some kind of nonaggressive response gets us what we want, we will learn to behave nonaggressively. Frustration leads to the disposition to be aggressive, but experience teaches us what kind of behavior works in dealing with this aggressive disposition. Readiness to allow for such learning on how to respond to feelings of frustration shows movement in the direction of accepting the social learning view, but proponents of this second approach continue to maintain that without frustration there wouldn't be aggression.

The third group of theories about individual human aggression emphasizes the role of social conditioning in aggressive behavior. According to this approach it is a mistake to assume that humankind has some fixed biological nature that makes people either aggressive or nonaggressive.[32] Human beings have the capability of learning to behave in many different ways depending on what kind of behavior is observed and consequently imitated, as well as on what kind of behavior is rewarded. Although this view is particularly associated with behaviorist psychologists such as John B. Watson and B.F. Skinner, many psychologists of other schools of psychology also favor the social learning theory. Anthropologists such as Margaret Mead, Ashley Montagu, and Geoffrey Gorer also are supporters of the social learning approach to explaining human aggressive behavior.

The evidence for the social learning view about the cause of aggressive behavior comes mainly from two sources: psychological studies which show how people's behavior and attitudes can be modified by conditioning and education, and anthropological studies which find very different behavior patterns in different cultures. Anthropologists can point to some societies, such as the Eskimos, where individuals are pugnacious but there is no group warfare; among others such as the Pueblo Indians, individuals are not pugnacious but there is group warfare.[33] This situation would suggest that both individual aggressiveness and group aggressiveness must be learned—separately. The social learning theory is supported also by the fact that adopted individuals reared from infancy in a culture different from that of their natural parents will display the attitudes and behavior patterns of the culture in which they are reared rather than that of their biological parents.

When the social learning theorists say that the environment causes the presence or absence of aggressive behavior, they mean that except in extreme cases of genetic abnormality or the like, the aggressiveness of an individual will be the result of the social conditioning to which the person has been exposed. The evidence about sex differences in aggressive tendencies mentioned in connection with the biological-instinctual theory cannot be ignored, but the social learning theorists claim that these inborn tendencies can be completely overcome by the proper training, as is demonstrated by the existence of many nonaggressive societies.

The casual observer might question the social learning approach on grounds that certain individuals, even offspring of the same parents, are very different in their aggressiveness though reared in the same environment. The social learning theorist responds that no two people, even children in the same family, have exactly the same environment. For example, there is a great difference between being a boy with a younger brother and being one with an older brother even when the boys are in the same family. It seems that, even though there may be some slight differences in the inborn tendency to aggressive behavior among individuals and even though people may be more likely to behave aggressively when frustrated, the most important factor determining the degree and kind of aggressive behavior displayed by individuals is their social conditioning.

The social learning approach is supported by evidence that aggressive behavior is displayed even in the total absence of any frustration or hostility by persons who are merely obeying orders to be aggressive. Such aggression would be classified as instrumental aggression, but it is still aggression. Furthermore, the context is somewhat similar to that which occurs during war. Stanley Milgrim conducted a classic experiment on aggression in the early 1960s which showed that people will administer what they believe are very strong injurious electric shocks to others just because they were told to do so. He concluded:

> Although aggressive tendencies are part and parcel of human nature, they have hardly anything to do with the behavior observed in the experiment. Nor do they have much to do with the destructive obedience of soldiers in war, of bombardiers killing thousands on a single mission, or enveloping a Vietnamese village in searing napalm. The typical soldier kills because he is told to kill and he regards it as his duty to obey orders. The act of shocking the victim does not stem from destructive urges but from the fact that subjects have become integrated into a social structure and are unable to get out of it.[34]

Experiments by Milgrim and others indicate that the intensity of aggression displayed by individuals in these experimental situations is totally independent of how frustrated they are.[35] In fact, in some experiments the amount of aggression displayed seems to depend much more on (1) the strength of the attack which stimulated the aggressive response and (2) what kind of reaction those behaving aggressively expected from others witnessing their aggression.[36] Such evidence challenges the validity of the frustration-aggression theory. It may be that on some occasions frustration produces hostility which produces aggressive behavior, but that viewpoint neglects the fact that aggressive behavior may be brought about by other factors which have no connection to frustration.[37] People can behave aggressively without being angry, especially when taking orders from someone in authority as they do in the armed forces.

So what kinds of conclusions can we draw from these three different views about the source of human aggression? Each has something to contribute, and it is a grave mistake to assume that any of these views is false just because another one is true with regard to what it affirms. The *biological-instinctual view* seems to be correct in affirming that there is a biological basis for human aggression (just as for many aspects of human behavior). When people have been hurt, especially when badly hurt physically, their natural reaction is to either flee or strike back depending on their anticipation of how successful they would be in a fight. The less able they are to flee from aggression against them, the more aggressive they become. Other things being equal (which often is not the case), males are more likely to fight than females. But even the best known of the proponents of the biological-instinctual view such as Freud and Lorenz recognize that this genetic component of human behavior is modifiable by cultural and environmental factors.[38]

The *frustration-aggression view* is correct in noting that frustration increases aggressive behavior, especially when one recognizes that frustration is not merely a reaction to any failure to attain some goal but depends on what is expected. Think of the different reactions to losing a game when one expects to win as opposed to the reaction when one does not expect to win. On the other hand, the frustration-aggression view is demonstrably wrong if it holds that frustration is the only source of aggressive behavior. People can engage in very aggressive behavior simply because someone they regard as an authority has told them to do so.

The *social learning theory* is correct in recognizing that ultimately people's aggressive behavior along with their standards of approval or disapproval of it is the result of what has been learned from experience. This learning comes from observing and imitating the behavior of adults and from one's own experience of whether aggressive behavior has paid off or not. People can also be intentionally taught new ways to deal with conflict and aggressive behavior on the part of others. From their experience they learn when aggression is not appropriate as well as how much and what kind of aggressive behavior is acceptable. Consequently, they learn rules which are very important not only with regard to what kind of behavior is acceptable for themselves but also for others. Children learn such rules even while young and then tend to follow them and expect others to do likewise, even their parents.[39]

In 1986 an international team of biologists, psychologists, ethologists, geneticists, and others adopted a statement in reaction to the belief of some people that war cannot be eliminated because it is a biological necessity. It is known as the Seville Statement because the meeting where it was first adopted was in Seville, Spain. This statement, which reflects support for the social learning view on the basis of aggression, has subsequently been endorsed by many organizations of scientists around the world, and in 1989 was officially adopted by UNESCO. Here are a few excerpts:

> It is scientifically incorrect to say that we have inherited a tendency to make war from our animal ancestors....
> The fact that warfare has changed so radically over time indicates that it is a product of culture. Its biological connection is primarily through language which makes possible the coordination of groups, the transmission of technology, and the use of tools. War is biologically possible, but it is not inevitable, as evidenced by its variation in occurrence and nature over time and space....
> It is scientifically incorrect to say that war or any other violent behavior is genetically programmed into our human nature.... Except for rare pathologies, the genes do not produce individuals necessarily predisposed to violence....
> It is scientifically incorrect to say that in the course of human evolution there has been a selection for aggressive behavior more than for other kinds of behavior.... "Dominance" involves social bondings and affiliations; it is not simply a matter of the possession and use of superior physical power, although it does involve aggressive behavior.... When ... experimentally-created hyper-aggressive animals are present in a social group, they either disrupt its social structure or are driven out. Violence is neither in our evolutionary legacy nor in our genes.
> It is scientifically incorrect to say that humans have a "violent brain."... How we act is shaped by how we have been conditioned and socialized. There is nothing in our neurophysiology that compels us to react violently.
> It is scientifically incorrect to say that war is caused by "instinct" or any single motivation.... Modern war involves institutional use of personal characteristics such as obedience, suggestibility, and idealism; social skills such as language; and rational considerations such as cost-calculation, planning, and information processing. The technology of modern war has exaggerated traits associated with violence both in the training of combatants and in the preparation of support for war in the general population. As a result of this exaggeration, such traits are often mistaken to be the causes rather than the consequences of the process.[40]

Our own investigation of these issues is completely consistent with this very important statement about biology, violent behavior, and war adopted by scientists from around the world.

Individual Aggression and War

Having discussed various views about the basis of individual human aggression, let us turn our attention to the issue of how such *individual* aggression may be related to that violent *group* conflict we call war. Three rather different situations need to be considered. The first deals with the aggressiveness of group leaders who have a great deal of influence on the behavior of the groups they lead. The second deals with the ways in which hostility, built up in members of a group as a result of frustration, may be directed against other groups. The third deals with the way in which soldiers are conditioned to actually engage in acts of violence against the enemy.

There is a remarkable incident involving rhesus monkeys that gives support to the notion that a particularly aggressive individual leader can be a cause of war. Robert Ardrey relates[41] how ethologist C. R. Carpenter had transported several groups of rhesus monkeys from India to Santiago Island off Puerto Rico to observe their behavior in a natural environment. One matter which he wanted to study was the dominance relationships of the males in the various groups of monkeys. The usual pattern of dominance among these monkeys is such that the top male monkey prevails in disputes about four or five times as often as the bottom male monkey. While making his observations Carpenter was surprised to find that one group of monkeys began conquering territory from five neighboring groups. In such struggles between groups the usual pattern was much threatening, little actual fighting, and no exchange of territory; but this situation was different. Furthermore, there seemed at first to be no explanation for the expansionist activity since an adequate food supply was distributed to all the groups each day and the size of all the groups was roughly the same.

But Carpenter soon found an explanation. The conquering group was led by an extremely strong, courageous, and domineering male. His factor of dominance over the *second* male in the group was the 5:1 ratio usually found between the top male and the *bottom* male. This commanding leader had a dominance factor of about 50:1 over the bottom male in his group. It was he that led his group on the warpath against the neighboring groups. When Carpenter removed the master monkey from the group, it went back to its own territory and stopped attacking its neighbors. When he returned the master monkey to the group, it again began imposing on the territory of its neighbors. One could not ask for a more striking case of the effect of an aggressive leader on the behavior of a group. In this case the master monkey was both the neces-

sary and the sufficient condition for aggressive behavior on the part of the group as a whole. This incident suggests that the individual aggressiveness of leaders may be a very relevant factor in the causation of war.

When we look at human history, we are struck by the names of individual aggressive leaders who led their people along the path of conquest — Alexander the Great, Genghis Khan, Napoleon Bonaparte, Adolf Hitler, and so on. It may be too simplistic to believe that a single aggressive human leader makes all the difference as was the case with the rhesus monkeys, but the role of the individual leader in determining whether a given human social group will go to war deserves more attention than it usually gets. Having made seven case studies of wars fought in the twentieth century, John Stoessinger in *Why Nations Go to War* concludes:

> With regard to the problem of the outbreak of war, the case studies indicate the crucial importance of the personalities of leaders. I am less impressed by the role of abstract forces, such as nationalism, militarism, or alliance systems, which traditionally have been regarded as the causes of war. Nor does a single one of the cases indicate that economic factors played a vital part in precipitating war. The personalities of leaders, on the other hand, have often been decisive.[42]

Bruce Bueno de Mesquita in *The War Trap* succinctly describes the critical role of the leader for initiating war as follows: "the approval of the key leader is necessary for war, while his disapproval is sufficient to prevent his nation from starting a war."[43] Since the aggressiveness of the individual leader may be a significant factor in whether a society goes to war and since it seems that women generally are less aggressive than men, an interesting question is whether having more women leaders might mean less war.[44] On the other hand, perhaps even women would need to be somewhat aggressive in order to get into leadership positions.

A second way in which individual aggression may be related to the problem of war involves the psychological phenomenon called "displaced aggression."[45] A person who is frustrated may not be able to direct his hostility toward the real source of his frustration and may, consequently, take it out on others. The typical example of displaced aggression is the man who is frustrated in his job by his superiors. He may become angry, but he cannot direct his hostility toward his superiors without losing his job or damaging his chances for promotion, so when he gets home he acts aggressively toward his wife, who then acts aggressively toward her children, who then act aggressively toward the pet dog.

The phenomenon of displaced aggression can be related to war in the following way. If there is widespread frustration among the members of a society, possibly because economic conditions are bad, a leader may be able to direct the resulting hostility toward some particular group, possibly toward some minority within the country or toward some foreign nation.[46] When economic conditions were very bad in Germany in the early 1930s, Hitler's attacks on the Jews gained a considerable following while just a few years earlier, during prosperity, very few persons paid any attention to him. Today we can expect that when the anticipation of rapid economic advancement in less developed countries is disappointed the hostility toward the richer nations will be great, but since the people of these poorer nations are unable successfully to attack these rich countries their hostility is likely to be directed toward their own leaders or toward their poor neighbors.[47] In fact, the leaders of these frustrated nations may deliberately direct their people's hostility toward neighboring countries in order to keep it from being directed toward themselves. It is an old device of political leaders to protect themselves from troubles at home by starting a crisis abroad, but the 1982 experience of Argentinian leaders with regard to the Falkland Islands–Malvinas indicates why political leaders adopting such a strategy ought to make sure they take on a weak enemy rather than a strong one.

All of the above suggests that prosperity is likely to make peace more probable while economic adversity is likely to produce hostility and war, even though the hostility and war may not be directed against the real source of frustration. It should be noted, however, that this phenomenon of displaced aggression seems to be more closely related to the issue of how leaders get their followers to participate in a war than to the issue of how the wars get started. Still, persons who call for aggressive action are more likely to make their way into leadership positions when the population as a whole is frustrated, and leaders are much more likely to embark on a course of action which will lead to war when they feel their followers are ready and eager for the effort.

A third way individual aggressiveness is related to war is in the preparation of soldiers to do the actual fighting of a war. This matter has nothing to do with how wars get started, but only with how individuals are induced to engage in violent behavior once the leaders have decided to go to war. Both the frustration theory of aggression and the social learning theory of aggression are relevant. Much of military training, especially basic training, is based on the principle that a frustrated soldier is more likely to be a hostile person and therefore an aggressive person. The task then becomes one of directing this aggression against the enemy rather than the military leaders in charge of the training or the political leaders who have been responsible for pulling the young person away from his personal pursuits to fight for the glory of his country. A frequently used device is to describe atrocities committed by the enemy. There is also an effort to get the soldiers to view the enemy soldiers as less than human and thus not deserving of the respect usually accorded to humans. A concerted effort is made to get these soldiers to follow orders without questioning them. Of course this military training is supported by a long prior period of social conditioning leading the young soldiers to identify with their country and to place a positive value on the idea of losing their life for their country.[48] This identification with the national group, nationalism, is one of our subjects to be addressed in the next chapter.

5.   Group Competition and Group Identification

The question of what causes war is an extremely complex one. Part of the complexity is generated by the different meanings of the word "cause" discussed in the previous chapter. But an even more important part of the difficulty is that war itself is a complex social phenomenon. We have defined war as "large-scale violent conflict between organized groups which already are governments or which seek to establish their own government over some territory." Thus our question about what causes war can mean (1) "What causes *individual persons* (both leaders and followers) to be so aggressive that they will engage in violent behavior as they do during war?" We discussed that question in the previous chapter. Or the question about what causes war can mean (2) "What causes groups to come into conflict with each other?" that is, *what kinds of things might groups fight about?* That is the first issue we will discuss in this chapter. Or the question about what causes war can mean (3) "What causes individuals *to identify with a group* so completely that they are ready to risk their lives fighting for the group?" (because if that didn't happen, modern wars couldn't occur). Why that identification occurs is the second issue we will discuss in this chapter. Our question about what causes war can also focus on other aspects of the social situation which may contribute to the outbreak of violent conflict between groups. We will focus on those possibilities in the next chapter.

Arenas of Group Competition

The kinds of things about which groups may come into conflict with each other are the same things about which individuals may come into conflict with each other: (1) survival (Who gets to continue existing?), (2) acquisition of goods (economic factors — Who gets what goods?), (3) wider acceptance of their beliefs (religious/ ideological factors — Whose beliefs are to be accepted and taught to future generations?), (4) status (Who is to be more admired to and imitated?), and (5) power (Whose orders will be obeyed?).

The lowest level of competition is for *survival,* to just keep on existing. If an individual is threatened with death, we can expect that person to struggle to survive. Similarly, if a group is threatened with extinction as a group, we can expect that group to struggle to survive. This desire for group survival interacting with the broader environmental situation helps explain why *primitive war* is so different from *civilized war.* Our nomadic ancestors, with plenty of unoccupied space in the world, could usually move into some unoccupied territory if their survival were threatened by some stronger group. They might at first put up some kind of resistance in order to continue hunting and fishing and gathering where they already were, but if defeat seemed likely they could just move to some other place. Societies which never developed a military-type organization to defend themselves against other groups survived by migrating to isolated less desirable places where they would no longer be pushed aside by other groups.[1]

Sooner or later, depending on the terrain and the rate of population growth, empty territory into which a group could escape would no longer be available. In this case the defeated group would either be completely exterminated or made into a permanent slave class within the victorious society. In that latter case we would have the start of a hierarchical coercive government characteristic of civilized peoples.[2] We would also then begin to have *civilized warfare* among the various triumphant groups for control of even more good land and other kinds of wealth. That is the second level of conflict or competition among societies, *economic conflict*.

For most of the "civilized" period, *economic* competition among groups has been focused on acquiring the goods provided by nature: land, good soil and a favorable climate for growing food, access to water, and supplies of raw materials such as wood and then metals like copper and tin. In the modern world, the desired things include material resources such as iron ore and bauxite for aluminum and energy sources such as coal and petroleum. The wants of human beings are virtually limitless and the numbers of them are ever increasing while the goods provided by nature are limited. Over thousands of years humans have used their ingenuity to get more of what they want from nature than nature would have provided without human management. The introduction of agriculture and the domestication of animals are two of the earlier developments in this process while the use of fertilizer for crops and the production of energy from uranium and plutonium are more recent developments. There is a continuing contest between how much is available and the ever increasing desires of an ever expanding population.

Thus there is a sense in which population growth is relevant to the problem of war. When production does not increase as fast as population, the conflict for available goods will become more intense. Eventually, the economic problem becomes a survival problem. In a particular place there can be just too many people to survive on the available resources, so some must die — if not in war then by starvation or even ritual human sacrifice. We have actual historical examples in particular places of this kind of ecological collapse. Two of them are isolated Easter Island in the Pacific Ocean and the Mayan Empire in central America.[3] A crucial contemporary issue is whether the same kind of ecological collapse might happen on a global scale within a few hundred years. The flourishing of science and the resulting technological revolution of the last two and a half centuries has generally allowed the production of goods to more than keep pace with population growth, but it re-

mains to be seen whether that rate of increasing productivity per person will continue in the future for the world as a whole. We have been helped considerably by the fact that people in more industrialized societies tend to have fewer children because children are no longer perceived as an asset (low-cost labor and old-age security) as they were in an agrarian society, but many of the world's people are still living in primarily agrarian societies and are still having large numbers of children.

Even if the global population were to grow faster than the supply of goods, however, it is not necessarily the case that the increasing tensions would result in war.[4] There might be great resentment on the part of those who are in danger of not surviving. Nevertheless if they believe there is no chance of getting what they need by group violence because they would simply be technologically outgunned, they are not likely to resort to group violence. If there is some other way of getting what they need (producing and selling addictive drugs, selling stolen goods, engaging in prostitution, making simple objects that can be sold to those with money, and so on), then that is what these "left-out" people will do rather than trying to fight a war which they know they will only lose. It is worth remembering that wars are usually fought by groups which believe they will gain something by engaging in them.[5] To fight a war, people must believe that in some way they will be better off if they fight than if they don't use violence. The rich and powerful who control the weapons and military forces set the rules for what the non-powerful can and cannot do in order to survive, much as parents set the rules for what young children can and cannot do in order to survive. When there is not enough for everyone, resentment is likely to grow and probably produce violent acts of protest by some individuals and small groups (such as occurs with terrorism), but it is not likely to produce organized war. Any remedial action by the rich and powerful to help the poor and weak is more likely to be motivated by compassion than by fear of violence by the "left-out." Any kind of violent revolt typically just produces more vigorous repression.

When governments were first established, the leaders of these societies used their commanding positions in the government to pursue their aim of increasing the quantity and kinds of goods available to themselves. Three strategies could be adopted by these leaders. One strategy would be to tax people of their own society in order to get goods for themselves. A second strategy would be to promote the development of technology within their society so that more and better goods are produced, either for their own use or for trading to other societies for goods which they have. A third strategy would be to organize an army composed of members of their society in order to take goods from other societies by force.

The first strategy is limited by the fact that if the people in the society are very poor the leaders will not be able to get much by taxing them. There is also the danger of an organized rebellion if the discrepancy between the supply of goods available to the leaders and that available to others in the society becomes too great and the police are not strong enough to prevent such an uprising. The second strategy of using technology is much more attractive in a scientific-industrial age than it was when human knowledge and technology were more limited, but still today, especially in conflicts among less developed countries, technology may not be able to produce what is wanted more cheaply than it can be obtained by force. Thus the third strategy, war, has been widely used by government leaders throughout "civilized" history as a way of getting more goods, even though the cost can be very high when the opposing society is equipped to put up a good fight to keep its goods for itself.

Originally the goods acquired in a successful war (the "spoils of victory") belonged to the leaders and the soldiers who took part in the fighting, but eventually with the development of more democratic societies the government was expected to look out for the welfare of the citizenry generally. Competition between ruling groups in different societies was transformed into competition between nation-state and nation-state, with the government of each seeking to enhance the standard of living of its whole society. Even au-

thoritarian governments now usually state their goal as generating more goods for everyone in the society, not just more for the leaders.

A great deal of ancient war was motivated by the desire to seize the goods of another society, but war for economic gain is by no means confined to the ancient world. From the sixteenth through the early part of the twentieth century there were continuing imperialistic wars in which the technologically advanced European nations were able to gain control over the territory of the less advanced peoples in the Americas, Africa, and Asia. These wars usually did not last very long because the military forces of the European nations were equipped with guns and other modern weapons unknown to the inhabitants of these less developed countries. Conquest by the more advanced nations gave them access to raw materials and to good agricultural land which they could control for their own purposes. The advanced nations were also able to restrict the flow of technological know-how to the native populations of the less developed countries, consequently preserving the arrangements whereby natural resources flowed into the hands of Europeans rather than being converted into manufactured goods within the less developed countries.

Since taking control of the natural resources of less developed countries was a very profitable operation, a new kind of economic competition developed among the imperial nations themselves. Each advanced nation wanted to control as much territory as possible in order to have access to whatever natural resources might be found there. Sometimes nations worked things out peacefully, such as when Spain and Portugal accepted the Pope's decision on how to divide Latin America between them or when Britain and France and some other European nations ended up apportioning large segments of Africa and Asia among them, but eventually the competition for colonial territory led to war. Thus competition for the goods of the Earth led to wars not only between technologically advanced countries on the one hand and less advanced countries on the other but also among the advanced countries themselves as each tried to expand its holdings at the expense of the others.

As some of the people in the less advanced countries gradually acquired some of the weapons produced by the more advanced countries and as the advanced countries became embroiled in wars among themselves (especially the Second World War), a new kind of war caused by economic competition became possible. People in the less developed countries were able to fight "wars of national liberation" to gain political independence and control over their own natural resources.

At present economic competition among the nations of the world continues. Rich nations compete against other rich nations, but the rich nations as a group also compete against the poor nations as a group. And of course, the poor nations compete among themselves. But now these economic struggles usually take place in a nonviolent way. The more advanced nations for the most part no longer have political control over the less advanced nations, but they control the capital, the technological knowledge, and the markets needed by the less developed countries. Consequently, they are usually able to work out arrangements favorable to themselves. One outstanding exception to control by the advanced countries is OPEC, the Organization of Petroleum Exporting Countries. By forming a producers' cartel, the less developed nations which have petroleum within their territory were able, especially during the 1970s, to greatly increase the price of crude oil, to the great disadvantage of the more advanced countries, which generally were very dependent on imported oil. The cartel still exists, but its influence has been decreased considerably as the result of collective action by the developed countries, by the discovery of oil in territory controlled by the developed countries such as the North Sea and Alaska, and by squabbles among the members of OPEC themselves. The economic struggle to control resources such as oil does still sometimes lead to war, however, as in 1990 when Iraq conquered Kuwait. That conquest led to a military response in February 1991 when Iraq was driven out of Kuwait by a coalition of developed countries led by the United States. This Gulf War was the result of different viewpoints in Iraq and Kuwait about whether to sell oil at "reasonable prices" to the industrialized countries, about how to use the money acquired from the sales of oil, and the extent to which Kuwait should help pay for Iraq's war against Iran.

We should not neglect economic competition as a contributing factor to war *within* nations. We earlier mentioned the possibility of rebellion in a situation where a ruling elite has a great deal more wealth than the rest of the people in the society. The ruling elite are usually able to hire a superior police force armed with superior weapons to maintain control over the rest of the society in much the same way that a technologically advanced nation is able to control its colonies. But a split may occur among the ruling elite which would present opportunities for others in the society to gain some power by agreeing to support one or the other faction of the ruling group. Or some other nation may provide military assistance to the poorer, less powerful people so they have a chance to successfully rebel against the military and economic domination practiced by the elite in that society. In either case it is possible that a civil war will occur due at least in part to the economic competition between groups within that nation-state.

A word should be said here about the way in which a depression or other economic difficulty can intensify the readiness to use violence as goods and resources become more difficult to obtain. This applies to both international and intranational strife. During economic hard times, especially when they are not anticipated, there is more frustration and consequently people are more ready to resort to violence to try to change things. A cycle of disaster can be established where poverty stimulates war which then leads to more poverty and thus even more violence. The other side of this situation is that prosperity makes war less likely because people aren't frustrated and compromises can be worked out more readily.

A *third kind of competition* that may lead to war is the effort by groups *to spread their own religious or political beliefs.* A group may have a set of accepted beliefs — about the ultimate nature of reality, about how individuals should behave, and about what kinds of institutions a society should have — which they think should also be adopted by other groups. This "Truth" which they desire to spread may be resisted by other groups, which typically have their own ideas about what is true and good. In modern societies the central issue in this type of conflict is control of information generally (the media) and control of the formal education system in particular. People's beliefs and values depend on the information available to them. Children tend to believe whatever ideas they are taught first, and any conflicting ideas they hear later will usually be viewed as false and wrong. Most adults will be influenced in their beliefs by what is believed by others around them. Thus control of the media and education is crucial for promoting a religion or ideology. Competition between groups for control of information and the formal educational system may lead to war. The increasing amount of information exchanged throughout the world because of satellite television and especially the internet is making it more and more difficult for authoritarian leaders to keep their people ignorant of what is happening in the world and even in their own country. At the same time, as a greater divergence develops between the traditional beliefs of some groups and the new scientifically based information becoming available, there can be an even greater determination to use violence if necessary to protect a group's traditional beliefs from "contamination" from outsiders.

If the aim of the leaders of a society were simply that people should come to believe what is objectively true and to approve of whatever is objectively good, the appropriate means of accomplishing this aim would be the exposure of both children and adults to the whole range of views that might be held on any topic. The study of philosophy, where people are stimulated to think things through for themselves, would be a central feature of the educational system. There would be a constant effort to challenge prevailing beliefs and

values so that mistaken views would gradually be corrected through investigation and debate.[6] Unfortunately, some people, including the leaders of some groups and some societies, do not want other people to explore ideas and reach their own conclusions. They want their children and other members of their group, and even members of other groups, to believe what they believe and to value what they value. Consequently, in some societies there is an effort to control education and information so that people will come to the "right" (acceptable) conclusions about what is true and what is good. Those who question the accepted beliefs and practices are discouraged, ignored, silenced, or even actively persecuted.

The goal of promoting the views approved by the decision-makers in the society and discouraging those which they disapprove is often not limited to their own society. Two societies with different religions or opposing ideologies are each likely to make efforts to promote their own views in the opposing society as well as in other countries not directly involved in the ideological conflict. Each may even try to make its religion or ideology the prevailing religion or ideology in the whole world. Such ideological conflicts may ultimately lead to war. The war between Communist forces and the United States in Vietnam (1954-1973) is an example of a war in which ideological conflict was a major factor.

Intense religious or ideological differences may also lead to war *within* a society. People of different religious or ideological persuasions may come to believe that they just cannot continue to live together in the same society. Sometimes a single issue such as the abolition of slavery may become a focal point for intense feeling that contributes to the outbreak of a civil war. A group which advocates a greater sharing of political power or economic wealth may find itself persecuted by the leaders of the society who would be losers if those views were widely accepted. If this group recommending changes uses force to defend itself, a civil war may develop. When groups with different religious/ideological views can find no compromise on how to live together, war breaks out. The continuing battles between Catholic and Protestant Christians in Northern Ireland, the Korean War (1950-1953), the 1978 revolution in Iran, the war between the Sandinistas and the Contras in Nicaragua during the 1980s, and the fighting in Bosnia-Herzegovina which followed the break-up of Yugoslavia in 1991 are just a few examples of how religious or ideological conflict can produce war within a country.

It might be supposed that people would fight more vehemently for physical goods than for abstract doctrines and ideals, but in fact religiously or ideologically motivated wars seem to be especially bloody and unrestrained. Each side believes that it has a holy mission to bring the other side to the "Truth," no matter what the cost or sacrifice. It may be firmly believed by people on both sides that it is better to die than to be forced to live in a society where the religion or ideology of the opposing side prevails. This viewpoint was succinctly expressed in the United States during the Cold War by the slogan "Better dead than Red." The vehemence of wars motivated largely by religious or ideological differences is evidenced by the nature of the fighting between Christians and Muslims during the twelfth and thirteenth centuries and between Protestants and Catholics in the sixteenth and seventeenth centuries. It has been argued that the destructiveness of modern war makes it likely that if there is a World War III the primary cause will probably be ideological conflict rather than hope of material gain.[7] It seems also that many wars taking place *within* nations during the past 25 years involve some kind of religious or ideological conflict.

To anyone who thinks carefully and impartially about the matter, conducting a war to resolve differences in belief about what is true and what is good is as ridiculous as having a fistfight between two individuals to discover whose ideas are best. Beliefs which are true and values which are good will come to prevail if given a chance to be expressed in open inquiry and debate. The notion that the ideas of the winner of a war are closer to the truth and that their values are superior to those of the loser cannot be accepted by any-

one who knows how often in human history the speakers of truth have been silenced and the toilers for good imprisoned or killed by those with greater physical force at their command. Violence may be a temporarily effective way of extending one's control over others, but it is not an appropriate method for advancing truth and goodness.[8] The search for truth and goodness requires open discussion of alternative views rather than coercion designed to promote the views of those who happen to be physically in charge at the moment.

A *fourth arena* of competition between groups is for *status*. Status or standing or rank is an abstract concept, but it is also a very real thing. Status is the result of a combination of fear, respect, and admiration. Among countries status or rank depends on things such as military power, economic power, and scientific or cultural achievements. As in the case of individuals, a country with high status will be acknowledged to be superior and will be deferred to and admired and imitated. Having status means having influence even when that influence may not be formally recognized in legal or political institutions. An example of having high status but still lacking recognized power is the situation of Japan, a country which has acquired a great deal of prestige because of its economic successes and helpful international contributions while (as of the year 2000) it still hasn't been made a permanent member of the U.N. Security Council.

Let us consider an example of how status may be gained in international affairs. Suppose that two nations are negotiating a trade agreement. The richer nation intends to export manufactured goods to the poorer nation while the poorer nation intends to export raw material to the richer nation. As the negotiations proceed the richer nation proposes that all goods moving in either direction be transported in its vessels. The poorer nation does not want to accept such arrangements, but the rich nation takes the position that if the goods are not shipped in its vessels it will simply stop negotiating with this poor nation and work out something with another more cooperative nation. At this point the poorer nation often is trapped because this rich nation is one of the few which can afford to buy large quantities of its raw materials and also supply some of the manufactured goods it needs. Thus the poorer nation is coerced into accepting a trade agreement where all the goods involved will be shipped in the vessels of the richer nation. There has been a struggle concerning which nation will get its way, and the rich nation has prevailed because the poorer nation needs what the rich nation has more than the rich nation needs what the poorer nation has. But this particular trade agreement also means that a situation of dominance has been established. Having yielded to the demands of the rich country on this occasion, the poorer country can expect to be coerced into accepting similar demands in the future.

The example just cited focuses on economic coercion in a struggle for dominance, but one nation might also establish its dominance over another on the basis of military superiority. A militarily weaker nation might be coerced into accepting trade agreements or other policies which it really does not want because of the threat of being invaded if it does not go along with the demands of the militarily stronger country. In international affairs coercion on the basis of the military superiority is just as likely as economic coercion. Military superiority is also even more crucial in a head-to-head confrontation. Since the ultimate test of a nation's strength lies in its capability of defending itself in a war, military superiority is the most crucial factor in national status.

A good example of competition for status outside the economic and military spheres was the contest between the United States and the Soviet Union with regard to accomplishments in space during the Cold War. Many aspects of the space race such as the size of satellites which can be kept in orbit and the length of time a person can stay in space before returning to Earth have military implications. But one event which had very little to do with military needs was the landing of men on the moon. The Soviets had launched the first satellite in 1957, an event that generated a perception throughout the world that Soviet science was ahead of American science.

The United States was losing status. In response to that situation, in 1961 President Kennedy issued a public challenge to the Soviets to see which country could be first to place a man on the moon. The United States accomplished that in 1969. The Soviet space scientists never did. The landing of men on the moon demonstrated the capability of American science and counteracted the earlier notion promoted by the Russians that "socialist science and technology" was superior to "capitalist science and technology." The American effort was motivated purely by a concern for status.

So far we have noted that economic coercion or military coercion or superior scientific accomplishment may be used by one nation or group to establish its superior status or dominance over another. Competition between countries also occurs in other areas such as cultural achievements or winning the most medals in the Olympic Games. Having status means being recognized as superior in some area of competition. But in international affairs there is a general consensus that being "Number One" militarily is much more important than being "Number One" in other ways because ultimately the question of status comes down to who could win a war. That is the ultimate competition. Violent contests of physical force for dominance occur among animals to determine which one is "top dog" of the pack. Similar violent contests of physical force for dominance may take place between nations or between groups within a nation. They are called wars.

In the end, however, the dominant nation or group within a nation wants not only status but also *formal recognition of that status* by means of a treaty or other formal political document. It wants others to formally acknowledge its *authority to determine what policies will be followed* in a particular territory and over a particular population. That is, the dominant group wants not only status but *political power*. Regardless of what other ultimate goals are being pursued, acquiring political power is the immediate aim of warfare. Political power (authority to act as a government for all the territory at stake) is what the winner wins.

It should be noted that although political power may sometimes seem to be *an end in itself,* in fact it is essentially *a means* by which other things can be accomplished. A group which has acquired power is able to give orders to accomplish whatever it is that it wants to accomplish, but having power to make decisions for the whole society still leaves open the question of what policies will be adopted. In this respect the quest for political power resembles the quest for money by individuals. Persons who accumulate a great deal of money will be able to buy whatever they want or to give away as much as they want to whomever they wish, but having the money simply provides a means to some other ends. Those who have acquired large amounts of money must still decide how to use it. Similarly, a country or group which wins a war, thus establishing its right to decide what will be done, must still decide how to use that power.

There is another similarity between the quest for money and the quest for political power. People whose aim is to acquire more and more money may at the beginning of their quest have some idea of what they want to use the money for, but after a while the aim of acquiring more money may itself become a goal. While trying to acquire more and more money, these persons may have no idea of what to do with it once it is in their hands. Similarly, leaders of nations or of groups within nations usually aim to acquire more and more political power. At the beginning they usually have some idea of what they want the power for, but in time the aim of acquiring more power may itself become a goal. These leaders may want more power but have no idea of what to do with it once they have it.

The fact that some leaders may not know what to do with their political power once they have it does not stop them from trying to get more power as the recognized decision-makers over more territory and more people. Having gained control over their own country, they may try to expand their control to include other countries. These other countries may decide that they will fight rather than just

yield their decision-making authority to this power-seeking leader. Thus the desire for political power simply for its own sake on the part of some leaders may itself become a cause of war. Joseph Schumpeter in his book *Imperialism and Social Classes* argues that "objectless" expansionism (expansionism with no reasonable objectives in terms of the welfare of the nation involved) occurs regularly and in fact may even be the cause of a majority of international wars that have occurred.[9]

At the same time it should be remembered that power typically is used to get other things. Beyond assuring survival, power can also be used with regard to the other arenas of competition we have discussed. The nation or group which has political power will be able to use that power to get a larger share of the available goods for its own people, to promote the acceptance of its religion or ideology, and to further enhance its own status. Whether the struggle for political power happens to be instrumental to these other ends or is an end in itself, getting more political power is the *immediate* goal in all warfare, as our definition of war has noted.

Group Identification and Nationalism

Groups could not carry out sustained violent conflict with each other if individuals did not commit themselves to fighting for those groups. In earlier times participating in a war may have involved a personal commitment on the part of the soldiers to the king or to some nobleman, but in modern warfare commitment to be ready to engage in battle for some group usually depends on a psychological phenomenon called "identification." People are said to identify with a group when they feel that what is good for that group is good for them and that whatever harms that group harms them. To put it another way, if the group experiences some type of success it will make them personally feel better because the group's welfare is perceived as an extension of their own.

The phenomenon of identification is a common part of human life. For example, students tend to identify with their school and its athletic teams. If the team wins, they feel good. If the team loses, they feel bad. People identify with the religious or ideological group to which they belong, with the racial or ethnic group to which they belong, with their labor unions or professional organizations, with the company which employs them, with their age group, with their gender group, with the local community where they live, with their state, with their nation, and so on. Whenever people think in terms of "we" (for example, "We won" or "We got recognized"), they are identifying with some group.

Group identification seems to be increased by competitive situations, especially when the group or its representatives are experiencing success or confronting a particularly crucial struggle. Winning athletic teams produce increased school or community loyalty. When a representative of a racial or religious group wins a prize, other members of that group experience a greater pride in their racial or religious identity. When a religious or ethnic group faces persecution, other members of that group feel a special awareness of being members of that group. Group identification usually continues at some level, however, even in losing situations and noncritical confrontations.

Since members of a group identify with the success or failure of the group, leaders of any group are under a great deal of pressure to advance the interests of the group. They have a role to play: to do what is best for the group. If they do not succeed or if they seem not to be aggressive enough in pursuing the interests of the group, they are likely to be replaced by other leaders who promise to do better. All groups want to be gainers, winners, the best of their kind. Such a situation necessarily fosters competition and group conflict. If this group conflict degenerates to the point that the members of both groups start using violence, we have a war.

One of the more obvious ways of lessening conflict between two groups is to persuade them both to see themselves as members of the same larger group which is united against some other group. Thus, Catholics and Protestants may experience less tension if they perceive themselves as Christians struggling against Muslims. In turn Christians and Muslims may have less conflict with each other if they view themselves as believers in God struggling against atheistic Communists or some other anti-religious movement. Perhaps believers and atheists could in turn see themselves as humans struggling together for survival against the forces of nature, including the psychological forces (habits, prejudices) within themselves, which threaten their continued existence.

Of all the various types of identification, the one most relevant to the war problem in recent times is nationalism.[10] Nationalism is not a *necessary condition* of war since prior to the last quarter of the eighteenth century wars were fought to a great extent by mercenaries, that is, men who hired themselves out as soldiers. They fought for the king who paid them and felt no nationalistic sentiment. In many wars people were motivated by identification with a religious group rather than a nation. Neither is nationalism a *sufficient condition* of war since it is possible for people to have strong nationalistic feelings and yet not engage in warfare; the Swedes and Swiss are both good examples. Yet nationalism seems to be an important contributory factor to war, especially in the last 350 years.

To clarify the issue of nationalism as it relates to war, however, we must distinguish three different ways in which this term is used.[11] The first two meanings both involve the psychological phenomenon of *identification* we have just discussed. The third meaning of nationalism is very different. It refers to a *doctrine* or *belief* about how governmental arrangements should be based on racial and ethnic considerations.

In order to distinguish the first two types of nationalism we must note the difference between a *nation* and a *nation-state,* a difference which requires special attention because of our tendency to use the term "nation" when we in fact mean "nation-state." A *nation* (or *people*) refers to a group of people who are of the same racial stock, use the same language, share the same religious and cultural traditions, and perceive themselves as a homogeneous group. In this racial-ethnic sense of "nation" there is no reference to any political unit or nation-state; some nations lack nation-states of their own. Thus we use the term "nation" when we speak of American Indian groups such as the Mohawk nation or the Lakota nation. Another good example is the Jewish nation after the destruction of ancient Israel and before the creation of the modern state of Israel in 1948.[12]

A *nation-state,* on the other hand, refers to a population living in a certain territory under the authority of a government. This meaning of "nation" differs from the first meaning. In some nation-states the people are *not* a homogeneous group. Switzerland is a particularly good example of such a nation-state. It is a political unit, even though it is composed of several different cultural groups with different languages and traditions. Russia and the United States are also examples of nation-states whose populations are composed of several different cultural groups.

Nationalism in the first sense, *racial-ethnic nationalism,* refers to a person's identification with a homogeneous nation or people.[13] This type of nationalism develops naturally when one is reared in a homogeneous group. We tend automatically to identify with other people who look like us, act like us, use the same language we do, and have the same religious and cultural heritage we have. Within a homogeneous ethnic group an intense feeling of group solidarity develops. There is a strong tendency to view people who look different, act differently, use a different language, or who have different religious beliefs and cultural traditions as "strange," "odd," and "uncivilized" or perhaps not even human.

Nationalism in the second sense, *loyalty to the nation-state* (also called *patriotism*), refers to a person's identification with a nation-state and the people who live within it. This type of nationalism does not develop naturally but comes about as the result of a deliberate effort to inculcate loyalty to the nation-state and its institutions. Symbols such as a flag, a national anthem, and a pledge of allegiance are used as a focus of loyalty. Education of the children emphasizes the history, heroes, and glories of the nation-state and the value of sticking together against outsiders. National holidays are celebrated. A national military force maintains allegiance to the national government, and persons in this force as well as those who hold office in the national government are accorded honor. By such devices the "we" perspective of the people is extended beyond their own cultural group to the heterogeneous nation-state as a whole.

The third definition of the term *nationalism,* what we will call *"doctrinal nationalism,"* is very different from the previous two meanings of the word, both of which are related to the notion of identification with some group. In this third sense, *nationalism* is not a matter of identification at all. It refers rather to a *doctrine* or *belief,* namely the viewpoint that *each racial-ethnic group has a right to have its own independent political nation-state and that all members of this racial-ethnic group should live together in a single political nation-state.* This idea is often called "national self-determination" and has generally been associated with nationalistic democracy. The ideal according to doctrinal nationalism is for each racial-ethnic group to be united in its own independent at least somewhat "ethnically pure" country.[14] This doctrinal version of nationalism is often associated with the 19th-century Italian political writer and activist Giuseppe Mazzini, who used it as the theoretical underpinning for promoting the unification of Italian city-states into the single nation-state of Italy. The basic idea was that the people living in the separate city-states in Italy at that time were all one people (Italians) and thus should have their own nation-state just as the Spanish and the French and the English had. Doctrinal nationalism has also served as a theoretical support for separatist movements among minority racial-ethnic groups within nation-states and for independence movements which promote "wars of national liberation" in territories ruled by foreign colonialists.

Doctrinal nationalism or national self-determination has been behind various movements, earlier in Europe but now also on other continents, which have been intimately connected with violent conflict. In a general way, doctrinal nationalism will almost certainly produce dissatisfaction wherever there are various racial-ethnic groups intermingled in particular geographical areas. Suppose, for example, that there are some enclaves of Italians living within the boundaries of France and some French people living in enclaves within the boundaries of Italy. According to doctrinal nationalism or national self-determination, how is this situation to be handled? Should some small areas of land within France become part of the nation-state of Italy and some small areas of land within Italy become part of the nation-state of France? What should happen to those areas that are about 50 percent French and 50 percent Italian? If these Italians surrounded by French people want to be under the political control of Italy, why don't they just move into territory that is already part of Italy? And a similar question could be addressed to the French living in Italy. But why should any people be forced to move to a different geographical area because of a doctrine about "pure" nation-states and national self-determination?

We need to examine the presuppositions of doctrinal nationalism. Why is it desirable that each racial-ethnic group have its own "ethnically pure" nation-state? Why can't many different racial-ethnic groups live together in a heterogeneous nation-state? The assumption seems to be that in a heterogeneous nation-state one racial-ethnic group (usually but not always the majority) will be in control and will use its political power to discriminate unfairly against other racial-ethnic groups which are less powerful. Undoubtedly, such situations do occur (consider the apartheid system which existed in South Africa), but there may be other remedies besides doctrinal nationalism. Why not have ethnically heterogeneous nation-states which aim to protect the rights of *all* individuals regardless of their racial-ethnic group? Why not have multi-ethnic nation-states where all individuals, regardless of race or ethnic background, have an equal opportunity to get into positions of economic and political power?[15] That seems to be an attractive alternative to doctrinal nationalism.

The main force working against this proposed alternative is the widespread uncritical acceptance of the legitimacy of doctrinal nationalism or national self-determination. This situation has become painfully obvious with regard to the break-up of the former multi-ethnic nation-state of Yugoslavia (see map on page 46). Some Serbs, motivated by the nationalistic vision of a "Greater Serbia," want to unite all Serbs into a single nation-state. Other ethnic groups in the former Yugoslavia such as the Croats don't want to remain a part of a state where the Serbian majority is motivated by doctrinal nationalism rather than the ideal of a multi-ethnic state as existed in Yugoslavia under the Slovene-Croat leader, Marshal Tito. A great tragedy occurred in the former Yugoslav republic of Bosnia-Herzegovina. In that state, which declared its independence from Yugoslavia in 1991, the population was 44 percent Muslim, 31 percent Serb, and 17 percent Croat. Some Bosnian Serbs wanted to become part of "Greater Serbia," and some Bosnian Croats wanted to become part of the newly independent state of Croatia. But that is not true of *all* of the Serbs and Croats in Bosnia-Herzegovina. Some of them wanted Bosnia-Herzegovina to be a separate multi-ethnic state. In many cases families and close friends of different ethnic groups have lived together in harmony in the former Yugoslavia. Some of the Bosnian Serbs were in fact fighting in the Bosnian army against other Bosnian Serbs even though they themselves were Serbian! They wanted to prevent the break-up of Bosnia-Herzegovina into separate ethnic states. But the uncritical acceptance of doctrinal nationalism by people on all sides makes their position almost impossible. Other Serbs view them as traitors because they do not share the vision of a "Greater Serbia." (There is an obvious parallel here to the situation for Jews who oppose Zionism or Quebecois who do not want Quebec to secede from Canada or Chechens who oppose the secession of Chechnya from Russia.) At the same time some uninformed Bosnian Muslims treat these Serbs who want a multi-ethnic Bosnia-Herzegovina as enemies just because they are Serbs.[16] It is sad to see how the defenders of a multi-ethnic Bosnia-Herzegovina have been sacrificed on the altar of doctrinal nationalism by a world that seems unable to free itself from this war-engendering ideology.

Returning to our examination of the assumptions underlying doctrinal nationalism, why is it essential that all persons of the same racial-ethnic nation live in a single nation-state? The assumption here seems to be that in unity there is strength to be better able to compete militarily and economically against other racial-ethnic groups. The British and French, who got themselves united earlier, were able to establish world empires by the beginning of the twentieth century. On the other hand, when the Italians and the Germans finally got themselves united in the last part of the 19th century there were few new areas of the world to colonize. But it becomes obvious here that this side of doctrinal nationalism is based on the assumption that the international system is to remain forever a battleground of different aggressive racial-ethnic groups each in control of a particular state and doing all it can to promote the welfare of this state at the expense of other nation-states. Perhaps that will be the model for the future as it has been for Europe in the past. On the other hand, it is possible that a post–World War II global system will evolve where it is no longer the case that military power is the accepted means by which ethnically pure nation-states battle for domination over each other. In such a revised world order it would no longer be so important for each racial-ethnic group to be united in its own nation-state. Another possibility is that, even if the global system as a whole does not change, the really powerful actors in the international system will be large multi-ethnic nation-states rather than ethnically pure ones. Certainly the outcome of World War II suggested that things are moving in this direction.

Before leaving the topic of nationalism we need at least to make mention of the situation of "indigenous peoples," those "native" or "tribal" peoples scattered all over the globe whose very survival is endangered by the spread of industrialized nation-states.[17] Earlier it was noted that the struggle to survive is the most basic kind of competition among groups and that groups which have not been able to prevail militarily have usually migrated to isolated areas to avoid further conflict. There are large numbers of these pre-civilized or pre-industrialized peoples who are being threatened because more civilized industrialized peoples are now pushing into these previously isolated areas. Of the 6,000 cultures in the world 4,000–5,000 are indigenous cultures,[18] and they include 300 million persons living in more than 70 different countries.[19]

It has been noted above that one alternative to doctrinal nationalism or national self-determination is the establishment of multi-ethnic nation-states where the rights of minority groups are protected. The fate of indigenous peoples will be determined not just by what protection they are given by the governments of individual nation-states but also by what protection they are guaranteed by the world community. A U.N. Declaration on the Rights of Indigenous Peoples is currently being drafted by a working group under the auspices of the U.N. Human Rights Commission in connection with the International Decade for the World's Indigenous Peoples (1995–2004).[20] The adoption of such a declaration would be an important development for the preservation of both these indigenous groups and of the ecological systems where they live.[21]

Nationalism as a Cause of War

We have distinguished three different meanings of nationalism: (1) identification with one's racial-ethnic group, (2) patriotism, or loyalty to one's nation-state, and (3) doctrinal nationalism, the belief that each racial-ethnic group has a right to have all its members living in its own ethnically pure nation-state. There are four different contexts in which doctrinal nationalism, with its heavy emphasis on racial-ethnic nationalism as the proper basis for political structures, may produce tensions and eventually war. At the same time, the aspect of nationalism that has probably been most significant in modern *international* war is loyalty to the nation-state or patriotism. Let us consider in more detail the ways in which nationalism may be a cause of war.

According to our definition of war, wars always involve government in some way or other. Consequently, *nationalism as identification with the racial-ethnic group* becomes a causal factor in war only when it is combined with political aims as occurs in doctrinal nationalism. Undoubtedly, racial-ethnic nationalism is a factor in many uprisings and riots and "racial incidents" within countries, but unless there are some political aims these events should not be classified as wars.

As noted above, there are four different contexts in which *doctrinal nationalism* may be causally involved in war. First, doctrinal nationalism may provide theoretical support for a *liberation movement* against a country which has conquered a group and made its members into a colony. According to doctrinal nationalism or national self-determination each racial-ethnic group has a right to have its own nation-state rather than being ruled by some other nationality. Thus it follows that this conquered and colonialized racial-ethnic group has a right to become an independent nation-state.[22] The conquered people are likely to develop an intense hatred for the people who have kept them in subjection. They will also tend to regard members of their own nation who cooperate with the conquerors as traitors. When the time is right, the nationalistic feeling of the oppressed people will support a *war of liberation* to throw off the control of the other nation. Since the end of World War II this set of events has occurred in many nations which were once colonies, such as India, Kenya, Algeria, Vietnam, Zimbabwe, Angola, and Mozambique. The same type of resentful nationalism may also be manifested in situations where the foreign political control is more indirect or where the foreign domination is more economic than political. In these cases nationalistic feeling may support a revolutionary movement directed against those native leaders who are viewed as being too cooperative with the foreign oppressor. In Cuba in 1959 and Nicaragua in 1979 such wars of liberation had

some success, while both the 1965 uprising in the Dominican Republic and the 1968 uprising in the former Czechoslovakia failed.

The second way that doctrinal nationalism may become a cause of war is by spawning *separatist movements* within a politically unified nation-state. One example of this possibility is the effort of some French-speaking Canadians to get Quebec to secede from Canada and form a separate nation-state. The French-speaking Canadians resent the pro–English bent of the national government and most Canadian business operations. They fear the gradual elimination of French culture and use of the French language. The Canadian government has responded with efforts to try to protect French culture and use of the French language, but there is constant tension because of the two languages. According to doctrinal nationalism French-Canadians should have their own nation-state rather than trying to survive in a multi-cultural Canada.

Separatist movements have actually led to war in many situations because the central government is often ready to fight in order to prevent loss of some of its territory. Two million people lost their lives during the late 1960s when the Ibos of Nigeria unsuccessfully tried to establish a separate nation-state of Biafra.[23] In 1971 the Bengalis of what was then East Pakistan fought a successful separatist war, with help from India, to establish the new country of Bangladesh.[24] In May 1993 Eritrea won its independence from Ethiopia after a 30-year armed struggle in which over 570,000 people died.[25] Chechens, who declared their independence from the Russian Federation in 1991, have been engaged in a continuing separatist war to win that independence since the Russians invaded in 1994 in an effort to reestablish their control over Chechnya. Still additional examples of separatist wars could be cited.[26]

In some situations a racial-ethnic group which wants to have its own independent nation-state is not located within a single nation-state but within the territory of two or three nation-states. An example of this situation is the Kurds, some of whom are living in northern Iraq, some in northern Iran, some in eastern Turkey, some in Armenia, and some in Syria.[27] Some Kurds hope to have an independent Kurdistan someday, but that would require a successful separatist movement in at least one of the first three countries mentioned, something which is not likely to happen since the other nation-states in which some of the Kurds live would probably use their influence to prevent it for fear that a wider separatist movement would also take some of their own territory.

The third kind of movement generated by *doctrinal nationalism* that might lead to war is *irredentism.* This term comes from the 19th century. After the nation of Italy was politically unified, the new Italian national government claimed that there were other areas containing cultural Italians which were *not yet redeemed* (in Italian, *irredenta*), that is, which were not yet incorporated into the new Italian nation-state. These areas were within the boundaries of other nation-states. The Italian government did not invite the cultural Italians in these areas to come and live within the political boundaries of Italy but instead claimed that the areas where they lived should become part of Italy. The other political nation-states in which the cultural Italians lived did not look kindly on this effort to take some of their territory. It is easy to see how this kind of conflict can lead to a violent confrontation. Some examples of irredentism leading to war are the moves by Germany to control Austria and parts of Czechoslovakia and Poland, which led eventually to World War II, and the claim of Morocco to the Tindouf area of Algeria. In some cases one country claims that culturally and historically the whole of another country belongs to it. Examples are the claim of China to Tibet (which was conquered by China in 1951 and put more directly under its control in 1959) and the claim at one time of Ghana to all of Togo.

The fourth kind of movement generated by *doctrinal nationalism* that might also lead to war is that in which an ethnic group within some independent nation-state seeks to have itself absorbed into another nation-state which it culturally resembles. This type of effort is a *reintegrationist* movement. It is similar in a

way to irredentism, but here it is the people in the "unredeemed" territory who are actively seeking to be reattached to what they regard as their homeland, rather than the homeland actively seeking to annex the area in which they live. The resistance in this case comes from other ethnic groups in the independent nation-state who do not want to be absorbed into the larger political unit. Cyprus is a good example of this type of situation. Cyprus is presently an independent nation-state, having won its independence from Britain in 1960. Many of its 80 percent ethnically Greek population would like to see it become part of the nation-state of Greece. On the other hand, the 20 percent of the population which is ethnically Turkish is adamantly opposed to such a move. With the nation of Greece ready to defend the interests of the Greek Cypriots and the nation of Turkey ready to defend the interests of the Turkish Cypriots, the potential for violent conflict is obvious. The United Nations peacekeeping force on Cyprus has been able to keep the situation under control most of the time, but there have been many violent outbreaks including an invasion by Turkish troops in 1974 in response to fears of the Turkish Cypriots that the island was about to be annexed by Greece. Cyprus remains divided with a Turkish-controlled "autonomous republic" in the north and the rest of the island under the control of Greek Cypriots. The desire of Catholics in Northern Ireland to reunite that state with Ireland may be viewed as another example of a reintegrationist movement which has led to violence.

We can now turn our attention to the way in which *patriotism or nationalism as loyalty to the nation-state* is related to war. It is this kind of nationalism that comes into play in most international conflicts. During conflict situations the people of the countries involved are urged not only to love their own country but to hate some actual or potential enemy. During World War II, for example, propaganda in the United States urged Americans not only to love their own country but also to hate the Germans and Japanese. After that war was over and the Cold War had begun, Americans were told that the Germans and Japanese are not really such bad people after all but that the Russians and Chinese, our allies in World War II, are the people we should hate. Since the end of the Cold War in 1990 for some Americans and at certain periods the Russians have no longer been automatically regarded as enemies, but the U.S. national attitude toward Russia is still in flux.

Nationalistic group hatred gets people ready to kill if there is a war. It also distorts people's perceptions of events so that war becomes more likely. Nationalism is nourished by focusing on the good things done by one's own nation and the evil things done by "the enemy," simultaneously ignoring the bad things done by one's own nation and the good things done by "the enemy." It tends to accentuate the differences between "us" and "them" and to dismiss the similarities. In this way, the members of the opposing nations are led to be proud of their own nation and to be indignant about all of the horrible things done by "the wicked enemy."

A particularly good example of nationalistic hatred is the 150-year antagonism that developed between the French and the Germans as the result of being opponents in one war after another from the time of Napoleon through World War II. It became difficult for either group to see any virtue in the other. They even accentuated their differences in food, drink, language, and so on. Under such circumstances it was relatively easy for the German and French governments to mobilize their people for war against each other.

But in this relationship between Germany and France there may be an encouraging lesson concerning the connection between nationalism and war. It seems that nationalism in the sense of hatred of another group is more an effect of war and preparation for war than a cause of it, though it may certainly be both. Because the Cold War created a political situation requiring the Germans and French to cooperate against a possible invasion from the Russians, the nationalistic hatred between these two nations diminished considerably. The shift in American attitudes since World War II toward Germans and Japanese also supports the notion that nationalistic ha-

tred is more the result of wars and indoctrination dictated by political interests than it is a cause of wars. It appears that nationalistic hatred is produced deliberately by leaders and propagandists to prepare their own people for a war against another country. It is not the result of some inherent hatred of the people of one nation for the people of another.

Still, we should not overlook the important role that nationalism plays in building support for national policies which lead to war. People want their own nation-state to have a high status; they feel good when their country has the highest gross domestic product or the highest per capita gross domestic product or the largest number of nuclear warheads. People feel bad when their country falls behind others in these and other categories. They feel good when their country expands its territorial holdings and bad when the extent of territory controlled by their country is reduced. People feel especially good when their country wins military battles or is successful in getting another nation to back down in a head-to-head confrontation, and they feel bad when their country loses a military battle or retreats in a head-to-head confrontation.

These nationalistic feelings support national leaders who aggressively defend the nation-state's economic interests and lead the country to increased military strength and dominance over other countries. The difficulty is that status is a relative thing. It is impossible for all nation-states to be first, or even near the top, with regard to wealth or military power. Struggles for superiority and "honor" (not backing down) thus take place between country and country. It is nationalism which generates public support for those national leaders who behave aggressively in these struggles. This support for aggressiveness certainly does not decrease the likelihood of international war. What promotes peace is appreciating the interests of groups other than one's own (what does the situation look like from their point of view?) and being ready to be somewhat conciliatory rather than aggressive in dealing with these other countries.

In summary, we see that nationalism contributes to war in several ways. Doctrinal nationalism supports liberation movements, separatist movements, irredentist movements, and reintegrationist movements, all of which may lead to war. Loyalty to the nation-state or patriotism supports aggressive national leaders in their struggles for power. It would be difficult to point to any war in the 19th and 20th centuries in which nationalism in one or another sense has not been a significant factor.

6. Other Views About Causes of War

So far we have discussed the hypotheses (1) that war is caused by individual human aggression; (2) that it is caused by groups competing for survival, for goods, for control over the distribution of ideas, for status, and for political power; and (3) that it is caused by group identification, especially identification with the nation. Now we will consider some other views that have been advanced on why wars occur.

Arms Races as a Cause of War

If the ultimate test of a nation's strength is its capacity to defend itself in a war, then any nation which anticipates war seems to have little choice but to build up its military forces to be superior to those of the anticipated enemy. It could even be argued that, in the face of a possible attack from another nation, failure of a nation to increase its military forces might in fact encourage attack because the other nation would be led to expect a quick and easy victory. On the other hand, if two nations confront each other and each aims to make its military forces superior, a steady increase of arms on both sides will result. This escalation of arms construction and deployment will be further intensified if military planners on each side engage in an extra build-up just in case the potential enemy's forces are stronger than estimated.

This situation in which two potential enemy nations (or groups of nations) each try over a period of time to gain armed superiority over the other is called an arms race. Such a race seems to contribute to the likelihood of war between the nations involved. The temptation to start a war seems to be especially great when one nation possesses a newly developed, significant weapon which its potential opponent does not yet have but will probably acquire in the near future. Under these circumstances, why not start a war when the prospect of victory is greatest? Why wait, when waiting might eventually result in the enemy gaining military superiority?

To get a better understanding of what it is like to be a leader of a nation involved in an arms race, the reader is invited to play a simple game.[1] Ideally there should be three participants, but with the proper arrangements and understandings, two can play. When there are three persons, one acts as supervisor, referee, timekeeper, and scorekeeper while the other two represent the heads of nations involved in an arms race. The players should each have a small piece of paper or cardboard which can be concealed under their hand on a flat surface. This piece of paper should have a plus-sign on one side and a minus-sign on the other, so the players can indicate whether they have chosen to increase or decrease the military spending of their own nation.

To begin the game, the timekeeper tells the players that they have 30 seconds before they will be required to render their first arms decisions (which can be considered the first annual budget). The players are permitted to communicate with each other and to make "treaties," but as in actual international situations no one enforces any agreements that might be made. As the 30-second deadline approaches, the players place their pieces of paper on the table with either the plus-sign or the minus-sign face up, but conceal it until the timekeeper says, "Now." Players then uncover the papers allowing the others to see the decisions. The timekeeper calculates, records, and announces the score and then informs the players that the next decision is due in 30 seconds. The entire sequence is then repeated. The game can be as long or short as players desire, but for the first game the recommended duration is about 20 decisions.

The scoring of the game is crucial, and the players must understand it before beginning play. Each player receives 20,000 points at the start of the game. This figure represents the average standard of living of the people in each player's country. The object of the game is to score as high as possible, that is, to improve the average standard of living of one's nation as much as possible. Each time a decision is made, scoring depends on the combination of the decisions of the two players. If both players put the minus-sign up, indicating a cutback in military spending, each is awarded 100 points increase in average standard of living. If both put the plus-sign up, indicating an increase in military spending, each loses 100 points on their average standard of living. But if one puts the plus-sign up and the other the minus-sign, they receive different scores: the player with the plus-sign gains 500 points while the one with the minus-sign loses 500 points. This scoring reflects a situation in which the military superiority of one nation allows it to make coercive arrangements with other nations to the disadvantage of its opponent. The game illustrates the logic of arms races and the difficulty of controlling them even when both parties realize objectively that it would be best for both to disarm.

What strategy should a player use in this game? One might adopt a tit-for-tat strategy, opting each time to do what the opposing player had done on the previous turn. One could adopt a hawkish strategy and increase arms spending every turn, regardless of what the opponent does, on grounds that this would maximize gains and minimize losses whatever decision the opponent makes. A player might adopt a dove-like strategy and consistently decrease arms expenditures regardless of what the opponent does on grounds that this seems to be the only way of ending the arms race. (Empirical evidence suggests that this strategy does not work in many situations and in fact often encourages the opponent to be more aggressive.[2])

Players could also adopt different strategies with regard to communication with the opponent. For example, they might decide to announce what strategy they intend to use and then use it, or they might decide to *say* that they will use one strategy and then actually use another. They must decide whether or not to abide by agreements entered into with the

other player. Games like this (usually called the "prisoner's dilemma" game) have been played and observed with a view to determining which strategies different kinds of people do actually use and which strategies are most likely to succeed in bringing an arms race under control.[3]

In what sense, if any, are arms races a cause of war?[4] It seems that arms races themselves are always an *effect* of some other "cause of war" such as a struggle for power. Nations do not simply fall into arms races against some nations and not against others; there is always some other cause such as economic or ideological conflict which leads to the arms race. For example, leading up to World War I there was an arms race between Britain and Germany but not between Britain and the United States. Why? The difference can be explained in part by the conflict of ideology between Britain and Germany while Britain and the United States were ideological allies. There were also other factors such as Germany's readiness to challenge British dominant status not only in Europe but in the world as a whole. When the Germans began to build a large navy, the British, who at that time had the biggest and most powerful navy, felt they had to stay ahead in the naval arms race or sink to number two. At the same time, the Germans were determined to show that they could outdo the British in building warships. The arms race obviously did not by itself cause World War I, but it may well have served as a contributory cause.

It has been argued by Lewis Richardson that the behavior of nations involved in an arms race can be described by a mathematical model.[5] According to this model there are only two circumstances where arms races could be kept from going out of control and ultimately resulting in war: (1) the capability for building more arms is overcome by resistance to military spending, or (2) one side decides to drop out of the arms race and accept domination by the other. Richardson believed that neither of these things would be likely to occur in the twentieth century.[6] Of the wars that occurred between 1820 and 1929, Richardson concluded that arms races were a significant factor in the outbreak of war in about one-ninth of the cases.[7] That result suggests that arms races are sometimes a contributory factor to the beginning of war even though they are also the effect of other causes.

The end of the long Cold War arms race between the United States and the Soviet Union in 1989 supports the correctness of Richardson's mathematical model. Richardson had specified two circumstances where an arms race could come to an end rather than going out of control: (1) resistance to more military spending and (2) the readiness of one side to accept domination by the other. Although he believed it unlikely that in the 20th century either of these circumstances would be realized, in fact both were. The Soviets under Gorbachev decided that they just could not continue to spend so much for the military while their domestic economy was failing, and they also decided that they could accept domination by the United States. But it was not generally expected they would do that. In fact, for those who lived through the end of the Cold War it was difficult to believe that the totally unanticipated changes were actually occurring. We were very lucky in 1989. Many would say, "Thank heaven that somehow the reform-minded Gorbachev got to be the top leader in the Soviet Union." What all this means is that improbable events do occur. As anyone familiar with probability theory can testify, improbable events are occurring all the time.

It is still the case, however, that arms races can contribute to the outbreak of war and that once an arms race gets going it is very difficult to stop it. Can either side accept a secondary status and not do everything possible to win the arms race? To give up is tantamount to losing a war, as is evident from what happened to the Soviet Union from 1989 to 1991. The development of some new kind of weapon during an arms race can be particularly dangerous because the side that does not have it may be tempted to start a war immediately on grounds that they will have a better chance to win if they attack before the enemy has produced very many of its new weapons. At present there are arms races in

various parts of the world that indicate the existence of tension which may give way to all-out war including that taking place between India and Pakistan. That arms race is especially dangerous now that both sides have the capability of producing and delivering nuclear weapons. Don't forget the arms race game.

Military Planning as a Cause of War

Somewhat related to arms races as a cause of war is the idea that war can be the result of contingency plans made by the military on how to fight a war. The job of the military of any country is to be ready to fight and win a war if war comes. In order to do this well the military must constantly make plans concerning what could be done and, in some cases what must be done, if war breaks out. Once a war begins, you cannot afford to lose. Also, you must plan ahead in order to have the right kinds of weapons on hand and the right kinds troops properly trained in advance and so on. Furthermore, in such military planning one typically starts from a worse-case analysis in order to avoid being unpleasantly surprised by the enemy's capabilities. When both sides do this, something similar to an unrestrained arms race occurs. Each side feels threatened by the other's preparations because the extent of those preparations and capabilities is exaggerated by their own worse-case estimations.[8]

The classic case of how military planning can serve as a contributory factor to the beginning of a war is the connection between Germany's Schlieffen (or von Schlieffen) Plan and the outbreak of World War I.[9] The German plan was worked out as a strategy on how best to fight a two-front war against France on the west and Russia on the east. The thinking was that since France was the more technologically advanced country and Russia was only slowly becoming industrialized it would be best to attack France first while implementing a holding action against the Russians until the French were knocked out of the war. Then the German forces could be moved to the eastern front for a longer fight against a larger but less technologically advanced Russia.

The Schlieffen Plan included the strategy of going around the main French defenses by going into France through Belgium, even though the Germans had signed a treaty guaranteeing Belgium neutrality. It also relied on the supposition that it would take the Russians several weeks to mobilize their forces while German mobilization would be accomplished quickly once it was decided that war would be fought.

The assassination of Austrian crown prince Franz Ferdinand by Serb nationalists in June 1914 was followed by the "blank check" pledge of Germany to help Austria in a war against Serbia even if Austria attacked first. This pledge of support went beyond what was required by the defensive alliance between Austria and Germany. The Russians wanted to be ready to help their Slavic-brother Serbs if they were attacked by Austria so Russia began to mobilize its forces. This mobilization endangered the Schlieffen Plan with its supposition that it would take the Russians some weeks to mobilize, so the Germans demanded that the Russians stop their mobilization. The Russians, noting that mobilization of one's forces is not an act of war, refused to stop. As a result, the Germans were pushed to ask the French whether they intended to honor their alliance with the Russians. When the French did not renounce their commitment to Russia, the Germans launched their attack against France and World War I was on. The French were being attacked by Germany because of a squabble in southeastern Europe between Austria and Serbia. Why? Because the German Schlieffen Plan for a two-front war required attacking France first.

There are of course other cases where military planning has been a contributory factor to the outbreak of war. For example, the Japanese attack on American forces at Pearl Harbor in Hawaii in December 1941 was the result of Japanese military planning on what was supposed to persuade the Americans to retreat from the western Pacific. Another example is the preventive war started by the Israelis against their Arab opponents in 1967. Military planning is critical to winning a war. As long as international conflicts are to be re-

solved by military superiority, political leaders cannot afford to lose a war. Consequently, the political leaders are often guided in their actions by what the military leaders tell them must be done in order to win a war. That can include actually initiating the fighting.

Particular Villains as a Cause of War

If we look at the problem of crime within a society, it seems reasonable to believe that a good portion of it is caused by a few antisocial people. It seems that the best way to eliminate, or at least greatly reduce, crime is to lock these criminals away so they can no longer harass the rest of society. Some see an analogy between crime and war and believe that the basic cause of war is the existence of a few villains who are ready to use force and violence to exploit the rest of society in order to get wealth and power for themselves. Wars are caused by these war-mongers, it is claimed, and the way to reduce the likelihood of war is to get rid of this relatively small number of troublemakers.

Different versions of this approach point to very different types of villains. One view focuses on power-hungry aggressive individuals (totalitarian dictators) who gain control of a top position in a nation or another group and then lead that group to use violence to extend its control over others. A second view says that the villains who cause war are the military leaders and weapons manufacturers (the military-industrial complex) who stand to realize substantial personal gains as the result of war or preparing for war. A third view sees the culprits as the elite of a society (the ruling class) who are ready and willing to use violence to try to halt the inevitable social changes which will eventually eliminate their positions of privilege.

The importance of the aggressiveness of the group leader was discussed earlier in connection with the relation of individual aggressiveness to the outbreak of war. As was noted then, it would be difficult in the human context to defend the view that these aggressive leaders are a necessary or a sufficient condition for war, but the more limited contention that power-hungry leaders are a contributory factor is quite plausible.[10]

A related thesis claims that particularly aggressive individuals are more likely to get into leadership positions in an authoritarian political system while liberal democratic political systems are less likely to allow such individuals to get to the top or to carry out inordinately aggressive policies when they do get to the top. According to this view, if all governments were democratic rather than autocratic the danger of war would be reduced considerably.[11] Woodrow Wilson's slogans during World War I, that it was "the war to end all wars" and at the same time "the war to make the world safe for democracy," are based on this viewpoint. The difficulty for this thesis is that democratic nations have had their share of aggressive leaders and oppressive foreign policies. It seems that the British, French, and Americans have been just as imperialistic as the Germans, Spanish, and Russians. One can hardly review the policies and practices of the U.S. government toward American Indians, toward Filipinos during and after the Spanish-American War, and toward Central America in the twentieth century and conclude that democratic governments are not aggressive toward other societies. The claim that liberal democracies do not fight wars with other liberal democracies has evidential support, but that happy situation may be explained by the different principle that countries where the leaders have similar cultural backgrounds and ideological commitments tend not to fight wars with one another.[12]

In evaluating the relationship between democracy and war it should not be forgotten that Hitler came to power in Germany in accord with democratic procedures and that he had public support as long as his various military adventures were succeeding. It is questionable whether democracies have any special advantages in keeping aggressive individuals from gaining positions of leadership. Any restraint on aggressiveness may be due more to the checks on the power of the leader that exist within a democratic system, and even here it must be remembered that there is not much of

a check as long as military action results in quick victory. Vietnam was a public relations disaster for the U.S. government, but the positive reaction to quick military victories in Grenada, Panama, and the 1991 Gulf War shows that the public does not generally disapprove of aggressive military action. In fact they seem to enthusiastically support it as long as victory is achieved quickly and with few casualties.

A second view about the particular villains who cause war is that war is made more likely by munitions makers, high-ranking military officers, and others who profit from war and war preparations. The expression *military-industrial complex*[13] is used to refer to that relatively small group of people who benefit from war and preparation for war, a group that includes not only the professional military and the arms manufacturers but also others such as bankers who finance the arms industry, labor unions whose members produce arms, scientists and engineers engaged in weapons research, politicians eager to promote government spending in their political districts, and veterans' organizations. The fact that the U.S. military budget keeps going up despite the fact that the United States already accounts for over one-third of the world's military spending suggests that something other than security needs is promoting this spending.[14]

The thesis that arms manufacturers and their allies in the military, the government, and the newspaper-publishing business might deliberately promote war scares to stimulate military spending seems to have been first seriously argued by Richard Cobden in Britain in 1861.[15] He noted the repeated occurrence of a series of events beginning with expressions of concern by high-ranking naval officers (widely publicized by the newspapers) that France was preparing to invade Britain. An increase in naval appropriations soon followed, and then the threat disappeared. One event which provides a particularly good piece of evidence to support the view that arms manufacturers have deliberately stimulated arms races occurred a few years before World War I. H.H. Mulliner, the managing director of a British shipbuilding firm, told his friends in the military that he had secret information that the Germans had suddenly accelerated the building of battleships.[16] The story was leaked to the press, who cooperatively published it. The British public demanded that more battleships be built to meet the German challenge. The Germans denied having increased their efforts, but once the British speeded up theirs the Germans felt they had to do the same. After this naval arms race was in motion, Mulliner wrote a series of letters which were published in the London *Times* indicating how he had started the whole thing, but the arms race did not stop and Mulliner himself was fired. Another incident worthy of mention occurred in 1927 when American steel companies sent William Shearer to the Geneva Disarmament Conference for the express purpose of disrupting it.[17]

In the United States the notion that the U.S. munitions manufacturers had been responsible for involving the United States in World War I became popular in the 1930s as a result of public investigations by a Senate committee chaired by Senator Gerald Nye, although the committee failed to prove the allegations.[18] The idea that the military-industrial complex is a possible source of danger to U.S. policy-making was brought to public attention again by President Eisenhower in his 1961 farewell address.[19] During the Vietnamese War some opponents of the war claimed that the military-industrial complex was responsible for U.S. involvement. The notion that the arms race between the United States and the Soviet Union during the Cold War was largely due to the activities of the American military-industrial complex was widespread.[20]

Some observers claim that there was also a military-industrial complex which promoted war and preparation for war in the Soviet Union.[21] Even though there were no owners of arms industries in the Soviet Union, there were managers of such industries whose influence was greatly affected by the importance ascribed to their work. The military and the hawkish members of the political leadership had the same interests as their counterparts in the United States. It was even suggested that the military-industrial complexes of the Soviet Union and the United States kept the arms race going as an informal cooperative enterprise which was very profitable to both of them.[22] With the Cold War ended it has been suggested that the U.S. military-industrial complex is searching for some new "enemy" that will keep its services in demand. For example, the proposed new missile defense system is supposedly being designed in part to protect the United States against a missile attack from North Korea, but by the time the system gets deployed it is quite possible that North Korea will no longer be an enemy nation.

What about these claims? Do certain people who profit from war actually cause wars to occur? Even Senator Nye claimed only that American munitions makers had caused the United States to be dragged into World War I, not that they had caused the war in the first place. And even if one took seriously the idea that there was an informal cooperative effort between the American and Soviet military-industrial complexes in support of a gigantic arms race, it does not follow that these groups actually wanted to cause a war or that they could have done so if they had so desired.

The claim that the military complex is a contributory factor to war is quite credible. Before the age of the long-range bomber and the intercontinental ballistic missile, high-ranking military officers and owners of arms-producing facilities could be relatively sure that they would not personally be hurt by war and that they stood to gain a great deal by it. But even in an age of intercontinental missiles certain kinds of war can be very profitable for military-industrial complexes in the richer countries as long as the danger of an all-out nuclear war is avoided. Furthermore, these are just the kinds of wars that have been occurring since the end of World War II. The fact that these situations are profitable for the military-industrial complex does not of course prove that they bring them about, but it does raise doubts. One such profitable situation would be for the country where a military-industrial complex is located to engage in a limited war with an enemy which has no chance of directly hurting the wealthier country. This was exemplified by U.S. engagements in Korea, Vietnam, and Kuwait and Russian involvements in Hungary, Czechoslovakia, and Afghanistan. A second type of profitable situation for the military and arms producers is a war involving smaller allies of their own country in which the wealthier country supplies military know-how and weapons which need to be replaced again and again as they are destroyed in the fighting. Wars such as those in the Middle East during the Cold War period provided an excellent opportunity for the United States and Soviet Union to test some of their military equipment under actual battlefield conditions. Add to these wars the arms races which occurred in various parts of the world and it is evident that the *post*–World War II era was a very profitable one for the military-industrial complexes in the United States, Britain, France, and the Soviet Union. Even though the Cold War is over, huge amounts of public money continue to flow into the military-industrial complex of the United States and its allies in order to be militarily prepared to fight any "enemy" which may appear on the scene.

Nevertheless, it is more plausible to suppose that national governments struggling for power with each other create the military-industrial complexes than to believe that the military-industrial complexes control the governments. The decision to spend large amounts of government money for military purposes so that arms-making is profitable is a political decision. Governments could make it equally profitable for industry to make computers and tractors to donate to less developed countries. Then a products-for-development complex would come into being which would be as self-perpetuating as the military-industrial complex. Why isn't there an influential products-for-development complex? It is because governments are willing to spend large amounts for weapons to use in the struggle for power against other national governments while they are unwilling to spend large amounts to assist people in less developed countries.

As long as crucial international conflicts are to be resolved by force and threats of force, governments of nations likely to be challenged by others seem to have little choice but to try to make their military forces "second to none." Once a military-industrial complex is created to produce this military superiority, it tends to be self-sustaining and to encourage attitudes and policies which will work to its own advantage. This probably contributes to the existence of arms races and to the outbreak of limited wars, but like the arms race itself, the military-industrial complex seems to be an effect of other, more fundamental causes rather than an ultimate cause of war.[23]

A third view about villains who are responsible for war is associated with the names Karl Marx, Friedrich Engels, and V.I. Lenin. According to this view the villains are the elite of a society who try by force to maintain their positions of privilege in the face of economic and social changes which threaten to eliminate the underpinning responsible for their status. This view which was championed by Communists in the Soviet Union, China, Cuba, Vietnam, and other parts of the world has obviously lost a great deal of influence since the end of the Cold War and the disintegration of the Soviet Union. Nevertheless it is worth reviewing because of its importance in understanding what motivated the Communists theoretically and because it still influences the thinking of some intellectuals — and not just Communists — throughout the world.

Understanding this Communist view will require a brief discussion of some of the basic ideas of Marx, Engels, and Lenin.[24] According to them the most important thing about a society is how its goods and services are provided. A society in which people hunt, fish, and forage for food will be much different from a society in which agriculture and domesticated animals provide the food supply. In fact, they believe that the whole social structure and cultural outlook will depend on the mode of production. In a feudal society where agriculture and domesticated animals are the basic sources of goods, those who own land will be the elite and the culture will develop around their outlook and interests. On the other hand, in a bourgeois society where small-scale manufacturing is the basic means of producing goods, those who own the shops will be the elite and the culture will reflect their concerns. (See the chart on page 119.)

According to this theory, if the mode of production continues to be the same, the society will be stable and violent conflict at a minimum. But if the basic mode of production changes, then the situation is different. Consider, for example, what happened at the beginning of the industrial revolution when simple machines were introduced which enabled one person to produce a great deal more than previously could be produced by several persons in the same period of time. The introduction of these machines changed the mode of production from one in which each family milled its own grain and wove its own cloth by hand to one in which machines did this work. Before the introduction of these machines wealth would depend basically on how much land you owned; afterward it would depend basically on how many of these machines you owned and how much money you could gain from selling what was produced. In the old feudal society the big landowners (the nobility) were the elite. A whole social structure and cultural outlook had been built around their interests. The newly rich bourgeoisie (the owners of businesses) did not fit into this structure and outlook. Consequently, a struggle for power resulted. The old landed aristocracy tried to preserve the social structure which supported their positions of privilege while owners of the machinery strove for more political power in recognition of their new wealth and power in the society.

If the old elite would have modified their social structure to allow the owners of machinery to gain more political power, a peaceful transition could have taken place, but the land-owners didn't make such a move. Why not? First, they did not intend to surrender their positions of privilege simply because some other group wanted them to do so. Second, the old social structure with which they were familiar was "natural," the only social structure they could imagine. On the other hand, the bourgeoisie had power represented by the productive capability of their machines. If the old nobility wouldn't step aside peacefully, there was no choice but to take political power from them violently. The French Revolution in 1789 is a good example of the violent overthrow of the old aristocracy by the new middle class.

One might be inclined to say that it was the new middle class rather than the old nobility which caused this violent upheaval. It was, after all, the bourgeoisie and their followers who were the active agents of the revolution. But according to Marx and Engels such a view of the situation overlooks the force used by the old order to try to prevent change. It is true that the repressive violence used by the police was authorized by the laws of the existing government, but that fact merely shows that the government was just one more part of the social structure controlled by the old nobility. The blame for the violence, according to the Marxists, should be placed not on the revolutionaries seeking to establish a social order based on the objective reality of the new dominant mode of production which they controlled, but rather on the old elite who were using force to try to preserve a social order which was no longer appropriate to the new situation.

What has been said so far may lead the reader to believe that Marx and Engels were supporters of bourgeois capitalism. In one sense they were. They thought capitalism was a great advance over feudalism and that it was desirable for the bourgeoisie to use force to overthrow the social structures of the landed aristocracy. But in another sense Marx and Engels were opponents of bourgeois capitalism. They opposed the capitalist society in which they lived because they believed that still another qualitative shift had taken place in the mode of production, a shift from the old small-scale individualistic manufacturing to the new social production of goods by cooperative effort in huge factories. The social structure (such as private ownership of factories and their output) and cultural outlook (such as rugged individualism) of the capitalists were built on the foundations of small-scale manufacturing, but Marx and Engels argued that the shift to mass production made these social structures and this cultural outlook obsolete. Thus the capitalists were now to be opposed by the new revolutionary socialists, just as the landed aristocracy had previously been opposed by the revolutionary capitalists. Now it was the capitalists who were using government-sanctioned force to obstruct needed social change. It may seem that the socialist revolutionaries are the instigators of war, but according to Communists the blame belongs to the capitalists who refuse to permit the social changes required by the shift to the collective production of goods. In the 19th and 20th centuries, according to the Marxists, the capitalists who resist the needed change to socialism have become the villains responsible for war.

In order to evaluate this view in relation to the issue of what causes war, let us return to our distinctions about the various senses of the word *cause*. According to this Marxist outlook, are the present capitalist leaders supposed to be a sufficient cause of war? That is, do they by themselves bring about war? The answer seems to be "No." They might, according to Communists, be responsible for the oppression which occurs, but war occurs only when there is also violent resistance to this oppression. Consequently, it does not seem that Marxists maintain that the capitalists are a sufficient condition for war.

Are the capitalist leaders a necessary condition for war at the present time? (Obviously at an earlier time the question would need to be raised concerning the landed aristocracy rather than the capitalists.) It would seem that Marxists answer this question in the affirmative, believing that if all members of the capitalist class were out of the way then war would be eliminated. At any stage in history, the Marxists seem to be saying, if the old elite would just step aside when their privileged positions are no longer objectively supported by the new prevailing mode of production, then there would be no wars.

Such an extreme claim seems difficult to defend. A survey of history reveals many wars in which one feudal society fought against another feudal society and one capitalist society against another. We can even find instances in recent history of one socialist society fighting against another socialist society. If the only basis for war is the unwillingness of the old elite to give way to the new order, why do these nonrevolutionary wars occur? It seems that Marxist thought focuses for the most part on wars *within* societies rather than wars *between* societies, and even *within* societies it is questionable whether the Marxist view adequately accounts for wars such as those resulting from nationalistically motivated separatist movements.

Recognizing that Marxist theory did not seem particularly relevant to the wars taking place between countries in the late 19th and early 20th centuries, Lenin extended Marx's analysis of social conflict to the international sphere.[25] The capitalist countries were engaged in two kinds of wars, he said: colonial wars against less developed countries and wars among themselves. The first type of war could readily be explained by an extension of Marxist principles. The capitalists were countering a possible revolution in their own societies by subjugating distant peoples, exploiting them, and giving some of the benefits to the workers in the home country. This arrangement allowed large profits to continue to flow into the pockets of the capitalists without objection from the working classes at home.

The second type of war, that kind due to economic competition between capitalist nations for control in colonial regions, introduces a cause for war not present in the original Marxist position. Lenin's revision of Marxism still ascribes blame to the capitalists for all wars but it *no longer* claims that *all* wars are conflicts between an old elite class and a new revolutionary class. Once Marxist-Leninists concede that economic competition between one capitalist nation and another may be a cause of war, then it would seem that they should also allow that wars may be the result of economic competition between one *noncapitalist* nation and another. They then should also admit that wars within countries can be caused by various kinds of competition between groups which are from the same economic class. Thus there can be *other causes of war* besides what is allowed by the older Marxist view, which claims that war is always due to the old ruling class not yielding political power to the people who control the new prevailing mode of production.

Furthermore, Lenin's revision seems unable to account for more recent wars between one socialist country and another. Were any capitalists involved in the border dispute which developed between China and the Soviet Union in the 1960s? Were any capitalists involved in the Communist Chinese invasion of Communist Vietnam or the Communist Vietnamese invasion of Communist Cambodia in 1979? Once it is admitted that other factors such as nationalism may be involved in these disputes, the question is raised whether nationalism might not be the crucial factor in other wars.

The Marxist-Leninist thesis that the capitalist class is the cause of all war depends on accepting a debatable theory of history which views the ruling class as the cause of all violence. Recent wars between socialist countries seems to refute the notion that the capitalists are a necessary condition of war. The most that can plausibly be claimed is that capitalists are a contributory cause of war, a claim that seems to be strongest in the case of colonial wars and efforts to squash liberation movements in less developed countries.[26]

War as an Effort to Suppress Internal Dissension

The famous German philosopher Hegel observed that "peoples involved in civil strife also acquire peace at home through making wars abroad."[27] There seems to be little doubt that when a group or society is engaged in a violent conflict with a common enemy, differences of interest within that group or society are temporarily ignored. For example, in revolutions to overthrow a government such as occurred in Iran and Nicaragua in 1979, the revolutionary forces were able to unite in the fight to overthrow the old regime even though they may have very different views about what

sort of new government is to be established after the revolution succeeds. In the same way quarreling groups within a nation tend to forget their grievances against each other when that nation is engaged in a war against another nation. Labor and management perceive that they must work together. Rich and poor see that they must join together in defense or go down to defeat together. Different racial or cultural groups will unite in the common effort even though they might be quite antagonistic toward each other in peacetime.

Under these circumstances it is easy to see that a leader who is being criticized by various factions within a movement or by various groups within a society might be tempted to begin using violence against a common enemy in order to quell the dissent. If internal strife is threatening, a war could be started to keep the internal disturbances under control. The leader must be subtle about accomplishing this outbreak of warfare, however, so that the other side can be blamed for it.

Has this sort of thing ever really happened? Has there ever been a war which was begun with the motive of overcoming internal dissension? One example frequently cited is that of Otto von Bismarck, Chancellor of Prussia and then Chancellor of the German Empire during much of the last half of the 19th century. At one time he observed that his various wars had undercut the influence of the left-wing revolutionaries in Prussia, but he never said that he started the wars to accomplish this aim. The wars he started in the middle and late 1860s aimed to bring the previously separate German states under Prussian control. One might be tempted to say that he started wars with external enemies in order to unify the German nation and that he succeeded in accomplishing this goal after peaceful efforts to unite the German states had failed.[28] But it can be asked whether this case is truly an example of wars being started in order to alleviate internal dissension. It seems rather to be a case of a leader being particularly clever at gaining new territory without arousing any resentment among the people who have been brought under his control.

The effort in 1982 by the government of

Argentina to take over the Falkland Islands–Malvinas from Britain is viewed by some as an example of a government starting an external skirmish in order to counteract domestic unrest. On the other hand, that effort may have been triggered by the desire of the Argentine government to have control over those islands when a treaty about ownership of resources located on the ocean floor around those islands would soon come into effect. In any case, the project failed because the British soon recaptured the islands. Furthermore, regardless of the motives in this particular case, attempts to discover any general correlation between internal discord or instability and the fighting of external wars have been inconclusive and subject to varying interpretations.[29] Consequently, it is questionable to what extent internal dissension should or should not be viewed as a contributory cause of war.

War as an Effort to Eliminate Injustice

The issue of the relation between peace and justice has previously been discussed. It was noted that peace may refer to the persistence of a situation in which some group or some nation is being treated unjustly. If this injustice is flagrant, the resentment may become so intense that people are ready to use violence to change the situation, especially if nonviolent efforts have proved to be unsuccessful.

It is interesting that both Thomas Jefferson and Karl Marx argued that violence is justified in such situations and that both the American and Russian revolutions are examples of wars fought to remove what were perceived to be injustices not removable in any other way. Jefferson even suggested that the use of violence to protect liberty would need to be repeated with some regularity. He wrote in a letter to Colonel Smith in 1787:

> What country can preserve its liberties, if its rulers are not warned from time to time, that this people preserve the spirit of resistance? Let them take arms. ... What signify a few lives lost in a century or two? The tree of liberty must be refreshed from time to time with the blood of patriots and tyrants. It is its natural manure....[30]

Of course, the notion that violence should be used if necessary to combat injustice is not confined to Americans and Russians. In fact, almost all efforts to justify the use of violence, other than the rationale of self-defense, point to the need to remove some perceived injustice. For example, much civil strife has resulted from issues such as opposing claims concerning which person is the rightful ruler of a nation, and even Hitler's earliest aggressive actions were "justified" on grounds that the Treaty of Versailles ending World War I had been unfair to Germany.

A good contemporary example of war being waged in order to remove a perceived injustice is the battle of the Palestinian Arabs against the nation of Israel. Israel was established by Jews in 1948 with the aid of Britain and the United States on land inhabited largely by the Palestinian Arabs. When the British relinquished their control of the Middle East after World War II, these Palestinians wanted to establish a new independent nation. They had no objections to Jews already living there joining with them in a secular state, but they did object to the creation of a Jewish state which would be administered in accord with Jewish religious views and which would as a matter of policy try to attract more Jewish people to the area. Why, they asked, should Palestinians be required either to accept second-class citizenship in a Jewish state or to leave homes their families had occupied for generations? Why, they wondered, could they not have a secular state in which anyone would be welcome but no one would have special privileges? They used violence to try to prevent the establishment of a Jewish state, and they have continued to use violence against it after it was created. The Palestinians felt that it was very unjust for such a state to be created, without their consent, on territory which they regarded as their own. A comparable situation for Americans would be to have some groups of American Indians, assisted by other nations, reestablish their "nations" in the places where immigrants from Europe and other places now live, with the requirement that we abide by the Indian laws or get out. Of course, both the Jews and the Indians might feel that they were finally getting back what had unjustly been taken from them at an earlier time. Such are the intricacies of questions of justice. One great problem related to using violence to remove perceived injustices is that different parties have different perceptions of what is just. Will injustices be committed in order to "even the score" for prior injustices? Would there be any end to such a process of "correcting" previous injustices?

Questions of justice are even more likely to be the cause of war *within* nations. We have previously discussed the Marxist view that one cause of war is the unwillingness of the elite to give up positions of privilege when changed conditions indicate they should. We also noted earlier that governments tend to be more sensitive to the problems of people with wealth and power than to the poor and powerless. It is not surprising that sometimes people feel so oppressed that they believe the only viable action is to resort to violence.

Using violence to fight injustice constitutes a problematic situation. The use of violence will probably result in much injustice itself. There is usually a question of whether some nonviolent approach might be effective in alleviating the injustice. There is also a danger that the use of force by the oppressed will fail and make the oppressors even more oppressive. Finally, there is the problem of whether or not one's own perceptions of what is just or unjust are merely biased views reflecting self-interest. Regardless of these considerations, the desire to remove some perceived injustice has been a contributory factor in many wars, especially those taking place within countries.

The Absence of Peaceful Alternatives as a Cause of War

War comes about as a result of conflicts between groups, but such conflict situations need not be resolved by resort to violence. Bargaining, arbitration, agreed-upon rules and procedures for working out disagreements, and the institutions of government represent some other avenues for resolving conflict.[31] As John Vasquez puts it in his book *The War Puzzle*: "[W]ar comes with the progressive failure of non-violent games to resolve issues and the feeling that only a reliance on unilateral practices will get one what one wants."[32] There are some conflict situations, however, where none of these alternatives seems to be a viable option. The difficulty with bargaining is that it depends ultimately on threats of force and stubbornness. It rewards nonconciliatory attitudes. Arbitration depends on the availability of arbitrators perceived as fair by both parties and also as so strong and independent that they will not be intimidated by either. With agreed-upon rules and procedures there can be a problem of what to do if one side or the other just refuses to follow them. The institutions of government, which are able use force if necessary to enforce the rules, are barely beginning to be developed with regard to handling conflicts between nations. Even within a nation a fair resolution depends on the government being neutral between the parties to the conflict, a situation which often does not exist. Consequently, it frequently happens that the parties to a dispute decide on trial by force simply because there seems to be no other way.

Within a country, the belief that the conflict cannot be resolved by any approach short of violence produces new sources of antagonism on both sides. Groups intent on overthrowing the government or on establishing an autonomous state for some national minority cease to rely merely on propaganda and peaceful protests to promote their point of view. They inaugurate the use of violence against the police and sabotage against the government generally. On the other side, the government begins arresting and torturing anyone who might in any way be suspected of aiding the revolutionary or separatist forces. Tensions mount. Each incident involving violence calls for more violence by the other side. The perception that violence is the only way to settle the issue thus becomes itself a contributory factor to the outbreak and escalation of violence.

In international conflicts the same situation exists. Once it is believed that the use of violence is the only way to resolve the dispute, it follows that if either side momentarily gains a substantial advantage, it should strike at that moment. When it is believed that there will be a war anyway, why not fight it when one has the best chance of winning it? It is apparent that viewing war as inevitable can itself be a cause of war.[33] If such thinking had prevailed, the United States might have attacked the Soviet Union in the early 1950s when Americans had a marked superiority in atomic weapons and the means of delivering them against the enemy. This type of reasoning seems to have been the basis for the Soviet Union's plans to attack China in 1969 and for earlier American thoughts about attacking China during the Korean War. There is some hope for humanity in light of the fact that this thinking did not result in action on these occasions. Still there is no assurance that restraint and the possibility of third-party intervention will continue to inhibit military action in the international arena.

We must conclude that the absence of trustworthy nonviolent ways of resolving conflicts of interest at both the national and international levels constitutes an extremely important contributory factor to the outbreak of war. In the many nations where political and judicial institutions do provide relatively adequate nonviolent means for adjudicating conflicts, peace and a satisfactory degree of justice are maintained even when intense antagonisms exist. The absence of fair and nonviolent instruments for resolving conflict in other nations and at the world level is a particularly important cause of war, because the presence of such instruments would diminish the likelihood of war even in the face of the existence of the other causes of war previously discussed.[34]

It may not be immediately obvious that what is here being described as "an absence of

peaceful alternatives" to resolve conflicts is in fact ultimately the absence of a democratic political system that allows conflicts between various groups to be worked out through debating and balloting rather than by armed force. Such a system also allows the tension between those who emphasize peace and those who emphasize justice to be worked out through gradual changes based on hearing what the other side has to say and then reaching a temporary decision about what policy to adopt for the moment. Such a system provides an alternative to the existing international system as well as that which exists in some nation-states where the ultimate appeal is to force.

It is not appropriate to say that what is needed is *any* alternative to anarchy.[35] A totalitarian government could also provide an alternative to anarchy, but such a system would lack the positive features of nonviolent conflict resolution provided by a democratic political system. That is why we cannot say that *any kind of government*, on the national level or on the global level, would provide a satisfactory alternative to resolving conflicts by force. It must be a *democratic* government where the leaders are chosen by and are responsible to the people being ruled and where there are open debates and political parties to represent the ideologies and interests of the various groups. It is *the absence of such a democratic political system* that is a contributory factor to war, both within some nations and within the world. Furthermore, once such a system is in place, all the other causes of war can be overcome. Consequently, one could say, as Kenneth Waltz in his book *Man, the State, and War* has maintained, "Force is a means of achieving the external ends of states because there exists no consistent, reliable process of reconciling the conflicts of interest that inevitably arise among similar units in a condition of anarchy."[36]

7.   The Value of War

The general assumption of our inquiry about war is that human society is now faced with the problem of how to eliminate it. But is war really all bad? Hasn't war, at least in certain respects, been a good thing for human society? Although it would be a mistake to argue that wars occur *because* they serve good purposes such as controlling population and stimulating technological progress, still it might be claimed that we should not seek to prevent them because they do have some favorable results. Let us examine some of the alleged positive values of war to see if war may in fact have some redeeming qualities.

The Biological Value of War

At the end of the 18th century Thomas Malthus first published his thesis that there is a natural tendency for the population of humans to increase in a geometrical progression (or exponential pattern) (2, 4, 8, 16, 32, etc.), while food production tends to grow only in an arithmetic progression (2, 4, 6, 8, 10, etc.). Consequently, population will tend to outgrow food supply, and there must be some devices by which the population growth is checked. According to Malthus, disease, famine, and war are three such devices. Thus war, it is claimed, has a positive value: People are killed off so they and the children they would have produced need not face death from disease or starvation.

Has war been an important factor in controlling human population? The facts seem to suggest not. Even if as many as 51 million people were killed in World War II as some claim,[1] that would have been only 2 percent of the world's population.[2] The people killed in that war were replaced in a single year. In South Vietnam the population actually grew at a rate of 3 percent a year during three years (1964–67) while a war was being fought on its soil.[3] Statistics from earlier wars, all of which were considerably less lethal than World War II, indicate that "during the Christian Era, warfare has not been a major force controlling the size of human population."[4] It is disease, rather than war, which has been the major factor in controlling human population growth. The surge in population during the past 50–75 years is the result of modern medical knowledge, the use of DDT, and the development of public sanitation and water purification projects, not a lack of war.

A second view about the biological value of warfare claims that war improves the genetic quality of humans because it provides a means by which the less skilled and less cooperative members of human society are killed or disgraced, while the better warriors win mates and produce offspring. But since such a small proportion of the population is killed even in a war as tragic as World War II, there could be no significant selection of the fittest even if one grants the very debatable premise that war results in the less fit becoming less likely to produce offspring.[5] Anthropologist Frederick Thieme has observed that "racial discrimination, selective immigration policies, imperialistic exploitation of peoples, and a host of other forms of behavior have had a much more significant effect on demography or genetics of many populations than has warfare."[6] It seems then that during the last 5,000 years or so war has not been an important factor in either population control or genetic selection.[7]

What about the future? There has been a steady trend toward more casualties in each war, and the development of modern weaponry, both nuclear and nonnuclear, would not seem to promise any reversal of that trend. An all-out nuclear war between the big powers could in a few hours produce many times the fatalities that occurred during all of World War II, and subsequent deaths from radiation and burns and other causes would swell the death count even further. Conventional weapons are being greatly improved in accuracy and destructiveness so that a much higher number of deaths can be expected even in nonnuclear wars. Thus future wars will probably have a much greater impact on the population of the earth than even recent wars have had. Since the death from modern weapons is so indiscriminate, it is inconceivable that survivors in future wars would be genetically superior to those who get killed. Also, the possibility of genetic damage from radiation means that any war fought with nuclear weapons will surely be very detrimental to humanity from a biological point of view.

The Technological Value of War

Another alleged positive value of war is that it stimulates the pace of invention and social change. Societies tend to get into ruts and continue doing things in the same old way until some crisis, such as a war, forces them to adopt a more efficient social and production system, to do without some resources to which they are accustomed, or to be creative in the development of new weapons. Progress requires challenge, and war serves as the most intense kind of challenge to the society as a whole. Those who advocate this point of view may note the rapid development of aviation, electronics, medical technology, weather forecasting, synthetic materials, and so on during the past world wars. They may point to the large-scale government planning that was nonexistent before World War I and to the changed roles of women, largely a result of World War II. They may call attention to the changed situations of the former colonies of the Western European nations which have now become independent countries. Their claim is that all of this progress would not have occurred so rapidly without the stimulus of war.

But it is impossible to say what would have occurred without the world wars. Before World War I the world had been moving toward a global community with a minimum of trade barriers and parochial nationalistic feelings. Within a few decades inventions such as the telegraph, the telephone, the light bulb, the phonograph, the radio, the motion-pic-

ture camera and projector, the automobile, the airplane, and the agricultural tractor were brought forth with no stimulus from war. The technique of assembly line production was developed during the latter part of the 19th century when there were no significant wars. The Suez and Panama canals were built and put into operation. Remarkable advances were made in controlling malaria, yellow fever, and typhoid. Freud was publishing his theories about the psychological origins of various forms of mental illness, and X-rays were discovered. Einstein published his paper on the theory of relativity in 1905. What would have happened if there had been no World War I? Didn't World War I, with its demand for battleships, submarines, artillery pieces, tanks, and military aircraft, retard scientific progress with regard to the production of civilian goods? On the other hand, it was the necessities of war that led the Germans to pioneer the large-scale production of synthetic rubber and use of the Haber process to make the nitrates needed for explosives.

What was the situation between the world wars? New plastics were developed, along with synthetic materials such as rayon and nylon. The effectiveness of penicillin against bacteria was discovered. The basic principles of television, nuclear energy, and rocket propulsion were known before World War II broke out in 1939.[8] During that war, as during most wars, the scientific knowledge already available prior to the war was devoted to technological advancements for the military: nylon parachute cords, radar, V-2 rockets, atomic bombs, and the like. World War II caused a delay of at least five years in the development for consumer goods such as nylon clothing, television, and the use of nuclear energy for generating electricity. On the other hand, the war probably hastened the development of antibiotics, DDT, jet engines, helicopters, rockets, and substitutes for petroleum.

The thesis that war and preparation for war yield "spin-offs" that improve human life needs to be countered by the observation that similar investments of money and effort made with the direct aim of improving human life would undoubtedly yield even greater benefits.[9] If it is the case that scientific and technological progress increases during war, it seems due primarily to the willingness of governments to spend large amounts of money on the development of weapons and related research. Suppose that governments were willing to spend similar amounts on medical research, better transportation and communication systems, and eliminating crime. Suppose that governments were willing to undertake massive expenditures to improve the educational levels of their citizens and to research better ways of teaching and learning. It seems safe to predict that the resulting social progress would be several times greater than that which occurs as "spin-offs" from military programs. It is not war and preparations for war that produce technological change. Instead, massive public expenditures for research and development financed by government borrowing achieve this result. Most governments are willing to go into debt in order to pay these costs when stirred up by the threat of external attacks but are less willing to do so simply to improve the lives of their citizens.

Perhaps social changes might come more slowly without war. Change might be more evolutionary than revolutionary, but this seems to be desirable because revolutionary change tends to elicit more violence later. There is also the issue of whether change is always desirable, a question that especially needs to be considered with regard to the kinds of changes war brings. For example, during war there tends to be a greater concentration of power in the hands of a few government leaders, a situation which may continue after the war ends. Is that desirable? During war there tends to be less questioning of public policies and the decisions of those in command, which may also continue after the war is over. Is that desirable? Wars may accelerate social changes, but the changes may be undesirable.

Another aspect of this issue of technological and social progress as a result of war concerns the costs involved. Even if it were granted that more technological and social change takes place during war and that this change is desirable, one must still ask whether the cost of war exceeds the benefits. What might have been accomplished by those killed in a war? What additional things might have been accomplished even by those who survived the war uninjured but who had to devote several years of their early lives to fighting in it? Even in the simplest economic terms the public debt incurred for fighting a war (including assistance to veterans and their survivors) continues long after the war ends, contributing to inflation and taking funds that might be used instead for improving the quality of life. As the destructiveness and costs of war continue to escalate, it becomes more doubtful that war can be justified on the basis of any technological and social progress it might generate.

The Economic Value of War

Closely related to the issue of the technological value of war is the matter of the economic value of war. Especially among Americans there is a widely held view that war promotes economic prosperity. During World War I the U.S. economy did very well. Then, after ten years of peace (the "Roaring Twenties") came a depression, a depression which did not really end until the U.S. economy was stimulated by the outbreak of World War II in Europe. There were also boom times during the Korean and Vietnamese conflicts. Doesn't this history show that war means an abundance of jobs, high wages, and good profits? The situation is somewhat similar for other countries such as Sweden, Switzerland, Canada, Australia, and post–World War II Japan.

This perception that war is good for the economy depends, however, on the war's being fought on someone else's territory. For example, one could hardly say that the American Civil War was good for the U.S. economy of the southern part of the United States or that World War II was good for the economy of European countries such as Germany, Poland, and Czechoslovakia. Similarly, the wars occurring within some African countries at the present time are devastating to their economies, not something that helps them.

When some part of the world is being devastated by war and cannot produce the goods it usually does, there will obviously be a great opportunity for those countries not in the zone of destruction to produce and sell more to those who can no longer provide for themselves. Thus war will mean prosperity for those away from the war as they gain from the misfortunes of those at the center of the fighting. War destroys goods, and only those at a distance from the destruction will profit from it. A specific example of this truth is the devastation of Korea during the Korean War of 1950–53 while the Japanese economy boomed during this period.

Another reason that war seems to produce prosperity is that it leads governments to spend large amounts of money that they don't really have. War serves to excuse a level of government borrowing and spending which would not be tolerated in peacetime. That spending creates demand, thus stimulating the economy. But it should be noted that government borrowing and spending would have the same effect even if there were no war. It isn't only government spending *for war* which leads to more jobs and high profits. *Any* government spending financed by borrowing rather than higher taxes would produce the same results, at least temporarily. Later, of course, when the borrowed money needs to be repaid, there will be a drain on the economy, and that happens also whether the original spending was for the military or some other purpose.

If war isn't a stimulus to economic prosperity, what about military spending when there is no war but only a build-up of military forces? Doesn't that stimulate the economy? Once again, it isn't government spending *for the military* which leads to more jobs and high profits. Any government spending will do it. Large government outlays for education, for highways and public buildings, for medical research, for social welfare — for anything — will produce the same results, especially when it is paid for through deficit financing. Furthermore, government spending for other kinds of goods and services usually leads to increased productivity later while military products are essentially for destroying things.

In fact it is now a generally accepted principle that even in the short term more jobs would be created by nonmilitary spending than by military spending. According to various studies, government spending for military purposes actually causes a loss of jobs because more jobs could have been created if the same amount of money had gone to nonmilitary purposes.[10] It was estimated, for example, that back in 1974 state and local governments could have hired 30,000 more people per billion dollars of spending than could have been hired by the armed forces.[11]

It has also been pointed out that spending for the military is harmful to the economy in the long run. Even people who have benefited from military spending acknowledge that fifteen years ago the United States was technologically 20 years behind where it would have been if the money spent on military research between 1950 and 1980 had instead been put into those areas of science and technology promising the most economic progress.[12] In 1986 economist Lloyd J. Dumas, having studied the impact of military spending on the U.S. economy, concluded:

> The military system ... has diverted and continues to divert a substantial fraction of the United States' technological talent and enormous amounts of physical and financial capital, undermining the ability of U.S. producers to operate efficiently and thus to stay competitive with foreign producers.[13]

At that time it was also noted that among Western industrialized nations there was an inverse relationship between the amount the government spent on military research and the rate of growth of manufacturing productivity.[14]

If military spending is a burden on the economy, then a decrease in military spending should result in economic prosperity. Has that in fact happened? Consider this view of an expert on the issue.

> In February 1999, the House Banking Committee asked Federal Reserve Chairman Alan Greenspan to explain why he thought the U.S. economy had been doing so well. Among the probable reasons, Greenspan listed "the freeing up of resources previously employed to produce military products that was brought about by the end of the cold war." Congressman Barney Frank (D-MA) then led the witness through a series of follow-up propositions:

"I take it [that] what you are saying is that dollar for dollar, military products ... are there as insurance ... and to the extent [that] you could put those same dollars into other areas, maybe education and job training, maybe into transportation ... that is going to have a good economic effect." Greenspan affirmed all of this.[15]

This answer about what has caused the recent boom in the American economy from an acknowledged expert should be sufficient to silence those who say that we need military spending to boost the economy.

Military spending may be temporarily good for particular regions where the research and production of goods is taking place, but in the long run it is not good for the country, or even those particular regions, because other kinds of businesses do more to encourage continuing growth. If weapons are needed for defense, that is a separate issue, but the notion that military spending is good for the national economy is very mistaken. It just takes resources away from investment in more productive kinds of goods. Can anyone imagine leaders of less-developed countries being advised to increase their governmental military spending as a way to improve their long-term economic development?

The conclusion forced on us by the facts is that war, and even military spending without war, is not good for the economy. Similar government expenditures in nonmilitary areas would produce more jobs and more economic prosperity. Furthermore, using capital for military expenditures constitutes a real hindrance to long-term economic growth.

The Psychological Value of War

Another claim made for the value of war is that it provides a feeling of significance for the individuals who participate, challenging citizens to sacrifice for the welfare of the society as a whole rather than pursuing their own personal welfare. What else besides war can lead individuals to give up the pursuit of their own petty aims and devote their efforts to an endeavor which is crucial for human destiny? It is only during war, some claim, that the existence of the society and its values are really threatened. It is only then that citizens can

reasonably be called upon not only to forego certain amenities but perhaps to sacrifice their lives for the sake of a larger good. People are forced to think in terms of the overall course of history and the relative insignificance of their own personal goals and activities. As the German philosopher Hegel put it:

> War is the state of affairs which deals in earnest with the vanity of temporal goods and concerns — a vanity at other times a common theme of edifying sermonizing. ... War has the higher significance that by its agency, as I have remarked elsewhere, "the ethical health of the peoples is preserved...."
>
> In peace civil life continually expands; all its departments wall themselves in, and in the long run men stagnate.[16]

Similar sentiments are expressed by World War II Italian Fascist leader Benito Mussolini.

> War alone brings up to its highest tension all human energy and puts the stamp of nobility upon the people who have the courage to meet it. All other trials are substitutes, which never really put men into the position where they have to make the great decision — the alternative of life or death.[17]

That there is some truth in the general point being made by Hegel and Mussolini can be confirmed by talking with persons who have been involved in a war in which they truly believed. Among Americans such persons are more likely to be veterans of World War II than of the Korean or Vietnamese conflicts. These World War II veterans are likely to have fond memories of the war period, when the humdrum existence of everyday life was broken by a new feeling of the significance of every act which contributed to the war effort and thus to the victory of "our" values over "their" values. When discussing such a war, they are likely to tell of a feeling of being a part of something bigger and to confirm the insight that war not only requires self-discipline and self-sacrifice but also provides a psychological lift, a sense that one's life will make some difference in the course of the world.

What can be said in response to this claim concerning the psychological value of war? The American philosopher and psychologist William James recognized the need for self-discipline and self-sacrifice for a larger cause which is met by participation in war, but he also realized that war was becoming too destructive to be a satisfactory way of meeting this need. Consequently, he recommended an alternative. In his essay "The Moral Equivalent of War"[18] James advocated having the government direct a "war" against the injustices of fate and nature, a war for which the young people of the nation would be drafted, trained, and then supported as they attempted to right the wrongs of the world.

James's list of tasks to be performed suggests that he was thinking mainly of requiring the men of the upper classes to get their hands dirty doing the kind of work ordinarily done by people of the lower classes, but his basic idea could be modified by having youth from all types of backgrounds go to work in less developed countries or parts of their own country too poor to pay for their services. These young people would constitute an "army against injustice," something like the U.S. Peace Corps or the AmeriCorps VISTA (Volunteers in Service to America) program,[19] but James's proposal called for compulsory service for all young people rather than voluntary service for a few. These young people would thus be forced to dedicate themselves to problems beyond their own personal advancement and would find some significance in their lives as a result of being part of a general war on injustice. James realized that the task of establishing this battle against injustice as the moral equivalent of war would be difficult, but he thought it could be done. "It is but a question of time, of skillful propagandism, and of opinion-making men seizing historic opportunities."[20]

The psychological lift which comes from participating in war might also be duplicated by educating people to adopt a certain attitude toward their own lives. It is the awareness of being completely caught up in a good cause which transcends one's personal fate that makes participation in war such a significant experience. People should be able to become similarly involved in other efforts to advance the welfare of the human community. The problem of developing a human society which is both peaceful and just on the local, state, national, and global levels is a big enough

problem to absorb the energies of any who care to join. There may not be danger of losing one's life in the sense of being killed, but there is a challenge to lose one's life in the sense of making continuous personal sacrifices of time and money in order to promote the general welfare. Perhaps we should follow William James's suggestion and require all our young people to participate in such an endeavor for a couple of years; but an even better approach may be to try to open the eyes of all, young and old, to the challenge and rewards of serving humanity, letting them respond as they will. In either case, it is to be hoped that the psychological lift generated by participation in war can be replaced by a similar satisfaction from sharing in the never-ending battle to eliminate injustice, violence, and ignorance.

The Social Value of War

Two different theses about the social value of war need to be considered. The first, called "international Social Darwinism," maintains that war is an instrument of struggle among various societies which, like the struggle for surviving among individual organisms, results in the survival of the fittest societies. War is thus an instrument of social evolution. The second thesis maintains that warfare functions as a safety valve allowing the hostility among members of a society to be directed toward an external enemy.[21] War thus promotes social cohesion.

The thesis that war is a useful device by which more advanced societies eliminate less fit societies was popular with Europeans from the 15th through the first part of the 20th centuries. It provided a rationale for subjugating native populations in the Americas, Asia, and Africa. The question which must be raised is whether technological superiority in weaponry proves social or cultural superiority. Were those societies which first used iron weapons socially and culturally superior to those which during the same period fought with weapons of bronze? Is the Spartan society to be judged culturally superior to that of Athens simply because it was victorious in the Peloponnesian

War? Making weapons and winning wars is but part of the business of a society; an inferiority in this activity does not imply an inferiority in other respects. It seems as inappropriate to evaluate societies on the basis of their capacity to win violent conflicts as to evaluate individuals on this basis.

What about the thesis that war has the positive value of promoting social cohesion by allowing hostility to be displaced onto an external enemy? Other crises such as earthquakes or tornadoes also stimulate group cohesion but do not provide the outlet for hostility that war does. Thus the challenge is to find some other activities which promote group cohesion while at the same time providing a legitimate outlet for aggressive feelings. One obvious substitute for war in this regard is participation in amateur and professional athletic contests, either actually or vicariously through observation. For example, an American basketball team composed of individuals from different racial groups competing against teams from other nations does wonders for reducing domestic tensions between these racial groups. At the same time, however, these contests, like war itself, may stir up antagonisms between nations. In 1969 a three-game series to determine who would represent Central America in the World Cup soccer championship touched off a short "Soccer War" between El Salvador and Honduras,[22] and in 1985 there was a "soccer riot" in Belgium when British fans attacked supporters of an Italian team.[23] Athletic contests should be a substitute for war, not a stimulus to it. Another possible alternative to war is competition among societies in scientific activities such as the exploration of space or the conquest of disease. Among less developed countries there could be contests to increase the literacy rate, reduce the infant mortality rate, or raise agricultural production.

The possibility of implementing alternative forms of competition is not the only way to respond to the thesis that war is desirable because it creates internal cohesion. It can be noted that even if war was once valuable as a means to this end, it no longer is. The destructiveness of modern warfare is so great that the cost now exceeds any benefits to be expected in terms of group cohesion. Another response is that group cohesion is not always a good thing. Internal dissension is somewhat better than the conformity and uniformity of expressed opinion which is typical of a society at war with an external enemy. Such considerations undermine the notion that war is desirable because of the internal cohesion it maintains within a group.

The Moral Value of War

We earlier noted that a possible cause of war is the desire to eliminate injustice. We have also observed that there is a tendency for people with power to establish institutions by which their privileged positions can be maintained and that this situation exists both within national governments and among national governments at the global level. Frequently political institutions will be used not only to protect power but to extend it. Thus government itself may become an instrument of exploitation. In such a situation ordinary citizens cannot effectively appeal to the government for protection because the government itself is controlled by the exploiters. History is full of instances where people have used violence to overthrow an oppressive government. One of the positive values of war, it is claimed, is its use to gain freedom from tyrannical government. The threat of such a possibility is also useful in checking governments that otherwise might be more oppressive. This same principle seems to apply in the international sphere. If weaker nations possessed no possibility at all of resisting the more powerful nations by some use of force, they would probably be exploited even more than they are.

The use of violence and threats of violence has probably had some influence at times in reducing or eliminating tyranny and the exploitation of weaker nations by stronger ones. An evaluation of the thesis that war and the threat of war is therefore desirable, however, requires taking account of the whole picture. The possibility of violence against the government may serve to keep the government from becoming tyrannical, but a tyrannical government may react to threats of violence by becoming even more oppressive. It may establish secret police to ferret out even the beginnings of protest. It may try to control every facet of life so that no revolution can even get started. The possibility of violence against the government thus can be used as an excuse for even more tyranny. The same situation exists on the international level. One nation may try to dominate another one completely on the grounds that even a little freedom in the subordinate country could be used later to move to total independence. Then the previously dominant nation would lose some of its power.

Suppose that a different approach were adopted both by the rulers and the ruled. Suppose that a tradition were established, as has been done in Western-style democracies, that on the one hand there would be no armed revolt against the government and that on the other hand the government would allow some gradual peaceful change even if it opposed the interests of the privileged people of the society. In this situation the government probably would not be very tyrannical since it would not be fearful of being overthrown. A new balance could be brought into existence in which distortions of justice and exploitation of the poor are kept under control while those not in power would be permitted to publicize their views and even gradually change the social structure. On the international level, a less powerful nation which appears to be somewhat cooperative toward a more powerful nation would probably be allowed more freedom than a smaller nation which constantly rejects all cooperation. The balance here again requires the more powerful nation to control its desire to exploit while the weaker nation foregoes making too strident demands for recognition of its rights.

It is distressing to realize that in these situations power is only partly restrained by considerations of justice and that the claims of the less powerful for justice must be tempered by a recognition of the realities of power. This type of compromise, widely practiced, is not the morally perfect situation. Yet these situations seem immensely preferable to an unrestrained, violent struggle for power between the privileged and the underprivileged. In this latter situation, the success of a violent revolution may in fact produce a new group of leaders who will themselves become a new privileged group even more oppressive than those they replaced. Cognizant of how it was able to come to power, this group will seek to prevent others from overthrowing its rule. On the other hand, if there is absolutely no possibility of violent resistance by the have-nots regardless of the level of exploitation and oppression, a real danger of tyranny exists.

The ideal situation seems to be a system of governance with built-in checks against tyranny. Nevertheless, it must be admitted that sometimes, despite efforts to put restraints on what the leaders of government can do, the injustice perpetrated by those in power may become so gross and the exploitation of the weak so outrageous that resort to violence may be the only reasonable course of action. Peace is desirable, but so is justice. Ideally governments should be vehicles of both peace and justice, but experience shows that government power can become merely another instrument used by privileged groups to extend their dominance over the have-nots.

This analysis suggests that the proper way to eliminate the resort to violence as a legitimate means of securing justice is to establish governments which are truly impartial and which allow for peaceful change in the direction of a more just society. To the extent that this kind of system is realized, resort to violence as a means of eliminating injustice becomes inappropriate.

Will War Be Missed?

The thesis of this chapter is that none of the claims for the alleged positive values of war are defensible. We don't need war to keep the population growth rate down or to eliminate genetically inferior people. We don't need war in order to stimulate new technological developments or social change. We don't need war to avoid economic slowdowns or to guarantee long-term economic growth.

We don't need war in order to have something meaningful to do with our lives. We don't need war in order to weed out unfit societies or to sustain social cohesion. We don't need war in order to eliminate injustices in society. There is nothing for which we need war.

Suppose that we could abolish war. Suppose that military careers and military technological challenges and military glory were no longer part of our life. Would we miss war? Would we be really glad that war was no longer part of human life? Undoubtedly some people would miss the challenges of the ultimate life-or-death contest which war is. Undoubtedly there would be some kind of military-like games and military-like recreational activities for those who miss the old ways. But on the other hand, there would be unparalleled progress in civilized life — in education, in science, in health care, in more participatory social institutions, in the arts. Society would no longer be subject to these spasms of killing and destruction, the periodic wasting of lives and property known as wars. Changes, both technological and social, might come more gradually and steadily. There would still be problems to solve and conflicts to manage, but the problems would be less of our own making and the resolving of the conflicts would be less violent and more enduring.

Will we miss war? I think not. It seems to me that the overwhelming response to the elimination of war will be "Good riddance."

Let me add a final word for those who might regard thoughts about abolishing war as totally unrealistic. If we take the long view of the history of humanity, I think that we can be somewhat optimistic. As Kenneth Boulding noted in 1964 in *The Meaning of the Twentieth Century: The Great Transition*:

> A strong case can be made for the proposition that war is essentially a phenomenon of the age of civilization and that it is inappropriate both to pre-civilized and postcivilized societies. It represents an interlude in man's development, dated 3000 B.C. to say, 2000 A.D.[24]

Boulding was obviously overly optimistic about the date when we can say that we have succeeded in moving into a post-civilized world where war is no longer part of our way of interacting with each other. Nevertheless his over-all point about how using war as a way of working out group conflicts is only an interlude in humanity's long-term historical development is worth taking seriously. Getting beyond our uncertainty about whether the elimination of war is an attainable and desirable state of affairs seems to be an important step in reaching that goal.

Part Three.
The Contemporary Situation

8. Ideological Aspects of the Contemporary Situation

Ideology is like religion except that its main concern is how to structure society rather than focusing on how the individual ought to live. An ideology consists of a set of beliefs about the human situation and the way society ought to be organized which guides the thinking and policy actions of a substantial number of persons, especially those who have political power. Knowing about ideologies is very important for understanding about politics and the conflicts which lead to war. *Politics* is concerned with what *policies* a society as a whole will follow. An ideology or a religion is often a very basic part of what guides political parties and national governments with regard to what policies they are trying to promote. Consequently, understanding various ideologies is very important to understanding what wars (and also elections) are all about. Groups usually have other interests besides just promoting a particular ideology or religion, but in many conflicts it is the ideology or religion that is a particularly important part of the conflict.

Our goal is a better understanding of the ideologies most relevant to the social conflicts occurring in our world in the 20th and 21st centuries. There will be no effort to propagandize for one point of view or another. The aim is to understand the differences in various ideologies and the thinking behind those differences. After reviewing some basic distinctions in the first section, we will focus our attention on the predominant ideology in the

United States, Western Europe, and Japan: capitalistic democracy or democratic capitalism. Then we will deal with the basic tenets of Communism (Marxism-Leninism and Maoism), an ideology which has provided the motivational base for twentieth century revolutions in Russia, China, Cuba, and Vietnam and which still influences critiques of capitalistic democracy. In the fourth section we will focus on Fascism and related ideologies which are opposed to the egalitarianism of both democracy and socialism. In the fifth section we will review the ideologically-relevant "end of history" thesis of Francis Fukuyama. In the sixth section we will discuss the role of religion and religious movements in war and peace.

Some Basic Distinctions

In our earlier discussion of justice we noted that there are two opposing principles which must somehow be reconciled or balanced in order to have a just (or fair) society. These two principles are *the principle of merit* (that some people deserve to have more than others because they contribute more or are more qualified in some way) and *the principle of equality* (that everyone should have roughly the same amount because how much one can contribute depends ultimately on many factors outside one's own control). The *principle of merit* suggests that people should be able to keep whatever they have already acquired, while the *principle of equality* suggests that those who have more should be expected to share with those who have less. These two opposing principles of justice or fairness are so fundamental in social philosophy that adherence to one or the other view is typically used to determine the seating arrangements in the legislative bodies of the world. Legislators who tend to emphasize the principle of merit are usually seated on the right, while those who tend to emphasize the principle of equality are seated on the left. Consequently, to describe someone as a *rightist* indicates that that person emphasizes the principle of merit with regard to what constitutes a fair distribution of wealth and political power within the society, while to describe someone as a *leftist* means that that person is a champion of the principle of equality. It should be evident that rightists will have a high regard for competition and for hierarchical systems, while leftists will have a high regard for cooperation and compassion for the less fortunate.

In order to get a better appreciation of this distinction between a rightist view and a leftist view and a better understanding of the strengths and weaknesses of these two kinds of views, let us consider how they could be applied to the problem of giving grades in school. Suppose that we wanted to develop a *rightist grading system which promotes competition by rewarding merit*. If we really want it to be competitive, we should have not just five possible grades or even ten possible grades. We should have *rank-order grading* on each test or assignment. In a class of 30 students, papers would be marked "#1 out of 30" or "#16 out of 30" or "#29 out of 30." In order to further stimulate competition the grades would be posted for all to see. It is not difficult to imagine what would happen with such a rightist system of grading. Competition would be fierce, especially between those at the top of the class. As we know from the rental-car ads, "#2 tries harder." So would #3 and #4. The motivation to work harder to get a better grade would be very great. Much studying would take place, and it could be expected that much learning would occur.

On the negative side of this competitive system we might notice those ranking at or near the bottom of the grading scale dropping out. They would just quit. Who needs constant public reminders that they are near the bottom of the class? The intense competition might also have an adverse effect on human relations. Those who are at the top of the class would be likely to feel "superior," while those who are not doing so well even though they are trying as hard as they can are likely to be frustrated. They are likely to resent the fact that others are able to get better grades without spending as much time studying. They would probably complain that the system "just isn't fair" because they are doing as well as they can under the circumstances but not getting much recognition for that effort. They would call attention to the fact that they weren't able to decide whether they would be born smart or not. With regard to the impact of this competitive system on personal relationships, who is going to help someone else to understand the material if that means possibly being one step lower in the class ranking on the next test? Finally, there might be secretive efforts to cheat in some way. Isn't getting the good grade the only thing that really matters much in this system? What difference does it make how much one learns if it doesn't help one get a better ranking?

For contrast, let us consider what a *leftist grading system* would be like where we are trying to *foster equality and cooperation*. If we want equality and cooperation, we should have a system which gives everyone a good chance to succeed and where the class gets graded as a group. We should have a system of *pass-fail grading for individuals* and possibly some kind of *group grade for collective achievement*. We would of course need to establish some minimum standards for individuals that must be met in order to get credit for the course, for example, that you could not be absent more than three times during the term. The grade for the group would be based on the completion of a project to be done by them collectively during the term. We can imagine what would happen with such a leftist or egalitarian system. Most of the class would probably do nothing but come to class. They might even bring games to play and music tapes to listen to during class time. Why do more than the minimum required for getting credit for taking the course?

On the other hand, a few conscientious students might try to get the class project organized and encourage others to join in and "do their share." Some people might even get very involved with the project, doing extra research in the library to make it better. Those working on the project would try to help each other with regard to whatever was needed to improve the project. An *esprit de corps* might develop as the project progresses, and enthusiasm might build about "our" project and what "we" have been able to do together. Some close friendships might blossom from the joy of working unselfishly together. Some who had not been participating earlier might get involved now in order to be part of what was developing into an exciting and worthwhile project. At the same time, those who had contributed much to the project might feel some resentment toward those slackers who were still not doing anything. They would probably complain that it "just isn't fair" that those who were doing nothing to help would nevertheless be getting the same credit as those who had worked hard. The others could respond that those with more talent and interest should do more and were getting their reward by being able to contribute more to and consequently getting more satisfaction out of the project. In contrast to the competitive system, with this egalitarian system it is evident that there wouldn't be any motivation to cheat in order to try to get a better individual grade.

This discussion about rightist and leftist grading systems provides an opportunity to comment on another aspect of the rightist-leftist distinction. The rightist emphasis on competition and merit resembles the "struggle for survival" and the "survival of the fittest" which we find in nature. Therefore we can say that the rightist viewpoint reflects a *"naturalistic"* approach to life. In nature different organisms are born with different inherited traits, and then they compete with each other to see which ones "have what it takes" to survive. Some individuals "luck out" and happen to be born with superior intelligence or supe-

rior athletic ability or superior musical ability. Some people are born of parents who happen to be rich or happen to live in a country where food and shelter and education and health care are readily available. In the competition of life these lucky people will fare much better than those who have not been so fortunate. As the saying goes, "Life isn't fair." That's just the way things are.

Charles Darwin (1809–1882) was a famous English naturalist who emphasized the long-term consequences of this process of "survival of the fittest" in nature, so this rightist way of thinking is sometimes called "Darwinism." The emphasis on the desirability of competition to see who "has what it takes" to survive can be applied to social policy (something which Darwin himself did not do), and then it is called "Social Darwinism." *Social Darwinism* maintains that the government should *not* sponsor welfare programs to help those individuals who are not doing so well in the competition for the goods of life or to help those business enterprises that are not doing so well in the competition to make money. This rightist outlook says that it is desirable in the long run that those who don't "have what it takes" to succeed not be given special assistance. Let them perish before they produce "less fit" offspring or other businesses like themselves. Let society follow the hard way of nature.

While the rightist approach is *naturalistic,* the leftist approach is *humanistic* or *moralistic.* The rightist is correct in saying that nature is not fair, but according to the leftist it is not appropriate for society to merely follow nature's unfair way. Instead human society should intervene in order to counteract the injustice of an unthinking natural order. If someone is born blind or deaf, the rightist attitude is, "If they can't hack it, too bad." The leftist view is that human society should equalize things by giving special assistance to those who are less fortunate. Society should correct the inhumaneness and harshness and randomness of nature. Just as in a family those who happen to have disabilities or debilitating accidents are usually given extra help, so in the community as a whole those who have not been treated so well by fate should be given extra help by the whole human family.

Here one sees clearly the contrast between the competitive, naturalistic, scientific, realistic, hard-hearted outlook of the rightist and the compassionate, humanistic, ethical, idealistic, tender-hearted outlook of the leftist. The rightist believes that nature's way is best, especially in the long run. Besides there is no point in trying to change the unchangeable. The leftist agrees that nature is often cruel but believes that the "survival of the fittest" approach must be replaced by a more humane process in which human civilization creates its own just and rational order. This contrast can be applied directly to attitudes toward the problem of war where rightists are more likely to say that "War is nature's way, so why try to change it" while leftists are more likely to say "Let's work to replace nature's cruel way of war with a just, humane social order based on human reason and compassion."

Let us return to our discussion of the difference between a rightist system of grading and a leftist system of grading in a classroom situation. To get a better appreciation of these two different outlooks you need to think of these alternative systems of grading first in terms of something you are naturally very good at and then in terms of something that you are *not* very good at. You might consider various sports, artistic projects, playing a musical instrument, public speaking, selling things, making things with your hands, fixing mechanical things, dancing, singing, playing chess, and so on. If you focus on something you are good at, the rightist system of grading will probably seem to be the best way. If you focus on something that you are not so good at, the leftist system of grading will probably appeal to you. In other words, we all like to compete in areas where we can expect to do well but would rather have a grading system which is not so focused on competition for those areas where we individually cannot do so well. Applying this point to ideological positions, we can see that those who are doing fairly well in the competition of life are probably going to have a great deal of sympathy

with the rightist approach while those who have not been so fortunate will probably have more appreciation of a leftist approach.

So which system is the best system in general? Is a rightist system or a leftist system of grading in the classroom better? Which system is better for encouraging athletic accomplishment? Which system is better for encouraging musical accomplishment? More relevant to the topic of ideology, which system is best for getting people to do the work which society needs to have done? Is it better to follow a rightist system or a leftist system for determining the distribution of goods in society? Is a rightist system or a leftist system better for determining who makes the decisions for the society as a whole? What are the strong points and weak points of each system? In view of the difficulties which occur when we have either a completely leftist system or a completely rightist system, policy decisions for particular situations probably should try to find a proper balance between these two alternatives.

Returning to our discussion of ideological terminology, there can be degrees of commitment to the rightist view or to the leftist view. (See chart on page 111.) A person who is intensely devoted to the principle of merit and who may even want to use violence to silence those who favor the principle of equality is an *extremist of the right,* while a person who is similarly committed to the principle of equality is an *extremist of the left. Moderates,* on the other hand, of both the right and left, believe in the use of persuasion and the right of the opposition to be heard. Thus extremists of both right and left often favor authoritarian forms of government while moderates tend to favor Western-style parliamentary democracies where freedom of expression by the opposition is an important part of the political process.

We have noted that social structures, including governments, are usually controlled by the rich and powerful in the society and are consequently usually designed to maintain the privileges which these people and their families enjoy. We have also noted that people in these top positions tend to believe that they hold these positions because they deserve to have them. Thus those at the top of a society are usually defenders of the principle of merit and will want to preserve the *status quo,* that is, they will want to conserve the present values and structures of society which have allowed them to get into the top positions which they occupy. When such rightists take a moderate stance, they are called *conservatives.* On the other hand, moderate leftists who want to reduce impediments to social change and create more opportunity and assistance for those who are not so well off are called *progressives.* (These moderate leftists are sometimes called "liberals," but this term "liberal" is ambiguous because it can also be used to describe all moderates — rightists as well as leftists. The term "liberal" — especially when used by economists or when qualified as *"classical* liberal" — can also be used in a third way to describe those who oppose any kind of government interference with the market forces of supply and demand. Thus the term "progressive" is the most appropriate term for moderate leftists.) Extreme rightists who strive for even more privileges for those who are specially talented and otherwise well off are called *reactionaries,* while extreme leftists who want to completely uproot the present privileges and existing hierarchical structures of the society are called *radicals.*

The word "radical" comes from the Latin word for "root." The term "radical" has now come sometimes to be used as equivalent to *extremist,* so one may hear the expression "radical rightist." Nevertheless, when used this way, the term begins to lose its connection with the original idea that a "radical" is someone who wants to *uproot* or *fundamentally change* the accepted way of doing things or the existing social order. Thus it is better to use a different term "reactionary" for an extremist of the right, someone who wants to give even more power to the rich, dominant, and naturally talented individuals or families or groups who have been or who currently are in control of the society.

These ideological terms are widely used to refer to politicians and others with regard to their views about how society should be organized, but we still must make one further distinction. This is the distinction between people's *economic ideology* (their views on how the goods of society should be distributed) on the one hand and their *political ideology* (their views on how the political decision-making power in society should be distributed) on the other. (See chart on page 111.) This distinction is useful because it is possible for a given individual to have a rightist view with regard to economic ideology (that is, to believe that goods should be distributed on the basis of merit) and a leftist view with regard to political ideology (that is, to believe that political power should be distributed on the basis of equality). It would also be possible for a person to be a leftist with regard to economic ideology (that is, to believe that goods should be distributed on the basis of equality) and a rightist with regard to political ideology (that is, to believe that political power should be distributed on the basis of merit). The significance of this distinction becomes more evident when it is noted that the first combination mentioned is precisely what we find in the capitalistic democratic ideology prevalent in the United States and Western Europe while the second combination is characteristic of the Marxist-Leninist view which guided the Soviet Union during the Cold War and which still guides the thinking of leaders in Communist countries such as Cuba.

This distinction between *economic ideology* and *political ideology* raises another very important issue in social philosophy — the influence of a nation's economic and political systems on each other. One possible view is that the economic system is basic and that the political system is merely a reflection of it. According to this view economic wealth necessarily creates political power. Another possible view is that the political system is basic and that the influence of excessive wealth can be held in check by the government. According to this second view political power assisted by the police power of the state may be used to control and even redistribute economic wealth. Marxist philosophy theoretically opts for the first alternative while Western-style democratic theory has been based on the latter alternative, though in actual practice both

Ideological Terminology

	Leftists emphasize the desirability of *equality* and *cooperation* and tend to rely on an *inclusivist* or *collectivist* system.		Rightists emphasize the desirability of *merit* and *competition* and tend to rely on a *combative* or *individualistic* system.	
Degree of Emphasis	*Extremist* Opposition may be silenced.	*Moderate* Use persuasion; let the opposition be heard.	*Moderate*	*Extremist* Opposition may be silenced.
General Term	*Radical* End all distinctions of rank.	*Progressive* Gradually get more equality.	*Conservative* Preserve present ways & rankings.	*Reactionary* Increase privileges of elites.
Economic Ideology (distribution of goods)	*Communism* People get what they need without regard to how they worked.	*Socialism* People get only what they earn by their own labor.	*Capitalism* People get money by investments, ingenuity, and their own labor.	*Monopolism* Wealth is concentrated in hands of one small group of persons.
Political Ideology (who makes the laws)	*Pure or Direct Democracy* Everyone votes on everything.	*Representative Democracy* Elected reps make the laws.	*Oligarchy or Aristocracy* An elite group makes the laws.	*Absolute monarchy or Dictatorship* One person makes the laws.

*Note: The term "**liberal**" was not used on the chart because that word has different meanings. (1) It may simply mean "moderate" (the opposite of "extremist"). (2) The term "**liberal**" may mean "**progressive**" (the opposite of "conservative"). (3) The term "**classical liberal**" refers to someone who favors freedom of individuals and opposes government control. Thus a classical liberal is someone who supports capitalism along with a representative democracy in which the powers of government are very limited. Since the word "liberal" can be understood in so many different ways, it is advisable not to use it in discussions about ideology.*

Communist states and democratic countries have often acted contrary to their own philosophical foundations. For example, if Marxists want to increase the political power of the working classes and political power depends on economic power, it would seem that they should focus their efforts directly on raising the wage levels of the workers rather than trying to take control of the government through revolution. In the case of democracies, it would seem that they should do more to prevent economic power from being so influential in the political process since such economic influence keeps the state from fulfilling its theoretical function of acting as a check on economic power.

In the chart above the various economic and political ideologies are arranged from the most egalitarian on the left to the most hier-archical on the right. With regard to *economic ideologies,* the most leftist distribution of goods is represented by *communism,* aptly characterized in the famous expression, "From each according to his ability; to each according to his need."[1] It is the kind of situation found in a closely knit family where each member contributes as much as he or she can and where each one gets what he or she needs. But the communists want to extend that kind of familial thinking to the whole of humanity. The next step toward the middle is *socialism,* the view that one's only source of income should be wages for one's labor. That is, one should *not* be able to make money from assets already accumulated as one does when acquiring profit in a capitalistic system, possibly from inherited wealth. In a socialist system, factories and other things like rental property which can be used as a source of income are to be owned by society collectively, that is, controlled by the government. There may be differential pay, however, on the basis of the quantity and quality of work done or on the basis of how critical the work is to the society. Consequently, some people may be a little richer than others, but the huge disparities in wealth which come as a result of inherited wealth, ingenuity, and other kinds of good fortune in a capitalist system will be eliminated. The next step across the center line into the area of the moderate right is *capitalism.* Here factories, rental property, patented inventions, and the like which can be used to make money (profit) are owned by private individuals. In a capitalistic system people can earn income from wages as in a socialist system, but there also exists the opportunity to make large amounts of money from investments and patents on inventions and figuring out new, more efficient ways of doing things. As a result there may be greater discrepancies in the amount of wealth different individuals have. The final step to the right is *monopolism,* a particular variation of the capitalist system where wealth comes to be concentrated in the hands of just a few families. As a matter of fact, monopolism is just as likely to be found in an agrarian society where wealth is concentrated in land holdings as in an industrialized capitalistic society where wealth is usually related to ownership of large businesses. In a monopolistic system a small group of rich families is able to control or eliminate all potential competitors so there is no chance that the concentration of wealth will be changed. As we move from left to right there is less and less equality in the distribution of the wealth within the society and a smaller and smaller group of persons in whose hands the wealth of the society is concentrated.

With regard to *political ideologies,* which focus on the issue of who the decision-makers for the society will be, the most leftist or egalitarian system is a *pure or direct democracy,* where every person in the group gets to vote on each social issue to be decided. The model here would be the New England town meeting where all the citizens of the town come together and can adopt laws by a vote of those attending the meeting. Every member of the community is a legislator (lawmaker) for the group. The next step toward the middle is a *representative democracy.* Here the whole community of citizens elects a more limited number of persons who will be the decision-makers for the whole society. The system is still democratic, however, since those legislators holding political office must get reelected from time to time by the whole group they are representing. ("Democratic" means "rule by the people.") Crossing the center line and continuing to the right we have either *"oligarchy"* (rule by "the few," that is, by a small group composed of the well-to-do) or *"aristocracy"* (rule by "the best," by the nobility). Here only a small number of persons are the decision-makers for the whole society, and they do not need to worry about getting elected. The ruling group is viewed as above the level of the poor, ignorant, and uninformed masses and therefore more qualified to make decisions for the whole society. The final step to the right politically is represented by *absolute monarchy* or *dictatorship,* where one person, unrestricted by anyone or anything else, makes the decisions about what the whole society will do. All the political power is vested in the hands of that one person. As we move from left to right there is less and less equality in the distribution of decision-making authority and a smaller and smaller number of supposedly "more qualified" and "better informed" people who make the decisions for the whole group. As the number of decision-makers is limited, there is more efficiency in the decision-making process. One person can make a decision much more quickly than a group of twenty or a group of two hundred or the whole society. The critical question, however, is what system of decision-making is best for the whole society in the long run.

Capitalistic Democracy

The prevalent ideology in the United States, Western Europe, Japan, and many other parts of the industrialized world is capitalistic democracy or democratic capitalism. As already noted above, capitalism refers to an economic system in which the instruments of production are owned by private persons rather than the government, while democracy refers to a political system in which the decision-making political power is ultimately in the hands of the people as a whole.

The term *capitalism* is derived from the term *capital,* which in this context refers to things such as the machines and factories which can be used to produce more wealth. These "capital goods" which get used to produce things are to be distinguished from "consumer goods," those items which people use to satisfy their own needs and desires. A person who owns some capital goods is a *capitalist,* and the income derived from owning these capital goods is called *profit.* To be able to earn profit people must save some of their wealth and use it for investment in capital goods rather than buying consumer goods and services for immediate gratification. Thus profit ideally represents a reward for saving rather than spending. Of course, saving money rather than spending it will not automatically produce a profit. The money must be invested, either directly or by an intermediary such as a bank, in something which increases productivity, such as machines. Suppose, for example, that some new machine enables a group of employees to produce five times as many consumer goods as they could have produced without it. This larger quantity of goods can then be sold, and part of the money received can be used to pay the workers' wages while another part can provide profit to the investor whose money made it possible to buy the machine in the first place.

A capitalistic system depends on the existence of some kind of capital goods such as machinery that will increase productivity (which is why capitalism comes along with industrialization) as well as on there being some people who are willing to assume risk and invest their money in productive capital goods rather than spending it on consumer goods for themselves. It also depends on the manufacturer's ability to sell the goods which are produced and on having workers who know how to operate the machines. To be able to sell the goods produced, the capitalist must make things of the type and quality which will appeal to potential buyers. A capitalist must pay workers enough that they will work for him or her rather than someone else. Consequently, in theory a system of competition develops among capitalists (or groups of capitalists who have merged their savings to form an enterprise such as a joint-stock company or a corporation). Each capitalist tries to give potential buyers a better bargain than they can get from others. Each capitalist competes for the best workers. Since income depends on the quality and quantity of goods sold, capitalists will pay higher wages to more highly skilled and more efficient workers. Capitalists will also be eager to purchase more efficient machines, which in turn motivates inventors and other capitalists to provide such machines.

The resulting *market economy* rewards inventiveness, good business management, and useful skills. Investing one's money in capital goods rather than spending it on consumer goods will be rewarded with profit. Inefficient and inept businesses will go bankrupt while efficient and proficient ones will prosper and earn more money with which to make further investments and expand their operations. While each person, capitalist and worker alike, aims only to better his or her own personal situation, the system as a whole works naturally to increase productivity and efficiency as well as the quality and variety of consumer goods available. At the same time prices, wages, and profits reflect the supply of and demand for goods, labor, and funds for investment.[2]

The capitalistic system fits well with the view that humans are inherently selfish and lazy but also able to calculate what will be best for themselves in the long run. They will work hard to acquire more for themselves. In a smoothly functioning capitalistic system there is no great need for people to be altruistic or even concerned about the welfare of others. They can be confident that acting in accord with their long-term self-interest will do more to help advance human welfare in the long run than any deliberately charitable acts. Furthermore, the competitive system of "survival of the fittest" assures that in the long run those capabilities and those ways of doing things which are productive will be preserved and passed along to posterity while those which are not will perish. The capitalistic system motivates people to work hard and be inventive because that is how one acquires wealth in order to be able to survive. Another imperative to be followed in a capitalist system is to save rather than spend, since saving can produce profit which will result in having more goods in the long run. One critical aspect of the capitalist system is that stealing and wanton destruction of the property of others must be prevented. If people can't be assured of keeping and enjoying what they have earned, then their motivation to work rather than stealing from others or loafing will be destroyed. The capitalist system has proved to be very effective in motivating people not only to work hard but also to invent and use new more efficient ways of doing things. Economic growth (progress) and capitalism go hand in hand.

In actual practice, however, there may be some drawbacks in the operation of the capitalistic system. Sometimes one capitalist or a small group of capitalists manages to gain a monopoly in the production of goods of a particular kind; then the competition, which had previously kept prices down, disappears and the prices go up. Another difficulty is that, even in the absence of monopolies, competition is imperfect. Those with very large assets generally have an inherent advantage because they can take greater risks, invest more on the development of new products, buy more expensive machinery, spend more on advertising, and wait longer to realize profits on their investment. Since larger companies and corporations have these competitive advantages, there is a built-in tendency in capitalism toward the development of those very monopolies which can destroy the competitive system.

There are also several other difficulties for the capitalist system. In setting wage levels, the greater assets of the capitalists put them in a much better bargaining position than that of the poor laborers looking for a job, since the laborers need work immediately to get money for food and shelter while the capitalists can wait until someone is found to work at the wages they are willing to pay. Another concern is that unscrupulous capitalists may produce unsafe products whose defects are not visible to the buyer. Capitalists can hire advertisers, who may be able to persuade people to buy products or services which they really do not need. Also, since products can be sold only to those who have money to pay for them, there is a tendency to produce luxury items which appeal to the whims of the wealthy rather than to make things which meet the basic needs of those who have little or no money. Furthermore, the intrinsic advantage for the richer in bargaining situations, as well as their opportunity to gain money from savings and investments, produces a strong natural tendency throughout the system for the rich to get richer while the poor are left out.

It has sometimes been claimed that capitalism is racist and imperialist. It may well be the case that some capitalists have been racists, but that is not an inherent characteristic of the capitalist system. In fact, racism is totally foreign to it since the only things which matter in a capitalistic system are competence as a worker or manager or investor plus the possession of money in order to be able to buy as a consumer or to invest as a saver. The race, religion, sex, and age of the individual employee or consumer are irrelevant. It may also be the case that some capitalists have been imperialistic, but nationalistic imperialism is directly contrary to the theoretical basis of capitalism. Capitalists want to be able to make the biggest profit possible on their investments regardless of where that might be. Theoretically they should favor a worldwide "free-trade" market economy rather than a system of national tariffs and regulations.

There is only one type of discrimination which is an inherent part of the capitalist system, and that is discrimination against the poor. The poor are discriminated against because they do not have enough money to serve as potential buyers or to be able to invest and earn profits. Capitalism works on the basis of the market forces of supply and demand, and demand is *not* the same as need. *Demand is want plus the money to buy what is wanted.* The poor may be in need but their needs will not constitute part of the demand because they lack money to buy. The other side of this situation is that capitalism won't work well if wealth is too concentrated in the hands of too few persons because then there won't be enough demand to keep buying the products being produced.

For the capitalists themselves the biggest problem is the tendency for the whole economy to undergo a continuing cycle of boom followed by bust. During the boom period when goods are selling well, the capitalists invest more in production, hire more workers, and pay each worker more as the competition for labor, especially for skilled labor, increases. Since the workers are getting paid more, they are ready to spend more for consumer goods. Demand increases. The capitalists respond by building more factories to produce still more goods. But the collective value of all the wages paid to all the workers will never be as great as the collective value of all the goods being produced by them. (If it were, there would be no profits left over for the capitalists who own the factories and other capital goods.) Consequently, there is no way the workers can buy all the consumer goods being produced. More goods have been produced than can possibly be sold. Then the bust phase of the cycle begins. The capitalists start laying off workers since there is already an over-supply of what is being produced. These workers no longer have any money with which to buy goods. Others who still have jobs try to keep their expenditures down as much as possible since they fear that they may soon also be laid off. Even lower prices and easy credit eventually are not enough to sell all that is being produced. This cutback in purchasing causes sales to decrease even further, leading to more layoffs and even more reluctance to buy. Capitalists may then try to sell their machines because they are sitting idle, but no other capitalists will want to buy them when there is no demand for goods. Production eventually

comes to a virtual halt. Workers are unemployed, machines are sitting idle, and capitalists are not making any profits. Finally the oversupply of consumer goods is eliminated and then the boom part of the cycle can begin again.

In order to deal with the various problems of a completely unregulated or *laissez-faire* capitalistic system, an alternative system has been developed, *government-regulated capitalism*. Under this system the government undertakes certain tasks such as regulating or breaking up monopolies, or establishing laws to protect smaller firms against unfair competition from larger ones, or enacting laws to protect the right of laborers to join unions and bargain collectively with the employer. Agencies are established to protect the public from unsafe products, to protect workers from unsafe working conditions, and to keep industries from polluting the environment. The government institutes progressive rates of taxation on income and adopts other measures to try to mitigate to some extent the natural tendency in a capitalistic system for the rich to get richer. Social assistance programs are adopted so the unemployed, the disabled, the very old, children, and others will be able to provide for their basic needs. The government also tries to moderate the boom and bust cycles by controlling the money supply, interest rates, tax rates, and the amount of government spending. Thus the system of government-regulated capitalism aims to preserve the positive values of capitalism — productivity, efficiency, variety of products, and personal freedom — while controlling its less desirable features.

Let us now turn to the political part of the capitalistic democratic ideology. Democracy refers to a political system in which decision-making power rests ultimately in the hands of the people as a whole. The people get to choose who their lawmakers and leaders will be. They do this through a system of representatives and elected leaders chosen for limited terms of office. The only way these legislators and leaders can continue to stay in power is to be reelected when their term of office ends. The political leaders need not be of any particular family, economic class, gender, nationality, religion, occupation, or political party. In the well-known words of Abraham Lincoln, democracy is "government of the people, by the people, and for the people."

The political ideology of Western-style democracy includes not only the notion of majority rule but also the principle of minority rights. The right to vote is worthless if there is no chance to be informed about the issues or to hear the arguments offered by persons promoting various points of view. Opposition candidates as well as those representing the group in power must be on the ballot, and the voting must be secret so that it is impossible to determine how any individual voted. People must be free to give their opinions, ask questions, hear the opinions of others, form voluntary associations to promote one or another point of view, travel about, and so on. People must be educated about history and philosophy and economics so that they can evaluate the arguments being used to advance various proposed policies. These rights or freedoms are rooted in the notion that in a democracy public policy should be the outcome of rational discussion, debate, and deliberation rather than the dogmatic pronouncements of some individual or small group.

The previous paragraph should make it clear that a democratic political system is more than just voting for candidates. There are a whole set of values and practices that must accompany that voting. That is why many countries who try to implement democracy are not successful in implementing it immediately. Also those who try to institute a democratic political system where none existed previously must realize that the real test for democracy is not just the first balloting but even more whether there is a second and third and fourth election. Those who lose an election must know that another election will be coming where they will have another chance to try to persuade the voters to give them the power to rule.

A fundamental asset of the democratic political system is that it allows for peaceful change over time. People who don't like a public policy must be free to speak out against it. They must be free to enlist the help of others and even to run for political office themselves. Democracy requires that officials be elected for a limited term of office and that they will not be allowed to stay in office unless re-elected. In such a system there is no point in trying to start a violent revolution. It could succeed only if one had the support of many people, and with such massive support one should be able to win an election. At the same time those in authority will have no need to use force except in the case of an attempt to use violence to try to overthrow the government.

Sometimes the question is raised whether in a democracy persons ought to be permitted to openly advocate the overthrow of the government. It is clear that democratic theory requires that such a viewpoint be allowed to be openly expressed. If those who espouse this view can gain enough followers to win elections or to pose a real threat to the government, then the government itself has failed to persuade many people of its value. On the other hand, to try to silence those who advocate overthrow of a democratic government is to resort to an undemocratic approach, which is inconsistent with the rational defense of democracy. Such a course of action would leave this dissatisfied group with no option but to turn to violence to promote their views, the very sort of thing which democracy is designed to make unnecessary.

Capitalistic democracy is sometimes attacked on grounds that, although there are formal freedoms such as expressing a point of view and running for public office, there are in reality only a few wealthy or otherwise influential persons who can take advantage of these freedoms. It is noted that participation in politics requires time both for keeping oneself informed and for the actual political activities and that such time is not equally available to all persons in the society. Such participation also requires at least minimal amounts of money. There is undoubtedly a great deal of truth in these criticisms. It is obvious that some people are able to exert a great deal more influence on the political process than others. There is the continuing danger that money will exert too much influence on the democratic process and that the leftist democratic political system will no longer be able to hold the rightist capitalist economic system in check.[3] Nevertheless the freedom to participate does exist and many people do participate in various ways that go beyond voting. Furthermore, most people find plenty of time and money for recreational activities and a great deal of time to watch television. It seems that the biggest factor lacking in many cases of non-participation in the political process is not so much the opportunity but the inclination. People may complain about the influence of special-interest groups on government policy, but often it is their own non-participation that permits these groups to have so much influence.

Communism (Marx, Lenin, and Mao)

The ideology followed by the former Soviet Union, by China, by Cuba, by North Korea, by Vietnam, and by many Marxist-Leninists and Maoists throughout the world is popularly known as "Communism." The basic ideas of this ideology were formulated by Karl Marx and Friedrich Engels in the 19th century and then supplemented or modified by V. I. Lenin and Mao Zedong in the 20th century. Marxism-Leninism is one particular variety of *socialism*. The central thesis of socialism is that capital goods, the machines and other means of production, should be owned jointly by the whole society and used to promote the general welfare rather than being owned by individuals or private corporations for their private benefit as is the case in capitalism. Marx and Engels called their view *scientific socialism* to distinguish it from earlier socialist views which they regarded as utopian or unrealistic. The *utopian socialists* believed that socialism could be brought into existence merely by convincing people (especially capitalists) of how desirable it would be to have such a system. Marx and Engels, on the other hand, claimed that significant social change

could come about only as the result of the operation of inexorable and inevitable historical forces. Having a few good-hearted capitalists turn the ownership of their factories over to their workers would not be enough to bring about a fundamental transition from capitalism to socialism.

What are these historical forces? The answer to this question is provided by the *materialistic interpretation of history* developed by Marx and Engels.[4] According to this theory the basic factor in understanding historical change is neither divine intervention as Christians believe nor philosophical thought as Hegel had taught, but rather the manner in which the goods of a society are produced, that is, material or economic factors. This *"historical materialism"* or *"economic determinism"* maintains that the predominant mode of production determines all the other aspects of society. Most importantly, the class of people who control the means of production will be in positions of power while those who do the actual physical work required will be the exploited class. If the primary mode of production is small-scale agriculture as in a feudal society, then the landowners will be the ruling class and the serfs who do the physical labor of farming will be the exploited class. If the primary mode of production consists of using machinery as happens after industrialization, then those who own the machines will be the class in control while the workers who run the machines will be the exploited class. (See chart on page 119.) The predominant mode of production and resulting social relations will also determine the nature of the whole social "super-structure," that is, the kind of government, the legal concepts of the society, the philosophical views, the nature of the religion, and the nature of art. According to this analysis, it is especially important for understanding the history of conflict to note that the ruling or dominant class will always establish governmental structures and laws which protect its own interests.

According to the Marxist point of view, violent social conflict arises when the predominant mode of production changes and the old ruling class refuses to give up control of the government to those who control the new means of production. Consider, for example, the transition from feudalism to capitalism that took place in Europe in the 16th, 17th, and 18th centuries. The feudal kingdoms, complete with archdukes, dukes, marquesses, earls, viscounts, and others, had established a system of government by the king and nobility to serve their purposes and to solve their problems. The commercial and productive activities of the up-and-coming bourgeoisie (or burghers, so called because they lived in the towns) did not fit in with the land-centered, manorial system of the feudal lords. In cases of conflict between landowners and merchants, the laws and government structures always favored the landed aristocracy. The bourgeoisie wanted more power and more government concern about the kinds of problems they faced (such as the need for free roads to get from one place to another), but the old dominant class would not willingly surrender control. Although the bourgeoisie in a few cases were able to gain some political power peacefully, the usual course of events was a large-scale violent revolution (a war, such as the French Revolution) to overthrow the well-established feudal government. It is important to see that for Marx, the supporters of the feudal system were not wicked individuals deliberately doing harm to others. They were driven by their social situation to do what seemed to them natural and good, although that also naturally meant doing what was good for themselves and their families.

Marx and Engels argued that by the middle of the 19th century a new transition was taking place. Once again a shift in the prevailing mode of production was taking place and again the old ruling class was refusing to step aside graciously. Now, however, it was the capitalistic bourgeoisie that had created laws and government structures to promote their interests; their focus was on protecting private ownership and individual enterprise. But the prevailing mode of production had now shifted from privately owned machines in workshops employing only a few people to corporately owned machines in large factories employing hundreds of workers and often managed in part at least by people other than the owners. Nevertheless the owners were still appropriating for themselves all the "surplus value" of the goods produced. That is, as raw materials were converted into more valuable manufactured items, the owners of the factories sold what was produced, paid the bills (including wages), and kept all the difference for themselves rather than sharing some of that gain in value from the manufacturing process with the workers who ran the machines. The production of the goods had become a social enterprise in which many workers and managers participated, but the owners of the machines still viewed the goods produced as belonging completely to themselves. The increased value produced during the manufacturing process was treated as belonging solely to the owners of the machines with the workers getting only the minimal wages required to keep them employed.

The factory workers, the proletariat, were viewed by Marx and Engels as the new up-and-coming productive class whose interests were being neglected and thwarted by the laws and governments controlled by the bourgeoisie. Although it was conceivable that in some cases the proletariat might be able to gain political power peacefully, in actuality the proletariat would usually need to have a violent revolution to overthrow the bourgeoisie-controlled state just as earlier the bourgeoisie usually had to use violence to overthrow the governments controlled by the landed nobility. Once the capitalist-controlled government had been overthrown, then the working class would establish its own new kind of government, a "dictatorship of the proletariat." Marxists, however, do more than just predict that this will happen. Their aim is to make it happen. As might be expected, the Marxists' eagerness to push history along by promoting violent revolutions against bourgeois governments caused such governments to view them as mortal enemies.

Marx and Engels claimed that the system of private ownership which was suitable for the small-scale enterprises of the early bourgeois period was no longer appropriate

Marx's Five Stages of Civilization					
Name of Stage	*Primitive Communism*	*Ancient Slavery*	*Feudalism*	*Capitalism*	*Socialism*
Prevailing Mode of Production	Hunting, gathering, and fishing	Slave labor to increase private property	Peasant labor and use of animals for farming	Commerce and small-scale manufacturing	Mass production
Measure of Wealth	Group welfare	Number of slaves and amount of land	Amount of land	Amount of money	Satisfaction of human needs
Ruling Class	None	Slave-owners and Emperor	Land-holders and King	Entrepreneurs and capitalists (Bourgeoisie)	Workers (Proletariat)
Oppressed Class	None	Slaves	Peasants	Factory workers and unemployed persons	None
Government	Communal rule	Emperor and open coercion	King and Court of Lords with personal loyalty to immediate superior	Capitalistic democracy or fascism	People's State governed by Worker's Party
Prevailing Philosophy	Collectivism (What is good for the group?)	Pragmatic obedience to those with power (What is commanded?)	Loyalty to immediate superior in exchange for protection (What is expected by my overseer?)	Individualism or totalitarianism (What is good for me?)	Collectivism (What is good for the group?)
Prevailing Religion	Tribal gods and personified natural forces	Worship of God who is powerful and demanding	God works through the Church, His intermediary (Catholicism)	God deals directly with individuals (Protestantism)	No Divine Master (atheism)
Prevailing Art Form	Decoration of everyday objects	Palaces and monuments for emperors	Art for worship and for the pleasure of the King and Court	Snobbish art for those with money and leisure	Art to advance collectivist attitudes and for edifying the life of the masses

for the large-scale enterprises of mass production. When a large number of people work together to produce an object such as an automobile, that product should belong to the workers, not to the small group which happens to have enough extra money to buy stock in the company. Capitalists may argue that those who bought stock made it possible to purchase the machines which in turn provided employment for the workers, but according to Marxists these capitalists were able to accumulate the extra money for purchasing stock only by some kind of previous exploitation. How do these capitalists get their money? They do not need to work but rather merely make money from the money their families accumulated from earlier exploitation or good fortune. Suppose a person inherits $1,000,000 from rich parents. Without any special talent for investing wisely, the heir should be able to get an 8 percent a year return on the money. That income of $80,000 per year, year after year, is much more than factory workers can hope to earn, no matter how hard they work. As Marxists see the situation, the laws of the capitalist society protect this continued exploitation of the workers by the capitalist class generation after generation. At the same time, in the 19th century when Marx was formulating his ideas, the capitalist-controlled governments had not shown much concern for the problems of the proletariat such as the need to continue surviving during periods of unemployment, the need for income after retirement, the availability of affordable health care, and an assured minimum supply of the basic necessities of life such as food and housing regardless of one's financial situation. Even basic education for young children was available only to those who were well-off financially.

The Marxists also claim that the capitalistic free enterprise system, even when regulated by government, is unable to take full advantage of the productive capabilities of mass production. Although each individual enterprise plans its operations with a view to making as much profit as possible over the next few years, there is little or no effort to coordinate the productive capabilities of the whole nation or the whole world for the long-term welfare of the society. During the bust part of the capitalist business cycle, factories sit idle and workers are unemployed even though there are plenty of unmet needs in the society. Even when the system is working rather smoothly, production is geared to what people with money will buy, not to the needs of the general population. As a result factories regularly operate well below their maximum capabilities.

Marx and Engels addressed themselves primarily to criticizing capitalism. Workers were encouraged to overthrow capitalist governments, but they were not provided with much guidance about what to do after they gained control. They were told that a transition period would be needed before they could move to the higher phase of Communist society when the slogan "from each according to his ability, to each according to his need" could be implemented. During this transitional "socialist" period private ownership of the means of production would be eliminated but differential pay on the basis of one's contribution to society would continue.

The theories of Marx and Engels are certainly not free of difficulties. They accepted the labor theory of value from earlier writers, a theory which maintains that the value of any product depends completely on the amount of labor required to get it out of nature and into usable form. Even when patched up with questionable notions such as the idea that machines represent stored labor, the labor theory of value has difficulties. Labor is undoubtedly a big factor in the value of most things, but supply and demand seem to be even more crucial factors. Scarce but very useful materials such as petroleum are very valuable even if relatively little labor is required to take them from nature, and the value of a beautiful art object often bears little relation to how long the artist labored in order to create it.

Also, even if we were to accept a large part of the Marxist materialistic interpretation of history, we could still raise some questions about how it applies to recent history. Marx and Engels seem to assume without argument that the dominant class in a mass-production society should be the factory workers (the proletariat). They fail to consider an interesting alternative possibility, namely, that the new dominant class is the managers. The important role played by managers in both capitalist and socialist economies gives some plausibility to this alternative view. Such a view would also make the transition from individualistic capitalism to the collectivist type of production analogous to what Marx and Engels claim happened during earlier transitions. In no earlier shift did the oppressed class of the previous stage become the new ruling class. Instead the new dominant class (such as the capitalist class) was a totally new class brought into existence by the new mode of production. In the shift from small-scale manufacturing to mass production the new class which arises with decision-making power upon which both stockholders and factory workers depend is not the proletariat but rather the managerial class. Thus according to this alternative version of Marxism, the interesting question is how this up-and-coming managerial class will be able to wrest social power away from the capitalist class. Will a violent revolution be necessary for the transition, or will the new managerial class somehow manage to take control of the society without resorting to violence to accomplish it?

Marx made several specific predictions which have turned out to be wrong. For example, he predicted that as capitalism progressed the middle class would become smaller and smaller. In fact, it has become larger and larger. For another example, he expected that the proletarian revolutions would occur first in the most advanced industrialized nations such as France and Germany while in fact the first successful revolutions occurred in Russia, at that time one of the least advanced countries of Europe; in China, a predominantly agrarian and feudal nation; and in Cuba, a semi-colonized agricultural country. Furthermore, the revolutions which have occurred seem to be more the result of Marxist philosophy than of any objective historical forces. For a third example, he predicted that capitalists would amass such an abundance of capital that they would be searching around for places to invest. In fact, just the opposite has occurred.

Everywhere there is a shortage of capital for investment. From a purely objective point of view, so many wrong predictions necessarily raise serious doubts about the correctness of the theory.

We have already mentioned, in connection with the discussion of the causes of war, that Lenin made some amendments to Marxist theory in order to use it to explain international war. According to Lenin, capitalists are necessarily going to be engaged in imperialistic ventures as they seek to take over other areas for raw materials and markets.[5] He argues that the workers' revolutions did not occur first in the most industrialized countries as Marx had predicted because the capitalists in these countries "bought off" their workers by sharing some of the profits from exploiting their colonies. But, as noted earlier, Lenin's view that capitalists can get into wars (such as World War I) as a result of nationalistic economic competition among themselves undermines Marx's contention that all wars are the result of class conflict and opens up the possibility that nationalism may be as important a factor in war as the change in the mode of production emphasized by Marx.

Since Marx and Engels had not provided much guidance on what the proletariat should do after they gained power, Lenin had to work out his own program of action after the Bolshevik Revolution in Russia in 1917. He decided to base the government on the soviets — councils of workers, soldiers, and peasants who had been elected by their fellows to serve as representatives. These soviets had been the prime movers in the overthrow of the czar. Nevertheless, it was claimed by Lenin that the soviets needed the leadership of professional intellectual revolutionaries for guidance, so the Communist Party of the Soviet Union was organized in such a way that it could be controlled by the intelligentsia ("the Vanguard of the Proletariat") who had led the revolution.[6]

The procedural arrangement which governed the operation of the Communist Party in the Soviet Union is called *democratic centralism*. The basic features of democratic centralism are that representatives are elected at the local level; that these lower level representatives then elect higher level ones who elect higher level ones, and so on; that decisions are made by majority rule; that after a decision has been made no further dissent or questioning of that matter is permitted; and that decisions of higher level organs are binding on all lower level organs.[7] It is the last two features which gave the central decision-making bodies so much power in the Soviet system. It is also these two features, plus the fact that the Communist Party was the only political party allowed to exist in the country, which made the political structure in the old Soviet Union so different from Western-style democracies. Despite the existence of elections at the lower levels, the "centralized" political system actually functioned as a kind of oligarchy or aristocracy where a small group of individuals in the upper echelons of the Communist Party were the all-powerful decision-makers as well as administrators of the whole society.

When Mikhail Gorbachev became the top leader of the Communist Party in 1985, he introduced the ideas of "glasnost" (openness), "perestroika" (restructuring), and "demokratizatsiya" (democratization) into the Soviet Union. The whole social system was radically changed, motivated in part by the desire to encourage changes in the failing centrally controlled economic system. Decisions of the top leaders could now be debated and criticized. Persons not members of the Communist Party could participate in the discussion of political issues. The system of democratic centralism was modified to be much more like Western-style democracy. But once freedom of expression became the accepted style, Gorbachev could no longer keep the political and economic changes in check, and the Soviet Union itself eventually came to an end in December 1991. Somewhat paradoxically, Gorbachev was able to introduce these big changes toward a more open and democratic society rather rapidly just because he was at the top of a political system which was authoritarian.

While discussing Communism, we must also take account of the theoretical modifications introduced by China's Mao Zedong. While Marx and Lenin had focused attention on the class conflict between workers and cap-

italists as industrialization was taking place, Mao emphasized the conflict between the poor rural peasants and the more affluent elite of the cities, a conflict which existed even before industrialization. From his point of view, one didn't need to wait for industrialization and the development of a proletariat in order to have a revolution to stop exploitation. The peasants could use their superior numbers to take control of the countryside and then strangle the cities which depended on the rural areas for food. Military power was critical, but peasants armed with guns and familiarity with the terrain would be able to outmaneuver troops sent from the cities to subdue them. Furthermore, people living in the rural areas could be recruited for the revolution both by giving them land confiscated from the aristocrats and by threatening them with violence if they did not cooperate.

Mao's focus on the rural poor versus the urban rich extended to his analysis of international affairs. He saw the world as divided between the rich, developed "urban" countries and the poor, undeveloped "rural" countries. He thought that the thrust of Communism on the international level should be to get the poor rural areas to revolt and throw off the control exercised over them by the rich urban areas, just as his revolution in China had begun with the rural areas throwing off the control of the cities. Mao disagreed with Lenin's view that all imperialism was due to capitalism. He claimed that the two superpowers at that time, the capitalistic imperialistic United States and the socialistic imperialistic Soviet Union, were vying with each other for hegemony over the whole world. These two nations constituted what he called the First World. The other developed countries he called the Second World, while the undeveloped countries were called the Third World. Mao believed that the best hope for the Third World countries was to unite under China's leadership and then get assistance from some of the Second World countries to keep the two superpowers in check.

Mao had great faith in the ordinary, unsophisticated, powerless people of the society and was always on guard against any elitist tendency even within the Communist Party of China. He made a special effort to place university students and professors in the fields working beside the poorest peasants, and at the same time he championed the idea that hard-working peasants should be given priority in access to education. One of his main fears was that an elitist group, out of contact with the hard life of the peasants in the rural areas, would again gain control of China and overturn the revolution of the dispossessed which he had led. That concern led him to promote the primacy of ideological training over the learning of skills and also the notion of a continuing revolution by the younger members of the society against anyone who had acquired some status. A specific manifestation of this latter idea was his "Great Proletarian Cultural Revolution" of 1966–69, which turned out to be a major disaster for China in both economic and human terms.

At the moment Communism seems to be an ideology with a past but little hope for the future. The republics of the former Soviet Union, with the possible exception of the Ukraine, seem to have given up on that ideology. All of the former Soviet satellite countries of eastern Europe are eager to develop market economies and Western-style democracy. During the past two decades China seems to be moving toward more acceptance of a market economy but still remains under the control of a one-party political system. Even Castro in Cuba allows some private enterprise, and North Korea seems ready to admit that its socialist system has been a failure, a fact made obvious to all because of the dramatic contrast with what South Korea has been able to accomplish. In fact there seems to be a general consensus throughout the world that Communism hasn't worked. Nevertheless there are still a few Marxists and Maoists in various countries who believe that Communist ideology is basically correct and that the difficulties experienced have been due to administrative mistakes and the persistent opposition, both overt and covert, of the powerful United States of America and its allies. Still others have little sympathy with the positive program of the Communists but think that the Communist critique of capitalism is a good stimulant to further reform of that system.

Fascism (National Socialism)

For many people the ideology of Fascism seems even less worthy of attention than that of Communism. Fascism (also called "National Socialism" or "Naziism") flourished in the 1920s and 1930s led by Mussolini in Italy, a cluster of rebel military leaders in Japan, Hitler in Germany, and Franco in Spain. It was the motivating ideology of all the Axis powers which were defeated in World War II. There is a widespread belief that the Fascist way of thinking was destroyed by that defeat. Nevertheless Fascism has recently received some public attention again because of active *neo–Nazi* movements in some countries such as Germany and the United States. Because of its relationship to Hitler's Aryan racism in the past, Fascism is usually associated with white supremacy movements, but the basic idea of displaying strength through collective aggressive actions coordinated by a leader against other groups can be adopted by any national or ethnic group. One can have yellow racism or black racism as well as white racism. The basic rationale for these various racist or nationalist campaigns are the same.

What are the central ideas of Fascism or National Socialism? It may be best to begin by considering what a *fasces* is. It is a bundle of rods around an ax handle with the blade of the ax protruding. It was used by ancient Roman magistrates as a badge of their authority. The point of this symbol is that there is strength in unity, that the sticks in the fasces cannot be broken as a single ax handle could. The message is that the members of a nation-state or some ethnic group must be bound together in order to be able to overpower outsiders.

The Fascist movement can best be understood as a reaction against both Western-style democracy and Marxism. The Fascists accept the Marxist criticism of Western-style democracy that such a government is basically a facade behind which big corporations fight for their private economic interests. These democratic governments have no real decision-making power and no specific aims. They are necessarily wishy-washy and lacking in determination because they must try to be responsive to the views and interests of many different constituencies. At the same time the Fascists are utterly opposed to the internationalistic loyalty to the proletarian class throughout the world which is promoted by the Communists. The Fascists regard it as treasonous to try to arouse violent conflict between one part of the nation and another part of it. One's loyalty should be to one's nation and race and culture so that it can prevail in its struggle for dominance against other nations. Fascism is an extreme rightist ideology firmly opposed to both the multi-culturalism and moderation of Western-style democracy and the egalitarianism and internationalism of Marxist socialism.

Since Fascists are rightists, one might expect them to promote the value of competition, and they do. But their focus is not on the competition of individual against individual as one finds in Western capitalism but rather on the competition between one nation-race-culture and the others. That is why it is sometimes called "National Socialism." It focuses on the struggle of one national society against other national societies. It sees the world as a struggle between societies not just for survival but even more for dominance. Fascists emphasize power and feeling and will rather than law and reason and restraint (which are the values promoted by Western-style democracy). Fascists emphasize loyalty to nation and race rather than loyalty to economic class and the oneness of the whole human family (which are the values promoted by Communism). Furthermore Fascists glorify war, discipline, aggressiveness, and violence. Peace is regarded as both boring and contrary to nature. Moderation and a tendency to be conciliatory are regarded as weaknesses, and tolerance for different races and cultures is regarded as stupidity and the source of national disintegration.

Fascism is in a sense even more Darwinian than unregulated capitalism since in the Darwinian theory of evolution it is not individuals who survive but rather species. Fascism, however, ignores the fact that all members of the human race belong to one species. It presupposes the thoroughly unscientific view that particular ethnic groups or races or nations are like species competing with each other for survival. Thus for Fascists the fate of individual members of the nations are not important. It is the survival of the whole nation that counts. Furthermore, the struggle is ruthless. There are no constraining rules. What matters is survival of the nation and its dominance over other nations. Warfare is the natural condition of these competing national groups.

Thus, Fascists or National Socialists believe in the organic unity of their nation and the superiority of their own group. They glorify their own national history, their racial characteristics, their military successes, their language and customs and cultural achievements. The individual is to be totally subordinated to what is good for the national group. Each individual is like a cell in the organic whole. In actual practice what this means is that the national society is organized like a military organization, and all members are to do their duty as determined by those of higher rank. The government manages the economy through bureaucratic control although the actual ownership of capital goods often remains under private control. (In Fascist Italy, however, more than in Germany and Japan, the government actually owned some important businesses.) Loyalty to the nation and to the national leader ("Il Duce" or "Der Führer") is supreme and absolute. Individual deliberation about whether the leader might be mistaken is the height of immorality.

One might consider how readily the widespread feelings of patriotism, loyalty to one's nation (whether "nation" means ethnic group or nation-state), hatred of foreigners, and impatience with the deliberative discussions of a democratic government can be used by a charismatic leader to promote a Fascist outlook. This is especially true if economic conditions are bad or other important social problems are not getting resolved. Although Fascism as a recognized ideological movement seems to have been destroyed by World War II, it is easy to see how a dynamic leader in almost any nation facing intractable economic and social problems might try to create the kind of militaristic, aggressive, obedient, intolerant, almost mystical nationalistic movement which could be described as Fascism, whether it is called by that term or not.

The "End of History" Thesis

Former U.S. State Department official Francis Fukuyama is the author of a widely discussed article entitled "The End of History?" published in the Summer 1989 issue of *National Interest,* a quarterly journal of foreign policy.[8] That article is very relevant to the issue of ideology and war. In fact, it seems that the article could have been titled "The End of Ideological Wars." Fukuyama builds on the Hegelian view that history is a reflection of the conflict among ideas. His thesis is that during the past two centuries or so the significant wars have been a reflection of a deeper struggle among different ideologies. The American Revolution (1775–1781) and the French revolution (1789–1799) were the historical embodiments of Western-style democracy with its ideals of "natural rights" such as life, liberty, and property for all citizens; liberty of action so long as the rights of others are respected; limited government legitimized by consent of the governed; a free economy based on market forces with a minimum of government regulation; equality of opportunity; freedom of thought; and tolerance for individual differences. During the past 175 years this democratic capitalistic ideology has been challenged by the ideologies of Communism and Fascism, but the 20th century has seen the defeat of both of these opposing ideologies, especially in World War II and the Cold War. Democratic capitalism has by no means completely triumphed in Russia and China yet, but Fukuyama is confident that the direction of the flow of events toward acceptance of Western democracy will not be stopped. The implication is that there are no more ideological challengers to democratic capitalism in sight anywhere. Consequently,

the ideological struggles which are embodied in history seem to have come to an end.

Fukuyama points out that he is not saying that there will be no more wars of any kind. There will still be some less advanced areas of the world where ideological struggles and other kinds of conflict will continue for a while, but the situation among the powerful states that might get involved in a major war is different. These advanced areas have reached "the end of history" in the sense that there will no longer be large and violent international struggles about the correctness of some ideology. As Fukuyama himself says:

> There would still be a high and perhaps rising level of ethnic and nationalist violence [in less advanced nations], since those are impulses incompletely played out, even in parts of the post-historical [more advanced] world. Palestinians and Kurds, Sikhs and Tamils, Irish Catholics and Walloons, Armenians and Azeris will continue to have their unresolved grievances. This implies that terrorism and wars of national liberation will continue to be an important item on the international agenda. But large-scale conflict must involve large states still caught in the grip of history, and they are what appear to be passing from the scene.[9]

It must be remembered that Fukuyama's thesis is by no means accepted by everyone. One widely-discussed alternative viewpoint is Samuel Huntington's thesis that the world is going to witness a "clash of civilizations" which will challenge the present hegemony of Western civilization.[10] But Fukuyama's thesis is one that Americans and West Europeans like very much to hear. After all, it says that democratic capitalism (our ideology) has triumphed throughout the world. It says that, at least for a century or so, there will be no major ideological challenges to Western-style democracy. Huntington, however, notes that as some non-Western cultures modernize they eventually become less Western.[11] Other critics point to factors such as ethnic strife and religious fundamentalism and unresolved tensions within the Western world itself as reasons to be skeptical about Fukuyama's optimism. Doubters note that the apparent triumph of democratic capitalism may be due more to the military and economic power of the U.S. being used to undermine new social experiments in places such as Nicaragua than to the attractiveness of the ideology itself. Other skeptics point to the tension between rightist capitalism and leftist democracy which exists within Western ideology and to the growing gap between the rich and the poor both within Western societies and in the world as a whole. There is also the problem of how to balance globalized universalistic Western-style democratic ideology against the supposed psychological need of people to belong to some national cultural community which is differentiated from humanity in general.[12] Still, Fukuyama's article has aroused a great deal of interest and has made a forceful statement for the view that the ideological struggles of the last two centuries have for a while at least been worked out and that a period of ideological stability lies ahead as Western-style democratic capitalism gets concretely embodied in more and more particular societies throughout the world, and possibly eventually even at the global level.[13]

Religion and War

This topic of the relation between religion and war is a very difficult topic to address because of the great variety of religions and their different views about involvement in social issues in general and in the problem of war in particular. Religions also differ greatly in the degree to which they are tolerant or intolerant of other religious and philosophical views. Furthermore, there may be differences in beliefs and degrees of tolerance even among the individual members within a particular religious group. Finally, it is important to realize that religions can change or evolve. Consequently, what was true about religion in general or a particular religion in the past may no longer be the case.

Even though most religions have taught the desirability of peace and the need to practice the Golden Rule of doing unto others as you would have them do unto you, many of them have also taught that it is important to defend one's faith, using violence if necessary. Indeed religions often promise special rewards to those who lose their lives defending the faith. Many religions teach that there are just wars, and that for the most part a just war is any war that one's religious (and political) leaders say is a just war. (Religious leaders have often cooperated with political leaders in order to be in a good position to get assistance from the government in prosecuting heretics or proponents of other religions.) The message of the religious leaders is that violence is usually not acceptable but that in this particular "just war," violence is not only acceptable but even obligatory. It is said that "God" (whose will the religious leaders claim to know) not only approves participation in this war but requires it. The result of this situation is that we sometimes have soldiers motivated by "obedience to God" fighting on opposite sides in the same war. Thus religions may serve a key role in "justifying" the use of violence by individuals in warfare. The world's religions talk about peace and compassion, but they nevertheless often provide the impetus for the most ruthless and unrestrained violence.

Over the long term religions do evolve even though by their very nature they tend to preserve parochial beliefs and traditions. They begin in a particular place at a particular time and become an integral part of a particular culture. It is only as this culture comes into contact with other cultures that an awareness develops that other groups have their own religions. Sometimes this interaction with other views generates a greater determination to preserve one's own religion uncontaminated by the views of others, but often the result is a recognition of the value of the insights of others and even a borrowing from them. One of the important developments of the past few centuries is the increasing contact among different religious groups. Although some still react by insisting on the unique value of their own religion, there has been a general trend of more tolerance of and accommodation to the views of others. The widely accepted Golden Rule of doing unto others as you would have them do to you leads to a diminished insistence that others must accept the views and practices of any particular religion.

Some religious groups have come to sponsor dialogues among open-minded leaders of the various religions to show by example that people of different religious traditions can nevertheless be good friends with one another. Many dialogues among different religious groups are arranged locally, but international meetings of religious leaders are also important. The first Parliament of the World's Religions was held in Chicago at the World's Fair in 1893. The second such Parliament was again held in Chicago but not until 100 years later. The Third Parliament of the World's Religions convened in Cape Town, South Africa in December 1999 and attracted leaders from most of the world's religions. At the end of August 2000, two thousand religious leaders from all over the world came together for the four-day Millennium World Peace Summit at the United Nations in New York.[14] These international conferences of religious leaders typically produce statements of support for peace and tolerance among religions and among all the peoples of the world.

Are some religions more likely to support wars than others? It has been suggested that the mystical religions (like Hinduism and Buddhism) which are based more on personal mystical experiences are less supportive of war than the prophetic religions (like Judaism, Christianity, and Islam) which are based more on acceptance of the message of some prophet or prophets.[15] In these latter religions there is a definite tendency to divide people into two groups, those who accept the message and get saved and those who do not and get condemned. Consequently, it becomes very important to determine exactly what the message is, which in turn tends to produce internal divisions in these religions. If one's religion has the Truth which must be accepted in order to be saved, then there is a real temptation to use violence if necessary to convert others for their own salvation. People must be convinced "for their own good" to accept the Truth even if they resist. Thus these belief-based religions can more readily be used to promote war than is the case with the mystical religions, where what is important is having certain kinds of experience rather than believing certain ideas.

But the issue of tolerance of differences is not just a matter of what religion is being practiced or what ideas are believed. Even more important is the *manner* of believing. As John Stoessinger has pointed out, one can distinguish, even within the prophetic religions, between the dogmatic or authoritarian way of believing and the humanistic or democratic way of believing. To quote Stoessinger:

> The dogmatic or authoritarian way insists that religious belief has a monopoly on truth. The believer possesses the truth and no one else really does. Secondly, God is all-powerful and man powerless, with man's greatest virtue obedience to this all-powerful God. Conversely, the humanistic way of believing is the more democratic one. Religious beliefs are not viewed as having a monopoly on truth. In fact, other belief systems also are recognized as having a part of that truth. Moreover, man is not totally powerless but is a kind of (forgive the banality) junior partner, together with the deity, in the building of a somewhat better world. Whether one is a Jew, Christian, Moslem, or anything else, if he believes in a dogmatic way, he will tend to contribute to war; if he believes in the humanistic or the more democratic way, he will tend to contribute to peace.[16]

This same general outlook is put forth by well-known Christian theologian Hans Kung in his effort to promote dialogue among the world's religions. He suggests that Christians need to be self-critical about their own religion. They need to prepare themselves to really conduct dialogue with other religions (as well as other denominations of Christians) rather than viewing these others as merely pagans from whom nothing at all can be learned about religion. Such dialogue among religions is essential to peace, since "there will be no peace among the peoples of this world without peace among the world religions."[17] Kung carefully notes that he is *not* saying that *all* war can be stopped by the proper input from religion but only that the right kind of contribution from religion can reduce the amount of war.

> Let me say it once more, unmistakably: Religions, Christianity, the Church, cannot solve or prevent all the world's conflicts, but they can lessen the amount of hostility, hatred, and intransigence. They can, first, intervene concretely for the sake of understanding and reconciliation between estranged peoples. And second, they can begin to do away with at least the conflicts of which they themselves are the cause and for whose explosiveness they are partly to blame.[18]

During the last three decades or so, it seems that religious groups have become more active in the political arena.[19] One obvious example was the takeover of Iran in 1979 by Shi'ite Muslim fundamentalists led by the Ayatollah Khomeini. Another is the takeover of Afghanistan by the Sunni Muslim Taliban group in 1996. (Recently there has been some concern about the possibility of a war between these two Muslim groups.[20]) But religious groups are also a major factor in the violent social conflict between Jews and Muslims in the Middle East, between Shia and Sunni Muslims in the Persian Gulf and Pakistan, between Hindus and Buddhists in Sri Lanka, between Catholic and Protestant Christians in Northern Ireland, between Christians and Muslims in Sudan, and between Hindus and Sikhs in India. During the ten years from 1990 to 2000, more than 100 new conflicts erupted where religion was a major contributory factor.[21] But religious leaders can also be promoters of peace. In South Africa Nobel Peace Prize winner Bishop Desmond Tutu has been a leading spokesman for reconciliation between blacks and whites.

What is behind this greater social activism of religious groups? It would be rash to try to make generalizations which cover all these cases. In some cases, such as the Catholic Christians in Poland, the Sikhs in India, and the various groups in the former Yugoslavia, religions serve as vehicles for national ethnic groups seeking political independence. In other cases, such as the Catholic Christians in Latin America and the Muslim fundamentalists in Iran, the religious fervor reflects a struggle for social justice against an earlier pattern of docile compliance with the dictates of the politically powerful. In cases such as Iran and Afghanistan as well as the United States the religious groups are protesting against modernist secular ideas which are viewed as promoting immorality and shamelessness. Sometimes the religious fervor is heightened by frustration engendered by repeated defeats and continuing subordination. In Iran and Afghanistan, however, the previously suppressed religious fundamentalists have gained power, and Christian reformists had some success against a right-wing dictatorship in the Philippines. In countries such as Algeria, Tunisia, Egypt, and Turkey Islamic fundamentalism is a vehicle of the dispossessed to challenge the political and economic elite now in power, and in Haiti some activist Christians are playing a similar role. Whether these various religious groups focused on acquiring political power will be able to gain and retain that power and then use it to develop societies which reflect their religious ideals remains to be seen.

In conclusion, we can reiterate our point made at the beginning of this discussion of religion and war, namely, that there is a wide variety of religions and a great diversity in their tolerance for alternative views. Some religious leaders are urging their followers to engage in violence against all those who hold other views while at the same time many other religious leaders, sometimes in the same religious group, are doing everything they can to get their members to be more tolerant and more supportive of peaceful resolution of conflicts.

9.   National-Historical Aspects of the Contemporary Situation

National governments are the main agents relevant to the war problem. They are motivated not only by their ideologies (discussed in the previous chapter) but also by national interests and a national perspective which each has developed as a result of its own history. These diverse national outlooks may contribute to war. From within a given national perspective the actions of the leaders of that country usually appear rational and praiseworthy, while from the perspective of another country those very same actions may seem offensive and detestable. A sensitivity to these different outlooks can help to keep conflicts from becoming so intense that people are ready to resort to violence.

The aim of this chapter is to examine the national perspectives of those countries or groups of countries whose policies are most important in contemporary international politics. We will begin with the viewpoints of the United States and Russia. Then we will turn our attention to Western Europe, Japan, and China. Finally, we will consider briefly how the world looks to the group of nations known as the less developed countries.

The U.S. Perspective

The ideological outlook of the United States is capitalistic democracy or democratic capitalism. But the American dedication to the economic freedom of a market system and to the political freedom of Western-style democracy is not just an abstract philosophical commitment. It is embedded in and reinforced by the American historical experience.

In the Revolutionary War (1775–1781) the newly settled American colonies won their political independence from Great Britain. Although some people of that day may have questioned the wisdom of that rebellion, no American citizen today doubts that that fight for independence was a good thing. The consequence has been a readiness on the part of Americans to identify with others struggling for their political independence. The Monroe Doctrine (1823) proclaimed U.S. opposition to any recolonization of Latin America by European powers. After World War I (1914–1918) U.S. President Wilson included "national self-determination" as one of his "Fourteen Points" for a peaceful world. After World War II (1939–1945) the United States championed the independence of British and French colonies even though those European countries had been allies in the war. What was viewed as Soviet colonization of Eastern Europe after World War II was a central factor in the development of the Cold War. One element of domestic opposition to U.S. involvement in the Vietnamese War (1964–1973) was the idea that the people of Vietnam should be allowed to have a Communist system if that was what they wanted.

Knowledge of the early fight for independence also leads to an uneasiness in most Americans about the United States having any colonies, and in fact there were none until 1898. The Philippines, acquired as a result of the Spanish-American War, were an American colony for nearly half a century but were given their independence in 1946; and Cuba was given its independence in 1902 when it could also have been made a colony. The former territories of Hawaii and Alaska have been converted to full-fledged states, and many Americans believe that the same move should be made with regard to Puerto Rico if the Puerto Ricans so choose. Nevertheless it must be noted that U.S. advancement to the level of a world power has come into conflict with the principle of "no colonies." For example, several islands in the Caribbean and others in the Pacific are U.S. colonies, though they are called "self-governing territories" because they are allowed to elect their own governors.[1] It also should be noted that the concern of Americans is generally limited to *political* independence. The problem of continuing *economic* dependency after achieving political independence, not having been part of the American experience, does not get much attention. Just as it is generally believed that individual persons who have political freedom should be able to take care of their own economic problems, so it is generally believed that nations that have their political independence should be able to take care of their own economic problems.

The confidence that an independent country should be able to take care of itself also grows out the American experience. Starting with 13 former colonies along the Atlantic coast, the United States expanded to take control of the land all the way to the Pacific Ocean. This expansion came through the pioneer spirit of people ready to literally break new ground as they extended their farms and towns into the vast area previously inhabited only by native Americans, who lived more by hunting, trapping, and fishing than by agriculture. The American settlers also realized the value of buying land from other Europeans when available at a good price — Florida from Spain, the vast Louisiana Purchase from France, and eventually Alaska from Russia. These rough-and-ready outdoorsmen also did not hesitate to resort to arms to take land from the native Americans and other settlers such as the Mexicans, taking half of Mexico's territory from that land in the Mexican-American War of 1846-1848. Their consistent winning of wars against less well-trained and less well-armed opponents resulted in a readiness to resort to arms that generally worked well for them as they realized their "Manifest Destiny," to extend the country "from sea to shining sea."

The commitment of Americans to a Western-style democratic political system is supported by their very satisfactory experience with their original Constitution, created by the Founding Fathers in 1787. American history shows that stable but nevertheless changing governance is possible without tyranny or armed revolution. The main blot on an otherwise good record of stability and internal tranquility was the very bloody Civil War or War Between the States (1861–1865) fought over the issues of slavery and the right of states to secede from the Union. Over the years many persons of diverse national, cultural, racial, and religious backgrounds have been somewhat peacefully integrated into a single pluralistic but generally harmonious national community. This experience has led Americans to be very unsympathetic to political violence. It is apparent to them that differences regarding public policy should be resolved by debating and voting. If people in other countries don't have such a system for resolving their differences, Americans believe that they should institute a government by which that can be done. The same outlook applies at the world level with regard to disputes among nations. Both the League of Nations and the United Nations were proposals of American presidents, and just after World War II almost two-thirds of the American public supported the idea of a federal world government modeled on the democratic constitutional U.S. federal system.[2]

Experience has also confirmed for Americans the value of a capitalistic economic system. Even though there have been depressions from time to time, the overall trend has been toward more and more abundance. New inventions, encouraged by the free enterprise system, have kept the United States in the forefront of technological change and increasing productivity. Recent "rags-to-riches" success stories of new immigrants demonstrate that the opportunity for anyone to succeed still exists. Undoubtedly the outstanding economic record of the United States has been due in part to the presence of good agricultural land, vast natural resources, and the general absence of destruction from war, but most Americans believe that the competition engendered by the market system is a crucial ingredient in the nation's prosperity. They tend to view the spread of U.S. business enterprises into other parts of the world as a good thing, not just for the businesses but also for the people who will get jobs as a result (though some

Americans are concerned that U.S. businesses are now creating too many jobs in other countries while closing down their factories in the United States).

The foundations of U.S. culture are based on the philosophical ideas of the Enlightenment of 18th century Europe. These ideas include a reliance on reason as opposed to trusting authority and tradition. In government this meant trusting in debate and voting by the common people while distrusting kings, aristocrats, and bureaucrats. In religion it meant trusting philosophical reasoning and scientific research rather than religious authorities such as the Church and the Bible. Most of the first settlers in what is now the United States were Christians who came from England to escape religious persecution and religious authority. They often had a Calvinist faith that earthly wealth was a sign of heavenly favor. But freedom of thought in religion also meant that some had even abandoned traditional Christianity in favor of Deism, the notion that God created the world but no longer intervenes in its workings. Since the world always operates in accord with the scientifically discovered laws of nature, said the Deists, there were no miracles. People had to rely on their own efforts to make a "heaven on Earth" by understanding how nature works and then using that knowledge to transform the world. Even those who retained their Christian belief in miracles tended to accept the idea that "God helps those who help themselves."

A related Enlightenment idea that became an important part of American culture was the notion of progress. After the stagnation of the Middle Ages and the revival of the values and ideals of the Classical Period of the Greeks and Romans which was central to the Renaissance, the new Enlightenment view carried to the New World by the early Americans was that things are not only changing but are getting better. Humanity had not only discovered the glories of Athens and Rome but was moving ahead to new heights. The knowledge and culture of the ancients had indeed been recovered, but beyond that there was newly discovered scientific knowledge and a new kind of society where everyone, not just the nobility, could enjoy the good things of life. A better life was possible, and the New World was a place where these dreams could be realized.

Another important aspect of the American outlook is the insistence that there be a moral basis for political and military action. The first Americans felt that it was necessary to issue a "Declaration of Independence" to morally justify to the whole world their use of violence to achieve independence. The reasoning in that document is based on "natural law" theory, especially as that theory was spelled out by the English philosopher John Locke (1632–1704).[3] Locke, following ancient Stoic philosophers as well as more recent thinkers, argued that there is a moral law based on reason (that is, a "natural law") which serves as an unwritten standard of justice to be used by the individual conscience in evaluating governments and the written laws they may adopt. This "natural law" exists as a rule for correct behavior even in a situation where no government has yet been established to make laws and enforce them.

When philosophers explore social obligations and the moral basis of government, they try to imagine what rights and obligations people would have even if there were no government. Such a situation is described as a *state of nature*. Any rights people have in such a situation are called "natural rights," and any obligations are called "natural obligations." These "natural rights" and "natural obligations" together make up the "natural law."

Some "realistic" philosophers such as Thomas Hobbes (1588–1679) maintained that in a *state of nature* people would have a "natural right" to keep whatever they could acquire for themselves but would have no "natural obligations" whatsoever to anyone else.[4] The state of nature would be a constant war of everyone against everyone, and the only way out of such a situation would be to establish a very strong government that would adopt some "civil laws" (written laws adopted by a government) and enforce them. According to Hobbes, only after a government had been established would it make any sense to talk about any obligations to others, and even then the government itself would decide what was obligatory and what was not.

The Americans adopted Locke's much more "idealistic" view of the moral situation in the *state of nature*. As noted, Locke said that even in the state of nature there would be a "natural law" which would bestow on everyone some "natural rights" and "natural obligations." Locke claimed that everyone has a natural *right* to (a) life, (b) liberty, and (c) property. Consequently, it is also the case that everyone has a natural *obligation* (a) not to kill others, (b) not to enslave others, and (c) not to steal from others. That means that life in the *state of nature* would not be nearly as "lawless" as Hobbes had portrayed it. With regard to the question of how the "natural law" would be enforced, Locke maintained that everyone would be entitled to enforce it, and in the end God would make sure that violators of it would get punished.

Since these rights and obligations exist even in a *state of nature,* no government can take them away. Borrowing from Locke's view, Jefferson wrote in the Declaration of Independence that there are certain "unalienable rights" (rights that could not be taken away), "that among these are life, liberty, and the pursuit of happiness" that no government, including the British government, could nullify. So Locke's ideas about the existence of a "natural law" became the basis of the Declaration of Independence adopted by the Continental Congress of the American colonists in 1776 while they were fighting for their independence.

The "natural law" theory borrowed from Locke has continued to influence American thinking with regard to the relations among individual citizens, but it has also been extended to the relations among nation-states. There is no world government over the national governments, but that does not mean that there is no law governing what it is right and wrong for nation-states in their relations with each other. Nation-states have a "natural right" (a) to exist, (b) to be free, and (c) to control their own natural resources. That means that they also have "natural obligations"

(a) not to attack or destroy other nation-states, (b) not to subjugate or colonize other nation-states, and (c) not to unfairly exploit the natural resources of other nation-states. This "idealistic" or "moralistic view" of international relations which is so central in American political thinking means that there is a general antipathy to the Hobbesian "realistic" view of international relations prevalent among many political scientists and political leaders.

Guided by this "idealistic" perspective as well as by pragmatic considerations, the foreign policy of the United States from the end of the War of 1812 until the time of World War I (1914–1918) was to stay out of European power politics. In the Monroe Doctrine of 1823 the Americans also made it clear that they expected Europeans not to try to recolonize the parts of Latin America that had become independent during the Napoleonic Wars. These policies worked partly because of the geographical separation between Europe and the Americas provided by the Atlantic Ocean and partly because they were acceptable to the British, who had the most powerful navy during this period. These policies also proved to be beneficial for the overseas interests of American enterprises which had an inside track for doing business in Latin America while facing minimal nationalistic antagonism in the rest of the world.

American business also prospered greatly within the United States as the nation expanded its control across the continent. The need for transportation to the ever farther west frontier was met by building canals and the railroads. The warning of George Washington to stay out of European struggles for power did not preclude driving the Spanish out of Cuba and the Philippines in the Spanish-American War (1898). Having defeated the Spanish, the next step was a war against the natives in the Philippines (1899–1901) in order to acquire the use of those islands for American business interests as well as to bring civilization to the savages.

It was also because of American business interests that the isolation from European power struggles ended in 1917. Especially after

World War I broke out in 1914, there was a great demand in Europe for American products, including arms and ammunition. American businesses were willing to sell to anyone who would buy, but geographical factors plus the British navy made it easier to sell to the Allies.

German submarine attacks on U.S. ships triggered U.S. entry into World War I, but U.S. sympathies were already with the British and French, partly because of evidence that the Germans were secretly encouraging Mexico to attack the United States and also because the Germans were perceived as aggressors who had immorally invaded neutral Belgium. Americans have an animosity toward aggressors[5] that is directly linked to the general acceptance of natural law theory discussed previously. According to that view, nation-states, like individuals, should follow moral principles. They should not physically attack others who have done no harm to them. They should not violate their contracts and treaties. They should respect the property of others. The Germans had violated all these precepts. As aggressors they deserved to be punished. If the British and French could not accomplish that alone, then it would be completely appropriate for the United States to join the effort to enforce the "natural law."

After the war Woodrow Wilson proposed a League of Nations where the whole community of nations could collectively determine whether some nation had committed aggression against another. But the U.S. Senate did not provide the two-thirds majority needed to ratify the Versailles Treaty containing the League's Covenant, so the United States did not participate in the League. In the Senate it was argued that since the United States didn't want other nations "meddling" in the Americas, it likewise should not get involved in the affairs of other nations. Subsequent events might have been different if the United States had joined the League, but as it was the League did not take forceful action against aggressors, and by 1939 the big powers were at war again in both Asia and Europe.

Through 1940 and most of 1941 the U.S. public was not ready to support military action against the all-too-obvious aggression of the Axis powers. That changed quickly when the Japanese attacked the U.S. Pacific Fleet at Pearl Harbor in Hawaii on December 7, 1941. Since that day Americans have been urged to "Remember Pearl Harbor" and to be prepared for an unexpected attack. Pearl Harbor marks the end of an era in American foreign policy. The United States could no longer afford to be indifferent to world affairs. Furthermore, the rapid advances of the Japanese military forces during the first six months after Pearl Harbor made it clear that in the future the United States would need a bigger, better-prepared military force in place before any actual fighting begins. The United States had become a full-fledged participant in world power politics.

Even before World War I had ended another event took place which had a great impact on subsequent U.S. foreign policy, namely, the Bolshevik Revolution in Russia in 1917. From the beginning the Communists were perceived as enemies. The opposition of Americans to Communism has three separate but very powerful roots. First, those who are well off financially will obviously be opposed to a movement whose avowed aim is to take their wealth from them and probably even exterminate them. Second, those who are committed to Western-style democracy oppose Communism because of its authoritarian politics and its readiness to use violence to achieve its aims. Third, those who have traditional religious commitments oppose it because of its militant atheism. It is not surprising, then, that U.S. military forces, along with those of Britain, France, and Japan, intervened in Russia in 1918-1919 to help the pro–Western White Army try to prevent the new Communist regime and its Red Army from taking control of the whole country.

Despite the negative attitude toward the Communists, in World War II Americans found themselves fighting on the side of the Communist Soviet Union against the Axis powers, who were enemies of both Communism and Western-style democracy. During the war the United States sent much-needed materiel to the Soviets. Exactly three months after the war in Europe had ended (May 8, 1945), the Soviets launched an attack on Japanese positions in Manchuria as they had agreed to do. At the end of the war the relations between the Soviet Union and the United States were reasonably good. The United Nations was organized on the basis that these two nations together with Britain, France, and China would work together to preserve world peace. But the mood of cooperation changed quickly. From the American point of view the Soviets used their military presence in Eastern Europe to establish Communist governments there instead of permitting free elections. The former U.S. ally *talked* about supporting democracy but its actions seemed all too similar to the authoritarian Germans who had just been defeated.

In response in March 1947 U.S. President Truman announced that the United States would provide military assistance to those resisting attempted subjugation by revolutionary minorities or by outside pressures. This "Truman Doctrine" marked a great shift in U.S. policy. It indicated that the United States would be getting involved even in the internal affairs of other countries if military force rather than the ballot box was being used to take control of a country. The policy seemed to work in Turkey and Greece, where U.S. assistance helped anti–Communist regimes to stay in power. A second part of the U.S. response was the Marshall Plan, a program of economic assistance to European countries so they could rebuild quickly and consequently be less susceptible to Communist-inspired uprisings. A third part of the U.S. response, instigated by a Communist takeover in Czechoslovakia (February 1948) and a Soviet cut-off of Western ground access to West Berlin (June 1948), was the creation of the North Atlantic Treaty Organization (NATO). In that alliance the United States, Canada, and the countries of Western Europe agreed that an attack on any one would be regarded as an attack on all. As a result the Communist expansion in Europe was halted. The U.S. program of "containment" seemed to be working.

But the situation was different in Asia.

Mao Zedong's Communist forces gained control of all of mainland China in 1949. That most populous nation in the world had come under Communist control. In 1950 the Communist North Koreans attacked non–Communist South Korea, and President Truman, already under attack for having "lost" China by not giving enough support to the anti–Communist forces there, quickly sent U.S. forces to Korea. He also got the United Nations to declare North Korea an aggressor, so other nations joined the effort to stop the aggression. After much fighting and long negotiations a truce was signed in 1953. Again Communist expansion efforts had been halted.

In Vietnam, however, a more complicated situation existed. During World War II the French colony of Indo-China had been taken over by the Japanese. After the war the French tried to reestablish their colonial control, but their efforts were resisted by local forces led by Ho Chi Minh. Ho had worked with agents of the U.S. Office of Strategic Services (OSS) against the Japanese during the war and considered himself to be the George Washington of Vietnam. At the same time he was a committed Communist who had spent many years in Moscow. In Vietnam, the American sympathy for national independence movements came into conflict with its opposition to Communism. At first the United States refused to help the French against Ho, but after unexpected gains by the Communists in China the United States changed its policy and started providing materiel to the French. After the French were forced by military defeat to leave in 1954, the part of Vietnam north of the 17th parallel came under Communist control. At this point the United States began to offer assistance to the non–Communist Vietnamese left in control in the south. The number of U.S. advisers was gradually increased in order to help the South Vietnamese government deal with Communist guerrillas. In 1964 the United States sent military forces into South Vietnam. A long, indecisive war with many casualties ensued. In 1973, partly in response to domestic protests, U.S. forces left. Very shortly thereafter the South Vietnamese government surrendered. The Communists had gained control of all of Vietnam. Soon they also solidified their control over the neighboring countries of Laos and Cambodia.

What was the United States to do in situations like Vietnam? The "hawks" had argued that the Communists had to be stopped in Vietnam or they would soon take over all of Southeast Asia. Military containment had worked in Europe and Korea, and it should also work in Indo-China. The "doves," on the other hand, argued that there was overwhelming support for Ho Chi Minh among the people of Vietnam and that the United States had no business intervening on the side of a small non–Communist minority. There is still strong disagreement in the United States about what should have been done in Vietnam, and the same conflicting views were evident in debates about U.S. involvement in places such as Nicaragua where apparently popular movements for progressive change had Communists in key leadership positions.

Latin America became a focal point for U.S. resistance to Communism in the late 1970s and 1980s. Fidel Castro had made Cuba a center for exporting Communism to all of Latin America, and especially to Central America and the Caribbean. Many Latin American governments were controlled by right-wing military dictatorships opposed to any kind of liberalization. Opposing them were revolutionary "democratic" forces, many of whom were inspired by Castro's success in Cuba. Democrats and Republicans had very different ideas about what strategy to use to stop the spread of Communism in this area. Democratic President Jimmy Carter tried to persuade the ruling regimes to adopt reforms while simultaneously trying to wean the revolutionary forces away from Communism by showing them that the United States was interested in human rights and progressive change. In 1978 he persuaded the Senate to ratify the Panama Canal Treaties which would eventually return the canal to the Panamanians. This agreement was to send a message that the United States was becoming more sensitive to the concerns of Latin Americans. In 1978-1979 a civil war in Nicaragua led to

the overthrow of the corrupt leader Somoza, but a substantial proportion of the Sandinista forces which engineered that revolution were Marxists and their biggest supporter was Castro in Cuba. Even though Sandinista leader Daniel Ortega included non–Marxists in his government, many Americans were convinced that the Communists had taken control in one more country, which would serve as a base to promote Communist takeovers in other countries such as El Salvador. When Republican Ronald Reagan became president in 1981, he adopted a totally different strategy of giving military and financial support to the counterrevolutionary "Contras" in order to overthrow the Sandinistas. In 1983 Reagan sent U.S. forces to invade the island nation of Grenada after a Communist take-over had occurred there. The message was obvious. No leftist revolutions would be allowed in the Western Hemisphere.

President Reagan also decided to take a more aggressive stance against the Soviet Union, which in 1979 had already shown its disdain for Carter's conciliatory approach by intervening to help Communist forces in Afghanistan's civil war. In the early 1980s Reagan launched a massive military build-up of nuclear forces culminating in the proposal for a Strategic Defense Initiative which supposedly would provide a protective shield against any Soviet nuclear attack. Reagan had made it clear that the United States was going to try to gain military superiority rather than being content with nuclear parity with the Soviet Union. It is still a matter of debate to what extent this Reagan policy of building up U.S. military forces was what led the Soviet Union to decide to drop out of the arms race and to what extent Gorbachev wanted to end the arms race anyway because of the sad shape of the Soviet economy.

One can hardly exaggerate the significance of the changes which took place in the international situation between 1986 and 1991. During these five years the United States went from the Cold War stance of matching the placement of Soviet medium-range nuclear missiles in Europe to seeing its long-time enemy, the Soviet Union, actually go out of existence as a country. The Cold War, which lasted over 40 years, ended with the United States as the sole superpower in the world.

In 1991, when a U.S. organized coalition of military forces defeated the Iraqi forces which had invaded Kuwait, U.S. President George Bush could speak of a "New World Order." The Cold War was over, and now the United States would lead in establishing a world where aggression would not be allowed, where all nations would follow the principles of natural law in their relations with one another. This American ideal, which had been behind the creation of the League of Nations and the United Nations, was now going to be realized under the political and military leadership of the United States. The other major Western-style industrialized democracies (Britain, France, Germany, Italy, Canada, and Japan) would have special consultative status. The U.N. Security Council would be used when feasible, and NATO or the Organization of American States (OAS) or other organizations would be used when suitable. The United States would be leader, not an autocrat, in the "New World Order."

During the Clinton administration (1993-2001) the United States increased its domestic economic strength and military dominance over all other countries. At first there was a readiness to support U.N. peacekeeping efforts in Haiti and Somalia, but after the loss of 18 U.S. troops in Somalia in a U.N.-led peacekeeping effort in 1993 (even though those troops were not under U.N. command but were a separate U.S. commando unit acting without U.N. knowledge or authorization[6]), there has been a reluctance to commit U.S. troops or much money to U.N. efforts. The reluctance to support any kind of substantial U.N. involvement resulted in a massacre in Rwanda in 1994. When tensions and fighting arose in the former Yugoslavia in 1998, the threat of a veto in the U.N. Security Council by Russia led to the decision to rely on NATO to do the military intervention in Kosovo. The United States also wants to encourage regional peacekeeping in places such as Africa. Even with regard to U.N. peacekeeping, the United States seems to be searching for a way to keep control of any international interventions while avoiding any great risk to U.S. military personnel and minimizing any commitment of U.S. money.

At the beginning of the 21st century the United States is very much the dominant power in the world. It seeks to direct events by a wide variety of approaches all the way from bilateral diplomacy to using international institutions as long as it can control them. The goal seems to be to extend the American way of doing things, including both the economic ideology of capitalism and the political ideology of liberal democracy, to the whole world. At the same time in particular situations there can be a real conflict between what advances U.S. ideological principles at the global level and what promotes short-term U.S. national interests.[7] Nevertheless Americans generally are very confident that the United States has discovered the best way to organize a society and that the rest of the world will come to see that it cannot do better than to imitate the American model.

The Russian Perspective

It is important to understand the distinction between "Russia" on the one hand and "the Soviet Union" or "Union of Soviet Socialist Republics (U.S.S.R.)" on the other. The country of Russia (sometimes called "the Russian Empire") was ruled by the czars up to 1917. Czarist Russia came to an end with the Menshevik revolution in the spring of 1917. Then the short-lived pro-Western Kerensky government was overthrown by the Bolshevik or Communist revolution in the fall of 1917. The Communists combined the various parts of the old Russian Empire to create the new Soviet Union in 1922. It is not easy to distinguish between the Soviet Union and the part of it called the Russian Federation because they overlap in some ways. The "Russian Federation" is the largest of the 15 republics that made up the Soviet Union before its dissolution in 1991. Before that disintegration, Moscow served as the capital of both the Soviet Union and the Russian Federation. The Russian Federation comprised 75 percent of the territory of the former Soviet Union. Even after the break-up of the Soviet Union, the Russian Federation remains the largest country in the world in terms of territory. The Russian Federation also contains over 50 percent of the population of the former Soviet Union. The Soviet Union was a federation of 15 republics, while the Russian Federation is itself a federation of 88 identifiable political subunits. After the Soviet Union was dissolved, the Russian Federation took its place in the United Nations, including occupying its permanent seat on the U.N. Security Council.

The history of the western part of Russia from the tenth century on follows essentially the same series of social patterns one finds in the rest of Europe: kingdoms established by traders over the areas they were exploiting, then feudal kingdoms based on land holdings, then urban-centered kingdoms based on merchant capital, and then a larger "national" kingdom with an autocratic leader supported by the nobility.[8] But there were some differences. First, these developments in Russia occurred considerably later than in Western Europe. Secondly, and partly as a consequence of the first point, in Russia the landed aristocracy eventually was joined by the new industrial capitalists as rulers of Russia rather than being overthrown by them as happened in the Western European countries. As a result, Russia did not become the kind of capitalistic democracy which had developed in England and France, though it was moving in this direction in the decades just before the 1917 revolution.[9]

A third significant difference between Russia and the countries of Western Europe is the size of the country which eventually came to exist. In Western Europe the expanding populations of the flourishing countries not only came up against each other but before long also reached the shoreline. At this point some of them took to ships and the New World. For the Russians there was land and more land to be taken, especially to the east, and the Russians became "land-sailors" moving ever onward to new lands. The greatest geographical expansion of the borders took place in the 17th and 18th centuries when all

of Siberia and even Alaska were brought under Russian control, and the border to the west and southwest was extended to approximately its present location. In the 19th century large numbers of Russians migrated into these new areas, and additional territory was added in the south central region between the Caspian Sea and China. Efforts to expand still farther south brought the Russians into conflict with the British, but in 1907 an agreement on spheres of influence was reached which put Afghanistan into the British orbit.[10]

Although Russian expansion has continued over a long period of time, it also needs to be noted that Russia has been invaded on several occasions from the west, where there are few natural barriers to assist in the defense of the country. In 1812 Napoleon invaded. In 1916 the Germans and Austrians invaded. In 1920-1921 the Poles invaded. In 1941 the Germans under Hitler invaded again. On the first and the fourth occasions, after sustaining massive losses the Russians drove the invaders back and eventually were victors in the war. On the second occasion the Russian government collapsed and was forced to accept a punitive peace settlement. The land lost during the third invasion was taken back in 1939. But at the end of World War II the Soviets believed it was time to put an end to these invasions from the west. Consequently, they were determined to create a row of friendly "buffer" states in Eastern Europe through which any potential invader would need to pass before reaching the Soviet border.

Another important aspect of the Russian historical experience has been the seemingly never-ending effort to catch up with Western Europe. The Renaissance, the commercial revolution, and the industrial revolution all began farther west and only later reached Russia. The result, as perceived by both Western Europeans and some Russians, has been a long history of Russian "backwardness." During the rule of leaders such as Peter I (1689–1725), Catherine II (1762–1796), Alexander I (1801–1825), and Alexander II (1855–1881) efforts were made to promote Western ways of thinking and acting in Russia, but they only partly succeeded. Russian "backwardness" was most evident in warfare. The Russians had done rather well in their wars during the first half of the 19th century, but the Crimean War (1853–1856) showed they were no match for the British and the French. Their rate of industrialization lagged behind that of the Western Europeans. The Russo-Japanese War (1904–1905) and the first part of World War I (1914–1918) demonstrated that they couldn't even hold their own against Japan or Germany. This history of inferiority is important in realizing how important it was for the Soviets to win in their competition with the West during the Cold War, whether the contest was athletic, artistic, scientific, ideological, political, economic, or military. In this context one can appreciate the great concern of Soviet leaders like Gorbachev that in the 1970s and 1980s the Soviets had fallen decisively behind the West with regard to computers, robotics, and other new technologies even though the Russian space program had led to the launch of the first artificial satellite in 1957.

Some other aspects of pre–Revolution Russia are worth mentioning briefly. One is that Russians had been accustomed to an autocratic political system, a system which the 5th-century leaders of Moscow borrowed from their Mongol overlords and which was not softened much until the decade before the Bolshevik Revolution. A second is that religiously inclined Russians traditionally thought of Moscow as the center of World Christian Orthodoxy, "the Third Rome," the successor to Rome and Constantinople as *the* holy city of Christendom.[11] The czars and patriarchs served together as protectors of "the Truth" until such time as the rest of the world would be ready to receive it. As custodians of "the Truth" they felt it was altogether appropriate to regulate what the people could read and hear so that they would not be lured away from the true faith. Both of these phenomena have interesting parallels with what happened in the Soviet Union under the Communists.

The Bolshevik Revolution in 1917 brought massive changes in the social order. The leader of the Revolution was Vladimir Ilyich Ulyanov (1870–1924), better known by his adopted name of Lenin. He was a Russian Marxist whose involvement in revolutionary activities got him exiled to Siberia in 1895 and then chased out of the country in 1907. In 1917 he returned by train from Switzerland, aided by the Germans, who rightly anticipated that his revolutionary activities would lead to Russian withdrawal from the war. Lenin's writings had served as inspiration to the revolutionaries, and when he arrived in St. Petersburg, the Russian capital, he was recognized as leader of the Bolshevik (majority) faction of the Russian Social-Democratic Workers Party. He persuaded that group not to participate in Kerensky's liberal democratic provisional government which had been set up after the abdication of Czar Nicholas II in March of 1917. The Kerensky government refused to quit the war even though Russian soldiers were being slaughtered wholesale because of their inferior weapons. Using the slogan "Peace, Land, Bread," Lenin then led the Bolsheviks in their own revolution to take control of the Russian government in November (October according to the old Russian calendar) of 1917. Under his leadership the new government agreed to peace with Germany; fought to victory against a group of counter-revolutionaries who received assistance from British, French, American, and Japanese military forces; and established the first Marxist state.[12] A Russian government whose aim had been to protect the interest of the nobility and well-to-do was replaced by a Soviet government whose aim was to advance the interests of the workers and the peasants.

Just as Americans generally believe that their historical experience has confirmed the value of their ideology of capitalistic democracy, so Soviet citizens during the Cold War period generally believed that their historical experience had confirmed the value of the Marxist-Leninist ideology. When they compared the Soviet Union with pre–Revolution Russia, they were proud of the differences. Not everything had been perfect, but certainly significant progress had been made, especially in view of the great losses suffered in World War II.

One of the most obvious improvements

was the quantity and quality of industrialization which had taken place. Although some progress had been made in the late 1800s and early 1900s, Russia at that time was still a backward country, as the fighting in World War I had demonstrated. During the Cold War the Soviets were able to challenge the United States in the development of the most technologically advanced types of weaponry — nuclear weapons, long-range missiles, surveillance satellites, attack helicopters, nuclear-powered submarines, and so on. Though the Soviet Union was not at the top in the production of consumer goods, still its position relative to the rest of the world was certainly much better than it had been before the Revolution. The Soviet citizenry were convinced that the industrialization pushed so relentlessly by Stalin in the 1930s had given them the capability to defeat the Germans in World War II and that the continued emphasis on industrialization and arms production had enabled them to neutralize postwar U.S. efforts to dominate the world.

A second great improvement was the increased opportunity for nearly everyone in the country except the old nobility, the bourgeoisie, and the kulaks. Under the czars many children never learned to read or write, and access to university-level education was generally restricted to the upper classes. National minorities often were not allowed to use their national languages in schools. Health care for peasants and the poor in cities was virtually nonexistent. Taxes on peasants were ten times as high as taxes on landlords.[13] Sports and museums were only for the wealthy. Under Communism all that had changed. All children had access to education. There was no discrimination against anyone because of her or his nationality.[14] All people could get adequate medical care and participate in the cultural life of the society. Taxes were fair for all. Things such as special training for sports and the arts were provided free to everyone by the government.

A third kind of improvement, according to the Communists, was the kind of personal outlook developed by individuals living in a socialist system. In pre–Revolution Russia either people would learn to selfishly compete to get all they could for themselves or they would be brought under the influence of the Church, in which case all critical and scientific thinking would be subordinated to the acceptance of superstition and ancient ways of thinking. Under the socialist system people were directed toward social cooperation and progressive thinking directed toward improving the lot of all humanity.

Somewhat related to the above was the Communist understanding of the situation with regard to war and peace. It was claimed that under the czars Russia got involved in wars in order to advance the interests of its own elite or the interests of foreigners with investments in Russian industry. After the Bolshevik Revolution, it was no longer necessary to fight wars in order to control markets and raw materials for the capitalist class. The wars the Soviets had to fight and get prepared to fight were responses to capitalistic nations which wanted to eliminate the one socialist state strong enough to help protect successful revolutionary movements in other countries from externally supported counter-revolutions.

After World War II the Soviet Union believed that its forces were obliged to help the progressive socialist groups in the Eastern European countries maintain control against pro-capitalist groups, groups who not only wanted to put a reactionary government back in control in their own countries but who also would eventually cooperate with other capitalists in trying once again to overthrow the socialist regime in the Soviet Union. Assistance had also been given to progressive groups in other countries, but it was noted that in no case had Soviet forces ever invaded a capitalist state unless that state had first invaded the Soviet Union, as Hitler did. Soviet military forces were sent into another country only after the proletariat there had launched a revolution with some possibility of success and had requested Soviet assistance to prevent a counter-revolution. Communists pointed to the existence of a capitalist state like Finland right on the Soviet border to show that capitalist countries did not need to fear invasion from the Soviet Union.[15]

The Communists in the Soviet Union proclaimed that their ultimate goal was a world in which all nations had adopted a socialist system. According to their understanding, that was the only way in which capitalist exploitation of some countries by others could be halted. But the Communists' proclaimed strategy was never to use force to take over a country which generally wanted to remain a capitalist country. From their point of view a proletarian revolution would necessarily be a revolution by the majority against an entrenched elite minority, and it could not possibly succeed unless it had widespread public support.[16] After a proletarian revolution had succeeded, as in Cuba, then it would be the task of the Soviet Union to help that regime set up a new socialist society and to prevent any attempted counter-revolution. The Soviets did not perceive themselves as threatening to the United States or any other capitalist country because their aim was limited to supporting leftist revolutions which had come about with majority support.

According to the Soviets, the attempt by the United States to portray the Soviet Union as an aggressive country was only a way of diverting attention from what the United States itself was doing, namely, maintaining military forces all over the world in order to protect U.S. economic interests as they exploited the raw materials and low-paid workers of the less developed countries.[17] From the Soviet point of view that was the significance of U.S. interventions in Iran in 1953, Guatemala in 1954, Vietnam in 1955–1973, Lebanon in 1958, Cuba in 1961, the Dominican Republic in 1965, Chile in 1973, Grenada in 1983, Nicaragua in 1985, and Panama in 1989. According to the Communists the United States proclaimed itself the champion of democracy but in fact was always intervening to prevent revolutions by "the people" against the capitalists.

But one issue that the Soviet Union eventually had to face was how "democratic" that country itself was. Although there were elections, there was only one party which could nominate candidates, the Communist Party. The system of democratic centralism where the decisions of higher level bodies were binding on the lower levels meant that ultimately the real power was in the hands of a very small group of leaders at the top. The Communist Party was supposedly the party of the common people running government for the sake of the masses, but in fact the party itself became the home of a new elite with its own special privileges. They had their own stores for shopping, their own hospitals, their own vacation spots, and so on. They had limousines and chauffeurs at their disposal. They used their positions to get special privileges for themselves and to help their family members and their friends.

Government policy in the Soviet Union reflected the views of the leadership group, and often a single individual. Under Stalin (1924–1953) ruthless terrorism was used to keep the population completely under the control of the leaders. Control of the national economy was centralized, and there was a focus on the development of heavy industry and armaments. Not everyone was enthusiastic about the Communist system, but during World War II the population worked hard for "Mother Russia" in order to defeat the Germans. After the war Stalin's heavy-handedness against those who did not totally obey him became evident again. It is estimated that Stalin was responsible for the deaths of more than 42 and a half million Soviet citizens,[18] an average of about one and a half million for each of the 29 years when he was head of the Soviet Union.

After Stalin died in 1953, Georgy Malenkov became Senior Secretary of the Party for one year. Then came a 9-year period of de–Stalinization and reform under the leadership of Nikita Khrushchev. The Soviet space program delivered the first artificial satellite in 1957, an event used by Khrushchev to promote the idea that Communism was proving its superiority over capitalism. On the other hand, the Soviets built the Berlin Wall in 1961 to prevent East Germans from escaping to the freer and more prosperous West. The Cuban missile crisis in 1962 resulted from Khrushchev's push for Soviet military parity with the U.S. Having led the world to the brink of nuclear war, Khrushchev and Kennedy tried to ease the tensions by signing the Partial Nuclear Test-Ban Treaty in 1963. In 1964 Khrushchev was removed from power for making decisions without first consulting with the rest of the leadership, for supporting unscientific theories about the biological inheritance of acquired characteristics which had had a negative impact on agricultural production, for advocating organizational reforms that threatened the position of many people in the party bureaucracy, for inappropriate public behavior such as banging his shoe on a desk at the United Nations and inordinate bragging about the accomplishments of Soviet science, and for being unreasonable in his disputes with the Chinese Communists (such as threatening to launch a nuclear strike on their nuclear facilities if they exploded a nuclear weapon, which they did the day after he was removed from his position[19]).

The Leonid Brezhnev years (1964–1982) saw a return to stable and traditional bureaucracy, a praising of Stalin's accomplishments, a steady growth in military spending, greater assistance to Communist Vietnam in its struggle against U.S. forces while simultaneously following a path of "peaceful coexistence" with the United States itself (including signing nuclear arms control agreements like SALT I and SALT II), an effort to develop more technology relevant to the production of consumer goods, and a reigning in of cultural freedom. In Eastern Europe Romania managed to defy the Soviets by trading with the United States, Western Europe, and China instead of trading exclusively within the Soviet bloc. In 1968 a liberal regime in Czechoslovakia was squashed by an invasion of Soviet and other Warsaw Pact forces in accord with the "Brezhnev Doctrine," the idea that the Soviet Union and its allies reserved the right to use military force to intervene militarily in any Soviet bloc country that seemed to be wavering from orthodox Marxism, thus endangering the whole bloc. In 1979 Soviet forces were dispatched to Afghanistan to help the Marxist faction in a civil war there.

When Brezhnev died in 1982, there was a struggle within the Party leadership between hardliners who wanted to maintain the Stalin-Brezhnev conservative bureaucratic approach and reformists who wanted to open up the system to new ideas in the Khrushchev anti–Stalin fashion. None of the contenders was young, so it seemed obvious that no one would be in power for long. Yuri Andropov, a reformist, won the contest and used his 15 months in office to promote more discipline in the workplace in order to increase productivity. One of the more significant things he did was to move fellow reformist Mikhail Gorbachev up rapidly in the Party bureaucracy. In fact, when Andropov died it seemed that Gorbachev would be one of the contenders for the top post even though he was much younger than the others at the top. The hardliners, however, were committed to Konstantin Chernenko. At this point Gorbachev apparently struck a deal that he would step aside for Chernenko if it was clear that he would become leader when Chernenko died. The result was that the 73-year-old Chernenko became the Party Secretary for 13 months, but Gorbachev then became the new leader with little resistance when Chernenko died in March 1985 .

Gorbachev was aware that some in the higher echelons of the Party and the government were not enthusiastic supporters of his reform ideas, but he used his position to rapidly replace those people with others who would support him. He started out echoing the ideas of Andropov that there was a need for more commitment to work hard on the job so that the Soviet economy could progress and produce a standard of living more like that found in the West. He initiated penalties for absenteeism and launched an attack on alcoholism. In June 1987 he presented proposals for giving local enterprises more autonomy and having local factory managers elected by the workers. In the international arena Gorbachev indicated strong support for the United Nations and urged diplomats to be more sensitive and less dogmatic in their interactions with other countries. He noted that the Soviet Union was not going to attack anyone and wanted to work out arms agreements to reduce both nuclear and conventional weapons. Domestically he promoted *pere-stroika* (restructuring), *glasnost* (openness), and *demokratizatsiya* (democratization). The highly centralized bureaucratic structures were to be decentralized. The media and artists were no longer to be censored for saying things critical of the government. Eastern European countries were to be free to do things in their own way. In elections within the Soviet Union several candidates would be allowed, not just one as in former years. In the West there was considerable suspicion that Gorbachev was pretending to be "nice" so that he could catch them off guard.

Looking at the situation in retrospect, it seems that Gorbachev was being completely honest. If he was deceiving anyone, it was only himself in believing that he could start a reform process which would not result ultimately in the break-up of the Soviet Union. Once people were free to speak out, it became obvious that many of the different nationalities which had been under Russian authoritarian control did not like that situation. Lithuania was the first to declare its independence from the Soviet Union in March 1990. Gorbachev, now holding the newly created post of President of the Soviet Union, tried to stop this move that might break up the whole Soviet Union by arguing that the separation and its terms would need to be negotiated by both sides. Gorbachev also began to hold back on some of his economic reforms in order to get more support from conservatives, but the result was a negative reaction from Boris Yeltsin, President of the Russian Federation. On August 19, 1991, one day before a Union treaty was to be signed that would end effective control by the Soviet Union over the republics, there was an attempted coup d'etat by conservatives in order to oust Gorbachev and then try to maintain the existence of the Soviet Union by the use of military force. That attempt was foiled at least in part due to the actions of Yeltsin in Moscow when he daringly and successfully pleaded with the Soviet military forces not to fire on their fellow Russians. The coup attempt failed for lack of support by the military forces, and Yeltsin's courageous actions resulted in his popularity among re-

formers greatly surpassing that of Gorbachev. The failed coup led to a rash of declarations of independence by the republics. The 15 former republics of the Soviet Union became the independent countries of Estonia, Latvia, Lithuania, Russian Federation, Belarus, Ukraine, Maldova, Georgia, Armenia, Azerbaijan, Turkmenistan, Kazakhstan, Uzbekistan, Kyrgyzstan, and Tajikistan (the last two are just east of Uzbekistan). On December 8, 1991, the leaders of the Russian Federation, Belarus, and Ukraine, three of the largest republics, issued the "Declaration of Minsk," which declared that the Soviet Union no longer existed and which invited other former republics of the Soviet Union to join them in creating the Commonwealth of Independent States (CIS). On December 24, 1991, the Russian Federation was accepted as the successor of the Soviet Union in the United Nations, and on December 25, 1991, Gorbachev resigned from the meaningless position of President of the no longer existent Soviet Union.[20]

Thus Yeltsin, the first democratically elected President of the Russian Federation, became the man in charge. He was regarded as a popular reformer who with support from the West would lead Russia into becoming a part of the capitalistic democratic world. But the difficulties for accomplishing this goal were formidable. Under the new 1993 constitution elections produced a Russian parliament controlled by former Communists, who resisted economic change, and patriotic nationalists, who opposed reconciliation with the West. Fortunately for Yeltsin, the new constitution put most of the power in the hands of the President. A second difficulty was the danger that the Russian Federation might itself dissolve into its many parts just as the Soviet Union had done. The greatest danger in that respect was the province of Chechnya, which launched a secessionist war in 1994-96 that humiliated the Russian army and temporarily established Chechnyan autonomy. A third difficulty was the problem of trying to establish a capitalistic economic system after 70 years of a socialist system which had demonized all capitalists as crooks. Yeltsin relied heavily on economic advisors from the United

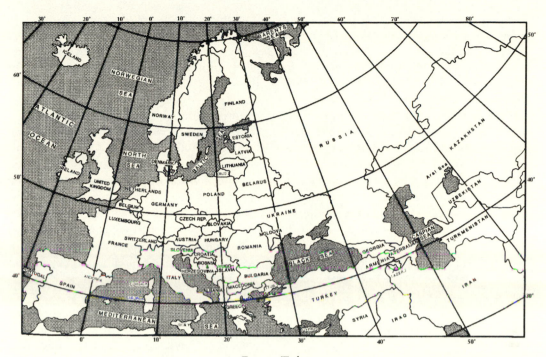

Europe Today

States, but Russia did not get as much economic assistance from other countries as had been expected and most plans for economic reforms did not work as anticipated, often because of large-scale corruption.

In an effort to bring about some reforms while playing off his opponents against each other, Yeltsin ended up having to appoint seven prime ministers in a nine-year period. None of them were very successful. The effort to privatize the Russian economy ended up with many managers of the old Soviet era getting fabulously wealthy by taking over ownership of what they had previously just managed. They then used their wealth and positions to take over the government bureaucracy. These "oligarchs" who took control of the Russia discouraged the formation of other businesses which might compete with them. The new capitalism also did not eliminate the bureaucracy and indifference to the consumer so pervasive in the old socialist system. Furthermore, now organized crime was out of control, and anything connected with the government went downhill rapidly as taxes were not collected. Bribery became more profitable and efficient than abiding by the

law. Pollution was totally out of control. Even the average life-span of Russians declined as medical facilities deteriorated and drinking mushroomed. Many older citizens longed for the old days of stability and security. Yeltsin himself suffered from health problems undoubtedly aggravated by his heavy drinking. As the end of the no longer competent Yeltsin's term approached nearly everyone was more than ready for a change.

Even before the scheduled end of his term at the end of 1999, Yeltsin resigned and appointed former secret-service agent Vladimir Putin[21] to be acting President. In May 2000 Putin became the elected President, having captured over half the votes in an election with many candidates. Putin was aided by his image as a serious, competent, dedicated man who would make Russia strong again, beginning by defeating the Chechens (although the Russians were being criticized in the campaign on grounds that they were just killing innocent civilians in the cities rather than the rebels hiding in the hills).[22] Putin appears to be determined to return Russia to its great power status by internal reforms to get laws obeyed and taxes collected and by developing better external diplomatic relations with other countries such as China and India. His policy stance toward the United States does not seem to be antagonistic, but he does seem eager to develop alternatives to just going along with whatever the United States wants. He also apparently wants to stop putting so many resources into nuclear weapons so that more money will be available for building up Russia's conventional military readiness to deal with its immediate neighbors. Even though Russia's economy did not do well during the Yeltsin years, it seems to be gradually improving under Putin. Russia's potential is great. It has abundant natural resources, a large territory with a substantial population, and a good knowledge base for future industrial expansion.

The Western European Perspective

"Western Europe" refers, of course, not to a single nation but a group of nations of which the largest are Germany, Italy, the United Kingdom, and France. To be able to discuss their outlook in a collective manner is an indication of how much the world has changed since 1945. Before then it was the conflicts among these European nations which led to one war after another, culminating in the two World Wars. These countries still have their national differences, but in today's world such variations are minor in comparison to their common situation and outlook. All of them are capitalist democracies united in the European Union and officially allied with the United States in the North Atlantic Treaty Organization (NATO).

For all of these European countries the past was much more glorious than is the present. In the 16th century, Spain, by virtue of its exploitation of the New World, was the chief power in the world. During the next century France became dominant. England challenged France for supremacy in the 18th century and became dominant after the defeat of Napoleon in 1815. In the 1880s and 1890s the imperial European powers, led by Britain and France, divided most of Africa and

Asia among themselves. By the end of the 19th century the British could boast that "the sun never sets on the British Empire," while a recently united Germany was searching for its place in the sun. In 1900 a military force composed of contingents from eight different countries (though almost half the troops were from Japan) was sent into China to put down the Boxer Rebellion there. These industrialized European nations viewed themselves as carrying civilization to the savages of the rest of the world. In China the main point of dispute among them was whether each nation should have its own area of control or whether there should be an "open door" policy so that the whole of China would be available for exploitation by any trader regardless of nationality.

Though these European countries were heavily armed with new weapons of war made possible by modern industry and though they were organized into two opposing alliances, it seemed in the early 1900s that they were keeping their competition for power and new colonies under control. But in 1914 they stumbled into World War I. The war came to a conclusion only after the military forces of the United States put an end to the deadlock on the battlefield. After the war, despite the efforts of President Wilson, the United States declined to become actively involved in the power struggle among industrialized nations, so Europe remained the center of world affairs.

Twenty years later the European countries were at war again, and again the United States intervened. By the end of that war in 1945 the European countries were in shambles. The United States and the Soviet Union were clearly the new powers in the world, and though they could not agree on much else they did concur in the view that the European nations should give up their colonial empires. Nevertheless attempts were made by the European nations to regain control over some of their colonies. These efforts often led to battles against local nationalist forces seeking independence. By 1960 most of the former colonies had become independent nations.

After having battled and battered one another for centuries, since the end of World

War II the countries of Western Europe have been cooperating with one another and even taking some steps toward unification. The United States helped turn things in this direction when it decided that its postwar economic assistance to European countries (the Marshall Plan) would be coordinated through the Organization for European Economic Co-operation (OEEC). After the rebuilding of Europe was completed, this organization did not go out of existence but continued to give advice concerning economic problems. In 1961 it was expanded beyond Europe into the Organization for Economic Cooperation and Development (OECD) which included all of the industrialized democracies.

Another significant development contributing to the unification of Western Europe, also promoted by the United States, was the creation in 1949 of the North Atlantic Treaty Organization (NATO), a military alliance aimed at preventing any further expansion by Communist military forces in Europe. It provided not only for an integrated military command but also for a Council which discussed political issues. In 1993 membership in NATO included Belgium, Canada, Denmark, France, Germany, Greece, Iceland, Italy, Luxembourg, Netherlands, Norway, Portugal, Spain, Turkey, the United Kingdom, and the United States. In 1994 NATO began a program called Partnership for Peace (PfP) so that countries formerly controlled by the Communists, including the republics of the former Soviet Union, could work with NATO in peacekeeping and humanitarian programs in Europe. In March 1999 the Czech Republic, Hungary, and Poland became full-fledged members of NATO. Despite its largely European base, however, NATO is not just a European organization because it includes also the United States and Canada.

But the Europeans have done some cooperative institution-building on their own. In 1947 France and Britain signed the *Treaty of Dunkirk,* pledging military assistance to each other in the event of another war with Germany and agreeing to strengthen economic relations. The *Brussels Treaty* of 1948, which supplanted the Treaty of Dunkirk,

specifically mentions the goal of progressive unification of Europe. The 1954 modification of this treaty produced the Western European Union (WEU), composed of seven countries: United Kingdom, France, Belgium, Netherlands, Luxembourg, Italy, and West Germany. This Union still provides an arena for discussing political issues, military policy, and the administration of military forces. It is a forum in which, unlike NATO, Canada and the United States are not involved. In January of 1948 the *Benelux Economic Union* (Belgium, Netherlands, and Luxembourg) initiated an economic program in which customs duties among the three nations were abolished and a common tariff was levied on goods coming into the three-nation region. In 1949 the *Council of Europe* was formed as an effort to promote the political unification of Europe, but it subsequently has focused on the protection of human rights. It established a *European Court of Human Rights* (based in Strasbourg) which acts as an appeal court on civil liberties and which in a couple of cases has even nullified national laws that it found to be inconsistent with its principles. A restructured full-time *Court of Human Rights* was established in November 1998, and 41 European countries now accept the compulsory jurisdiction of that court.[23]

Of greater political significance than the bodies mentioned above is the *European Community* (EC), which developed out of the *European Coal and Steel Community* (ECSC) created in 1952 by the Treaty of Paris signed by France, West Germany, Italy, and the Benelux countries. The success of the ECSC led to agreements in 1957 to create two other organizations, the European Atomic Energy Community (Euratom) and the European Economic Community (EEC or "Common Market"). These organizations began operating in 1958. In 1967 the three separate European organizations (ECSC, Euratom, and EEC) were merged into a single *European Community* (EC). In 1993 the European Community was transformed into the *European Union* by ratification of the Treaty on European Union (Maastricht Treaty).

The European Union (EU) has several

elements. (1) *The Commission of the European Communities* or *European Commission* (located in Brussels) functions as the administration of the Union. It has the task of implementing the various treaties adopted by the member states as well as the rules adopted by the Council of Ministers. It is headed by 20 commissioners and has a staff of over 15,000 persons. (2) *The Council of Ministers of the European Union* (which meets in Brussels) is composed of one appointed representative from each of the 15 member states. It is the EU's decision-making body which has the responsibility of determining how treaties are to be applied to particular situations and how the economic policies of the various member-states are to be coordinated. (3) *The European Council*, composed of the governmental heads of the member-states, determines high-level policy. (4) *The European Parliament* (meets in Strasbourg and Brussels) is the legislature-in-the-making composed of over 500 directly elected representatives (though from its beginning in 1958 until 1978 they were elected from the national parliaments). The number of representatives for each country is based on its population. The European Parliament does not yet have law-making power but the present law-making Council of Ministers is supposed to confer with the Parliament. The Parliament also has the responsibility of reviewing the budgets, and it has the right to discuss anything, even matters not addressed in the treaties. (5) *The European Court of Justice* (located in Luxemburg) is the judicial branch of the EU. (6) *The European Monetary Union* (EMU) and its *European Central Bank* (ECB) (located in Frankfurt) along with the *Eurosystem of Central Banks* (ESCB) have the responsibility of establishing a new European currency called the "euro." The third stage of economic unification started at the beginning of 1999 with the setting of irrevocable exchange rates between the euro and the national currencies. In 2002 the new European banknotes will be issued to replace the national money in the eleven participating countries: Austria, Belgium, Finland, France, Germany, Ireland, Italy, Luxemburg, Netherlands, Portugal, and Spain. The four remaining EU countries, which are not participating in the monetary union, are Denmark, Greece, Sweden, and the United Kingdom.

Does all this organization mean that there is movement towards a United States of Europe? Possibly, but not without difficulties. Ironically the end of the Cold War and the reunification of Germany in September 1990 raised new questions about European unification. During the Cold War Western European countries had a militarily powerful common ideological enemy against which they needed to unite, but with the end of the Cold War the only "outsiders" against which the Europeans must unite are the economic competitors of the United States, Japan, and China. Now the question of the inclusion of Eastern European countries into a united Europe must be addressed. Also, the reunification of Germany has ended the earlier relative equality of population and influence in the European Community among Britain, France, Italy, and West Germany. Previously, all four countries had populations between 55 and 61 million, but a united Germany with a population of more than 80 million as well as the largest economy and a central geographical location now has a preeminent position.

The decisions facing the European Union are sometimes couched in terms of focusing on "deepening" the community or on "widening" it.[24] "Deepening" refers to making the existing community of 15 nation-states more integrated. This could mean giving more powers to the central authority such as the establishment of a Union policy on agricultural subsidies and regulations or welfare payments to new immigrants.[25] "Widening" refers to extending formal membership in the European Union to other European countries. Some obvious candidates are Iceland, Norway, and Switzerland which were formerly in the European Free Trade Association along with Finland, Austria, and Sweden before the latter countries joined the European Union in 1995. But beyond that there are several other countries which would like very much to become part of the European Union: Poland, the Czech Republic, Slovakia, Hungary, Slovenia, Croatia, Lithuania, Latvia, and Estonia.

Turkey, which is already a member of NATO, also wants to become part of the European Union as its first non–Christian member. There is a definite concern on the part of these countries that not being included in the European Union could present some real economic difficulties for them later. It might be noted in passing that if these "outsider" countries (other than Norway and Iceland) are admitted to the official "Europe," Germany's position would become more central while that of France and Britain would become a more peripheral than is the case in the existing European Union. In fact, some Europeans are concerned that the Germans will in fact take over in Europe, thus succeeding in doing economically and politically what they were not able do militarily in World War II.

Before the end of the Cold War and the reunification of Germany, the focus was on "deepening" the community. Jacques Delors, president of the European Commission, pushed hard for more deepening. One of his successes was adoption in 1991 of the Treaty of Maastricht which established the European Union in 1993. A major problem for a real European Union is the reluctance of the national governments and their citizens to transfer national sovereignty to a supranational body, to become Europeans rather than Frenchmen, Englishmen, and Germans. There is a struggle between seeking true integration into an economically, politically, militarily, and culturally unified community on the one hand and creating a collection of separate international functional coordinating agencies on the other.

It is still unclear what direction Europe will take. There is a desire for economic integration in order to be better able to compete against the United States and Japan, but there is considerable reluctance to bring about the political integration on which economic integration must be based if it is to be enduring. The Germans are especially eager to have an EU through which they can exercise their influence in the world without overtly arousing the fears of others about a resurgent Germany. But the notion of a unified Europe dominated by the Germans is exactly what

scares many non-Germans. Now that the Cold War is over there is also that difficult question of just where the eastern and southern borders of the European Union should be. Does it make sense to exclude such former Communist countries as Poland, Hungary, and the Czech Republic which now want very much to be part of a democratic capitalistic Europe? Why should Mediterranean states like Malta be excluded from a united Europe? Why shouldn't Turkey, which has been a faithful member of NATO, be allowed into the European Union?

In the long run might it not be more sensible to aim to integrate Europe (including the former Soviet republics) into a wider whole-world community than to try to separate Europe from the rest of the world? Or if uniting the whole world seems too unrealistic at this time, why not at least integrate all the industrialized democracies into an Intercontinental Community of Democracies which would include all the NATO countries, Japan, Australia, and New Zealand?[26] Such a proposal should be especially attractive to the British, who are reluctant to develop stronger ties with continental Europe if that eventually comes to mean weaker ties with Canada, the United States, Australia, India, and other former British colonies.

The Japanese Perspective

Japan is the only non–Western nation other than Israel which is generally listed as belonging to the 24-nation class of "industrial countries." Instead of becoming a colony of the Western nations as most of the nations of Asia and Africa did or a semi-colony as China and many of the nations in Latin America did, Japan itself became a colonial power. Though considerably smaller geographically than the United States and though having less than half its population, in 1998 Japan's Gross National Product (GNP) was second in the world, exceeded only by that of the United States, and its Per Capita GNP ($32,380) exceeded that of the United States ($29,340).[27] Consequently, Japan must be regarded as a major actor in international affairs.

The critical period for Japan's future occurred between the last years of the 16th century and the beginning of the 20th century.[28] The Japanese reaction to the West during this period can be characterized as readily accepting Western technology while fighting off the intrusion of Westerners themselves into Japan as long as possible. A long period of internal peace in Japan under the Tokugawa shoguns (1600–1868) produced a unified and basically successful opposition to European efforts to forcibly enter the country. The virtual exclusion of Westerners was broken in 1853-54 when Commodore Perry and his fleet of U.S. ships forced the Japanese to agree to the return of shipwrecked sailors, the opening of fuel ports in Japan for foreign ships, and the development of economic and political relations. During the period called "the Meiji Restoration" (1868–1912) the Japanese worked out compromises which surrendered as little control to the Westerners as possible. At the same time they studied Western science and technology and industrialized their own society. As a result, just over 40 years after the Perry "opening" to the West, the Japanese had so developed their economic and military capabilities that they were able to defeat the Chinese in the Sino-Japanese War (1894–1895) and thus take control of the island of Taiwan (also called "Formosa"), the Pescadores Islands, and the Kwantung peninsula in southern Manchuria. Ten years later the Japanese were able to defeat Russia, one of the major powers of Europe. While the Chinese, convinced by their superior culture that they had nothing to learn from foreigners, remained under Western domination, Japan had rapidly borrowed Western ways and quickly become a world power.

As a world power, Japan embarked on the task of collecting more colonies just as Britain, France, and the other European powers had done. In 1910 Korea was formally annexed and put under Japanese military control. In World War I (1914–1918) Japan sided with the Allies and used the opportunity to take control of German holdings along the coast of China and some islands in the Pacific which had belonged to Germany. In the years 1918 to 1920 Japanese forces joined the British, French, and American troops fighting against the Communists in Russia, but the Japanese didn't leave eastern Russia until 1922. After World War I in the Treaty of Versailles (1919) the Allies gave limited recognition to Japanese influence in China, but a Japanese demand that the Treaty include a declaration of racial equality was rejected. Nevertheless, in the League of Nations established by that Treaty, Japan was recognized as one of the five big powers and thus granted a permanent seat on the League Council.

The imperialist drive of Japan slowed momentarily in the 1920s when a liberal government agreed to limitations on the size of the Japanese navy relative to that of the United States and Britain in accord with the Naval Limitation Treaties of 1922 and 1930. The Japanese already exercised indirect control over mineral-rich Manchuria, but in 1931 the military, ignoring the civilian government, took direct control of that region. In 1933 Japan withdrew from the League of Nations because that organization had recommended sanctions in response to the takeover in Manchuria. Undeterred, Japan continued taking control of additional pieces of Chinese territory, and open warfare between the two nations began in 1937. The outbreak of war in Europe in 1939 allowed the Japanese to move into what had been French-controlled Indo-China (now Vietnam, Cambodia, and Laos). They then prepared to attack Burma and the Dutch East Indies (now Indonesia) in pursuit of what they called the "Greater East Asia Co-Prosperity Sphere," a scheme for Japanese hegemony throughout Southeast Asia. The United States refused to accept this militaristic expansion, and the cutting off of U.S. exports of oil and scrap metal to Japan led to the Japanese attack on Pearl Harbor in the Hawaiian Islands in December 1941. The Japanese aim was merely to deter the United States from interfering with their expansion into southeast Asia. They had no intention of conquering the United States. Unfortunately for them, the American reaction to their attack was more uncompromising than they had anticipated.

World War II ended with the dropping of atomic bombs on Hiroshima and Nagasaki and the subsequent surrender of Japan.[29] The United States imposed a democratic political system, at first under strict U.S. supervision but operating on its own after the Peace Treaty of 1951. The new Japanese constitution prohibited armed forces but permitted a national police reserve, which later became a "self-defense force" as the United States came to see Japan less as a past enemy and more as an ally in the Cold War. Nevertheless the Japanese themselves were not eager to rearm. The experience with nuclear bombs had produced a strong anti-militaristic sentiment among the Japanese which still persists.

Having failed in its effort to develop an empire by military means, Japan decided to follow a different path. As Ezra Vogel put it, "Like the Venetians and Dutch in their heydays, the Japanese conceived a vision of economic power without military power."[30] The U.S. use of Japan as a base of operations during the Korean and Vietnamese conflicts provided an additional boost to Japanese economic growth. Between 1960 and 1981 Japan's GNP increased 3.3 times as fast as the average of the other leading industrialized countries.[31] In terms of the value of the U.S. dollar in 1975, Japanese per capita income went from $146 in 1951 to $395 in 1960 to over $2000 in 1972.[32] It should be remembered too that during this period Japan had the burden of paying reparations to countries in Southeast Asia for damages done during World War II.[33] Japan was an industrialized country even before World War II, but this post-World-War-II "economic miracle" means that Japan has become a model to be imitated by other countries, especially in Asia.

An important factor in Japan's economic expansion is its relatively small investment in the military sector. During the Cold War when the Soviet Union was spending 13 to 14 percent of its GNP for the military and the United States 5 to 6 percent of its GNP, Japan was devoting about 1 percent of its GNP to the military.[34] As a result Japan had a great deal more of its assets available for capital investment and nonmilitary research and development, two items which are very important for economic growth. These spending figures should not be taken to mean that Japan is militarily weak, however, because Japan's GNP is so large that an expenditure of only 1 percent still makes Japan's military budget the third or fourth largest in the world.[35]

A current issue for Japan is whether to make an increased investment in the military. The United States has been urging the Japanese to do so in order to counter Russian and Chinese military power in the Pacific area and to assist in U.N. peacekeeping efforts. Of course, it would also be helpful to the United States and Western Europe from the standpoint of economic competition if the Japanese would spend more of their governmental expenditures on the military. On the other hand, a Japanese increase in outlays for the military might be viewed by the Chinese as a threat to them, and presently one of the most promising situations for the Japanese economy is their blossoming relationship with China. In that country there are over a billion customers for Japanese products, plus raw materials which the Japanese need. Also, the Japanese have thrived under the U.S. nuclear umbrella, so why change anything? Furthermore, even apart from popular opposition, it would not make sense for Japan to try to develop nuclear weapons of its own. Japan would then become a threat to China and a prime target for the nuclear weapons of both China and the Russian Federation. Because of Japan's small size and its concentration of population and industry in a very limited geographical region, it is difficult to find a major power more vulnerable to a nuclear attack than Japan.

At the same time Japan needs to protect itself against interruptions in trade. The Japanese economy depends on importing raw materials and exporting finished products. Japan has no oil of its own, and 80 percent of what it imports comes from the often unstable Middle East; it also must import close to 100 percent of its iron ore, bauxite for aluminum production, wool, rubber, and phosphates and about 90 percent of its wheat and soy beans.[36] With no colonies to rely on and no military power that can be readily projected to other parts of the world, Japan desperately needs world peace.

Japan has suffered from the 1997-98 economic crisis in the newly developing countries of Asia because of its heavy investment in that area. In 1990 writers were pointing to the Japanese economy with its close cooperation between government and big corporations as a model to be followed by everyone, including the United States. That view has changed, however, because of the great performance of the U.S. economy during the 1990s along with the recent economic problems of the southeast Asian countries which have been following the Japanese model. Now it is Japan's turn to learn from the more open, more competitive, more individualistic, more experimentalistic economic practices of the United States.[37] It remains to be seen to what extent the Japanese will make modifications in the way that their political and economic systems function. Thus far deficit spending by the Japanese government has not been able to bring the country out of the decade-long recession, which is exacerbated by mountains of bad loans in the banking system. Nevertheless there is every reason to believe that Japan will eventually adapt to the new globalized economy and will remain one of the main economic powers in the world. Japan's central role will become even more important as the developing countries of southeast Asia also make the needed modifications and recover from the 1997-98 economic crisis.

We have already noted that Japan's economy is second largest in the world. Japan's need for peace in order to trade with the rest of the world was also mentioned. The Japanese are steadily becoming more involved with the United Nations and with U.N. peacekeeping. If the U.N. Security Council ever gets modified, Japan probably will become a permanent member, though without a veto. Japan's great dependence on international trade and its tragic history with nuclear weapons provide that country with strong motivation to try to develop more effective world-level political and judicial institutions. The development of such institutions coincides perfectly with Japan's national interests.

The Chinese Perspective

If Japan is the "mighty midget" of the world, China is the "awakened giant." Twenty-two percent of all the people in the world live in this country, and only the Russian Federation and Canada are larger in land area. China also represents one of the oldest continuous civilizations in the world, with a recorded history going back 4,000 years.[38]

For our purposes the history of China can be divided into three periods: (1) the long classical period up to the 19th century during which China was the center of Asian culture, (2) the period between 1840 and 1945 when China was dominated by other nations which had already industrialized, and (3) the period of new independence and development since 1945.

During the many centuries of the first period China was known as "The Middle Kingdom." Although the degree of centralization varied from time to time depending on the independence or subservience of the local "warlords," there was always a Chinese Emperor, the son of Heaven, who was the center of power. His dominion extended over the surrounding national groups, who were regarded as inferior peoples, as barbarians whom the Chinese would try to civilize. A "tribute system" existed whereby the leaders of these other peoples would send gifts to the Chinese emperor in recognition of his superiority. Those who presented these offerings would be required to kowtow (kneel and touch their heads to the ground) several times in front of the Emperor, who then would give them some even more valuable things in return as his way of showing that his wealth was greater than theirs. It is important to realize that Chinese superiority was based not primarily on military domination but rather on cultural accomplishments such as literature, philosophy, art, government, and the production of fine goods.

There were some sporadic contacts between China and Europe at least as early as the first century C.E., and Venetian Marco Polo made a well-publicized 25-year journey through the Orient in the late 13th century.

But more sustained contact did not occur until the 16th century when Portuguese traders established a trading colony in Macao just off the Chinese coast. Spanish, Dutch, and British traders followed shortly thereafter, and some Spanish missionaries were even appointed to positions in the Chinese government during the 17th century.[39] Nevertheless their impact on Chinese civilization was not lasting.

The rude awakening which marks the beginning of the second major period of Chinese history, the "century of humiliation," came in the form of the Opium War (1839–1842). British traders had opened a base of operations in Canton. They were eager to acquire silks, porcelain, spices, and other goods to take to Europe, but they had difficulty figuring out what to sell the Chinese in return. There was some minor interest in clocks, telescopes, and similar gadgets but not enough to keep the trade going. The Westerners had found, however, that they could supply the Chinese with opium, and once they were addicted they became good customers. The Chinese government had prohibited the sale of opium, but despite continuing efforts could not enforce the prohibition. When a large cache of British opium was seized and destroyed by Chinese officials, the British, arguing that such action constituted interference with their right of free trade, launched an attack and destroyed the Chinese fortifications at Canton. This Opium War ended with the signing of the Treaty of Nanking (1842), which gave the British the right to sell opium, huge reparations for British losses, and the colony of Hong Kong. It also provided for the opening up of four more "treaty ports" for European traders where the principle of "extraterritoriality" would apply, that is, where Westerners accused of violating laws could be tried only in Western courts.

The Opium War was followed by other battles between Westerners and the Chinese government which was trying to control their activities. Each time the military power of the small groups of Europeans enabled them to prevail. New "unequal treaties" were signed giving the Europeans and Americans the right to operate in even more places. Some Chinese, influenced by the teachings of Christian missionaries, tried to overthrow the imperial government. The result was the extremely bloody civil war known as the T'aip'ing Rebellion (1851–1864) in which it is estimated that ten million people were killed. The government, eventually assisted by the Westerners who were not sure they would be able to continue their activities if the rebels were to gain control, put down the rebellion. In 1884 and 1885 the French gained control of Vietnam, which had been one of the states paying tribute to China. A new level of humiliation was reached in 1894 and 1895 when the Japanese, an Asian people, used their newly developed Western-style military forces to remove Korea from Chinese control.

In 1900 a group of Chinese called the "Boxers" decided that it was time to use physical force against the Europeans, but their "Boxer Rebellion" was suppressed by a collective force from eight other nations. In 1911 Sun Yat-sen, "the Father of Modern China," led a successful rebellion against the Empress, but his Nationalist Party could not maintain control of the government and real power remained in the hands of the "warlords." In 1920 the Chinese Communist Party was organized. They adopted the policy of working within the Nationalist Party, but not all of the Nationalists wanted their help. Feuding between the two factions continued throughout the 1930s and 1940s even as they both fought against the Japanese.

The third period of China's history begins with the end of World War II in 1945. The Japanese had taken over the European holdings in China, and now the Japanese were defeated. The way was open for the Chinese to take control of their own country, but which faction would rule? Even before the war ended the United States had been trying to get the Nationalists, led by Chiang Kai-shek, and the Communists, led by Mao Zedong, to come together in a coalition government, but these efforts failed. In the fighting that ensued it seemed at first that the Nationalists would win; but by the end of 1949 the Communists, aided by mass defections from the military because of promises of land from the Communists, had gained control over all the mainland part of the country. The Nationalists had retreated to the island of Taiwan, where they remain today, still outside of Communist rule.

The Communists' top priority for the new People's Republic of China was industrialization, and with assistance from the Soviet Union the effort moved ahead rapidly. In the countryside the redistribution of land and the establishment of cooperatives were pursued. Education was expanded, and a Marxist-Leninist ideological emphasis was instituted. The aim was to develop the "new socialist man," a person who would be unhesitatingly loyal to the country and the proletarian revolution and who would put those loyalties above pride or self-advancement or love of family and local community.[40] Many people, especially the well-off and the well-educated, resisted these changes. In fact, over 35 million people (compared to over 20 million killed by the Nazis in Germany) were killed by the Communist regime in order to establish its new social order.[41]

A top priority in foreign policy was to overcome the image of weakness, of being able to be pushed around by other countries. When China's 1950 warning to the United States that U.N. forces in Korea should stop advancing toward the Chinese border was ignored, a million Chinese "volunteers" entered the fighting to help the North Koreans. At the same time the Chinese sent troops into Tibet to bring that territory under Chinese control. An uprising there in 1959 was suppressed, and in 1962 the Chinese established their control over some border territory near Tibet which had also been claimed by India. In the early 1950s the Chinese were also able to get the Soviets to return various concessions in Manchuria which had been granted to Russia under coercion at earlier times. Nevertheless the Chinese were thwarted by the United States from achieving their top priority, control over Taiwan.

One of the most amazing developments in recent world affairs is the break between China and the Soviet Union which took place between 1958 and 1972. There had always been some conflict between Stalin and Mao, and after Stalin died in 1953 things did not improve, partly because Mao believed that he deserved a higher status in the world Communist movement than the new Soviet leaders, who had not themselves participated in a revolution. Nevertheless in the period 1956–1958 a compromise seems to have been worked out in which Mao agreed not to challenge Khrushchev's doctrine of "peaceful coexistence" in exchange for help in the development of nuclear weapons.[42]

The first serious break between China and the Soviet Union occurred in 1958-1959. Mao sought but did not receive Soviet support in his struggles against the Chinese Nationalists on Taiwan in 1958 and in his border disputes with India in 1959. Khrushchev encouraged opposition to Mao within the Chinese leadership, and in June of 1959 he unilaterally canceled the treaty in which the Soviets had promised assistance for the development of nuclear weapons.[43] After a friendly meeting with U.S. President Eisenhower later that year in which the cancellation of the treaty with China on nuclear weapons development probably played a significant role, Khrushchev stopped to see Mao in China. Apparently they quarreled bitterly not only about the Soviet approach of "peaceful coexistence" with capitalists but also about Khrushchev's request to set up a radio transmitter in China for contacting Soviet submarines, about Soviet hegemony over Outer Mongolia, and about the location of the Sino-Soviet border. Mao was irked because the Soviets refused to treat the Chinese as equals, while Khrushchev was concerned that the Chinese would pull the Soviets into a nuclear war. In 1960 the Soviet Union withdrew all forms of aid to the Chinese.[44]

Apparently a new compromise was reached by the end of 1960, but the dispute broke out again at the October 1961 Soviet Party Congress. In 1962-1963 the clashes along the border escalated, though mutual public accusations were not made until the fall of 1963. In 1962 the Soviets did not confer at all with the Chinese during the Cuban missile crisis, and the 1963 Soviet-U.S.-British agreement not to test nuclear weapons in the atmosphere may have been aimed at embarrassing the Chinese, who were about to conduct their first nuclear test.[45] In 1964 Khrushchev threatened to destroy the Chinese nuclear facilities if they did detonate a nuclear device, and the Chinese responded that they would then invade the Soviet satellite state of Outer Mongolia.[46] On October 15, 1964, Khrushchev was removed from his leadership position in the Soviet Union, and the next day the Chinese exploded their first nuclear weapon.

The new Soviet leaders continued their struggle against the Chinese, however, by trying during the next several years to get international meetings of Communists to expel China, but they were unable to accomplish this. In 1968 the Soviets invaded Czechoslovakia, a move which suggested that they might also intervene in other Communist nations such as China. In March of 1969 the Soviets and Chinese reached an agreement on the nonuse of force and continuation of the present boundaries. Nevertheless both sides continued to build up their military forces just in case the agreement was not observed.

The other half of the shift in China's outlook at that time concerns its relationship with the United States. During the 1960s the Chinese viewed the United States as their archenemy. The Americans were the defenders of the Nationalists on Taiwan, the instigators of the military advance toward the Chinese border during the Korean War, and the leaders of the anti–Communist effort in Vietnam. So why did the Chinese suddenly become friendly with the United States in the early 1970s? The Chinese conflict with the Soviets was certainly not sufficient by itself to throw them into the arms of the Americans. The key event in the change of the Chinese attitude toward the United States was the 1969 warning by U.S. President Nixon to the Soviets that an attack on Chinese nuclear facilities would be regarded as an unfriendly act because the radioactive fallout would land on Americans stationed in Korea and Japan.[47] At the same time the United States made sure that the Chinese knew about evidence from U.S. satellites which indicated that the Soviets were prepared

to make such an attack if the United States had not intervened. The Chinese responded not only by changing their policy toward the United States and having Nixon come to China but also by inviting Nixon for a second visit even after he had resigned in disgrace from the U.S. Presidency as a result of the Watergate scandal. The Chinese wanted to show their gratitude; they realized that Nixon's strong protest to the Soviets had saved them from an attack on their nuclear facilities. Without nuclear weapons they would have remained at the mercy of a nuclear-armed Soviet Union which had already used its power to impose its will on Communist "comrades" in other countries.

Another important development for understanding the current Chinese perspective is the dramatic shift in outlook which took place after Deng Xiaoping took over the leadership in 1978. In an effort to combat the rise of a new upper class and an "elitist" mentality among them, Mao had implemented the "Great Leap Forward" (1958–1959) and the "Great Proletarian Cultural Revolution" (1966–1969). Both of these ideologically-inspired projects proved to be overwhelming impediments to the growth of Chinese productivity.[48] The possibility of war against the Soviet Union made it clear that China needed modernization, not ideologically motivated exercises designed to keep everyone equal. The "four modernizations" to be implemented in the post-Mao regime were agriculture, industry, science and technology, and defense. The new leadership claimed that individual effort could be rewarded and decentralized decision-making could be encouraged even in a Communist state. The guiding principle was to be, "What works?" As Deng put it, "What difference does it make what color the cat is as long as it catches mice?" It was also decided that the building up of Chinese society required peace with the other nations of the world and a decrease in military spending except in the area of new weapons development.

China's leaders seem to be following the program started under Deng Xiaoping even though he died in February 1997. There has been a continuing effort to stimulate economic development while still maintaining the ultimate political control of the Communist Party. Under this "socialist market economy," China has been experimenting, at times permitting fairly unrestrained capitalism and even foreign investment, especially along its southeast coast, but also intervening from time to time with measures of restraint imposed by the Communist Party–controlled central government.

The trend toward less restriction and more freedom started to get out of control in May of 1989 when university students in Beijing organized a huge demonstration and hunger strike in response to the death of Hu Yaobang, former Communist Party leader who had been removed from office for refusing to take action against a student demonstration in 1986. The previously scheduled visit of Soviet reformer Mikhail Gorbachev to Beijing deterred the Chinese government from clamping down immediately, but on the night of June 3, 1989, the Chinese military moved forcefully against the students with their large plaster-of-Paris and styrofoam statue of the "Goddess of Democracy." The resulting "Tiananmen Square massacre" was a demonstration to the whole world that the Chinese leadership under Prime Minister Li Peng and Communist Party General Secretary Jiang Zemin was not going to tolerate that much democracy.

When allowed to operate in an open market system, the Chinese show themselves to be very good entrepreneurs. By early 1993 over 70 percent of the economy was outside the centrally controlled state system, and during 1992 the GNP increased by 12.8 percent.[49] For the decade of the 1990s the average annual rate of growth in the Gross Domestic Product (GDP) was 11.1 percent, best in the world.[50] The rate of growth of GNP was less in 1997-1998, but it was still a healthy 7.4 percent even at a time when most of the rest of Asia was experiencing negative growth.[51] In 1998 the total GNP of China, not including Hong Kong, had climbed to $928.9 billion, seventh largest in the world.[52]

When individuals become successful in business, their wealth can then be used to undermine the control of the central government. Their businesses not only make them economically independent and politically powerful but also provide jobs which allow their employees to become less and less dependent on state subsidies. As Elizabeth Perry and Ellen Fuller pointed out in their 1991 article "China's Long March to Democracy" in the *World Policy Journal,* "Increasingly, economic wealth is being translated into political capital."[53] The trends seem to point to a growing tension between the kind of authoritarian political system the Communist leadership wants to maintain and the more open political environment the vigorous economy is likely to produce.

With regard to the problem of war, the two main issues to be worked out between China and the United States are (1) the desire of the Communist leadership to establish its control over the island of Taiwan and (2) the desire of the United States to bring China into the world community as a more Westernized country. China regained control of Hong Kong on July 1, 1997 on the basis of a treaty (the Basic Law) which calls for a semiautonomous government and the continuation of capitalism in Hong Kong for at least 50 years. This compromise is called the "one country, two systems" arrangement. If it works, it could serve as a model for the incorporation of Taiwan into China. Whether the Hong Kong model is working very well is debatable. Residents of the island are becoming gradually more dissatisfied with the control exercised by Beijing. Furthermore, developments within Taiwan indicate an increasing opposition there to the "one China" idea and a greater desire for independence, especially as the mainland Chinese resort to threats of military action to stop any such move toward independence.[54] With regard to prompting China to become more Westernized, one of the main issues is respect for human rights, especially the rights of religious groups and of ethnic groups such as the Tibetans. The strategy of the West seems to be to bring China into the World Trade Organization and similar international organizations with the expectation that when the Chinese see the value of the Western way of doing things they will choose to imitate it. The Chinese, on the other hand, are quite confident that their cultural traditions focused on communal welfare and maintaining the social order are superior to the very individualistic, competitive ways of the West. They believe that their task is to demonstrate this superiority to the whole world. Their perspective is still influenced by the distant past when all of East Asia learned from China how to be "civilized."

The Chinese are building up their military capabilities both by their own production and by buying planes, missiles, submarines, and the like from the former Soviet Union. Their aim is to make China not only the leading economic power in the world but also one of the leading military powers so that they never again will experience anything like the "century of humiliation." There is little doubt that China will be an increasingly important player on the world scene. The very different ideological views of the Chinese and the Americans suggest that there is likely to be ongoing conflict between them. A crucial issue for the whole world as well as for the island of Taiwan is whether that conflict will proceed nonviolently or whether at some time it will degenerate into war.

The Less Developed Countries

The process of industrialization, the change to relying on energy-using machines to help us do our work, began in Britain in the 18th century. As already noted, it represents what Kenneth Boulding in *The Meaning of the Twentieth Century* calls "the second great transition" in human society.[55] The first great transition was the agricultural revolution which began about 10,000 years ago when our distant ancestors changed from their nomadic life-style to relying on agriculture and domesticated animals and to living in permanent settlements. The second equally great transition, industrialization, is based on scientific knowledge of how nature works which is then incorporated into new technology for manipulating the physical world. Industrialization transforms humanity's relationship with nature and with other people because of the incredible new power it puts in the hands of humankind.

Industrialization spread from its starting place in Britain to North America and northern Europe, then to southern and eastern Europe and Japan, and then to Russia and China. Countries which became industrialized earlier used their new power, especially evident with regard to weaponry, to dominate those who had not yet industrialized. At the end of World War II in 1945, one could distinguish between the industrialized or developed countries of Europe and North America plus Japan and Australia and New Zealand on the one hand, and the less industrialized or less developed countries in the rest of the world. Because most of the developed countries were in the northern hemisphere while most of the less developed countries were in the southern hemisphere, one could speak of the "North-South" division in the world. But the spreading wave of industrialization has not stopped; it is still breaking on new shores. That transformation of society that began in Britain over two hundred years ago is now reaching the most remote corners of the world. However, it is still not arriving in all places at the same time.

This section on national-historical perspectives deals with the outlook of that large group of very diverse countries which began the process of industrialization much later than the current big powers. They have been known collectively as the *"poorer countries,"* the *"less developed countries"* (LDCs), *"the South,"* or the *"developing countries."* Even though times have changed, it should be noted that during the Cold War these countries were described as the *"Third World"* or the *"non-aligned countries"* because they were not allied with either the United States and NATO or with the Soviet Union and its Warsaw Pact Organization. They sought to do what they could to mitigate that East-West conflict, that Communism-vs.-Capitalism contest which they feared could bring a nuclear holocaust which would end their existence as well as that of the protagonists. One of their more widely publicized efforts was their 1995 "five-continent peace initiative" to halt the testing of nuclear weapons and to stop any effort to put nuclear weapons in outer space.[56]

How can one characterize this collection of very diverse LDCs, which together have over 80 percent of the world's population? The *typical* LDC is a poor nation in Africa or Asia and a former colony of some European country, but not all of them fit this description. The oil-rich LDCs of Kuwait, Qatar, and the United Arab Emirates, for example, have comparable per capita GDPs to Italy or New Zealand.[57] Argentina, Brazil, Costa Rica, and Albania are not in Africa or Asia and have not been colonies for a very long time. Many LDCs are very small with populations of less than a million, while India has a population of about a billion. Some are richly endowed with natural resources, while others have virtually none. What they all have in common is that in 1950 they could not be said to be industrialized countries. Except for a few "Newly Industrialized Economies" (NIEs) such as Singapore, Taiwan (technically part of China), and South Korea they *still* cannot be described as having attained the category of industrialized societies. Of course, becoming industrialized happens gradually, so it is difficult to say exactly when a country has arrived at being a developed country. For example, it is debatable whether South Korea should be classified as "industrialized." According to a widely accepted list there are only 24 countries (out of the 160 countries in the world included in the data) which were classified as "developed countries" in 1994.[58]

Traditionally, when dealing with world affairs only the views of a few more powerful countries have been considered. The views of the less powerful, less developed countries have been largely ignored. The establishment of the United Nations has made it technically possible for the less powerful countries to be recognized as legally sovereign nation-states when they become members of that organization. Nevertheless the question of how much influence these less powerful countries can actually have on world affairs is still to be answered. A new experiment in international affairs is being tried, largely within the U. N.

framework. Through collective action the leaders of the less powerful nations of the world are making a heroic effort to influence policies adopted at the international level to deal with global issues. The final outcome of that struggle is not yet clear, but its unfolding merits at least a brief review.

The effort of these LDCs to exert some kind of collective influence on world events has been carried out mainly through a series of international conferences. Although the national representatives of the various LDCs had earlier informally conferred with each other at the United Nations, the first formal meeting for these "Third World" nations was the Bandung Conference held in Bandung, Indonesia, in 1955.[59] All the nations of Asia and Africa were invited, and 29 sent representatives. The conference condemned all forms of racism and colonialism and called for peaceful co-existence among all nations regardless of ideological commitment or social system. Plans to convene a second conference of African and Asian countries 10 years later fell apart, largely because of disputes about whether China and the Soviet Union should be allowed to participate.

Nevertheless the Bandung Conference spawned other meetings. In 1961 President Tito of Yugoslavia organized a Conference of Non-Aligned States in Belgrade. His aim was to organize the countries which were not allied with either the United States or the Soviet Union regardless of their geographical location. Twenty-five governments were represented. They agreed that non-aligned nations should work together in opposing colonialism of any kind and should seek to reduce tension between East and West. In 1964 Egyptian President Nasser convened the Second Conference of Non-Aligned States in Cairo. This time 47 governments attended, many of the new ones being black African countries.

The Belgrade Conference in turn inspired another significant meeting for the LDCs, the 1964 U.N. Conference on Trade and Development (UNCTAD) held in Geneva, Switzerland. In advance of this U.N.–sponsored conference, representatives of the LDCs developed a Joint Declaration indicating what they hoped the meeting would accomplish: tariff reductions, opening of markets in the rich countries for products from the poor countries, stabilization of the prices of raw materials, more financial assistance to the LDCs, and a greater share of shipping revenues and the like for the poorer countries. Seventy-five countries signed this declaration. Later three more countries signed and one which had signed withdrew, leaving 77 signers. The association formed by these 77 LDCs was later joined by others but is still called the "Group of 77." For the most part this group works within the U.N. framework.

That 1964 Geneva Conference was the first major forum for negotiations on economic issues between North and South. The North refused to grant the LDCs the kinds of changes they were seeking, but the South did manage to make UNCTAD a continuing subsidiary organ of the U.N. General Assembly, where negotiations would be carried on at subsequent conferences. These conferences have for the most part been exercises in futility for the LDCs because of the adamant opposition of the North, especially the United States.

After 1965 the LDCs solidified their two basic associations, the Non-Aligned Movement (NAM) and the Group of 77.[60] The NAM was gradually transformed into a permanent organization with a standing Bureau which meets regularly while summit conferences are held once every three years. An important theme of the 1992 meeting in Jakarta, Indonesia was that the end of the Cold War did not end the need for the NAM because the polarization between North and South still had to be addressed. The eleventh summit was held in Cartagena, Colombia, in 1995. In 1998, for the first time the United States sent an observer to the NAM summit, which was being held in Durban, South Africa.[61] The Non-Aligned Movement, whose chair from 1998 to 2001 is President Thabo Mbeki of South Africa, has 112 national members plus the Palestine Liberation Organization.[62]

While the Non-Aligned Movement is an independent organization separate from the United Nations, the Group of 77 has become the bargaining agent for the LDCs within the United Nations in New York and at meetings of UNCTAD, the World Trade Organization (WTO), the Food and Agriculture Organization (FAO) in Rome, the United Nations International Development Organization (UNIDO) in Vienna, the United Nations Educational, Scientific, and Cultural Organization (UNESCO) in Paris, and the United Nations Environmental Program (UNEP) in Nairobi.[63] Despite its name, retained for historical reasons, the Group of 77 now includes 133 countries. On April 10-14, 2000, it held its first South Summit of the heads of state in Havana, Cuba.[64]

Besides their own conferences, the LDCs can use their voting power in the U.N. General Assembly to convene U.N. conferences on various issues which they believe require some attention, even if the richer countries would rather not address them in such an open forum. Since these conferences are arranged by the U.N. General Assembly rather than the Security Council, all countries are represented and there is no veto power for the big powers. One example of a conference where the LDCs were able to have an impact on global policy was the third U.N. Conference on the Law of the Sea (UNCLOS) which met for one or two sessions each year from 1973 until 1982. The task of that conference was to work out a treaty for the oceans which would embody "the common heritage principle," the principle that the resources of the ocean floor should belong to all of humanity collectively and not just to the rich countries that had the technology to exploit those resources. Despite opposition from the United States, that treaty came into effect in 1994 and the new institutions of the Law of the Sea regime began operating in 1998. Another example was the U.N. Conference on the Environment and Development (UNCED) or "Earth Summit" held in Rio de Janeiro, Brazil, in June of 1992. The LDCs wanted such a conference in order to focus attention on the responsibilities of the rich countries to put some restraints on their pollution of the environment and also to provide more economic and technological assistance to the LDCs so that they would not need to despoil the environment in order to get the resources they need for economic development.

A good example of how the LDCs are trying to influence world politics, but also of how they get restrained by the more powerful countries from making much headway in this direction, is the adoption by the U.N. General Assembly in November of 1989 of a resolution declaring the period 1990–1999 to be a Decade of International Law.[65] Traditionally, the LDCs had looked upon international law as merely a facade by which the rich and powerful countries maintained a legal pretense for their exploitation and domination of the poorer countries. But in September 1988, at the NAM ministerial meeting in Nicosia, Cyprus, it was announced that the following June a special NAM ministerial meeting focused on international law would be convened at The Hague, The Netherlands, seat of the International Court of Justice. This change of attitude on the part of LDCs toward international law apparently was inspired by the fact that in June of 1986 the International Court of Justice had rendered a judgment against the United States and in favor of Nicaragua in a case involving U.S. mining of the harbors of Nicaragua and U.S. support for the "Contras" against the Sandinista government of Nicaragua.[66]

The June 1989 NAM meeting at The Hague adopted "The Hague Declaration on Peace and the Rule of Law in International Affairs" which called for a decade focused on strengthening international law and the International Court of Justice plus convening a peace conference in 1999, the 100th anniversary of the 1899 Hague Conference which had established the Permanent Court of Arbitration. The Hague Appeal for Peace conference was held May 11-15, 1999, in the Netherlands, but because of opposition from the United States it was not officially sponsored by the United Nations. Instead it was organized by over 1,000 nongovernmental organizations with over 8,000 persons attending. U.N. Secretary-General Kofi Annan was one several dignitaries who addressed this "Largest Peace Conference in History."[67] The nongovernmental organizations and the LDCs as well as

the governments of some developed countries had just scored an even more important victory for international law with the adoption of the Rome Statute for an International Criminal Court in July 1998. That event and its significance will be discussed in more detail in Chapter 12 on "Legal Aspects of the Contemporary Situation."

Thus the LDCs have managed to maintain their associations for collective bargaining against the rich countries, and they are continuing to use the U.N. General Assembly and U.N.–sponsored international treaties and conferences to try to get more "global justice." While the Cold War was on, they were sometimes able to play the Russians and Americans off against each other, but that is no longer the case. Arab oil money gave them a lift in the mid-1970s, but the threat of using the cut-off of oil as a weapon against the rich countries has been nullified, partly because the oil-rich countries themselves have invested much of their savings in the stable economies of the West. The situation is that these LDCs need what the developed capitalist countries have much more than the developed capitalist countries need what they have. It seems that about the only way for these LDCs to have any input in global decision-making is to pass non-binding resolutions in the U.N. General Assembly and set up more international conferences where all national governments are equally represented. Furthermore, just keeping their own LDC associations together is a major challenge in view of the diversity of interests and even some wars among themselves. Past experience has engendered considerable pessimism about what can be expected from negotiations with the rich countries, especially the United States. There has been some attempt to focus more attention on what can be done cooperatively among themselves without help from the North (including establishing their own development bank with paid up capital of $2 billion[68]), but so far the results are minimal. Nevertheless, the LDCs are trying to use the U.N. and their own organizations (together with support from some peace-and-justice non-governmental organizations) as a means of having some influence on the world scene.

10. Military Aspects of the Contemporary Situation

When nations confront each other in war, military power determines the outcome. Economic power, technological capability, size of population, and morale of the people are relevant only insofar as they can be converted into military power. Military power depends on military leadership, the quality and quantity of their personnel in the armed forces, and, most importantly, on the weaponry available. Our discussion of the military aspects of the contemporary situation will focus on this last ingredient.

The Post–World War II Struggle for Power

The end of World War II in 1945 left two major powers with strong military forces: the United States and the Soviet Union. The Americans were in a much stronger position than the Soviets, having come through the war without any destruction to their homeland and also having developed the first atomic bombs. The Soviets, on the other hand, had lost 9 percent of their population during the war, and the most densely populated part of their country had served as a battlefield for more than two years. The United States was eager to forget war and bring its troops back home, but the Soviet Union under Stalin's leadership maintained some military forces to ensure that the newly established governments of Eastern Europe would be friendly to the Soviet Communists. Although the possession of nuclear weapons by the United States allowed American President Truman to be somewhat tough in dealing with the Soviet Union, it should be remembered that the victorious Soviet military forces were concentrated in Europe with a devastated Western Europe before them while the United States had many of its forces scattered throughout the Pacific area. Furthermore, in 1945 the United States had built only three atomic bombs, one by one, and the last two had been dropped on Hiroshima and Nagasaki.[1] Thus no atomic bombs were available for use against the Soviets had war broken out. It is unlikely, however, that the Soviets or anyone else except the highest American officials knew this.

Soviet efforts to create a buffer of friendly governments in Eastern Europe and American efforts to spread Western-style democracy throughout the world soon came into conflict in Poland, Czechoslovakia, Hungary, Romania, Bulgaria, Greece, Turkey, and conquered Germany. A Communist coup d'état in Czechoslovakia plus a Soviet move to cut off Western access to Communist-controlled Berlin led to the creation in 1949 of the North Atlantic Treaty Organization by the Western nations to prevent any further Communist expansion. The detonation of an atomic device by the Soviets and the takeover of China by Mao's Communist forces in 1949 added to American fears of further expansion by the Communists. The United States detonated a thermonuclear device (a hydrogen bomb) in November of 1952, and the Soviets followed with theirs in August of 1953. In 1957 the Soviets successfully tested an intercontinental ballistic missile and launched an artificial satellite called "sputnik." These events greatly shocked Americans, who for the most part had assumed that American technology was vastly superior to that of the Communists in the Soviet Union. Three months later Americans launched a much smaller satellite, which Soviet leader Khrushchev ridiculed as a "grapefruit." It had now become evident that these two opposing powers would soon be capable of attacking each other with nuclear weapons carried by long-range missiles.

Deterrence Theory

This state of affairs where each side could directly attack the homeland of the other with weapons of mass destruction delivered by virtually unstoppable missiles presented a totally new military situation. Imagine that you are responsible for the military defense of your country. Previously, you could always protect your nation from attack by defensive military efforts. A protective buffer of other allied countries could be maintained, territory through which the enemy must proceed before striking, or there might be bodies of water which the enemy must cross before being able to inflict any damage on your homeland. You could count on having some time to launch a defensive effort against attacking enemy forces. Even if the enemy used airplanes, it was at least possible to try to shoot them down before they were able to drop bombs on your cities. With long-range missiles carrying nuclear warheads, however, everything was different. How could you hope to stop missiles which are guided to their targets by gravitational and inertial forces and which travel so fast that they can go a sixth of the way around the earth in half an hour? Furthermore, since these missiles are carrying nuclear warheads, one hit could destroy a whole city! If the enemy fired 100 missiles and you could somehow destroy 90 percent of them, you would still lose 10 of your cities!

Although the notion of some kind of anti-missile missile enjoyed popularity for a time, the prevailing view came to be that there simply was no dependable defense against an attack which used ballistic missiles armed with nuclear warheads. The only conceivable military strategy seemed to be to try to prevent such an attack in the first place. The aim became one of *deterring* the potential enemy from launching a missile attack by threatening a similarly unstoppable retaliatory attack of equal or greater magnitude. It was necessary to persuade the enemy that you had the capability to launch a retaliatory attack even if a surprise attack was launched first, and also that you had the "guts" to launch a purely vengeful destructive attack once your strategy of deterring an attack had failed. Emphasizing a quick retaliatory attack meant that you needed radar units and spy-in-the-sky satellites to detect a missile attack by the enemy, not because anything could be done to stop the incoming missiles, but so that you would know when to launch your own missiles in return.

But the military must consider all the possibilities. What if the enemy were able to somehow knock out or neutralize your radar units and spy satellites? How then could you protect your own missiles from destruction by a surprise attack? One solution would be to build hardened silos for your land-based missiles so they would not be destroyed except by a direct hit. Another solution would be to put at least some of your missiles aboard submarines so that the enemy would not know where they are. You might also keep some bombers carrying nuclear bombs in the air at all times so that they could respond to an attack which was able to wipe out your military air fields. With your own nuclear weapons thus protected, you would have what is called *second-strike capability*. That is, you could absorb a first strike by the enemy and still retaliate. You would desperately want to prevent a situation where an enemy could destroy or neutralize all your own retaliatory capability; that is, you would want to be sure that the enemy does not acquire a *first-strike capability*. If the enemy were to develop systems which could defend against your bombers and detect the whereabouts of all your submarines while at the same time making its own missiles so accurate that they could score direct hits on your missile-launching silos, radar sites, and spy satellites, you would be in deep trouble. Still it would be difficult for the enemy to launch an attack so swiftly and with such a fine degree of accuracy and timing that you would have no chance to launch at least some missiles. Thus what would pose a particularly great threat to your capacity to retaliate would be the development by the enemy of a truly effective anti-missile-defense system because then, even if you were able to launch several missiles in retaliation, those missiles could be knocked out by that defense system before they did any damage.

The doctrine of deterrence through the threat of massive retaliation required that your own missiles be targeted on the enemy's population centers. The enemy theoretically would be deterred from making an attack for fear of suffering a tremendous number of casualties in return. But, asked the military, what if there were some type of limited military engagement and you wanted only one or two of your nuclear weapons to knock out a few of the enemy's military installations? Then you would need to have your missiles targeted on missile sites and military bases rather than on population centers. Such targeting represents what is called *counter-force* targeting rather than *counter-population* targeting. The notion of *limited nuclear war* presumes that you could announce to the enemy that you are not launching a full-scale nuclear attack but are merely going to knock out one or two military bases. According to this way of thinking, you would warn them that if they try to respond to your limited attack, an all-out attack will then be launched in response. It is hard to see why the enemy would do anything but lash back with an all-out attack under these circumstances,[2] but during the Cold War some military planners on both sides continued to think in terms of the possibility of a limited nuclear war. The knowledge that some missiles were aimed at military targets which one might want to destroy in a so-called *surgical strike* increased the tension during the Cold War because of the fear that such missiles might in fact be used as part of a general first strike. Missiles aimed at population centers, on the other hand, would be useful only in a retaliatory strike.

There is no reliable defense against a large attack using ballistic missiles armed with nuclear warheads. Up to the end of the Cold War, and even now, the Americans and the Russians both remain vulnerable to a nuclear missile attack by the other. The use of hardened silos for land-based missiles plus the use of submarine-based missiles meant that both sides retained a second-strike capability against the other and that neither could achieve a first-strike capability. Such a situation had a certain stability in it, but it was realized by both parties that the development of an extensive, reliable anti-missile defense by either side would upset this stable situation. That is why the Soviet Union and the United States agreed as part of the 1972 SALT I Treaty to limit the development and deployment of anti-missile missiles. This arrangement for international stability based on each side remaining vulnerable to nuclear retaliation by the other side was called *mutual assured destruction* or *MAD*.

The Cuban Missile Crisis

The closest the world has come to a nuclear holocaust was the Cuban missile crisis of October 1962. Fidel Castro had established a Communist government in Cuba. An invasion attempt by non–Communist Cubans who had fled to Florida was conducted with some U.S. support in 1961, but this effort at the Bay of Pigs to prompt an anti–Castro uprising failed miserably. Apparently in an effort to discourage future invasion attempts against Cuba as well as to give the Soviets a chance to counter U.S. missiles based in Turkey, the Communists decided to put some Soviet missiles in Cuba. Reconnaissance flights by U.S. planes spotted the building of the missile sites. The United States claimed that this presence of a non–American nation's military forces in the Americas was a violation of the long-established Monroe Doctrine, which stated that non–American nations should stay out of American affairs. The United States also succeeded in getting the Organization of American States (OAS) to endorse this viewpoint. The Soviets could have responded to American complaints by noting that the Monroe Doctrine is simply a U.S. pronouncement which is not international law, even if it had been endorsed by the U.S.-dominated OAS. They might have argued that Cuba was a sovereign state which could legitimately invite the Soviets to put missiles on its soil if it wished to do so. Instead, when confronted with the American accusation, the Soviets denied that they were installing missile bases in Cuba. At a dramatic meeting of the U.N. General Assembly, U.S. Ambassador Adlai

Stevenson displayed aerial photos proving to the whole world that the Soviets were liars. President Kennedy sent American ships to intercept the Soviet ships bringing parts needed to complete the missile sites. The world held its breath as the Soviet freighters neared the U.S. Navy ships. It seemed that a nuclear war might begin at any moment. But Khrushchev directed the Soviet ships to turn back, and a nuclear holocaust was averted.

Why did Khrushchev direct the Soviet ships to turn back? It may have been because the two nations had reached an understanding that the United States would not assist any further efforts to overthrow the Castro regime. There may also have been other factors such as an "unrelated" commitment to remove U.S. missiles from Turkey, but an important consideration undoubtedly was the fact that at that time the United States had about a 5 to 1 superiority in the number of nuclear weapons which could be delivered by long-range missiles and bombers. The Soviet Union had been coerced into ceasing its missile-building efforts in Cuba even though the Soviets had some missiles capable of delivering atomic warheads onto U.S. cities. It was the overwhelming superiority of the United States in the quantity of available nuclear warheads and delivery systems which had been decisive.

The notion that a country needs only a minimal deterrent force was severely damaged by this incident. The Soviets saw that it was not sufficient merely to have some missiles with nuclear warheads which could strike the United States. They began a massive missile-building effort and increased their defensive capabilities against U.S. bombers. It was the stimulus of the Cuban missile crisis and its outcome that led the Soviets to conclude that military power was necessary not just to deter an attack on the homeland but also for success in international bargaining. In an anarchic world a nation which is obviously second in military power will be coerced into accepting terms dictated by the nation which is first in military power. Since most American leaders also recognize the validity of this principle, as long as world anarchy continues there will be a virtually unlimited arms race to develop ever

more destructive weapons and a technological race to try to create some kind of defense against a missile attack. This desire to be able to coerce the other side when negotiating is a more important motive for building nuclear weapons than any intention to actually use them. It has been noted that U.S. presidents have used the threat of nuclear strikes in at least 20 crisis situations.[3] It has also been argued that Israel's possession of nuclear weapons has persuaded its enemies to give up on the possibility of using force to overcome Israel and that the possibility of Arab nuclear weapons in the future has been encouraging Israel to negotiate now.[4]

Modern Nuclear Weaponry

Humankind's first weapons, the club, the spear, and the bow and arrow, could kill one person at a time. The invention of the exploding grenade in the 15th century meant that a single weapon might kill four or five persons at once. By the beginning of World War I in 1914, artillery shells and torpedoes made it possible for one weapon to kill 10 or 20 people at once, and by the end of that war a single shell from the Germans' "Big Bertha" cannon might kill 40. During World War II, the large bombs dropped by the Allies might kill 60 or 70 persons. But the atomic bomb dropped on Hiroshima in 1945 killed at least 75,000 persons! The first thermonuclear bombs were 20 times as powerful as the Hiroshima bomb, and now some nuclear warheads are available which have more than 1,500 times the explosive power of that first nuclear bomb.[5] Since some of the explosive power will necessarily be wasted because of the physical principles involved in large explosions, it doesn't follow that these newer thermonuclear weapons would kill 1,500 times as many people, or even do 1,500 times as much damage, but there is little doubt that one of these super bombs could kill millions of people in a big city. In fact, atomic weapons generally are so powerful that the primary military problem has been how to make them smaller so that they won't be more destructive than desired.

The quantity of nuclear warheads generally increased during the period of the Cold War. It was not until the late 1950s that nuclear warheads of many different sizes and kinds came rolling off the assembly lines. By 1960, the United States had 7,000 nuclear warheads in Europe.[6] In 1975 it was estimated that the United States had 8,000 nuclear warheads on its strategic (long-range) weapons and 22,000 on its tactical (battlefield) weapons.[7] The chart on page 164 compares the destructive power of 1981 nuclear arsenals with the total firepower used in World War II.

Nuclear Weapons

Since the radioactive material in nuclear warheads gradually decays so that eventually there is not enough available to trigger an explosion, the weapons must eventually be disassembled and the still-active material recycled into new weapons. Thus, even though new warheads are constantly being produced, the quantity of them is not always increasing.[8] Here are the figures for the estimated stockpiles of nuclear warheads, including both those actively deployed and those in reserve, possessed by the five acknowledged nuclear powers in 1986, 1993, and 2000.[9]

Country	1986	1993	2000
United States	23,400	16,750	10,500
Former Soviet Union*	45,000	32,000	20,000
Britain	300	300	185
France	355	524	450
China	423	434	400
TOTAL	64,478	50,008	31,535

*Includes Russia, Belarus, Ukraine, and Kazakhstan.

In addition to the acknowledged nuclear powers listed above it is generally believed that Israel has as many as 100 nuclear warheads.[10] At one time South Africa had six nuclear weapons, but they were dismantled and melted down before South Africa signed the Nuclear Non-Proliferation Treaty in July 1991.[11] It is now evident that India and Pakistan have nuclear weapons, but how many they have is unknown.[12] There is some suspicion that North Korea and Iran may be trying to develop nuclear weapons, but there is no evidence that they have succeeded.[13]

Nuclear warheads are not very useful for strategic military purposes, however, unless a nation has some means of delivering them to the target. It is the existence of long-range bombers and ballistic missiles as much as the availability of nuclear warheads which make today's military situation different from that of World War II. The first delivery system for nuclear warheads was the airplane. By 1948 the United States had produced bombers with intercontinental range. Then in 1957 came the Russian development of the intercontinental ballistic missile (ICBM). A ballistic missile is started on its way by a rocket engine which does not need oxygen from the atmosphere. The missile goes high above the atmosphere and then free falls onto its target; it is in effect a space shot which does not quite go into orbit. Since it goes so high, its launching is readily detectable by radar, but its speed is so great that the distance between the Soviet Union and the United States can be traversed in half an hour. The first intercontinental ballistic missiles were liquid-fueled, making it difficult to keep them ready for launching on a continuous basis, but before long they were equipped with solid propellants. Solid propellants also made it possible to develop submarine-launched ballistic missiles (SLBMs) which could be launched even while the submarine was submerged. Nuclear warheads have also been placed on artillery shells and bazooka rockets and developed for use as aerial bombs, depth charges, and demolition munitions.[14]

Eventually strategic missiles were armed with more than a single nuclear warhead. At first these separate warheads launched by a single missile simply separated a bit from each other while descending so that the target area would be sprayed with several warheads rather than a single one. Then a system was developed for guiding the separate warheads from a single missile onto different targets: that is, multiple independently targetable reentry vehicles (MIRVs) were developed. The next effort was to try to develop maneuverable reentry

U.S. Senate staff have reviewed this chart
and found it an accurate representation.

Nuclear Weapons

The dot in the center square represents all the firepower of World War II — total, 3 megatons. The other dots represent the firepower in existing nuclear weapons (in 1981): 18,000 megatons (equal to 6,000 World War IIs). About half belonged to the Soviet Union, the other half to the United States. The top left circle represents the weapons on just one U.S. Poseidon submarine — 9 megatons — enough to destroy more than 200 of the largest Soviet cities. The lower left circle represents one Trident submarine — 24 megatons — enough to destroy every major city in the northern hemisphere. (Chart reprinted by permission of James Geier, 2 Howard Street, Burlington, VT 05401.)

vehicles (MARVs) which could evade anti-missile devices. Later developments relative to long-range ballistic missiles were the use of a mobile rather than a stationary launching pad for land-based missiles and the development of substantially increased accuracy.

In the late 1970s came the development of cruise missiles. They differ considerably from ballistic missiles in that they depend on continuous power after launching until they strike their target. They are in fact pilotless jet aircraft with very small wings. Cruise missiles do not travel nearly as fast as ballistic missiles, but they can fly very close to the surface of the earth, a feature which makes them difficult to detect with radar. Thus they may give an enemy less time to respond than the much speedier ballistic missiles. Cruise missiles are also very maneuverable and can even be called back after they are part way to their target. In addition, they are smaller and much less expensive to build than ballistic missiles. Cruise missiles also pose a special problem for arms limitation agreements because they are much more easily concealed than ballistic missiles and because it is difficult (though perhaps not impossible) to distinguish between short-range and long-range versions of the weapon.[15]

Research and development on new weapons continued in many areas. The range of submarine-launched ballistic missiles was steadily extended. Both land-based and submarine-launched ballistic missiles became much more accurate because of new guidance systems based on the use of more satellites, and the average number of warheads on each long-range missile was increased. Air-launched cruise missiles (ALCMs) were joined by sea-launched (SLCMs) and ground-launched cruise missiles (GLCMs), and long-range "stealth" bombers were developed which because of their design and construction are very difficult to detect by radar. Neutron bombs which produce a great deal of deadly but short-lasting radiation were developed for possible use against military forces, especially those inside armored vehicles such as tanks.

Changes in weaponry required changes in strategy too. For example, before long-range missiles were so accurate, it was feasible to harden ICBM launch-sites and expect that a substantial proportion of them could survive a nuclear attack by the enemy because they could be destroyed only by direct hits. This situation permitted a nation to wait until after an enemy's nuclear weapons actually exploded before launching a retaliatory attack. Now the situation has changed. If a nation waits that long, it may have very few land-based ICBMs left to fire back at the attacker. Consequently, a new strategy was needed, namely, to launch one's own missiles as soon

as a warning is received that the enemy has launched its missiles. Since it takes only a half hour at most for the enemy missiles to strike a nation's launching sites, the response needs to be quick. Unfortunately this "launch-on-warning" strategy substantially increases the likelihood of a nuclear war beginning by accident, especially in tense situations.

Missile Defense Systems

We have already noted that nuclear weapons and ballistic missiles caused many military planners to conclude that one could no longer rely on defense but must focus instead on deterrence. But some planners disagreed with this conclusion. They thought that it might be possible to develop a reliable defense against ballistic missiles. Their proposal was the Strategic Defense Initiative (SDI) or "Star Wars Defense" proposed by U.S. President Reagan in 1983. It was believed that the Soviet Union was working on a similar system to defend itself against a ballistic missile attack.

The basic idea of such a strategic defense system was to have an alternative available in case the goal of deterring an attack failed. According to the earlier widely accepted deterrence strategy, the aim of one's nuclear arsenal was to keep the enemy from attacking, but if an attack did nevertheless occur, there seemed to be no point in actually launching a retaliatory strike. You could wreak destruction on the enemy, but your action would no longer be a means to any sensible end. If the United States were attacked, the President would be obliged to order a retaliatory attack which would kill millions of people for no purpose except revenge. Strategic defense was designed to give the President an alternative if an enemy nuclear attack were launched; the incoming missiles could be destroyed. At the same time, however, each side viewed the development of a strategic defense by the other side as provocative since it would allow them to launch a first strike and then wipe out any attempted retaliatory strike. That is, the development of an effective defense system by one side would mean the end of the deterrence capability of the other side. The provocative-ness of a defense system is especially great if it is not likely to be able to successfully ward off an attempted first strike by the enemy but *is* capable of providing a rather good defense against a retaliatory strike from an enemy significantly disabled by one's own first strike. Unfortunately, the technology is such that it is just this level of capability that a strategic defense system is likely to have. It wouldn't be much good for defense, but it would be very useful as a supplement to a first offensive strike.

The operation of a space-based strategic defense system can be understood only if one first understands how ballistic missiles work.[16] The flight of a ballistic missile has four phases. During the "boost phase," which usually lasts about three minutes, the rocket engines get the missile underway. The second phase, the "post-boost phase," begins as the last rocket booster is detached and falls away and the post-booster vehicle (called the "bus") with its low-thrust rocket engine carries the load of nuclear warheads still upward but at a less steep angle. During its five-to-eight-minute trip the "bus" drops off as many as ten reen-try vehicles (each with a nuclear warhead) at just the right time and angle to aim them to-ward their intended targets. It may also drop off decoys and debris to make it more difficult for the enemy to locate the real warheads. This "post-boost phase" is followed by the "mid-course phase" or "coast phase" which lasts about 20 minutes for an intercontinental mis-sile. At this point the reentry vehicles are being carried through space simply by inertia, and gravity eventually begins pulling them back toward earth along a rainbow-like path. The fourth and final phase, called the "terminal phase," begins when the reentry vehicle de-scends into the atmosphere of the earth. Dur-ing this phase, which lasts less than two min-utes, the reentry vehicle plunges at extremely high speed toward its target, while decoys, which lack the specially hardened protection given the reentry vehicles, burn up or break apart in the atmosphere.

The strategic defense system is multilay-ered, that is, it is designed to destroy missiles in each of the four phases. Different detection devices and weapons systems are required for each phase of the missile's trajectory. The cru-cial phase is the boost phase because at that point each missile is carrying up to ten reen-try vehicles which later will become separate targets. The problem is that hitting the mis-siles during this phase requires hypervelocity guns, chemical rockets, or directed energy weapons like lasers based on satellites (called "battle stations") orbiting the earth. Further-more, the period of time for detecting the launch, locating the missiles, and destroying them is very short. The sensing system used to track the enemy missile during the post-boost phase is a bit different, but the weapons used against it are essentially the same as those used during the boost phase. In the mid-course or coasting phase, sorting out the reen-try vehicles from the decoys and debris be-comes a major problem; but the time period is longer and the defense can begin to rely on ground-based interceptor rockets. In the ter-minal phase, one can use the same type of ground-based anti-ballistic missiles previously developed by both the United States and the Soviet Union. Even then, however, one is con-fronting a problem similar to trying to hit a bullet with a bullet.

There was much controversy about the Strategic Defense Initiative. Besides the main aim of supplementing deterrence with de-fense, it was claimed that SDI would also permit the United States to protect itself in case of an accidental launch of a nuclear mis-sile. It also could stop an attack from some "crazy" leader who would not be deterred by the threat of retaliation. Even if the system were only partly effective, it was argued, it would be very helpful in a limited nuclear war and would greatly limit the amount of dam-age from an all-out attack. On the other hand, opponents argued that the technological prob-lems are insurmountable, that countermea-sures could readily make the system ineffec-tive, that a much simpler system could deal with accidentally launched missiles, and that the many satellites on which the system de-pends would be very vulnerable if the enemy did in fact want to launch a first strike.[17] It was argued that a strategic defense system would in fact increase the likelihood of a nuclear war in tense situations because accidental damage to sensitive satellites might be interpreted as the beginning of an attack. There was also the problem that the system would pose a definite offensive threat to any potential enemy since the space-based weapons could be used even if no enemy launch had been attempted. Finally, even if it were possible to make each of the three parts of the defense system 90 percent effective, a launch of 1,400 enemy missiles each carrying ten warheads would result in 14 targets being hit.[18]

The United States did a great deal of research on SDI, but the system was never implemented because the Cold War ended in 1989 and the Soviet Union itself disintegrated in 1991. Nevertheless the issue of whether to try to build some kind of defense against enemy missiles did not disappear, partly because Russia, even though now led by non-Communists, still has many of the nuclear weapons and long-range missiles which belonged to the Soviet Union. In fact, U.S. focus on the issue of missile defense has become even more intense. With a single enemy who also had a big stake in avoiding an all-out nuclear war, the strategy of deterrence seemed reasonable. But now there are several potential attackers who have or will have ballistic missiles, and some of them might not be deterred by concerns about what they would lose in a retaliatory attack. Even countries or terrorist groups which lack nuclear weapons might be able to launch some ballistic missiles carrying chemical or biological weapons. The threat to launch such an attack against the United States or one of its allies such as Japan might be a way of persuading U.S. not to intervene in a particular conflict such as one between China and Taiwan. Consequently, an important issue in current U.S. defense policy is, Should the country try to build a missile defense system, and if so, should it be a *national missile defense (NMD) system* using very high-speed missiles that could defend the United States itself from any kind of missile attack, short-range or long-range, or should it be a *theater missile defense (TMD) system* using slower missiles that could defend a fairly small area such as Taiwan from an attack by short-range missiles?[19]

Opponents of the NMD system ask, Where might such a missile attack on the United States come from? Potential enemies (with the exception of Russia) do not have missiles of sufficient range to reach the United States. Ships sent to attack from shorter range could readily be detected and, if necessary, destroyed. The huge expense of such a system (estimated to be at least $30 billion) raises the question of whether there might be some better way of promoting national security at lower cost (maybe even using that amount of money to create an environment where no one would have any reason to attack the United States). Besides, U.S. development of a NMD would be likely to goad the Chinese into trying to develop more long-range nuclear weapons in order to have the capability to overcome the U.S. defense system, and this development, duplicating what happened during the Cold War confrontation with the Soviet Union, would decrease, not increase U.S. security. Also, if deterrence worked against the Soviet Union, why won't it work against other enemies? Furthermore, any enemy planning to attack the United States with biological or chemical weapons (or even nuclear weapons if available to them) would be more likely to sneak them into the United States by way of trucks or small boats or airplanes (as drugs get smuggled in) than to launch a missile attack. A missile attack would give a clear indication of who the attacker is and a ready target for retaliation, but in a sneak attack the identity of the attacking group might remain concealed.

In response, advocates of the NMD system note that even though potential enemies like China, North Korea, Iraq, and Iran do not yet have such long-range missiles, they might develop such a capability in the near future. The Chinese are likely to develop and build the best missiles and weapons they can regardless of what the United States does. Also, potential enemies would not even need to develop particularly accurate missiles in order to deliver biological weapons somewhere onto U.S. territory. Consequently, now is the time to develop the capability to counter such threats.

Advocates of a *theater missile defense system* rather than a national missile defense system point to the need to be able to defend U.S. allies such as Taiwan, Japan, and Israel against an attack using relatively short-range missiles. These friends of the United States are susceptible right now to threats of a short-range missile attack, and a U.S.-engineered missile defense system designed to counter such an attack could be used to defend them. Another argument for developing a theater missile defense system is that the Pentagon's national system to protect against long-range missiles arouses the opposition of the Russians who want to maintain the bilateral commitment to mutual deterrence which was put into place by the 1972 anti-ballistic missile (ABM) treaty. This treaty permits both the United States and Russia to develop one missile-defense site, but the previously selected U.S. site at Grand Forks, North Dakota would not be able to protect parts of Alaska and Hawaii.[20] The Russians do not object to the development of theater missile defense systems as long as enemy missiles are destroyed only during the boost phase. In fact, they have even indicated a willingness to work with the United States to develop a TMD system,[21] but the United States has rejected that proposal because it wants a defense against high-speed long-range missiles. Nevertheless even some U.S. advocates of a national missile defense system suggest that in the long run a NMD system probably would be less expensive to build and more versatile if it were to evolve from the theater defense systems already being developed by the U.S. Navy.

On September 1, 2000 President Clinton indicated that he had decided to postpone deployment of the Pentagon's proposed national missile defense system because it has not yet proved that it will actually work.[22] His decision also took into account its cost, the low level of the existing threat to which it was addressed, and implications for international relations. A major concern about NMD is the reaction of other countries. Even U.S. allies in NATO are distressed by the focus on a system which can protect the United States from a missile attack but which provides no protection for other countries. Nevertheless, the United States plans to continue its effort to improve the technology so that eventually this national defense system will work. In essence, the United States is saying to its allies, if you want a missile defense system, develop your own. At the same time U.S. efforts to improve the theater missile defense systems also are continuing but so far with much less public attention.

Modern Non-Nuclear Weaponry

When discussing the destructive potential of modern war, there is a tendency to think mainly of nuclear weapons and the missiles needed to deliver them. In some arms control agreements special attention is given also to chemical and biological weapons. All the remaining weapons tend to be lumped together into a miscellaneous category called "conventional weapons." But a separate class of "chemical and biological weapons" is not always easy to distinguish. For example, is napalm a conventional weapon or a chemical weapon? Are incendiary bombs conventional weapons or chemical weapons? This section will deal with all kinds of non-nuclear weapons. These are the weapons typically used in warfare, and they are rapidly becoming more sophisticated and deadly.[23] At the same time it should not be forgotten that even in World War II more people were killed in Tokyo in a May 1945 raid using "conventional" incendiary bombs than were killed ten weeks later at Hiroshima by an atomic bomb.[24]

In Vietnam, the U.S. introduced many new weapons designed mainly to kill or seriously impair individual persons.[25] Besides using napalm and white phosphorus, which had been developed earlier, the U.S. used fragmentation bombs loaded with difficult-to-detect plastic fragments and also asphyxiation bombs that released a cloud vapor which, when ignited, quickly consumed all the oxygen in the area. Such new antipersonnel weapons, plus others being developed, promise that the number of injured people and the severity of their wounds will be much greater in future wars than has been the case in the past. Lasers being used to guide weapons may accidentally blind enemy soldiers, and weapons are already being produced and sold at international arms markets which will not only nullify optical sensors being used to find targets but also deliberately blind enemy personnel, either temporarily or permanently.[26]

A big difference in the new high-tech weapons is the improved range and accuracy of projectiles made possible by radar, television cameras, heat-seeking devices, infrared devices, radio beams, radio control, and tiny computers as well as the lasers just mentioned. In earlier times soldiers practiced for hours to be better able to hit what they were aiming at. A huge proportion of the firepower delivered in battle did not hit the target. But that situation is rapidly changing. The new precision-guided munitions (PGMs) or "smart weapons" are much more likely to hit the target. The targets at which these devices are aimed are very unlikely to escape destruction. For example, during the Vietnam War two bridges which had escaped destruction during many regular bombing attacks were knocked out in the first effort when smart bombs were used.[27]

The great accuracy of these new precision-guided munitions means that during future battles it will not be safe to be in an airplane or a tank or a ship or anything else that is easy to locate. The military answer to this situation is to have pilotless aircraft and eventually crewless tanks. An airplane equipped with television cameras and the proper control systems can be flown by a "pilot" on the ground and can take greater risks of being shot down than would be reasonable with a pilot aboard. On September 27, 2000, Boeing Corporation announced in St. Louis that it has already produced such an Unmanned Combat Air Vehicle (UCAV).[28]

The automated battlefield is the prospect of the future.[29] It can be expected that we will even see robotic killing machines, "weapons programmed to kill without reference to human authority."[30] The outcome of battle will depend on the technological capabilities of the weapons, which will necessarily have been designed and produced well before the war begins. The development of the automated battlefield and the training of personnel to use such equipment will be very expensive for nations that want to participate in preparing for such battles, but any nation that does not get involved in the use of the new weaponry will be as helpless against this military technology as primitive peoples with bows and arrows were against Europeans equipped with guns. The cost of developing and producing these new weapons will obviously be high, and the contest for superiority will be unending.[31] The military has never been particularly enthusiastic about nuclear weapons, since they are too powerful to require much need for complex strategy, but with the new electronic, unmanned conventional weapons the game of war becomes very challenging. The military-industrial complex will also gain new significance because the outcome of battles is likely to depend as much on the weapons available as on the ingenuity of the military leaders.

Chemical and biological weapons are likely to be important in the future not so much because of their likely use on the battlefield (they are difficult to control) but because of their possible use against large populations by those countries (and terrorist groups) which lack the capability or the financial resources to build nuclear weapons. These kinds of non-nuclear weapons are much less expensive to build than nuclear weapons, and the facilities for building them are much easier to hide from "enemy" inspectors. Retired Green Beret commander Colonel William Wilson observes:

> Biological weapons come cheap. A panel of experts told the United Nations that in a large-scale operation against a civilian population, casualties might cost $2,000 per square kilometer for conventional weapons, $800 for nuclear weapons, or $600 for nerve gas, but only $1 for biological weapons. In the not-too-distant future, countries throughout the world will learn how to produce [through genetic engineering] an enormous variety of large biological molecules, including toxins, on a scale that was previously inconceivable.

Gene-splicing's potential to facilitate the large-scale production of biological and toxin weapons raises another danger — proliferation. Unlike the complex and expensive technological infrastructure required to design and produce nuclear weapons, a sophisticated recombinant-DNA facility can be set up without a large capital investment. Since 1982, U.S. Army scientists have made increasing use of gene-splicing to study and prepare defenses against extremely hazardous biological toxins. Between 1980 and 1984 the number of Pentagon-funded projects using recombinant-DNA technology grew from zero to more than forty, including eleven projects under way in army and navy laboratories and thirty-two others contracted out to universities and private technology firms in Israel, Scotland, and the United States.[32]

It seems that biological weapons, and to a lesser extent chemical weapons, are likely to become the weapons of choice, especially for poorer countries and terrorist groups which can't afford long-range ballistic missiles, nuclear weapons, precision-guided munitions, and unmanned combat air vehicles.

Weapons and War

Will the weapons of war ever become so destructive and inhumane that people will be deterred from engaging in warfare? Probably not. In the past the development of various weapons such as the long bow, cannons fired by gunpowder, dynamite, and nuclear weapons have led some people to suggest that the availability of such horrific devices of death and destruction would mean the end of war, but that hasn't happened. Maybe such weapons have intimidated some people to refuse to participate in wars but others have still been willing to do so. The main result has been the decision of various groups that military superiority is crucial and that it is better that they have the new horrible weapons than that their adversaries have them. Consider the efforts of the present nuclear powers to keep other countries from acquiring nuclear weapons rather than supporting efforts to eliminate them entirely.

One feature of the more destructive and more accurate weapons being developed at the end of the 20th century is that they allow war to be fought successfully by an ever smaller proportion of the population (though it may

take a substantial number of others to create their weapons). A military force with modern weapons can overwhelm a much larger force which lacks such weapons. The fact that these weapons are very destructive does not inhibit their use. It merely allows a smaller force equipped with them to be able to overcome a larger one. The capability of developing the new weaponry and learning how to use it becomes much more important than the size of the fighting force. In a way that lesson was clear even at the time of the Opium War when a small British military force was able to impose its will on the much more numerous Chinese population because of its technologically superior weaponry.

War by its very nature is destructive. The goal of warfare is for one group to impose its will on another group by threatening them with destruction if they don't yield. If one side's weapons are destructive and horrible enough, won't they be better able to impose their will of the other side? Furthermore, the newer weapons such as long-range missiles and unmanned combat aircraft make war even more impersonal and more like a game in a video arcade. Any human inhibitions about injuring other people are benumbed.

What counts in war is whether "we" have the weapons to coerce "them" into yielding to "our" will or "they" have the weapons to coerce "us" into yielding to "their" will. The production of ever more destructive and inhumane weapons is not likely by itself to move us toward ending war. Abolishing warfare requires eliminating the notion that one should use physical force in order to decide who gets to make policy for the larger community. The selection of who decides the policies for the community must be decided in a different way, by elections, whether the community is a country or the whole world. The increasing destructiveness of weapons may help to persuade a few more people that such a fundamental change in how leaders and policies are selected is necessary, but to make a difference they will need to focus on instituting the new system rather than just bemoaning the existence of ever more horrible weapons.

11. Institutional Aspects of the Contemporary Situation

There are many kinds of international institutions, but the one most obviously relevant to the problem of war is the United Nations. It will be our first topic, and we will address it in four sections: (1) its structure, (2) its peacekeeping and nation-building activities, (3) the dominant influences during its history, and (4) its accomplishments. Other international institutions will then be discussed even though the relation of some of them to the war problem may be less direct. For example, there are many government-sponsored *global administrative or functional agencies* which are important to our study because of their roles throughout the world in solving social problems. We also need to consider *regional functional and political organizations* formed by national governments. (An administrative or functional organization is limited to dealing with one particular kind of problem, such as regulating the use of a river or controlling diseases, while a political organization addresses any kind of issue of interest to the member nations, including peacekeeping.) Finally, we need to discuss international *nongovernmental organizations,* that is, international organizations formed by individuals and citizen groups rather than by representatives of national governments.

The Structure of the United Nations

The first effort to create a global political institution was the formation of the League of Nations after World War I. Forty-two nations were original members of the League, and 20 others became members at one time or another, including all the major powers except the United States. The three main organs of the League of Nations were the Assembly (one representative from each nation), the Council (permanent representation for the Great Powers and elected rotating representa-

tion from some other nations), and a Secretariat (civil servants employed by the League). Associated with the League but not formally part of it were a number of specialized functional agencies handling particular international problems. All of them in one form or another have now become specialized agencies associated with the United Nations. One of the basic principles of the League was that no nation surrendered any of its sovereignty over its own affairs when it became a member. Measures other than those dealing with procedural issues required unanimous support in both the Assembly and the Council.

World War II seems to have come about partly as the result of the League's failure to act decisively when powerful nations such as Japan and Italy began to engage in expansionist military activities. Great Britain and France in particular seem to have been guided more by balance-of-power thinking than by the provisions of the Covenant of the League, which they tended to regard as good for public relations with their citizenry but too idealistic for dealing with international relations in the real world. In 1933 the Assembly of the League adopted a resolution condemning Japan for its invasion of Manchuria, but Japan responded by quitting the League. In 1936, when the League did nothing to protect Ethiopia from being conquered by Italy, several countries withdrew, and Italy itself withdrew near the end of 1937. The Soviet Union was expelled in 1939 for attacking Finland. After the German conquests of 1939–1940 (which included conquering France), Great Britain was the only great power still in the League and few other nations continued as members. For all practical purposes the League ended in June of 1940 when Secretary-General Joseph Avenol resigned, though a final "funeral session" was held in 1946 after the United Nations had been formed.

The formation of the League's successor, the United Nations, began while World War II was still being fought. U.S. President Franklin Roosevelt, aware of the fate of Wilson's plan for U.S. participation in the League of Nations, decided not to wait until the war was over to involve the United States in an organization to preserve the peace. In January of 1942 representatives from 26 nations met in Washington, D.C. They adopted a "Declaration by the United Nations" to fight together against Germany, Italy, and Japan as well as to accept the democratic and anti-imperialist principles enunciated in the Atlantic Charter, which had been signed by Roosevelt and Britain's Prime Minister Winston Churchill in August of 1941. A resolution calling for the creation of a general international peace-keeping organization was adopted by the United States, the Soviet Union, the United Kingdom, and China at the Moscow Conference in October of 1943. At Washington in August of 1944 and at Yalta in February of 1945 representatives of the big powers agreed on the general structure of the United Nations. The actual final wording of the Charter of the United Nations was worked out by delegates from 50 nations[1] in San Francisco in April, May, and June of 1945. (Germany surrendered, ending the war in Europe, on May 8, 1945.) The Charter was signed on June 26, 1945, and acquired sufficient ratifications to go into effect on October 24, 1945, the date generally recognized as the beginning of the United Nations. (Japan surrendered, ending World War II, on August 15, 1945.) The first session of the U.N. General Assembly was held in London in January 1946. Among other things, it decided to establish permanent headquarters in or near New York City. Most of the subsequent meetings of the United Nations were held in temporary facilities at Lake Success in the New York City area until 1952, when the organization moved into its present building along the East River in Manhattan.

The structure and principles of operation of the United Nations are similar to those of the League of Nations.[2] Each nation retains its national sovereignty; that is, each nation decides for itself what it will or won't do and can withdraw from the organization whenever it so desires. Disputes between nations are to be resolved by negotiation rather than war. Aggression by one nation against another is to be stopped by collective security, that is, by collective action of all the other nations against the aggressor, using economic measures primarily but including military action if necessary. In both the League of Nations and the United Nations, the primary bodies have been the all-inclusive Assembly and the smaller Council in which the big powers have more influence. The greatest differences are that the United Nations has more machinery devoted to promoting economic and social progress in the poorer nations of the world and that decisions do not need to be unanimous.

The main body of the United Nations is the General Assembly, in which each member nation may have up to five representatives but only one vote. The General Assembly (GA) has the power to make decisions concerning the operation of the United Nations, such as determining the budget of the organization and electing representatives to various U.N. bodies including the Security Council, but with regard to other matters it can only make recommendations to the member governments. Actions are taken on the basis of majority rule (two-thirds majority on certain important issues) rather than requiring unanimity as in the League of Nations. The General Assembly cannot pass laws for the world as a legislature could, but neither is the Assembly merely a "debating society" as it has sometimes been called, for it does govern the operation of the U.N. organization itself including approving its budget. The number of nations in the United Nations has increased from the original 51 members to 189 in 2000.

The primary function of the U.N. Security Council (SC) is the maintenance of peace. The five major powers who fought together to win World War II were expected to work together to preserve the peace. Thus the United States, the Soviet Union (the Russian Federation after December 1991), the United Kingdom, France, and China are permanent members of the Security Council. Any one of them can prevent Security Council action by casting a veto. Originally the Security Council had six additional nations elected to it by the General Assembly, but in 1965 the Charter was amended to increase that number to ten. A measure can be enacted by the Security Council only if it receives an affirmative vote of nine of the 15 members and no permanent member is against it. All members of the United Nations, upon joining the organization, commit themselves to accepting and carrying out the decisions of the Security Council. From a legal point of view, then, decisions of the Security Council are binding in a way that resolutions passed by the General Assembly are not.

A third major organ of the United Nations is the Economic and Social Council (ECOSOC). Its main function is to coordinate efforts to promote economic and social welfare throughout the world. It does this by working with the many specialized agencies of the United Nations and by establishing its own committees and commissions. For example, it has commissions on the status of women, on statistics, on population, on social development, on narcotics, and on human rights. Originally the Economic and Social Council consisted of 18 representatives selected by the General Assembly, but the number was increased to 27 by an amendment which became effective in 1965 and then to 54 by another amendment which came into effect in 1973.

The fourth main organ of the United Nations, the Trusteeship Council, has been very successful in its task of supervising the transition of Trust Territories from being dependent territories under the control of larger nation-states to being independent nation-states. All of the original eleven Trust Territories have become independent countries and member states of the United Nations. Since the Trusteeship Council has now discharged all its responsibilities, it could conceivably in the future be converted into a Council for the Rights of Indigenous Peoples[3] or into a wider-scope Human Rights Council.

The fifth main organ of the United Nations is the International Court of Justice (ICJ), the revised version of the Permanent Court of International Justice which had been created by the League of Nations. Like the earlier Court, the International Court of Justice meets in the Hague, Netherlands, and has 15 judges. Every three years five new judges are selected for nine-year terms, and no country may be represented by more than one judge. The aim of the Court is to render legal decisions in cases involving international law involving national governments, such as how treaties between countries are to be applied in particular disputes. Although the Court can give advisory opinions when asked to do so by the General Assembly or the Security Council, only nation-states can be parties in any actual case to be decided by the Court. Furthermore, all nations which might be directly affected by a decision of the Court must agree in advance to abide by the decision before the Court will consider a particular case.[4] As one might expect, it is usually difficult to persuade an alleged violator to make such a commitment.

The sixth main part of the United Nations is the Secretariat, which encompasses the employees of the United Nations under the directorship of the Secretary-General (SG). The SG not only is in charge of all the personnel employed by the United Nations but also has special responsibilities such as making an annual report to the General Assembly and bringing to the attention of the Security Council any matter which he believes threatens world peace. The SG is elected by the General Assembly after being recommended by the Security Council. Although no term of office is stipulated in the U.N. Charter, the first General Assembly decided that a Secretary-General should serve for five years and could then be reappointed for another five years. The Secretaries-General of the United Nations have been (1) Trygve Lie of Norway (1946–52), (2) Dag Hammarskjöld of Sweden (1953–61), (3) U Thant of Burma (1961–71), (4) Kurt Waldheim of Austria (1972–81), (5) Javier Pérez de Cuéllar of Peru (1982–91), (6) Boutros Boutros-Ghali of Egypt (1992–96), and (7) Kofi Annan of Ghana (1997-).

The United Nations is funded solely by

contributions from the member states. The amount each country is to pay is determined by the General Assembly and is based on how rich a country is, in terms both of its total economy and the average income per person of its citizens. The total regular budget of the United Nations for the year 2000 is just under $1.1 billion.[5] The U.S. share is 25 percent or about $.275 billion ($275 *million*). There is a separate budget for U.N. peacekeeping operations and another one for the war crimes tribunals. In 1998 U.S. payments for the regular budget, for peacekeeping, and for the tribunals totaled $.586 billion ($586 *million*) (compared to $265.890 billion for the U.S. Department of Defense).[6] It should also be noted that the *U.N. system* (discussed later in this chapter) includes thirteen separate functional international organizations plus five others associated with the World Bank Group. Each of these functional agencies has its own separate headquarters and budget. They report to the United Nations about their activities but are distinct from it, some of them having been created long before there was a United Nations.

U.N. Peacekeeping and Nation-Building

According to the U.N. Charter, international peace is to be maintained by a system called *collective security*. According to this strategy if any member nation of the United Nations is attacked, all the other member nations are to help the victim nation against the aggressor. This approach to keeping the peace goes beyond the traditional alliance system in which a particular group of nations agree that if any one of them is attacked by a potential enemy state or alliance they will all fight together. With a system of collective security, on the other hand, it is assumed that all member nations of the *whole international community* will work together, militarily if necessary, against *any* country or group of countries that attack any one of them. For such coordinated action to take place, some person or body must be able to indicate when aggression has taken place and what kind of action (for ex-

ample, diplomatic sanctions, economic sanctions, deployment of military forces) should be taken against the aggressor. In the United Nations the responsibility for indicating when aggression has taken place and coordinating the effort against the aggressor belongs to the Security Council.

The League of Nations had been committed to this same collective security approach to peace, but the strategy had failed miserably when Japan attacked Manchuria in 1931 and again when Italy attacked Ethiopia in 1935. Even when there is agreement that aggression has occurred and that military action should be taken, it is difficult for national leaders to act in accord with the collective security principle. Each nation-state realizes that military action is risky and that some of the soldiers involved in the fighting will probably be injured and killed. At the moment of truth national leaders and their citizenry are likely to ask themselves, "Why should soldiers of *our* country get killed to help protect some *other* country?" The answer to that question is that participating in military action against an aggressor is part of one's responsibility as a member of the United Nations, because that is the system by which the U.N. is supposed to keep the peace. But that is a hard answer to sell to the public. The leading members of the League of Nations were not ready to make the required commitment in 1931, nor in 1935, nor in the critical years after that leading up to World War II. Nevertheless the United Nations was based on trying that same strategy of collective security again. Near the end of World War II the United States, at that time the undisputed leading world power, believed that Woodrow Wilson's League of Nations had failed only because the United States had not become a member. The Americans were confident that under U.S. leadership collective security would work for the United Nations.

During the first few years of the United Nations, the United States and Britain tried to use the organization to oppose Communist moves in Eastern Europe, but these efforts often failed because the Soviets simply used their veto in the Security Council to prevent any action by the United Nations. When Communist troops from North Korea invaded anti–Communist South Korea in 1950, however, the U.N. Security Council, prodded by the United States, declared North Korea to be an aggressor and called on U.N. members to help the South Koreans and their U.S. allies. This action was possible only because the Russians were boycotting the Security Council at the time in order to protest China's being represented at the United Nations by Chiang Kai-shek's appointees, even though Communist revolutionary forces led by Mao Zedong had conquered all of mainland China. Sixteen other nations sent troops in response to the call of the Security Council, but the brunt of the fighting was borne by South Korean and U.S. forces. Nevertheless this action by the United Nations marked the first time in history that an international organization had organized a collective military force to resist armed aggression.

At first the forces defending South Korea were driven back almost into the sea, but then a daring counter-attack was launched. The U.N. forces, commanded by U.S. General Douglas MacArthur, pushed northward past the 38th parallel, which had been the boundary between North and South Korea. As they pushed farther north, the Chinese Communists warned that they would enter the war if the northerly advance was not halted before it reached the Chinese border. The warning was not heeded. The large number of "volunteer" Chinese troops pushed the U.N. forces back toward the 38th parallel. After two years of indecisive fighting, a truce was worked out in 1953, and the boundary between North and South Korea was set not far from where it had been before the war.

An important procedural development took place at the United Nations during this Korean conflict. After the Security Council had declared North Korea to be an aggressor, the Soviet Union returned to its seat in the Security Council in order to veto any further resolutions for U.N. action. The U.N. General Assembly responded by passing the "Uniting for Peace Resolution." This resolution declared that the General Assembly can make recommendations to the member nations (including recommending the use of armed forces) whenever the Security Council fails to act in cases where peace is threatened or aggression has occurred. This tactic of taking action in the General Assembly when the Security Council fails to act has been utilized on two other occasions. It was used in 1956 with American and Russian approval after an attack by Britain, Israel, and France against Egypt; and it was used again in 1960 to authorize the continued use of U.N. troops in the Congo when the Security Council, which had originally authorized the mission, failed to support its continuance.

The only time that a heavily armed military force has been used in a U.N.-supervised collective security action against a specified aggressor was in Korea, but during the Gulf War in 1990-91 the United Nations played a less direct legitimizing role in a military "collective security" effort to stop aggression. In August 1990 the military forces of Iraq under the leadership of Saddam Hussein invaded and conquered the small neighboring oil-rich country of Kuwait. Iraq had several complaints against the Kuwaiti leadership, some of them related to repayment of Kuwait's loans from Kuwait to Iraq during the Iran-Iraq War of 1980–1988. Saddam Hussein decided to use military force to incorporate the independent country of Kuwait into Iraq to which he claimed it rightly belonged. Western countries, led by the United States, were concerned that Saddam was gaining control over more of the world's oil supply and might try to acquire even more by taking over the oil fields of Saudi Arabia too. Furthermore, the Iraqi conquest of Kuwait was the very kind of naked aggression that the United Nations was supposed to stop, and it was quickly condemned by the U.N. Security Council. U.S. President Bush immediately sent American military forces to Saudi Arabia to stop any further advances by Iraqi forces. He then proceeded to organize a large-scale multi-national "collective security" effort to take economic and, if necessary, military action against Iraq. The U.N. Security Council passed a resolution authorizing member states to use "all necessary means"[7] to get Iraqi forces out of Kuwait. It also set a deadline of January 15, 1991, for those forces to be removed. When the deadline passed without an Iraqi withdrawal, massive air attacks by the U.S.-led coalition were carried out against Iraq for the rest of the month and into February. On February 24, 1991, a ground attack began which ended only 100 hours later with a very one-sided victory for the coalition forces. The fighting ended when Saddam Hussein agreed unconditionally to all U.N. demands. The aggression against Kuwait had been stopped under the authority of the U.N. Security Council, but the military action itself had been directed by the United States and only "legitimized" by the U.N. Security Council.

Most of the U.N.'s efforts to keep the peace, however, have *not* involved military action in accord with the principle of collective security. The main response of the United Nations to conflict situations has been to implement what has come to be called a *"peace-keeping operation."* Such an operation traditionally consisted of sending an observer mission to some area of tension or sending lightly armed soldiers to police a truce between previously warring parties. These peacekeeping operations, especially since 1988 (when U.N. peacekeepers were awarded the Nobel Peace Prize) and the end of the Cold War in 1989, have expanded in concept to include a wide range of activities such as monitoring elections and protecting those providing humanitarian assistance to refugees.[8] These activities are often described as "nation-building" activities because they usually take place *within* a country in turmoil rather than dealing with disputes *between* countries. It should be noted that even though setting up peacekeeping and nation-building operations has become the usual U.N. response to conflict situations, such operations are not explicitly mentioned in the Charter of the U.N. Indeed, no one had even thought of carrying out such activities in 1945 when the Charter was written.

Several U.N. peacekeeping operations have been established in the Middle East. On November 29, 1947, the U.N. General Assembly adopted a resolution calling for the partition of Palestine into a Jewish state and an Arab state with international status for Jerusalem. Even before the withdrawal of British forces, Arabs and Jews were engaged in war with each other as the Arabs tried to prevent the establishment of a Jewish state. On April 23, 1948, the Security Council established a Truce Commission for Palestine to try to prevent violence. On May 14, 1948, the General Assembly voted to appoint a Mediator for Palestine to try to work out a peaceful solution of the conflict. On that same day the Israelis proclaimed the independence of the state of Israel. Fighting erupted the next day as Arab countries in the area mobilized their armies to try to put an end to this new state of Israel. The Security Council called for a cease-fire, but it lasted only four weeks. Then the Security Council called for another cease-fire and made an effort to use its own U.N. Truce Supervision Organization (UNTSO) to enforce it. This mission, created by the Security Council on May 29, 1948, is usually taken to be the beginning of U.N. peacekeeping.

Despite UNTSO, a second Arab-Israel war (involving also Britain and France) broke out in 1956. After the fighting ended, the U.N. Emergency Force (UNEF), wearing blue berets for the first time, was established to supervise a cease-fire, but Israel refused to allow UNEF troops on territory it controlled. Consequently, they were stationed only on the Egyptian side of the border. In 1967 Egyptian leader Gamal Abdel Nasser, having asked U.N. Secretary-General U Thant to remove the U.N. troops from Egyptian territory, inaugurated a blockade of the Gulf of Aqaba, Israel's only access to the Red Sea. The Israelis responded by attacking Egypt, Syria, and Jordan and quickly gaining control of the Sinai Peninsula, the Gaza Strip, the West Bank, all of Jerusalem, and the Golan Heights. The U.N. Security Council arranged a cease-fire to end this "Six-Day War," but Israel maintained control over the territory it had taken. In November 1967 the Security Council passed the crucial Resolution 242, setting down principles for the solution of the Middle East conflict. It called for withdrawal of Israeli forces from territory taken in the recent war, an end to all war in the area, free navigation for all ships through international waterways such as the Suez Canal, resolution of the problem of what to do with the Palestinian Arab refugees, and maintenance of the territorial integrity and political independence of all countries in the area. The U.N. viewpoint is that Resolution 242 is still operative as the basis for peace in the area.

After the October 1973 war, the Security Council once again called for an end of military activities and sent in a U.N. force to supervise the truce. The new U.N. Emergency Force (UNEF II) was stationed between Israeli and Egyptian forces, while the U.N. Disengagement Observer Force (UNDOF) was stationed between Israeli and Syrian forces. The establishment of these U.N.-sponsored peacekeeping forces was significant because for the first time the Soviet Union actively supported a U.N. peacekeeping effort and troops from a Communist country (Poland) were a part of the peacekeeping force.

Near the end of 1976 Syrian forces took over much of Lebanon in an effort to stop fighting between Muslims and Christians in that country. The Israelis did not want these hostile Syrian forces along their northern border, however, and gave strong military support to the Christian, anti–Muslim forces in the southern part of Lebanon. In 1978, after over a year of civil war in Lebanon, the U.N. Security Council voted to create the U. N. Interim Force in Lebanon (UNIFIL) to try to maintain some public order in the southern part of that country. The Israelis complained that terrorist attacks were still being launched by Palestinians in Lebanon, and in June 1982 they invaded Lebanon in an effort to eliminate all military activities of the Palestine Liberation Organization (PLO) in that country. In June 1985 Israeli forces were pulled out of Lebanon except for a narrow strip of land just north of the Israel-Lebanon border and south of the area in Lebanon patrolled by UNIFIL. In May 2000 even those forces were removed.

In 1988, despite intense opposition from the United States, the U.N. General Assembly recognized the right of the Palestinians to have an independent nation-state. Nevertheless for at least the past two decades the United States has played a larger role than the United Nations in trying to bring the Israelis and Palestinians together. Actually both have to be involved in the process. The Israelis view the United Nations as biased in favor of the Palestinians while the Palestinians view the United States as biased in favor of Israel.

The Middle East is not the only place where the United Nations has been involved in peacekeeping and nation-building. On May 29, 1998, when the U.N. Department of Peacekeeping Operations celebrated the 50th anniversary of U.N. peacekeeping, it was reported by Bernard Miyet, U.N. Under-Secretary-General for Peacekeeping Operations, that during those 50 years there have been 49 different operations. He noted then that "14,000 troops, military observers, civilian police, and civilian personnel are serving in 17 different peacekeeping missions."[9] He pointed out how U.N. peacekeeping had evolved from the days of the Cold War when most of the missions were to deal with conflicts between states to the situation in the last decade where the task has usually been to assist individual newly-independent countries in resolving civil wars and nation-building.

U.N. peacekeeping efforts peaked in 1993 when there were 70,000 persons involved and the expenditure was over $4 billion.[10] The low point was 1998 when those figures had declined to 12,000-15,000 persons deployed and an expenditure of about one billion dollars. In the year 2000 the figures are back up to 35,000 persons and a $2.2 billion budget.[11] The low 1998 figure can be attributed in large part to the withdrawal of U.S. support since the mid-1990s for the United Nations in general and for U.N. peacekeeping in particular. As of December 31, 1999, accumulated arrearages for U.N. peacekeeping amounted to about $1.35 billion, over two-thirds of it owed by the United States.[12] This lack of financial support from the member states for the United Nations is the biggest threat to the future of U.N. peacekeeping. The United States seems generally to have turned away to some extent from supporting U.N. peacekeeping, relying instead on other regional organizations such as

NATO, the Organization for Security and Cooperation in Europe (OSCE), and the Economic Community of West African States (ECOWAS) and its Military Observer Group (ECOMOG).[13]

Some of the current U.N. peacekeeping operations were instituted since the end of the Cold War in 1990, but others were started long ago.[14] Three of the missions still existing in 1999 were mentioned in the discussion above of the conflicts between Israel and its Arab neighbors. As already noted, the U.N. Truce Supervision Organization (UNTSO) established in 1948 was the first peacekeeping effort. It has continued to supervise the various agreements and cease-fires which have been reached for that area. It assists the other two still-existing peacekeeping operations in the Middle East, namely, the U.N. Disengagement Observer Force (UNDOF) created in 1974 to monitor the cease-fire between Israel and Syria on the Golan Heights and the U.N. Interim Force in Lebanon (UNIFIL) created in 1978 to confirm the withdrawal of Israeli forces from Lebanon, which still has not been completed.

The U.N. Military Observer Group in India and Pakistan (UNMOGIP) was established in January 1949 to monitor a cease-fire in the state of Jammu and Kashmir between Pakistan and India worked out through the efforts of a commission appointed by the U.N.[15] In 1972 India claimed that its agreement with Pakistan meant that UNMOGIP's mandate had been fulfilled, but Pakistan objected. The Secretary-General then declared that this peacekeeping mission can be ended only by action of the U.N. Security Council. With fighting flaring up from time to time in Kashmir, it is not likely that this will happen very soon.

Another still-existing U.N. peacekeeping mission is the U.N. Peacekeeping Force in Cyprus (UNFICYP). Near the end of 1963 fighting broke out between the Greek and Turkish residents of the newly independent nation of Cyprus, and in March 1964 UNfiCYP was sent there to control the violence. These mainly British forces have remained, though they were unable to do much except to maintain control of the Nicosia Airport during the 1974 conflict when armed forces from Turkey invaded the island in response to a Greek-led attempted *coup d'etat* against the government of Cyprus. The United Nations has tried to promote a unified demilitarized Cyprus, but in November 1983 the "President" of the Turkish Cypriots, who comprise 18 percent of the population living on the island, proclaimed an independent Turkish Republic of Northern Cyprus. The U.N. Security Council called on all member states not to recognize such a state, and none has except Turkey.[16] The U.N. peacekeeping force continues to occupy an east-west buffer zone across the island.

A more recently established but still continuing U.N. peacekeeping effort is the U.N. Iraq-Kuwait Observer Mission (UNIKOM) established in April 1991 after the Gulf War to patrol the demilitarized zone between Iraq and Kuwait. In view of the ongoing problems with Saddam Hussein in Iraq, it is not likely that this U.N. mission will soon be ended, especially since Iraq is paying two-thirds of the cost of the operation.

One current U.N. peacekeeping mission, the U.N. Observer Mission in Georgia (UNOMIG), is related to the break-up of the former Soviet Union. It began in July 1993 in order to monitor a cease-fire agreement between the Muslim rebels in the northern region of Abkhazia in Georgia and the forces of the central Georgian government. Its main aims are to allow refugees to return to their own homes and to preserve the integrity of Georgia. Russian forces authorized by the Commonwealth of Independent States (CIS) are helping to maintain order.[17]

The U.N. Mission for the Referendum in Western Sahara (MINURSO) was established in April 1991 to hold a referendum to determine whether the area known as Western Sahara (formerly a colony of Spain) should become the separate independent country of the Sahrawi Arab Democratic Republic (SADR) or whether it should be a part of Morocco. In April 1976 Morocco and Mauritania had entered into an agreement to divide the Western Sahara territory with the northern two-thirds going to Morocco and the southern third to Mauritania. The Polisario Front (Popular

Front for the Liberation of the Saguia el Hamra and Rio de Oro) guerrillas, fighting to make the area their independent country, convinced Mauritania to abandon its claims in August 1979. A U.N.-monitored cease-fire between the Moroccans and the Polisario guerrillas was implemented on September 6, 1991. The decade-old problem is to determine who will be eligible to vote in the agreed-upon referendum.[18]

Four other current U.N. peacekeeping missions are in Africa, two of them established in 1998. The U.N. Mission in the Central African Republic (MINURCA) was established in April and the U.N. Observer Mission in Sierra Leone (UNOMSIL) in July. In the Central African Republic, successful presidential elections in September 1999 led to the replacement of MINURCA by a new unit, the U.N. Peace-Building Office in the Central African Republic (BONUCA). In Sierra Leone a half-hearted and poorly organized effort led to a series of disasters, including the much-criticized, U.S.-supported July 7, 1999 Lomé Accord between the government of Sierra Leone on the one hand and the atrocity-committing Revolutionary United Front (RUF) led by Foday Sankoh on the other. On February 7, 2000, the U.N. Security Council authorized a much larger military force, and on June 7, 2000, the U.S. Senate agreed to release $50 million to pay for the operation. Efforts being made to get better trained and equipped forces and to throttle the illicit trade in diamonds being used to fund the RUF as well as to create a tribunal to prosecute those guilty of committing atrocities.

The two other existing U.N. operations in Africa were established in 1999. The U.N. Organization Mission in the Democratic Republic of Congo (MONUC) was established by the Security Council on November 30, and the U.N. Observers in Angola (UNOA) was established on October 15 in order to replace the U.N. Observer Mission in Angola (MONUA) which had been disbanded in February 1999. In the Congo the effort to get foreign forces out of the country in accord with a peace plan adopted in Lusaka in July 1999 ran into trouble at first because Congo President Laurent Kabila would not allow the U.N. observers into the parts of the country controlled by his forces. An increase in the size of the peacekeeping force in February 2000 plus a determined effort by Richard Holbrooke, U.S. Ambassador to the United Nations, resulted in pledges of support for the U.N. effort from the warring parties plus pledges of more peacekeeping troops from Nigeria and South Africa. In Angola the problem is a long-lasting battle between the Angolan government now led by President José Eduardo dos Santos and the UNITA Party rebels led by Jonas Savimbi. The rebels use diamonds and other businesses connected with the exploitation of natural resources and the illegal trading of weapons to finance their military activities. Thus the United Nations is working with the existing governments in Africa to establish and maintain order in the face of well-organized and well-financed armed groups seeking to carve out their own spheres of influence and money-making.

Two other present U.N. operations are related to the break-up of the former Yugoslavia. One is the U.N. Mission in Bosnia and Herzegovina (UNMIBH), whose work is carried out by the International Police Task Force (IPTF) created by the U.N. Security Council in December 1995 in accord with Dayton Peace Accords. The other is the U.N. Interim Administration Mission in Kosovo (UNMIK). In the former, the IPTF is merely commissioned to act as a civilian police force, but UNMIK, supported by NATO and Russian forces, has been given the unprecedented responsibility to act as a government in the Yugoslav province of Kosovo.

This same kind of authority to administer an entire government was given to the U.N. Transitional Administration in East Timor (UNTAET). Developments in the former Portuguese colony of East Timor began with the announcement in January 1999 by Indonesian President B. J. Habibie that a referendum would be held to determine the future of this territory. The U.N. Mission in East Timor (UNAMET) was established in June 1999 to provide support for holding the referendum. The referendum was held on

August 30, 1999, and the result was an overwhelming vote against autonomy within Indonesia. That result was equivalent to a vote for independence from Indonesia. Afterwards vengeful local pro-Indonesian militias opposed to the independence of that region began killing and looting and destroying what little property the East Timorese had. Almost half the population was rounded up and forced into West Timor where they would still be under the jurisdiction of the Indonesian government. The suggestion to put a U.N. peacekeeping force into the area at the time of the referendum had been rejected by the government of Indonesia, and U.N. policy has always been not to put U.N. peacekeepers on the territory of any country that doesn't want them. Finally the government of Indonesia was persuaded to change its stance, however, and on September 15, 1999, the U.N. Security Council authorized "Interfet," a multinational force under the command of Australia, to restore order and protect those trying to provide humanitarian aid. In February 2000 UNTAET was authorized to run East Timor for a year (or more if necessary) under Chapter VII of the U.N. Charter, meaning that military force can be used to maintain control.

Having reviewed these existing U.N. peacekeeping operations, let us also briefly consider some earlier U.N. peacekeeping operations of note. A very important early effort was in the Congo. In 1960 the Security Council authorized the establishment of the U.N. Congo Force (ONUC) to assist the newly independent nation of the Congo in suppressing a rebellion in the mineral-rich province of Katanga. This rebellion was not merely an internal affair, however, because many of those fighting for Katanga's secession from the new government were European mercenaries flown into the area to keep foreign mining operations out of the control of the new national government. The first aim of the U.N. forces was to get all foreign mercenaries out of the country. After several military battles lasting until 1963, the local leaders of the rebellion were finally persuaded to accept control of the province by the national government of the Congo, but the U.N. forces were not completely removed from the country until 1964. It was during this operation in September 1961 that U.N. Secretary-General Dag Hammerskjöld was killed while on a mission to try to end this fighting.

Namibia (formerly called Southwest Africa) represents one of the most successful of all U.N. nation-building operations. It began in 1966 when the U.N. General Assembly voted to take over administration of Southwest Africa from South Africa, to which it had been entrusted by the League of Nations. In May 1967 an 11-nation Council for Southwest Africa was established, but nothing much happened other than authorizing a change in the name of the country to "Namibia" in 1968. The project of establishing a whole new country began with a Security Council resolution in September 1978, but implementation did not occur until April 1989 after Cuban and South African forces were removed from Angola and the United Nations took on the task of supervising the withdrawal of South African forces from Namibia. Then the U.N. team, called the U.N. Transition Assistance Group (UNTAG), brought together the opposing racial and ideological groups to establish a new democratic regime for that country.[19] A Constituent Assembly was elected in November 1989, a new constitution was adopted by the Constituent Assembly in February 1990, and independence was declared on March 21, 1990. The next month Namibia became a member of the United Nations. This successful effort may have played a role in encouraging the positive developments which subsequently occurred in South Africa.[20]

Having successfully put a government together in Namibia, the United Nations decided to try to do it again in Cambodia.[21] There the process started with the small U.N. Advanced Mission in Cambodia (UNAMIC) moving into the country during November 1991 to supervise a truce agreed to by the three warring factions the month before. The U.N. Transitional Authority in Cambodia (UNTAC) set up its operations in March 1992 and then conducted elections in May 1993. Eventually the two opposing sides who had participated in the election process agreed to serve as co-chairmen of a transitional government under the leadership of former monarch Prince Norodom Sihanouk.[22] Ninety percent of the registered voters participated in the parliamentary elections of 1998 which resulted in no clear victory for any party. After some violent clashes, a compromise was worked out. Hun Sen of the Cambodian People's Party was to be Prime Minister while his main opponent, Norodom Ranariddh of the National Unified Front for an Independent, Neutral, Peaceful, and Cooperative Cambodia, would be President of the Assembly. The difficult issue to be addressed in Cambodia now is how to bring to justice the leaders of the Khmer Rouge who were responsible for killing so many people while in control of the country from April 1975 to January 1979. It must be determined to what extent the international community should be involved. Some Cambodians argue that the prosecutions should be carried out by the Cambodian government, but that alternative is not acceptable to others because the current leader Hun Sen was once part of the leadership of the Khmer Rouge.

The approaching end of the Cold War in 1988 meant that the operation of the U.N. Security Council was no longer hampered by the threat of vetoes from the Soviet Union/Russia on the one hand or the United States on the other. The result was that 17 new U.N. peacekeeping operations were authorized from 1988 through 1993.[23] To better understand the scope of past U.N. efforts, in addition to those U.N. operations already mentioned, the following should also be noted: (1) the U.N. Good Offices Mission in Afghanistan and Pakistan (UNGOMAP) created to monitor the Afghanistan/Pakistan border as the Soviets withdrew their forces in 1988; (2) the U.N. Iran-Iraq Military Observer Group (UNIIMOG) established to monitor the Iraq-Iran border after their war ended in 1988; (3) the U.N. Angola Verification Mission (UNAVEM I) set up in Angola as the Cubans were withdrawing their forces in 1989, and then UNAVEM II established in June 1991 to supervise peace accords between two opposing domestic factions in Angola and subsequent elections; (4) the U.N. Observer Group in Central America (ONUCA), set up in 1989 to verify on-site inspections in the carrying out of the Guatemala Agreement (Esquipulas II) to stop cross-boundary shipping of arms to guerrilla groups in El Salvador, Honduras, and Nicaragua; (5) the U.N. Observer Mission in El Salvador (ONUSAL) set up in El Salvador starting in July 1991 to oversee the stalled peace process there and to provide a civilian-controlled military force for El Salvador; (6) the U.N. Operation for Mozambique (UNUMOZ) set up in Mozambique in 1992 not only to monitor an agreement ending the civil war there but also to prepare the way for elections conducted by the parties themselves; (7) the U.N. Observer Mission Uganda-Rwanda (UNOMUR) set up along the Uganda/Rwanda border in July 1993 to prevent military assistance coming into Rwanda from Uganda; and (8) the U.N. Observer Mission in Liberia (UNOMIL) established in September 1993 to oversee a July peace agreement signed between the warring opposing political factions in that country.

The United Nations has also been called on more and more often to monitor elections where there is an international dimension relevant to the stability or security within that region of the world. In addition to the operations already discussed, we can note three others, two of them in the Western Hemisphere. (1) In 1989 the U.N. Observation Mission for the Verification of Elections in Nicaragua (UNOMVEN) was set up to monitor the important February 1990 elections in Nicaragua in which the leftist Sandinistas lost control over Nicaragua. (2) In December 1990 and January 1991 observers from the U.N. helped monitor the two-stage elections in Haiti, but some of the military leadership in that country prevented the newly elected Jean-Bertrand Aristide from taking office. As a result in September 1993 the U.N. Mission in Haiti (UNMIH) was authorized to operate in that country. (3) Elections supervised by U.N. personnel (UNAVEM II) were held in Angola in September 1992, but the UNITA Party would not abide by the results. Thus one can see that a major problem for the United Nations and the international community generally has been that in some cases rebellious armed factions refuse to accept the results of U.N.-monitored elections.

The peacekeeping/nation-building idea (including monitoring elections) has now become so popular that other international organizations and even specially created *ad hoc* multinational groups are conducting similar operations, sometimes under legitimizing resolutions passed by the U.N. Security Council. In 1999 such operations were being carried on by the North Atlantic Treaty Organization (NATO), the Organization for Security and Cooperation in Europe (OSCE), the Economic Community of West African States (ECOWAS), and the Commonwealth of Independent States (CIS) as well as independent groups of countries focused on dealing with a particular conflict. It seems that the United Nations has started a useful kind of activity that will continue even without the United Nations itself always being directly involved.

Dominant Influences in the United Nations

If we look at the United Nations not just from the viewpoint of what the structures are but from the viewpoint of who actually influences what happens within the organization, we can delineate three periods in its history. The first period, the time of U.S. dominance, lasted from the signing of the "Declaration by the United Nations" in 1942 through the San Francisco Conference to draw up the Charter in June 1945 to the crucial vote in 1971 which decided that the Chinese Communists would finally be allowed to appoint China's representatives at the U.N. The second period, the late Cold War period during which the United States and the Soviet Union nullified each other's efforts in the Security Council while the less developed countries increased their membership and influence in the General Assembly, came to an end in 1989 with the end of the Cold War (marked by the tearing down of the Berlin Wall) and the end of proxy wars between the superpowers throughout the Third World. The third period has been characterized by U.N. involve-

ment in peacekeeping efforts throughout the world with general support from the whole international community but with new questions arising about lack of support from the United States, about limited financial resources, and about the extent to which the world community can legitimately involve itself in intranational conflicts. Of course, these transitions from one period to the next occurred gradually and the shifts did not take place all at once.

At the beginning the United Nations was basically a child of the United States. It was conceived by U.S. President Franklin Roosevelt as a replacement for the League of Nations. The United Nations was brought into existence during World War II by the United States, with major support from Britain and acquiescence by the Soviet Union. When the United Nations was formally created in 1945, Europe and Japan had been devastated by World War II, and the United States had about 40 percent of the gross world product and a monopoly on nuclear weapons. Of the 51 original member nation-states of the United Nations, two-thirds (Western European countries, Latin American countries, members of the British Commonwealth, China, Iran, Iraq, Lebanon, Liberia, the Philippines, Saudi Arabia, and Turkey) could usually be expected to vote in accord with whatever the United States wanted. The United States could get anything it wanted passed in the General Assembly (such as the Universal Declaration of Human Rights in 1948), and in the Security Council its desires were blocked only by Soviet vetoes (though as already noted the Security Council was even able to declare Communist North Korea an aggressor in 1950 because the Soviets were absent at that meeting). During that early period the Soviet Union cast veto after veto while the United States never had to cast a veto because what it opposed never even came up for a vote.

A big change occurring in the United Nations during this first period was the admission of a large number of new members, many of them former colonies of European countries. Because of Cold War animosity, only nine countries were allowed to become members of the United Nations between 1945 and 1955, but in 1955 there were 16 new members in one year. In 1960 U.N. membership reached 100 countries with the admission of 17 new members, all but one being former African colonies. The United States and the Soviet Union both strongly supported this official recognition of the end of colonialism, so it was not difficult for the newly independent countries in 1960 to get the U.N. General Assembly to pass a resolution supporting the idea that all territories have a right to self-determination which overrides any claims advanced by colonial powers.[24]

But this increase in the number of U.N. members from Africa and Asia together with new Marxist-inspired attitudes of opposition to U.S. economic domination on the part of most less developed countries culminated in the crucial 1971 vote on China which marks the end of the first period of U.N. history. The Chinese Communists under the leadership of Mao Zedong had taken control of all of mainland China in 1949. The Soviets argued that Mao's Communist government should now appoint the Chinese representatives at the United Nations, but the United States argued that the Chinese Nationalists led by anti–Communist Chiang Kai-shek were still the legitimate government of China. The issue of who should appoint the U.N. representatives from China came up regularly in the General Assembly, but year after year the U.S. position prevailed. In 1971, however, things were different. In 1969 the United States under President Nixon's leadership had shifted its own policy toward China in an effort to get the Chinese Communists to side with the United States against the Soviet Union. At the same time, the United States did not want to abandon its old ally, Chiang Kai-shek and his Chinese Nationalist Party. A good compromise seemed to be to allow Taiwan to become a separate member of the United Nations, an approach that was called the "two Chinas" policy. But both the Chinese Nationalists and the Chinese Communists opposed that proposal. Consequently, the United States, in an effort to keep its Nationalist Chinese ally from losing its representation at the United Nations,

opposed the 1971 resolution which said that the Chinese Communists should appoint China's delegates at the United Nations, just as it had opposed similar resolutions previously. But this time the General Assembly voted in favor of the resolution to unseat the representatives of Nationalist China to make room for representatives appointed by the Chinese Communist regime. For the first time in the history of the U.N. General Assembly, an important resolution opposed by the United States had been adopted. But it is worth noting that the United States had been so dominant at the United Nations during this first period that the Chinese Communists had to wait 22 years before they were permitted to appoint China's delegates at the U.N.

That 1971 vote made it evident that the United Nations was into its second period marked by the control of the General Assembly by the less developed newly independent anticolonial countries while the Security Council was immobilized by the U.S.-Soviet confrontation where one or the other would veto every significant resolution. Having an international organization dominated by the poorer, less developed countries was definitely a new kind of situation in international affairs. The General Assembly could not pass binding resolutions as the Security Council could, but it did control the operation of the United Nations itself, including the adoption of the budget for the organization. On the other hand, during this period the prevailing attitude of the big powers was to ignore the United Nations, to try to keep it poor and powerless, and to conduct their business with each other bilaterally or through other international organizations such as NATO and the Warsaw Treaty Organization (WTO or Warsaw Pact).

The big problem for this new controlling group of less developed countries at the United Nations was that they lacked economic power. Contributions to the United Nations are assessed by the General Assembly on the basis of ability to pay, and none of these former colonies made very large contributions to the support of the U.N. In fact, in 1971 over a third of the U.N. budget came from the United States on grounds that the United

States had over a third of the world's gross income. The United States managed to score a point against the less developed countries in response to the 1971 vote on China. In 1972 the United States successfully requested that the General Assembly set 25 percent of the U.N. budget as the maximum any single nation could be assessed. The United States did nothing to counter rumors that if this proposal to reduce its own contribution was not passed it might just quit the United Nations altogether. The message from the United States was clear: Don't push your voting advantage too far, or you may lose a substantial portion of the money coming into the United Nations. On the other hand, the less developed countries realized that neither the United States nor the Soviet Union was likely to withdraw from the United Nations because this would clear the way for the other to maintain a close working relationship with those very nations in which the ideological battle between Communism and democratic capitalism was being fought.

The financial threat to the United Nations from the United States was temporarily diminished at the end of 1973 when the Organization of Petroleum Exporting Countries (OPEC) quadrupled the price of oil. This event not only demonstrated the vulnerability of the developed countries to economic pressures; it also meant large amounts of money in the coffers of those oil-rich Arab nations with sparse populations on which to spend their new-found wealth. These countries could now provide some of the foreign aid which the United States might threaten to withhold from nations which voted against it in the United Nations. They could replace U.S. contributions to the United Nations if the United States were to withdraw from the organization. This new situation provided the impetus for the less developed countries to become even bolder in the United Nations. In 1974 they passed a resolution calling for a New International Economic Order to replace the existing system of trading arrangements which favored the developed countries, and in 1975 they adopted another resolution declaring that Zionism is a form of racism. The passage of

this last resolution shows how Arab oil money was able to influence U.N. voting. Since the United States had always supported the existence of Israel and now Arab countries opposed to Israel were using their financial influence to get anti–Jewish resolutions passed by the United Nations, some Americans who had previously supported the United Nations began to have doubts about the organization. The United Nations was perceived by many to have become an anti–U.S. organization controlled by less developed countries overly sympathetic to Communist ideology and readily swayed by Arab oil money to thumb their noses at the United States.

During this Cold War period there was little the United Nations could do to end armed conflicts along the borders of and within the less developed countries. Every conflict in these poorer countries became an opportunity for the opposing superpowers to pour in weapons and military assistance to try to gain some increased influence in that part of the world. U.N. involvement was not welcome. In places such as Ethiopia and Somalia, there were even switches with regard to which superpower was giving assistance to which fighting group. In 1987 there were 22 wars where more than a thousand people a year were dying, and all of them were in less developed countries.[25] In 1990 it was observed that "without exception, the wars of the last two decades have all been in the developing world."[26] The situation seemed to be that the superpowers did not want peace but rather victory in war for whichever group they were supporting.

The transition to the third period in U.N. history has come as a result of the end of the Cold War between the United States and the Soviet Union. It is difficult to say precisely when that conflict ended, but one significant point indicating that the international situation had changed was the December 1987 signing of the INF Treaty to eliminate all medium-range missiles from Europe. Then came the April 1988 agreement leading to Soviet withdrawal from Afghanistan. In November 1989 the Berlin Wall was torn down. In December 1991 the Soviet Union ceased to exist. During this rapid transformation of the international landscape, the United Nations was being called on to monitor truces or elections in Afghanistan, Angola, Guatemala, and Nicaragua, thus bringing an end to conflicts where one side had been supported by the Communists and the other side by the U.S. The plan to create a new government in Namibia also started moving forward at this time.

For Americans the existence of a "new" United Nations became evident during the 1990–91 crisis in the Persian Gulf when U.S. President Bush used the U.N. Security Council, no longer hampered by the threat of a Soviet veto, to condemn Iraq's invasion of Kuwait and to authorize U.S.-led military action against Saddam Hussein's Iraq. The President talked of a "new world order" where international aggression would no longer be permitted. After the Gulf War ended, the United Nations was called on to make sure that Iraq lived up to the terms of the truce and also to assist with temporary humanitarian assistance to the Kurds being attacked by Saddam Hussein's forces in northern Iraq. New U.N. peacekeeping operations were being established all over the world. Many people, both within the United States and elsewhere, were voicing the opinion that the United Nations "is finally working as it was designed to work."[27]

Buoyed by the quick, one-sided victory in the Gulf War and by successful U.N. peacekeeping/nation-building operations in Namibia and Cambodia, Americans were ready to support more participation in U.N. efforts in places such as Somalia. But the U.S. domestic budget crisis, the existence of obviously difficult and dangerous situations such as that in the former Yugoslavia, and the deaths of 18 Americans in Somalia in October 1993 combined to raise questions about how much the United States should support the United Nations. All these new peacekeeping operations had caused the U.S. portion of the expenses for U.N. peacekeeping to skyrocket, from $61.1 million in 1987 to $794 million in 1993.[28] That seems a miniscule amount compared with the $278 *billion* budgeted for U.S.

national military expenditures in 1994,[29] but American leaders seemed to be more ready to cut millions from international peacekeeping than to cut billions from national military spending. From their viewpoint too much of the U.N. peacekeeping was not relevant to U.S. national interests.

Despite the reluctance of the United States to pay its share for U.N. peacekeeping or other U.N. activities, the United States still dominates the United Nations. Since all the real power in the United Nations is vested in the Security Council and since the United States has a veto in the Security Council, it is evident that the United Nations cannot do anything without the approval of the United States. Furthermore, the power wielded by the United States in the United Nations is not purely a negative one. When one looks back over the various peace-keeping efforts of the United Nations, it is evident that the United Nations got involved when the United States wanted it to get involved and the United Nations got out when the United States wanted it to get out. This influence of the United States can be seen in all cases, but it is particularly evident with regard to Somalia, Haiti, Iraq, and the former Yugoslavia. In all these cases the United Nations followed the desires of the United States.

The most obvious incident showing the power of the United States in the United Nations, however, is the selection in 1996 of Kofi Annan to be the U.N. Secretary-General even when *all* the other members of the United Nations wanted Boutros Boutros-Ghali to serve a second five-year term. In the process of selecting a new Secretary-General the Security Council provides nominees (so far there has always been only one) and the General Assembly elects one of them. In 1996, the United States indicated that it would use its veto to keep Boutros-Ghali from being nominated for a second term. Great pressure was put on other countries to support the U.S. position. Eventually even France, which had threatened to veto any nominee except Boutros-Ghali, was coerced into supporting Kofi Annan.[30] When Annan was elected by the General Assembly, the United States alone had prevailed over all the other 184 members of the United Nations in its goal of getting rid of Boutros-Ghali. This incident all by itself provides overwhelming evidence of how completely the United States dominates the United Nations.

Despite the dominant position of the United States, the international community has nevertheless been able to accomplish some things opposed by the United States. One example is the creation of institutions and organizations related to the Law of the Sea Treaty such as the International Seabed Authority, the International Tribunal for the Law of the Sea, and the Commission on the Limits of the Continental Shelf despite the failure of the United States Senate to ratify this treaty, mainly because of provisions related to mining of the ocean floor which were regarded as unfair to privately owned corporations.[31] Another is the adoption in 1998 of the Rome Statute for the creation of an International Criminal Court (ICC). This treaty has not yet been ratified by enough countries to bring it into effect, but that is likely to happen by the year 2003 despite U.S. obduracy.[32] International treaties such as the Convention on the Rights of the Child and the Convention to Eliminate All Forms of Discrimination Against Women have been ratified by most of the countries of the world. The United States has signed them but has not ratified them because some influential domestic religious groups are opposed to some of their provisions.[33] Thus, the agenda of the United Nations spelled out in its Charter is moving forward despite the foot-dragging of its dominant member.[34]

In this post–Cold War period one of the big questions to be answered is the extent to which the United States will focus its attention on its own domestic problems while ignoring the much greater problems of people living in other parts of the world. Countries such as China, Iraq, Iran, Pakistan, and Afghanistan would undoubtedly be happy to see the United States and its "Westernized" allies being less supportive of U.N. involvement in international issues such as peacekeeping in support of democratic approaches to governance, defending human rights, and protection of the environment. Their concern is that their own national sovereignty may be compromised by an active United Nations engaged too much in "humanitarian interventions" based on Western values. They are very concerned by statements such as those of U.N. Secretary-General Kofi Annan in his 2000 Millennium Report that

> national sovereignty must not be used as a shield for those who wantonly violate the rights and lives of their fellow human beings. In the face of mass murder, armed intervention by the Security Council is an option that cannot be relinquished.[35]

At the same time conservative groups in the United States are very much concerned that such "humanitarian interventions" could set a precedent for involvement by the international community in what they regard as U.S. domestic issues such as U.S. treatment of native Americans and African-Americans.

Accomplishments of the United Nations

The United Nations came into existence on October 24, 1945. It has not been particularly successful in its announced aim "to save succeeding generations from the scourge of war." Yet the rest of that first sentence of the U.N. Charter makes reference to the two world wars, and the fact is, regardless of whether the United Nations by itself is responsible for it or not, there has been no World War III. The League of Nations was formed in 1919, and twenty years later another world war was being fought. The United Nations has already existed for 55 years without another world war. Furthermore, a look at its record reveals that it not only has accomplished several of its aims to some degree but also has brought about other desirable developments.

One of the major accomplishments of the United Nations is that it has managed to maintain its existence and even to extend its membership to practically all the nations of the world. Survival is no small task for a large political organization. Even a national-level political institution which maintains its existence for over 50 years is considered a stable institution. Well over half the nations which now belong to the United Nations did not have independent national governments at the time the United Nations was formed; the United Nations is older than they are! Continuing existence by itself produces expectations and traditions. The longer the United Nations survives as an organization with almost universal membership, the more difficult it becomes for anyone to conceive of a world without it or for national leaders to conceive of their own nations as nonmembers.

With regard to the war problem, the United Nations has been the agency by which multilateral arms control agreements have come into existence as well as the vehicle for many peacekeeping operations.[36] The United Nations has established various committees to further arms control. With regard to peace-keeping efforts, one can only conjecture about whether any of the situations in which the United Nations intervened might have otherwise developed into a large-scale war. The U.N.'s role in Korea should not be forgotten, even if it is unlikely that there will ever again be a similar operation. At least the precedent was set for an international organization coordinating an effort to resist aggression in accord with the idea of collective security. One should also consider whether in the absence of the United Nations there could be a situation such as the one that occurred at the time of the Gulf War when the major military power in the world sought the approval of the international community before launching a military attack to punish an aggressor nation and then turned over the task of enforcing the truce to the international community.

A third area of achievement for the United Nations consists of providing opportunities for formal and informal exchanges between diplomats in times of crisis and for planning cooperative efforts to resolve conflicts. The existence of the United Nations makes possible meetings in the hallway or the lunchroom which may produce important diplomatic exchanges that would never have taken place if formal arrangements for such meetings had been required in advance. Especially diplomats from smaller countries may

be able to take part in discussions to which they otherwise would not have been invited. The Secretary-General and other U.N. personnel can participate in negotiations as representatives not of this or that nation, but of the world community. How much difference this opportunity for ready contact between diplomats has made toward preventing war cannot be determined with precision, but it is hard to believe that it hasn't helped greatly.

Fourth, the United Nations has been developing a whole new tradition in international politics, one of conferring and debating and appealing to disinterested third parties rather than making military threats and issuing ultimatums. This new tradition involves a shift from a situation where interaction between nations was only bilateral and coercive to one where it is also multilateral and persuasive. The United Nations is thus serving as a school where national governments and their leaders are learning how to participate in a democratic parliament. Even representatives from nations with autocratic governments are learning that different points of view must be allowed to be expressed, that the opinions of third parties are important, that appeals to reason rather than force can be influential, and so on.

Unfortunately, the United States, which prides itself on being a democratic nation, seems to have trouble at times functioning within this democratic forum. As a nation Americans have yet to learn the very important lesson that on the world scene they are a minority, less than 5 percent of the world's population. They have yet to learn that democracy means listening as well as talking, appealing to reason rather than being coercive, and taking the opinions of others seriously even when one doesn't agree. They need to learn that there are others in the world who care about freedom and justice just as much as people in the United States.

A fifth area of achievement for the United Nations is its supervision of the relatively smooth transition from a world of colonizing nations and their colonies to a world of independent sovereign countries. We have already noted that the Trusteeship Council has completed its monitoring of the shift to independence of many lands and that over half the nations of the United Nations were colonies at the time the United Nations was formed. Even if the United Nations had accomplished nothing else, its supervision and legitimation of the decolonization of much of the world makes it one of the greatest success stories in human history. Furthermore, the leaders of these newly independent countries are very conscious of the important role the United Nations has played in their history.

Obviously one cannot claim that the United Nations accomplished this transition alone. There can be no down-grading of the sacrifices made in the wars that sometimes had to be fought for independence. At the same time, it can be noted that the process would undoubtedly have been much slower and much bloodier without the United Nations. Many nations have won their independence without bloodshed, and the existence of the United Nations has often facilitated this development. The United Nations provides a ready means by which the independence of a nation can be registered as an objective fact. A country may declare itself to be independent, but that independence is publicly recognized by the rest of the world when it becomes a member of the United Nations, equally sovereign with every other nation.

The United Nations has not only helped these new nations to achieve recognized independence; it has also helped them to survive once they have become independent. This is its sixth area of success. Most of these former colonies are poor and short of the skills needed to run businesses, schools, hospitals, and governments. They need loans and other forms of development assistance. The United Nations has helped to provide these necessities. The less developed countries have been successful in the past in using the United Nations as a vehicle to procure and secure their *political independence*. Their expectation now is that it will also assist them in their *economic and social development*.

A seventh area of accomplishment for the United Nations is its progress in carrying out the aim stated in the second paragraph of the Charter, namely, "to reaffirm faith in fundamental human rights." The various declarations and covenants on this subject serve as an ideal for the world's governments and peoples to pursue even though they are often far from being actualized. Their role in the development of standards may be compared to that played by the Declaration of Independence and the Bill of Rights in the formation of public opinion in the United States. The three main U.N. human rights documents (the Universal Declaration of Human Rights adopted by the General Assembly in 1948; the Covenant on Economic, Social, and Cultural Rights passed by the General Assembly in 1966; and the Covenant on Civil and Political Rights also passed by the General Assembly in 1966) were all adopted without a dissenting vote.[37] Even national governments which do not honor these rights in practice feel bound not to vote against them as public statements of the ideals toward which humankind should be moving.

The Covenant on Civil and Political Rights contains an optional Protocol which nations may also adopt when they ratify that Covenant. The Protocol indicates that the nation acceding to it recognizes the right of its citizens to file complaints about violations of their rights directly to the U.N. Human Rights Committee, a committee formed of representatives elected by those nations who have ratified the Covenant. As more and more nations accede to this very special Protocol, the pressure on the others who have not adopted it should mount. The accusations of human rights violations made against each other by potential enemies do not carry much weight because each is known to be merely attacking an opponent, but failure to ratify the Protocol of the Covenant on Civil and Political Rights should be viewed as a self-accusation before the whole world. Unfortunately, the media in most of the world have not paid much attention to these Covenants and the all-important Protocol, so the pressure of world public opinion has not yet been brought to bear on this issue.

In addition to the three basic documents on human rights, the United Nations has also adopted several treaties on specific human rights such as the prevention of genocide, protection of refugees, political rights of women, abolition of slavery, the nationality of married women, the status of stateless persons, consent to marriage, elimination of racial discrimination, elimination of religious intolerance and discrimination, and the rights of children. Most of these efforts to further human rights would not have occurred without the United Nations.

An eighth accomplishment of the United Nations is directing the attention of the whole world to crucial global problems so that action can be taken toward solving these problems. The technique which has been used to focus attention on an issue is the convening of a world conference devoted to that problem. Experts from all over the world, governmental representatives, and sometimes private citizens too, get together to discuss this problem and possible solutions to it. The first of these world conferences was on the environment. It was held in Stockholm in 1972 and led eventually to the creation of the U.N. Environmental Programme (UNEP) with headquarters in Nairobi, Kenya. In 1973 the first session of the U.N. Conference on the Law of the Sea was held in New York. Many subsequent sessions were held in Caracas, Geneva, and New York over a period of nine years, and the UNCLOS treaty on the governance of the oceans was signed in 1982 by 117 nations. In 1974 the World Conference on Population was held in Bucharest and the World Food Conference met in Rome. Starting in 1975 and continuing into 1977, the Conference on International Economic Cooperation in Paris dealt with the relationship between the developed and the less developed countries. In 1976, Vancouver (British Columbia, Canada) and Geneva were the sites of conferences on human settlements and employment. In 1977 the World Water Conference was held at Mar del Plata, Argentina, and a conference on the nuclear fuel cycle was held in Salzburg, Austria. In 1978 the Conference on Technical Cooperation among Developing Countries was held in Buenos Aires. In Vienna in 1979 a conference was held on Science and Technology for Development. In 1981 a conference was held in Nairobi on New and Renewable Sources of Energy. Vienna was host again for the 1982 Conference on the Peaceful Uses of Outer Space. In July 1985 a Conference to Review and Appraise the Achievements of the U.N. Decade for Women was held in Nairobi, Kenya, with an even more influential Conference on Women being convened in Beijing ten years later. In June 1992 the widely publicized U.N. Conference on Environment and Development (also called "the Earth Summit") was held in Rio de Janeiro, Brazil. In 1994 there was the Social Summit in Copenhagen and the Conference on Population in Cairo. This list of U.N.-sponsored world conferences is by no means complete. The success of the earlier conferences in drawing attention to a given problem led to such a multiplication of conferences in the mid-1990s that some of them no longer attracted much attention in the media. Furthermore, opposition from the United States has led to a situation where the United Nations has been restricted in its support of such conferences. The 1999 Hague Appeal for Peace had to be organized by nongovernmental organizations, though U.N. Secretary-General Annan did support that conference and gave the closing plenary speech.[38] The U.N.-sponsored conferences have served to alert the public to pressing global issues and have also encouraged experts to address them. Perhaps the U.S. viewpoint will change in the future and the United Nations will again be freer to convene conferences on problems confronting the global community.

A ninth area of accomplishment of the United Nations is most evident to social scientists and government officials. The United Nations secures and maintains data on societies all over the world and publishes yearbooks and statistical records containing comparative information from these societies. For years information-gathering capabilities and kinds of measurement varied widely from country to country, but the data has gradually become standardized. These data about what has happened and what is happening all over the world are indispensable for planning for the future, and it is satisfying to note that this worldwide information gathering which was once done mainly by an under-funded United Nations is now also being done on an even larger scale by private parties, nongovernmental organizations, and national governments.

The tenth contribution of the United Nations is actually a large number of achievements accomplished by (1) a collection of special programs, entities, and institutes of the United Nations itself plus (2) a group of fairly autonomous organizations and specialized agencies which report to the U.N. Economic and Social Council. All of these collectively are known as "the United Nations System." The second group will be discussed separately in the next section under the heading "Worldwide Functional Agencies." In order to convey the wide range of activities carried out by this U.N. system, here is a listing of the special programs, entities, and institutes of the United Nations itself.[39]

Programs and Funds:

U.N. Conference on Trade and Development (UNCTAD)
U.N. Drug Control Programme (UNDCP)
U.N. Development Programme (UNDP)
U.N. Environment Programme (UNEP)
U.N. Fund for Population Activities (UNFPA)
U.N. Office of the High Commissioner for Refugees (UNHCR)
U.N. Children's Fund (UNICEF)
U.N. Relief and Works Agency for Palestine Refugees (UNRWA)
World Food Programme (WFP)

Other U.N. Entities:

Office of the U.N. High Commissioner for Human Rights (OHCHR)
U.N. Centre for Human Settlements (Habitat) (UNCHS)
U.N. Office for Project Services (UNOPS)
U.N. University (UNU)

Research and Training Institutes:

Int'l Research & Training Institute for Advancement of Women (INSTRAW)
U.N. Interregional Crime and Justice Research Institute (UNICRI)
U.N. Institute for Training and Research (UNITAR)

U.N. Research Institute for Social Development (UNRISD)
U.N. Institute for Disarmament Research (UNIDIR)

Worldwide Functional Agencies

National governments are one of the most prominent features of social life on the earth. The boundaries of their control often mark the limits within which a certain language or a certain currency is used. But national boundaries are not inscribed on the surface of the earth, and they do not stop the flow of air and water and animals and radio waves and goods and people from place to place. As a result, problems frequently arise which cannot be handled by national governments acting separately. The League of Nations and the United Nations represent two different efforts to create a supranational organization dedicated to dealing with world problems *in general*. On the other hand, each of the *international governmental organizations* (IGOs) now to be discussed aims to perform a *specific function*. These IGOs are called "governmental agencies" because they consist of persons appointed by national governments to serve in organizations dealing with international problems. Thus they need to be sharply distinguished from those organizations to be discussed a bit later, namely *international NON-governmental organizations* (INGOs), which are staffed by volunteers or persons paid by contributions from private citizens. The IGOs to be discussed now are called international *functional agencies* or *specialized agencies*. They are also sometimes called *administrative agencies* because they aim to do what needs to be done to solve a particular kind of international problem without getting involved in political and ideological issues.

The first permanent functional international governmental organization (IGO) was the Central Commission for the Navigation of the Rhine, created in accord with the Final Act of the Congress of Vienna in 1815. This Commission contained representatives from all countries which border the Rhine, and its task was to facilitate and regulate river traffic.

It established the first group of international civil servants and even provided pensions for them. Except for periods of war the Rhine Commission has continued to function to the present day.

The next permanent functional international government organization (IGO) was the European Commission of the Danube, created in 1856. It developed a system of tolls and licenses which permitted the lower Danube to be kept navigable without all the expense being borne by Romania. It also provided a single licensing agency for all users of the river regardless of what country they might be in or go through. The Commission proved to be a success, lasting until World War II. After that war a new Danube Commission was formed. Similar international commissions have been established to supervise navigation on other waterways which flow through more than one country. These functional agencies for waterways are *regional* rather than worldwide in scope, however, and consequently are more directly related to the next section below, which deals with regional functional agencies.

The first of the worldwide functional international governmental organizations (IGOs) which eventually became a part of the present U.N. system was the International Telegraphic Union (ITU) established in 1865. This agency was created by a multilateral convention which enunciated the general principles of the organization and set the rules to be followed by those signing the convention. The International Telecommunication Convention of 1932 brought together the International Telegraphic Union and the International Radiotelegraphic Union, which had been established by a separate convention in 1906. The new International Telecommunication Union (ITU) started operating in 1934 and became a specialized agency affiliated with the United Nations in 1947. Its task is to encourage international cooperation in the use and further development of communication by telegraph, radio, cable, telephone, and television. Regulation of the use of various radio and television frequencies, which is especially important for small countries or in areas near borders of large countries, is one of its main functions.

One of the better known worldwide functional international governmental organizations is the Universal Postal Union (UPU). To facilitate international postal communication without each nation trying to throw the burden of postal charges for this international mail on the other, the General Postal Union was formed in 1874-75. A single scale of charges for all international mail was to be established, and transit charges through any given nation were to be based on weight and mileage. The legislative body is the Postal Congress which meets every five years. New policies are adopted by majority vote, but each nation must then separately ratify its concurrence with the change. It is so advantageous to each nation to belong to the Union that a tradition has been established of virtually automatic ratification of any changes proposed by the Congress. The name of this organization was changed to the Universal Postal Union (UPU) in 1878, and it became a specialized agency of the United Nations in 1948.

There are so many worldwide functional international governmental organizations (IGOs) that it would be tedious to try to discuss each one. We can, however, mention those that are officially part of the U.N. system. Most of these specialized agencies are funded through assessments on their members. Two of these discussed above are (1) The International Telecommunication Union (ITU) and (2) the Universal Postal Union (UPU). Here is an alphabetical list of the others (except for the five which make up the World Bank Group, which are at the end of the list):

(3) The Food and Agriculture Organization (FAO) aims to improve the quantity and quality of the world's food supply by assisting in agricultural research programs, irrigation projects, pest control activities, development of fishing techniques, and the like.
(4) The International Atomic Energy Agency (IAEA) aims to promote the safe and peaceful use of atomic energy.
(5) The International Civil Aviation Organization (ICAO) aims to promote safe and efficient international air travel by regulating aircraft operation, safety equipment, pilot training, and language use for communications related to international flights.
(6) The International Fund for Agricultural

Development (IFAD) aims to provide resources for agricultural and rural development in the poorest rural areas.

(7) The International Labor Organization (ILO) aims to improve the workplace environment for laborers by setting international standards for safety and working conditions so that employers in one country cannot argue that they are disadvantaged compared to employers in another country who need not meet the same standards.

(8) The International Maritime Organization (IMO) aims to improve ship safety and navigation procedures on the high seas, minimize environmental damage from shipping activities, and insure that damages to private property or the environment are paid for by those who do the damage.

(9) the International Monetary Fund (IMF) aims to promote the stability of exchange rates between different national currencies and to promote international cooperation with regard to monetary policies.

(10) The U.N. Educational, Scientific, and Cultural Organization (UNESCO) aims to increase international cooperation in the areas of education (especially literacy programs), scientific research, and the preservation and exchange of culturally and historically important buildings and objects.

(11) The U.N. Industrial Development Organization (UNIDO) aims to assist the less developed countries of the world in their efforts to industrialize.

(12) The World Health Organization (WHO) aims to prevent the spread of disease (especially across national boundaries), to promote health education, and to encourage medical research.

(13) The World Intellectual Property Organization (WIPO) aims to promote international cooperation in respecting copyrights, patents, and trademarks.

(14) The World Meteorological Organization (WMO) aims to coordinate the gathering and exchange of weather information from all over the world.

(15) The World Trade Organization (WTO) is the successor organization of the General Agreement on Tariffs and Trade (GATT), which grew out of a treaty designed to lower tariffs and reduce restrictions on international trade. The WTO aims to develop free trade throughout the world and has a rigorous mechanism for adjudicating complaints of noncompliance.

(16) The World Bank system as a whole provides a means by which richer countries can provide foreign assistance to less developed countries without needing to worry about whether the projects being proposed are in fact promising and without getting into the position of funding worthless projects just because of the political consequences of not funding them. The World Bank Group (WBG) consists of:

(16a) The International Bank for Reconstruction and Development (IBRD) provides loans and other assistance for economic development.

(16b) The International Development Association (IDA) helps the poorest nations by arranging loans at extremely low rates of interest.

(16c) the International Center for Settlement of Investment Disputes (ICSID) aims to resolve international disputes related to investment.

(16d) The International Finance Corporation (IFC) tries to promote private business in less developed countries.

(16e) The Multilateral Investment Guarantee Agency (MIGA) serves to attract international investments to poorer countries by insuring investors against non-commercial risks such as takeovers by national governments or destruction of property by revolutionary groups.[40]

In a sense, all these global functional agencies which form part of the U.N. system (as well as the programs and entities and institutes directly related to the United Nations previously discussed) constitute what would be departments or bureaus if a fully developed world government existed. For example, WHO would be the Department of Health, FAO would be the Department of Agriculture, and UNESCO would be the Department of Education. These agencies are busy solving real world problems and improving the quality of life for the whole human race. For example, as the result of the work of WHO, smallpox has been eliminated from the face of the earth.[41] It has been noted that famine and disease have killed many more people than war, and these are the problems being successfully addressed by the functional international organizations such as FAO and WHO.[42]

Regional Functional and Political Organizations

Although our discussion of functional agencies has so far been directed mainly to those which are *global* in scope, we did mention the commissions for the Rhine and Danube rivers, which are examples of *regional* functional organizations. There are many more of these international regional functional organizations than those which have a worldwide scope.[43] Although regional functional organizations carry on many different specific kinds of tasks, the most important ones fall into two classes. First, there are those regional organizations whose primary function is military cooperation against a prospective opponent. Second, there are those regional organizations whose primary function is economic cooperation. In addition to these regional *functional* organizations there are also regional *political* organizations which aim to peacefully resolve any kind of conflict among their members and to adopt a common policy toward nations outside the organization.

Regional *military* organizations may look at first glance like simple military alliances, but there is a difference. A regional military organization includes a governing council, which meets on a regular basis, and an integrated military staff, which functions at all times, not just during crises or war. In other words, an actual organization is created to implement a military agreement rather than just having a commitment to join in the fighting in case of an attack. The most obvious example of such a regional military organization is the North Atlantic Treaty Organization (NATO). NATO is involved in peacekeeping efforts in Albania [NATO Albania Force (AFOR)], Bosnia [NATO Stabilization Force (SFOR) II] and Kosovo [NATO Kosovo Force (KFOR)]. At the same time the Commonwealth of Independent States (CIS) dominated by the Russian Federation has been supplementing U.N. peacekeeping in Georgia (UNOMIG) while forces from CIS nations as part of the Organization for Security and Cooperation in Europe (OSCE) are involved along with NATO forces in SFOR and KFOR. It is evident that these regional military and political international organizations are actively engaged in peacekeeping.

Regional *economic* organizations usually seek to develop a free trade area where tariffs and quotas between member states are eliminated or to go beyond that to a common market where a common tariff policy is adopted toward nations or groups of nations outside the regional group. These regional economic organizations also seek to promote economic cooperation and development among their members. In the case of Benelux (an economic union of Belgium, the Netherlands, and Luxembourg which preceded the European Community/Union) cooperation included provisions for the free flow of capital and labor across national boundaries and for common tax laws, welfare policies, and postal and transport rates.

The outstanding example of regional economic integration is Western Europe. The European Coal and Steel Community (ECSC) was created in 1952 to integrate the coal and steel industries in France, West Germany, Italy, and the Benelux countries. The European Economic Community (the EEC or "Common Market") was created by the same countries in 1957 to establish a common market among themselves and a common economic policy toward other nations. Denmark, Ireland, and the United Kingdom joined in 1973, Greece in 1981, and Portugal and Spain in 1986. In 1993 the EEC was changed into the European Union (EU).

The success of the EU in promoting economic growth in Europe has encouraged the formation of other international economic organizations such as the Andean Community of Nations (CAN) established in 1969, the Caribbean Community and Common Market (Caricom) established in 1973, the Latin America Economic System (LAES) established in 1975, and the West African Economic and Monetary Union (WAEMU) formed in 1994. There are also several regional development banks modeled on the World Bank such as the Inter-American Development Bank (IADB) established in 1959, the African Development Bank (AfDB) established in 1963, the Asian Development Bank (AsDB) established in 1966, the Caribbean Development Bank (CDB) established in 1969, the West African Development Bank (WADB) established in 1973, and the Arab Monetary Fund (AMF) established in 1976.[44]

Some economic international organizations are less than global in scope but also are not regional. One example is the Commonwealth of Nations (also known simply as "Commonwealth") established in 1931 by Britain and many of its former colonies. Another example is the Organization for Economic Cooperation and Development

(OECD). That organization began in 1948 as the Organization for European Economic Co-operation (OEEC) whose aim was to coordinate American assistance to a devastated Europe. The United States, Canada, and Japan joined with these Western European countries in that organization, whose name was changed in 1961 to the Organization for Economic Co-operation and Development (OECD) and whose aims included the further development and economic stability of the developed capitalist countries, the coordination of aid to the less developed countries, and the promotion of world trade. Still another example of an economic international organization which is not global but which is also not regional is the Organization of Petroleum Exporting Countries (OPEC) formed in 1960. Its aim is to stabilize the price of crude oil by limiting production by its members to agreed-upon levels.

Usually increasing economic cooperation within a group of countries will eventually lead to problems of a political nature. For example, there are frequently differences among member countries with regard to tax policies, agricultural subsidies, and benefits for the unemployed. As economic integration proceeds, it becomes necessary to decide how to reconcile these different policies. Economic cooperation reaches a point where it cannot be expanded without some type of political integration. The European community seems to have reached this point.

Consequently, it should not be surprising that when we turn our attention to international *political* regional organizations, it is Western Europe which is farthest along the path to significant political integration. The European Union (EU) (formerly called "the European Community (EC)") has a decision-making Council, a Commission, a Court of Justice, and a Parliament. At first the members of the European Parliament (EP) were selected by the national legislatures, but in the spring of 1979 the people of Western Europe for the first time were able to directly elect their representatives in the European Parliament. The powers of the European Parliament are quite limited now, but they can be expected to grow as this institu-

tion matures and as demands for a more democratic EU continue to be made.

Although Europe leads the way in political integration, there are several other regional political organizations which are much weaker in nature but are nevertheless dedicated to dealing with the problems of the region in a general way and not serving as merely functional or administrative organizations. The basic aim of these organizations is usually to keep nations outside that region from intervening in what are viewed as regional matters. If the nations in the region are able to settle any disputes among themselves, then action by other nations or by the United Nations will be unnecessary.

For example, the Organization of American States (OAS), which includes all the countries of the Americas except Cuba, serves to continue the Monroe Doctrine of the United States, according to which nations in other parts of the world are to refrain from interference in American affairs. It also promotes development and observance of human rights in the nations of the Western hemisphere. Similarly, the newly independent nations of Africa have created the Organization of African Unity (OAU) not only to work together in moving out of their colonial status but also to try to settle conflicts within and among African nations without the involvement of outsiders. The Arab League was established to foster Arab unity but has found little agreement except in *anti*–Israel sentiment, and even on the issue of how to deal with Israel there has been much disagreement. One regional international political organization which seems more interested in promoting cooperation among its members than in keeping outsiders out is the Nordic Council, composed of Denmark, Finland, Iceland, Norway, and Sweden. That Council, established in 1952, aims to promote more uniform legal and economic practices among its members. The Association of Southeast Asian Nations (ASEAN) formed in 1967 is another example of a group which is focusing more on cooperation than opposing outsiders. Still another Asian regional international organization is the South Asian Association for Regional Cooperation (SAARC) formed in 1985 and composed of Bangladesh, Bhutan, India, the Maldive Islands, Nepal, Pakistan, and Sri Lanka. With the Cold War ended an organization which is likely to become a focus for cooperation between all states of Europe, the republics of the former Soviet Union, the U.S., and Canada is the Organization on Security and Cooperation in Europe (OSCE) established in 1995 as the successor to the Conference for Security and Cooperation in Europe (CSCE) or Helsinki Group. It now has 55 members and a Secretariat in Vienna.

It is possible that one or another of these or other regional international political organizations will become more significant in the future, but so far only the European Union seems to have developed a higher level of integration than that found at the global level in the United Nations. Meanwhile, it is distressing to see that in many regional organizations the motive of keeping outsiders out usually seems to be as important as furthering positive cooperation among the nations of the region.

International Nongovernmental Organizations

When we look at the international institutions which reflect a developing global community, the focus tends to be on those institutions created by and for national governments which we have been discussing up to this point. The world is changing, however, and one of the significant changes is the increasing influence of international organizations created by individuals and groups other than national governments, what is sometimes called "civil society,". These international *nongovernmental* organizations (INGOs) play a crucial role in promoting those attitudes and perspectives which are essential if there is ever to be peace and justice and conservation of nature on a global scale. And as Hilary French notes in the Worldwatch Institute's *State of the World 2000*, their number is growing rapidly. She says,

> The number of NGOs working across international borders has ... soared over this century, climbing from just 176 in 1909 to more than 23,000 in 1998.[45]

Although her primary interest is in groups working globally to preserve the environment, her point about more international groups being formed applies also to organizations focused on peace and justice issues.

The first known international non-governmental organization was the International Red Cross. This organization grew out of the efforts of Jean-Henri Dunant, a Swiss humanitarian who had organized emergency aid services for both French and Austrian wounded soldiers at the Battle of Solferino in 1859. The Geneva Convention of 1864 committed the nations who signed it to caring for war wounded, whether friend or enemy. National Red Cross Societies (or Red Crescent Societies in Muslim countries) have been created to provide humanitarian assistance not only in time of war but also during peacetime, especially when natural disasters occur. Global coordination is now provided by the International Red Cross and Red Crescent Movement (IRCM) and its secretariat in Geneva.

The United Nations has recognized the importance of these international nongovernmental organizations (INGOs) by permitting many of them to have a special affiliation with the United Nations and its agencies through the U.N. Economic and Social Council as provided in the U.N. Charter.[46] Among the INGOs affiliated with the United Nations, the ones most directly relevant to the problems of peace and justice are those whose efforts are focused on issues such as human rights and disarmament. Amnesty International, which won the Nobel Peace Prize for 1977, conducts independent investigations of violations of human rights and consequently has even been permitted to present its findings to the U.N. Human Rights Commission (UNHRC). The same privilege has been extended to another INGO, the International League for Human Rights. In fact, these two organizations were so successful in bringing violations of human rights to the attention of the public that a few national governments retaliated by trying (unsuccessfully) to deprive them of their consultative status with the Economic and Social

Council. In the disarmament area it was the nongovernmental U.S. National Resources Defense Council which worked out an agreement in May 1986 with the Soviet Academy of Sciences whereby scientists were allowed to set up monitoring stations near where the other side conducts nuclear tests.[47] This arrangement proved to suspicious national governments and their military establishments that adherence to governmental agreements restricting nuclear tests could be verified.

A very important event for INGOs occurred at the United Nations when, during the 1978 Special Session on Disarmament, representatives from some of the nongovernmental organizations interested in disarmament were allowed to address the Assembly.[48] These representatives seemed much more eager to move toward a disarmed world than the government representatives of many of the nations. This is why the INGOs are so important. They speak for the welfare of the whole human community. They are really committed to promoting peace and justice. Many of the national governments and their representatives, on the other hand, are interested primarily in protecting national interests, the interests of powerful groups in their countries, and the status quo.

U.S. President Eisenhower once remarked, "I like to believe that people, in the long run, are going to do more to promote peace than are governments. Indeed, I think that people want peace so much that one of these days governments had better get out of the way and let them have it."[49] A good example of the relevance of this observation was what one INGO was able to accomplish in 1997. The International Campaign to Ban Landmines was able to generate enough public concern that the national governments were pushed to adopt a treaty banning the mines even when some of the influential national governments at the United Nations were opposed to such a move. The campaign began at the end of 1991 as an idea in the mind of Robert Muller of the Vietnam Veterans of America. He himself had been the victim of a landmine, and while working with civilians in Cambodia he realized that something more

had to be done than just fitting victims with prosthetics. The International Red Cross and Red Crescent Movement (ICRM) (another INGO as noted above) helped with a worldwide publicity campaign in 1995. Jody Williams of Vermont coordinated the effort and got important support from admired public persons such as Diana, Princess of Wales, and President Nelson Mandela of South Africa. The crucial moment came at an international conference on landmines in Ottawa in October 1996 when Canadian Foreign Affairs Minister Lloyd Axworthy announced that there would be another conference 14 months later when a treaty would be ready for action.[50] The Ottawa Treaty banning anti-personnel mines was adopted on December 3, 1997, and went into force on March 1, 1999. The Campaign to Ban Landmines and its coordinator Jody Williams received the Nobel Peace Prize on October 10, 1997, in a move which the Nobel Committee admitted was designed to induce the national governments into signing the treaty at the December meeting.[51]

Another huge victory for the INGO community occurred in Rome in July 1998.[52] The United Nations General Assembly had decided to convene a conference to consider adopting a treaty to create an International Criminal Court (ICC) where individuals who violate certain international laws would be subject to trial by an international court. The result was adoption of the Rome Statute by a vote of 120 to 7. Its adoption was viewed as a great victory for INGOs in part because the United States, after originally being supportive of the ICC, had become rather opposed to it. The push from the INGO community was crucial in persuading other national governments not to yield to the resistance of the U.S. government.

During this same period the idea was proposed at the United Nations that a world conference on peace should be convened on the occasion of the 100th anniversary of the first Hague Peace Conference of 1899, but some governments such as the United States were opposed. As a result it became doubtful whether there would be such a conference.

Several peace-and-justice groups decided to convene their own conference. The result was the very successful Hague Peace Conference of 1999 sponsored by about a thousand INGOs. More than 8,000 people attended. In his address to the conference U.N. Secretary-General Kofi Annan said:

> The United Nations, as you know, is an association of States. Some unkind people have even called it a trade union of governments. But I have always believed it needs to be much more than that if it is to make any real difference in the world. Not for nothing did our founders begin the Charter of the United Nations with the words "We, the Peoples." They knew that States exist to serve peoples, and not the other way round.[53]

It seems that the INGOs need to push the national governments to do what serves the peoples.

One large group of INGOs affiliated with the United Nations consists of the international religious organizations. These affiliated religious groups include representatives from Catholic and Protestant Christianity, Judaism, Islam, Buddhism, and Hinduism as well as smaller groups such as the Baha'is, the Friends, and the Unitarian-Universalists. Religious groups are important to peace because of their role in the development of attitudes. An important event for peace-supporting religious groups was the Millennium World Peace Summit of Religious and Spiritual Leaders at the United Nations in New York August 28–31, 2000.[54]

Another group of international nongovernmental organizations consist of professional or vocational groups. Still others focus on special hobbies and interests. Many service organizations such as the Rotarians or the Lions have an international scope. There are also athletic organizations which transcend national boundaries. Only a minority of these numerous INGOs are formally related to the United Nations, but they nevertheless are global institutions which tend to break down the nationalism and parochialism which have been such prominent factors in modern warfare.

Still another very important kind of nongovernmental international institution is the transnational business enterprise. These "multinational corporations" tend to promote feelings of human unity. National differences in regulations, tax laws, systems of measurement, language, and the like are nuisances to these international companies. Although transnational businesses are motivated by a desire for profit and may in some ways be perceived as instruments of imperialism, in other ways they facilitate the development of a global perspective and a positive attitude toward human cooperation which is free from nationalistic biases.

A significant problem for many international organizations is the absence of a common neutral global language. Governmental organizations and some transnational business enterprises are able to provide the equipment and personnel to make quick translations available to the participants at their meetings, but this is not true for most of the INGOs. Such organizations are usually not able to afford translations and copies of written material in several different languages. Generally the leaders of the national governments have not shown much interest in this problem, but in 1954, 1985, and 1993, UNESCO passed resolutions urging national governments to teach their students about the world language problem and the international language Esperanto which has been developed to deal with it.[55] Nevertheless it seems that solving the problem by adopting a neutral easier-to-learn language for the global community will depend primarily on the work of a nongovernmental organization, the Universala Esperanto-Asocio.

INGOs have been helped immensely by the development of e-mail and the Internet. It remains to be seen how much impact this new electronic communication technology will have and whether the global community will have more peace and justice because of it.

12. Legal Aspects of the Contemporary Situation

We are likely to suppose that laws can exist only when there is some authorized person or body to make the laws and see that they are enforced; that is, we may believe that there cannot be law without government. Since there is no government above the nations (the United Nations is not a full-fledged government even though it is a political organization), we may conclude that there cannot be anything such as international law which nations are obliged to obey. But such a conclusion would not be correct. International law exists and is recognized as such by national governments even though it is not always obeyed. Our discussion of the legal aspects of the contemporary situation begins by reviewing how international law has evolved. We then turn to the laws of war as an example of international law. After considering the sources of international law, we will discuss the issue of how effective international law can be expected to be in regulating the behavior of nations.

The Nature of International Law

International law rests on the presumption that the relations between nations are somewhat different from the relations between individual persons. Individual persons are not self-sufficient. They need other persons to bring them into existence, to care for them when young, to exchange goods and services with them (no person can take care of all his own needs), and to keep them company. They have sexual desires which lead them to mate with others and parental feelings which cause them to care for their offspring. Until very recently nations, especially larger nations, were presumed to be relatively self-sufficient "organisms." They could be expected to survive if necessary without any interaction with other states. Unlike individuals, states do not need

other states to bring them into existence or to take care of them when young. They do not need other states to help them provide for their needs or to keep them from being lonely. They do not have sexual desires which lead them to interact with other states, nor do they produce son and daughter nations which must be cared for. People must live in societies, but until recently it was supposed that nations do not need to live in a society of nations; they were considered to be able to survive in relative isolation from other nations.

Since people must live in societies to survive and meet their various needs, they can be expected to abide by certain restrictions on their behavior in order to remain members of that society. As societies evolve, these restrictions are codified as the law of the society, and the laws are maintained by religious and political authorities. This law of a society over its own citizens is called *municipal or domestic law* as opposed to the very different type of law, *international law,* which regulates the behavior of nations in their mutual relations. Because of their different situations, individual persons are born into a society and are subject to the laws of that society, while nations are viewed as being subject to no laws except those which they have explicitly accepted as binding on themselves. Another way of saying that states are subject to no externally imposed law is to say that they are *sovereign.*

Although nations are not subject to any laws but those to which they have deliberately and explicitly subjected themselves, they may nevertheless be conquered and destroyed by other nations. Many nations that once existed no longer do. Thus a struggle for survival and power exists among the various nations presently existing. In this contest for survival and power, nations may find it advantageous to enter into agreements (treaties) with other nations. For example, consider a situation where there is an aggressive state more powerful militarily than each of two other neighboring states but not more powerful than both of them together. In this situation the two weaker nations may enter into an agreement not to attack each other and to fight together if the stronger one should attack either one.

What assurance is there that these two nations will live up to their agreement with each other? The situation is somewhat different from a contract between two citizens of the same state where the government will use its power to penalize any party which fails to fulfill its agreement. There is no international or world government over the states to enforce the agreement if either side should try to back out. Still nations make such agreements, and most of the time they live up to them. Why? Because it is in the self-interest of each state to do so. Let us consider the situation in detail. Suppose that you are the leader of the state which finds its treaty partner being attacked. It is in your self-interest to abide by your agreement even though it means going to war. That is because if the more powerful enemy state overcomes your partner, which is likely if you refrain from fighting, then that victorious nation will probably attack you after it has solidified its conquest of your former partner. Consequently, it is better to join in the battle as soon as your partner is attacked than to wait and let the more powerful state conquer your partner and you, one at a time.

There is also some motivation to join in the battle in accord with the treaty merely to establish the fact that your country can in general be counted on to live up to its agreements. If your country should get a reputation for not fulfilling its treaty obligations, then other nations will be reluctant to make other treaties with you in the future. Furthermore, since each nation enters into only those treaties that it wants to make, your country need not make any commitments which it does not intend to keep. Of course, there are cases where states have not lived up to their agreements, but in such cases the governments involved are very eager to provide some justification for not keeping their commitments, thus preserving their honor as treaty-keeping countries. States tend to abide by the treaties into which they enter because it is in their own long-term self-interest to do so.

One of the most basic kinds of agreements nations make with each other is that which provides for reciprocal benefits; that is, each nation agrees to do for the other exactly what the other one agrees to do for it. For example, Nation A may agree to allow the citizens of Nation B to travel through Nation A unhindered if Nation B allows the citizens of Nation A to travel through Nation B unhindered. A good deal of international law depends on this principle of reciprocity. It is the basis, for example, of the law of diplomatic immunity, whereby each nation agrees not to harm or arrest or otherwise interfere with diplomats sent into its territory by other nations. Without such an agreement diplomats might be harassed, put in jail and held for ransom, or even killed. Under such circumstances no diplomats would go to other countries and international communication among nations would be severely handicapped. The principle of reciprocity is also the basis of the laws of war to be considered below. Such rules governing conflict are obeyed because each nation finds it beneficial to abide by them, because only then can the other side also be expected to abide by them.

Certain agreements, such as that providing for the immunity of diplomats from arrest, have become so common that nations may feel it is no longer necessary to stipulate that such an agreement exists when they begin dealing with each other. These and similar widely accepted arrangements in the dealings of countries with one another have come to be viewed as the rules of international *customary law*. To avoid possible misunderstandings about exactly what these customary rules are, however, they were codified in 1961 in the Vienna Convention on Diplomatic Relations.

The sovereignty of the nation is basic in all international law. Even though the rules of international customary law have the weight of wide acceptance and tradition behind them, any country which wishes to renounce them or to join with another nation in some agreements which are not consistent with the customary law may do so. As sovereign, any nation can decide which other nations it will recognize. It can decide to take on obligations to another nation or to an international body such as the United Nations. It can unilaterally declare a previous agreement with another state to be void if in its own opinion the other party has not fulfilled its obligations under the agreement! Furthermore, no nation can be bound by the agreements of other nations. Consequently, even if all nations but one agreed to follow certain principles (for example, that all should completely disarm), that single sovereign nation could still refuse to go along. If other countries were determined to make the agreement universal, their only option would be to physically subdue the recalcitrant country, consequently depriving it of its existence as a sovereign nation. This example also illustrates how some nations may be subject to coercion by other more powerful nations even though, in principle, all nations are sovereign. The reality is that nations are sovereign, but only so long as they can maintain their existence as independent nations.[1]

The Evolution of International Law

It should be evident that international law is not static, but is instead a changing body of obligations which may even differ from nation to nation. Although the counterpart of modern international law was developed among the Greek city-states, present international law has grown out of the dealings of European states with each other in the Middle Ages when nations were generally much smaller than those of today. At one time it was supposed that nations were at war with each other unless they had specifically entered into an agreement to be at peace. Unless there were specific agreements to the contrary, rulers could do as they pleased with any foreigners in their territory. To assure that a treaty would be kept, one party frequently provided the other with hostages who could be killed or otherwise abused if the provisions of the agreement were not fulfilled.

As the European community grew in wealth and technology, certain traditions and expectations with regard to international behavior developed. Frequently, principles of municipal law were extended by analogy to the international situation, especially when the ideologies and institutions of the nations involved were similar. Different views about the nature of international law were used to support efforts to argue for or against the adoption of certain proposed rules. Some philosophers appealed to *natural law*, that is, to the dictates of reason, as a guide to what is required of nations in their relations to each other. Others took what has come to be known as the *positivist position*, maintaining that countries had no obligations to each other except what they had specifically agreed to do in formal treaties. Still others appealed to *custom and tradition* as the basis for determining present obligations of one nation to another.[2]

Regardless of what philosophy of law might be used to provide a rationale for the principles of international law which came to be followed in the European system, the principles adopted were those which were acceptable to the more powerful nations. Thus, freedom of the seas became an accepted principle. Likewise the notion that the discoverer of a land was entitled to claim it for his own country was generally accepted. Any kind of claim which was not challenged by other nations would be regarded as legitimate. The right of conquest over "inferior" native peoples was accepted without question. As these European nations extended their control over the Americas, Africa, and Asia, they took these concepts of international law with them. Needless to say, if the peoples being subdued could have learned about this "international law" which was being used to justify their subjugation, they would not have regarded it as very desirable. It merely served as a device by which the powerful could exploit the weak, all the while maintaining that this was done by a legal process. It also functioned, however, to regulate the dealings of the European countries with each other, so that the danger of war between the colonizers would be minimized.

By the 19th century Europe had become

a society of nations where interactions were not just between one state and another but frequently among several countries. After World War I, President Wilson persuaded the Europeans of the desirability of an international organization to regulate international affairs. The creation of this League of Nations, which was intended to include not only European nations but also nations of other parts of the world, was conceived as being completely consistent with the notion of national sovereignty on which international law was based. Any nation which wanted to join could do so without giving up any of its sovereignty, since all decisions of the League were to be unanimous. No nation could be compelled to join the League or to remain in it once it had joined.

Although the League of Nations in no way encroached on the principle of national sovereignty, it did develop a new principle in international relations, the notion of collective security in the face of an aggressive attack. Until the creation of the League, war had been regarded as a natural and legitimate way of expanding national power and any nation that was attacked was expected to defend itself. The League introduced two very important new ideas into international law, (1) that launching a military attack against another nation was a reprehensible act and (2) that it was the responsibility of sovereign nations to assist other sovereign nations in the enforcement of this principle, even when they were not themselves victims of the aggression.[3] It is obvious from history that nations found ways of avoiding this responsibility when it did not serve their own interests, but nevertheless the principle of the illegitimacy of military aggression and of the responsibility of all nations to act against an aggressor had been stated and at least nominally accepted by the nations which joined the League.

Another important development in international law came when the League of Nations adopted a treaty to create a Permanent Court of International Justice (PCIJ) in 1920. The treaty was ratified in 1921, and the Court started to operate in 1922. For the first time an international tribunal was established to interpret international law as it applied to particular conflicts between countries. If there were any dispute about what was required by international law in a particular situation, the nations now had a third party to which they could turn for an answer if all the disputants involved agreed to do so. This development also meant that there would be some pressure on every nation to accept principles of international law that had been accepted by most other nations. It was still true, however, that no legal principles could be applied by the Permanent Court to any nation which had not accepted the Court's jurisdiction in that particular case.

The establishment of the United Nations after World War II also marked important new developments in international law, at least in terms of what nations committed themselves to doing. The U.N. Security Council, composed of representatives from a small group of countries, was authorized to decide what kind of action should be taken with respect to threats to the peace, breaches of the peace, and acts of aggression. It was also given the right to determine what actions member nations and their military forces should take in such circumstances![4] Although any countries supplying forces must ratify arrangements made by the Security Council, there was an important move away from the notion of national sovereignty in these provisions. The principle enunciated in the U.N. Charter is no longer simply that of collective defense as found in the League Covenant, but rather *internationally organized* collective defense under the direction of the Security Council and its Military Staff Committee. To be sure, no country is compelled to join the United Nations, but once it has signed the Charter it takes on a new kind of obligation not previously found in international law. The existence of such a commitment has led Switzerland to stay out of the United Nations itself, even though it belongs to most of the U.N.'s specialized agencies.

A second new development in international law ushered in by the United Nations concerns the commitment to human rights mentioned in the Charter and developed by the Universal Declaration of Human Rights (1948) and two later treaties, the International Covenant on Economic, Social, and Cultural Rights and the International Covenant on Civil and Political Rights (both entered into effect in 1976). Especially significant for the development of international law is the Protocol to the Covenant on Civil and Political Rights.[5] Nations which adopt this Protocol give their citizens the opportunity to appeal directly to an international body, the U.N. Human Rights Committee, if they feel their human rights are being violated by their own national government. Here, for the first time, the possibility exists of a nation entering into an international agreement which restrains the sovereignty of that government over its own citizens.

A third development in international law since the end of World War II has been the much greater emphasis on violations of international law by individual persons. There has been an effort to delineate and prescribe penalties for those individuals who have broken international law. The wide and early acceptance of the principle of the freedom of the seas resulted in pirates being considered international criminals, and the problem of piracy at sea was almost eliminated in the 19th century (though it has recently become a problem again). Newer kinds of problems are piracy in the air in the form of hijacking airplanes, taking of international hostages, crimes by individuals against diplomats and citizens of other countries, and terrorism by individuals. International conventions have been adopted defining these crimes and indicating what national governments may do when such crimes are committed.

The effort to penalize individuals for breaking international law got a big boost from the Nuremberg trials after World War II, where Nazi leaders were tried as individuals for war crimes. In 1950 the U.N. General Assembly accepted the report of its International Law Commission setting out the seven principles recognized and used in the Nuremberg trials.[6] These principles define what is meant by terms such as "crimes against peace," "war crimes," and "crimes against humanity,"

and they indicate that committing such crimes *cannot be excused* on grounds that one is a Head of State or some other government official or that one is just following orders of the Government or one's superior. Although there continue to be differences of opinion about whether the persons tried at Nuremberg (or later in the similar trials for Japanese leaders in Tokyo) were guilty of breaking some existing law or whether these trials were simply a device used by the victors to humiliate the vanquished, one can also see them as part of a trend toward singling out for punishment those individuals who break international law. In regard to this issue it is worth noting that a couple of the German defendants at Nuremberg were found *not guilty* of violating international law.[7]

The Nuremberg example has not been forgotten. In May 1993 the U.N. Security Council decided to establish an international war crimes tribunal in The Hague, The Netherlands, to prosecute war crimes and human rights violations committed after January 1, 1991, in the former Yugoslavia. In November of 1994 another international *ad hoc* tribunal was created to investigate the genocide which occurred in Rwanda. The U.N. General Assembly held a conference in Rome in July 1998 to work out a treaty for creating a permanent International Criminal Court which would be able to try individuals suspected of committing war crimes, genocide, and crimes against humanity (and also aggression once a definition has been worked out on how this might apply to individuals). The treaty, known as the Rome Statute of the International Criminal Court, was adopted by that UN conference by a vote of 120 to 7 and is now open for signing and ratifying by national governments.[8] It goes into effect after being ratified by 60 countries. As of 31 December 2000 the Rome Statute had been signed by 137 countries and ratified by 27.[9] The United States wants the treaty modified so that U.S. officials and military personnel could not be subject to trials by an international tribunal. But if that principle were to hold for the United States, by the priniciple of reciprocity it would also have to apply to all the other nations of the world, in which case the very idea of an international tribunal to deal with individuals who transgress international law would be nullified. If such a permanent International Criminal Court were created, it might serve to deter leaders from committing these crimes such as genocide much more effectively than just trying to set up *ad hoc* courts after the crimes have been committed. A problem which still needs attention is how to get individuals, especially national leaders with control over military forces, into court for trial or for sentencing after they have been indicted with an appointed lawyer representing them.

This brief survey indicates that international law is developing gradually in the direction of world law, a law which is above the national governments and which puts some restrictions on national sovereignty.[10] Consider the changes that have taken place. While it was once assumed that nations are at war with each other unless they had explicitly signed a truce, it is now assumed that nations are at peace unless they have declared war on each other. Furthermore, fighting a war is now viewed as unacceptable behavior unless it is in response to aggression launched against the nation itself or against some other nation.

The old presuppositions on which international law was based no longer hold. In a modern technological world, nations are no longer self-sufficient. Even a large and powerful nation such as the United States must import large amounts of oil and other raw materials from abroad, and it must sell some of its goods to other nations. In the present world the behavior of every nation makes a great deal of difference to all the others, whether it consists of testing nuclear weapons, adopting high tariffs to protect domestic production, adjusting the exchange rate of its currency, raising the prices on its exports, broadcasting propaganda, putting CFCs which destroy the ozone layer into the atmosphere, or building up its armed forces. Consequently, it no longer makes sense to conceive of nations as essentially isolated "organisms" which once in a while come into contact with their immediate neighbors. A society of nations has been developing and, along with it, a code of conduct suitable for such a society.[11]

Laws of War

One of the most interesting aspects of international law is that even when nations are engaged in open hostilities against each other they still follow rules, the laws of war, which restrain their behavior. How is this possible? It stems from the same principle as all international law, namely, mutual self-interest. For example, in war both sides will experience situations where some of their military forces are so outnumbered that they will want to surrender rather than be slaughtered. Consequently, a rule of war exists by which armed forces are permitted to surrender rather than being killed. Furthermore, it is to the advantage of each side to keep observing this rule. If one side starts slaughtering opponents who have surrendered, it can expect the same to happen to its own personnel who are captured. The rules of war are designed to keep war from becoming even more brutal than it otherwise would be.[12]

A fundamental distinction made in the rules of warfare is that between military personnel (combatants) and civilians (noncombatants). It is presumed that the contest in war is between the military forces of the nations involved and that the aim of warfare is military victory. According to this way of thinking, there is no point in killing civilians because it does not contribute to military victory to do so. Since the governments on both sides want to preserve their civilian populations from any more harm than necessary, the rules of war indicate that it is acceptable to try to kill military personnel (as well as to destroy the armaments they use or could use) but that it is improper to try to kill civilians (or to destroy the equipment they use for farming or other civilian pursuits). Trains and ships and airplanes carrying military personnel or military supplies are fair game, but others are not. Following this same outlook, prisoners, wounded military personnel and those who care for them, pilots who have parachuted from their aircraft, survivors of sunken ships, and the like are not to be attacked since they no longer constitute a military threat.[13]

In modern warfare the distinction between military and civilian sectors of a nation's wartime efforts has become very blurred. Whole nations are mobilized for warfare. The high school student of today is the soldier of tomorrow, so why wait until he gets into uniform before trying to kill him? Some of the food which the farmer grows may go to civilians, but part also goes to the military, who would have a hard time continuing the war without it. The workers who are producing tanks, airplanes, ships, and ammunition are civilians, but the goods they produce are as crucial to the continuation of the fighting as the soldiers who use them. The wounded soldier of today is the already-trained functioning soldier of tomorrow, so why wait until he has recovered before trying to kill him?

Also, if we look at war carefully, we see that it is the governments rather than the military forces which are ultimately responsible for carrying on the war. If the civilian population is bombed and otherwise intimidated, won't they eventually pressure their own government to stop the war by surrendering? Why not make the population of the other side suffer just as the other side will cause suffering to one's own population if the area where they are living were to be conquered? Such questions came to the fore especially during World War II when aerial bombing made it possible to attack far behind the front lines. Furthermore, now that nuclear weapons with their extensive destructiveness are available, it becomes hard to see how an attack could any longer be pinpointed on military targets even if the attacker wished to do so. The present planning for the use of strategic nuclear weapons is not inhibited very much by any wish not to harm civilians. On July 8, 1996, the International Court of Justice (ICJ or World Court) responded to a 1994 resolution of the UN General Assembly asking for an advisory opinion on the legality of using or threatening to use nuclear weapons. The result was a 7-to-7 vote that such action "would generally be contrary to the rules of international law applicable in armed conflict" but that "the Court cannot conclude definitely whether the threat or use of nuclear weapons would be lawful or unlawful in an extreme circumstance of self-defense, in which the very survival of a State would be at stake."[14] Whether the issue is nuclear weapons or other weapons and strategies of war, the traditional distinction between military targets on the one hand and civilian areas and personnel on the other is being completely subordinated to the question of what war aims are being pursued. Yet, if this distinction between military and civilian targets is eliminated, then those international laws protecting prisoners and the wounded on grounds that they are not presently active members of the enemy's military forces would seem to lose their justification too.

If there cannot be humane war, why not try to prohibit war itself as inhumane? An effort to renounce war as an instrument of national policy was made in 1928 in the form of the Treaty for the Renunciation of War (also called "The Pact of Paris" and "The Kellogg-Briand Pact"). Unfortunately, this treaty did not stop World War II from occurring (though it did serve as a basis for some of the indictments of German leaders at the Nuremberg trials). The U.N. Charter also contains statements renouncing war, and even renouncing the *threat* of using force![15] The trouble is that international laws of war have not always been obeyed during war, and there is no basis to expect that an international law against starting a war would be observed any more faithfully. In the final analysis, nations tend to act in terms of their perception of their own national interest; and when obeying international law comes into conflict with national interest, it is national interest which prevails.

The Sources of International Law

We have already noted that international law differs from municipal law in that there is no authorized person or body which enacts or enforces it and that international law evolves as other things change. We have mentioned in passing some of the sources of international law, but will now explore this issue in more depth. Suppose that you were a member of the International Court of Justice hearing a case. Since there is no world legislature whose acts would produce world law, where can you turn to discover what the international laws are that might bear on the case at hand?

Article 38 of the Statute of the International Court of Justice spells out precisely what sources are to be used.[16] First, you could turn to "international conventions [including treaties], whether general or particular, establishing *rules expressly recognized by the contesting states*." Note that it does not matter what principles of international law may have been accepted by other nations. All that counts are the principles explicitly acceded to by the parties involved in the present dispute.

Second, you could refer to "international custom, as evidence of a general practice accepted as law." As we noted earlier, there are certain principles involved in the relationships between nations which have become so common that they are assumed rather than being written into treaties. Many of these rules which make up international customary laws were codified in the 1961 Vienna Convention on Diplomatic Relations.

Third, you could use "the general principles of law recognized by civilized nations." An example of such a general principle is the idea of reciprocity, the principle that whatever rights a nation claims for itself must also be recognized as rights for other nations too. It is understood that this source of law is to be used only when the matter cannot be resolved using the first two sources. It is only the very general principles of law which are accepted by all the major legal systems of the world that are relevant. The main point of specifying this source of international law is to preclude a situation where the Court could not decide an obvious issue because the principle involved had not come up for consideration in earlier treaties or conflicts.

Fourth, appeal could be made to "judicial decisions" previously rendered by international, and even national, courts and to "the teaching of the most highly qualified publicists of the various nations." Scholars of international law are constantly publishing arguments for one or another position, and if there were a consensus among these experts on international law from various legal traditions, then their opinions might be used to support a judgment. Still, it must be remembered that appeals to previous judicial decisions and to the opinion of experts are "subsidiary means for the determination of rules of law" and consequently become significant only when the first three sources leave the issue unresolved.

One of the most interesting sources of international law is that which grows out of treaties and covenants in a secondary way. For example, states which have joined the United Nations have signed a treaty (the U.N. Charter) upon entering the organization. The Charter establishes the whole U.N. structure, including the General Assembly. Suppose the General Assembly unanimously passes a resolution dealing with a particular aspect of international law, for example, that the oceans are "the common heritage of mankind" rather than the property of any nation. If none of the nations protested or voted against this principle when given the opportunity to do so, it can be assumed that all have accepted it, just as if they had signed a treaty containing this declaration. No nation could later claim during a judicial proceeding that it had not accepted it. On the other hand, if a given nation had voted *against* that declaration, it would *not* be obliged to conform to that declaration no matter how many other nations in the General Assembly had voted for it. Thus, there is no assumption that the General Assembly can make international law. The situation is rather that nations put themselves on record when they cast their votes in the U.N. and that these votes might later be taken by the International Court of Justice to indicate acceptance of a measure acted on by the General Assembly.

Enforcing International Law

Just as there is no legislature or other authority to make international law, so also there is no police force or other agency to enforce it. What is to be done if a decision has been rendered by the International Court of Justice and a nation refuses to abide by the decision? Ideally, the UN Security Council should coordinate enforcement efforts, but it is also conceivable that the UN General Assembly might recommend measures to the member states of the United Nations or that individual nations might act on their own. In any case, efforts to enforce the decision might include cutting off trade, severing diplomatic relations, eliminating international exchanges with regard to mail or transportation, or initiating military action.

How effective would such UN enforcement efforts be? It seems to depend a great deal on the power and self-sufficiency of the "outlaw" country and the level of support among the more powerful nations for enforcing the sanctions. If the country which refused to abide by the Court's decision was a weaker nation and there was enthusiastic support for enforcement among all the big powers, the actions suggested above would undoubtedly be effective; there probably would be no need to go beyond the imposition of economic sanctions. On the other hand, if the country which refused to abide by the Court's decision was a powerful country or had even a single powerful ally who would not support sanctions against it, efforts to enforce the decision would be vetoed in the Security Council or thwarted in some other way. Another aspect of trying to enforce a decision against a nation-state is the fact that carrying out sanctions, such as cutting off trade, might be more disadvantageous to the other nations than to the nation supposedly being punished. Such sanctions might also turn out to be much more harmful to the innocent members of the country than to the leaders, who might well be able to live comfortably despite the sanctions. Consider the situation in Iraq under Saddam Hussein in the 1990s.

Even though we might abhor the fact that international law will be much more of a constraining factor on weak nations than on strong ones, we should not forget that unfortunately the same thing is true to some extent even within domestic legal systems. Very wealthy individuals, politically influential people, corporations, labor unions, and the like have enough power that legislatures and courts are much more protective of their interests than of the interests of poor, powerless, unorganized people. What makes the national political and judicial systems as workable as they are is that even the most powerful individuals and groups constitute only a small proportion of the nation as a whole and thus their capacity to resist the dictates of the common interest is restricted. On the other hand, on the international scene the United States alone accounts for over a quarter of the world's production of goods and services. Its allies in Western Europe and Japan account for another quarter. How could any world organization hope to endorse decisions to which the United States and its allies were intensely opposed? Perhaps the only hope for either international law or world law is to deal with individual persons rather than large groups or nations. Then the problem of enforcement becomes much more manageable.

We should not suppose, however, that the only motivation which national governments have for obeying international law is the possible coercive activities of other nations. As noted previously, another important motive is long-range self-interest. International law has been built on the basis of agreements which are mutually satisfying to the nations entering into the treaties. Any loss which may come from the application of international law in one situation will probably be small compared with the gains that can be made in the long run by making use of international law. Consequently, although nations can be expected to struggle to their utmost to advance their national interests, they can also be expected to exercise some restraint instead of openly violating international law. For the smaller, less powerful nations the gains from a strengthened system of international law will be even greater than for the more powerful countries. In this connection it is worth mentioning that the UN General Assembly, at the instigation of the less developed countries, declared the 1990s to be "The Decade of International Law."

A third motivation which national governments have for obeying international law is furnished by the relation of such governments to their own citizens. In many democratic nations, and even in some non-democratic ones, there is a concern for the morality of law which will be marshaled against any national government which blatantly transgresses it. In the 1930s when the governments of Great Britain and France were making deals with Mussolini to try to lure him onto their side against Hitler, even though the Covenant of the League of Nations required them to resist Italy's aggression in Ethiopia, they had to keep what they were doing secret from their own people.[17] They knew that a substantial proportion of their own citizenry backed the League and its principles of collective defense against nations engaging in aggression. In 1974, when OPEC quadrupled the price of oil, there was some talk of using military force to conquer the oil fields of the Middle East, but such a blatant use of force and indifference to international law would probably have generated mass protests in the United States and other Western democracies as well as among the allies of the conquered countries.

National governments must also keep up at least the appearance of abiding by international law because of the dangerous example they would provide to their own citizens if they openly defied established principles of international law. Although there is a considerable difference between municipal law and international law, the subtleties of this distinction will not be apparent to most of the citizenry. Consequently, most national governments will do everything they can to avoid being perceived as violators of international law because they do not wish to provide an example of lawlessness to their own people.

Finally, it should be kept in mind that there is one way in which the enforcement of international law is not as much of a problem as the enforcement of municipal law, namely, that in international law each nation is subject only to those rules which it has explicitly accepted as binding, while in municipal law individual persons are subject to rules which they did not personally consent to obey but which were imposed on them by the government. A nation need not commit itself to any rule that it doesn't intend to follow. This situation means that nations will have fewer legal obligations but will usually abide by the ones to which they have committed themselves. An obvious exception, however, is the situation where nations have just lost a war and are coerced into signing agreements which they would not make voluntarily. Under these circumstances they may not feel obliged to fulfill the terms which have been imposed on them. Germany's readiness to follow Hitler in ignoring the Versailles Treaty would be a good example of such an exception.

Regardless of theoretical considerations, however, one cannot be very optimistic about the enforcement of international law after what happened with regard to Iran in 1979. The Iranian government acquiesced in the seizure of American diplomatic personnel and property by some of its own citizens in direct violation of the principle of diplomatic immunity, one of the oldest principles of international law. The International Court of Justice ruled unanimously that Iran had violated the 1961 Vienna Convention on Diplomatic Relations, which Iran had signed. Nevertheless, no international sanctions were adopted against Iran, even though it was not a superpower or the close ally of a superpower and all diplomats everywhere were threatened by the weakening of this particular international law. The fact that many countries were dependent on Iran for oil may have also been an important factor. Nevertheless, the failure of the international community to enforce the decision of the International Court against Iran was a disaster from the point of view of promoting future reliance on international law and the International Court of Justice. At the same time it should be recognized that the decision of the Court may have been a factor in Iran's being persuaded by Algeria to eventually release the American hostages they had taken.

From a historical point of view we can see how international law is gradually becoming more important in international affairs and in the behavior of nation-states. We are witnessing a momentous shift to a readiness to deal with individual persons who violate international law. At the same time there is a great resistance to any rapid movement in the direction of a global legal regime. The less developed countries are very fearful that it would be a means by which the rich and powerful countries could control even what goes on within the boundaries of other countries while the powerful countries such as the United States fear that such a regime would provide a means by which the poor and weak countries might be able to limit what the rich and powerful can do.

Part Four.
Proposals for Solving the War Problem

13. Reforming the Attitudes of Individuals

In Part Four we are making an important shift from focusing on facts about what has happened and is happening to a new kind of question: What *should be done* to deal with the war problem? It seems that any *prescription* about the proper remedies should be based on a *diagnosis* of why wars occur. We have already discussed the causes of war in Part Two. The information in Part Three should help to evaluate those various theories about why wars occur. In a general way, we can classify the various alleged causes of war into four groups: (1) wars begin in the minds and the ensuing attitudes of those *individuals* who decide to participate in or support wars; (2) wars result from the *basic structure* or *ideological foundations* of some war-prone, unjust *national governments;* (3) wars occur because of the *policies,* foreign and domestic, followed by national governments; and (4) wars are due to the law-of-the-jungle *nature of the international system* in which national governments must operate. Of course, wars are very complex events and there are probably many different kinds of causes of war in the sense of being contributory factors. Consequently, dealing with the war problem will probably require several different kinds of actions. One's *prescription* for what should be done to deal with the problem should be based on one's *diagnosis* of why wars occur.

The four chapters which make up Part Four are arranged according to four general *classes of prescriptions* on how to deal with the war problem, each related to one of the classes of alleged causes mentioned in the previous paragraph. Within each class or group of pre-scriptions are *particular proposals,* some of which might be combined with each other and some of which are blatantly incompatible with each other. Our aim is to explore all the alternatives so that you are in a better position to evaluate particular proposed prescriptions. In fact, examining these various prescriptions may even lead you to reexamine your thinking about the causes of war. As noted above, there should be a direct relation between what you maintain causes wars and your prescription(s) for moving toward a solution of the war problem.

This present chapter is focused on modifying the *attitudes of individuals* as a way of dealing with the war problem. There are different specific proposals about what attitudes need to be developed, and you might very well agree with some proposals and disagree with others. You might agree with all of them, or you might think that none of these proposals are worthwhile because you might believe that the *attitudes of individuals* are not a very important factor in war. In that case, you will be more interested in the subsequent chapters on what should be done to promote peace. Chapter 14 discusses three specific prescriptions which are quite different from each other but all of which fit into the general category of prescriptions addressed to changing the *basic structure* or *ideological basis* of *some national governments* which are alleged to be the trouble-makers who cause war. Chapter 15 contains a wide range of proposals, some of which are diametrically opposed to each other but which nevertheless all fit into the category of prescriptions focused on what *policies national governments should follow* in order to avoid war. Chapter 16 also contains a variety of proposals, but they have in common the fact that they are addressed to the issue of changing *the way the international system works* as the key to having a peaceful world.

The preamble of the constitution of the United Nations Educational, Scientific, and Cultural Organization (UNESCO) states: "Since wars begin in the minds of men, it is in the minds of men that the defenses of peace must be constructed." In one way or another, education seems to be at least part of the solution to almost any social problem. But when we speak of education, we must beware of jumping to the conclusion that education is only for young people or that it refers only to what happens within school classrooms. Education refers to all teaching of some by others in all kinds of situations. Most of our attitudes come from our parents, our close associates, and the mass media. Teachers are close associates of their students only for a brief period of time. Consequently, although it is to be hoped that teachers and the formal educational system of which they are a part can be instrumental in furthering the objectives discussed below, it would be a gigantic mistake to believe that the institutionalized educational system, by itself, can do a great deal to reform the attitudes of individuals. If the attitudes of individuals are to be reformed in a manner that will make war less likely, many persons in the society will need to take part. The efforts of the mass media will be especially important, and several kinds of attitudes will need to be addressed. Furthermore, it is not only the attitudes of the masses which need to be reformed but even more importantly the attitudes of the leaders.

Interest in Social Issues Including International Affairs

Attitudes about the importance of certain kinds of events are affected by how much we know about them. It is true that when we think that something is important we make an effort to find out about it, but it is also true

that we tend to regard as unimportant anything about which we know very little. Consequently, the development of attitudes and interests depends to some extent on the knowledge we acquire, especially when young. If this knowledge is only about our own immediate family and close friends, we may unconsciously come to believe that what is happening to others in other places is unimportant. If we know about what is happening in a series of television programs but have no knowledge about or interest in what is happening in the real world around us, we may form the mistaken opinion that such a real world doesn't matter much. The same principle holds at another level, too: If we learn only about our own nation and its history and traditions, we may unconsciously come to believe that what has happened and is happening to people in other lands is unimportant. Interest in the problems of the larger society and of the global community is not inborn. It must be developed in younger people and nurtured in older people.[1]

Most injustice that exists in society is the result not of a deliberate intent to harm others but of indifference. People are very much aware of their own personal and family problems, but a special effort is required to develop a sensitivity to the problems of others and to the problems faced by the society as a whole. The root cause of much social injustice is the widespread attitude of indifference to the difficulties of others. Consequently, a just society requires that its members acquire an interest in the problems of other individuals and in the problems which confront the group as a whole, whether that group is one's town, one's country, or one's planetary community.

It is important for peace and justice at the global level that this interest go beyond domestic issues.[2] People need to be informed about international affairs and about the problems faced by other nations as well as those confronting their own country. They need to know about governments and other institutions and about the various ideas and ideologies that motivate people. If we never learn about the competing interests and the various outlooks which guide social decision-making, we probably will never understand the significance of the individual events which are reported in the news. Also if we have never been encouraged to think of war as a problem for humanity to solve, we will probably not be aware of how particular political decisions help or hinder the solution of this problem.

Skepticism and Tolerance

Developing awareness about social issues, the problems of different nations and different groups, social philosophy, and the war problem is not sufficient, however. It is also important that certain attitudes be developed if the war problem is to be solved. A crucial one is an attitude of skepticism toward what others tell us and toward the beliefs we have already adopted. We are credulous creatures. We tend to believe whatever we are told unless there is some good reason to doubt it, and sometimes we believe what we are told even when there is reason to doubt it. We are also creatures of habit. If there should be a conflict between one idea and another, we tend to believe whichever idea we happened to have heard first. We find it difficult to discard any belief we have once held, and the longer we have held it the harder it is to give up for another one, even one which may be more logical.

It is because of our natural credulity and our natural dislike for changing our views that we must make a special effort to develop a skeptical outlook in ourselves and others. Although what people tell us is generally a reflection of what they believe to be true, no one is infallible. Consequently, at least part of what we are told by others is false. We are not infallible, either. Thus it follows that at least some of our own present beliefs are mistaken. Of course, if we knew which of our ideas are false, we would discard them. The only rational procedure is to be somewhat skeptical both about our own beliefs and the beliefs conveyed to us by others.

Skepticism is especially important for solving the problem of war because wars often have an ideological basis. There is usually an effort by the leaders of each nation or social

group to impose their "obviously correct" views about religious, economic, political, or other matters on the rest of their own group as well as on other societies. In each nation or group, people come to be convinced of the correctness of their own beliefs because those beliefs were the ones they heard first and most often from persons very dear to them. They just *know* that their own views about religion and about the ideal political and economic arrangements in a society are true. The views of others, on the other hand, have come to their attention only late in life, if at all. These views are unfamiliar and are often conveyed by strangers or books written by unknown authors, so it is assumed that they are mistaken. Thus each side, being composed of people who are credulous creatures of habit, is sure that it is fighting for truth and justice. Most people in each nation or social group believe themselves to be the agents of good and the enemy to be the embodiment of evil. Even violence seems justified since the issue is perceived as a struggle of truth and justice against falsehood and wickedness.

One way of trying to prevent this situation is for all people everywhere to develop skeptical attitudes toward all their own beliefs and toward the "information" which is being conveyed to them. Prejudices which differ from our own and the propagandistic nature of devices used to spread ideas with which we disagree are obvious to us. What is necessary is that we be alert to the fact that we also have our own prejudices (most of them learned in our earliest years), and that the ideas which we have been led to accept may also have been spread by propagandistic devices. We need to examine even our most basic beliefs to determine whether they have a sound foundation or are merely reflections of prejudices. Even after we have critically examined our beliefs, we must continue to keep in mind that we may be mistaken.

Closely related to the attitude of skepticism is the attitude of tolerance for beliefs and practices which are different from our own. If we are absolutely sure of the correctness of our own beliefs and practices, then it may seem appropriate to impose these beliefs and practices on others even if they are not willingly accepted. If we happen to be in a position where we cannot impose them on others, we still are tempted to make fun of different beliefs and practices. But we need to combat these inclinations. Just learning about the various beliefs and practices of others at an early age will help to make them seem less strange, but special efforts should also be made to develop an attitude of appreciation of the different perspectives of others. Such an attitude does not develop automatically. It is the natural inclination of people to be intolerant of beliefs and practices different from their own, and this tendency supports a readiness to engage in wars against foreigners or others who differ in some way. Consequently, the deliberate development of an attitude of tolerance for those who are different is one instrument for making wars less likely.[3]

Taking Personal Responsibility

In social situations, we often feel that we must do something because it is expected of us or because that is what everyone else is doing, even though we know that we shouldn't do it and wouldn't do it if it weren't for the social pressure. Even in very serious situations we may feel constrained to do something we really don't want to do because our role requires us to do it. An important attitude to be developed is the conviction that I am personally responsible for what I do and that such accountability can never be nullified by excuses such as "everybody else was doing it" or "that's what was expected of me."

In the previous chapter we briefly talked about the seven principles used at Nuremberg in the war trials after World War II. Those principles make it clear that all individuals are accountable for their behavior and that one cannot be excused on the grounds that someone else (even someone in authority) told me to do it or that I had to do it because that was what was expected of me. If the behavior is such that you will not be ashamed of having done it later, then it is O.K. to do it. Following orders may be a good thing or a bad thing. The crucial question is not whether someone told you to do something or whether everyone else was doing it. The crucial question is whether the action was right or wrong, whether it is something that you will be proud of or ashamed of when you think about it later.

Anyone who doubts the importance of this attitude of taking personal responsibility and its relation to the problem of war must read the last chapter, "Epilogue," of the seventh edition of John Stoessinger's *Why Nations Go to War*.[4] Although the general thesis of this book is that individual leaders and their decisions are the critical factor in the outbreak of war, in that final chapter Stoessinger switches the focus to other individuals and the importance of their decisions. He tells how, as a young Jew seeking to escape from Prague in the early 1940s, his life was saved on two different occasions because some individual did what was right rather than just following orders or doing what they were expected to do or doing what everyone else was doing. Professor Stoessinger concludes that chapter as follows:

> As a teacher of young college students, I see now that I must teach a most important truth: that there is no such thing as collective guilt, and that, in dark times, there are always men and women who will confront evil, even in its most absolute form, and reaffirm our humanity. In the depths of the abyss, moral courage still survives, and at times even prevails.[5]

Stoessinger's story is not unique. Other Jews were also saved by the heroic actions of non-Jews who risked their own lives to do what was right. In fact, at Yad Vashem, the holocaust museum in Jerusalem, there is a long avenue of trees, each of which honors some person or couple or family who risked death to save Jews. In December 1995, there were 1172 such trees, and more are added from time to time as new information becomes available.[6] It is a sad commentary on human nature, however, that there are so few of them.

Reluctance to Use Violence

Another attitude which needs to be fostered to promote peace is the reluctance to resort to violence in situations of disagreement and conflict. Each of us has ideas of what is true and right and good (with what is good often being taken as equivalent to what is good *for me*). We regularly find others disagreeing with us. When we are in a position to do so, it is tempting to coerce the other party into following our point of view. The mistreatment of children, old people, minority groups, and women testifies to the readiness of people to use violence to impose their will on others. But the attitudes of skepticism and tolerance just discussed imply another way of handling conflict situations. The use of violence overlooks the possibility that our own ideas may be mistaken. It also neglects the consequence that resentment is aroused in those who are coerced into acting against their own will.

A nonviolent approach to conflict situations will involve a recognition that one's own beliefs about what is true or right may need to be corrected, as well as an effort to appreciate the point of view of the other party. The conflict situation can thus be viewed as an opportunity for learning and developing a wider range of concern. The opportunity for learning can best be exploited if each party can state not only its position but also the grounds or reasons for this position. Each party to the conflict should be free to raise objections to beliefs which it thinks are mistaken. Ideally, the parties would become aware of the weaknesses in their own positions and the strengths in those of their opponents. Eventually a compromise of some sort may be possible. Each party should also develop a sensitivity to the concerns of the other. In conflict situations it is desirable to engage in role-playing where each party argues for the opponent's position. This exercise helps develop an awareness of the interests of the other party. Undoubtedly, this nonviolent approach to conflict situations is not one which will occur automatically. If we want life to be more peaceful, we will need to make an effort to have both children and adults learn about it and want to use it.

Although peace requires that people learn to develop a reluctance to use violence in conflict situations, many young people today are being taught just the opposite.[7] Boys are still often told that the "manly" way of resolving differences of opinion is to use their fists against those who disagree. Propagandists urge their followers to stop at nothing in promoting their cause. On television and in movies violence is glorified as the quick and proper way of resolving conflict, and the long-term consequences of using violence in conflict situations are conveniently neglected. In discussing international relations, many government leaders and media representatives assume without even considering alternatives that the use of force and threats of force is the only proper way to handle conflicts between nations. The question of what is right or just is often not asked; the only issue is how to coerce the other party into accepting one's own terms. When many people feel that violence and threats of violence are the proper way to resolve differences among them, there is little hope of avoiding war and eliminating arms races. On the other hand, if there were a general feeling that conflict situations should be resolved by nonviolent means, the chance for peace would be much greater.

One way of reducing the readiness to use violence in social situations would be to expand public knowledge about the philosophy and techniques of nonviolent resistance and to promote a wider awareness of some of the situations where nonviolent actions have brought about social change. A widespread familiarity with the teachings and lives of Mohandas Gandhi and Martin Luther King, Jr., would provide a good beginning.[8] It would also help if people had more information about other political conflicts where people used nonviolence to protect themselves against attempted coercion.[9] Peace on all levels will be furthered if people develop a negative attitude toward using violence to deal with conflict situations.

Unselfishness

It is a commonplace that warfare would be greatly reduced if people were less greedy and selfish. It seems that no matter how much people have, they always want more. The situation is aggravated in a society where advertising creates wants in order to sell goods and services to those who have the money to buy them. People who never thought about a midwinter vacation of a week or two in Hawaii or the Caribbean may, as the result of advertising, find themselves not only wanting such a vacation but positively needing one. Furthermore, the vicissitudes of life are such that it is impossible for most people to have enough insurance and savings to take care of all the emergencies that might arise. Faced with what appears to be unlimited "needs" for our own welfare, it is difficult for most people to be much concerned about the welfare of others. The expenditure of $1,000 or more for a vacation seems sensible, while a gift of half that amount to educate illiterate people in other parts of the world might lead some to think that the giver had lost his sense of the worth of money. Our own "needs" seem pressing and urgent, while those of others seem insignificant and remote. It is certainly natural to be more concerned about ourselves than others, but a peaceful world will require people to develop more concern for others and a more realistic appraisal of their own needs than what is generally found at present among the affluent persons of the world. Those who are well off need to remind themselves regularly that no one has chosen where to be born or whether to be rich or poor. Any one of us might just as well have been born in a poor country where the threat of starvation and death from disease is a daily reality.[10]

It is not only individual selfishness which must be tempered but group selfishness as well. One of the interesting aspects of society is the existence of small groups, such as families, whose members display the greatest unselfishness toward each other but who are reluctant to assist those outside this group. For example, parents may sacrifice so that their children can acquire a college or university education but will be reluctant to give a penny so that other children can learn the very basic skills of reading and writing. They will make sure that their own parents are cared for but at the same time display complete indifference toward other old people who may be in much more desperate need of help. In this situation, the individuals may be very unselfish, but the family group could well be described as selfish.

While generosity confined to the family group is a natural human trait, peace will be much more likely when not just individuals but also families (and other larger groups such as nations, too) become much less selfish.

Globalism and Humatriotism

We have just considered the needs for families and other groups to become less selfish not only as individuals but also as groups. Another way of handling what is essentially the same problem is to expand the "we" group, the group with which we identify. The attitude of identifying with members of our family and with close friends seems to develop naturally. With a bit of effort, nations are able to extend considerably the group with which the individual identifies. When there is a single language, a single cultural heritage, and a racially homogeneous group, the identification with the nation is likely to be easily established, but even in nations such as Switzerland, where a variety of languages and cultures exists, it is possible to develop a sense of "we" which extends to the whole country.

An obvious question arises. If people can be taught to identify with all the others in a heterogeneous nation, why can't the same devices be used to stimulate identification with all the people of the world? If a national flag can be used in helping to develop a sense of identification with the nation, why not use the U.N. flag to help develop a sense of identification with the whole global society? If nationalism can be furthered by a pledge of allegiance to the national government, why not use a pledge of allegiance to the whole world in order to further a commitment to the global community?[11] If nationalism can be developed by celebrating national holidays, why can't a sense of globalism be developed by celebrating world holidays?

A step in the direction of a world holiday has already been taken by the United Nations General Assembly. In December 1971, a resolution was adopted 63 to 6 proclaiming U.N. Day, October 24, to be an international holiday and recommending that it be observed as a public holiday by all nations which are members of the U.N. Dorothy Schneider of St. Louis, who was instrumental in persuading delegates from various nations to introduce this resolution, has now shifted her efforts to getting the United States to follow the recommendation and make U.N. Day a national holiday in the United States.[12] A somewhat related annual event in the United States and some other countries which helps to develop an attitude of globalism is the annual collection for the U.N. Children's Fund (UNICEF) conducted near the end of October.

Of course, the fact that such devices *can* be used to develop a sense of globalism does not mean that they *will* be used. In fact, the persistence of the system of sovereign nations and the enduring possibility of war mean that national governments, schools, and mass media which are directly or indirectly under their control will probably continue to try to develop *patriotism* (loyalty to the homeland) rather than *humatriotism*[13] (loyalty to the human race). National governments can't afford to have their soldiers hesitating to kill enemy soldiers just because they are also human beings. In case of war they need young people who are unquestioningly loyal to them, not to the whole human race. If a world government were instituted over the national governments, the situation would be different. Then an effort could more readily be made to develop humatriotism because national governments would no longer have a potential need for soldiers. It is worth noting, for example, that the state governments in the United States formally control the educational system but do not need to develop intense loyalty to their own state governments because they have no need for soldiers to fight against other states. The irony of the situation is that a world government probably will not be feasible until there are large numbers of people who have already adopted an attitude of loyalty to the world community. It seems then that the development of humatriotism cannot wait until after a world government is formed. Loyalty to the whole human race is needed now.

It is sometimes argued that creating a sense of globalism will not work in the same way as creating a sense of national loyalty because there will be no out-group or enemy to serve as a stimulus for group cohesion. It is claimed that the love for one's own group (amity) must be accompanied by the hatred of some enemy group (enmity). For example, Robert Ardrey says, "The primate amity-enmity complex cannot exist without enemies."[14] Earlier, Sigmund Freud had observed, "It is always possible to unite considerable numbers of men in love towards one another, so long as there are still some remaining as objects for aggressive manifestations."[15] Historically, nationalism seems to have been strongest when there has been a traditional enemy, such as occurred when Germany and France confronted each other in the 19th and first half of the 20th centuries. On the other hand, there are cases where national pride and patriotism are strong even in the absence of any recent external enemies; Switzerland and Sweden are but two examples. Also, in a study directed specifically to the topic of loyalty, Harold Guetzkow concluded: "Although an out-group is often useful in serving as a foil in the development of in-group solidarity, it is not a necessary condition for the development of group loyalty."[16] It is at least possible that people can learn to view war, huge military expenditures, wasted resources, pollution, diseases, and natural disasters as "the enemy" of the human race against which they can direct their aggressive tendencies.[17]

In our earlier discussion of nationalism, we noted that the existence of different languages within a country, though not an insurmountable obstacle to building a sense of national identity, nevertheless constitutes a hindrance to that goal. Not being able to communicate directly with other people because of language differences tends to block the process of identification. If people cannot read the same materials or listen to the same radio and television broadcasts, they may develop very different attitudes and beliefs about the world. There is also a basis for suspicion when some people are speaking to one another and others cannot understand what they are saying. It follows that one thing which might help a great deal to develop a sense of community among all the peoples of the world is the use of the same language everywhere.

It is unlikely that people will stop using the language with which they are familiar and start using another. What seems more realistic is that people all over the world could concentrate on learning the same second language. In that way people everywhere could retain their own native languages but at the same time speak directly with people from other countries without the assistance of a translator. It is possible that everyone in the world could learn to use a national language such as Chinese or English or Spanish, but the ideal situation would be a world language which is no one's native language. In the late 19th century, with this very thought in mind, a Polish oculist named Ludwig Zamenhof developed an international language called Esperanto. This artificially constructed language is based on a vocabulary drawn from a mixture of European languages and has an easily learned, completely regular grammar and phonetic spelling. Interested individuals and groups worldwide have devoted themselves to spreading the use of Esperanto. It is also used in some international broadcasting and international publications.[18] The efforts at the League of Nations in the early 1920s to have Esperanto adopted as an official language did not succeed. Similar efforts at the United Nations have so far met with a similar fate, but UNESCO has passed resolutions commending the work of the Esperantists in 1954 and 1985.

Whether it be Esperanto or some other language, it would be helpful in the long-term development of the world community if the United Nations would take action, declaring some single language to be the one official language of the future.[19] It could be determined that at some definite future date (perhaps 25 or 50 years hence) this language would be the only one to be used at the United Nations and in official international communications. Starting immediately, young people all over the world could be taught this language in addition to their own. Costly translation facilities and multiple printings of all documents could then be avoided.[20] Maximum use of the technological capabilities of worldwide communication and transportation systems would no longer be hindered by the absence of a single language. Everyone in the whole world could communicate directly with everyone else.

In the absence of such deliberate action by the United Nations it is still possible that some single world language may develop. In fact, English is rapidly becoming such a language not only because it is the official language in many countries but also because of the present influence of American technology and business. The difficulty with English as the world language, in addition to its eccentric spelling and other irregularities, is that such a development carries with it overtones of cultural imperialism. Not only the English language, but also the cultural traditions and values which are carried in the language, would be thrust on everyone. A global ethnically neutral language like Esperanto would avoid this problem. Even though its vocabulary is fundamentally European, Esperanto has from the beginning carried with it a spirit of international cooperation and has been accepted enthusiastically by Japanese, Chinese, Koreans and other non–Europeans.

The crucial point, however, is the central role that a single world language, whether Esperanto or some other language, would have in creating a sense of world community. If somehow a single world language could be decided upon, the development of a sense of "we"-ness which includes the whole world would develop much more rapidly. It is a sad commentary on the absence of vision of the political and educational leaders of the nations that so little attention has been directed to this significant problem of a single language for the whole human family.[21]

Before leaving the topic of patriotism and humatriotism, we should take note of how perceptions of international affairs would be different if nationalism were subordinated to globalism. Such a change could be expected to at least partially erode the double standard of morality which now is frequently manifested in the perception of foreign relations. For example, at the time of the Cuban missile crisis in October of 1962, Americans generally believed that it would be very wrong for the Soviets to install missiles there even though the Cuban government wanted them and even though the United States had its own missiles in Turkey not far from the Russian border. For another example, Americans generally believe there is something wrong about some other countries having nuclear weapons, but at the same time feel it is quite proper for the U.S. to have thousands of them. On what basis can it be argued that it is bad for these other countries to have nuclear weapons but that it is good for the U.S. to have them? If the predominant nationalistic point of view is replaced by a global perspective, this double standard of morality will no longer go unquestioned.

Of course, it is not only American nationalism that leads to the adoption of a double standard of morality in international affairs. Russian nationalism, Israeli nationalism, Palestinian nationalism, Vietnamese nationalism, and so on — all of the nations find it easy to excuse themselves for the very things they find reprehensible if done by other nations. Such a distortion of perceptions provides a fertile ground for wars. An attitude of globalism could serve as a welcome corrective to the double-standard mentality of nationalistic thinking in international affairs.

Even many of those involved in the academic study of international relations could benefit from adopting a global framework which would override the nationalistic perspective which is so automatically assumed in their work. Many scholars in the field of foreign affairs have been unable or unwilling to see world politics from a perspective where the problem to be addressed is one of governing the whole world for the welfare of the whole human race. They tend to consider global issues strictly from the standpoint of how knowledge of international affairs can be used to help their own national leaders to promote the welfare of their own particular nation. Some scholars do not even ask how a human problem such as the problem of war can be solved. Fortunately, there are others who have adopted a global perspective and have come to see that political science need not forever remain the handmaiden of national governments. Humatriotism is needed by everyone, including scholars in the field of international relations.

World Citizenship

It is not sufficient, however, that people begin to identify with all other human beings. People need to take on a readiness to work for the world community and its further development. Such an attitude would lead to more citizen support for globally minded organizations in their efforts to solve global problems. An acceptance of one's role as a world citizen would lead to personal actions such as learning a global ethnically neutral language, conserving resources, eating less meat (which would free more grain for use as human food), and making financial contributions to international agencies such as the International Red Cross and UNICEF and to the international relief organizations of churches and other groups. A good example of what can be done by committed world citizens is the still-celebrated "Live Aid" global rock concert and telethon telecast from Philadelphia and London July 13, 1985.[22] It featured well-known rock artists from all over the world and introduced new songs such as "Do They Know It's Christmas?" and "We Are the World." The program was watched by 1.4 billion people in over 170 countries. That event not only raised millions of dollars to aid famine victims in Africa but also greatly increased awareness of the reality of a single world community.

The development of a positive attitude toward world citizenship does not preclude taking on responsibilities at the local or national level of community. Just as a good citizen of Illinois or California or Texas can also be a good citizen of the United States, so a good citizen of the United States can also be a good citizen of the world. In fact, citizenship at the various levels of community is important.[23] It would be inappropriate for a citizen of Illinois or California or Texas to seek to promote the interests of that state in a manner detrimental to the larger community of the United States. In the same way, it is inappropriate for a citizen of any nation to seek to promote the interests of that nation in a manner detrimental to the larger world community. A good national citizen will also be a good world citizen, and a good world citizen will also be a good national citizen.

Looking Forward Rather Than Back

When dealing with social problems, human beings have a tendency to look back rather than forward. Consider how often in a conflict between individuals one person says, "You started it; you did X" while the other says, "It's not my fault, you did Y." This same thing happens in social conflicts: Group A remembers that at some time in the past Group B did this dastardly thing to their ancestors while Group B focuses on some other unforgivable deed done by the ancestors of Group A.

Looking back to what has been done is a sure formula for *not* solving problems. A most obvious fact is that no one can change the past. The most that one could do under such circumstances is to say "I'm sorry," but that is going to be very hard to say if the action was not yours but something done by some group of your ancestors. Looking back also involves making both sides return to the very frame of mind which produced the antagonistic actions. That makes it more difficult to resolve the conflict. Digging into the past to try to get more information about who was right and who was wrong may be appropriate in a courtroom where guilt or innocence must be determined, but in a social conflict situation it just accumulates more facts from the past that can't be changed and generates more antagonistic feelings that make resolving the conflict more difficult.

In order to deal with problems constructively, people should learn to focus on *what can be done in the future* rather than what was done in the past. In conflict situations, the best approach is to consider not merely what one party can do (although that may be necessary in some situations) but rather to have both parties to the conflict work together with

the attitude "What can *we* do to get from the present situation to another situation which will be better for both of us?" The notion of "clearing the air" by discussing the past is totally wrong-headed. What is past is past and can't be changed. The appropriate approach is to rule out talk about the past and focus on the present and the future. Attend not to feelings about the past but to goals for the future.

There is no doubt that looking toward the future is in some ways more difficult than focusing on the past. When one looks at the past, there are details and realities. When one looks toward the future there are only imprecise goals and shadowy ideals. With reference to the earlier proposal that there should be world holidays to celebrate global events comparable to national holidays to celebrate significant events in the nation's history, how can one establish holidays to celebrate goals that are yet to be realized? How can one decide on an appropriate date for celebrating something that is going to happen in the future? It is difficult, but it is not impossible. It does require a shift from our usual way of thinking, but it can be done. This proposal says that if we can get more people to make that shift from focusing on the past to focusing on the future, it is more likely that we can do something constructive in the way of solving the war problem.

Overcoming Defeatism and Apathy

One attitude which needs to be overcome not only for solving the war problem but for solving all kinds of social problems is the attitude that the problem is so big that there's nothing anyone can do about it. Many people regard it as practically impossible to make any significant social changes, even in a small community. They tend to think that it would be even more difficult to make such a major change as abolishing war. Therefore they do nothing to even help with such an effort.

A number of observations can be made to counteract this kind of attitude. First, it can be noted that some very significant social changes have been made in the past, so social change is possible. From 1787 to 1789 the United States of America was created through the adoption of a totally new constitution. The persons mainly responsible for that change numbered less than a hundred. Non-governmental organizations such as the International Red Cross, Amnesty International, and Greenpeace which have had a significant impact on society were originally started by a handful of persons. Religions which have influenced millions of people have usually been started by one individual or a very small group. We see the tremendous impact of these efforts and tend to think that there was not much effort required and that their success was more or less a sure thing; but if we see the world as it was when those movements were just getting started, we can readily imagine almost everyone predicting that the effort could never succeed. After changes have occurred, they seem completely natural and almost fore-ordained; but at their small beginnings success seems to be impossible. Modern chaos theory tells us that the flapping of the wings of a butterfly may eventually influence the weather in a major way halfway around the world, so we can conclude that what one person does or doesn't do also may have a significant impact. All too often people get off track by asking, "What about others? They don't seem to be doing anything to help solve this problem." The proper response to that comment is that what other people do is their business, and what you do is your business. Are you as an individual doing what is helpful, or are you part of the problem?

Second, we should note that there is a big difference between concluding, "I can't do anything that will make much of a difference" and "I can't do anything at all." We need to keep in our minds the oft-quoted words of Edward Everett Hale:

I am only one, but still I am one.
I cannot do everything, but still I can do something.
And just because I cannot do everything
I will not refuse to do the something that I can do.

Along the same lines we have the verse "Stubborn ounce person" by Bonaro Overstreet:

You say the little efforts that I make will do no good,
That they will never prevail to tip the hovering scale where justice hangs in the balance.
Well, perhaps I never thought they would,
But I am prejudiced beyond debate in favor of my right to choose which side the scale shall feel the stubborn ounces of my weight.

Third, when thinking about dealing with the war problem, one can discard the *predictive* mode of thinking in favor of the *prescriptive* mode of thinking. Instead of focusing on the question *"Will* war ever be abolished?" (as if what we do could never have any bearing on the outcome), people could learn to ask *"Should* war be abolished?" and *"What needs to be done* in order for that to happen?" If we do not think of ourselves as agents whose actions can make a difference, then we are not likely to make a difference. On the other hand, if we view ourselves as free agents who can decide what should be done and who can then act to bring about what should be, then we are likely to make a difference. We need to promote that outlook reflected in the words of Robert Kennedy (borrowing from George Bernard Shaw's *Man and Superman*): "Some people see things as they are and ask 'Why?' I dream things that never were and ask 'Why not?'"

14. Reforming the Internal Operation of National Governments

We have considered one general approach to promoting peace, modifying the attitudes of individuals. A different strategy is that of focusing on reforming the internal operation of national governments.[1] National governments are crucial to the war problem, whether we consider international wars or civil wars. With regard to international wars, the national governments not only carry on the wars but also implement the policies which generate the conditions which may result in war with other nations. In civil wars the national government will almost always be one party in the war, and its policies will have been instrumental in producing the conditions which lead to revolt. Consequently, it is plausible to argue that if national governments operated properly, the problem of war would be solved. There are various proposals about how the internal operation of national governments should be changed in order to make war less likely. We will examine three of them.

"The Western approach" assumes that war is due to the existence of nondemocratic national governments. If all national governments were democracies, it is claimed, warfare, both international and intranational, would be eliminated or greatly reduced. On the other hand, "the Marxist approach" assumes that the existence of war is due to capitalist-controlled national governments. If all national governments were structured in accord with Marxist principles, it is claimed, warfare, both international and intranational, would be eliminated or greatly reduced. A third view, the Gandhi-King approach, assumes that war and violence are the result of injustice. Furthermore, any kind of government is likely at times to perpetrate injustices, and the proper way of countering unjust governmental decisions is to mobilize large-scale nonviolent protests. The Gandhi-King view claims that if people everywhere could be organized and trained in the techniques of nonviolent resistance, then not only warfare, but also the gross injustice which foments it, would be eliminated or greatly reduced.

The Western Approach

Defenders of the idea that democracy in every nation is the way to peace generally suppose that international wars are caused by power-hungry dictators who want to expand the area of their domination. As noted in our discussion of the causes of war, the aggressiveness of leaders may be a significant factor in whether the groups they lead will behave aggressively toward other groups. It is claimed by supporters of this Western approach that (1) extremely aggressive persons are more likely to gain control of the government in a dictatorship than in a democracy, because when people elect their leaders they will not vote for persons who (a) advocate war or (b) follow aggressive policies against other countries which are likely to lead to war or (c) continue fighting a wasteful war that is already being fought. Also, (2) in a democratic government there will be more institutional restraints on what an aggressive leader can do. Furthermore, (3) in a democratic government leaders are accustomed to resolving differences through discussion and compromise rather than by resorting to force. Authoritarian leaders, on the other hand, do not need to pay any attention to the views of their people, and they are accustomed to using ruthless force to subdue dissenters even in their own countries. Such individuals, it is argued, can be expected to use military force to try to increase the area of land and the number of people over which they have control, and there will be no internal constraints to prevent them from doing that. Consequently, it can be concluded that democratic nations will tend to have governments which seek peace and compromise, while countries with authoritarian rulers will tend to be militaristic, aggressive, and imperialistic.[2]

In the eyes of most Americans, World War II was a perfect illustration of the correctness of this view. Hitler established his authoritarian rule within Germany before being able to use his militaristic approach to subdue people in other countries. Mussolini began by silencing dissenters in Italy. The Japanese military allowed no public criticism of its policies in Japan. These nations thus were able to launch aggressive attacks on their neighbors without worrying about objections from their own people. If there had been a democratic government, it is argued, at least some of the people in Germany would have protested against Hitler's military expansion into Austria, Czechoslovakia, Poland, the Low Countries, France, Denmark, and Norway. Some persons would have protested against attacking Britain and Russia and declaring war on the United States. If there had been a democratic government in Japan, surely there would have been some protests against the attack on the United States at Pearl Harbor. Also, the Soviet Union headed by the dictator Stalin was able to reach an agreement with Hitler to divide Poland between them. Would the Russian people have approved that move if they had been allowed to openly express their views?

According to the adherents of this view, it is not only international war which would be ended if all nations were democracies. Such a change would also mean an end to wars within countries. If people can change their rulers at the ballot box, there seems to be no point in engaging in a violent struggle against the government. Dissenters can simply wait until the next election and try to generate enough support for their views to vote a different government into power. Under such a system, it is claimed, there is no justification for forceful action against the government in power. Even the motivation for trying to organize a violent revolution against the government is removed because it seems to be easier and less dangerous to exert the effort needed to win an election than to launch a successful military revolt.

But historical realities raise some questions about the theory that the institution of democratic governments everywhere would mean the end of war. Democratic governments in Great Britain, France, and the United States seem to have been as imperialistic and to have fought as many wars as the authoritarian governments in Spain, Portugal, and Russia. The involvement of the United States in the Mexican War and then the Spanish-American War can hardly give support to the notion that democratic governments don't engage in expansionistic, aggressive wars. There may have been a few protesters, but they did not prevail. Even disregarding American interventions against allegedly pro-Communist governments in Cuba, Vietnam, Chile, Nicaragua, and Angola, there were also interventions against democratically elected non-Communists in Latin America (Guatemala in 1953 and the Dominican Republic in 1965), western Asia (Iran in 1954), and Africa (Ghana in 1966). Such interventions in other countries raise doubts about the inherently pacifist nature of democracies. Furthermore, even if it were the case that democratic governments do not deliberately seek to bring about wars, they might still inadvertently make war more probable because of the policies they follow in international affairs as a result of their voters focusing on domestic affairs and fearing entanglement in the affairs of other nations.[3] Also, regardless of the apparent cogency of the argument about the needlessness of revolutions in a democracy, the historical reality is that even democratic governments do experience violent revolutions and civil wars. One of the bloodier examples is the American Civil War.

Another issue that is relevant to testing this hypothesis is the difficulty of determining exactly when a country is a democracy. Americans often begin by assuming that the United States is a model of democracy, but is it? Although the public gets to vote in elections, how much influence do they have in determining who the nominees will be, especially for lower positions? How much chance do people with unpopular views have to publicize such views or get their names on the ballot?

How much chance do poor people have to distribute their views compared to rich people? To what extent are elections in the United States basically determined by who has money themselves or rich friends? There are obviously degrees of being democratic, and that makes it difficult to determine the truth or falsity of the thesis that democracies do make wars, even on each other.[4] The issue of whether extending democracy to more countries will automatically produce a peaceful world (which seems to be a viewpoint adopted by the U.S. government over a long period of time but especially since the end of the Cold War) is a major point of controversy between scholars with those in opposition arguing not that democracies are more aggressive but only that the policies of national governments depend more on the international situation than on the domestic character of the national government.[5]

The historical record thus forces us to re-examine the argument that the institution of democratic governments would mean the end of war. A basic assumption of the argument was that ordinary people want peace. The problem is that the people of a nation also want other things. They want a high standard of living and will support policies that give it to them, even though these policies may arouse antagonism in other countries. Furthermore, the identification of people with their nation leads them to support wars which add to the territory and glory of the nation. What the people generally oppose is not war but a losing war or a long drawn-out indecisive war.[6] A war which can be won quickly without many casualties and which adds to the national territory or prestige will generally have popular support.[7] Even in Germany in World War II, Hitler was quite popular as long as the German forces were winning. In the United States, President Reagan's invasion of Grenada in 1983 was quite popular within the country though widely protested in the rest of the world as a most blatant violation of international law.

With regard to war within a country, the "revolution through the ballot box" argument neglects the fact that a minority group may suffer from the tyranny of the majority. In such a situation, an appeal to the ballot box is almost certain to end in defeat for the mistreated minority. The minority may have no wish to rule over the majority, but may simply want to withdraw and form a separate government in order to be free from domination. Having no chance of winning an election or of seceding peacefully, they may feel that resort to violence is the only means of changing the situation, even in a democracy. Consider the situation of the Basques in Spain or the Chechens in Russia.

A Marxist reading this discussion would object that the whole presentation has been incredibly naive. It is based on the assumption that there are democratic governments where the people really have the power to elect the leaders they want and to follow the policies they approve. In reality, says the Marxist, so-called democratic governments are in fact controlled by capitalists and politicians who are subservient to them. Decisions on whether or not to engage in war are made on the basis of whether it would be advantageous to the capitalists who control the political system. Imperialistic wars against weaker nations will be "sold" to the public through an appeal to nationalism, even though the real motivation is to give capitalists access to cheap raw materials and labor. As for a revolution through the ballot box, the capitalists will make sure that the process by which candidates are nominated will be under their control. They will make sure that the mass media and the educational system indoctrinate people to admire capitalism and hate socialism. People who openly advocate socialist ideas will be harassed by the FBI and the local police and ignored by everyone else. Consequently, the Marxist argues, the so-called democratic system can be changed only if working classes use violence to remove the capitalists from their position of behind-the-scenes control. Furthermore, says the Marxist, socialist societies such as Cuba will be able to demonstrate their superiority only when they exist in an environment where they cannot be hassled and undermined by rich and powerful capitalist countries determined to show that a socialist society cannot be better than a capitalist one.

Even though the argument that democracy in all countries would reduce warfare apparently has some deficiencies, perhaps something can still be said for it. The Marxist critique can actually be used to help undercut the historical cases used previously to show that democracy doesn't stop war. If the Marxist analysis is correct, then the cases cited do not refer to truly democratic nations but only to pseudo-democratic national governments. It could be argued that it was a small ruling clique that sold the American public on the Mexican War and then on the Spanish-American War, and that the protesters of those wars were not given sufficient opportunity to express their views. What would have happened in a "true" democracy? It is hard to say. Nevertheless, it is worth noting how so-called democratic governments have had to keep some of their militaristic adventures secret from their own citizens. One distressing illustration of such secrecy occurred prior to World War II, when the governments of Britain and France suppressed their secret agreements with Mussolini concerning Ethiopia.[8] Another example is the U.S. government's concealment from its citizens of events during the Vietnamese War. These cases of government secrecy suggest that government leaders in democracies realize that some of their war-oriented policies would not be generally approved by their own people. Perhaps leaders in truly democratic governments would be less inclined to follow militaristic, aggressive policies than those national leaders who are not obligated to explain or defend their policies before the public.

Peace researcher R. J. Rummel wants to take this argument in favor of democracy and against dictatorships (what he calls "absolutist" governments) one step further. He agrees with the thesis that absolutism is "the major factor causing war,"[9] but more important than that is the fact that the toll of deaths resulting from *absolutist governments killing their own citizens* has been much greater than the total number of people getting killed in wars, both international and civil! To quote from Rummel himself:

And the worst type of these absolutist governments is communist. It is a killing machine, responsible for the massacre, executions, starvation, deaths from forced exposure, slave-labor, beatings, and torture of at least 95,153,600 people in this century or 477 people per 10,000 of their population. By contrast, the number of battle casualties from all wars in this century is 35,654,000 or 22 per 10,000 people of the populations involved. On a per capita basis, communism is at least 20 times deadlier than war. Communism in this century has killed even more people, aside from the communist wars, than the 86,000,000 that perished in all the wars and revolutions since 1740.[10]

The problem, however, is not only Communism but any kind of totalitarianism and absolutism.

Hitler killed from 4,200,000 to 4,600,000 Jews, but he also killed (aside from military action) 425,000 Gypsies, 2,500,000 Poles, 3,000,000 Ukrainians, 1,400,000 Belorussians, and 2,500,000 to 3,000,000 Soviet prisoners of war.[11]

The absence of democratic procedures regularly brings disaster and death.

Where the government is totalitarian, as under Soviet communism or the current Muslim ayatollahs of Iran, or absolutist as under Idi Amin of Uganda or Francisco Macias of Equatorial Guinea, the ruling elite have the same effective power over their people that slave masters have over the slaves. Mass killing, executions, forced privation, and the like then become a practical means to maintain power, eliminate opposition, punish disobedience, and pursue political, economic, social, and religious policies. Without the restraints of opposing power foci, regular competitive elections, free speech, and a pluralistic social system, it is natural that human life will be secondary to a regime's desire for self-preservation, power, and the success of its policies.[12]

So, concludes Rummel, not only is democracy effective in avoiding war but even more importantly it saves lives within one's own society during what is supposedly "peacetime." On the other hand, one of the most embarrassing facts for advocates of democracy is that notorious dictator Adolf Hitler originally came to power in Germany as a result of an election in which his Nazi Party got more votes than any other party.

The Marxist Approach

Even though many scholars and others believe that after the end of the Cold War it is no longer appropriate to use much space to discuss Marxist ideas, this ideology in fact had a great deal of influence on events in the 20th century. In a few places, it is still influential. Consequently, it deserves to be explained and understood. From the Marxist point of view, it is not authoritarian national governments that cause war, but rather countries where control is in the hands of capitalists. It is assumed that people who make investments will subordinate all other interests to that of making money from those investments. According to Marxist theory, capitalists make money by exploiting the workers who operate their machines. As more goods are produced and sold, the capitalists make more profit. Consequently, the Marxist sees capitalists and their managers as desiring to gain control over more and more resources, workers, and consumers. The capitalists in the more technologically advanced countries are able to extend their control over less developed countries either directly by turning them into political colonies, or indirectly by supporting native leaders who will be cooperative. Capitalistic or imperialistic wars break out between capitalistic countries as they compete with each other for control of these less developed countries. Wars of national liberation break out when less developed countries struggle to rid themselves of control by foreign capitalists and their native lackeys. Even after less developed countries gain their political independence, they are likely to remain economically dependent on foreign investment and thus can be manipulated as they compete with one another for this investment from outsiders. During the Cold War there was also the possibility of war between capitalist and Communist countries if the capitalist country were to intervene to try to prevent a Communist revolution or to try to reestablish capitalism by force in a Communist country.

According to Lenin, World War I was a good example of a war fought between advanced capitalist countries as they struggled with each other for control of colonies in Africa and Asia. By then the British and French had worked out agreements with each other regarding colonial holdings, but Italy,

Japan, and Germany were just getting ready to go colony hunting. In World War I, both Italy and Japan correctly determined that they would better extend their territorial holdings by fighting against Germany and Austria-Hungary and with the French, British, and Russians. Although that war was touched off by conflict in the Balkans, it was Germany's rapidly increasing military power that had led to the opposing alliances which caused the war to spread rapidly once fighting began. World War II was also viewed by Communists as primarily a struggle between the capitalist classes in Germany, Italy, and Japan on the one hand and those in France, the United Kingdom, and the United States on the other. The battle in eastern Europe between Germany and the Soviet Union, however, was taken to be the result of capitalist Germany trying to eliminate socialism in Russia. Examples of wars of national liberation were the Algerian War, when the French were expelled, and the Vietnamese War, in which the Vietnamese Communists drove out first the capitalists of France and then the U.S.-supported Vietnamese capitalist government of South Vietnam.

Marxists also claim that capitalists are to blame for civil wars, because capitalistic governments make laws which justify the exploitation of workers, and workers have no opportunity to gain fair treatment other than through a violent revolution. "Democratic procedures" may be devised to create the illusion that it is possible for the masses to inaugurate changes in policy, but the capitalists ensure that anticapitalist candidates have virtually no chance of getting elected. If such a candidate should somehow be elected, the capitalists will use the military to engineer a *coup d'état* to remove the elected anticapitalist from power. Events in Chile in the years 1970–73, when the Marxist Allende was democratically elected and then overthrown by a rightist military group, follow this pattern exactly. These events, say the Marxists, show that the possibility of a lasting peaceful socialist takeover of a capitalist country by a revolution at the ballot box is an illusion. Consequently, according to the Communists, revolutionary war is the only course open to those who desire social justice for the masses. Castro's more enduring revolution in Cuba illustrates the proper Marxist way to get rid of an oppressive capitalist regime and then establish a socialist society, but the capitalists are still using their economic power to try to undermine Castro's experiment in socialism in Cuba.

Once again, however, there are historical realities that raise doubts about the correctness of the Communist doctrines put forth. If simply instituting socialist governments will end war, why is it that the Communist regimes in Russia and China engaged in battles with each other along their border in 1962-1963 and again in 1969? Why is it that Vietnamese and Cambodian Communists fought each other in Cambodia in 1978? Why did the Chinese and Vietnamese Communists engage in warfare against each other in 1979? According to Communist doctrine socialist regimes should never have such wars.

Also, civil disorders do not seem to cease when Communist governments take over. Consider the revolts in Hungary in 1956, in Czechoslovakia in 1968, and in Afghanistan in 1979-1989 as well as the uprisings that occurred at various times in East Germany and Poland. If Communism ends the problem of injustice within a society, why was it necessary to take extreme measures to prevent large numbers of people from fleeing these nations? Even very repressive totalitarian governments weren't able to completely silence dissenters or to completely stop defectors from finding asylum in other countries.

The historical record thus suggests that there is something wrong with the Marxist argument. Where does it go awry? A basic assumption of the Marxist view is that capitalists want profits and nothing else, but in fact capitalists are people with other interests, too. They can be, and sometimes are, interested in political freedom and the welfare of the human race as well as their own profits. Marxists also assume that workers always identify with other members of the working class from all over the world, as if nationalism were nonexistent. In fact, the ineffectiveness of the

socialist pacifist movement at the beginning of World War I, the conflicts between the Russians on the one hand and the Yugoslavs and Chinese on the other, and the conflict between Vietnam on the one hand and Cambodia and China on the other all indicate that nationalism is a stronger social force than any anticipated class solidarity among the workers of the world.

With regard to civil war, it seems a mistake to assume, as the Marxist does, that a government will be dedicated to justice simply because it is controlled by noncapitalists. Why suppose that socialists will be completely unselfish leaders, dedicated only to the welfare of the society? The Marxist tends to neglect the fact that the desire for personal privileges and political power can make a person indifferent to the concerns of others as surely as the desire for profit from investments can.

The defender of democracy would object that the Marxist analysis concentrates too much on the economic aspects of the social system without paying enough attention to political aspects or to the psychological principles which apply to the behavior of leaders. Some Marxists think that the rise to power of autocratic leaders such as Stalin and Mao was merely an accident, while in fact the system of centralized political control which is practiced in Communist countries may make the concentration of power in the hands of one authoritarian person almost inevitable.

Even though the Marxist view that ending capitalism will end war has been shown to be questionable, we should note that the desire of those with wealth to expand their profits and their area of control has been an important factor in many past wars. It is the capitalistic part of Western ideology, rather than the democratic part of it, which has led the European peoples to exploit others who had less technological knowledge. It is the capitalistic part of Western ideology which has led to wide differences in income, wealth, and power within Western societies and within the world wherever capitalism is practiced. The Marxist criticism that capitalism has not been particularly concerned about social justice seems to some extent correct. But so far, there is little evidence that the socialist systems controlled by Communists abound in justice or freedom, and in the international sphere socialists seem to be as subject to nationalistic enmities as capitalists are. Furthermore, past experiences in the Soviet Union and Maoist China as well as contemporary developments in Cuba suggest that a socialist-type planned economy is much less productive and progressive than a capitalist-type market economy, and the resulting shared poverty is still misery.

The Gandhi-King Approach

A third approach to reforming the internal operation of national governments focuses on the problem of justice rather than directly on the problem of war. It assumes that a major cause of war is the resort to violence or threats of violence by those who want to eliminate the injustices perpetrated by those in power. Injustice stems from the fact that, both within nations and on the global level, people with economic, military, and political power use that power to advance their own personal and group interests at the expense of those who lack such power. This unjust behavior on the part of the powerful, for the most part, is not the result of a conscious and deliberate effort to harm other people, for they, like all people, are merely more aware of their own interests than of the interests of others. Injustice is usually the result of indifference to the interests of those being exploited.

The natural reaction of exploited people is to feel resentment and hatred toward those who exploit them. They become disposed to use violence to overthrow and destroy their oppressors. Whether that disposition will lead to action depends greatly on whether they believe that such action might lead to success. But, argued Gandhi, even if one can succeed in hurting and forcefully overcoming the oppressors, to react in such a resentful, hateful, and aggressive manner is to become a perpetrator of injustice oneself. Reducing the situation to a mere struggle for power between oppressors and oppressed leaves no room for moral considerations. The side which wins the contest of force will simply impose its will against the other side. Even if the formerly oppressed group wins the struggle for power, it will simply become a new ruling group using threats of violence to control those who lost the fight. It is unlikely that there will be any more justice than before.

In order to escape from round after round of conflict in which oppression begets violence which begets counter-violence, an entirely different approach is required.[13] Committing injustice in order to try to eliminate injustice is inappropriate. As Gandhi once put it, "An eye for an eye makes the whole world blind." A means must be found which is appropriate to the goal of furthering justice. Instead of relying on physical force, Gandhi believed that the champion of justice must appeal to a different kind of power, the power of love and commitment to truth. *"Satyagraha"* means "the power of truth," and a person committed to using that power is called a *satyagrahi. Satyagrahis* will feel no ill will against those whose interests conflict with their own, no matter how oppressive and unjust they may seem to be. Instead of seeking a situation in which they can impose their will on those who have coerced them, they will try to do what will be beneficial for everyone. *Satyagrahis* will dedicate their whole being to the removal of injustice, but they will not hate anyone, even the perpetrators of the most gross injustices. Their attitude will be one of trying to help oppressors to rid themselves of their insensitivity to the concerns of others.

What technique might the victims of social oppression use to stop the injustices being committed against them without in turn becoming oppressors? In the development of his own thinking, Gandhi's first response to this situation of injustice was to try to use reason. He thought that if the oppressed party could state its case so clearly and dispassionately to the oppressors that the injustice would be evident to any rational observer, then the oppressors would see their error and change their ways. But while practicing law in South Africa, Gandhi discovered by personal experience that this appeal to reason accomplished virtually nothing toward changing the oppressive policies of the ruling groups. Something else was needed.

The new technique Gandhi developed to give power to truth is known as *nonviolent resistance.* Sometimes his approach is mistakenly called "passive resistance," but the technique he advocated is anything but passive. Gandhi insisted that those who were suffering from injustice must be active in their resistance to it. If they did nothing, the oppression would continue. The oppressed must be committed to the removal of injustice by an appeal to the oppressor's sense of justice. They must act to dramatize their plight and show their willingness to suffer even more, if necessary, to change the situation. Although individuals should do whatever they can to protest injustices, the likelihood of success in changing unjust conditions is much greater when large numbers of people are willing to unite their efforts in nonviolent resistance. Some particular techniques of collective nonviolent resistance are demonstrations, boycotts, strikes, and refusals to comply with orders given by the ruling group. An important part of the Gandhi approach is the openness of the planning for nonviolent resistance. Those whose injustices are being protested are permitted to give their side of the story and are told in advance what types of nonviolent activities will be undertaken, as well as details of when and where they will occur.

It is claimed that nonviolent resistance can end war because it provides a means other than violence by which oppressed people can eliminate injustice. The case of India shows how it can be used by the people of a nation to rid themselves of domination by the government of another nation. The civil rights movement in the United States, led by Martin Luther King, Jr., shows how it can be used within a nation as a substitute for violent revolution. But the big question for nonviolent resistance is whether it can succeed in eliminating government-supported oppression when there is no threat of violence in the background. The detractors of the nonviolent approach argue that in the cases of India and the United States, there was a real threat of violent action if the nonviolent approach didn't work. Without the threat in the background, it is claimed, neither Gandhi nor King would have succeeded. Furthermore, it is argued that the British and American governments are not among the more ruthless and oppressive governments the world has ever known. Could the Jews have used nonviolent resistance against Hitler's Nazi government? Could Russian dissidents have used nonviolent resistance against Stalin's ruthless rule? Can massive nonviolent resistance even get started when there is a government which prevents potential dissenters from meeting with each other? Such questions arouse skepticism about how effective nonviolent resistance can be against an extremely determined oppressive government.

The defenders of nonviolent resistance respond that even ruthless governments eventually become reluctant to use violence against nonviolent protesters because the ruthlessness becomes so evident, even to the people who have previously not been protesting against it.[14] Gandhi believed that there is a basic decency about most people that would rebel against obvious oppression. The task is for oppressed people to make their oppressed state obvious to people who are otherwise indifferent. Members of the oppressed group who have been indifferent to trying to change the situation and even some others outside the oppressed group will join the resistance effort once the unjust situation is sufficiently dramatized. To be sure, organizing nonviolent resistance so that it can be effective is not easy. Gandhi liked to compare the need for strategy and for courage required for nonviolent resistance to that required in a military confrontation. The "soldier" of nonviolent resistance needs to be trained and disciplined and should be regarded as just as much a hero as any guerrilla fighter who uses violence to try to eliminate oppression. In fact, participants in nonviolent resistance would be even more worthy of admiration than the guerrilla fighters because they would not be drawn into defiling their own human nature by killing and injuring others in the name of justice.[15]

In the end, however, it seems that the basic assumptions of the Gandhi-King approach can still be called into question. Even if people do have some basic sense of justice, it seems to be a weak motive for action compared with self-preservation. It seems almost self-evident that sufficiently ruthless government leaders can keep most dissenters silent by the use of threats of death and injury, if not to the individual then to those that person loves. It is also very questionable whether all or even most wars are the result of the use of violence to eliminate the oppressive policies of some dominant group. In fact, in international affairs it seems that wars are usually fought between one powerful nation or group of nations and another powerful nation or group of nations. The truly poor nations, economically and militarily, realize that any attempt to use force will bring on defeat. Even within countries wars are between groups which already have some power or status. It could be argued that groups which use nonviolence do so simply because they realize that violent resistance would make matters worse. It seems that nonviolent resistance may offer an alternative to violence as a way to remove some injustices in some particular kinds of situations, but it is debatable whether even the widespread use of nonviolent resistance to protest oppression by ruling groups would do much to reduce the frequency of war. In fact, such activity might even lead to more ruthless oppression by those in power.[16]

Nevertheless in some situations nonviolent resistance has been an important factor in bringing about change. The overthrow of the Shah in Iran in 1979 was largely nonviolent.[17] The February 1986 expulsions of Duvalier from Haiti and Marcos[18] from the Philippines were both largely the result of nonviolent efforts. The nonviolent movement led by Bishop Tutu in South Africa was instrumental in calling world attention to that country's continuing policy of *apartheid*. In 1989 the uprisings against the Soviet army in eastern Europe showed how successful nonviolent resistance can be.[19] The overthrow of Ceausescu in Romania in 1989 and of Milosevic in Yugoslavia in 2000 are also testimonies to the effectiveness of large-scale nonviolent movements in overcoming oppressive dictators.[20] The impact of the Gandhi-King approach on world events is gradually growing. On the other hand, the suppression of the nonviolent "Democracy Movement" by the Chinese Communist armed forces in Tiananmen Square in Beijing in June 1989 seems to have been at least a temporary defeat for nonviolence, but it remains to be seen what will happen in the long run. Iraq may also be another difficult testing place for the efficacy of nonviolence against a ruthless dictatorial regime.

15. Reforming the Policies of National Governments

In the previous chapter, we considered various ideas about how the *internal operations* of national governments might be changed to lessen the likelihood of war. In this chapter we will examine proposals concerning the *policies* national governments might adopt to reduce the likelihood of war. Most people interested in politics and international relations believe that it is in this area that solutions to the war problem must be found, even though they might disagree about which of these policies are the right ones to follow. A wide range of policy options will be discussed, some of which are diametrically opposed to each other. The aim is not to recommend one policy or another but to call attention to the range of options available and to suggest points to consider in evaluating them. Although our focus will be mainly on courses of action which might be adopted in relation to other national governments, in many cases a national government might apply similar approaches to relations with antagonistic groups within the country.

National governments and the policies they follow are crucial to the war problem. International wars are the result of interactions between various national governments, and wars within nations are usually the result of reactions of various groups to the policies of their own national governments. It seems that war could be eliminated if national governments followed the proper policies. Of course, there may be contextual factors which make it difficult for national governments to follow ideal policies, but a discussion of that point must be postponed to the next chapter.

As we discuss these various proposals, we need to keep certain points in mind. *First,* our point of view is to consider policies that might be adopted by any national government. There will be a natural tendency to think only in terms of policies that might be adopted by one's own country, but our aim is to maintain a broader perspective. For example, some policies that might not seem very attractive to a superpower may make a great deal of sense for other nations. *Second,* we are engaged in a normative or evaluative enterprise, not a descriptive or factual inquiry. Our focus is on what *should be* done, not on what policies leaders *are* pursuing. We may refer to cases where a particular policy is being used or was used by way of example, but the fact that a policy is being used or was used does not settle the issue of whether such a policy is a desirable one. *Third,* it is not to be supposed that these various policies which we will be considering are mutually exclusive of one another. Some of them are basically incompatible with others, but others could be pursued simultaneously. *Fourth,* we need to remember that the war problem has four aspects: (a) the threat of nuclear war between big powers, (b) the threat of conventional war between nations, (c) the threat of war within nations, and (d) the expenditure of huge amounts of money and effort for military purposes. Certain proposals may be directed primarily to one or another of these aspects of the war problem. Even a proposal which promises to deal successfully with one aspect of the problem will probably need to be supplemented by other proposals to deal with other aspects of the problem. *Fifth,* some of these proposals have received a great deal more attention than others. There may be an unconscious tendency to think that proposals which are unfamiliar are for that reason insignificant. Readers are advised to be on guard against the natural tendency to dismiss new ideas as unworthy of serious consideration just because they have not previously heard of them.

Peace Through Military Strength

The most common national policy for avoiding war is to be so strong that no potential enemy will risk an attack. The Latin phrase *si vis pacem, para bellum* (if you want peace, prepare for war) succinctly describes this approach. This "para bellum" approach can be applied both to international relations and to the situation within a nation. War with other countries breaks out, it is maintained, when stronger nations let weaker ones entertain the hope that they might win in a contest of force. War within a country breaks out when some revolutionary group comes to believe that it might be able to succeed. According to this view, the secret of preserving peace is for those with power to have such an overwhelming amount of it and such an obvious resolve to use it that no other government or group will be tempted to test their strength.

In order to fully appreciate the attractiveness of the peace-through-strength position, it is important to realize that wars very seldom, if ever, happen by accident. Wars occur when the leaders of at least one government or organized group estimate that they will gain more from fighting a war than they can gain by any other means.[1] If a national government is weak, other governments outside and organized groups within are likely to try to take advantage of it. A weak government will regularly be in a position of either (a) being forced to peacefully yield some of its interests to aggressive enemies or (b) being attacked militarily if it does not yield enough to placate its stronger opponents. The only way of avoiding such an unpleasant situation is to be strong. In the modern world being strong means not only having well-trained and well-equipped military/police forces but also supporting research to develop new and better weapons and tactics.

In the United States, many advocates of the peace-through-strength approach are very critical of the policies followed by the U.S. government at the very end of World War II. At that time the United States had a monopoly in nuclear weapons, an overwhelming superiority in arms production, and well-trained armed forces. It was a great mistake, claim the supporters of this view, to disarm so rapidly when it should have been obvious that the Communists would be making aggressive

moves all over the world to try to expand the territory under their control. If U.S. military power had been maintained rather than dismantled, U.S. forces could have saved at least some of eastern Europe from falling under Communist domination. An all-out effort in China from 1945 to 1949 could have kept that country from falling under the control of Mao's Communist forces. In the Korean War, the United States should have used its superior military might to attack China itself (as General MacArthur wanted to do) when the forces from that country began assisting the North Koreans. If the United States had given more aid to the French in Indo-China when the war first started and had put more resources into the struggle after the French pulled out in 1954, the Communists would not have gained control of that area. According to this view the United States was consistently too restrained and too reluctant to use its military power. The only time that Communist expansion was halted was when the United States indicated its readiness to use all its military force, as in Europe after the formation of the North Atlantic Treaty Organization and as in Cuba in 1962 when the Russians were coerced into removing their missiles.

Supporters of the peace-through-strength approach maintain that the Cold War came to an end because of U.S. President Reagan's commitment to this approach. Reagan made it clear that the United States was willing to spend more and more on "national security" in order to gain overwhelming military superiority rather than continuing to have a standoff with the Soviets. He realized that if the Soviets could neutralize U.S. strategic nuclear weapons, they might think they could use their superior conventional forces in Europe to take over Western Europe or at least engage in coercive diplomacy against the countries of that region. Consequently, he launched the "Strategic Defense Initiative (SDI)" or "Star Wars" program to gain strategic superiority. When the Russians started deploying medium-range missiles that could strike Western Europe, Reagan responded by deploying U.S. Pershing II missiles based in Europe and aimed at the Soviet Union. He insisted that the only thing that would halt deployment of the U.S. missiles was the "zero" option, that is, absolutely no medium-range missiles anywhere for the Soviets or the United States. After much bluster the Soviets backed down and accepted the "zero" option. The Soviets also began to realize that it would be impossible for them to match the kind of buildup of military forces that Reagan had planned. According to this outlook, that is why the Cold War ended with the Soviets in effect capitulating to the United States.

So far we have been considering this policy of peace through strength only from the U.S. point of view, but it is a policy that could be pursued by any nation. During the Cold War, it was being pursued by the Soviet Union as well as the United States. That is exactly why there was such an intense arms race between those two superpowers. But also in regional disputes such as those between Israel and its Arab neighbors or between India and Pakistan, both sides typically put as many resources into building up their military forces as they think they can afford, not only to defend themselves but also to be able to be tough in negotiating sessions. Nations do not want to find themselves in a position where their critical interests must be sacrificed because the opponent is militarily stronger. In a world where conflicts of national interest are ultimately settled by force and threats of force, being militarily strong is a good way to avoid being forced into accepting "agreements" which you don't really like.

There are some problems, however, with the peace-through-strength approach. The nation which is very strong militarily can be fairly confident that it won't be attacked, but can other nations be confident that they won't be attacked by it? Strong military forces may make a nation more secure from attack, but its forces then constitute a threat which makes other nations less secure. The leaders who build up the military might of their countries may be thinking in terms of using those forces to deter an attack on their own country, but once the forces are available it is very tempting to use them to launch an attack on another country. Following a peace-through-strength

policy may thus lead to attempted conquest through war even though that was not the original intent.

A second problem for the peace-through-strength approach concerns the actions required of a national government which pursues this policy to its final logical implications. If all conflicts are ultimately to be decided by force, then force should be used to eliminate competitors while they are weak. In the international sphere, this approach would require a dominant nation to seek to extend its control over potential enemies by attacking them and conquering them before they become militarily strong enough to offer much resistance. Within a country, a peace-through-strength approach would require a national government to seek to silence all criticism and dissent before it has a chance to spread and possibly lead to a revolution. A peace-through-strength policy ultimately requires maintaining the status quo by means of the forceful suppression of any efforts to challenge the power of those who presently are in control. Such an approach seems fitting only for a totalitarian regime bent on eliminating all opposition, whether from some other country or from within.

A third problem for the peace-through-strength approach concerns what happens when rival parties both adopt this approach. In the international arena, the result is an unrestrained arms race which consumes more and more of the resources of the countries involved. When the contending nations have nuclear weapons, a balance of terror results which is threatening even to other countries. Rather than solving the war problem, the peace-through-strength approach intensifies one aspect of the problem, the huge cost of preparations for war. The same result occurs within nations when opposing groups commit themselves to the use of military force to resolve their differences. Guns and ammunition are stockpiled by those not in power for the day when they may be able to revolt against the government. The government, on the other hand, builds up its forces and tries to imprison anyone who might participate in a revolt. Ruthlessness begets more ruthlessness in the continuing struggle for power. Even those who would prefer to remain neutral and stay out of the struggle cannot escape the violence. Nations which had been peaceful thus become battlegrounds in which both their human and material resources are consumed. This tragedy has occurred in recent decades in countries such as Lebanon, Angola, Afghanistan, Cambodia, El Salvador, the Congo, and Sierra Leone.

Thus, the view that peace should be preserved by building up military strength runs into some significant difficulties. It seems to be more a policy for trying to maintain the power of those who now have it than a policy which promotes peace. Leaders using the peace-through-strength approach must be ready to resort to more and more force to try to thwart any effort to modify the present social order, both international and domestic. This attempt to prevent peaceful change may in fact be a major contributory factor to the eventual outbreak in violence. The leaders may begin with some sensitivity to issues of justice and the possible need for change, but the logic of their reliance on force pushes them to assume that their own control must be maintained. Furthermore, when opposing groups both adopt this same approach, an all-out race for military superiority is the result, aggravating rather than solving the war problem. The peace-through-strength approach, when carried to its logical conclusion, even encourages violent attacks against potential enemies while they are weak. A proposal which is put forth as a policy to promote peace turns out in the end to be a policy which blocks efforts for peaceful change and leads to arms races and encourages the opportunistic use of force.

Nevertheless seeking peace and security through strength is the prevalent approach among the national governments of the world. In a world where conflicts of national interest may ultimately be settled by war, there seems to be no substitute for military strength. How else can a country keep from becoming coerced by other nations which have built up their strength? Though the peace-through-strength approach has some real deficiencies from the point of view of solving the war problem, it seems destined to remain one of the most popular policies for national governments to follow unless there is a modification of the international system.

Peace Through Alliances

A country which seeks peace through strength need not rely solely on its own military forces. It can turn to forming alliances with other countries which will provide military assistance if war comes. States with a common interest can enter into a mutual defense pact which declares that an attack on either will be considered an attack on both. By such an alliance both nations have strengthened their power relative to others. Weaker countries will be much less vulnerable to an attack from a potential enemy if they have formed an alliance with a much stronger nation. This situation is not unlike that of a small boy who finds a big, strong friend who will help him resist a bully who has been harassing him. The idea of increasing one's strength by making alliances also applies in the case of conflicting groups within a country. It is not unusual for a revolutionary effort to succeed because of an alliance of dissatisfied groups which nevertheless begin fighting against each other once the old regime has been toppled. At the same time, ruling governments may themselves be the result of an alliance of groups working together to preserve the basic structure of the present order.

Though a country which has alliances with other countries may be stronger as a result, the question remains whether it will be less likely to get involved in a war. Some potential enemies that might otherwise consider attacking will probably be deterred, but the stronger nation in the alliance may try to control the policies of the weaker, possibly even resorting to military force to do so. There is also the possibility of a country being dragged into a war if its ally is attacked or of being attacked simply because it has entered into the alliance with the other country (as happened to France at the beginning of World War I). Finally, there is a danger that a country's ally, knowing that it will have assistance, will deliberately act in a confrontational way (as Austria did with Serbia after getting the "blank check" from Germany before World War I). Thus, entering into an alliance does not necessarily mean that a nation will be more likely to remain at peace. Consequently, upgrading national strength through alliances has drawbacks not found in the strategy of increasing strength by building up one's own military forces. Strength through making alliances, however, will usually be much less expensive.

Separate from the issue of whether a country entering an alliance is more or less likely to get into a war is the issue of whether alliances in general make peace more probable or less probable. It can be argued that alliances are *undesirable* on grounds that World War I became a major war rather than a minor war because of the system of alliances existing before the war began. At the same time, a widely held contrary view maintains that alliances are *desirable* because they can promote peace by preserving a *balance of power*.

There are several different kinds of situations where the balance of power concept is relevant. (1) There may be two opposing nations (or blocs of nations), neither of which has obvious military superiority over the other. This two-sided situation is called a *bipolar balance of power*. Each of the sides is likely to try to gain superiority by various means including recruiting new allies; but peace will be maintained, according to the balance of power view, as long as neither side gains a great superiority over the other. (2) A second type of situation is the *tripolar system* where three opposing nations (or groups of nations) are contesting for dominance. In this situation the two weaker parties can form an alliance against the more powerful one. Or if two of the three parties are nearly equal in power, then the third party may act as a "balancer," shifting its support from one bloc to the other to make sure that neither bloc gets too powerful. Many historians believe that Britain played just such a role as "balancer" in Europe between the opposing blocs on the mainland from 1815 to 1914, thus keeping most conflicts from degenerating into wars

during this period of the *Pax Britannica*. (3) A third situation is a *multipolar system* where there are many different nations and groups of nations which keep shifting alliances with each other, thus keeping any nation or group of nations from gaining an overwhelming military superiority. Similar balance of power situations can also be found in the struggles among partisan groups within countries.

The basic premise of the balance-of-power view of maintaining peace is that wars occur when one side has overwhelming superiority over the other. It is assumed that under such circumstances the more powerful side is likely to start a war because it is confident it can win. A balance of power, on the other hand, should help to preserve peace because the outcome of a war would be more uncertain and the opposing parties would be more cautious. But this basic supposition of the balance of power view is very questionable. When a nation or group of nations has obvious military superiority, other nations and groups of nations tend to be conciliatory and even subservient in order to try to avoid a war they know they can't win. Of course war might still occur if they concluded that they had to fight to try to keep what they still had. On the other hand, when there is a balance between powers, it might well be that a crucial conflict situation will develop and neither side will back down because neither perceives itself as weaker than the other. War then seems a likely result. It is surprising that the balance of power view is so popular when it is doubtful that war is more likely when there is an imbalance between powers than when there is a balance.

As a matter of fact, nations can be expected to form alliances with other nations, especially against nations and groups of nations which seem threatening, but this behavior is more readily understood on grounds that the nations are protecting their own national interests by getting help against a potential enemy than on grounds that they are trying to preserve peace by maintaining a balance of power. The most common path for protecting national security has been building up the country's own military forces, but entering into alliances has also been a popular alternative way of preserving peace through military strength, especially for smaller countries.

Peace Through Neutrality and Economic Self-Sufficiency

A very different approach which national leaders may adopt to try to keep out of wars is to concentrate on solving the domestic problems of their own nation while seeking to isolate themselves from the conflicts of other nations. Following this approach means avoiding all alliances and refraining from military interventions. One's military forces will be such that they pose absolutely no threat to any other nation. At the same time a country pursuing this strategy will usually be committed to using research, technology, and conservation measures to avoid economic dependency on other countries. For example, a country which is very dependent on imported oil for energy could be expected to make a massive effort to develop alternative energy sources on the assumption that in the long run this approach will be less expensive than building up military forces in order to try to guarantee the availability of oil.

A good example of a nation which has followed a policy of neutrality for some time is Switzerland. The Swiss have steadfastly refrained from entering into any kind of military alliances. They even obtained an explicit exemption from participation in any military sanctions against other nations before joining the League of Nations, and they have been reluctant to join the United Nations because it requires all members to abide by the resolutions of the Security Council. They have tried to mind their own business, not developing any close ties with any other particular nations, but not making any enemies either. Under this policy they have managed to stay out of both world wars. They have military forces, but these forces are single-mindedly devoted to defending the homeland against any possible invasion. For the Swiss this policy has worked well, and they presently have the world's highest per-capita income.[2] Swe-

den is another example of a country which has done very well by following a neutralist policy.

The success of a neutralist policy, however, may depend on factors outside the control of the national leaders. Switzerland and Sweden are countries where much of the land is mountainous. For the most part they do not provide good travel routes for armies of other nations bent on conquest, and the Swiss and Swedes could fairly readily blow up their bridges and tunnels, thus frustrating would-be invaders. The situation is quite different for countries such as Belgium and Poland. These nations have also tried to stay out of wars, but with little success. Their relatively flat land is very inviting to militant leaders looking for good routes for getting at their enemies. Switzerland and Sweden also have been assisted in their policies of neutrality by their lack of readily exploitable scarce natural resources. It would seem that a small country with crucial natural resources such as the oil-rich United Arab Emirates would be well advised not to try to defend itself without relying on any allies.

For a good part of its history, the United States tried to follow a policy of neutrality with regard to Europe. Nevertheless it found itself dragged into both world wars. After World War II, the United States followed just the opposite of a neutralist or isolationist policy, forming alliances and intervening militarily all over the world in an effort to stop the spread of Communism. The Vietnamese War raised some doubts about the desirability of playing "world policeman," but the success in the 1991 Gulf War has led to renewed support for the "world policeman" role. With the Cold War over, some are calling for a return to isolationism, but it is unlikely that the United States will or can go back to that policy. If a country imports many items from other parts of the world and its corporations are investing and exporting all over the world and its economy comprises over one-fourth of the world total,[3] it can hardly pretend that it has no interest in what is happening in the rest of the world.

A country may also find it difficult to

follow a strategy of neutrality and self-development if it is very short of resources. Japan is a good example, for it must import almost all the oil it uses. Development of hydroelectric, solar, and nuclear energy can provide a bit of self-sufficiency, but the need for energy and other natural resources is too great to be met by current technology. Japan's objective situation seems to preclude a policy of national self-sufficiency and noninvolvement in international conflicts.

It seems then that the desirability of a policy of neutrality and economic self-sufficiency depends on particular circumstances. A country which is a major power may find it hard to refrain from helping ideological allies when they are in danger of being conquered by a powerful ideological enemy. A country which depends greatly on others for resources must take an interest in the outlook of those nations. A small country with readily exploitable resources is likely to be quickly conquered by aggressive powers if it relies only on its own defensive efforts. A country which provides a good route for conquering armies may not be able to stay out of wars. And the fact that a nation decides not to intervene in the affairs of other nations does not automatically assure that other nations will forego the use of force to conquer it or damage its vital interests.

Do neutrality and isolationism promote peace? It certainly seems that a country which is following a policy of neutrality will not be a threat to other nations. Consequently, it is less likely to be attacked. Its lack of alliances means that it is also less likely to be dragged into wars between other nations. On the other hand, if there are other nations committed to the use of military force in expanding their power, a policy of neutrality may play right into their hands by allowing them to conquer one country at a time. Even the case of Switzerland needs to be reexamined from this point of view. If Hitler had been successful in maintaining control for some time over all of the rest of continental Europe, would not Switzerland sooner or later have been converted by one means or another into a German-speaking fascist country swearing its al-

legiance to *der Führer?* If so, Switzerland was saved not by its isolationist policy but by the Allies who put an end to Hitler's rule. Similarly, other countries following an isolationist policy may escape from war for a time, but they face the possibility of being swallowed up by those interested in expanding their power by military means unless they are saved from disaster by others. If there are powers bent on spreading their control without limit by military means, it seems prudent to join with others in resisting such expansionism at its beginning. Isolationism would be a good policy if all other nations would always mind their own business, but there often are national leaders who feel that they should control more than they already do. The same kind of considerations apply to groups within countries which seek to stay out of political issues. Whether they can preserve their own interests and ideology by noninvolvement in political conflicts will depend on the policies pursued by the other groups in that society. The fate of the Baha'is in Iran shows that political noninvolvement does not always save a group from being persecuted.

Peace Through Strictly Defensive Strength

We have noted that a national policy of neutrality does not necessarily prevent a country from being attacked. Such a country may thus need some kind of defense. Nations not committed to neutrality may also want to adopt a system of defense which will not be threatening to their neighbors. There are two possible approaches to a purely defensive program for national security.[4] The first relies on a *strictly defensive military capability for the armed forces*. The second, discussed in the next section, is a radically different approach called *civilian-based defense* which involves training the whole population in techniques of nonviolent resistance to be used against an invader.

The approach of relying on purely defensive military forces for national security builds on the fact that some kinds of weapons will be threatening to other nations while others will not. For example, weapons such as bombers and tanks will make other countries feel less secure because such weapons have an offensive capability. On the other hand, if a country refrains from building offensive weapons while nevertheless stockpiling defensive weapons such as landmines and anti-tank weapons, other nations will not feel threatened by its military capability. Of course, countries typically say that *all* their weapons are defensive. The crucial test of whether a weapon is really defensive, however, is whether the potential adversary views it as defensive.[5] The basic idea of the purely defensive military approach is that relying on weapons that have only a defensive capability allows a country to acquire a very strong military defense without leading other countries to become concerned that they may become victims of an attack.

What are some of the main characteristics of a strictly defensive military effort? Obviously one would need to build obstacles and protected weaponry which an invader would need to get past in order to get into the country. Any weapons which are mobile would need to be small and have limited range so they would not be threatening to neighboring countries. A purely defensive force would not contain any nuclear weapons because there is no way to use these weapons in one's own territory without destroying what one is trying to protect. An effective defense force would need to be dispersed throughout all parts of the country rather than concentrated in certain areas which could be readily destroyed by a few nuclear weapons. In fact, defensive forces should be especially well trained in guerrilla fighting (paramilitary defense) so they would be able to continue to harass an invader even if the conventional defensive forces were defeated.

A great asset of a policy which shifts away from offensive weapons and builds up defensive capabilities is that a country can increase its own security without needing any kind of prior agreement with the adversary. The elimination of all offensive weapons means the availability of more resources for defensive weapons while the adversary becomes less threatened and therefore less likely to remain antagonistic.

It is to be noted that this defensive military approach in effect seeks to deter the enemy from attacking, but *not* in the sense of threatening retaliation as in the doctrine of nuclear deterrence. Rather one deters the enemy by decreasing the likelihood that an attack will be successful because one has strengthened one's defensive capabilities. To apply this defensive approach to the area of strategic nuclear weapons a country would need to dismantle all its nuclear warheads and delivery systems and rely completely on a missile defense system. Needless to say the Strategic Defense Initiative proposal of U.S. President Reagan did not fit this model because it did not call for getting rid of all U.S. offensive weapons.

Would such a strictly defensive military effort be a good way of promoting peace and security? There might be some minor problems such as determining whether certain defensive weapons might not be able to be used offensively in some situations and making sure that widely dispersed and somewhat autonomous defensive units remain loyal to the central government. One's capability of helping friendly countries would be severely limited. An even bigger problem, however, is that restricting oneself to defensive weapons means that enemies could attack repeatedly knowing that no counterattack on their territory would occur. They could continue to build newer offensive weapons while destroying the defensive weaponry the other country already has and its capability to build more. They would know that they could never lose more than their own attacking forces. How long could a purely defensive effort be successful under these circumstances?

The response of the advocate of the strictly defensive approach would be to raise the issue of why the enemy would want to attack. Doesn't one country attack another because it fears being attacked itself? If the opponent has no offensive weapons, wouldn't that fear be eliminated? So why would a country attack another country which has purely defensive forces?

Here we reach the questionable assumption on which the proposal for a strictly defensive system is based, namely, that the only reason one nation would attack another is the fear of being attacked itself. The whole history of war indicates that some groups attack others even though there is no fear whatever of being attacked by them just as some individuals attack others even though there is no fear of being attacked by them. To secure valuable assets, to spread an ideology, to gain status, to dominate — these are the reasons one group attacks another. It is naive to suppose that these motives will disappear just because other groups have decided to rely on strictly defensive weapons. It is true that we would have a more peaceful world if *all* nations would give up their offensive weapons and rely instead on strong defensive forces, but some groups have expansionist aims and will continue to build up their offensive capabilities until they can overcome the defenses of others. This offensive capability will make other groups feel insecure, but that is exactly what the expansionist group intends. It can then coerce other groups into accepting a situation which they don't like but can't resist. If they do try to resist, the aggressive group will resort to war and force compliance.

If no other groups actively challenge the aggressive group, it can be expected to continue its aggressive ways, probing here and there to find places where the defense of some other group is not sufficient to resist it. In a system of collective defense, other groups could come to the assistance of the weak; but if each group is relying only on its own defensive efforts, a strong aggressor will be able to overcome them one resisting group at a time. Even if the nonaggressive groups unite in a common collective-security effort, they will be at a great disadvantage because they can do nothing to destroy the capability of an aggressor to build even more powerful offensive weapons while the aggressor is able to destroy their capability of building defensive weapons. Groups which rely on strictly defensive efforts are destined to be overcome eventually by aggressive groups with superior offensive capabilities. It just isn't true that groups prepare for and engage in war only because they are fearful of being attacked by others.

Peace Through Civilian Defense

The second kind of purely defensive effort which has been proposed as a way of promoting peace is to rely on the civilian population of the society rather than military forces. This civilian-based system of defense could be used as a backup for the strictly defensive military strategy just discussed, but it could also be used by itself. The basic idea of a civilian-based system of defense is to train all the citizenry of a country in techniques of nonviolent resistance which can be used to frustrate invaders. Gene Sharp, the primary spokesman for this idea, notes that the people of a society need to be equipped with a means of fighting so that they can defend themselves rather than relying solely on that small part of the population which constitutes the armed forces of the country.[6] Even if a country has an army of professional soldiers, the people of that country should not be defenseless if their army is defeated. And once a nation dedicates itself to developing a full-fledged system of civilian defense, it may find that building up traditional military forces is superfluous. Such a system of national defense also has the advantages of not being threatening to one's neighbors and of being useful for resistance even to an internal group which attempts to take over the government by force. Consequently, its supporters claim, it is an especially appropriate type of defense for a democratic country.

Exactly how could a civilian population defend itself nonviolently against an invading army? It might begin by destroying anything that would be useful to the invaders. Explosives might be used to blow up key bridges, harbor facilities, airports, mines, factories, radio broadcasting towers, and the like. Automobiles could be parked in rows to block highways and streets. Human chains 20 or 30 people deep, unarmed but backed up by reinforcements and determined not to move, could be formed to stand in the way of the advancing enemy. Work which the enemy wanted done simply wouldn't be done. The people would obey no commands but those given by their own leaders, and the leaders would give no commands that would assist the invaders.

The strategy of civilian-based defense depends on the principle that invading military leaders can succeed in accomplishing their goals only if others cooperate by following their orders. If the whole civilian population just refuses to do what they are told, if they refuse to work or provide supplies, then the invading army will be stymied. The army will be in the country but they will have no control over it. They may make threats and even carry some of them out in order to try to get their commands obeyed; but if the whole population stubbornly refuses, then they cannot be subdued regardless of the violence that may be used against them. If their resistance is completely nonviolent, the commanders of the invading army may eventually even have difficulty trying to get their own troops to follow orders to use violence against these nonviolent people.

It may be argued that once the invading force kills a few people the others will be frightened into obeying, but that reaction is precisely what training in civilian defense must overcome. Soldiers do not stop fighting just because some of their comrades have been killed. In fact, such an event may make them more determined than ever to fight. Civilian defenders need to be taught to react in the same way except that their resistance must be nonviolent. They must also realize how important it is that no one turns traitor and cooperates with the invader and that no one begins to use violence, thus undermining the nonviolent resistance. Most important of all, they must be taught to keep firmly before their minds the truth that no matter how many of their friends and family are killed or tortured, the number of casualties would probably have been even greater if they had tried to rely on military resistance and thus invited massive destructive attacks.

The notion of civilian-based defense as an alternative to a traditional military defense system may not seem a very attractive possibility to countries which have nuclear-tipped missiles to launch at any country which attacks them. But what about countries such as Sweden, Thailand, Mexico, and Nigeria, not to mention smaller countries? They do not have a nuclear deterrent. What sort of defense can they hope to develop against a possible attack by a nuclear power? Even if they could develop nuclear weapons and missile launchers, they might not want to do so since the presence of such weapons in their country might invite a nuclear attack. Even a big buildup of conventional weapons might make them a target for attack when they otherwise might not be bothered. Consequently, the civilian-based defense system constitutes an attractive possibility. The governments of Sweden, Norway, Lithuania, Latvia, Estonia, and the Netherlands have sponsored official studies of the possibilities of this approach.

Would a system of civilian-based defense work? Advocates point to the partial success of resistance movements in the Ruhr Valley in 1923 when the German population resisted a French-Belgian takeover attempt, in Norway and in Denmark where Hitler's forces were shunned and ignored during World War II, and in the Czechoslovak uprising against the Russians in 1968. In 1920, the German Weimar Republic was saved from an attempted internal takeover (the Kapp Putsch) by strikes and refusal of the population to cooperate. In these cases there had been no advanced preparation for the resistance effort. It is claimed that a civilian population trained in advance and equipped with hidden resources such as duplicating machines and radio transmitters and e-mail networks could be much more successful. If there can be partial successes against military forces without advanced preparation, one could expect even better results with planning and special training in civilian defense.

The skeptics remain unconvinced, however.[7] The crucial issue is human nature. Will people refrain from reacting violently when under violent attack? Will people stand up to threats of violence when they see their own family members being threatened and tortured? If some people yielded to threats and revealed secret hiding places and secret codes, it would become more and more difficult for others to keep up their resistance. There might even be some persons who for ideological or other reasons would want to help the invaders. Another problem is that the enemy would also be in a position to use nonviolent techniques against the population of the invaded country. For example, the invaders could shut off supplies of electricity, food, petroleum, medical care, and so on if the captured citizenry would not cooperate. The approach of civilian-based defense, its detractors argue, does not have enough respect for the influence of physical force, especially in an age of mind-altering drugs and brainwashing techniques. The mind is too dependent on the body, too much a part of the body, too vulnerable to biochemical manipulation, too dedicated to the continuation of one's own personal existence. Some people may be committed enough to suffer greatly and possibly die, but it is doubtful that such commitment would be the prevalent response regardless of advance training and preparations. Furthermore, there is always the gruesome possibility that the invading nation would simply slaughter huge numbers of people and then move some of its own population into the conquered country. Some domestic revolutionary movements as in Cambodia have massacred substantial proportions of their own people, so the possibility of murdering large numbers of foreigners should not be too readily dismissed.

The advocate of civilian-based defense might still maintain that, especially for smaller countries, this system of defense makes more sense than other alternatives. But is this true? Doesn't an alliance with other countries offer more security than civilian-based defense? Furthermore, even though a traditional military buildup might not constitute much of a deterrent to a big power, it might nevertheless be a good policy to follow for opposing other small and middle-sized countries, especially when one considers the influence of military power on international negotiations. Also a civilian defense system won't help much to assist in the defense of an ally. It seems that relying on a civilian-based defense system alone is not a particularly attractive strategy though it may be worth planning in advance to follow such an approach if and when one's mili-

tary forces have been subdued. If all nations were committed to using civilian-based defense rather than building up their military forces, war might be less probable; but it seems that few nations are ready to rely for their security solely on a type of defense whose success seems so questionable.

Peace Through Arms Control

As previously noted, two rival nations pursuing a policy of peace through military strength are likely to find themselves engaged in an arms race. We earlier noted that arms races are sometimes a contributory factor to the outbreak of war. It would seem that anything which could keep arms races in check would make war less likely. It is the aim of arms control agreements to promote peace by slowing and possibly even reversing arms races.

One of the main problems for those contemplating arms control agreements is being able to know whether the other side is keeping its part of the bargain. Treaties governing the testing of nuclear weapons and limiting the number of strategic weapons were possible during the Cold War because of technological developments which permitted each side to know what the other was doing without needing to rely on "on-site" inspections. Probably the most important advance in this regard has been the development of spy-in-the-sky satellites which carry sophisticated photographic equipment. By means of these satellites it is not difficult to locate the complex of radars and antiballistic missiles which constitute an ABM site or the launching pads for intercontinental ballistic missiles.

The problem of inspection can still be a major obstacle, however, with regard to smaller weapons such as cruise missiles. Consequently, agreements limiting these smaller weapons are not to be expected unless some system of on-site inspection can be worked out. Such a system is not likely, however, as long as the parties fear that the others will use such inspections not merely to make sure that agreements are being kept but also to gain valuable information about military installations which could be used when planning an attack. Even the notion of a neutral on-site inspection team is not likely to be acceptable in a tense situation because the adversaries may not trust neutral observers to be clever enough not to be duped or neutral enough not to pass valuable information to the other side.

Another problem for arms control agreements is that new kinds of weapons are always being deployed. This situation is especially acute in the age of modern science. Arms control agreements are addressed to the kinds of weapons which exist at the time the agreements are made. As new kinds of weapons are developed, they generally are not restricted by earlier agreements. For example, agreements to limit nuclear weapons, possibly even prohibiting the testing of them, do not restrict laser weapons or bacteriological/viral weapons and the research directed to their future development.

Somewhat related to this problem of new-weapon development is the probability that arms control agreements will only serve to divert military spending and research from one kind of weapon which is restricted to another kind which is not. Consider what happened with the 1972 SALT I agreement between the Soviet Union and the United States. That treaty put limits on the number of long-range nuclear weapons launchers each side could have, but it did not put any limits on the number of warheads each missile could carry. The treaty was successful in diverting efforts away from building more launchers but at the same time it simply increased the effort to put multiple warheads on each missile. Also both SALT I and SALT II limited only intercontinental range missiles, so both sides were free to engage in a new arms race focused on building medium-range missiles.

A cynic will note that during the Cold War the arms agreements between the United States and the Soviet Union put restrictions on weapons which both sides had decided wouldn't be very effective anyway or on weapons which both sides decided they already had in more than adequate quantity. Also when many tests had already been done with large-yield nuclear weapons and when it became apparent that the military needed smaller, not larger, nuclear weapons, then an agreement was made to ban the testing of large nuclear devices with a yield of over 150 kilotons. Furthermore, there was always some consideration given to the situation of other countries. After the United States, Britain, and the Soviet Union had learned how to test nuclear weapons underground in 1963 but the French and Chinese did not yet have that capability, a treaty was adopted banning nuclear explosions in the atmosphere. In fact, part of the motivation for that treaty probably was a desire to embarrass the Chinese if they tried to explode a nuclear device, but they did it anyway in 1964. The treaty to ban large nuclear explosions may have had somewhat the same kind of motivation since the United States and the Soviet Union no longer needed more information about such large weapons but newer nuclear powers would. The Non-Proliferation Treaty is obviously an effort to keep countries which do not already have nuclear weapons from obtaining them.

The positive value of arms control agreements, however, should not be disparaged too much. With the Cold War having ended, START I has actually led to the dismantling of large numbers of nuclear weapons. The CFE (Conventional Forces in Europe) Treaty has provided the framework for large cutbacks in weaponry and forces along the previous battle line between East and West in Europe. Without the tradition of earlier arms control agreements during the Cold War it would have been difficult to move suddenly to these very significant agreements for backing away from war readiness. Also procedures and traditions were established that could serve as a basis for other agreements such as a Comprehensive Test Ban Treaty (CTBT).

Nevertheless, arms control agreements are directed more to controlling the symptoms of conflict than to preventing war. The arms control agreements during the Cold War played only a tangential role in ending that tense situation. They may have kept arms expenditures and weapons development somewhat under control, but perhaps they didn't even do much to restrain military spending.

The restrictions established by the agreements may have merely resulted in larger expenditures for the research and development of unprohibited kinds of weapons. With the Cold War ended, the arms control agreements provide a good device for winding it down. But the Cold War ended because of other factors, not because of arms control agreements. The new arms control agreements that have led to a decrease in the numbers of weapons are an effect of the end of the Cold War, not a cause of it. Arms control agreements are undoubtedly more desirable than not having them, but they do not seem to have had much bearing on preventing war.

The major difficulty with arms control agreements as a road to peace is that even if successful in slowing arms races they do very little to eliminate the danger of war. Suppose, for example, that through arms control agreements all of the nuclear weapons and all the ballistic missiles which now exist could be eliminated. Suppose that even the knowledge of how to build such weapons were eliminated. Would such a development mean the end of war? Obviously not. We would simply regress to something like the pre-nuclear world of 1945. Almost 40 million people were killed in World War II, and nuclear weapons accounted for less than 250,000 of the deaths. And the nonnuclear weapons of today are much more destructive than those available in the 1940s. In fact, one could even argue that the elimination of nuclear warheads and ballistic missiles would make war *more* likely. Without the threat of such weapons, we might already have had World War III. Those who want to eliminate all nuclear weapons need to ask themselves whether the goal they seek is really desirable.

Peace Through Renunciation of War

If agreements limiting certain kinds of weapons do not do much to reduce the likelihood of war, perhaps national governments could go further and renounce any use of force or threats of force to settle their differences. The most obvious example of an effort in this direction was the General Treaty for the Renunciation of War, commonly called the Kellogg-Briand Pact, of 1928. In it the signing parties agreed to renounce war "as an instrument of national policy in their relations with one another."[8] It stated further that "the high contracting parties agree that the settlement or solution of all disputes or conflicts, of whatever nature or of whatever origin they may be, which may arise among them, shall never be sought except by pacific means."[9] Sixty-one nations had signed this pact by the end of 1930, the only important nonsigners being Argentina and Brazil. However, the agreement did not state what should be done if some nation did violate the agreement, which Japan, Paraguay, and Italy had all done by 1936. It is questionable whether the agreement had any influence on the behavior of the nations which had signed it. Still, at the Nuremberg Trials after World War II, this treaty was appealed to as setting forth international law which had been violated by the Nazi leaders.

Another example of an international agreement renouncing the use of force is the Charter of the United Nations. Article 2 says in part:

> 3. All Members shall settle their international disputes by peaceful means in such a manner that international peace and security, and justice, are not endangered.
> 4. All Members shall refrain in their international relations from the threat or use of force against the territorial integrity or political independence of any state, or in any other manner inconsistent with the Purposes of the United Nations.[10]

But once again there is no indication of what should be done if this pledge is violated. It is also doubtful whether national governments act much differently because they have joined the United Nations. By becoming members of the United Nations, however, nations do indicate that they accept these principles as international law.

A more recent example of the use of this approach to peace is the 1973 Agreement Between the United States and the Soviet Union on the Prevention of Nuclear War. In this agreement

> The Parties agree ... to proceed from the premise that each Party will refrain from the threat or use

of force against the other Party, against the allies of the other Party, and against other countries, in circumstances which may endanger international peace and security.[11]

This agreement also indicates that whenever there seems to be a risk of nuclear conflict, the two governments "shall immediately enter into urgent consultations with each other and make every effort to avert this risk."[12]

How much either side felt bound by this agreement is a matter for speculation. Still, it seems pointless to sign such an agreement unless there is at least some expectation by each side that the other will abide by it.

The technique of maintaining peace by renouncing the use of force suffers from a number of deficiencies. The most obvious one is the absence of provisions for enforcement. No punishment is stipulated for those who violate the pledge, no arrangements are made for deciding whether punishment is warranted, and no structure is established to oversee the punishment of violators. Agreements not to use force to resolve disputes cannot be expected to work until there is also agreement on some alternative trustworthy way of settling differences. About all that can be said for pledges by national governments not to use force is that it is probably better for them to make such pledges than to refuse to make them.

The approaches of arms control and the renunciation of force can be joined in a single effort to try to achieve general and complete disarmament. The reader may be surprised to learn that in 1961 the United States, represented by John McCloy, and the Soviet Union, represented by Valerian Zorin, reached an agreement on principles to govern negotiations aimed at general and complete disarmament. Among them were the following:

(1) The aim of negotiations should be general and complete disarmament accompanied by the establishment of reliable procedures for the peaceful settlement of disputes.

(2) When the process is completed, all armed forces will be disbanded, all stockpiles of weapons will be destroyed, all military training will be ended, and all military expenditures will cease.

(3) The disarmament programme should take place in stages with verification of compliance at each stage by an international disarmament organization created within the framework of the United Nations.

(4) During the disarmament process institutions for the peaceful settlement of international disputes should be strengthened and a U.N. international peace force should be developed to keep the peace.[13]

These principles were also approved by the U.N. General Assembly.

Unfortunately, there was a significant difference of opinion concealed in the agreement about having verification concerning compliance. The Soviets took this to mean that the process of destroying weapons would be verified, while the United States insisted that the verification must extend also to what arms still remained. This difference received more attention than the areas of agreement. It seemed that the governments involved did not really want to reach a workable agreement. The leaders of national governments have difficulty imagining a world where they will have no military forces to try to protect their national interests, and their distrust of possible enemies is too great to allow them to seriously consider the notion of complete disarmament. Part of the difficulty, of course, is the lack of any clear idea of how international disputes would be resolved in the absence of those military forces which at present give the more powerful nations a superior position in bargaining situations.

Peace Through Conciliatory Moves and Confidence-Building Measures

Arms control agreements and eventually general and complete disarmament seem to be moves in the right direction in the struggle against war, but sometimes tensions and distrust are so great that negotiations between opposing parties cannot even get started. What, if anything, can be done to move toward peace in situations where neither side trusts the other enough to even contemplate the possibility of arms control agreements?

One of the best known and earliest proposals for action in this kind of situation of mutual distrust is the 1962 GRIT proposal made by psychologist Charles Osgood.[14] GRIT stands for "Graduated Reciprocation in Tension Reduction" or "Graduated and Reciprocated Initiatives in Tension Reduction."[15] The aim of GRIT is to convert a situation of intense tension and distrust into one where it is possible to have negotiated settlements made in good faith. The general idea is for one party to make a series of conciliatory moves announced in advance with a public invitation for the other party to make reciprocal gestures of its own choosing. At the same time defenses continue to be maintained in case the opposing party misinterprets the moves as signs of weakness.

Osgood's very detailed proposal was addressed specifically to the Cold War confrontation between the United States and the Soviet Union. He suggested that even while making conciliatory moves the United States would need to maintain its capacity to launch a nuclear retaliatory attack and be ready to meet an attack using conventional weapons with adequate conventional weapons of its own. He proposed that the announced conciliatory gestures be carried out regardless of whether the other side indicated it would reciprocate, and they would need to be continued over a long period of time, not just for a month or two. Conciliatory moves were to be planned which would promote cooperative enterprises, which would encourage the transfer of sovereignty from the national to the international level, which would reduce the imbalance between have and have-not nations, and which would strengthen democratic ways of life. If successful, this strategy would lead to reciprocal conciliatory moves by the Soviets, a lessening of tension, and some serious bilateral negotiating.

Would such a policy of unilateral conciliatory moves work? At the height of the Cold War would the United States even be willing to try such a policy in its dealings with the Soviet Union? It seems that a policy of this sort was attempted by President Kennedy in 1963 and with some good results, the most obvious one being the adoption of the treaty to stop nuclear testing in the atmosphere signed in August of 1963.[16] The main conciliatory moves consisted of a unilateral U.S. halt to nuclear tests in the atmosphere and U.S. approval of the sale of a large amount of wheat to the Soviet Union.

> For each [conciliatory] move that was made, the Soviets reciprocated. ... They participated in a "you move–I move" sequence rather than waiting for simultaneous, negotiated, agree[d]-upon moves. Further, they shifted to multilateral-simultaneous arrangements once the appropriate mood was generated. ...
>
> A danger that seems not to have been anticipated by the United States Government did materialize: the Russians responded not just by reciprocating American initiatives but by offering some initiatives of their own ... Washington was put on the spot: it had to reciprocate if it were not to weaken the new spirit, but it could lose control of the experiment.[17]

Why was such an apparently successful move for peace which began in June of 1963 not continued past November of 1963?

> The reasons were many: the Administration felt that the psychological mood in the West was getting out of hand, with hopes and expectations for more Soviet-American measures running too high; allies, especially West Germany, objected more and more bitterly; and the pre-election year began, in which the Administration seemed ... [to want to make sure that] even if all went sour — if the Soviets resumed testing, orbited bombs, etc. — no credible "appeasement" charge could be made by Republicans.[18]

Another relevant factor may have been President Kennedy's assassination on November 22, 1963, but some additional conciliatory moves were made by President Lyndon Johnson after he was elected in 1964. He continued them for about a year. Increasing U.S. involvement in Vietnam may have made the Russians less ready to respond to conciliatory moves on other fronts. It is also relevant that Khrushchev was removed from his leadership position in the Soviet Union in 1964. Kennedy and Khrushchev had gone through the Cuban missile crisis to the brink of nuclear war in October of 1962 and then led their countries through the détente of 1963, but by the end of 1964 neither man was any longer part of the international decision-making process.

Another example of a unilateral conciliatory move to resolve a conflict was Anwar Sadat's dramatic trip to Jerusalem to address the Israeli Knesset in December 1977. The long-term consequences of that move are still not complete, but there is no doubt that it led to negotiations and an agreement between Egypt and Israel in 1979 that would otherwise have been unthinkable. Strictly speaking, Sadat's move does not fall within the strategy outlined by Osgood, however, because there was not a series of moves but simply one dramatic gesture. Also Sadat was not operating from a position of military strength, and he seems to have been motivated partly by the hope of influencing public opinion in the United States, a country which could be expected to act as a mediator in the dispute. Still, Sadat's act was an example of making a conciliatory move to loosen a deadlocked confrontation.

It would be a mistake to assume that unilateral conciliatory moves will always be successful. The success of Kennedy's initiatives in 1963 may have resulted from the fact that Kennedy and Khrushchev had come face-to-face with the possibility of nuclear war during the Cuban missile crisis a few months earlier. The success of Sadat's move seems to be due to the fact that he gave the Israelis what they had wanted all along: the recognition of Arab countries that Israel had a right to exist. It is quite conceivable, however, that conciliatory moves could have other results. When the stronger party in a conflict situation makes a conciliatory move, the other party may view this as an opportunity to catch up or surpass the other side in strength. When the weaker party makes a conciliatory move, the stronger may view this as an act of desperation which signals that a complete victory can be won by becoming more aggressive.

Advocates of the gradual-tension-reduction approach can reply that there is some risk in any situation. One must also take account of the risk involved when tensions continue to mount and actual fighting breaks out using today's devastating weaponry. Furthermore, the GRIT proposal as worked out by Osgood preserved a retaliatory capability. The gradualist is not suggesting unilateral disarmament, only unilateral conciliatory moves which may induce the other party to reciprocate. The other party may not reciprocate, but how can this be known until the attempt is made? Although our discussion of the peace through tension-reduction approach has been focused on international relations, this same type of strategy could also be applied to group conflicts within nations.

Osgood's GRIT proposal was addressed to a situation where trust had to be established where little existed. More recently the idea has been developed that treaties worked out between previously hostile parties should contain confidence-building measures (CBMs) so that the trust that has been built up can be continued. These measures include efforts to build transparency, that is, to let the other side know what is being done. Examples of CBMs are regular reporting about the quantities of various kinds of arms one has, providing information about the military exercises one is planning, and establishing periodic conferences to discuss whether there are any problems that need to be addressed.

Peace Through Good Relations, Morality, and Cooperation

Although there are obvious differences between international relations and interpersonal relations, there may nevertheless be some principles operative in the interaction between individuals which can also be applied to the interaction between nations. The GRIT proposal discussed in the previous section is a case in point. It was developed not by an expert in international relations but by psychologist Charles Osgood. The presumption made by Osgood is that some principles effective in reducing interpersonal conflict might, with suitable modification, be applicable to reducing international conflict. Undoubtedly one must be careful in making such a move. Nevertheless certain kinds of behavior which tend to keep interpersonal conflict under control should be considered in terms of what they may suggest for more peaceful international relations.

One kind of behavior which seems to promote good interpersonal relations is regularly *communicating* with others and especially responding to messages received from them.

In international affairs, the parallel of such politeness would be the maintenance of diplomatic relations with all other countries which indicate a desire to have them. Even if their interests and ideologies are different, nothing is to be gained by refusing to have official dealings with them. Such a response can only create bitterness and almost guarantee unfriendliness in return. Communicating with another person does not mean that one approves of that person's life-style, and in a similar way maintaining diplomatic relations with other countries need not indicate approval of the governments or policies of those countries. In both interpersonal and international relations, the frank and open exchange of views seems more fruitful for preventing violent conflict than the refusal to maintain communication. The courtesies and rituals of diplomatic exchanges can take some of the edge off even the most bitter disputes. One way of promoting peace would be the maintenance of proper diplomatic relations with all other governments that desire them, regardless of their ideologies.

At the same time sometimes in interpersonal relations strong antagonistic feelings develop, and then peace may best be achieved by a separation of the feuding parties. If two persons have found they cannot tolerate each other, perhaps the best course of action is for each to have nothing to do with the other. Similarly, in international relations peace may be furthered if two antagonistic countries simply ignore each other. Unfortunately, such a solution often is not possible in international affairs because of geographical proximity or other factors.

Another important aspect of interpersonal behavior which may provide some ideas about how to solve the problem of violent international conflict is *morality*. In interpersonal relations morality provides a basis for individual restraint. It is based on notions of reciprocity (don't do things to others that you wouldn't want them to do to you) and the benefit to each person of a peaceful social order (rather than having a situation where each person pursues his own self-interest without any regard to the interests of other individuals or the welfare of the group as a whole). Similarly, in international relations morality based on reciprocity and the benefit to all nations of a peaceful international order can serve as a welcome restraint on the actions of national governments.

Many, perhaps most, scholars of international affairs would consider any attempt to apply moral principles to the behavior of nations as completely misguided.[19] They would contend that nations are quite different from individual persons. They would argue that the very purpose of national governments is to promote the interests of the nation while people do not exist merely to promote their own interests. Individuals are necessarily part of a social order while nations are not necessarily part of a community of nations. Leaders of nations, they contend, must think purely in terms of the preservation of their own nation and the furthering of its interests. To determine policy on the basis of some notion of international morality, it is claimed, would be to act contrary to their duty to the nation they lead.

Regardless of how widespread this view is, it must be questioned. The view that the national governments should be concerned only about the people of their own nation neglects the fact that nations are composed of people who have a species-kinship with people of other nations. Those living in other countries are people too, and our empathy with them does not end at the nation's borders, no matter how much some national governments may try to promote such a limitation of concern. Furthermore, nations more and more *do* live in a community of nations. Only a few of the larger nations of the world are even close to being self-sufficient communities. The main point to be made in connection with the view that national governments should not be restrained by any kind of moral considerations, however, is that widespread acceptance of this doctrine of the absence of morality in international relations is itself at least partly responsible for the prevalence of war in the world. If individuals were to be guided in their behavior by a like principle that each person should pursue only personal interests regardless of the effects on others, then the same kind of animosity and violence which is sometimes found in international relations would be observed in interpersonal relations. A recognition of the need for morality among nations based on the principle of reciprocity and the value to all nations of a peaceful international order would undoubtedly reduce the amount of war in the world. National leaders would be free to promote the interests of their state, but only within the limits permitted by international morality.

Has there ever been anything like moral behavior on the part of nations? A few examples may help to refute the notion that moral behavior is completely unheard-of in international affairs. One case occurred in 1956 when U.S. allies Britain, France, and Israel attacked Egypt, then ruled by Nasser and supplied with military equipment by the Russians. Surely expediency dictated that the United States would support its allies against a nation generally regarded at that time as being at least partly in the Communist camp. But the United States, following principle rather than expediency (and also eager to keep the Soviets from having an excuse to put their military forces into Egypt), worked with the Soviet Union in the United Nations to stop the attack made by its own allies on grounds that it violated the U.N. Charter's prohibition against aggression. One could also point to the Marshall Plan undertaken by the United States after World War II to assist Western Europe in rebuilding itself economically. This plan was undoubtedly motivated in part by a desire to keep the Communists from gaining control in these countries, but the United States might have tried to achieve that aim by continued military occupation and policies similar to those followed by the Soviets in eastern Europe. Economic assistance to the less developed countries of the world should also be mentioned, especially that which comes through the United Nations with no strings attached, as well as international disaster relief efforts and the acceptance of refugees from other countries. It seems that humanitarian concerns at least sometimes extend beyond national boundaries.

The debate in the United States concerning the ratification of the Panama Canal treaties in 1978 reveals the kinds of arguments which can be advanced for and against a foreign policy based on moral restraint. The Carter administration's morally oriented policy was based on the assumption that the United States should be sensitive to the national interests of Panama and to the attitudes of Latin Americans toward the United States. The heavy-handed manner by which the United States had gained control of the Canal Zone in the first place was considered somewhat questionable. The opponents of Carter's moral approach regarded that historical point as irrelevant and appealed instead to the current national interest of the United States. They argued that the United States was a powerful nation and should not yield anything to a small Latin American country ruled by a dictator. Furthermore, they argued, the decision on the Canal treaties should be evaluated strictly from a military point of view and in the Cold-War context of the worldwide struggle against the Soviet Union.

These two views on the Canal treaties dramatize how a moral or idealistic approach which takes account of the interests of other countries differs from a so-called realistic approach which appeals solely to national self-interest and militaristic considerations. The realistic approach is consistent with the peace through military strength strategy previously discussed, but it tends to arouse resentment. The other nation may not respond militarily at that moment, but a readiness to use violence has been created and may be manifested when the opportunity presents itself. The moral or idealistic approach, on the other hand, tends to stimulate friendship and increase the long-term prospects for peace. It may, of course, also encourage the oppressed to be more vocal about their other complaints, but in the long run this reaction seems preferable to ongoing suppressed indignation. These same kinds of considerations enter into more recent debates about U.S. policy toward Communist China. Should China be treated with respect as a country which has its own cultural values and perspectives, or should the United States use its economic and military might to try to coerce China into conforming to our standards and interests?

Another principle from interpersonal relations that seems applicable to international relations is that *working together* on mutually beneficial projects tends to promote friendship.[20] Of course, it is possible that such joint efforts may also produce tension, so it is important to choose the right kinds of projects. An example of the wrong kind of project was the Apollo-Soyuz Test Project in 1975 in which American and Russian spacecraft were joined in space. The Russians and Americans involved shook hands in space as well as conducted a few joint experiments, and the events were jointly televised to the peoples of both countries and to the rest of the world. Nevertheless, this joint space venture was not a particularly good choice for a cooperative project because of the close connection between space technology and military technology. There were those in both nations who suspected that the other side was using the project to find out more about its technology.

There are many places in the world where relations could be improved by carrying out joint projects. In the Middle East the Israelis and Arabs could undertake joint development projects which cross their national boundaries. Such joint projects might also be worked out by India and Pakistan. On the island of Cyprus, projects could be undertaken which would help both the Greek and Turkish communities. This strategy can be used within countries when the leaders of groups between whom there is tension can establish some projects on which the opposing groups can work together. It is undoubtedly difficult to get such projects started, but experience shows that when carefully planned and implemented they do work to decrease tension.

Closely related to the idea of joint projects is the idea of the mutual exchanges of people between communities. An extreme example of this approach is the practice of exogamy among some primitive peoples. Since young people are required to marry outside their own group, kinship relations are built up among individuals in the different groups.

Under such circumstances the likelihood of war among these groups is greatly reduced, especially since even the leaders then have these extra-group kin. Exogamy does not seem very workable in the modern world, but something like it was practiced not too long ago among European royalty. It is still possible, however, to encourage exchanges of entertainers, athletes, artists, teachers, engineers, students, and other groups. Such exchanges promote an awareness that foreigners have skills, interests, and attitudes which are not unlike those of the people in one's own country. As more and more individual friendships are built up across national boundaries and between ethnic groups, there is more and more resistance to the possibility of war between them.

Another kind of exchange is the exchange of information. Governments can encourage the exchange of books and magazines, films and tapes, lecturers and educators. One possible development would be for news broadcasters and journalists from different countries to have regular programs on local stations. With modern communication equipment it is possible to hear radio broadcasts from other countries and to communicate by phone or e-mail with people in other countries. When people travel to other countries, as is now possible for an ever increasing number of people, there is a two-way exchange of information between travelers and local residents.

Our discussion of cooperative projects and exchanges has now gone from dealing with *government-to-government* relations to dealing with *person-to-person* relations. Modern communication and transportation systems, the existence of a global economy, and increasing interest in matters beyond the borders of one's own country mean that more and more individuals not connected with the government are meeting other individuals from different countries and different ethnic groups. Deliberate efforts by groups of individuals to "build peace" by reaching out personally to "enemy" groups, independently of what their national governments or ethnic leaders might want to do, have become widespread enough to be given a name. It is called "Track-Two Diplomacy," a term first used by Joseph

Montville of the U.S. State Department in 1981.[21] Not all of these "citizen-diplomacy" efforts are as highly structured as his own version of how such an exchange between "opposing groups" should be organized. Montville's model contains three key components: (1) an informal problem-solving three- to five-day workshop composed of small numbers of politically influential members from the "opposing" groups mediated by a small cadre of psychologically sensitive trained facilitators, (2) a "grand strategy" worked out in the workshop to influence public opinion to be supportive of efforts to move toward more harmony, and (3) the implementation of a project which is economically advantageous for both of the "opposing" groups. Even though Montville is from the U.S. State Department, he does not propose this as a government-sponsored activity but rather as one that non-governmental groups can promote.

Citizen diplomacy to promote cooperative projects and exchanges seems to be a worthwhile approach to peace whether it is sponsored by governments or by non-governmental groups. If it were promoted by governments it would fit nicely into our present subject of policies national governments might follow to promote peace. On the other hand, if it were promoted by nongovernmental groups, it would seem to require a different place in our discussion of proposals for solving the war problem, probably in the chapter on reforming individual attitudes. Montville himself ties citizen diplomacy to the idea of functionalism as a road to peace, a topic which we will discuss in the next chapter. Track-Two Diplomacy has been placed in this chapter because it is so closely tied to the idea of cooperative projects as a way of improving relations between societies in conflict, even though the exchange may be sponsored by nongovernmental groups as well as by governments.

The great difficulty for joint projects and mutual exchanges as a road to peace is how to get them started when tensions are high. Even if it becomes possible to work out such projects or exchanges during a period of high tension, they might well be sabotaged in one way or another by a few individuals, leading to more antagonism than if there had been no joint project or exchange efforts in the first place. But once there is a break in a confrontation situation, these joint projects and mutual exchanges can do much to solidify the new spirit of cooperation, either in the international situation or between groups within a country. Respect for the other group, a sensitivity to the interests of the other group and to the advantages of peace, and the implementation of cooperative projects can be expected to promote peace. On the other hand, coerciveness, hard-nosed selfishness, and a refusal to undertake joint projects can be expected to increase the probability of violent conflict in the long run.

Peace Through Third-Party Involvement

When a conflict arises between two parties, there are various devices for trying to resolve it. One, of course, is a contest of force. But in most situations the parties can agree in advance that they do not want to use force to settle the disagreement if another way can be found. One of the most common approaches is to bargain. When both parties have a great deal to lose if they cannot come to some kind of agreement, there is a great deal of pressure to be conciliatory. On the other hand, in most negotiating each side tries to get the best bargain it can, and this factor tends to make each party unconciliatory. A bargainer who is "hard-nosed" tends to be rewarded while one who is too conciliatory gives up more to the other side than necessary. Consequently, the bargaining process itself is usually very tense as each side tries to get all it can. Most of the interaction between nations takes place by bargaining. In some situations, however, bargaining does not resolve the issue and the conflict continues. Is violent conflict the necessary outcome? Not necessarily. There are other ways of trying to resolve the dispute. One important alternative is the introduction of a third party to try to help the two sides come to an agreement. This third party may intervene on its own because it wants the dispute settled or it may be invited to participate by the parties in the conflict.

We can distinguish four different roles a third party might play in trying to resolve a conflict: (1) provider of "good offices," (2) mediator, (3) arbitrator, and (4) adjudicator. To *provide "good offices"* means to assist the parties in a conflict to communicate with each other in a situation where bargaining has not even begun or where it has ceased because of its apparent hopelessness. The "good offices" may consist of conveying messages between parties who have refused to talk to each other or of providing a neutral meeting place for representatives of the two sides so neither one needs to agree to meet at a place favorable to the other.

Mediators do more than facilitate communication. They actually make proposals which they then encourage both sides to accept. In their proposals they are able to bring in an outside perspective about what seems to be a fair agreement. When there is a mediator on the scene, negotiators for the opposing sides can explain any conciliatory actions to their constituents on grounds that they are merely reacting positively to the efforts of the mediator while still being adamantly opposed to the other party. This point is important because the negotiators need to be able to assure the people they represent that they are getting everything they can for their own group. Sometimes mediators may even offer some rewards of their own to the disputing parties to try to get them to accept the proposed solution. Still, the mediator must get both sides to accept explicitly all aspects of the proposed agreement before the conflict is resolved.

In arbitration, the two parties who can't reach an agreement on the issues which divide them are at least able to agree in advance that they will abide by the decision of an *arbitrator* they both view as neutral. They each present their case to the arbitrator, who then renders a judgment about how all aspects of the dispute are to be resolved. The obvious difficulty for this approach is to find an arbitrator whom both sides can really trust.

Adjudicators differ from arbitrators in that they limit themselves to the legal aspects of the case. They are concerned not with making a decision that will be perceived as acceptable by both parties involved but only with rendering a judgment about what the law dictates in this particular case. Some sorts of disputes are best handled by an arbitrator while others, where laws are already prescribed to govern the situation, may best be handled by an adjudicator or judge.

How does this discussion apply to conflicts between nations and between groups within nations? Sometimes one national government will act as provider of good offices, mediator, or arbitrator in a dispute involving other national governments. On other occasions a particularly respected individual or group of individuals may be called on to act as a third party to help settle a dispute between nations or between groups within a nation. International organizations may also serve as third parties in dispute settlement, especially in the areas of mediation and adjudication, but discussions of their role will be postponed to the next section in which the use of international organizations to promote peace will be the theme.

A good example of third-party intervention on the initiative of the third party itself is U.S. participation in the conflict between Israel and its Arab neighbors. The U.S. would like to see this dispute completely resolved. The U.S. has been the main supporter of the state of Israel since its creation in 1948, but it also wants to be on good terms with the Arabs because of how much oil they supply to the United States and its allies. The United States has been in a good position to act as a mediator in this dispute because both the Israelis and the leaders of most of the Arab governments regard the United States as a friend. President Carter offered large financial incentives to both sides in order to bring about the Camp David accords between Israel and Egypt in 1978. That led to a formal land-for-peace treaty between those countries in 1979. In 1982 the U.S. played a major role in preventing a fight to the finish between the Israelis and the Palestine Liberation Organization in Beirut, Lebanon. More recently the United States has been pushing the Israelis to settle their differences with the Palestine Liberation Organization. An important "Declaration of

Principles" was signed by both parties in September 1993 in Washington, but the effort to reach a final settlement in the dispute between the Israelis and the Palestinians is still being pursued. Some Arabs have raised the issue of whether the United States really is a neutral third party in this conflict and have suggested that there should be more reliance on other third parties such as the European Union or the United Nations.

Of course, many other instances of efforts to settle international disputes through the efforts of third parties can be cited. In 1871 the U.S. and Britain signed the Treaty of Washington which established the Geneva Arbitration Tribunal to settle what was known as the *Alabama* claims. These claims of the United States against the British were made on grounds that the British had illegally sold warships, including the *Alabama,* to agents of the Confederacy during the American Civil War. The arbitration panel decided that Britain should pay the United States $15,500,000 in damages, the British paid it, and the dispute was ended. In 1904 Russian warships fired on some British trawlers in the North Sea. The British demanded reparation. A Commission of Inquiry, consisting of naval officers from Britain, Russia, France, the United States, and Austria-Hungary, was formed to settle the dispute. It decided that the Russians should pay the British 65,000 British pounds. Once again the payment was made and the dispute was over. In 1905 U.S. President Theodore Roosevelt offered to assist in ending the Russo-Japanese War. His offer was accepted, and the United States played a major role in mediating the conflict, which ended with the signing of a peace treaty.

More recent cases of successful third-party intervention can also be cited. In 1949 Egypt and Saudi Arabia successfully mediated a dispute between Syria and Lebanon which arose from the killing of some Lebanese civilians by Syrian soldiers and which had led to a harmful cessation of trade between the two countries.[22] Turkey and Iran served as mediators in a border dispute between Pakistan and Afghanistan which began in 1947, when Pakistan gained its independence from Britain, and which lasted until 1963.[23] In 1967 President Hamani of Niger successfully mediated a dispute between Chad and Sudan which had occurred as a result of Sudanese assistance to Muslim insurgents in Christian-ruled Chad.[24] In 1958, a conflict flared up between Chile and Argentina concerning the possession of three islands at the southern tip of South America, and the British were called upon to act as arbitrators but without much success.[25] In 1977 Queen Elizabeth II rendered her judgment, based on the opinion of expert legal advisers, that all three of the disputed islands belonged to Chile, but the Argentinians refused to accept this judgment even though they had earlier agreed to abide by whatever decision was made.[26] In 1984, however, the dispute was resolved through the mediation of the Pope with the three islands still going to Chile but with Argentina getting control over most of the ocean around them.[27] In 1980 Algeria played a key role in getting U.S. hostages out of Iran.

The strategy of third-party settlement of disputes can also be applied to conflicts within a nation. Sometimes the third party in such disputes may be another nation. For example, a civil war in Yemen from 1962 to 1970 which saw Egyptian and Saudi Arabian intrusion to help the opposing sides was eventually settled with the assistance of Sudan and Saudi Arabia. At one point, representatives from Iraq and Morocco also helped oversee the withdrawal of foreign troops.[28] For another example, the United Kingdom took an active role in negotiating between blacks and whites in its former colony of Zimbabwe in order to work out a constitution acceptable to both groups and to supervise the first elections.[29] Of course, the mediators in intranational conflicts are not always, or even usually, persons from another country. Individual arbitrators acceptable to both sides can sometimes be found within the society involved.

From a broader point of view, in democratic societies where there is a large middle class, this class in effect functions as an ongoing mediator between the rich and the poor, between the ultraconservatives and the revolutionaries. In fact, it can be argued that in many less developed countries the situation is explosive just because there is no sizable middle class to serve as mediators. Consequently, the rich, who want to preserve their positions of privilege, and the poor, who are pressing hard for a more equal sharing of wealth and power, may both feel that only violence and the complete domination of one group by the other can bring the conflict to an end.

It should be evident that third-party mediation has proved to be an effective approach for resolving some difficult conflicts. In order to be successful, the third party must be perceived as impartial and as having a real desire to have the conflict resolved. When the third party also has power and influence which it is willing to use to help enforce an agreement and economic resources which it is willing to use to "sweeten" the agreement, success is even more likely. Of course, there is always the possibility that the third party who seeks to resolve a conflict may end up being viewed as an enemy by both the disputing parties. Nevertheless, it is to be expected that third-party involvement will become more widely used in the future to try to keep conflicts, both international and intranational, from becoming wars.

Peace Through International Conflict Management

During the past century an approach to peace which has attracted increasing attention is that of controlling or managing conflicts through the use of international organizations such as the United Nations and the International Court of Justice. The use of regional international organizations such as the Organization of American States (OAS), the Organization for Security and Cooperation in Europe (OSCE), and the Organization of African Unity (OAU) to control conflict among members is also part of this approach, but our discussion will focus on the use of the United Nations and the International Court of Justice.

This idea of peace through international conflict management began with the development of the League of Nations after World War I and has become much more widespread with the development of the United Nations after World War II. In a very general way one could say that this approach to peace uses an international organization as a third party to deal with conflicts between members of that organization. An organization such as the United Nations can be used in many different ways: to allow for a public airing of differences between disputants, to furnish trained individuals for private mediation, to send special commissions to determine the facts of a conflict situation, to provide armed forces to guard against violations of agreements that have been reached, and so on. The International Court of Justice (ICJ) can render legal judgments about the application of international law to particular conflict situations. In using this approach nations surrender none of their national sovereignty, but yet they make use of the forum and the machinery of international organizations in order to resolve their conflicts.

On the basis of past experience with the League of Nations and the United Nations, the strategy of collective security does not seem to have been a very trustworthy system for stopping aggressive attacks. Nations want the benefit of collective security if they are attacked, but they don't want to take on the costs of making their contribution to collective security if some other nation is attacked. Although the United Nations has solved the very difficult problem of working out a very precise definition of "aggression," the even more difficult problem remains of determining in a particular situation whether a given nation is an aggressor or not. Furthermore, even if there is general approval of the notion that a given country is an aggressor, there still may be little response to an appeal for help to fight against that aggressor.

As already noted, the United Nations has in actual practice developed an approach to controlling conflict not envisioned at the time of its founding, namely, the policing of agreements arrived at by the parties to the conflict after the Security Council (or in some cases the General Assembly) has passed a resolution calling for a cease-fire supervised by U.N.

forces. Our earlier chapter on the United Nations included a discussion of this type of effort called *peacekeeping* and described the many peacekeeping operations presently being carried out by the United Nations. In peacekeeping there is no effort to brand one country or another as an aggressor. The attempt rather is to stop the fighting and persuade the countries to resolve their differences in a nonviolent way. It should be evident, however, that this approach can be used only in those circumstances where all the big powers in the Security Council agree or where the General Assembly, in view of inaction by the Security Council, passes a resolution calling for a cease-fire under U.N. supervision. Of course, in situations where emotions run high, appeals by the United Nations may simply be ignored.

The formal peacekeeping operations of the United Nations are not the only means by which that organization can promote peace. Peacekeeping activities come into play only after a situation has become tense and fighting has broken out. Ideally, other kinds of U.N. efforts can keep a potential conflict from reaching the fighting stage. The Secretary-General may confer privately with parties which seem to be heading for a conflict. Fact-finding commissions can be appointed. The General Assembly or the Security Council can pass resolutions which serve as indicators of international public opinion. As a result, national governments may be more restrained than they otherwise would be. The existence of the international organization serves at least to some extent to inhibit its members from pursuing their national interests without regard to consequences for other nations and for the international community as a whole.

It is not possible to evaluate exactly how successful the United Nations has been in defusing conflict situations because some potential conflicts are kept from even coming to public attention by behind-the-scenes meetings of diplomats at the United Nations. It is possible, however, to look at the U.N.'s record in handling disputes which have reached the stage of public awareness. In a 1978 study of the effectiveness of the United Nations in managing conflict in various types of situa-

tions R. L. Butterworth concluded that "the U.N.'s effectiveness was strongly linked to American leadership."[30] As we noted in our previous discussion of U.N. peacekeeping, that conclusion is still relevant. When the United States leads the way and supports U.N. peacekeeping as it did in the period 1990-1993, then it tends to be successful. When the United States withdraws from active involvement and support as it did in the period 1994-1998, U.N. peacekeeping tends to decline both in quantity and quality (although the peacekeeping operations of other international organizations such as NATO and OSCE which get U.S. support may substitute for U.N. peacekeeping). The future success or failure of U.N. peacekeeping will depend greatly on the degree to which the United States decides to support it.

It would seem that if nations were really interested in promoting peace, they could make greater use of both the United Nations and the International Court of Justice (ICJ) than they do now. Instead of thinking simply in terms of how they can use the United Nations to advance their short-term national interests, they could focus their attention on how to make the United Nations more effective as a peacemaking and peacekeeping organization.

A beginning point for discussing how U.N. peacekeeping could be improved is U.N. Secretary-General Boutros-Ghali's *An Agenda for Peace* issued June 17, 1992.[31] One of the most important ideas the Secretary-General put forth in this report was the idea of *preventive diplomacy*. Until now official U.N. efforts have generally been confined to what happens after fighting has already taken place and a truce has been worked out. The Secretary-General said that the United Nations should become involved in crises *before* fighting occurs. Such an outlook means that the U.N. would be engaged in more of its own information gathering. There would be greater use of U.N. fact-finding missions. There would be the possibility of the deployment of U.N. peacekeeping forces within the boundaries of a country which believes that it may be attacked by another country. The U.N.

forces would go in, with the approval of the Security Council, to forestall an anticipated attack. Or in a situation where two countries are mutually suspicious of each other, there could be a demilitarized zone between the two possible adversaries with U.N. forces in that zone. The big difference from the present situation is that the U.N. peacekeeping forces would be put in place *before* any actual fighting breaks out. Another aspect of preventive diplomacy is that the Secretary-General would be authorized to go to the ICJ to get an advisory opinion on the legal aspects of a conflict before any military action occurs.

An Agenda for Peace also called on member nations to earmark particular national military units for U.N. peacekeeping. It recommended the pre-positioning of military equipment needed for peacekeeping operations so that when peacekeeping forces are created the needed equipment will be ready. One of the more controversial ideas in the report is that the United Nations should have a new type of enforcement unit, more heavily armed than the lightly armed units which have thus far taken part in U.N. peacekeeping. Such forces would be ready to go into more volatile situations where U.N. forces have not previously been prepared to go such as the former Yugoslavia. The report also called for cooperative peacekeeping operations where the United Nations and regional organizations such as the OAS, the OAU, and the OSCE work together. Such cooperation between the United Nations and regional organizations has already begun in Latin America and the former Yugoslavia. In addition the Secretary-General proposed that humanitarian relief be coordinated by the United Nations, not just where fighting is already occurring but also where there is a danger of armed conflict as a result of starvation or the absence of adequate housing or adequate health care, and so on.

With regard to the financing of U.N. peacekeeping, one suggestion was the creation of a Peacekeeping Reserve Fund so that money would be available during the initial stages of a peacekeeping operation. Then starting up a new peacekeeping operation would not be hindered by a lack of financial resources ex-

actly when they are most desperately needed. Another recommendation was that a U.N. Peace Endowment Fund of a billion dollars be created with the proceeds from the fund being used to finance various facets of peacekeeping. Another recommendation was that U.N. member nations start paying for U.N. peacekeeping out of their national military budgets instead of their foreign affairs budgets. It was also suggested that money could be raised for peacekeeping by some kind of a tax such as a levy on arms sales or a levy on international air travel. (But it was this very idea that led the United States to oppose a second term for Boutros-Ghali as U.N. Secretary-General.)

An Agenda for Peace also indicated that all member nations should accept the compulsory jurisdiction of the International Court of Justice — without reservations. Many countries have not even committed themselves to accepting the jurisdiction of the Court. Of those that have made such a commitment, many have hedged their commitment with reservations. For example, the U.S.'s commitment to the authority of the Court is compromised by the "Connolly Reservation" attached to U.S. acceptance of the Court's authority. The "Connolly Reservation" says that the United States will decide for itself what is and what is not a domestic issue and will not accept the authority of the ICJ to make that determination. The report of the Secretary-General recommended that all countries withdraw their reservations so that such loopholes to accepting the decisions of the ICJ can be closed. When some countries make such reservations to their acceptance of the Court's authority, then other countries feel that they also can adopt their own particular reservations. As a result the ICJ's utility for resolving international legal disputes is undermined.

An Agenda for Peace also called for more fact-finding by the United Nations. What the Secretary-General did not specifically say is that the U.N. needs its own "intelligence" agency, including its own satellites for information-gathering. At present the United Nations is dependent on being given information from national satellites operated by a very few countries. As early as the 1978 U.N. Special Session on Disarmament France proposed that the United Nations should have its own U.N. surveillance system, but during the Cold War progress toward any kind of implementation was blocked by both superpowers.[32] Such an information-gathering agency might be integrated into a U.N. Arms Control and Disarmament Agency that could verify compliance with arms control agreements using the satellites as well as random on-site inspections.

An Agenda for Peace called for some heavily armed U.N. units that could be used in situations where armed resistance is expected. Events in the former Yugoslavia and Somalia suggest that there is a real need for such forces. But this proposal is not likely to be effective unless it is modified a bit. The Secretary-General seems to be thinking of contingents from national armed forces that would engage in this dangerous mission, but national governments are not likely to send their soldiers into such a situation when their own national interest is only remote. What is needed is a standing force of individually recruited volunteers directly under U.N. control.[33] With this arrangement national leaders would not be put on the spot for risking the lives of the soldiers in their national armed forces. A force of individually recruited soldiers could operate in dangerous places to promote the world interest rather than being restrained by concerns of short-term national interest.

With regard to the use of courts as a way of dealing with international conflict, we should mention again the current effort to create an International Criminal Court (ICC) where individuals can be held accountable for violations of international law. In the 1991 Persian Gulf War U.S. President Bush said that the United States had nothing against the people of Iraq but only Saddam Hussein. But what happened? The coalition forces led by the United States killed a hundred thousand Iraqis, but Saddam Hussein is still in charge of the country of Iraq. Economic sanctions have been imposed on the country of Iraq for not allowing inspections for the building of weapons of mass destruction, but they are harming the people of Iraq rather than Saddam Hussein and his supporters. Where is the problem? The difficulty comes from trying to punish the country of Iraq rather than Saddam Hussein, the individual. The focus should be on individuals who are violating international law rather than on this or that country. The current effort to create an ICC means that we may be on the way to focusing on violations of international law by individuals rather than focusing just on national governments.

Peace Through Peace Research and Peace Education

In 1998, even though the arms race of the Cold War is past, worldwide expenditures for military purposes still amount to over two billion dollars a day.[34] The United States accounts for over one-third of it.[35] As weapons become ever more sophisticated, the cost of developing and producing them can be expected to continue to increase. Also, it can be supposed that other countries, including the allies of the United States, will decide to increase their military spending in order not to be left so far behind the United States technologically. Under these circumstances it seems that the national governments should be interested in promoting peace research and peace education to find alternatives to war so that these huge outlays of resources for the military would become unnecessary. It also seems that they would be motivated to do this because of how horrible any future wars will be due to the increasing destructiveness and accuracy of new high-tech weapons.

From the point of view of cutting their own future costs, it is hard to imagine what better investment could be made by national governments than support of peace research, especially when it is recalled that national governments are responsible for maintaining peace among opposing groups within their own society as well as preventing wars with other countries. It seems that nations cannot afford not to invest more of their resources in learning better how to promote peace.

Despite the desirability of supporting peace research, national governments are not contributing much to such efforts. Fortunately, financial support for peace research comes from many other sources such as foundations, trust funds, special prizes, membership contributions, and university budgets. Also some national governments have provided some direct support to peace research. Two outstanding examples of nationally supported institutions devoted strictly to the study of peace from an international point of view are Sweden's Stockholm International Peace Research Institute (SIPRI) and Norway's International Peace Research Institute in Oslo (PRIO). In 1984 the U.S. Congress authorized the creation of a U.S. Institute of Peace, and the Institute began functioning in 1986.[36]

What specific kinds of problems might peace researchers consider? One obvious task would be the evaluation of proposals for solving the war problem such as those discussed in this book. Research could try to determine how various approaches could be made more effective and to learn how particular approaches could best be applied to particular kinds of situations. Peace researchers could examine periods of peace as well as the beginnings of wars in order to try to learn what factors promote peace and what factors undermine it. The problem of how to educate people to promote peace could be investigated. The various topics discussed in this book provide only a beginning list of the issues which peace researchers need to study.

Peace research can also develop new proposals and techniques for resolving group conflicts and then test their effectiveness. One rather new technique which has been developed to be used when an arbitrator has been enlisted to try to resolve a conflict is the *last-best-offer technique.* After the regular bargaining process has gone as far as it can go, each side is asked to give its "last best offer" to the arbitrator, that is, to indicate the most conciliatory agreement it can bring itself to make. The arbitrator must choose one or the other proposal, whichever one is felt to be most fair, as the final settlement. It is not permissible to "split the difference" between the two offers, a different mediating technique which has the

adverse effect of encouraging each side to be more excessive in its demands so that it will be better off after the difference is split evenly. With the last-best-offer technique, each side is encouraged to be as conciliatory as possible in hopes that its proposal will be the one accepted by the arbitrator. Peace researchers could investigate how this and other techniques might be applied both to international disputes and to disputes between groups within countries.

Although peace research involves discovering and evaluating techniques which are immediately applicable to current conflicts, it must also deal with the more general issue of the relation between justice and peace. It needs to focus on the problem of peace not merely from the point of view of how to preserve the *status quo* without violence, but also from the point of view of how to remove the injustices and resulting resentments which prompt people to resort to violence. If peace research is not to be simply another instrument in the hands of those with power and privilege, it must focus on the processes by which peaceful change can take place. It needs to address itself to investigating alternatives to violence for those who are presently being treated unfairly by the social system as a whole. On the international level, peace research must be concerned with the plight of the less developed countries and how the international order can be changed in a peaceful way to accommodate the interests of these countries without ignoring those of the more technologically advanced countries. On the domestic level, peace research must deal with the situation of the poor and dispossessed and how the social system can be changed in a peaceful way so that it takes account of their interests as well as those of the rich and powerful.

It seems obvious that supporting peace research would promote justice as well as peace both within nations and among them. In fact, economist and peace scholar Kenneth Boulding maintained that there is nothing that can be done that would more dramatically increase the probability of the survival of humanity than a massive effort in peace research.[37] Such an effort might make the difference of whether or not we all die in a nuclear holocaust. It could save governments large sums of money now being spent for military forces, weapons, police forces, prisons, and special personnel for suppressing riots. It is distressing to note that national governments are so wedded to resolving conflict by force that they are generally unwilling to fund the efforts to learn about other techniques of conflict resolution.

What about peace education?[38] Here national governments face a difficult problem. As much as they might like to educate their people to be more informed about and committed to peace, they realize that the present international system may require them to resort to force to protect their national interests. As Gwynne Dyer observes, "To be a state is also, in practice, to fight wars...."[39] Thus every nation must prepare its citizens so they will be ready to participate in wars. Under such circumstances it is not surprising that most national governments are less than enthusiastic about promoting peace education. Substantial support for peace education on the part of national governments is not likely until the system of sovereign nations is changed. How that system might be changed to promote peace is the topic of the next chapter.

16. Reforming the International System

We have reviewed proposals for promoting peace by reforming the attitudes of individuals, by reforming the internal operations of national governments, and by reforming the policies of national governments. We turn now to another set of proposals based on the view that, as helpful as some of these other proposals may be, there can be no lasting solution to the war problem until the present anarchy among nations is replaced by some kind of organization at the international level that puts some limits on national sovereignty.

The present international system consists of about 200 sovereign nations, each devoted to the pursuit of its own national interests. When we say that these nations are *sovereign,* we mean that there is no higher authority to which they are subject. As we have already noted, even the most significant international organization which presently exists, the United Nations, is based on acceptance of the principle of national sovereignty. Although there are some parts of the U.N. Charter which suggest that the Security Council can require member nations to do certain things, no nation can be forced to yield its sovereignty. If an effort were made by the United Nations to coerce a nation to do something it doesn't want to do, it could just withdraw from the organization and then would no longer be legally subject to its jurisdiction.

Those who believe that the system of sovereign nations must be changed before an enduring and dependable peace can be established argue as follows: There are bound to be conflicts of interest between different nations. These conflicts may be resolved by bargaining, mediation, arbitration, and adjudication; but if the conflict is intense and the nations involved have approximately equal military power, it can be expected that situations will arise in which each of these nations or groups of nations will insist on having its own way. So long as there is no higher authority which can settle the dispute, the opposing parties will use threats of force, and ultimately war itself, to try to resolve the conflict in accord with their own interests. The only way to avoid these wars and the military buildups which are related to them, it is claimed, is to place some restriction on national sovereignty. Those who want disarmament by the nations first and *then* a consideration of alternative nonviolent ways of resolving disputes are hoping for something that can never be. It is only *after* trustworthy nonviolent means of resolving disputes which limit the sovereignty of nations have been developed that one can expect the national governments to seriously consider disarming.

According to those who maintain that the international state system must be changed, part of the difficulty with the present system is the roles that national leaders are required to play. National leaders are expected to do everything possible to promote the national interest. Conciliatory moves with regard to the concerns of other nations may be taken as a sign of weakness and a betrayal of the nation they lead. A great deal of the power in the world is in the hands of national leaders who must play this role. On the other hand, who has the role of looking out not just for this or that nation or group of nations but for the whole human race? Who has the job of being concerned more about promoting world peace than about promoting national interests? The present international system lacks anyone with power to play this role. The Secretary-General of the United Nations comes closest to having such a position, but even he serves at the pleasure of the national governments and dares not say or do anything that might offend the more powerful ones. (Consider how the United States alone kept Boutros-Ghali from having a second term as U.N. Secretary-General.) The representatives of the national governments at the United Nations for the most part view themselves as having a responsibility not to solve world problems but only to protect the interests of the national governments they represent and who pay them. Under such a system, it is claimed, global justice and enduring peace are not likely. It is necessary to change the structure so that the power of those concerned about purely national interests is more limited while the power of those concerned about the welfare of everyone in the whole human community is strengthened.

Another difficulty with the present international system, it is argued, is that the notion of national sovereignty is not consistent with the realities of the modern world. National sovereignty is based ultimately on the two assumptions that nations are self-sufficient social units and that national governments are capable of protecting their citizens from any harm which might be done to them by those in other lands. But in today's world neither assumption is true. No nation exists which is not at least somewhat dependent on the events that take place in other national societies. Even the largest nations have needs which they themselves cannot meet. National governments also are no longer able to completely protect their citizens from any harm that might be done by people in other lands. It is obvious that the governments of the smaller and weaker nations are "sovereign" only in theory. Furthermore, even the superpowers cannot protect their own people completely. They cannot stop intercontinental missiles tipped with nuclear warheads from falling on their cities. Even if such an attack were deterred by threat of retaliation, governments cannot save their own citizens from the radioactivity of a nuclear war in which their own nation is not even involved. What could the United States do to protect its citizenry from radioactive fallout in the event of a nuclear war between Russia and China? All the deterrent weaponry in the world would not help. On another issue, might someone in another country manage to disable my computer when I look at a message which has been sent to me? How is my national government going to be able to protect me from that kind of harm? On longer-range issues, what can my national government do to pre-vent people in other lands from allowing CFCs to escape into the atmosphere, thus contributing to the destruction of the ozone layer which protects me from ultraviolet rays from the sun. It is no longer true that nations are self-sufficient and that national governments are capable of protecting their citizens from all dangers originating in other societies. As a consequence, it is argued, it is now necessary to move beyond an international system based on the obsolete idea of unlimited national sovereignty.

Does this proposal to establish a global system which limits national sovereignty reflect an idealistic or a realistic view of international politics? Typically it is the *idealists* who have thought in "utopian" terms of moral obligations beyond national borders and the need to adopt and abide by treaties rather than relying on military might and coercion. It is the *realists* who have thought in "hard-headed" terms of following enlightened self-interest and relying on physical force rather than just trusting nations to abide by treaties they have made. How does this proposal to move toward a global government fit into this idealist-realist distinction in thinking about international relations? It seems to reflect both viewpoints. On the one hand, like the *idealist* view, it supposes that we need to think in terms of what is good for the whole human community in the long run rather than just what is good for our limited national community in the short run. On the other hand, like the *realist* view, it says we cannot just rely on good intentions and people being nice to each other and keeping their promises. A system of enforceable world law needs to be established, says the world governmentalist, and individuals who violate it need to be tried and, if guilty, prosecuted.

It is significant that Hans Morgenthau, universally regarded as one of the great spokespersons for the realist viewpoint in international relations theory, very late in his life "stated that [because of the development of nuclear weapons] world government has become an historical imperative."[1] In commenting on this 1978 assertion, International Law professor Anthony Boyle says:

Those familiar with the work of both men [Morgenthau and Harvard Law Professor Louis Sohn] could not have been more surprised by Morgenthau's breathtaking answers. In the post–World War II study of international relations it had always been assumed that there existed a spectrum of view points ranging from the extreme realism of Hans Morgenthau, on the one side, to the extreme idealism of Louis Sohn, on the other, and with everyone else falling on the line somewhere in between. Morgenthau himself [by saying "Sohn and I might start from different principles, but we have arrived at the same conclusion"] had turned that line into a circle. By his own hands he had joined the two endpoints.[2]

The idea of a world government with its system of enforceable world law can thus be viewed as the synthesis which joins the seemingly opposed idealist and realist traditions in international relations theory.

How might a change from unlimited national sovereignty to a system of global law be carried out? One possibility would be limiting or bypassing national sovereignty with regard to specific international situations. A second possibility is the consolidation of groups of nations into larger but less-than-global political units on the basis of geography, culture, or ideological commitments. A third possibility would be the establishment of a world government over the national governments so that the kinds of political and judicial institutions for resolving conflict now found within nations would be created at the global level.

Those who prefer the third alternative, who would like to see the establishment of a world government, may still differ on which of three possible approaches is the best way to bring about such an institution. The *federalist approach* to world government advocates the deliberate decision by national governments to transfer certain powers (such as maintaining armed forces) to a world government while retaining other powers (such as establishing laws concerning the ownership of property) for themselves. The *functionalist approach* to world government advocates the creation of more and more global functional agencies (such as the World Health Organization, the Food and Agriculture Organization, and the Universal Postal Union) to handle particular global problems until such

agencies collectively constitute a world government handling all the problems of the global community. The *populist approach* to world government advocates a grass-roots people's movement to establish a democratic world government directly responsible to the people of the world. For them the strategy is to circumvent the existing obstructionist national governments and create a global political institution which would control national governments rather than being subservient to them.

Limiting National Sovereignty in Specific Situations

There are many particular ways in which national sovereignty might be limited or bypassed in order to reduce the likelihood of violent conflict. In order to give some organization to our discussion they will be considered under seven headings: (1) developing supranational agencies for governing territory not already controlled by nations; (2) modifying voting arrangements in the United Nations in order to diminish the influence of the principle of equal national sovereignty for all states regardless of size and economic power; (3) allowing the United Nations to have sources of revenue other than contributions from national governments, thus making the United Nations less financially dependent on national governments; (4) extending the powers of the International Court of Justice (ICJ) so that it can assist in the resolution of more conflicts; (5) allowing the United Nations and international judicial bodies to interact directly with private parties to help resolve international conflicts; (6) developing a standing autonomous international peacekeeping military force which could intervene in conflict situations; and (7) using direct nonviolent action by a nongovernmental group against the use of armed force by national governments. Thus this discussion aims to call attention to some ways in which the principle of national sovereignty might be gradually eroded in order to promote the peaceful resolution of conflicts.

One of the more promising approaches

to limiting national sovereignty is just to prevent it from spreading beyond its present limits. There are still parts of the world, such as the oceans, which so far have not been claimed to be under the jurisdiction of national governments. Traditionally international law maintained that the oceans could not be claimed by any nation or made subject to the laws of any country. "The freedom of the seas" meant that ships could go anywhere on the oceans. It meant that one could take out of the oceans fish, whales, or whatever else was wanted and dump into the oceans garbage, sewage, radioactive wastes, or whatever else wasn't wanted. In order to protect their coasts, nations were allowed sovereignty over an area out to three miles, called the "territorial sea" because it was regarded as the territory of the coastal nation. But beyond this three-mile limit, the seas belonged to no one.

Since World War II nations have been expanding their area of control of the oceans. In 1945 the United States, having discovered oil under the Gulf of Mexico in its continental shelf (the ground which slopes away from land but which is still under water), claimed ownership of all natural resources in the shelf, even beyond the earlier three-mile limit. In 1952 Chile, Ecuador, and Peru, not having much of a continental shelf but having many fish, upon which their economies depended, swimming in the waters off their coasts, joined together in the Santiago Declaration claiming ownership of the resources in the ocean itself out to a distance of 200 miles. Other nations also began claiming resources off their coasts beyond the three-mile limit.

To try to prevent further grabs of ocean resources and to eliminate possible violence from conflicting claims, the U.N. General Assembly in 1969 passed a resolution calling for a moratorium on efforts to exploit the resources of the sea-bed under the oceans until an international regime was established to control such exploitation. In 1970 it passed a resolution declaring the oceans to be "the common heritage of mankind" and another calling for a Conference on the Law of the Sea. The U.N. Conference on the Law of the Sea (UNCLOS) held its first session in New York

in December of 1973. Then one or two sessions met each year until the text of the Law of the Sea (LOS) Treaty was finalized in 1982. It was to go into effect one year after it obtained 60 ratifications. The sixtieth ratification occurred on November 16, 1993, so the LOS Treaty entered into force on November 16, 1994. The United States, having opposed the treaty in the 1980s, signed it in July 1994 after negotiating some modifications, but the U.S. Senate has not yet ratified it. The LOS Treaty provides for a territorial sea twelve miles in width instead of three; for the preservation of the international status of straits even as the width of the territorial sea is otherwise extended; for an economic zone under the control of the coastal state extending out to 200 miles; and for an International Seabed Authority (ISBA) to control exploitation of the resources of the sea bed beyond the economic zone of the coastal states. The General Assembly designated 1998 as the International Year of the Ocean (IYOTO), and in April of that year the ISBA began operating under its own budget.[3] In August 1998 the ISBA Council held its first meeting at its headquarters in Kingston, Jamaica. In July 2000 the International Tribunal for the Law of the Sea (ITLOS) opened its permanent headquarters in Hamburg, Germany.[4]

The creation of this legal governance system for the oceans is especially interesting from the point of view of the issue of national sovereignty. For the first time in human history a region of the earth is being placed under the control of an international regime with law enforcement capabilities. Now that such a supranational governmental organization is organized and functioning, it could serve as a model for the creation of similar agencies to govern other areas such as Antarctica and outer space, including the moon and planets.[5] At any rate, the effort to create an international agency to control the resources of the sea bed represents a first step in ending the expansion of territory controlled by national governments.

A second situation where national sovereignty could be eroded is in the voting arrangements in the Security Council and the

General Assembly of the United Nations. In the Security Council each of the five permanent members (the United States, Russia, China, the United Kingdom, and France) has the power to cast a veto, thus blocking action even if all other members of the Security Council favor the action. The extravagant degree of sovereignty granted these five nations could conceivably be trimmed if there were certain situations in which the veto could not be used. For example, the veto power could be eliminated on votes concerning the establishment of fact-finding commissions, the interposition of peacekeeping forces to preserve the status quo, or the admission of nations into the United Nations. The difficulty, of course, is that the five countries with veto power would all need to agree to the limitations being suggested before they could become a reality.

In the U.N. General Assembly at present, each nation, no matter how large or small, powerful or weak, gets one vote. The number of people in a nation and the amount of economic wealth and military power it has make a great deal of difference in the actual conduct of international relations, but these factors are not reflected in the voting of the General Assembly. It is theoretically possible that a resolution could be passed by a two-thirds vote in the General Assembly on the basis of votes of countries which have about 1.7 percent of the world's population or which pay less than 0.2 percent of the U.N. budget.[6] Under such circumstances, who is going to pay much attention to votes in the General Assembly? Resolutions have no binding legal authority anyway, but the one-vote-per-nation arrangement means that their moral influence is minimal too.

A change in the voting rules to take account of factors such as population and economic power could be viewed as putting some constraints on the notion of national sovereignty, especially that part of the doctrine which holds that every nation is equal to every other nation. One well-known proposal is that put forward by Grenville Clark and Louis Sohn in *World Peace through World Law*. Their system proposed in 1966 provides that the four most populous nations — China, India, the Soviet Union, and the United States — would each have 30 votes. The 10 next populous nations would have 12 votes each, the next 15 would have 8 votes each, the next 20 would have 6 votes each, the next 30 would have 4 votes each, the next 40 would have 3 votes each, and the others would have one vote each.[7] Clark and Sohn's *ad hoc* allocation of votes approximates a system of representation in which the number of votes is proportional to the square root of the nation's population, which itself is another possible system for allocating votes. On the other hand, if one were to rely on population alone (rather than the *square root* of the population) as a basis for allocating votes, in 1966 China with 22 percent of the world's population and India with 16 percent would have had considerably more votes than the Soviet Union with 6 percent and the United States with 5 percent. Such a system would have deviated too much from the realities of power in the world, so Clark and Sohn proposed that all four of these countries have the same number of votes. Under their proposal the General Assembly would become a law-making parliament with very restricted powers. An obvious difficulty for this Clark-Sohn proposal is that the *ad hoc* system of allocating votes would need to be changed from time to time as populations change or as nations divide or combine.

Another proposal for weighted voting in the U.N. General Assembly is Richard Hudson's "binding triad" idea.[8] Each country would continue to cast one vote as it does now, but the votes would be tabulated three times. On the first tabulation each nation would be credited with one vote as at present, but on the second computation the vote of each country would be multiplied by its population, and on the third computation it would be multiplied by that country's contribution to the U.N. budget. Any measure which received at least a two-thirds (or some other specified proportion) favorable vote on all three tabulations would become binding international law. Thus, the General Assembly theoretically would become a law-making body, though it might require considerable negotiating skills to work out measures which could garner the required number of votes on all three counts.

Still another system of weighted voting which can be applied to both the Security Council and the General Assembly has been proposed by Joseph Schwartzberg of the University of Minnesota.[9] In this proposed system each member nation of the United Nations has an Entitlement Quotient (EQ) based on the same three factors used by Hudson. The EQ is the average of (1) the nation's proportion of the world's population, (2) the nation's proportion of contributions to the U.N.'s budget, and (3) the nation's proportion of the total membership of the organization (which of course would be the same for each nation). Based on 1995 figures, the EQ of the United States would be its proportion of the world's population (4.71 percent) plus its proportion of contributions to the U.N. budget (25 percent) plus its proportion of the membership (1/188 or 0.53 percent) all divided by 3 (to get the average) yielding an EQ of 10.08 percent. Sample EQ's for some other nations would be 7.7 for China, 5.8 for India, 4.6 for Japan, 3.9 for Germany, 2.7 for France, 2.2 for the U.K., 1.8 for Italy, 1.6 for Brazil, 1.4 for Indonesia, and 0.18 for Nauru and other ministates. Requirements for adoption of a measure in the General Assembly would remain as it is now. With regard to the Security Council, the U.N. Charter would no longer need to specify the permanent members by name. Some threshold such as 4.0 could be set for membership on the Council. Any country which had an EQ of 4.0 or more would be on the Council. Also any bloc of countries whose EQs together total 4.0 would be entitled to a seat on the Council. On this basis about 17 blocs could be formed to acquire seats, and one seat could be reserved for countries that had not become part of any bloc. These modifications in the voting in the General Assembly and the Security Council would allow them to function as a bicameral law-making body for the United Nations.

Still other systems of weighted voting have been developed. The point here is not to argue for any one proposal but to show that several possible systems are available. Such weighted systems of voting would be a step away from the unrealistic notion of the sovereign equality of all states, that each state deserves equal influence in votes in the U.N. General Assembly regardless of its population (several states have populations of less than 25,000!) or how influential it is in international affairs. It should be noted that all of the proposed weighted voting systems described above have been joined with the notion that the United Nations should be able to make laws and not just pass resolutions as at present. To make that kind of change, however, would in effect be moving all the way to a world government, not just taking a step in limiting national sovereignty. If we make a distinction, we can see that it is possible to move to weighted voting in the U.N. General Assembly even if that body can only pass resolutions. It could be argued that with weighted voting at least the General Assembly's resolutions would carry some moral authority. The unrealistic notion of equal sovereignty for each country would have been overcome. That is why weighted voting is being discussed at this point. At the same time, it is a mistake to think that the U.N. General Assembly would or should be given any real authority beyond what it has now until some kind of weighted voting system is adopted. Until then the Security Council will remain the body where the critical decisions are made. Adoption of Schwatzberg's proposal for weighted voting in the Security Council would mean a real limitation on the present absolute national sovereignty possessed in that body by the five permanent members. It seems probable, however, that at least some of them will use their veto-power to keep any such change from occurring.

A third situation where national sovereignty might be eroded concerns the financial arrangements for the United Nations. At present the only source of funds for the United Nations is assessments and contributions from national governments. This arrangement means that those governments which make substantial contributions can exert considerable pressure on the United Nations by refusing to pay certain assessments or by trying to put conditions on their payments or by threatening to withdraw from the organization entirely if displeased. The United Nations would be much less susceptible to such threats if it had its own source of funds. When the International Seabed Authority (ISBA) created by the Law of the Sea (LOS) Treaty becomes operative, it could tax the resources being taken from the ocean floor and pass some of the revenue along to the United Nations. A small tax might also be levied on all resources taken out of the economic zones of the oceans on the principle that all parts of the oceans, even that part which makes up the national economic zones, have been declared to be the common heritage of mankind. It has been suggested that a small tax (usually referred to as the "Tobin tax" after James Tobin, the Nobel-prize winning economist who first suggested it) could be collected on profits made on short-term currency trading, a measure that would discourage speculation on rapid international currency fluctuations as well as providing a huge amount of income. In fact, on 23 March 1999 the Canadian Parliament even passed a motion in support of the idea. It might also be possible to tax arms that cross national boundaries or to assess a proportional tax on any nation's military expenditure that exceeds 3 percent of its GNP. Perhaps the United Nations could collect fines for violations of regulations it might adopt governing air or water pollution which crosses national boundaries. In any case, if the United Nations had its own source of funds, it would be less vulnerable to economic threats from national governments, so to that extent their sovereignty would be limited.

The fourth situation where national sovereignty could be eroded concerns the International Court of Justice (ICJ) and other international courts. At present only national governments can be parties in cases before the ICJ, and the Court will accept a case only if all parties to the dispute agree in advance to abide by its decision. Only the Security Council, the General Assembly, and other U.N. organs and agencies which first get the approval of the General Assembly can get *advisory* opinions from the Court. Under these circumstances the ICJ has not been very busy. Why not expand the powers of the Court? One possible change would be to allow the Security Council to get binding decisions from the ICJ rather than merely advisory ones. A second possible change would be to allow the U.N. Secretary-General and regional international organizations such as the Organization of American States to ask for advisory opinions. A third possible change, one which would have a much greater impact on national sovereignty, would be to allow national governments to get *advisory* opinions from the ICJ in a conflict situation even though the other governments involved have refused to accept the jurisdiction of the Court. Other changes of the same sort are possible. The point is that the ICJ would be able to take a much more active role in resolving international conflicts if such changes were made.

A fifth way of making national sovereignty less of an obstacle in international conflict resolution would be to permit greater interaction between individuals on the one hand and the United Nations and the ICJ on the other. As the United Nations was originally conceived, the only place in which there was to be any interaction between the United Nations and individuals was the Secretariat, where persons are hired as employees of the United Nations. Also the Economic and Social Council (ECOSOC) was permitted to consult with nongovernmental organizations concerned with matters related to its activities. Otherwise, the United Nations and the ICJ can do business only with national governments and their representatives. But some changes toward more direct interaction between the United Nations and private parties are already taking place. For example, at the U.N. Special Session on Disarmament in 1978 representatives of nongovernmental organizations interested in disarmament were allowed to address the session.

What further changes might be made in permitting the United Nations and the ICJ to interact directly with individuals and nongovernmental organizations? One idea is to let the United Nations directly recruit individuals to serve in U.N. peacekeeping forces rather than relying on contingents of armed forces from national governments.[10] Another idea is to have the General Assembly create a second, advisory assembly composed of representatives from national legislatures or nongovernmental organizations which could propose resolutions to the main assembly.[11] With regard to judicial issues, there already exist international conventions which prohibit certain activities such as hijacking airplanes on international flights or using violence against diplomats, criminal activities carried on by individuals rather than national governments. The ICJ could create a subsidiary International Court for Individual Crimes (ICIC) to deal with those individuals who are accused of violating these international laws less severe than the crimes over which the International Criminal Court (ICC) will have jurisdiction once it comes into existence. The ICJ could also establish international courts to handle civil cases between private parties from different countries or between a private party and a foreign government. Among other things, such courts would provide a setting for resolving legal disputes between governments and transnational corporations. The creation of such international courts would allow another venue for such cases, so that they would not need to be tried in national courts as is presently the case.

A sixth way to move toward limiting national sovereignty would be for some nations to join together to create their own separate Active Peacekeeping Organization[12] or Peacemakers Association of Nations.[13] The peacekeeping police force created by this new international organization would consist of soldiers drawn from all member nations, and they would serve as individuals in a unified force rather than as members of national contingents. In every member country there would be stationed some soldiers from all other member states. Each member nation of the peacekeeping organization would know that the newly created force would automatically provide assistance to it under specified conditions such as an attack by another country. Policies concerning the use of the peacekeeping force would be promulgated by the

political assembly of the new organization, and the force could also be used to assist peacekeeping efforts of the United Nations. Such a peacekeeping association of nations would allow its member states to reduce their expenditures for defense while increasing their national security and their participation in international peacekeeping. It would also represent a step away from world anarchy and reliance solely on one's own national military forces for security.

A seventh approach to limiting national sovereignty involves the use at the international level of the Gandhian idea of nonviolent resistance. A nongovernmental organization could be created composed of individuals from all over the world who are willing to participate in unarmed and nonviolent activities at points of conflict anywhere in the world. These people would be dedicated to direct nonviolent action to oppose the use of force by national governments. Such a World Peace Brigade was organized in 1962 but lost its momentum by 1964 because of financial difficulties and differences of opinion on whether to emphasize reconciliation of the opposing sides from an impartial point of view or confrontation to advance the interests of oppressed people. Another difficulty was that action seemed always to be related to issues of justice within a country rather than being addressed to international conflicts and concerns. Nevertheless, Robert Johansen proposed the creation of a nongovernmental, international nonviolent police force which would engage in mediation as well as nonviolent direct action, and the World Peace Brigade has been rehabilitated under the new title Peace Brigades International (PBI).[14] PBI carries on four kinds of activities: (1) providing protective accompaniment for those (such as leaders of human rights groups and oppressed groups) whose lives are threatened, (2) providing moral support for human rights leaders who may be getting discouraged, (3) fostering peaceful dialogue and reconciliation among conflicting parties, and (4) training in nonviolence. It has carried on activities in the Balkans, Mexico (Chiapas), Colombia, Guatemala, Haiti, Sri Lanka, and the United States (native Americans).[15] This international group committed to nonviolent intervention serves as a moral force which acts as a check on national armed forces when they are used for purposes such as suppressing people in their own countries. Increasing the size of this effort is one way of limiting national sovereignty when a national government is oppressing its own citizens.

We have considered a number of ways to limit or bypass the sovereignty of national governments in order to facilitate the peaceful resolution of conflicts, but all these approaches to eroding national sovereignty are quite modest compared to the grander schemes to which we now turn.

Consolidating Nations into Larger Units

When nations decide to associate with each other to carry on joint activities, they can work out different structural arrangements for their collective enterprise. They may decide on a looser organization called a "confederation" or "league," or they may prefer a tighter organization called a "federation" or "federal union." (See chart on page 266.) In a *confederation* or *league* each nation retains complete sovereignty. The central body composed of representatives from the member nations may make recommendations for collective action, but each country retains for itself the right to act or not act in accord with the recommendations of the central body. Each member nation is free to leave the association at any time and for any reason. Furthermore, the central body has no right to deal with the individual citizens of the member nations but rather must confine itself to dealing with the governments of the nations which belong to it. International organizations such as the United Nations and the Organization of American States are examples of this confederate type of organization.

In the tighter kind of organization called a *federation* or *union* the structure is different. In this system certain areas of decision-making are given to a new central "federal" government, and the member nations surrender their power to make decisions regarding these matters. However, the power to make decisions in all other areas is retained by the members. In a federal system there is, then, divided sovereignty. The central government has the authority to make laws concerning certain types of issues, while the member nations have the authority to make laws concerning all other issues. On those issues where the central government has authority, laws will be made on the basis of some agreed-upon procedure usually involving voting by representatives. Each member nation must abide by the decisions made by these procedures on these delegated issues regardless of its own interests. Furthermore, in a federal arrangement members are not free to dissociate themselves from the central government once they have joined. If they were free to leave, the central organization would be reluctant to make any decision which any member nation didn't like, and the result in practice would be similar to the loose association found in a confederation. Finally, in a federal structure the central "federal" government will have the authority to arrest, judge, and imprison individual persons who violate those laws made by the central government. The member nations, of course, will have their own particular laws and will have the authority to arrest, judge, and imprison individual persons who violate these laws. The governments of the United States and Mexico as well as those of many other nations are examples of this federal type of organization.

The history of the United States furnishes an excellent opportunity for appreciating the differences between a confederation and a federation.[16] Even though 1776, the date of the Declaration of Independence, is usually taken to mark the beginning of the United States of America, the fact is that there was no federal government uniting the colonies into one country until 1789, when George Washington became the first President. The Revolutionary War (1775–81) was fought by 13 sovereign states joined in a collective war effort against British rule. The participants thought of themselves as New Yorkers or Pennsylvanians or Virginians rather than Americans.

Comparison of Confederation and Federation

Confederation or League	*Federation or Union*
Each member state retains its complete sovereignty, including having its own independent armed forces.	Split sovereignty: member states possess authority in some areas while other powers are delegated to the central federal government.
Each member state has a right to withdraw at any time for any reason.	No seceding from the union is allowed; commitment is to stay in the central organization.
Individual citizens of member states have no right to interact with the central organization.	Individual citizens may interact with central government in those areas where it has authority.
Individual citizens of member states cannot be arrested or tried by the central organization or its officials.	Individual citizens can be tried as individuals in federal court for violating federal laws and in state courts for violating state laws.
Primary loyalty of citizens is to their own state; no expectation of loyalty to the central organization exists.	Primary loyalty is to the central federal government while secondary loyalty to one's state or province is permissible.
All financial resources for the central organization come as contributions from the member states.	The central federal government has its own independent sources of revenue, including authority to tax individuals.

During the period 1781 to 1788, they cooperated together under the Articles of Confederation with an organization structurally very similar to the present United Nations. Each state had one vote in the Continental Congress, and the Congress could pass resolutions making recommendations to the states but could not make binding laws. In 1787, at a meeting in Philadelphia whose announced purpose was to formulate amendments to the Articles of Confederation, a Federal Constitution was drawn up to replace the Articles. The Federalists, under the leadership of Hamilton, Madison, and Jay, led the state-by-state battle for ratification of the Constitution which would convert the confederate structure then existing into the federal structure of the United States of America. The main argument for federation was that many problems facing the states (maintenance of good currency, payment of war debts, restrictions on trade and travel between states, foreign relations with European countries, growing ten-

sion between some states, and threat of successful insurrections) could not be solved without a federal government.

After the creation of the federal government in 1789, the precise limits of the powers of the federal government had to be worked out in practice. Eventually the American Civil War (1861–65) was fought to determine whether states could secede from the federal union when they felt that the federal government was exceeding its authority. Those who favored secession claimed that states were totally sovereign and had the right to determine their own policies free from interference by the federal government. On the other hand, the defenders of the Union claimed that if some states were allowed to secede it would be the end of the federal government and the states of North America would revert to a confederacy. The outcome of the war was the preservation of the federal nature of the central government and the firm establishment of the principle that no state could secede from that union.

Returning to the present international situation, some thinkers claim that it would be desirable for various groups of nations of the world to join together in a common effort to advance the welfare of their people and to protect themselves from exploitation and conquest by outside nations. For example, how many countries in Africa or Latin America are in a position to defend themselves against exploitation and domination by more developed countries? For another example, how can the countries of Western Europe expect to compete economically with the United States if each acts separately in terms of its own national interest? It seems that the best hope for many nations of the world is to unite with other countries in a larger, more powerful organization. Such organizations may be based on geographical proximity, similarity of culture, ideological agreement, or some combination of these.

We have previously mentioned the existence of various regional political organizations such as the Organization of American States and the Organization of African Unity. All of them are examples of loose confederations formed basically to keep outside nations from intervening in their part of the world. Even the European Community, which has changed its *name* to "European Union" and which may someday become a real union or federation, is still basically a confederation. These confederate organizations do not basically alter the present system of sovereign nations because they do not limit the sovereignty of their members. Consequently, the following discussion about consolidating nations into larger units will be limited to the forming of federations.

The argument for such federations is that they alone in the long run will be strong enough to protect the nations involved from being dominated by others. The federal structure promotes peace by decreasing vulnerability from outside attack and by providing political and judicial institutions for the nonviolent resolution of conflicts among their own members. It also promotes justice by decreasing vulnerability to exploitation. A United States of Europe, for example, should be able to protect itself militarily even without U.S. assistance, and it should be more effective at preventing domination of its economy by the United States or Japan. It could also help manage conflicts among its own members.

The development of regional federations in Africa and Latin America would also be significant. A united Africa could be more effective in keeping non–Africans from intervening in African affairs, thus preventing both military and economic exploitation. It could help to keep peace among the various nations in the region and possibly even help control violence within nations. A united Latin America would be more effective in resolving conflicts among its members and in protecting itself from economic exploitation by American, Japanese, and European businesses as well as by drug traffickers operating within its own jurisdiction. In both instances, however, the nationalistic attitudes, the disparity in size and wealth of the countries involved, and the competition among the nations of the region with each other make the creation of such federations very unlikely. For example, in Latin America Brazil conceives of itself as a future superpower. It would be reluctant to join any Latin American federation unless it was given a commanding role in the organization, but the other nations of that region probably would not join any federation in which Brazil was given a commanding role.

Although federations are usually based on geographical proximity, they can also be based on other factors such as ideology. Some champions of capitalistic democracy have suggested that all "free nations" should join together in a federation in order to preserve their way of life from both Fascists and Communists. In 1938 when Hitler was threatening Europe, Clarence Streit advanced the idea of an Atlantic Union, a federation of the mature democracies on both sides of the North Atlantic plus the nations which at that time made up the British Empire.[17] In his proposed federation, other nations could be admitted as they demonstrated their capability for conducting their affairs in a democratic way. Streit and his followers saw this Union of the Free as a step toward eventual world government, since it could grow to include more and more nations. The Union of the Free can't *start* as a global government, however, since there are too many nations in the world which are not committed to or experienced enough in the system of democratic government. If a world government were to be established at such a time, the people who understand how democracy works could be outvoted by national governments with autocratic systems. But a Union of all the mature democracies would create an extremely powerful supernation which could dominate the world scene and the United Nations in the same way that the United States dominates the Western Hemisphere and the Organization of American States. This Union would be a much more effective way to stop the spread of totalitarianism, whether of the left or right, than the existing international system in which the sovereign national democracies often are competing with each other rather than working together. On the other hand, according to Streit, a federation limited to the European democracies would be a mistake, since it would tend to accentuate differences between the United States and Europe rather than bringing them together as the Union of the Free would do.

Streit's idea of a union of the Western democracies is still attracting attention. The organization promoting his view is now called the Association to Unite the Democracies. At the beginning of 1999 U.S. Secretary of State Madeleine Albright outlined her priorities for the coming year, and indicated that one of them was the creation of a new organization of democratic countries.[18] On June 25, 26, and 27, 2000, in Warsaw, Poland two meetings focused on cooperation among democracies were convened. One was the Community of Democracies (COD) meeting of over 100 *government representatives* and the other was the World Forum on Democracy (WFD) conference of over 250 delegates from *nongovernmental organizations*. These developments have given new impetus to the idea of a federation of democracies.

In response to the point of critics that

such a union might well provoke those left out of the federation to form a countervailing union of *nondemocracies*, defenders of the Union of Democracies note that any union of the states left out of the original nucleus would be very weak compared with the economic and military power of the advanced democracies. Also nondemocratic countries lack the bonds of shared values to support a federation. Their only motivation for uniting would be to oppose the advanced democracies, and that kind of negative goal cannot be an enduring basis for union. Furthermore, these other countries would know that once they individually adopted a democratic political system and a free market economic system, they would be eligible for acceptance into the Union of the Free. Finally, the 1991 demise of the Soviet Union has led to a situation where hardly anyone now believes that an authoritarian centrally controlled system is ideal. The Union of Democracies would have not only economic and military power but also the psychological power of an attractive ideal.

What can be said in the way of evaluating this proposal for a Union of the Democracies? First, it can be noted that the attempt to create such a union might in fact lead to some dissension among the advanced democracies because it would force them to focus on their differences as they tried to work out rules for the union. How many votes would each country have in the central parliament? Would the top leader be selected by parliament as is done in many of the countries of Europe, or would there be a separate election for a president as is done in the U.S.? What language or languages would be used? Might the union be dominated by one or two countries? Informal cooperation among the democracies might be a better approach than trying to get them formally integrated in a federation.

A second concern focuses on the situation of those newly democratic countries which might not be invited to be part of the original nucleus of the Union of Democracies. What would be the reaction of the poorer, non-Western newer democracies such as India and South Africa if they were told that they are not yet sufficiently "experienced in democracy" to be included? Might there be a split between the more mature, richer, Western, Christian democracies and the other newer, poorer, non-Western, non-Christian democracies? Might the less wealthy immature non-Western democracies even decide to create their own separate "more democratic" union of democracies rather waiting to be invited to join the "rich white man's" club?

Advocates of a Union of Democracies have gradually become more sensitive to this issue. In response to earlier criticisms, there is no longer any general inclination to exclude non-Western, non-Christian democracies such as Japan from being in the beginning nucleus. The proponents of a Union of Democracies now generally assume that even less affluent countries such as South Korea, Mexico, Namibia, and Bangladesh could be included in the original nucleus. The new criterion for inclusion in the beginning nucleus might even be just sincerely wanting to be part of the federation of democracies.

The proposal to create a federation of democratic countries seems worthy of serious consideration as a way of moving beyond national sovereignty toward a democratic world federation. It would have two big advantages over the current idea of trying to create a separate geographical European Federation. First, it would no longer be necessary to decide where the boundary of Europe is, that is, whether Cyprus and Malta and Turkey and Georgia and Russia are or are not part of Europe. Second, it would avoid the risk of a rift between Western Europe and the United States since both would be included in the Union of Democracies. Canada and Japan and South Korea and Australia and India and South Africa could all be included. A difficult but not insurmountable problem would be specifying exactly what the criteria are for a country to be able to join the Union of Democracies and then determining whether a particular country has in fact met them. It seems that not every country which *says* that it is a democracy should automatically be able to join. At the same time, there would be a real danger of unfairly excluding some countries for reasons other than not being democratic.

World Government Through Federation

In the previous section the difference between a confederation and a federation was discussed. It was also noted that the United States of America began as a confederation but was then converted to a federation by the states because the confederate structure was unable to adequately handle many of the problems facing the emerging American community. World federalists suggest that the national governments of the world should follow a similar course of action and convert the present United Nations into a federal-type central government because its present confederate structure does not adequately handle many of the problems facing the world community — problems such as environmental degradation, starvation and sickness that could be eliminated if resources were more equitably distributed, violation of human rights by national governments, huge and increasing disparities in wealth, international crime, and lack of financial support for international governmental organizations as well as the absence of dependable instruments for resolving international disputes nonviolently. This world federalist approach to world peace proposes that national governments delegate certain powers (such as the authority to own and control the production of weapons of war) to a central federal government while retaining for themselves other powers (such as the making of laws governing property ownership, education, and family relations). Some world federalists would like to see many powers shifted to the central government so that it could deal with all the various global problems facing the world community; they are called *maximalist* world federalists. Others would want to shift only those few powers directly related to the problem of war and disarmament; they are called *minimalist* world federalists. In either case there would be a drastic change in the international state system. National governments would transfer authority to deal with certain kinds of issues to a new global government, a government which would be quite different from present national governments, not only because of its extensive scope and the heterogeneity of the people it governed but also because there would be no external enemy against whom defense would be needed.

Instituting a federal world government involves a fundamentally different strategy than that of the federal union of democratic nations just discussed. The advocate of a federal world government maintains that a union of any part of humanity against any other part of humanity is going to leave unchanged the fundamental situation of sovereign entities which might go to war against each other. Force and threats of force would then still be the determining factors in conflict situations. The advocate of the Union of Democracies claims that Western-style democracy will prevail if the free nations will only unify their efforts and take advantage of their superior power. Peace will come as a consequence of that strategy. The world federalist, on the other hand, focuses on the need to change the method by which ideological and ethnic conflicts are resolved. The world federalist wants conflict to be settled within a global political and judicial structure which makes resort to violence unnecessary and unacceptable.

The world federalist believes that a democratic world federation can be established at the global level even if all the constituent nations are not democracies. For the world federalist, what is important is to apply the principle of resolving conflicts by debating and voting at the international level, even if some of the constituent member states are not democracies. It is assumed that seeing how effectively the democratic system works (replacing violent battling with nonviolent balloting) at the global level will encourage countries to adopt that same system within their countries. The world federalist says that democracy can spread from the top down as well as from the bottom up. The way to proceed is to begin with the virtually universal global political system which already exists, namely the United Nations, and convert it into a democratic federation. If particular nation-states do not want to adopt a democratic system within their countries, that is their affair. After all, part of the idea of federalism

is that the subordinate units solve their internal problems as they desire. Also, the democracy-at-the-global-level approach of the world federalists avoids the very difficult problem of determining whether a particular national government is or is not "democratic."

World federalists argue that the institution of government which has been somewhat successful at providing for the peaceful resolution of conflict within villages, within city-states, within provinces, and within nations should now be extended not merely to geographical regions or groups of nations with a common ideology but to the whole world.[19] They claim that modern technology has created a global community which needs global political and judicial structures. Relatively inexpensive air travel, satellite television, and other communications services such as the internet have linked people more closely with some individuals in other nations than with many in their own country. More and more the national boundaries marked on maps make less and less difference to the everyday lives of people and the associations they form. These national boundaries are already less significant for the world community than the boundaries between the states were at the time the federal government of the United States was created. The world is ready, the world federalist says, for world government.[20]

One obvious question to be raised is whether there is any hope that such a federal world government could possibly be brought into existence in the very near, or even the distant, future. We will turn to that issue shortly. For the sake of argument, however, let us suppose that such a federal world government could be created. Would it put an end to war? It should be recalled that there are two kinds of war, those between governments and those within a governed territory, that is, civil wars. If all the peoples and territory of the Earth were under one government, there would be an end to "external" wars (unless a violent conflict arose with visitors from another planet!). But the possibility of civil war within that politically unified global community would remain. In fact, the existence of civil wars within the world community would not be inhibited by a concern about an external enemy as is the case within nations. Even the United States, which the world federalist likes to point to as an ideal example of a federation which evolved from a confederation, had a brutal civil war. If federation did not prevent war among the states of the United States, what likelihood is there that it would prevent war among the nations of the world?

In response to this challenge, an advocate of a world federation would argue that one war in 200 years is a much better record than probably would have developed had there been no federal government in the area of the world that now makes up the United States. Even that one civil war might have been prevented if the time between the election of the President and the time of his inauguration had been shorter, as it was later made to be by a Constitutional Amendment. Also, the establishment of a federal government for the United States promoted a coordinated expansion to the West and led the various state governments to converge in their structure and ideology. Completely sovereign states probably would have competed with each other for control of the West and may well have diverged more and more from each other in their structure and ideology. Wars probably would have been as common as they have been in Europe. The American experience suggests that a world federation would probably greatly reduce the probability of war even if it would not necessarily eliminate it entirely.

But, the opponent of federal world government will argue, one cannot put much confidence in a generalization drawn from a single case. Furthermore, it is claimed, there are some instances which suggest that sometimes nations live more peacefully together under separate national governments than they would if an effort were made to bring them under a single central government. For example, Norwegians and Swedes seem to have had more peaceful relations with each other after they decided to establish separate governments than when they were under a single government. Canada and the United States, Sweden and Finland, Spain and Portugal, and many other neighboring but sovereign nations live in peace with each other with no expectation of war between them even though there is no government uniting them. It seems that where nations are peacefully inclined toward each other a government over them is not needed, while if they are not peacefully inclined toward each other it would be impossible to form such a government.

One response which the defender of world federalism would make to this point is that nations which are peacefully inclined toward one another at one time may not always be so inclined and that a common government over them would help to cement a community of interests between them and make it more likely that any conflicts which do arise are fought out in the political and judicial arena rather than with arms. Other federations such as Switzerland, Germany, Brazil, and Mexico show that the experience of the American federation in maintaining peace is not unique. Another response would be that most individual persons get along peacefully with others most of the time but no one would conclude from this situation that government over individual persons is unnecessary or undesirable. Government is needed not so much for the many who would live together in peace anyway but for the few who will go on a rampage if they are not stopped by force mobilized by the community as a whole. Also, the existence of the government as an agency for conflict resolution through its political and judicial processes tends to keep adversaries from thinking in terms of using violence to resolve their differences.[21] Furthermore, a world federation would make it feasible to enforce arms control measures since enforcement would involve action against those individual persons who possess and make weapons of war rather than seeking to regulate whole national governments as must be done in a confederation. That is why world government is the best hope, not only for ending actual war but also for ending the military buildups and intelligence-gathering agencies that are an important aspect of the war problem. Just as the state governments within the United States do not need to expend resources for armed forces and spying agencies to protect them against possible attack from other states, so in a world federation the national governments would not need to spend large amounts to have well-equipped and well-trained armed forces and security agencies to protect themselves from possible attack from other countries.

One of the main concerns voiced by opponents of a world government is the worry that such a government might become a vehicle for a world dictatorship from which there would be no escape.[22] This same kind of concern was voiced by those who opposed adoption of the Constitution of the United States of America as a replacement for the Articles of Confederation. The advocate of federal world government would use the same response used by the Federalists to argue for the creation of the American federation, namely, that tyranny can be prevented by creating a government with checks and balances both within the central government and between the central government and the member states as well as by incorporating into the constitution of the central government a Bill of Rights limiting its powers.

Another factor which could be expected to help keep a dictatorship from developing at the world level is the absence of any external enemies. If we look at national governments, we see that the restriction of the rights of citizens is usually justified on grounds that it is necessary to protect the nation from its external enemies. Such an appeal would not be available to the leaders of a world government because there would be no external enemies. With regard to this issue of protecting the rights of individuals, advocates of world federalism can even advance an additional argument for their position, namely, that the presence of a federal world government would tend to undermine national totalitarian and militaristic governments because they would no longer be able to victimize their own populations on grounds that such suppression is necessary for national security.

The opponent of world federalism might also raise the question of whether it is desirable to have still another layer of government when many people feel that there is already too much government spending and too much

government bureaucracy. The world federalist's response to this objection is two-fold. First, a large proportion of spending by the national governments is due to funding for military establishments in order to be prepared to fight wars and to maintain military superiority for diplomatic purposes. With a world federation these huge expenses would disappear, just as within the United States the state governments do not need to maintain military establishments. Second, the most efficient arrangement is to have social problems being tackled by the lowest level of government that can deal with that problem effectively. There are global problems such as destruction of the ozone layer and control of international drug-trafficking which by their very nature must be dealt with at the global level and which would involve less bureaucracy when addressed by a global agency than when they are addressed by many different national governments trying to coordinate their efforts by means of international treaties. The present international system where nation-states compete against each other economically, militarily, and in every other way has generated a situation where national governments are expected to deal with every kind of problem. A global-level government would not increase the total amount of government but would permit a better distribution of responsibility for dealing with social problems at the appropriate level.

Another problem which the advocate of world federation must address for people living in the Western-style democracies is whether the federal world government would be supportive of democratic capitalistic ideology. Might it not be sympathetic to authoritarian and socialist governments? Once again the response is two-fold. First, the federalist principle means that each nation-state would be free to have whatever kind of political system and whatever kind of economic system it wants *within its borders*. People do not need to have complete ideological agreement in order to live together in peace. They need only agree on what nonviolent procedures will be used to resolve their conflicts with each other. Second, the global system itself *would* have to be democratic and permissive of free enterprise. A world federation must be established by consent, not by conquest, and it can be expected that no nation-states will agree to enter a system which does not allow them an appropriate involvement in the decision-making for the world community. The particular kind of voting system to be established must be worked out, but it is assumed by all world federalists that at the global level there will be a democratic system based on voting. The democratic manner of operation at the United Nations also supports this expectation.

The question of whether the global government would allow free enterprise at the world level might have been a legitimate concern before the demise of the Soviet Union, but now there seems to be a consensus that a market economy is better than a centrally controlled economy. If particular nation-states want to have a socialist system within their countries they could do that, but the idea of a centrally controlled economic system at the global level is no longer an attractive possibility and would not be acceptable. In fact, another argument that might be marshaled in favor of world federation is that a worldwide system of free trade *requires* such a global government in order to establish common rules for the global system which cannot be eroded by some national governments having lax standards on environmental protection or worker safety.

One concern of many people in the richer countries is that a democratic voting system at the global level might result in legislation being adopted that would drain wealth out of the rich countries into the poorer countries. If there were a world federation, wouldn't the poorer countries use the global democratic political system to require a more equitable distribution of wealth in the world? At the same time, the poorer countries would be concerned that a federal world government would be controlled by the rich countries and used to solidify and institutionalize their current economically dominant economic position! The extent to which a world federation would be controlled by the poor or the rich would depend very much on the particular rules which are adopted, not only with regard to voting but also with regard to limitations on the powers of the government. The creation of a global political body, however, would probably result in greater equalization of wealth in the world. In fact, for some people, the need for greater economic equality at the global level and the improbability that it will become more equal without a world federation constitute yet another argument *for* a world federation. Economist James Yunker has argued that a world federation could function well only if accompanied by a "common progress" program to gradually equalize to some extent the distribution of wealth in the world.[23]

Assuming that the development of a federal world government might be desirable, is there any chance that such a government could be established? The general response to this question has to be, in view of the historical evolution not only of humanity but of all living things, the development of such a nonzero-sum governance system at the global level *in the long run is inevitable*.[24] From a more particular political point of view, the transition would involve a shift from resolving disputes on the basis of military power, where what counts is the size of armed forces and the destructive efficiency of weapons, to one of resolving disputes on the basis of political power, where what counts would be the number of votes and the skills of legislators. The crucial task would be to work out a voting system which would be fair to all and which would protect the interest of every nation-state at least as much as that interest is protected now. Since the smaller countries of the world are presently at the mercy of the larger, more powerful countries, they would have much to gain by joining a world federation which provides protection from exploitation by other nations. The middle-sized countries would also gain more control over their own destinies than they have under the present system, where critical issues may be decided without much input from them.

But what is the situation for the big powers with their nuclear weapons and formidable economic capability? The United States and its allies can pretty much determine what is going to happen in the international arena and how much opposition to their policies will be tolerated. Consider the response to the Iraqi invasion of Kuwait. On the other hand, the power of the big nations is not unlimited. They must consider the costs of military action as the United States learned in Vietnam and the Soviet Union in Afghanistan. During the Cold War the United States and the Russians also learned about the long-term adverse effects of huge military expenditures as their economies fell relative to those of other countries such as Japan which did not spend such a large proportion of its resources on the military. Under these circumstances it seems advantageous for the big powers to work out arrangements which would eliminate their arms races and also institutionalize to some extent their present predominant position in world affairs.

In fact, it would be only a slight exaggeration to say that a world government already exists. That reality is not immediately obvious because this world government is called "the government of the United States of America." If the United States were to decide to support the explicit conversion of the United Nations into a world federation, it would have the dominant role in determining the nature and rules of that government. It is amazing that some extreme conservatives in the United States are afraid that the United Nations might take control of this country when the actual situation is that the United States exercises overwhelming control over not only the United Nations but also over most of the other international organizations which in effect run the world. Somewhat ironically, the overwhelming global dominance of the United States at the present time is the very reason that at this moment the need to create a democratic world federation to manage international conflict does not seem to be very urgent.

Are we moving toward the development of a world federation? It can be noted that there has been interest in and support for "global governance" from very knowledgeable and experienced people in the area of inter-national relations. A specific example is the report of the 28-member Commission on Global Governance co-chaired by Ingvar Carlsson, former Prime Minister of Sweden, and Shridath Ramphal of Guyana, former Secretary-General of the Commonwealth. The title of the report is *Our Global Neighborhood*.[25] Although that report specifically says, "We are not proposing movement towards world government,"[26] the actual proposals very much suggest moving in that direction. Consider the following statements from that report:

> Sovereignty has been the cornerstone of the inter-state system. In an increasingly interdependent world, however, the notions of territoriality, independence, and non-intervention have lost some of their meaning. In certain areas, sovereignty must be exercised collectively, particularly in relation to the global commons....
>
> The principles of sovereignty and non-intervention must be adapted in ways that recognize the need to balance the rights of states with the rights of people, and the interests of nations with the interests of the global neighborhood. It is time also to think about self-determination in the emerging context of a global neighborhood rather than the traditional context of a world of separate states.[27]

In another place we find the following:

> The global neighborhood of the future must be characterized by law and the reality that all, including the weakest, are equal under the law and none, including the strongest, is above it.[28]

That may be less than world federation, but it is certainly indicative of a definite move in that direction.

But we should not limit ourselves to the contents of one report, even though it is very important because of the 37 internationally prominent persons who served on the commission or formally endorsed the report. There are other developments which indicate that we are moving in the direction of a global government. The most significant is development of the International Criminal Court (ICC) previously discussed.[29] The Rome Statute creating this court must be ratified by 60 countries before it goes into effect, but that should happen by the year 2003, despite efforts by the United States to delay it. The ICC is a giant step toward a federal world government because it allows a prosecutor of an international court to investigate and, when appropriate, to start prosecution of individuals, even national leaders, who have committed genocide, war crimes, and crimes against humanity — and, once the definition is worked out, aggression. Recall that one of the differences between a confederation and a federation is that in a confederation the central body does not interact with *individuals* in the member states but only with the *governments* of the member states. The ICC takes the world community beyond that limitation. National leaders will no longer be able to use their government position to avoid being prosecuted for violating international law. They will no longer be above the law. That change will be a giant step toward world federation — and world peace.

Other steps in the direction of a world federation are (a) the creation of the institutions established by the Law of the Sea (LOS) Treaty[30]; (b) the interventions by the international community in Bosnia, Kosovo, and Sierra Leone to protect human rights[31]; (c) the focus on developing a U.N. rapid response military force to allow the international community to react more quickly to crises,[32] and (d) the large public protests against the secret proceedings of the unelected representatives of the World Trade Organization suggesting the need for some kind of democratic political system to regulate the global economy rather than allowing multinational corporations to run the global economy for their own benefit without regard to impact on the environment or conditions for workers or absence of protection for consumers.[33]

Although no formal move toward a federal world government seems near at hand, some possibilities for action in that direction can be noted. It is conceivable that a coalition of countries such as Japan, India, Canada, France, Germany, Italy, Australia, Mexico, Nigeria, and Argentina could promote a democratization of the United Nations, or perhaps even the development of a new more democratic international organization, as a way of gaining more control over their own destiny. It is possible too that some U.S. President will lead the way toward the development of a world federation. It was U.S. Presidents, after all, who were responsible for the League of Nations and the United Nations. Another U.S. President, sincerely committed to world peace through world law and global democracy, might be able to make the seemingly distant dream of a democratic federal world government a reality in a rather short period of time.

Even the most optimistic advocates of world federalism do not see such a government coming into existence in the next 25 years. Yet many see such a development as inevitable. A crucial question is how best to structure such a government so that it will maintain peace and still allow for the peaceful change which is necessary if injustices are to be corrected. The various national governments need to be examined to learn which of the different existing political structures and procedures best promote justice and the nonviolent resolution of group conflicts. The strong emphasis on political justice embodied in the ideology of the West and the strong emphasis on economic justice embodied in the statements by those in the poorer countries both need to be incorporated into a future world federation. Advocates of world federation believe that the absence of real security in a world where national conflicts are resolved by force and threats of force combined with the ever increasing destructiveness of weapons will cause leaders to see that a change in the international system is necessary. They will have to take on the task of creating a democratic world federation where conflicts of interest are worked out by political and judicial means. That is what is in the long-term interest of all countries.

World Government Through Functionalism

Many of those who recognize the need to change the international system agree with the world federalists that problems need to be considered on a global basis but do not agree that a structured federal world government brought into existence by the deliberate action of the national governments is the best or most feasible way to make the shift away from international anarchy. These thinkers emphasize the interdependence of the nations of the world and the desirability of using functional agencies to manage various global problems on a problem-by-problem basis. They believe that many decisions on how to deal with global problems can be made on a consensual basis without much reliance on voting if discussions can be focused on solving specific global problems rather than on abstract principles. Most functionalists agree with world federalists that the eventual goal should be the development of a democratic world federation, but they believe that a direct attack on national sovereignty now would arouse too much emotional opposition. It is best, they say, to proceed incrementally through the establishment of more and more global functional agencies.

Earlier, when dealing with presently existing international institutions, we discussed the various functional agencies associated with the United Nations such as the World Health Organization, the International Labor Organization, and the Universal Postal Union. Functionalists believe that the best way to change the international system is to continue to create more and more such agencies to work on the various particular problems facing humanity. They claim that a functionalist approach would be much more likely to have some success in actually limiting national sovereignty than would any federalist effort to get the national governments to explicitly do that. If functional agencies are created, they will gradually develop the competence and authority to deal with the particular problems to which they are devoted. The national governments will find these functional agencies and the bureaucracies they have developed extremely helpful in carrying on the actual business of international problem-solving. Gradually, the functionalist notes, the agencies will make more and more of the decisions which need to be made concerning international issues while the national governments will find it less and less important to concern themselves with these matters. There will be no need for an explicit transfer of sovereignty be-

cause real power and authority will gradually have shifted to the global functional agencies.

The theory of functionalism as a basis of political integration was first worked out by David Mitrany in his book *A Working Peace System* published in 1943.[34] He urged leaders to shift their attention away from national security and political issues to the everyday problems with which a society must deal. Some of these problems are purely local, but others have an international dimension. Global problems such as disease, hunger, illiteracy, communications, transportation, and pollution should be addressed by international functional agencies focused on solving one particular kind of problem. Instead of viewing other countries as potential enemies, one should shift attention to *these social problems as the real enemies of humankind*. Mitrany felt that the inability to deal satisfactorily with these social problems was the underlying cause of war.

Mitrany argued that once these international functional agencies started dealing with these global problems, other benefits would also be derived. Success in one area would suggest the need to cooperate on other problems. National governments would be brought together to solve problems rather than struggling against each other for more political power. People from various countries working together to solve the problems would form transnational friendships. The loyalty of individual persons would shift from support for their national government to commitment to the problem-solving functional agencies. The problem of war would be solved because people would be more interested in working together to deal with specific global problems than in fighting for their government against other national governments.

Several years later Ernst Haas, a supporter of the general idea of functionalism, nevertheless offered a critique of Mitrany's presentation of the case for it. In his *Beyond the Nation-State*,[35] Haas argued that there are many causes of war and that economic deprivation, hunger, disease, and the like — though loathsome aspects of human existence which should be eliminated — are not usually relevant to the outbreak of war. He also argued that Mitrany was mistaken in believing that these international functional agencies could operate without reference to the political context. Haas rejected Mitrany's claim that success in one functional area would generate a readiness to work together in other areas and also his notion that there would be a shift in loyalty from national governments to functional agencies.

Haas then advanced his own arguments in support of functionalism. He claimed that working together on specific problems could develop habits of cooperating on the international level even if they wouldn't necessarily get transferred to any other particular area. He noted that interests of various national groups do sometimes provide a basis for international cooperation. There might be some common problems which they could better attack cooperatively than separately. It is not to be expected that loyalty to functional agencies will ever override loyalty to the nation-state, but when the functional agency also helps the national government to deal with its problems, then there will be a concurrence of feelings of support. The main value of functionalism, however, is not that it generates a new level of loyalty to the global community but that it depoliticizes issues so that national interest is no longer even a factor to be taken into account as one deals with the problem. Functionalism works especially well, Haas says, when there are national leaders and national interest groups with a common goal such as eliminating some communicable disease or preserving the environment. It is essential that the key decision-makers in the nations be supportive of the aims of the international functional agencies because politics determines the scope and level of involvement in functional activities and not the other way around.

To better understand this functionalist approach, let us consider what happens within national governments. Many important decisions are made by individual bureaucrats. In the United States, for example, the President and Congress cannot keep track of every decision concerning government action. The President delegates authority to Cabinet officers, who in turn delegate it to others, who in turn delegate it to others. Guidelines for action may be given by the President or a Cabinet member, but there are many decisions not governed by guidelines. With others there is considerable room for judgment about how the guidelines should be applied to a particular case. People at the bottom of the bureaucracy are likely to know more about some situations than those of higher rank. Consequently, they must often advise the higher-ups with regard to what should be done in specific cases. As long as things are running smoothly, those higher up in the bureaucracy don't want to be bothered with such decisions. In the same way, international functional agencies can build bureaucracies of experts to handle the practical problems of the international community. As long as these agencies adequately perform the tasks for which they were established, the national governments are not likely to intervene. As the functional agencies handle many of the real day-to-day problems of the global community, they will gradually become the "departments" of a developing world government.

Critics of the functionalist approach object that this proposed way of proceeding overlooks the areas of intense conflict between nations. They claim that national governments will use their power to keep functional agencies from carrying out any policies which they find contrary to their own interests and allow the agencies to do only what doesn't offend any national government. Otherwise, the offended national government will withdraw its support of the functional agency or try to obstruct its activities.[36] An actual example of this type of reaction was the withdrawal of the United States from UNESCO in 1984. But, functionalists will reply, in most cases the national governments will find the functional agency too useful to themselves to take such negative actions. For example, even a large and powerful nation would find it difficult to withdraw from the Universal Postal Union. It would then need to work out separate agreements for transfer of international mail with all the other countries in the world.

Furthermore, even if some nations don't want to belong to a particular international functional agency (for example, Communist countries did not want to belong to the International Monetary Fund), the agency can still serve others who do want to participate. International interdependence is such that nations which stay out or withdraw from an international functional agency will probably hurt themselves more than they will hurt the agency.

Will the development of global functional agencies help solve the problem of war? Even if these agencies successfully handle their particular assignments, won't arms races continue? Won't the issues vital to the interests of national governments still be resolved on the basis of force and threats of force? To this point functionalists make two responses. First, it may not be possible to do everything at once, but over a period of time the success of functional agencies will make it clear to all nations that they have more to gain by working together than by engaging in confrontation tactics. The number of issues considered to be worth fighting about will gradually diminish to zero. Second, the functionalists note that the problem of arms control and disarmament should be handled by a functional agency deliberately designed to take care of this problem. Such an agency might develop its own system of surveillance satellites to keep track of the military activities of all nations.[37] It might also develop proposals for arms reduction. The U.N. Register of Conventional Arms could serve as a model for self-reporting, a first step in the process of compiling an arms census (with some random verification checks) which could eventually provide a starting point for cutbacks. The representatives of the various nations on an International Arms Control and Disarmament Agency could work to develop arms control and disarmament policies on which they could all agree. Once policies were adopted, the functional agency could determine whether they were being implemented. If any nation failed to carry out its part of the arms control/disarmament plan, the International Agency could announce this fact to all other countries and

delay any further disarming until the offending nation complied. Obviously, if some powerful nation refused to continue to cooperate, the disarming could not go on. But what alternative could there be? Would the other nations of the world, or even a world government, try to use military force to persuade the reluctant country to disarm? Disarmament is possible only when all the nations, and especially the more powerful ones, are ready to take this action together.

We can imagine a debate between world federalists on the one hand and functionalists on the other concerning the functionalist approach to disarmament. Federalists would make two main points. First, they would go back to their basic thesis that disarmament cannot be expected until an effective political/judicial system is in place to provide a reliable alternative method for resolving intense conflicts of interest. To this point functionalists could reply that some kind of arms control might be possible even if the situation did not yet permit complete disarmament. Furthermore, they would argue, it is the existence of various kinds of functional agencies, including one for arms control, that would best prepare the way for a situation where formal political and judicial systems for resolving conflict could be developed and accepted.

The second argument of federalists would be to claim that a functional arms control and disarmament agency could not be as effective as a disarmament plan carried out by a world government because only under the federalist approach could the individual violators of the disarmament agreement be arrested and penalized. A functional agency could deal only with the national governments. Functionalists would reply that it is not individuals but national governments which purchase modern weapons and hire people to use them. As long as these governments want weapons and armies, they will not permit prosecution of their citizens who make them and practice using them. It may be true that national governments would not need arms to protect their interests if there were an effective world government which protected them, but, functionalists claim, it is also the case that the national governments would not need arms to protect their interests if the various functional agencies were successfully solving the various global problems to which they were addressing themselves. Functionalists argue that either the national governments would find cooperation more satisfying than military confrontation (in which case a formal world government is superfluous) or they would not (in which case even a federal world government could not prevent a war). Federalists would respond that there are possibilities between these extremes. Nevertheless, functionalists would reply, the gradual transfer of power to global agencies is much less threatening to national governments than the federalist plan for a sudden and explicit transfer of particular powers from national governments to a new central world government.

This hypothetical debate concerning the desirability and feasibility of trying to establish a functional International Arms Control and Disarmament Agency points up the basic differences between the federalist and functionalist approaches. Both have as their ultimate goal a governing structure for the world community, but they advocate different means for achieving that goal. Federalists want to make a frontal attack on unrestricted national sovereignty because they believe that national leaders, whose primary responsibility is to deal with international problems, should be able to see the desirability of transferring some of the powers of national governments to a central limited world government. That government could then use its powers to enforce a disarmament agreement by dealing with actual individuals who might try to violate it. This federalist approach seeks to create a world community from the "top down." Functionalists, on the other hand, maintain that the world community must become more accustomed to working together through the development of many different functional agencies before a full-fledged world government can be created. This functionalist approach maintains that one must work from the "bottom up," from a collection of functional agencies and a growing sense of world community to the development of a formal political structure to govern it. Of course, there is no reason that both of these approaches could not be used simultaneously. In fact, the very events which federalists pointed to in the previous section as showing progress toward a world federation such as (a) development of an International Criminal Court or (b) creation of the Law of the Sea (LOS) institutions or (c) intervention of the international community to protect human rights or (d) consideration of how to establish a U.N. rapid deployment force or (e) increasing awareness that the World Trade Organization needs to become more democratic are also the very kind of things that functionalists advocate as a way of moving toward a global governance system.

There does seem to be a problem with regard to how far integration can proceed on a functional basis until some kind of formal federation needs to be created. This seems to be the situation which the European Union is now approaching. Can European integration move beyond its present level without the creation of a formal political federation in which the division of powers between the national governments and the European federal union are clearly delineated?

World Government Through Direct Citizen Action

There are still other thinkers who agree with the world federalists and the functionalists that the present system of nations with unlimited sovereignty must be replaced by the development of some global institutions, but they differ concerning how this can best be accomplished. These "populists" think that the federalists are naive to believe that national governments are going to voluntarily and explicitly transfer even a few of their powers to a central world government. They also think the functionalists are naive to pay so little attention to power politics and the drive of national governments to promote their own interests at the expense of other nations. The more powerful nations will cooperate with the global functional agencies only so long as they can use them to preserve the advantages which they have over other nations. National leaders are too clever to allow their positions of superior power to be gradually eroded in those areas which are important in the struggle for goods, power, and status. It is true that there cannot be a transformed peaceful world until the national governments are made at least somewhat subordinate to a world government, but the national governments themselves will never initiate efforts which require them to give up any power. Consequently, the only hope for a peaceful world is for citizen action to create a globally oriented social and political system directly, that is, by somehow bypassing the national governments. There are several different ideas about how to do this.

One approach focuses on changing the attitudes and patterns of behavior of individuals without making any particular effort at present to construct a fully developed global political structure. Each person can be encouraged to think and act as a world citizen. Individuals who regard themselves as world citizens can meet together to carry out projects that encourage others to think of themselves as citizens of the whole world community. A recent book illustrating this general outlook is John Roberts' *World Citizenship and Mundialism.*[38] Some persons who regard themselves as world citizens even go so far as to say that any laws or rules of national governments which are inconsistent with this global outlook should be ignored.

A notable example of someone who advocates such an approach is Garry Davis. In 1948, he pitched a tent on the grounds of the Palais de Chaillot in Paris where the U.N. General Assembly was meeting and declared himself to be a world citizen and consequently not subject to the jurisdiction of national laws. Davis has also encouraged others (a) to adopt the view that their primary loyalty is to the whole of humanity rather than to a nation and (b) to openly declare themselves to be world citizens loyal to the "World Government of World Citizens" which Davis has established.[39] He says that 950,000 persons have signed statements indicating that they consider themselves to be world citizens, though only a few of them go so far as to totally reject the jurisdiction of national governments

as Davis has done. Davis has also organized a World Service Authority (WSA) which issues passports for use by stateless persons and refugees who often cannot get passports from any national government. Birth certificates, marriage licenses, and similar much-needed official documents are also available to those who cannot get them from any national government.[40]

The International Registry of World Citizens (IRWC, or RICM in French), founded in 1949, has its main office in Paris,[41] but it also works with other world citizen organizations. Its People's Congress consists of persons chosen by electors in over one hundred countries. At the end of 1999, twenty delegates and twenty deputy delegates had been elected. At the end of October 2000 the General Assembly of the IRWC/RICM consisting of the managerial counselor group and directors of registry centers met in Paris. Other assemblies and rallies of world citizens are held all over the world, but not on a regular basis.

The Association of World Citizens (AWC) is a U.S.-based related organization.[42] Its *World Citizen* magazine is published twice a year. This organization sponsored a World Citizenship Day rally in San Francisco on March 20, 2000, and its Eleventh World Citizens Assembly is scheduled to meet in Taipei, Taiwan from March 30 to April 5, 2001. The AWC, like most other world citizen organizations, is quite sympathetic to the United Nations as a beginning point for world government, but it maintains that the people of the world must move beyond an organization that is made up of representatives appointed by national governments and consequently tends to lack the global perspective needed in the 21st century.

Another strategy of the "world citizen" approach is to focus on cities and organizations rather than individual persons. An effort is made to get city councils or boards of aldermen to adopt resolutions declaring all people in their community to be world citizens.[43] A city which has adopted such a resolution is said to be "mundialized" (from the Latin word "mundus" meaning "world"). The adoption of a resolution of mundialization may include related provisions such as flying or displaying the United Nations flag, forming sister-city relationships with cities in other countries, making a regular contribution to the U.N. Secretary-General's Special Account in lieu of world taxes, and urging educational institutions in the community to promote a global outlook among their students. In Japan 306 cities have adopted resolutions declaring themselves to be world-cities![44] There are also 185 mundialized cities in France, 22 in Canada, and smaller numbers in other countries.

Especially in the United States the idea of adopting statements of mundialization has also been extended from city councils to other organizations such as universities, schools, churches, and lodges as well as to other political units such as state governments. For example, in the United States proclamations of world citizenship have been issued by political leaders in Minnesota, Illinois, and Iowa. The basic idea of the mundialization effort is to develop and give concrete expression to a global outlook without working through national governments. The Ninth International Meeting on Mundialization was held in San Francisco in June 1995. The mundialization idea is promoted by the various world citizen groups previously discussed. A related effort led by Lynn Elling and World Citizen, Incorporated in Minnesota is a program where schools, municipal governments, and even individual homes declare themselves "Peace Sites" committed to peace education and to promoting the "World Citizen" idea.[45]

Another general kind of populist approach to world government focused on the idea of creating some kind of council or committee of outstanding individuals from all over the world which would serve as a concrete embodiment of the conscience of the world community. This idea no longer seems to be attracting much attention, but in 1951 French philosopher Jacques Maritain suggested that a small council of persons deemed to be especially wise, disinterested, and trustworthy be selected to speak out as the conscience of humanity on social issues.[46] Such persons might be *nominated* by religious organizations, uni-

versities, and governments and then *elected* by the people of all nations. Those selected would lose their national citizenships and would have no power of any kind with which to enforce their judgments. Unlike a court, no individual or nation could bring issues before the council. It would simply issue moral judgments concerning what is just on issues of its own choosing. The problem, of course, is how many people would pay attention to such a world council of moral leaders even if it could be organized.

British philosopher Bertrand Russell went beyond proposing a council of this kind. He established the Bertrand Russell Peace Foundation to cast the public spotlight on institutionalized violence. This Foundation organized public tribunals to examine cases of gross violation of human rights by national governments.[47] In the 1960s and 1970s tribunals were held to hear evidence and render verdicts concerning matters such as war crimes committed by the United States in Vietnam, repression in Chile after the overthrow of the Allende government, and the exclusion of persons from public employment in West Germany on grounds of their political views. The Russell Foundation also held public hearings on the invasion of Czechoslovakia by Russian and East German military forces and the relationship between World Bank policies and problems of development in the poorer countries. The evidence uncovered and the verdicts rendered were published in the hope of influencing world public opinion.

Still another general approach for direct citizen action consists of having a worldwide assembly of "world citizens" draft a "World Constitution" which is then presented to the people of the world for their acceptance.[48] This effort derives from a World Constituent Assembly held in Interlaken, Switzerland and Wolfach, Germany in 1968. These groups began drafting a "Constitution for the Federation of the Earth." A subsequent Assembly held in Innsbruck, Austria in 1977 adopted the Constitution and also approved long-range plans for generating support for its ratification by votes of the people in national referendums. "Laws" have been adopted at sessions of the Provisional World Parliament held in Brighton, England (1982), New Delhi, India (1985), and Miami, Florida, USA (1987). Amendments to the Constitution were adopted at the meeting in Troia, Portugal in 1991. Efforts are being made to get universities, town councils, other organizations, and individuals to indicate their acceptance of this Constitution. Ultimately the success of this effort depends on the authorization of referendums by national governments for the ratification of the proposed Constitution and the bills which have been adopted. This plan of action differs from the traditional approach of world federalists because it contains a program for trying to push national governments into action, but there has been little success so far.

There are a couple of publications which should be mentioned in connection with this topic because they provide a communication link for those who adopt this focus on direct citizen action as the way to bring about world government. One is the bimonthly *World Peace News: A World Government Report*, an autonomous publication of the American Movement for World Government edited and published by Thomas Liggett in New York City.[49] The other is the bi-monthly *United World: WGOC* [World Government Organizations Coalition] *News & Views* edited and published by Gary Shepherd in Carbondale, Illinois.[50] Some of the material in these publications is very critical of the World Federalist Association and its efforts to work through regular political action at the national level to modify the United Nations into a federation instead of a confederation.

There are several efforts to promote citizen action based on a global approach but which do not specifically discuss the ideas of world government or world citizenship. One example is EarthAction Network, a worldwide coalition of organizations started at the Earth Summit in Rio de Janiero in 1992. It seeks to educate and mobilize its members about global issues, especially those related to the environment.[51] EarthAction provides "Action Kits" which go to parliamentarians and the media as well as its own members in an effort to mobilize public opinion and worldwide action on particular global issues. Another group is Global Action to Prevent War, a U.S.-based coalition-building effort to stop war, genocide, and internal armed conflict.[52] The distinguishing aspect of this effort is the development of a program with dates for accomplishing each step, a response designed to appeal to the feeling of some advocates of this direct-citizen-action approach that there is a need for some definite short-term accomplishments and not just long-term hopes.

Although the federalist, functionalist, and populist approaches to world government may seem to be in competition with each other, they can also be viewed as complementing each other.[53] Those who wish to avoid emphasizing one or another particular approach may even drop the term "world government" in favor of the term *world order*. This expression indicates that the desired global political order must promote the values of social justice, economic well-being, human rights, and ecological balance as well as peace.[54] Some advocates of world order are reluctant to use the term "world government" because they feel that such an expression suggests a political institution designed to protect the interests only of those who already have power. Nevertheless, they agree with the advocates of a democratic world federation that the present system of sovereign nations must give way to a new more democratic global political order.

The federalist, functionalist, and populist approaches all seem to be necessary if a new global political order is ever to become a reality. Since the national governments now have the highest level of political power, it seems that the federalists are right in saying that a global system of governance cannot be established without some degree of acquiescence, sooner or later, by these national governments. It seems that the functionalists are right in saying that, at least for the near future, it is easier to erode sovereignty by strengthening and multiplying global functional agencies than by launching a direct attack on unlimited national sovereignty. Finally, it seems that the direct-citizen-action advocates are right in saying that most national governments are not going to move toward a new world political order until they are pushed very hard in that direction by a substantial grass-roots movement.

A Note to the Reader

We have now come to the final step in solving the problem of war — action guided by the deliberation which has taken place in our inquiry thus far. There are many things you might do to be part of the solution. Some "proposals for solving the war problem" have been presented in the last four chapters of the text. As you review these proposals you should be able to find some that you find particularly worthwhile. One possible place to begin, of course, is with reforming the attitudes of individuals — including yourself.

Most of the proposals discussed deal with modifying social policies and institutions, however, and such changes are not likely to be accomplished by individuals working separately. Consequently, if you are really serious about doing something to help solve the war problem, you need to associate yourself in a formal way with some of the many organizations working against war and injustice. Most of these peace-and-justice organizations publish a regular newsletter and other literature as well as maintaining a website to keep interested persons up-to-date on relevant happenings and recent projects. Making the effort to actually join the organization is very important, however, because then you will be helping it to do its work as well as regularly receiving materials which will continue to keep you informed and motivated. You will be alerted about when to write letters to public officials in order to have maximum impact on public decision-making. You will be able to mesh your own particular talents with those of others in an integrated effort. Your membership will also help the organization you support to be noticed by political and media leaders. There would be a great deal more interest in dealing with the war-peace-justice issue if the membership of peace-and-justice organizations grew to four or five times its present level.

To find information about how to get in touch with particular organizations which interest you, go to the part of the text where the relevant topics are discussed and then look in the footnotes. Alternatively, you can search the Internet to get more information about organizations and topics of special interest to you.

There is no shortage of organizations and activities. What is needed is more people to support them. For most organizations the annual membership fee is $25 to $40, and most of them offer a reduced rate for students, retired persons, and others on limited income. The mention of contributing money, even a small amount, may dampen the enthusiasm of some people. Many people want a peaceful and just world, but not *that* much. Yet we must recognize that what we really value is indicated not primarily by what we say but by how we spend our time and money.

We are living during a momentous period in human history, a time of transition from a world of separate national communities to a new global community in which war may become obsolete. Our task is to help develop the attitudes and build the institutions which this new world community needs. Everyone's help is needed — including yours.

Notes

Chapter 1. The Nature of the War Problem

1. Simone Weil, "The *Iliad*, a Poem of Force," originally published in Mary McCarthy's English translation in *Politics* in November 1945 and reprinted in Peter Mayer (ed.), *The Pacifist Conscience* (Chicago: Henry Regnery Company's Gateway Edition, 1966), pp. 291–316. The quotation is from p. 292.

2. Gwynne Dyer, *War* (Homewood IL: Dorsey Press, 1985), p. xi. This book grew out of the making of a television series of the same title for PBS, available in video cassette form from Films, Inc., 1213 Wilmette Avenue, Wilmette IL 60091, (800)323–4222.

3. Worldwide military spending in 1998 amounted to $ 785.269 billion. Determining the percentage of the world's total production of goods and services in that year is somewhat complicated. If one takes the percentage of the gross national product being spent on the military *in each country* and then calculates the average, the result is 4.2 percent. If one instead does this calculation on the basis of the average of the percentages spent on the military *by each region* of the world, the result is 2.6 percent. Difficulties with evaluating different national currencies relative to each other means that percentage calculations are more reliable than trying to get some figure for gross world product and then calculating what percentage is spent on the military. These figures are from *The Military Balance, 1999–2000*, published by the International Institute of Security Studies (London: Oxford University Press, 1999), p. 305.

4. "Preparing for Peace" in Lester R. Brown (ed.), *State of the World, 1993* (New York: W. W. Norton, 1993), p. 140.

5. Barry Commoner, "Ecosystems Are Circular: Part II," *American Forests*, Vol. 80, No. 5 (May 1974), p. 60.

6. St. Louis *Post-Dispatch*, Apr. 12, 1985, p. 2.

7. Information downloaded September 27, 2000, from <http://www.projo.com/cgi-bin/story.pl/news/04283762.htm>(from *RI News*).

8. Ruth Leger Sivard (ed.), *World Military and Social Expenditures, 1991*, 14th ed. (Washington: World Priorities, 1991), p. 50. This figure reflects the value of a dollar in 1987.

9. Sivard, *World Military and Social Expenditures, 1991*, 14th ed. (Washington: World Priorities, 1991), p. 50.

10. Kenneth Boulding, *Stable Peace* (Austin, TX: University of Texas Press, 1978), p. 28. For a chart showing the share of the working population involved in the arms industry and in the armed forces as well as the share of the national income devoted to the war effort in 1943–44 for the Soviet Union, the United Kingdom, Germany, and the United States, see Michael Renner, *Ending Violent Conflict* (Washington: Worldwatch Institute, 1999, paper #146), p. 14.

11. International Institute of Security Studies, *The Military Balance, 1999–2000*, p. 301.

12. Joshua S. Goldstein, "How Military Might Robs an Economy," *New York Times*, October 16, 1988, p. F3.

13. Kenneth Boulding, *Stable Peace*, p. 29.

14. International Institute of Security Studies, *The Military Balance, 1999–2000*, p. 305. U.S. military spending of $265.89 billion accounted for over one-third of the world total and equaled 3.2% of the U.S. GDP (p. 300 of the same source). These figures reflect the value of the dollar in 1997.

15. In the middle of 1988 at the height of the Cold War it was reported by *The Defense Monitor* (published by the Center for Defense Information, 1500 Massachusetts Ave. NW, Washington DC 20005), Vol. 17, No. 5 (1998), p. 1, that the U.S. could "explode more than 16,000 nuclear weapons on the Soviet Union" while "the Soviets can explode over 11,000 nuclear weapons on the United States." These figures include more than 12,600 U.S. strategic (long-range) weapons (about half of which are on submarines) and about 10,500 Soviet strategic weapons.

16. For an insider's view of the Cuban missile crisis, see Robert F. Kennedy, *Thirteen Days* (New York: W.W. Norton, 1969).

17. Robert S. Norris and William M. Arkin, "Global Nuclear Stockpile, July 1998," *The Bulletin of the Atomic Scientists*, Vol. 56, No. 2 (Mar.-Apr. 2000), p. 79.

18. Robert S. Norris and William M. Arkin, "U.S. Nuclear Stockpile, July 1998," *The Bulletin of the Atomic Scientists*, Vol. 54, No. 4 (Jul.-Aug. 1998), pp. 69–71 (especially p. 71), and Robert S. Norris and William M. Arkin, "U.S. Strategic Forces, End of 1998," *The Bulletin of the Atomic Scientists*, Vol. 55, No. 1 (Jan.-Feb. 1999), pp. 78–80. On page 80 we read "The Navy continues to purchase Trident II SLBMS."

19. A history of the discussions of "nuclear winter" can be found in Thomas F. Malone, "International Scientists on Nuclear Winter," *The Bulletin of the Atomic Scientists*, Vol. 41, No. 11 (Dec. 1985), pp. 52–55. For a complete bibliography on the subject, see *World Armaments and Disarmaments, SIPRI Yearbook 1985*, pp. 127–29.

20. Willam M. Arkin, "A New Idea for Reductions," *The Bulletin of the Atomic Scientists*, Vol. 55, No. 11 (Jan.-Feb. 1999), p. 81.

21. Ruth Leger Sivard (ed.), *World Military and Social Expenditures, 1996*, 16th ed. (Washington: World Priorities, 1996), p. 19.

22. Sivard, *World Military and Social Expenditures, 1991*, p. 20.

23. See Pervez Hoodbhoy, "Myth-Building: The 'Islamic' Bomb," *The Bulletin of the Atomic Scientists*, Vol. 49, No. 5 (June 1993), p. 45. For a recent article on whether Israel should continue its policy of "opacity" on the issue of having or not having nuclear weapons, see Avner Cohen, "And Then There Was One," *The Bulletin of the Atomic Scientists*, Vol. 54, No. 5 (Sep.-Oct. 1998), pp. 51–55.

24. David Albright, "A Curious Conversion," *The Bulletin of the Atomic Scientists*, Vol. 49, No. 5 (June 1993), pp. 8–11.

25. David Albright, "The Shots Heard 'Round the World,'" *The Bulletin of the Atomic Scientists*, Vol. 54, No. 4 (Jul.-Aug. 1998), pp. 20–25. Almost all of this issue was about the tests of India and Pakistan.

26. Ayesha Khan, "Pakistan Joins the Club," *The Bulletin of the Atomic Scientists*, Vol. 54, No. 4 (Jul.-Aug. 1998), pp. 34–39.

27. David Albright, "A Proliferation Primer," *The Bulletin of the Atomic Scientists*, Vol. 49, No. 5 (June 1993), pp. 14–23. To understand why Iran is not included in this category, see Eric Arnett, "Iran Is Not Iraq," *The Bulletin of the Atomic Scientists*, Vol. 54, No. 1 (Jan.-Feb. 1998), pp. 12–14.

28. Albright, "A Proliferation Primer," pp. 16–18.

29. Michael Renner, *Ending Violent Conflict* (Washington: Worldwatch Institute Paper #146, 1999), p. 17. K. J. Holsti in *The State, War, and the State of War* (Cambridge: Cambridge University Press, 1996) has produced a summary of wars fought between 1945 and 1995 (see pp. 210–224) which shows that during that period "almost 77 percent of the 164 wars were internal" (p. 21) and that only 30 of them or 18 percent were "purely state-versus-state wars" (p. 23).

30. Michael Klare, "The Kalashnikov Age," *The Bulletin of the Atomic Scientists*, Vol. 55, No. 1 (Jan.-Feb. 1999), p. 19.

Chapter 2. The Conceptual Framework

1. For an historical overview of some attempts to define "war" see Donald A. Wells, *The War Myth* (New York: Pegasus, 1967), pp. 17–31. For a very thorough and helpful discussion of the issue of how to define "war," see John A. Vasquez, *The War Puzzle* (Cambridge: Cambridge University Press, 1993), pp. 21–50. My own definition of "war," however, was developed before I read this excellent discussion of the issue.

2. See Jane Goodall, "Life and Death at Gombe," *National Geographic*, Vol. 155, No. 5 (May 1979), pp. 592–621, and Jane Goodall, *In the Shadow of Man* [Fourth Distinguished Graduate Research Lecture, San Diego State University] (San Diego: San Diego State University Press, 1988), pp. 8-13.

3. Gwynne Dyer, *War*, p. 6.

4. Lewis Richardson in *Statistics of Deadly Quarrels* (Pittsburgh: Boxwood, 1960) used 317 (that is, $10^{2.5}$) deaths as the minimum. Quincy Wright in *A Study of War* (Chicago: University of Chicago, 1942) relied on the number of troops involved rather than the number of casualties and decided that a conflict would be counted as a war if at least 50,000 troops were committed to the fighting or if the war was recognized as a war in the legal sense (Vol. 1, p. 636). J. David Singer and Melvin Small in *The Wages of War, 1816–1965: A Statistical Handbook* (New York: Wiley, 1972) worked out very precise criteria for deciding whether to count an armed conflict as a war. An inter-state war is taken into account only if there were at least 1,000 battle fatalities (p. 35), while imperial and colonial wars are taken into account only if the imperialistic or colonial power suffered at least 1,000 battle fatalities per year (pp. 36–37). Small and Singer did not consider civil wars in their first study, but they did in their revised edition, *Resort to Arms: International and Civil Wars,*

1816–1980 (Beverly Hills CA: Sage, 1982). The same criteria for including a war in the study are given in the new edition on pp. 54–56.

5. On the relation between the society, the military, and war see Keith Otterbein, *The Evolution of War: A Cross-Cultural Study* (New Haven CT: Yale University-HRAF, 1970), pp. 17–23 and 63-64.

6. This quotation from Pascal is given along with brief observations and quips about war by many others in *The Christian Science Monitor*, February 5, 1991, p. 19.

7. Jean-Jacques Rousseau makes this point in *The Social Contract*, Book I, Chapter 4, where he says, "War is not, therefore, a relation between man and man but between State and State...." See Jean-Jacques Rousseau, *On the Social Contract with Geneva Manuscript and Political Economy*, Roger D. Masters (ed.), Judith R. Masters (tr.) (New York: St. Martin's Press, 1978), p. 50.

8. Kenneth Boulding in *The Meaning of the Twentieth Century* has suggested that moving from the civilized state to the post-civilized state should be a very desirable transition (p. 2) and could mean the end of imperialism and war (see pp. 11–12 and 77–103, especially pp. 77–84).

9. See all the articles but especially the editor's introduction in Yonah Alexander (ed.), *International Terrorism: National, Regional, and Global Perspectives* (New York: Praeger, 1976). A good collection of recent articles about terrorism is Bernard Schechterman and Martin Slann, *Violence and Terrorism, 99/00*, 5th ed. (Guilford CT: Dushkin/McGraw-Hill, 1999).

10. See Abraham D. Sofaer, "Terrorism and the Law," *Foreign Affairs*, Vol. 64, No. 5 (Summer 1986), pp. 901–22.

11. Margaret Mead, "Warfare Is Only an Invention — Not a Biological Necessity," *Asia*, XL (1940), pp. 402–05. That article has been reprinted in various books including Leon Bramson and George W. Goethals (eds.), *War: Studies from Psychology, Sociology, and Anthropology*, rev. ed. (New York: Basic Books, 1968), pp. 269–74; Charles R. Beitz and Theodore Herman (eds.), *Peace and War* (San Francisco: W.H. Freeman, 1973), pp. 112–18; and David Barash (ed.), *Approaches to Peace: A Reader in Peace Studies* (New York and Oxford: Oxford University Press, 2000), pp. 19–22. The quotations are from the second paragraph and then the last two paragraphs of her article.

12. In a book on the war problem, it may not be inappropriate to mention that it is regrettable that some of those who are so vocal about ending the killing of fetuses are not at the same time more vocal about ending the killing of children and adults in war.

13. Being servants of the society can also produce a greater reluctance to engage in wars with other countries. The issue of whether democracies are less likely to become engaged in wars with other countries is an issue that will be discussed in chapters 6 and 14. For a recent discussion of that issue in relation to the cause-of-the-war question, see Hidemi Suganami, *On the Causes of War* (Oxford: Clarendon Press, 1996), pp. 72–77.

14. Carl von Clausewitz, *On War*, edited with an introduction by Anatol Rapoport, translated by J.J. Graham (New York: Penguin Books, 1968), p. 119.

15. Clausewitz, *On War*, p. 405.

16. For an early example of the use of this distinction between negative peace and positive peace and favoring

the latter see Johann Galtung, "Violence, Peace, and Peace Research," *Journal of Peace Research*, Vol. 6 (1961), pp. 167–91.

17. See R.J. Rummel, *Death by Government: Genocide and Mass Murder Since 1900* (New Brunswick NJ: Transaction, 1994).

18. Thomas Hobbes, *Leviathan*, Chapter XIII in *The English Works of Thomas Hobbes*, edited by Sir William Molesworth (London: John Bohn, 1839, reprinted 1966), Vol. 3, p. 113.

19. Plato, *Republic*, Book I, pp. 331e and 332c.

20. Some complete books focused on the just war tradition are Michael Walzer, *Just and Unjust Wars: A Moral Argument with Historical Illustrations* (New York: Basic Books, 1977); James Turner Johnson, *Just War Tradition and the Restraint of War* (Princeton: Princeton University Press, 1981) and *Can Modern War Be Just?* (New Haven: Yale University Press, 1984); and Paul Christopher, *The Ethics of War and Peace: An Introduction to Legal and Moral Issues*, 2nd ed. (Englewood Cliffs NJ: Prentice Hall, 1998).

21. See John Brinsfield, "The Origins of the Just War Tradition," reprinted in Dick Ringler (ed.), *Dilemmas of War and Peace: A Sourcebook* (Madison WI: Board of Regents of Univ. of Wisconsin System and Corporation for Public Broadcasting, 1993), pp. 406–10. The original article "From Plato to NATO: The Ethics of Warfare" was published in *Military Chaplain's Review*, Spring 1991.

22. See James Turner Johnson, "Maintaining the Protection of Non-Combatants," *Journal of Peace Research* (Oslo), Vol. 37, No. 4 (July 2000), pp. 419–48, especially p. 427.

23. A summary of Grotius' criteria for a just war is given in Roy Gutman and David Rieff (eds.) *Crimes of War: What the Public Should Know* (New York: W. W. Norton, 1999), p. 224.

24. Gutman and Rieff, *Crimes of War*, p. 223.

25. For the contrary point of view, see Turner, "Maintaining the Protection of Non-Combatants," pp. 422–24. I confess to holding the view that Turner rejects, namely, that "war as an institution must be abolished" (p. 424). I think that Turner views war too much as a matter of actions by rather isolated individuals fighting against other rather isolated individuals instead of as a conflict between group and group. I am not opposed to restraint of the military during war as a necessary interim measure, but I am opposed to using the just war approach as a rationale for not taking more vigorous action to abolish war as a way of resolving social conflict, especially as more and more destructive weapons become available to ever smaller groups.

26. See for example Edward J. Laarman, *Nuclear Pacifism: "Just War" Thinking Today* (New York: Peter Lang, 1984) or William V. O'Brien and John Langan (eds.), *The Nuclear Dilemma and the Just War Tradition* (Lexington MA: Lexington Books, 1986).

27. For a book-length treatment of this decision, see Ann Fagan Ginger (ed.), *Nuclear Weapons Are Illegal: The Historic Opinion of the World Court and How It Will Be Enforced* (New York: Apex Press, 1998).

28. Ginger, *Nuclear Weapons Are Illegal*, pp. 75–76.

29. Ginger, *Nuclear Weapons Are Illegal*, p. 75.

30. Harrop A. Freeman, "Pacifism and Law" in Robert Ginsberg (ed.), *The Critique of War: Contemporary Philosophical Explorations* (Chicago: Henry Regnery, 1969), pp. 284–96, presents the interesting thesis that once government machinery is in place, the less powerful will gradually become able to make use of that machinery to protect themselves from oppression by the powerful. See especially pp. 291–93.

31. James A. Yunker has proposed a World Economic Equalization Program that would gradually but systematically shift some of the wealth of the richer nations to the poorer ones. He combines this program with a political Federal Union of Democratic Nations as a necessary strategy for getting global justice and global peace at the same time. He doubts that democratic political integration can come without greater economic equality in the world or that long-term peace can come without democratic political integration. For details of his proposal see his article "Rethinking World Government: A New Approach" in *International Journal on World Peace*, Vol. XVII (2000), pp. 3–33 or his recently published book *Common Progress: The Case for a World Economic Equalization Program* (Westport CT: Praeger, 2000).

32. For example, see Riseri Frondizi, "The Ideological Origins of the Third World War" in Ginsberg, *The Critique of War*, pp. 77–95, especially p. 89 and pp. 93–95.

33. Quoted by Frondizi in Ginsberg, *The Critique of War*, p. 94.

Chapter 3. The Historical Framework

1. Kenneth Boulding, *The Meaning of the Twentieth Century* (New York: Harper & Row, 1964), p. 1.

2. Dyer, *War*, p. 11.

3. William Eckhardt, *Civilizations, Empires, and Wars: A Quantitative History of War* (Jefferson NC: McFarland, 1992, pp. 195–97.

4. Maurice R. Davie, *The Evolution of War: A Study of Its Role in Early Societies* (Port Washington NY: Kennikat Press; originally published in 1929 by Yale University Press, reissued in 1968 by Kennikat Press), pp. 160–75, especially 174–75. For an in-depth discussion of this process and the importance of the ecological context, see Robert L. Carniero, "A Theory of the Origin of the State," *Science*, Vol. 169 (1970), pp. 733–38.

5. Dyer, *War*, p. 11.

6. Dyer, *War*, pp. 4–6 and 18–19. See also Charles S. Gochman and Zeev Moaz, "Militarized Interstate Disputes 1816–1976: Procedures, Patterns, and Insights," *Journal of Conflict Resolution*, Vol. 28 (1984), p. 615.

7. Frederick L. Schuman, *International Politics*, 7th ed. (New York: McGraw-Hill, 1969), p. 34.

8. Schuman, *International Politics*, pp. 38–39.

9. Boulding, *The Meaning of the Twentieth Century*, pp. 1 and 5–26, but in a sense the whole book is about the industrial revolution and its implications for the world.

10. For a listing of wars and war-related deaths from 1900–1995 in which there were 1,000 or more deaths per year, including these wars of national liberation, see Sivard, *World Military and Social Expenditures, 1996*, pp. 17–19.

11. John G. Stoessinger, *Why Nations Go to War*, 7th ed. (New York: St. Martin's, 1998), pp. 149–50.

12. Sivard, *World Military and Social Expenditures, 1996*, p. 19.

13. Boutros Boutros-Ghali, *Unvanquished* (New York: Random House, 1999), pp. 103–107.

14. The official name for the country is "Bosnia and Herzegovina" even though it is often referred to simply as "Bosnia."

15. For a detailed account of these events in Bosnia, see Stoessinger, *Why Nations Go to War*, pp. 190–200.

16. The Rome Statute creating the International Criminal Court is United Nations document A/CONF.183/9, English [98-28144(E), 250998]. It can be found on the internet at <http://untreaty.un.org/ENGLISH/notpubl/rome-en.htm>. For a thorough account of the negotiations leading up to the adoption of the treaty to create an International Criminal Court, see Fanny Benedetti and John L. Washburn, "Drafting the International Criminal Court Treaty: Two Years to Rome and an Afterward on the Rome Diplomatic Conference," *Global Governance*, Vol. 5 (1999), pp. 1–37.

17. Kenneth Boulding, *The Meaning of the Twentieth Century*, pp. 2 and 5–23. See also Harlan Cleveland, *Birth of a New World* (San Francisco: Jossey-Bass, 1993).

18. Robert Ardrey in *African Genesis* (New York: Dell, 1967) suggests that man should be defined as the weapon-making animal. See pp. 185–207. For a somewhat satirical treatment of the history of warfare and the development of new weapons see Richard Armour, *It All Started with Stones and Clubs* (New York: McGraw-Hill, 1967).

19. Our discussion is focused on the Western world because it is Europe "whose style of warfare has become the model for most of the world," Dyer, *War*, p. 54.

20. Dyer uses the title "Reductio Ad Absurdum: Total War" for the fourth chapter of *War*. He begins that chapter with a discussion of the American Civil War before moving on to World War I and World War II. Nevertheless, on page 178 he unambiguously says that World War I "was the first total war."

21. Dyer, *War*, pp. 19–52. On p. 32 he notes that "the pace of change was generally even slower in the five or six thousand years before the period I have arbitrarily called the 'middle passage'" (that is, 1500 B.C.E. to 1500 C.E.).

22. In *War* Dyer argues that the introduction of gunpowder was not the only factor that changed the nature of warfare in the 15th and 16th centuries and that "by the 17th century new kinds of fortifications were definitely winning the technological race against the cannons of the time" (p. 55). His view is that the real transformation to a greater reliance on firearms came as the result of the success of King Gustavus Adolphus of Sweden in the Thirty Years' War in the 17th century when he had his army rely on lighter weight muskets and light artillery because Sweden's small population limited the number of men who could be mobilized to serve as pikemen (p. 61).

23. Dyer, *War*, p. 62.

24. For a detailed account of the nature of war during this period see Dyer, *War*, pp. 62–66, and Michael Renner, "Ending Violent Conflict" in Lester Brown, Christopher Flavin, and Hilary French (eds.), *State of the World, 1999* (New York: W. W. Norton, 1999), pp. 151–56. Renner's chapter as a whole (pp. 151–68 is an excellent overview of the problem of war as it looks at the end of the 20th century.

25. For specific figures, see Renner, "Ending Violent Conflict" in *State of the World, 1999*, p. 153.

26. American military strategist Bernard Brodie noted that the creation of nuclear weapons had changed the mission of the military. Instead of having the task of winning wars, their new task would become how to avoid wars by deterring anyone from resorting to military force to resolve a conflict. See Bernard Brodie, *The Absolute Weapon* (New York: Harcourt, Brace, 1946), p. 76. For a more recent statement of this same point of view see Kalevi J. Holsti, *Peace and War: Armed Conflicts and International Order 1648–1989* (Cambridge: Cambridge University Press, 1991), p. 327.

27. For a good review of the thinking of American and Soviet leaders about nuclear weapons and their role in strategic planning see Kalevi J. Holsti, *Peace and War: Armed Conflicts and International Order 1648–1989* (Cambridge: Cambridge University Press, 1991), pp. 286–301.

28. Plinio Prioreschi, *Man and War* (New York: Philosophical Library, 1987). Relevant excerpts can be found in Melvin Small and J. David Singer (eds.), *International War: An Anthology*, 2nd ed. (Chicago: Dorsey Press, 1989), pp. 396–403.

29. Kenneth Waltz, *Man, the State, and War* (New York: Columbia University Press, 1959), pp. 235–36.

30. See Edward Rice, *Wars of the Third Kind: Conflict in Underdeveloped Countries* (Berkeley: University of California Press, 1988); Martin Van Creveld, *The Transformation of War* (New York: The Free Press, 1991); and Kalevi J. Holsti, *The State, War, and the State of War*.

31. International Institute of Security Studies (IISS), *The Military Balance, 1999–2000*, p. 305.

32. IISS, *The Military Balance, 1999–2000*, p. 300.

33. Center for Defense Information, *The Defense Monitor*, Vol. 28, No. 8 (1999), p.3. The military budgets given there (in billions of dollars) are United States — 288.8, Russia — 55.0, Japan — 41.1, China — 37.5, United Kingdom — 34.6, France — 29.5, Germany — 24.7, Saudi Arabia —18.4, Italy —16.2, South Korea —11.6, Taiwan —10.9. It is worth noting that of these nations only Russia and China could be considered potential enemies of the United States. On that same page we read that "[t]he United States and its close allies spend more than the rest of the world combined, accounting for 63 percent of all military spending."

34. The higher cost for military personnel in the United States is the result of having an all-volunteer professional military force, so that salaries and benefits must be competitive with those available in the rest of the society. In other countries such as China and Russia the military relies heavily on conscripts who receive much lower pay. High pay levels in U.S. civilian society also contribute to higher expenses for weapons and other military hardware.

35. IISS, *The Military Balance, 1999–2000*, pp. 301–304.

36. "Global Nuclear Stockpiles, 1945–2000," *The Bulletin of Atomic Scientists*, vol. 56, No. 2 (Mar/Apr. 2000), p. 79.

37. "Russian Strategic Nuclear Forces, End of 1998," *The Bulletin of the Atomic Scientists*, Vol. 55, No. 2 (Mar/Apr. 1999), pp. 62–63.

38. "U.S. Strategic Nuclear Forces, End of 1998," *The Bulletin of the Atomic Scientists*, Vol. 55, No. 1 (Jan/Feb. 1999), pp. 78–80.

39. "U.S. Strategic Nuclear Forces, End of 1998," *The Bulletin of the Atomic Scientists*, Vol. 55, No. 1 (Jan/Feb. 1999), p. 78.

40. See Greg Mello, "That Old Designing Fever," *The Bulletin of the Atomic Scientists*, Vol. 56, No. 1 (Jan/Feb. 2000), pp. 51–57. On page 52 he says: "Under [the Department of] Energy's current policy, *all* the nuclear weapons in the stockpile are to be replaced by modified versions or entirely new weapons."

41. John Somerville, "Scientific-Technological Progress and the New Problem of Preventing the Annihilation of the Human World," *Peace Research*, Vol. 11 (1979), pp. 11–18. The quotation is from page 17.

42. Sivard, *World Military and Social Expenditures, 1991*, p. 13.

43. Holsti, *The State, War, and the State of War*, pp. 14–28, 36–40, and 183–205, but especially pp. 21–23.

44. IISS, *The Military Balance, 1999–2000*, p. 300, gives the 1998 per capita defense expenditure for the U.S. as $982. When that is divided by 12 months, the result is just over $80 per month.

Chapter Four. The Cause of War: General Considerations

1. For an instructive recent review of viewpoints and issues related to how causality applies to the problem of war, see Hidemi Suganami's *On the Causes of War* (Oxford: Clarendon Press, 1996), chapter 4 on "Causation," pp. 114–52, as well as his comments on page 42. Suganami himself adopts the view that one should try to create an understandable narrative of how a particular war has come to occur. He contrasts this with J. D. Singer's focus on finding the causes of war in general, that is, with "the *regular* sequence of events which culminates in war" (p. 151). It seems to me that one will need something like what I call "contributory factors" or what Singer classifies as "correlated events" in order to decide what to include or not include in one's causal narrative about how a particular war got started.

2. This distinction between necessary and sufficient conditions on the one hand and contributory factors on the other can be approached in a different way. One can make the distinction in terms of explaining events by universal causal laws (which go with the first three meanings of "cause") or explaining them by probabilistic causal laws (which go with the notion of contributory factors). Daniel Geller and J. David Singer take this approach in *Nations at War* (Cambridge: Cambridge University Press, 1998), pp. 14–17. Whether one thinks in terms of contributory factors or probabilistic causal laws, as one must when dealing with a complex problem such as what causes wars, the difficulty is determining just how much the contributory factor is contributing in a particular case. The same kind of problem is encountered when one tries to apply probabilistic causal laws to particular cases: to what extent is the occurrence of this particular event explained by each probabilistic causal law. For an extremely valuable discussion of the problem of connecting empirical generalizations about war with causal theories about why wars occur, see J. David Singer, "From *A Study of War* to Peace Research: Some Criteria and Strategies" in J. David Singer and associates, *Explaining War: Selected Papers from the Correlates of War Project* (Beverly Hills: Sage, 1979), pp. 21–34, especially pp. 31–34.

3. The current status of this issue of whether we can find some necessary condition for war which is more than just a logical (definitional) necessity is discussed at length and in great detail by Suganami in *On the Causes of War*, the second chapter entitled "Prerequisites," pp. 43–79. His conclusions on pp. 77–79 are basically in agreement with my own.

4. Theodore Lentz, "Introduction," in Theodore Lentz (ed.), *Humatriotism* (St. Louis: The Future Press, 1976), p. 28. (Publisher's address: 6251 San Bonita, St. Louis, MO 63105.)

5. See for example Matthew Melko's *Fifty-Two Peaceful Societies* (Oakville, Ontario: Canadian Peace Research Institute Press, 1973). Melko has made some modifications of his original data as the result of comments received from others. See his "Note on the Dating of the Phoenician Peace" in *Peace Research*, Vol. 7 (1975), p. 108. For a more recent refinement of this effort see Matthew Melko and Richard D. Weigel, *Peace in the Ancient World* (Jefferson NC: McFarland, 1981). For a study of seven peaceful contemporary groups see David Fabbro, "Peaceful Societies: An Introduction," *Journal of Peace Research*, Vol. 15 (1978), pp. 67–83.

6. Using a statistical approach, R.J. Rummel claims that his research shows that democracies have fewer wars, external and *internal*, than totalitarian regimes. For an overview of his work see his chapter "Political Systems, Violence, and War" in W. Scott Thompson and Kenneth M. Jensen (eds.), *Approaches to Peace: An Intellectual Map* (Washington DC: U.S. Institute of Peace, 1991), pp. 350–70, especially pp. 351–52. Nevertheless, it is going too far to say that a democratic government is a *sufficient condition for peace* or that *its absence is a necessary condition for war*. Our conclusions must be limited to the category of *contributory factors*. See Hidemi Suganami, *On the Causes of War* (Oxford: Clarendon Press, 1996), pp. 66–67, 69, and 70.

7. For an example of such an inappropriate inference see Norman Alcock, *The War Disease* (Oakville, Ontario: Canadian Peace Research Institute Press, 1972), pp. 152–53. It is worth noting that Alcock nevertheless takes note of Lewis Richardson's care in concluding that arms races are only sometimes the cause of war. See pp. 70–71.

8. Much has been written about the causes of World War I. For an example of how probabilistic generalizations can be applied to this particular war, see Geller and Singer, *Nations at War*, pp. 156–90. Interestingly, when John Stoessinger considers World War I he argues that none of the factors mentioned by Geller and Singer were decisive but rather it was a result of the character and perceptions of the leaders. See John Stoessinger, *Why Nations Go to War*, 7th ed. (New York: St. Martin's, 1998), pp. 1–23.

9. Singer makes this same point in the next to last sentence of his "From *A Study of War* to Peace Research: Some Criteria and Strategies" in Singer and associates, *Explaining War*, p. 34.

10. The "Correlates of War" (COW) project is being carried out by J. David Singer and his associates. They attempt to find various factors that can be correlated with the occurrence of war. See J. David Singer (ed.), *Correlates of War I: Research Origins and Rationale* (New York: Free Press, 1979); J. David Singer (ed.), *Explaining War: Selected Papers from the Correlates of War Project* (Beverly Hills CA: Sage, 1979); J. David Singer (ed.), *Correlates of War II: Testing Some Realpolitik Mod-*

els (New York: Free Press, 1979), and Daniel S. Geller and J. David Singer, *Nations at War*. A list of 16 factors which the COW project has found to increase the probability of the onset of war are listed on page 27 of *Nations at War*.

11. A most valuable recent book on this whole topic is Suganami's *On the Causes of War*. On page 208 he says: "The best we can do by way of identifying the origins of any given war, then, is to construct a coherent and convincing narrative on the basis of available evidence and knowledge we have of the world." Such a narrative would depend greatly on our understanding of what sorts of things are contributory factors to the outbreak of war.

12. Leonard Berkowitz, *Aggression: Its Causes, Consequences, and Control* (Philadelphia: Temple University Press, 1993), p. 3. Berkowitz presents an excellent discussion of the precise meaning of the term "aggression," the varieties of aggression, and how to distinguish aggression from other concepts which are often mistakenly confused with it. See pp. 3–23. For a similar discussion of the precise meanings of the term "aggression" and other concepts related to it or likely to be confused with it see Robert A. Hinde and Jo Groebel, "The Problem of Aggression" in Jo Groebel and Robert A. Hinde (eds.), *Aggression and War: Their Biological and Social Bases* (Cambridge: Cambridge University Press, 1989), pp. 3–9.

13. Berkowitz, *Aggression*, p. 11.

14. See Irenaus Eibl-Eibesfeldt, *The Biology of Peace and War: Men, Animals, and Aggression*, tr. by Eric Mosbacher (New York: Viking Press, 1979), pp. 84–87.

15. See Robert A. Hinde and Jo Groebel, "The Problem of Aggression," p. 8. For a more extended discussion of the view that the causes of individual aggression are different from the causes of war see Ralph L. Holloway, "Human Aggression: The Need for a Species-Specific Framework" in Morton Fried, Marvin Harris, and Robert Murphy (eds.), *War: The Anthropology of Armed Conflict and Aggression* (Garden City NY: Natural History Press, 1967), pp. 29–48, especially pp. 29–30. For an earlier statement of this view, see Bronislaw Malinowski, "An Anthropological Analysis of War," *American Journal of Sociology*, Vol. 46, No. 2 (Jan. 1941), pp. 521–50, especially pp. 523–33.

16. A good collection of excerpts from selections relating individual aggression to warfare can be found in William A. Nesbitt (ed.), *Human Nature and War*. This booklet for students was published by the State Education Department of New York, 99 Washington Ave., Albany, NY 12210, in 1973. Individual aggression and warfare are often linked in magazine articles and books.

17. For a good collection of three selections, one dealing with each type of theory about human aggression, see Richard A. Falk and Samuel S. Kim (eds.), *The War System: An Interdisciplinary Approach* (Boulder CO: Westview, 1980), pp. 77–156.

18. Irenaus Eibl-Eibesfeldt, *The Biology of Peace and War: Men, Animals, and Aggression*, tr. by Eric Mosbacher (New York: Viking Press, 1979), p. 2.

19. Konrad Lorenz, *On Aggression* (New York: Harcourt Brace Jovanovich, 1966), p. 52. See also Berkowitz, a discussion and critique of this theory in *Aggression*, pp. 376–400.

20. Sigmund Freud, *Civilization and Its Discontents* (New York: Norton, 1930), p. 67.

21. Robert Ardrey, *The Territorial Imperative* (New York: Atheneum, 1961).

22. Robert Ardrey, *African Genesis*, p. 325.

23. Desmond Morris, *The Naked Ape* (New York: McGraw-Hill, 1967).

24. "Human Violence: Some Causes and Implications" in Beitz and Herman, *Peace and War*, pp. 119–43. This article contains a rather extensive bibliography on the physiological basis of aggression. Corning would probably object to being grouped with Lorenz, Ardrey, and Morris because his views are considerably different from theirs. Still, his emphasis on the physiological basis for aggressive behavior seems to require classifying his view as one that emphasizes the biological rather than the cultural or psychological aspects of aggression. At the same time it should be noted that for Corning, as well as for others such as Freud who emphasize the biological or instinctual basis of aggression, the solution to the war problem is to be found in politics rather than biology.

25. Berkowitz, *Aggression*, pp. 395–400.

26. Some research indicates that testosterone may not be so directly related to aggressive behavior as has been generally thought. For example, it has been found that men with a deficiency of testosterone are excessively aggressive and irritable and that testosterone replacement therapy made them less aggressive and more friendly. Testosterone is definitely related to male sex drive and possibly even to female interest in sex. It gives both men and women more vim and zest. On the other hand, it turns out that the female hormone estrogen may be a factor in aggressive behavior in both males and females. The enzyme aromatase in the brain converts testosterone into estrogen which then acts on the nerve cells through estrogen receptors, which are abundant in men. "Most of the effect of testosterone on the brain is paradoxically estrogenic in nature." See Natalie Angier, "Does Testosterone Equal Aggression? Maybe Not," *New York Times*, June 20, 1995, pp. A1 and B6.

27. See Robert Sapolsky, "Testosterone Rules," *Discover*, Vol. 18, No. 3 (March 1997), pp. 44–49.

28. For an ample collection of examples see Eibl-Eibesfeldt, *The Biology of Peace and War*.

29. Eibl-Eibesfeldt, *The Biology of Peace and War*, pp. 1–6, 60–77, 122–24, 188–196, and 221–39.

30. J. Dollard, L.W. Doob, N.E. Miller, O.H. Mowrer, and R.R. Sears, *Frustration and Aggression* (New Haven: Yale University, 1939). See especially p. 1.

31. Berkowitz, *Aggression*, pp. 44–47.

32. A recent collection of articles sympathetic to this view is found in Groebel and Hinde, *Aggression and War*. For a good general statement of this approach see John Dewey, "Does Human Nature Change?", *The Rotarian*, Feb. 1938, reprinted in Mary Mothersill (ed.), *Ethics* (New York: Macmillan, 1965), pp. 83–91. Another good general statement of this view is Mark A. May's "War, Peace, and Social Learning" in Bramson and Goethals, *War: Studies from Psychology, Sociology, Anthropology*, pp. 151–58.

33. Mead, "Warfare Is Only an Invention—Not a Biological Necessity," *Asia*, Vol. 40 (1940), p. 403.

34. Stanley Milgrim, *Obedience to Authority: An Experimental View* (New York: Harper and Row, 1974), p. 166.

35. Arnold H. Buss, *The Psychology of Aggression* (New York: Wiley, 1961), pp. 20–23.

36. Richard J. Borden, "Social Situational Influences on Aggression: A Review of Experimental Findings and Implications," *Peace Research*, Vol. 7 (1975), pp. 97–107.

37. William Eckhardt, "A Conformity Theory of Aggression," *Journal of Peace Research*, Vol. 11 (1974), pp. 31–39.

38. Eibl-Eibesfeldt, *The Biology of Peace and War*, pp. 2–3.

39. Eibl-Eibesfeldt, *The Biology of Peace and War*, pp. 100 and 116–21.

40. *UNESCO Courier*, Feb. 1993, p. 40. This Seville Statement is also reprinted in full at the front of Groebel and Hinde, *Aggression and War*, pp. xii–xvi. For more information about the Seville Statement see David Adams, "The Seville Statement on Violence: A Progress Report," *Journal of Peace Research*, Vol. 26, No. 2 (1989), pp. 113–21.

41. *African Genesis*, pp. 107–10.

42. Stoessinger, *Why Nations Go to War*, 7th ed., pp. 209–210.

43. Bueno de Mesquita, *The War Trap* (New Haven CT: Yale Univ., 1981), p. 21.

44. Peter A. Corning, "Human Violence: Some Causes and Implications," a paper prepared for the symposium "Value and Knowledge Requirements for Peace" at the 138th meeting of the American Association for the Advancement of Science in Philadelphia, December 1971. The paper is reprinted in Charles R. Beitz and Theodore Herman (eds.), *Peace and War* (San Francisco: W.H. Freeman, 1973), pp. 119–43. The discussion concerning women leaders occurs on pp. 129–30. For another discussion of the desirability of having women leaders because of sex differences in aggressiveness, see Melvin Konner, "The Aggressors," *New York Times Magazine*, Aug. 14, 1988, pp. 33–34. When Nobel Laureate García Márquez was asked in 1992 about what humanity needed for the future, he said "The only new idea that could save humanity in the 21st century is for women to take over the management of the world." This citation comes from a speech by Dr. Dessima Williams of Grenada in Dallas, Texas, at the National Assembly of the World Federalist Association in October 1999 as recorded in the *WFA Gender Equity Committee Collation #16* (January 2000), p. 5.

45. See E.F.M. Durbin and John Bowlby, "Personal Aggressiveness and War" in Bramson and Goethals, *War: Studies from Psychology, Sociology, Anthropology*, pp. 94–95. See also Edward C. Tolman, "Drives Toward War," pp. 165–68.

46. Ross Stagner, *Psychological Aspects of International Conflict* (Belmont CA: Wadsworth, 1967), pp. 109–10.

47. Stagner, *Psychological Aspects of International Conflict*, pp. 148–49, and Kenneth Grundy, "The Causes of Political Violence" in Beitz and Herman, *Peace and War*, pp. 50–68.

48. For a detailed description of the process by which young civilians are converted into soldiers, including the importance of patriotism in this process, see chapter 5, "Anybody's Son Will Do," in Dyer, *War*, pp. 101–29.

Chapter 5. Group Competition and Group Identification

1. Keith F. Otterbein, *The Evolution of War: A Cross-Cultural Study*, pp. 20–21, and Dyer, *War*, pp. 6–7.

2. Robert L. Carneiro, "A Theory of the Origin of the State," *Science*, Vol. 70 (1970), p. 735.

3. Michael Andregg, *On the Causes of War* (Minneapolis: Ground Zero, P.O. Box 13127, 2nd printing, 1999), cites these two examples on page 73 at the end of his outstanding chapter "Population Pressure" where he persuasively argues that current population growth is pushing us toward disaster and that one of the most needed programs for eliminating war is to stop further population growth, even by coercive legal restrictions if necessary. For the classical statement of the opposing optimistic view that human ingenuity will save us from ecological disaster just as it always has, see Julian Simon, *The Ultimate Resource* (Princeton: Princeton University Press, 1981).

4. For a good statement of the view that population growth is only tangentially related to the problem of war see Quincy Wright, *A Study of War*, abridged ed. by Louis Wright (Chicago: University of Chicago, 1964), pp. 278–95.

5. This thesis is demonstrated convincingly by Bruce Bueno de Mesquita in *The War Trap* (New Haven CT: Yale University, 1981).

6. Anatol Rapoport in *Fights, Games, and Debates* (Ann Arbor MI: University of Michigan, 1960), pp. 9–12 makes some excellent points about the differences between the three different activities mentioned in his title. He notes, however, that even in debates it is assumed that the aim is to get the other person to come over to accepting one's own opinion. The continuing search for what is true, which is our present concern, must take a different form. It must be what Rapoport calls an argument (p. 273). It consists of a dialectic of eliminating errors within one's own thinking rather than of defending a particular theory no matter what objections are raised. In his later work *The Origins of Violence: Approaches to the Study of Conflict* (New York: Paragon House, 1989), pp. 510–11, Rapoport again distinguishes between fights, games, and debates. His discussion of "Objective Criteria" on pp. 516–17 comes closer to the situation of trying to discover what is true but is still considered in the context of a conflict situation between opposing parties rather than in the context of a single individual trying to discover what to believe by considering all the facts and arguments which might be used to support various possible views. That dialectical process in which one argues within oneself to ferret out erroneous beliefs is the basis of philosophy and the appropriate alternative to militaristic ideological struggle among different social groups.

7. Risieri Frondizi, "The Ideological Origins of the Third World War," in Ginsberg, *The Critique of War*, pp. 77–95, especially pp. 81 and 87–88.

8. Harrop Freeman, "Pacifism and Law," in Ginsberg, *The Critique of War*, pp. 284–96, especially pp. 293–94.

9. Schumpeter, *Imperialism and Social Classes* (Cleveland: World, 1955), pp. 6 and 24–25.

10. For an outspoken attack on nationalism in general, see the ninth chapter, "The Burden of Nationalism," in Elliot Roosevelt, *The Conservators* (New York: Arbor House, 1983), pp. 124–30.

11. This issue of defining of nationalism can become very complex. For those who desire a more complete discussion of the issue I recommend Anthony D. Smith, *Theories of Nationalism*, second edition (New York: Holmes & Meier, 1983), especially pp. 153–91.

Smith says on page 168 that he plans to "reserve the term 'nationalism' for the doctrine and the movement" and to use "national sentiment" for what he had previously on page 160 called "Nationalism in the ancient world," but I am using the term "racial-ethnic nationalism" to cover what he eventually decided to call "national sentiment," and I am using "doctrinal nationalism" to cover what he on page 168 wants to call "nationalism."

12. For a recent book length treatment of the contemporary situation for nations which do not have a nation-state of their own, see Montserrat Guibernau, *Nations Without States: Political Communities in a Global Age* (Cambridge: Polity Press, 1999).

13. Smith, *Theories of Nationalism*, makes a very interesting distinction within what I am calling "racial-ethnic nationalism" between (1) *"ethnocentric* nationalism" and (2)*"polycentric* nationalism," with the first indicating a belief that the group has a special connection with the deity making it alone truly human while the second accepts the notion that it is but one among many human nations. The former viewpoint is pretty much restricted to the ancient world. See pp. 153–64, especially 158–59.

14. For some persons who address the issue of nationalism such as Lord Acton and E. Kedourie, it is this notion of "doctrinal nationalism" which constitutes the essential and proper meaning of the word "nationalism." See Smith, *Theories of Nationalism*, pp. 9–10 and 17–18.

15. For an article which supports this multi-ethnic viewpoint and cites India as a model to be followed by others see Shashi Tharoor, "The Future of Civil Conflict," *World Policy Journal*, Vol. 16. No. 1 (Spring 1999), pp. 1–11.

16. See Jonathan Landay's article "Loyal Serbs and Croats in Sarajevo See Woe in Partition of Bosnia," *Christian Science Monitor*, July 30, 1993, pp. 1, 4.

17. See Guibernau, *Nations Without States*, pp. 68–72.

18. See Alan Thein Durning, "Supporting Indigenous Peoples" in Lester R. Brown (ed.), *State of the World 1993*, pp. 80–100. The statistics are from p. 81.

19. See the statement by U.N. General Assembly President Theo-Ben Gurirab on 7 August 2000, U.N. Press Release GA/SM/184 OBV/153.

20. U.N. Association of U.S.A., *A Global Agenda: Issues before the 52nd General Assembly of the United Nations* (Lanham MD: Rowman & Littlefield, 1997), p. 185.

21. Durning, "Supporting Indigenous Peoples," in Brown, *State of the World 1993*, pp. 80–100.

22. It should be noted that on some occasions the group which has been subjugated is in fact a multi-ethnic group instead of all being of the same race and ethnic background, so that strictly speaking in some wars of liberation the appeal is not to doctrinal nationalism but rather to another principle, namely, that no potential territorial nation-state should be under the control of another nation-state.

23. Sivard, *World Military and Social Expenditures, 1991*, p. 25.

24. See Stoessinger, *Why Nations Go to War*, 6th ed. (1993), pp. 123–32.

25. Keesing's *Record of World Events*, 1993, p. 39450, and Sivard, *World Military and Social Expenditures, 1991*, p. 25.

26. For a valuable explanatory discussion plus a list

of separatist or irredentist wars motivated by doctrinal nationalism during the period 1945–1996 see R. William Ayers, "A World Flying Apart?", *Journal of Peace Research*, Vol. 37, No. 1 (Jan 2000), pp. 105–17.

27. For a brief account of the current situation of the Kurds, see Guibernau, *Nations Without States*, pp. 64–66.

Chapter Six. Other Views About Causes of War

1. This "Arms Race Game" is an adaptation of the "Prisoner's Dilemma" game. See Rapoport, *Fights, Games, and Debates*, pp. 173–74, and Ralph M. Goldman, "Political Distrust as Generator of the Arms Race: Prisoners and Security Dilemmas," from *Arms Control and Peacekeeping* (New York: Random House, 1982), reprinted in Burns H. Weston (ed.), *Toward Nuclear Disarmament and Global Security* (Boulder CO: Westview, 1984), pp. 90–94.

2. Alcock, *The War Disease*, pp. 169–70.

3. See Alan G. Newcombe, "A Foreign Policy for Peace," *Gandhi Marg*, Vol. 16 (1972), pp. 254–65. A slightly revised version of this article is reprinted in Israel W. Charny (ed.), *Strategies Against Violence: Design for Nonviolent Change* (Boulder CO: Westview, 1978), pp. 3–18. See also Alcock, *The War Disease*, pp. 164–73.

4. There have been several important studies of the extent to which wars have been associated with arms races. One of the most important and widely discussed is that done by W. D. Wallace, "Arms Races and Escalation: Some New Evidence," *Journal of Conflict Resolution*, Vol. 23 (1979), pp. 3–16. A review and analysis of the significance of Wallace's work is given by Suganami, *On the Causes of War*, pp. 89–99.

5. Lewis F. Richardson, *Arms and Insecurity* (Pittsburgh: Boxwood, 1960), pp. 12–36. See also Alcock, *The War Disease*, pp. 70–83 and 200–212.

6. Lewis F. Richardson, "Could an Arms Race End Without Fighting?" *Nature*, Vol. 168 (1951), pp. 567–68, and Richardson, *Arms and Insecurity*, pp. 35–36 and p. 76.

7. Richardson, *Arms and Insecurity*, p. 70.

8. For a specific example of how this situation developed between France and Germany before World War I see David W. Ziegler, *War, Peace, and International Politics*, 7th edition (New York: Addison Wesley Longman, 1997), pp. 238–39.

9. One very complete account of this connection is given by John Stoessinger, *Why Nations Go To War*, 7th edition (New York: St. Martin's Press, 1998), pp. 1–23, especially pp. 15–18. For a briefer account, see Dyer, *War*, p. 150. For a more general discussion of how military planning can be a contributory factor to the beginning of war, see Suganami, *On the Causes of War*, pp. 168–73.

10. Ziegler, *War, Peace, and International Politics*, 7th ed., p. 136, argues that the view that individual aggressive leaders are a cause of war cannot be correct because there are many wars in which there seem to be no villains. Ziegler's argument is cogent only against the view that individual aggressive leaders are a necessary condition of war. It does not apply to our thesis that individual aggressive leaders are a *contributory factor* to war. The view that national leaders play a key role in de-

termining whether or not their countries will engage in war is convincingly defended by Bueno de Mesquita in *The War Trap*, pp. 19–29.

11. See Kenneth Waltz, *Man, the State, and War* (New York: Columbia University, 1959), pp. 8–9. A primary advocate of the thesis that democracies are less likely to get involved in wars, especially with each other, is R.J. Rummel. A good statement of his view can be found in "Political Systems, Violence, and War" in W. Scott Thompson and Kenneth M. Jensen, *Approaches to Peace: An Intellectual Map* (Washington DC: U.S. Institute of Peace, 1991), pp. 350–70.

12. A recent book length treatment of the view that democracies do not war against other democracies is Spencer R. Weart, *Never at War: Why Democracies Will Not Fight One Another* (New Haven CT: Yale University press, 1998). For the opposing viewpoint on this issue see Steven Chan, "Mirror, Mirror on the Wall…," *Journal of Conflict Resolution*, Vol. 28, No. 4 (Dec. 1984), pp. 617–48. For an excellent balanced discussion of this issue see Suganami, *On the Causes of War*, pp. 101–111.

13. The term "military-industrial complex" was coined by Malcolm Moos and popularized by President Eisenhower when he used it in 1961 in his farewell address. See Alvin R. Sunseri, "The Military-Industrial Complex in Iowa" in Benjamin F. Cooling (ed.), *War, Business, and American Society: Historical Perspectives on the Military-Industrial Complex* (Port Washington NY: Kennikat, 1977), p. 158. For a booklet about the military-industrial complex in the U.S. see *Caution: Military-Industrial Complex at Work* published by the Council for a Livable World Education Fund, 110 Maryland Ave NE, Washington DC 20002, in December 1998.

14. International Institute of Strategic Studies, *The Military Balance, 1999–2000*, pp. 300 and 305. "The military-industrial complex that Eisenhower warned against is still powerful and entrenched" says Robert L. Borosage in "Let Them Eat Guns," *The Nation*, May 8, 2000, p. 38. See also "The Fiscal Year 2001 Military Budget" in *The Defense Monitor*, Vol. 29, No. 2 (2000), pp. 1–3.

15. Anne Trotter, "Development of the Merchants-of-Death Theory" in Cooling, *War, Business, and American Society*, p. 96.

16. Trotter, "Development of the Merchants-of-Death Theory" in Cooling, *War, Business, and American Society*, pp. 97–98.

17. Trotter, "Development of the Merchants-of-Death Theory" in Cooling, *War, Business, and American Society*, p. 94.

18. Trotter, "Development of the Merchants-of-Death Theory" in Cooling, *War, Business, and American Society*, pp. 101–103.

19. Benjamin F. Cooling, "Introduction" in Cooling, *War, Business, and American Society*, p. 3.

20. See for example Seymour Melman (ed.), *The War Economy of the United States* (New York: St. Martin's, 1971).

21. See C. Wright Mills, *The Causes of World War Three* (New York: Simon and Schuster, 1958), pp. 17–19, 47–50, and 86–89.

22. Stagner, *Psychological Aspects of International Conflict*, p. 137.

23. For a good critical discussion of the thesis that war is caused by a few individuals seeking personal gain,

see Bernard Brodie, *War and Politics* (New York: Macmillan, 1973), pp. 283–302.

24. The best source for these basic ideas is *The Communist Manifesto* by Marx and Engels. The *Manifesto* along with other relevant selections can be found in *The Marx-Engels Reader*, ed. by Robert C. Tucker (New York: W.W. Norton, 1972), and in *Karl Marx: Selected Readings* (Oxford: Oxford University, 1977), ed. by David McLellan. See also Frederick Engels, *Herr Eugen Düring's Revolution in Science*, tr. by Emile Burns (New York: International, 1939), especially pp. 292–310.

25. V.I. Lenin, *Imperialism: The Highest Stage of Capitalism* (New York: International, 1939), especially pp. 9–14 and 76–98.

26. It has been argued by a Chinese Marxist, Chen Qimao, that the presence of multinational corporations has generated a new situation where wars between capitalist countries have become very unlikely and that such wars are no longer inevitable as Lenin maintained. See Chan Qimao, "War and Peace: A Reappraisal," *Beijing Review*, Vol. 29, No. 23 (June 9, 1986), pp. 18–25, especially pp. 19–22.

27. Hegel, *Philosophy of Right*, tr. by T.M. Knox (Oxford: Clarendon, 1942), p. 295.

28. For a brief account of Bismarck's efforts and views see Ziegler, *War, Peace, and International Politics*, 7th edition, pp. 6–17.

29. For an attempt to show that there is a correlation between external war and domestic conflict in "polyarchic" (democratic) states see Jonathan Wilkenfeld, "Domestic and Foreign Conflict Behavior of Nations," *Journal of Peace Research*, Vol. 5 (1968), pp. 56–69. Wilkenfeld cites various earlier studies that had concluded that there was no correlation between foreign conflict and domestic conflict such as that reported by Rudolph J. Rummell, "Dimensions of Conflict Behavior Within and Between Nations," *General Systems*, Vol. 8 (1963), pp. 1–50. For a balanced review of the various studies on this issue see Suganami, *On the Causes of War*, pp. 85–88 and 200.

30. This letter is reprinted in John Somerville and Ronald E. Santoni (eds.), *Social and Political Philosophy* (Garden City NY: Doubleday, 1963), pp. 259–60.

31. For an excellent discussion of the various alternatives to violence, especially in the realm of international relations, see Vasquez, *The War Puzzle*, pp. 263–91, especially pp. 287–88. He says, "Only rarely in established states does war … become a way of resolving a political issue" (p. 263), thus showing how government tends to be more effective than the other alternative ways of resolving conflicts nonviolently.

32. Vasquez, *The War Puzzle*, p. 288.

33. Wright, *A Study of War*, abridged edition by Louise Leanord Wright, p. 428.

34. See Emery Reves, *The Anatomy of Peace* (New York: Harper & Brothers, 1945; republished by Peter Smith, Publisher, Gloucester MA, 1969), pp. 144–47. In 1995 this book was reprinted by Robert Betchov, 53 Avenue du Lignon, 1219, Geneva, Switzerland.

35. Suganami in *On the Causes of War*, pp. 46–53, 62–65, and 200–01 relates his discussion to the view of Kenneth Waltz in *Man, the State, and War: A Theoretical Analysis* (New York: Columbia University Press, 1959) that due to international anarchy there is nothing in the international system to prevent war. Suganami proceeds to show that, contrary to Waltz, international anarchy is not a sufficient condition for war

and that its elimination would not be a sufficient condition for peace. Nevertheless he concurs with John Vasquez's statement that "when power politics is a way of life, war is more likely to occur" (p. 53). I take this statement by Vasquez to be equivalent to my saying that the absence of peaceful alternatives to power politics is a contributory factor to war.

36. Kenneth N. Waltz, *Man, the State, and War* (New York: Columbia University Press, 1959), p. 238.

Chapter Seven.
The Value of War

1. Frank B. Livingstone, "The Effects of Warfare on the Biology of the Human Species" in Morton Fried, Marvin Harris, and Robert Murphy, *War: The Anthropology of Armed Conflict and Aggression* (Garden City NY: Natural History Press [Doubleday], 1967), p. 5.

2. Some nations suffered more than others with the Soviet Union losing 9 percent of its population during that war while Germany lost 5 percent of its population, England and France about 1 percent, and the U.S. only 0.2 percent. See Livingston, "The Effects of Warfare" in Fried, Harris, and Murphy, *War: The Anthropology of Armed Conflict and Aggression*, p. 5.

3. Livingstone, "The Effects of Warfare" in Fried, Harris, and Murphy, *War: The Anthropology of Armed Conflict and Aggression*, p. 5.

4. Livingstone, "The Effects of Warfare" in Fried, Harris, and Murphy, *War: The Anthropology of Armed Conflict and Aggression*, p. 5. Frederick P. Thieme, discussant of Livingstone's paper at the 1967 symposium of the American Anthropological Association on the effects of war on the human species, agreed with Livingstone's view. See p. 16 in the Fried, Harris, and Murphy book.

5. Livingstone, "The Effects of Warfare" in Fried, Harris, and Murphy, *War: The Anthropology of Armed Conflict and Aggression*, pp. 6–8. Interestingly, Livingstone is making the point that the genetic consequences are so slight that one need not be concerned that modern war has an *adverse* effect on the gene pool, an effect which might be expected when it is supposed that there is a tendency for the *better fit* persons to be called to serve in combat situations during war. Our concern in the text is the opposite view, namely, that war is *good* because then the *less fit* are less likely to survive and reproduce.

6. "The Biological Consequences of War" in Fried, Harris, and Murphy, *War: The Anthropology of Armed Conflict and Aggression*, p. 18.

7. The situation in earlier times among more primitive people may have been somewhat different. In fact, primitive warfare may have been an important factor in both population control and genetic selection. See Livingstone, "The Effects of Warfare" in Fried, Harris, and Murphy, *War: The Anthropology of Armed Conflict and Aggression*, pp. 8–11; Corning, "Human Violence" in Beitz and Herman, *Peace and War*, p. 126; and Stanislav Andreski, "Evolution and War," *Science Journal*, Vol. 7 (Jan. 1971), p. 91.

8. John Nef, "Political, Technological, and Cultural Aspects of War" in Ginsberg, *The Critique of War*, pp. 120–37, especially pp. 130–31.

9. "Military Research and the Economy: Burden or Benefit?", *The Defense Monitor*, Vol. 14, No. 1 (1985), pp. 1–8; and Lloyd J. Dumas, "The Military Burden on the Economy," *Bulletin of the Atomic Scientists*, Vol. 42, No. 8 (Oct. 1986), p. 24.

10. See for example Marion Anderson, *The Empty Pork Barrel*, a booklet published by Employment Research Associates, Lansing, Michigan, in 1978, especially page 1, where it was noted that one billion dollars spent by the government would, on the average, generate 58,000 jobs for defense but would generate 76,000 jobs for teachers. For a critique of this study and others which denigrate military spending as a means of stimulating the economy, see Gordon Adams and David Gold, "Recasting the Military Spending Debate," *Bulletin of the Atomic Scientists*, Vol. 42, No. 8 (Oct. 1986), pp. 26–32. For an extended discussion of the impact of military spending on the economy see Ann Markusen, "The Militarized Economy," *World Policy Journal*, Vol. 3, No. 3 (Summer 1986), pp. 495–516, especially pp. 499–503.

11. Anderson, *The Empty Pork Barrel*, p. 1.

12. See the statement of Simon Ramo, cofounder of TRW, Incorporated, a company with heavy military involvement, cited in Lloyd J. Dumas, "The Military Burden on the Economy," *Bulletin of the Atomic Scientists*, Vol. 42, No. 8 (Oct. 1986), p. 25. The original source is Simon Ramo, *America's Technology Slip* (New York: Wiley, 1980), p. 251.

13. Dumas, "The Military Burden on the Economy," p. 25.

14. "Military Research and the Economy: Burden or Benefit?", *The Defense Monitor*, Vol. 14, No. 1 (1985), p. 4.

15. Miriam Pemberton, "Sharing and Reducing the Military Burden," *Foreign Policy In Focus*, Vol. 5, No. 27, Aug. 2000, p. 1 (publication of Interhemispheric Resource Center, PO Box 2178, Silver City NM 88062).

16. Hegel, *Philosophy of Right*, tr. by T.M. Knox, p. 295.

17. From Mussolini, *The Political and Social Doctrine of Fascism* (tr. by Jane Soames) as reprinted in Somerville and Santoni, *Social and Political Philosophy*, p. 431.

18. This essay was originally published in *McClure's Magazine* in August 1910. It has been reprinted many times, including the complete text in David P. Barash, *Approaches to Peace: A Reader in Peace Studies*, pp. 65–69.

19. For more information about the U.S. Peace Corps see their website at <www.peacecorps.gov> or call them at 1-800-424-8580. For more information about AmericorpsVISTA see their website at <http://www.americorps.org/vista>. For information about other government programs for volunteers see the website for the Corporation for National Service at <http://www.cns.gov>.

20. William James, "The Moral Equivalent of War," in Barash, *Approaches to Peace*, p. 69. James seems a bit optimistic in supposing that a national government would have these young people disinterestedly pursuing justice rather than its own national interests. During the Cold War, American Peace Corps volunteers in less developed countries were frequently disillusioned to find that they had become agents of American foreign policy rather than disinterested workers for justice. It might be better to have these programs sponsored by the United Nations or some nongovernmental organization rather than a national government.

21. See Andrew Vayda, "Hypotheses About Functions of War" in Fried, Harris, and Murphy, *War: The Anthropology of Armed Conflict and Aggression*, p. 88.

22. *Newsweek*, Vol. 74, No. 4 (July 28, 1969), p. 54 and *Time*, Vol. 94, No. 4 (July 25, 1969), pp. 29–30.

23. Richard Lacayo, "Blood in the Stands," *Time*, Vol. 125, No. 23 (June 10, 1985), pp. 38–41.

24. Kenneth Boulding, *The Meaning of the Twentieth Century*, p. 77.

Chapter Eight. Ideological Aspects of the Contemporary Situation

1. This phrase from *Critique of the Gotha Program* can be found in David McLellan (ed.), *Karl Marx: Selected Writings* (Oxford: Oxford University, 1977), p. 569, and in Robert C. Tucker (ed.), *The Marx-Engels Reader* (New York: W.W. Norton, 1972), p. 388.

2. Adam Smith *(1723–1790) in An Inquiry into the Nature and Causes of the Wealth of the Nations* (ed. by J.R. McCulloch, Edinburgh: Adam and Charles Black, 1863), Book IV, Chapter II, p. 199, poetically describes this operation of the market system as the working of an "invisible hand." The basic ideas of capitalism and the implications of its natural international dimensions are described by Smith in this work.

3. That such a trend has developed in the 1980s is noted by Robert L. Heilbroner in *Visions of the Future: The Distant Past, Yesterday, Tomorrow* (New York: Oxford University Press, 1995), p. 88.

4. Although this view of history is fundamental in Marx's thought, the most sustained discussions of historical materialism occur in Frederick Engels, *Herr Eugen Düring's Revolution in Science*, trans. by Emile Burns (New York: International Publishers, 1939), pp. 292–310, and Frederick Engels, *Ludwig Feuerbach and the End of Classical German Philosophy* (trans. by Anonymous, Peking: Foreign Languages Press, 1976), pp. 38–59.

5. V.I. Lenin, *Imperialism: The Highest Stage of Capitalism* (New York: International, 1939), especially pp. 9–14 and 76–98.

6. David Lane, *Politics and Society in the U.S.S.R.* (New York: Random House, 1971), pp. 11–14.

7. Lane, *Politics and Society in the U.S.S.R.*, p. 129.

8. For a booklet which contains the original article plus a summary of the discussion of it held in July 1989 at the U.S. Institute of Peace see *A Look at "The End of History?"* edited by Kenneth M. Jensen, published by the U.S. Institute of Peace, 1550 M St. NW, Washington DC 20005.

9. This passage is on page 26 of the booklet mentioned in the previous note.

10. Samuel P. Huntington, *The Clash of Civilizations and the Remaking of World Order* (New York: Simon & Schuster, 1996). See especially pp. 36–78.

11. Huntington, *The Clash of Civilizations*, pp. 72–78.

12. See Francis Fukuyama's reviews of three recent books critical of liberalism in "The Sober Compromise: Does Liberal Politics Really Undermine Western Cultures?" *Times Literary Supplement*, No. 4858 (May 10, 1996), pp. 3–4. The review immediately following

Fukuyama's on pp. 4–5 of this number of *TLS* is also relevant to this issue. It is the review by Charles King of David Miller's *On Nationality* titled "Fellow-feelings: A New Defence of National Identity."

13. Fukuyama hints at this last point on page 34 of the booklet cited in footnote 8.

14. Jane Lampman, "World Religious Leaders Hold 'First' Summit," *Christian Science Monitor*, Aug. 28, 2000, pp. 1, 8.

15. Hans Kung, *Christianity and the World Religions* (New York: Doubleday, 1986), p. 353.

16. John G. Stoessinger, "The Great Religions in Peace and War," *Religious Humanism*, Vol. 15, No. 3 (Summer 1981), pp. 108–13.

17. Hans Kung, *Christianity and the World Religions*, p. 443.

18. Hans Kung, *Christianity and the World Religions*, p. 442.

19. See the *Journal of International Affairs*, Vol. 36, No. 2 (Fall/Winter 1982/83), pp. 187–328, which is devoted to the topic "Religion and Politics."

20. See the collection of excerpts from the print media about the "Taliban Virus" titled "Will Iran Spark an Afghan War?" in *World Press Review*, Vol. 45, No. 12 (December 1998), pp. 8–11.

21. Jane Lampman, "World Religious Leaders Hold 'First' Summit," *Christian Science Monitor*, Aug. 28, 2000, p. 1.

Chapter Nine. National-Historical Aspects of the Contemporary Situation

1. For details about islands controlled by the United States, see *World Almanac, 2000*, pp. 669–71.

2. David W. Ziegler, *War, Peace, and International Politics*, 7th ed. (New York: Longman, 1997), p. 170.

3. See Locke's *Second Treatise of Government: An Essay Concerning the True Original, Extent, and End of Civil Government*. It can be found as the second part of John Locke, *Two Treatises of Government*, edited by Peter Laslett, revised ed. (New York: The New American Library, 1965), pp. 305–477.

4. Hobbes's views on the absence of obligations to others in the state of nature are given in chapters 13–15 of his *Leviathan*. See *The English Works of Thomas Hobbes*, edited by Sir William Molesworth (London: John Bohn, 1839, reprinted 1966), Vol. 3, pp. 110–47. It should be noted that Hobbes maintained that even though one had no obligations *to others* in a state of nature, one did have an obligation to do what one could to get out of the very insecure state of nature by establishing a government which could provide protection from others.

5. Michael Walzer, *Just and Unjust Wars: A Moral Argument with Historical Illustrations* (New York: Basic Books, 1977), pp. 51–63.

6. Boutros Boutros-Ghali, *Unvanquished: A U.S.-U.N. Saga* (New York: Random House, 1999), pp. 103–07.

7. This conflict is apparent in U.S. failure to ratify several international treaties such as the Law of the Sea Treaty and the Comprehensive Test Ban Treaty and also in the U.S. voting record at the United Nations,

which runs contrary to the efforts of most other members to strengthen this organization created by the United States in accord with its own democratic ideology. See Steven Holloway, "U.S. Unilateralism at the UN: Why Great Powers Do Not Make Great Multilateralists," *Global Governance*, Vol. 6, No. 3 (Jul.–Sept. 2000), pp. 361–81.

8. See Mikhail N. Pokrovskii, *Russia in World History*, ed. by Roman Szporluk, trans. by Roman and Mary Ann Szporluk (Ann Arbor: University of Michigan, 1970), pp. 95–102.

9. Donald W. Treadgold, *Twentieth Century Russia*, 5th ed. (Boston: Houghton Mifflin, 1981), pp. 76–84.

10. Sergei Pushkarev, *The Emergence of Modern Russia, 1801–1917*, trans. by Robert H. McNeal and Tova Yedlin (New York: Holt, Rinehart, and Winston, 1963), p. 363.

11. Otto Hoetzsch, *The Evolution of Russia*, trans. by Rhys Evans (New York: Harcourt, Brace, & World, 1966), pp. 56–58.

12. Michael T. Florinsky, *Russia: A Short History*, 2nd ed. (Toronto: Collier-Macmillan, 1964), pp. 417–20, 435–37, and 446–73.

13. Pokrovskii, *Russia in World History*, p. 114.

14. Vladimir Mshvenieradze, *Political Reality and Political Consciousness*, trans. by Margot Light and Ludmila Lezhneva (Moscow: Progress, 1985), pp. 308–310.

15. See Pertti Pesonen, "Living Beside the Soviets," *World Press Review*, Vol. 33, No. 8 (Aug. 1986), pp. 34–36.

16. John Somerville, "Marxism and War," in Robert Ginsberg (ed.), *The Critique of War: Contemporary Philosophical Explorations*, pp. 138–51.

17. For a Cold War era presentation of the view that American foreign policy is based on U.S. economic interests see Harry Magdoff, *The Age of Imperialism: The Economics of U.S. Foreign Policy* (New York: Monthly Review, 1969).

18. R. J. Rummel, *Death by Government* (New Brunswick NJ: Transaction Publishers, 1994), p. 8.

19. Immanuel C.Y. Hsü, *The Rise of Modern China*, 2nd ed. (New York: Oxford University, 1975), p. 817.

20. See *Keesing's Record of World Events, 1991*, p. 38655. For a good review of five informative books dealing with the events leading to the end of the Soviet Union, see Michael Mandelbaum, "The Fall of the House of Lenin," *World Policy Journal*, Vol. 10, No. 3 (Fall 1993), pp. 97–109.

21. For an excellent article about Putin's life, see Michael Wines, "Putin Retains Soviet Discipline While Steering Toward Reform," *New York Times*, Feb. 20, 2000, pp. 1, 12.

22. See the series of press excerpts on the Chechnyan conflict in the *World Press Review*, Vol. 47, No. 2 (Feb. 2000), pp. 20–22.

23. Information acquired on 11 September 2000 from web-site for European Court of Human Rights <www.echr.coe.int/eng/INFORMATION%20NOTES>.

24. For a scholarly discussion of the issues involved see George Ross, "After Maastricht: Hard Choices for Europe," *World Policy Journal*, Vol. 9, No. 3 (Summer 1992), pp. 487–513.

25. See the collection of excerpts about European issues under the title "Continental Divide" in *World Press Review*, Vol. 47, No. 1 (Jan 2000), pp. 4–13.

26. For two excellent book length presentations of this proposal, see James R. Huntley, *Uniting the Democracies: Institutions of the Emerging Atlantic-Pacific System* (New York: New York University, 1980), and James R. Huntley, *Pax Democratica: A Strategy for the 21st Century* (New York: St. Martin's Press, 1998).

27. The World Bank, *Entering the 21st Century: World Development Report 1999/2000* (New York: Oxford University Press, 1999), pp. 230–31.

28. Edwin O. Reischauer and Albert M. Craig, *Japan: Tradition and Transformation* (Boston: Houghton Mifflin, 1978), pp. 74–76, 79–80, 89–91, 116–24, 128–30, 135–36, 142–89. See also Herschel Webb, *An Introduction to Japan*, 2nd ed. (New York: Columbia University, 1957), pp. 24–35.

29. It is worth noting that even after the two atomic bombs and the entry of the Soviet Union into the war there was still some opposition to surrendering among the Japanese leaders. See Reischauer and Craig, *Japan: Tradition and Transformation*, p. 277.

30. Ezra F. Vogel, "Pax Nipponica?" *Foreign Affairs*, Vol. 64, No. 4 (Spring 1986), p. 755.

31. Walter S. Jones, *The Logic of International Relations*, 6th ed. (Glenview IL: Scott, Foresman, 1988), p. 95.

32. Reischauer and Craig, *Japan: Tradition and Transformation*, p. 285.

33. Webb, *An Introduction to Japan*, p. 84.

34. U.S. Arms Control and Disarmament Agency, *World Military Expenditures and Arms Transfer, 1985*, pp. 68, 81, and 85.

35. According to the Center for Defense Information's *The Defense Monitor*, Vol. 28, No. 8 (1999), p. 3, Japan's military budget of $41.1 billion is third behind the United States and Russia. According to IISS, *The Military Balance 1999–2000*, pp. 300–05, Japan's military budget of $36.99 billion is also surpassed by that of France.

36. Reischauer and Craig, *Japan: Tradition and Transformation*, p. 323.

37. See Masaru Tamamoto, "The Privilege of Choosing: The Fallout from Japan's Economic Crisis," *World Policy Journal*, Vol. 15, No. 3 (Fall 1998), pp. 25–31 and "Fallen Idol," *The Economist*, June 20, 1998, pp. 21–23, reprinted in Robert M. Jackson (ed.), *Global Issues 99/00* (Guildord CT: Dushkin/McGraw-Hill, 1999), pp. 108–10.

38. Immanuel C.Y. Hsü, *The Rise of Modern China*, 2nd ed. (New York: Oxford University, 1975), p. 3.

39. Hsü, *The Rise of Modern China*, pp. 13, 1–41.

40. Hsü, *The Rise of Modern China*, pp. 709–92.

41. R. J. Rummel, *Death by Government*, pp. 91–110, and R. J. Rummel, *China's Bloody Century: Genocide and Mass Murder Since 1900* (New Brunswick NJ: Transaction Publishers, 1991).

42. Alberto Ronchey, *The Two Red Giants*, trans. by Raymond Rosenthal (New York: W.W. Norton, 1965), pp. 13–14, and Hsü, *The Rise of Modern China*, p. 794.

43. Ronchey, *The Two Red Giants*, p. 14 and Hsü, *The Rise of Modern China*, p. 815.

44. Ronchey, *The Two Red Giants*, pp. 17, 46.

45. Ronchey, *The Two Red Giants*, pp. 18–19.

46. Hsü, *The Rise of Modern China*, p. 817.

47. Hsü, *The Rise of Modern China*, pp. 821, 823–34. For more details see Joseph Alsop, "Thoughts Out of China—I: Go Versus No-Go," *New York Times*, March 11, 1973, Sec. 6 *(Magazine)*, pp. 31 and 100. It is interesting to note that the idea of launching an attack on China's

nuclear facilities may have earlier originated with U.S. President Kennedy! See page 31 of the Alsop article.

48. Hsü, *The Rise of Modern China,* pp. 786–89, 796–97, and 829–55.

49. Gerald Segal, "The Coming Confrontation between China and Japan," *World Policy Journal,* Vol. 10, No. 2 (Summer 1993), pp. 27–39.

50. World Bank, *Entering the 21st Century: World Development Report 1999/2000,* pp. 250–51.

51. World Bank, *Entering the 21st Century: World Development Report 1999/2000,* pp. 230–31.

52. World Bank, *Entering the 21st Century: World Development Report 1999/2000,* p. 230.

53. *World Policy Journal,* Vol. 8, No. 4 (Fall 1991), p. 676.

54. The situation on Taiwan is discussed as part of a review of two recent books about current China-United States relations by Steven Mufson, "Zigzagging over China," *World Policy Journal,* Vol. 16, No. 4 (Winter 1999/2000), pp. 97–103. Taiwan is discussed on pp. 100–01.

55. Boulding, *The Meaning of the Twentieth Century,* pp. 1–2.

56. See *New York Times,* Jan. 29, 1985, p. 1 (photo) and James Reston, "The Road to Geneva," *New York Times,* Jan. 30, 1985.

57. According to the CIA's *The World Factbook, 1999,* the estimated per capita GDP (purchasing power parity) in 1998 was $22,700 for Kuwait (p. 269), $17,400 for the United Arab Emirates (p. 504), and $17,100 for Qatar (p. 398), while it was $20,800 for Italy (p. 242) and $17,000 for New Zealand (p. 354).

58. Sivard, *World Military and Social Expenditures, 1996,* pp. 44–53 designates as "developed countries" the following: United States, Canada, Belgium, Denmark, France, Germany, Greece, Iceland, Italy, Luxembourg, Netherlands, Norway, Spain, United Kingdom (Britain), Austria, Finland, Ireland, Sweden, Switzerland, Israel, Japan, Australia, and New Zealand.

59. Robert A. Mortimer, *The Third World Coalition in International Politics* (New York: Praeger, 1980), p. 15, and Mario Rossi, *The Third World: The Unaligned Countries and the World Revolution* (New York: Funk and Wagnalls, 1963), pp. 6–9, 161.

60. Mortimer, *The Third World Coalition,* pp. 2, 24–42.

61. See the article "Nonaligned Movement Pities Moscow" by Andrew Selsky on the website <http://southmovement.alphalink.com.au/south-news/NBAM-ap-1.htm>.

62. The members are listed in U.S. Central Intelligence Agency, *The World Factbook, 1999,* p. 582.

63. For detailed information about the Group of 77 see "What Is the Group of 77?" on the website <www.group of 77>.

64. For articles about that South Summit see the website for Pakistan's *Business Recorder* at <http://www.brecorder.com/story/S0056/S5612>.

65. Dieter Heinrich, "World Federalists Welcome Adoption of U.N. Decade of International Law," *World Federalist News,* Nos. 14 & 15 (Dec. 1989), five-page "Special Report" inserted between pp. 6 and 7. (Published by WFM, Leliegracht 21, 1016 GR Amsterdam, The Netherlands. The new address of WFM is 77 U.N. Plaza, New York NY 10017.)

66. Lynn H. Miller, *Global Order: Values and Power in International Politics,* 2nd ed. (Boulder CO: Westview, 1990), pp. 85–86.

67. For a full report on this conference, see *World Federalist News,* Issue 34 (Summer 1999).

68. See the story "G-77 Nations to Set Up Development Bank with $2 Billion Capital" on the website for Pakistan's *Business Recorder* at <http://www.brecorder.com/story/S0056/S5612102.htm>.

Chapter Ten. Military Aspects of the Contemporary Situation

1. Sheldon Novick, "The Secret of the Atom Bomb," *Environment,* Vol. 18, No. 6 (July/Aug. 1976), p. 10. The first bomb had been used in the test at Alamagordo, New Mexico. Novick notes that two other bombs were made and then immediately exploded in 1946 (pp. 11–12). The U.S. had only a very few atomic bombs on hand in 1947 and didn't have a model suitable for mass production until 1948 (p. 16). This same information is presented by Novick in his book *The Electric War: The Fight Over Nuclear Power* (San Francisco: Sierra Club, 1976), pp. 15–17 and 24–30. The information that the U.S. had no atomic bombs in reserve after dropping two on Japan is also given by Bernard Brodie in *War and Politics,* pp. 51–52.

2. For a discussion of this point see Stockholm International Peace Research Institute, *World Armaments and Disarmament: SIPRI Yearbook 1981,* pp. 38–45.

3. Gwynne Dyer, *War* (Homewood IL: Dorsey Press, 1985), p. 181, quotes Marshal Oleg A. Losik of the Malinovsky Armored Forces Academy in Moscow as saying in 1982, "We know that since 1945 nineteen nuclear strikes have been considered in Washington — four against the Soviet Union." Joseph Gerson, *The Deadly Connection: Nuclear War and U.S. Intervention* (Philadelphia: New Society, 1986), p. 11, says, "The public record now reveals more than twenty occasions when U.S. Presidents threatened to resort to nuclear war during crises." The specific occasions are discussed by Gerson on pp. 10–13 of that book as well as by Barry M. Blechman, Stephen S. Kaplan, and others in *Force Without War: U.S. Armed Forces as a Political Instrument* (Washington: Brookings Institution, 1978), pp. 47–49.

4. Avner Cohen, "Did Nukes Nudge the PLO?" *The Bulletin of the Atomic Scientists,* Vol. 49, No. 10 (Dec. 1993), pp. 11–13, especially p. 13.

5. Nuclear weapons are measured in terms of the equivalent explosive power of a given number of tons of TNT. The Hiroshima bomb was equivalent to 12,000–14,000 tons (12–14 kilotons) of TNT. Some hydrogen bombs have been produced which have an explosive force equivalent to 25,000,000 tons (25 megatons) of TNT.

6. Novick, "The Secret of the Atom Bomb" in *Environment,* p. 16.

7. *The Defense Monitor,* Vol. 4, No. 2 (Feb. 1975), p. 1.

8. The U.S. total of nuclear warheads peaked at 32,000 in 1967. See William M. Arkin, Thomas Cochran, and Milton Hoenig, "The U.S. Nuclear Stockpile" in *Arms Control Today,* Vol. 12, no. 4 (April 1982), p. 2.

9. See Robert S. Norris and William M. Arkin, "Global Nuclear Stockpiles, 1945–2000," *The Bulletin of the Atomic Scientists,* Vol. 56, No. 2 (March/April 2000), p. 79.

10. International Institute for Strategic Studies, *The Military Balance, 1999–2000*, p. 135.

11. David Albright, "South Africa Comes Clean," *The Bulletin of the Atomic Scientists*, Vol. 49, No. 4 (May 1993), pp. 3–5; and David Albright, "A Proliferation Primer," *The Bulletin of the Atomic Scientists*, Vol. 49, No. 5 (June 1993), pp. 14–23, especially p. 20.

12. Robert S. Norris and William M. Arkin, "Global Nuclear Stockpiles, 1945–2000," *The Bulletin of the Atomic Scientists*, (March/April 2000), p. 79.

13. International Institute for Strategic Studies, *The Military Balance, 1993–1994*, p. 232.

14. "Science and the Citizen," *Scientific American*, Vol. 229, No. 4 (Oct. 1973), p. 47.

15. Kosta Tsipis, "Cruise Missiles," *Scientific American*, Vol. 236, No. 2 (Feb. 1977), pp. 20–29.

16. For a detailed description of the technological aspects of the strategic defense system see James C. Fletcher, "Technologies for Strategic Defense," *Issues in Science and Technology*, Vol. 1, No. 1 (Fall 1984), pp. 15–29; or John A. Adam and Paul Wallich, "SDI: The Grand Experiment," *IEEE Spectrum*, Sept. 1985, pp. 36–64.

17. For an informed but critical examination of SDI see Robert Bowman's *Star Wars: Defense or Death Star* published in 1985 by the Institute of Space and Security Studies, 5115 Hwy. A1A South, Melbourne Beach FL 32951.

18. Adam and Wallich, "SDI," *IEEE Spectrum*, Sept. 1985, p. 45.

19. For a thorough discussion of this issue, see Michael R. Gordon with Steven Lee Myers, "Politics Mixes with Strategy in Plan for Antimissile System," *New York Times*, June 23, 2000, pp. A1 and A10.

20. Gordon and Myers, "Politics Mixes with Strategy in Plan for Antimissile System," *New York Times*, June 23, 2000, p. A1.

21. See James Glanz, "Other Systems Might Provide a U.S. Missile Shield," *New York Times*, September 4, 2000, pp. A1 and A6.

22. "Clinton Won't Order Missile Defense System Deployment," *St. Louis Post-Dispatch*, September 2, 2000, p. 19. For the text of Clinton's speech, see <http://www.state.gov/www/global/arms/factsheets/missdef/000901_fswh_nmd.html>. For a skeptical article about how the system is supposed to work, see Mark Thompson, "Missile Impossible?" *Time*, July 10, 2000, pp. 30–33.

23. See Seymour J. Deitchman, *New Technology and Military Power: General Purpose Military Forces for the 1980s and Beyond* (Boulder CO: Westview, 1979).

24. Bernard Brodie, *War and Politics* (New York: Macmillan, 1973), p. 51.

25. See John Cox, *Overkill: Weapons of the Nuclear Age* (New York: Thomas Y. Crowell, 1977), pp. 62–66.

26. Barry E. Fridling, "Lasers Highlight Policy Blindspots," *The Bulletin of the Atomic Scientists*, Vol. 44, No. 6 (July/August 1988), pp. 36–39; and Nick Cook, "Chinese Laser 'Blinder' Weapons for Export," *Jane's Defence Weekly*, May 27, 1995, p. 3; and Peter Gelstead, "China Markets Blinding Laser," *Pointer, Jane's Intelligence Review*, Vol. 2, No.6 (June 1995), p. 1.

27. Philip Morrison and Paul F. Walker, "A New Strategy for Military Spending," *Scientific American*, Vol. 230, No. 4 (Oct. 1978), pp. 56–57.

28. Cynthia Wilson, "Boeing Will Unveil Unmanned Combat Air Vehicle Today," *St. Louis Post-Dis-patch*, Sept. 27, 2000, pp. C1–C2; and Cynthia Wilson, "Boeing Shows Off New Concept in Warplanes," *St. Louis Post-Dispatch*, Sept. 28, pp. A1, A4.

29. Morrison and Walker, "A New Strategy for Military Spending," *Scientific American*, pp. 55–60. See also "Battlefield of the 1990s," *U.S. News and World Report*, Vol. 83, No. 1 (July 4, 1977), pp. 48–50; and "One Shot, One Kill: A New Era of 'Smart' Weapons," *U.S. News and World Report*, Vol. 102, No. 10 (March 16, 1987), pp. 28–35.

30. See John Bell's review of Manuel De Landa's *War in the Age of Intelligent Machines* (MIT Press, 1992) entitled "Smart Kills" in *The Bulletin of the Atomic Scientist*, Vol. 49, No. 5 (June 1993), p. 54.

31. See graphs in Deitchman, *New Technology and Military Power*, pp. 60, 81, 106, 131, 225, 244, and 252.

32. William Wilson, "Chemical and Biological Welfare," *In Depth: A Journal for Value and Public Policy*, Vol. 3, No. 2 (Spring 1993), pp. 112–13.

Chapter 11. Institutional Aspects of the Contemporary Situation

1. Poland was unable to send a representative to the San Francisco conference but was permitted to sign as the fifty-first charter member.

2. For detailed information about the United Nations, see *Everyone's United Nations: A Handbook on the Work of the United Nations*, 10th ed. (New York: U.N. Dept. of Public Information, 1986, distr. by Bernan-Unipub, 10033-F.M.L. King Hwy., Lanham MD 20706). The United Nations also has its own website at <http://www.un.org>.

3. For information about the difficult situation of indigenous peoples see Alan Thein Durning, "Supporting Indigenous Peoples" in Lester R. Brown and others, *State of the World, 1993* (New York: W.W. Norton, 1993), pp. 80–100.

4. Even then problems may arise. For example, the U.S. has agreed to commit itself in advance to the jurisdiction of the Court, but the Connally Amendment to the Senate's acceptance of the Statutes of the International Court of Justice indicates that the U.S. will not accept this jurisdiction in cases which the U.S. (rather than the Court) decides fall within its domestic jurisdiction.

5. See U.N. Association of U.S.A., *A Global Agenda: Issues Before the 55th General Assembly of the United Nations*, (Lanham MD: Rowman & Littlefield, 2000), p. 272.

6. See U.N. Association of U.S.A., *A Global Agenda: Issues Before the 54th General Assembly of the United Nations*, (Lanham MD: Rowman & Littlefield, 1999), p. 299; and International Institute for Strategic Studies, *The Military Balance, 1999–2000*, p. 300.

7. For the wording of Security Council Resolution 678 see *Keesing's Record of World Events 1990*, p. 37870.

8. For a review of U.N. peacekeeping operations up to 1985 see U.N. Department of Public Information, *The Blue Helmets: A Review of United Nations Peacekeeping* (New York: U.N., 1985).

9. The contents of this speech can be found on the United Nations website for that 50th anniversary at <www.un.org/Depts/dpko/dpko/50web/4.htm>.

10. See the U.N. peacekeeping website at

<http://www.un.org/Depts/dpko/dpko/intro/finance.htm>.

11. See the U.N. peacekeeping website at <http://www.un.org/Depts/dpko/dpko/intro/finance.htm>.

12. See U.N. Association of U.S.A., *A Global Agenda: Issues Before the 55th General Assembly of the United Nations*, p. 272.

13. See Michael Renner, "UN Peacekeeping: An Uncertain Future," *Foreign Policy IN FOCUS*, Vol. 5, No. 28 (Sept. 2000).

14. For information on the existing U.N. peacekeeping operations being financed in 2000–2001, see U.N. Association of U.S.A., *A Global Agenda: Issues Before the 55th General Assembly of the United Nations*, p. 292.

15. See IISS, *The Military Balance, 1999–2000*, p. 293.

16. U.S. Central Intelligence Agency, *The World Fact Book, 1999*, p. 128.

17. IISS, *The Military Balance, 1999–2000*, p. 294 and U.N. Association of U.S.A., *A Global Agenda: Issues Before the 55th General Assembly of the United Nations*, pp. 42–44.

18. U.N. Association of U.S.A., *A Global Agenda: Issues Before the 54th General Assembly of the United Nations*, pp. 21–23; and U.N. Association of U.S.A., *A Global Agenda: Issues Before the 55th General Assembly of the United Nations*, pp. 30–31.

19. For a report on this successful project see U.N. Department of Public Information, *Everyone's United Nations*, 10th ed. (New York: U.N., 1986), pp. 350–57.

20. See Robert Rotberg, "Namibia Eschews Intolerance," *The Christian Science Monitor*, Aug. 2, 1993, p. 18.

21. For a view of this project just after the elections, see Kathy Chenault, "Large Voter Turnout Bodes Well for Cambodians Tired of War," *The Christian Science Monitor*, June 1, 1993, p. 7.

22. See Kathy Chenault, "Cambodia Agreement Eases Pressure on UN," *The Christian Science Monitor*, June 17, 1993, p. 7.

23. For a list of peacekeeping efforts that were being carried on in the middle of 1993, not only by the U.N. but also by other international organizations, see IISS, *The Military Balance, 1993–1994*, pp. 253–60.

24. Inis L. Claude, Jr., *Swords Into Plowshares: The Problems and Progress of International Organization*, 3rd ed. rev. (New York: Random House, 1964), p. 343.

25. Sivard, *World Military and Social Expenditures, 1987–88*, p. 28.

26. Sivard, *World Military and Social Expenditures, 1991*, p. 20.

27. Russell M. Dallen, Jr., "Curtain Rises on 48th General Assembly," *The Interdependent*, Vol. 19, No. 3 (Fall 1993), p. 1.

28. Steven A. Dimoff, "Congress's Budget-cutting Fervor Threatens U.S. Standing at U.N.," *The Interdependent*, Vol. 19, No. 3 (Fall 1993), p. 6.

29. "Cutting Unnecessary Military Spending: Going Further and Faster," *The Defense Monitor*, Vol. 21, No. 3 (1993), p. 1.

30. For a first-hand account of this incident see Boutros Boutros-Ghali, *Unvanquished: A U.S.-U.N. Saga*, pp. 258–335, especially pp. 313–331.

31. For details, see U.N. Association, *A Global Agenda: Issues Before the 55th General Assembly of the United Nations*, pp. 150–55.

32. For up-to-date information on ratifications of the Rome Statute, see *The International Court Monitor* published by the NGO Coalition for an ICC, c/o WFM, 777 UN Plaza, New York NY 10017, website <http:/www.igc.apc.org/icc>.

33. See United Nations Department of Public Information, *Millennium Summit Multilateral Treaty Framework*, DPI/2130, pp. 37–38 and 26–27.

34. For a review of how the United States has been an obstacle to global change, see Geoff Simons, "UN Reform: Addressing the Reality of American Power," *Global Dialogue*, Vol. 2, No. 2 (Spring 2000), pp. 40–51.

35. The quote is from the executive summary of the Millennium Report provided at the U.N. website <http://www.un.org/millennium/sg/report/summ.htm>.

36. For a recent valuable discussion on the achievements of the United Nations, including keeping peace, see Joseph Schwartzberg, "Needed: A Revitalised United Nations," *Global Dialogue*, Vol. 2, No. 2 (Spring 2000), pp. 19–31, especially pp. 21–24.

37. The texts of these documents can be found in Burns Weston, Richard Falk, and Anthony D'Amato (eds.), *Basic Documents in International Law and World Order* (St. Paul MN: West, 1980).

38. For an account of this conference and the text of Annan's speech, see *World Federalist News*, Issue 34 (Summer 1999), published by the World Federalist Movement (WFM), 777 UN Plaza, New York NY 10017. The text of the speech is on pp. 4 and 12. The website for WFM is <www.worldfederalist.org>.

39. This list is taken from the chart of the United Nations System provided by the U.N. Department of Public Information titled "DP/2079-March 2000."

40. This list is also taken from the chart of the United Nations System provided by the U.N. Department of Public Information titled "DP/2079-March 2000."

41. Donald A. Henderson, "Smallpox — Epitaph for a Killer?" *National Geographic*, Vol. 154, No. 6 (Dec. 1978), pp. 796–805.

42. See Joseph Schwartzberg, "Needed: A Revitalised United Nations," *Global Dialogue*, Vol. 2, No. 2 (Spring 2000), pp. 21–22.

43. For a list of some of the many international governmental organizations, many of which are regional, see Central Intelligence Agency, *World Fact Book, 1999*, pp. 550–601

44. Central Intelligence Agency, *The World Fact Book, 1999*, pp. 551–98.

45. Hilary French, "Coping with Ecological Globalization" (chapter 10) in Lester Brown, Christopher Flavin, and Hilary French (eds.), *State of the World, 2000* (New York: W. W. Norton, 2000), p. 202.

46. Article 71 of the U.N. Charter reads as follows: "The Economic and Social Council may make suitable arrangements for consultation with non-governmental organizations which are concerned with matters within its competence. Such arrangements may be made with international organizations and, where appropriate, with national organizations after consultation with the Member of the United Nations concerned." (*Everyone's United Nations*, 10th ed., p. 443.)

47. St. Louis *Post-Dispatch*, July 14, 1986, pp. 1, 12.

48. *United Nations Monthly Chronicle*, Vol. 15, No. 6 (June 1978), p. 27, and Vol. 15, No. 7 (July 1978), p. 4.

49. Friends Committee on National Legislation (245 Second St. NE, Washington DC 20002), *Washington Newsletter*, No. 397 (Nov. 1977), p. 6.

50. See the website of the *Landmine Monitor* for the report from Oct. 3, 1996, at <http://199.212.22.103/pages/lm/ldotta03.htm>.

51. Carey Goldberg, "Peace Prize Goes to Land-Mine Opponents," *New York Times*, October 11, 1997, pp. A1 and A6.

52. Information about the ICC is available on the website of the NGO Coalition for an International Criminal Court (CICC), <http:www.igc.apc.org/icc>.

53. "Kofi Annan's Address in the Hague," *World Federalist News*, Issue 34 (Summer 1999), pp. 4 and 12.

54. Jane Lampman, "World Religious Leaders Hold 'First' Summit," *The Christian Science Monitor*, August 28, 2000, pp. 1 and 8.

55. *Esperanto*, No. 960 (Dec. 1985), pp. 201–04; and *Esperanto*, No. 1054 (Dec. 1993), pp. 201–03. *Esperanto* is published monthly by the Universala Esperanto-Asocio, Nieuwe Binnenweg 176, 3015 BJ Rotterdam, Netherlands. For information about Esperanto see the website of the Esperanto League for North America at <http://www.esperanto-usa.org>.

Chapter Twelve. Legal Aspects of the Contemporary Situation

1. The discussion of international law in this chapter is confined to that part which deals with the relations between nations and which is called *public international law*. Not discussed here is that other part of international law, *private international law*, which deals with private persons and property in international situations where there are problems about which national government has jurisdiction and which national laws are applicable.

2. For a short discussion of the early development of international law, see Frederick L. Schuman, *International Politics*, 7th ed. (New York: McGraw-Hill, 1969), pp. 67–71. For a discussion of the principles of international law, see pp. 115–48 of the same work.

3. Article 10 of the League Covenant says: "The Members of the League undertake to respect and preserve as against external aggression the territorial integrity and existing political independence of all Members of the League. In case of any such aggression or in case of any threat or danger of such aggression, the Council shall advise upon the means by which this obligation shall be fulfilled." (From Schuman, *International Politics*, p. 711.)

4. The U.N. Charter reads as follows: *Article 41*. The Security Council may decide what measures not involving the use of armed force are to be employed to give effect to its decisions, and it may call upon the Members of the United Nations to apply such measures. These may include complete or partial interruption of economic relations and of rail, sea, air, postal, telegraphic, radio, and other means of communication, and the severance of diplomatic relations. *Article 42*. Should the Security Council consider that measures provided for in Article 41 would be inadequate or have proved to be inadequate, it may take such action by air, sea, or land forces as may be necessary to maintain or restore international peace and security. Such action

may include demonstrations, blockade, and other operations by air, sea, or land forces of Members of the United Nations. *Article 43*. 1. All Members of the United Nations, in order to contribute to the maintenance of international peace and security, undertake to make available to the Security Council, on its call and in accordance with a special agreement or agreements, armed forces, assistance and facilities, including rights of passage, necessary for the purpose of maintaining international peace and security. 2. Such agreement or agreements shall govern the numbers and types of forces, their degree of readiness and general location, and the nature of the facilities and assistance to be provided. 3. The agreement or agreements shall be negotiated as soon as possible on the initiative of the Security Council. They shall be concluded between the Security Council and Members or between the Security Council and groups of Members and shall be subject to ratification by the signatory states in accordance with their respective constitutional processes. See *Everyone's United Nations*, 10th ed.(New York: UN Department of Public Information, 1986) pp. 437–38.

5. Burns Weston, Richard Falk, and Anthony D'Amato (eds.), *Basic Documents in International Law and World Order* (St. Paul MN: West, 1980), pp. 210–11.

6. The seven Nuremberg principles can be found in 1950 UN Document UN GAOR, 5th session, Supp. No. 12 (A/1316), in *Yearbook of the International Law Commission*, 1950, Vol. II. They are also reprinted in many different books about international law including W. Michael Reisman and Chris T. Antoniou (eds.), *The Laws of War: A Comprehensive Collection of Primary Documents on International Laws Governing Armed Conflict* (New York: Random House [Vintage], 1994), pp. 335–36.

7. See Reisman and Antoniou, *The Laws of War*, pp. 332–333.

8. For details about this conference see *The International Criminal Court Monitor*, Issue 9, August 1998, published by the NGO Coalition for an ICC, c/o WFM, 777 UN Plaza, New York NY 10017, website <http://www.igc.apc.org/icc>. The text of the Rome Statute is U.N. Document A/CONF.183/9, 17 July 1998, and is available at website <http://www.untreaty.un.org/English/notpubl/rome-en.htm>. For information about the Rome conference as well as U.S. opposition to the treaty see Aryeh Neier, "Waiting for Justice: The United States and the International Criminal Court," *World Policy Journal*, Vol. 15, No. 3 (Fall 1998), pp. 33–37. For an extended discussion of how radical is the transformation marked by the International Criminal Court see David Fromkin, "International Law at the Frontiers," *World Policy Journal*, Vol. 15, No. 4 (Winter 1998–99), pp. 59–72.

9. For up-to-date information on signings and ratifications of the Rome Statute see the website <http://www.igc.apc.org/icc>.

10. For a comprehensive overview of the evolution of international law toward world law see Benjamin B. Ferencz, *A Common Sense Guide to World Peace* (New York: Oceana, 1985), pp. 1–42. For a book length discussion of how international law could become a basis for a global legal system using the U.N. Security Council, see Benjamin B. Ferencz, *New Legal Foundations for Global Survival: Security Through the Security Council* (New York: Oceana, 1994). For the argument that

there is a fundamental contradiction between national sovereignty and some kind of international law which military people should follow, see Donald A. Wells, *War Crimes and Laws of War* (Lanham MD: University Press of America, 1984).

11. For a book length argument for this thesis see Francis Anthony Boyle, *World Politics and International Law* (Durham NC: Duke University Press, 1985).

12. See Roy Gutman and David Rieff (eds.), *Crimes of War: What the Public Should Know* (New York: W. W. Norton, 1999).

13. Rules for warfare were first advanced by Hugo Grotius in his *On the Law of War and Peace* (1625). They have been developed by various conventions, the most important of which are the Geneva Conventions (developed at meetings in 1864, 1929, and 1949) and the two Hague Conventions (1899 and 1907). Other conventions such as the Convention on Genocide (1948) and the one protecting cultural property (1954) also apply to wartime situations. The laws of war also include rules about the treatment and obligations of neutrals. For a more detailed account, see "War, Laws of" in *Encylopaedia Britannica,* 15th ed. (1974), Vol. 19, pp. 538–42; and Schuman, *International Politics,* pp. 134–39.

14. For a very thorough treatment of this advisory opinion by the International Court of Justice about the legality of nuclear weapons see Ann Fagan Ginger (ed.), *Nuclear Weapons Are Illegal: The Historic Opinion of the World Court and How It Will Be Enforced*" (New York: The Apex Press, 1998). The quotations are from pp. 75–76.

15. See the Preamble and Article 2 of the U.N. Charter. *Everyone's United Nations,* pp. 429–31.

16. See *Everyone's United Nations,* p. 457.

17. Schuman, *International Politics,* pp. 220–21.

Chapter Thirteen. Reforming the Attitudes of Individuals

1. A moving plea for greater effort on the part of the U.S. in educating its people about other cultures and about world affairs can be found in Edwin O. Reischauer, *Toward the 21st Century: Education for a Changing World* (New York: Alfred A. Knopf, 1973).

2. For an eloquent and moving statement of this viewpoint, see Robert Muller, *The Birth of a Global Civilization* (published by World Happiness and Co-operation, P.O. Box 1153, Anacortes WA 98221, 1991).

3. A good example of the kind of material that can be helpful with children is the *Teaching Tolerance Magazine* published by Southern Poverty Law Center, 400 Washington Ave., Montgomery AL 36104, <www.teachingtolerance.org>.

4. John Stoessinger, *Why Nations Go To War,* 7th ed. (New York: St. Martin's Press, 1998), pp. 220–26.

5. Stoessinger, *Why Nations Go To War,* p. 226.

6. Martha C. Nussbaum and others, Joshua Cohen (ed.), *For Love of Country: Debating the Limits of Patriotism* (Boston: Beacon Press, 1996), p. 131.

7. David Grossman, "Trained to Kill," *Christianity Today,* August 19, 1998, pp. 1–8. See also his book *On Killing: The Psychological Cost of Learning to Kill in War and Society* (Boston: Little, Brown & Co., 1996).

8. A good brief introduction to the life and teachings of Gandhi is Louis Fischer's *Gandhi: His Life and Message for the World* (New York: New American Library, 1954). For an overview of Gandhi's thought see Joan V. Bondurant, *Conquest of Violence: The Gandhian Philosophy of Conflict* (Princeton NJ: Princeton University, 1958) and the selections from Gandhi's writings in *All Men Are Brothers,* ed. by K. Kripalani (Weare NH: Greenleaf Books, 1982). For an introduction to the life and teachings of Martin Luther King, Jr., one might well begin with his own *Stride Toward Freedom: The Montgomery Story* (New York: Harper and Row, 1958). On pp. 102–07, King gives his own presentation of the basic principles of the philosophy of nonviolent resistance. For current information about teaching nonviolence contact the Martin Luther King, Jr., Center for Nonviolence, 1707 Rodney Drive, Los Angeles CA 90027.

9. One academic source for such information is the last two chapters of Robert Holmes (ed.), *Nonviolence in Theory and Practice* (Belmont CA: Wadsworth, 1990), pp. 141–206. Another source is Peter Ackerman and Jack DuVall, *A Force More Powerful: A Century of Nonviolent Conflict* (New York: St. Martin's Press, 2000).

10. For a philosophical discussion of this idea see Herbert Spiegelberg, "Ethics for Fellows in the Fate of Existence" in Peter Bertocci (ed.), *Mid-Twentieth Century Philosophy* (Atlantic City Highlands NJ: Humanities Press, 1974), pp. 193–210.

11. One such pledge, composed by Lillian Genser of Wayne State University in Detroit, goes as follows: I pledge allegiance to the world, To cherish every living thing, To care for earth and seas and air, With peace and justice everywhere.

12. For more information, contact Dorothy Schneider, P.O. Box 78189, St. Louis MO 63178–8189.

13. The term "humatriotism" was formulated by Theodore Lentz of St. Louis and used as the title of the book he edited. *Humatriotism* was published in 1976 by The Future Press, 6251 San Bonita Avenue, St. Louis MO 63105.

14. Robert Ardrey, *African Genesis* (New York: Dell, 1967), p. 256.

15. Sigmund Freud, *Civilization and Its Discontents* (New York: Norton, 1930), p. 61.

16. Harold Guetzkow, *Multiple Loyalties: Theoretical Approach to a Problem in International Organization* (Princeton NJ: Princeton University's Center for Research on World Political Institutions, 1955), pp. 49–50.

17. An approach along these lines is suggested by William James in his essay "The Moral Equivalent of War" which is reprinted in David P. Barash, *Approaches to Peace,* pp. 65–69.

18. For more information about Esperanto, contact the Esperanto League for North America, Box 1129, El Cerrito CA 94530, phone 1-800-ESPERANTO, <http:www.esperanto-usa.org> or Universala Esperanto-Asocio, Nieuwe Binnenweg 176, 3015 BJ Rotterdam, Nederlando, <http://www.uea.org>. For a book length treatment of the history of Esperanto, see Peter G. Forster, *The Esperanto Movement* (The Hague: Mouton Publishers, 1982). For an argumentative article in support of Esperanto see Ronald J. Glossop, "Language Policy and a Just World Order," *Alternatives,* Vol. 13 (1988), pp. 395–409.

19. See Mario Pei, *One Language for the World* (New

York: Devin-Adair, 1958) for a book length treatment of this issue. For background information see also Humberto Eco, *The Search for the Perfect Language (The Making of Europe)* (Oxford: Blackwell, 1995).

20. For information on the costs of not having a common language just in Europe for the European Union, see Reinhard Selten (ed.), *The Costs of European Linguistic (Non)Communication* (Rome: Esperanto Radikala Asocio, 1996).

21. For example, consider the contents of the book *Many Voices, One World* (London: Kogan Page, New York: Unipub, and Paris: UNESCO, 1980), which is a report of the International Commission for the Study of Communication Problems appointed in 1977 by Amadou-Mahtar M'Bow, Director-General of UNESCO, and headed by Sean McBride. This Commission analyzed language and communication problems only from the point of view of national governments and did not mention Esperanto or even the idea of a single international language for everyone. It is unbelievable that an international commission set up by a U.N. agency to study communication problems could manage not even to address itself to this crucial issue.

22. The website for more information about this event is <http:www.herald.co.uk/local_info/live_aid.html>.

23. It is noteworthy that both the Boy Scouts and the Girl Scouts offer a merit badge for citizenship in the world to those scouts who fulfill the appropriate requirements as well as badges for citizenship in the community and citizenship in the nation.

Chapter Fourteen. Reforming the Internal Operation of National Governments

1. Those familiar with Kenneth N. Waltz's *Man, the State, and War: A Theoretical Analysis* (New York: Columbia University Press, 1959) may think that I have borrowed my classification of strategies for reducing war from that book. In fact, I had developed this classification before becoming familiar with Waltz's ideas. I regard the similarity of our views as an indication that the classification has some validity. Also, my view is not exactly the same as Waltz's because his analysis is focused on what *causes* wars while mine is focused on what *should be done* to make them less likely. That may be a minor difference, but it accounts for my dividing his second image (the nature of national governments is the key to war and peace) into two parts: (1) (discussed in this chapter) that what is required for peace is a change in *the basic structure* of national governments, and (2) (discussed in the next chapter) that what is required for peace is a change in *the policies* being pursued by national governments. I realize that my next chapter on national policies is not completely divorced from Waltz's third image (the nature of the international system is the key to war and peace), but obviously it is my 16th chapter that is more closely related to that third image. In general I find myself in agreement with Waltz's views and arguments.

2. Such views about the desirability of democracy as a way of reducing the likelihood of war go back at least to the 18th-century philosophers Rousseau, Montesquieu, and Kant. See Michael E. Howard, *War and the Liberal Conscience* (New Brunswick NJ: Rutgers University, 1978), pp. 23–28. This thesis was embraced whole-heartedly by Woodrow Wilson during World War I, and is sometimes even referred to as "Wilsonianism" or more recently "neo-Wilsonianism." For a more recent comprehensive but succinct statement of this view, see R. J. Rummel, "Political Systems, Violence, and War" in W. Scott Thompson and Kenneth M. Jensen (eds.), *Approaches to Peace: An Intellectual Map* (Washington: U.S. Institute of Peace, 1991), pp. 350–70. For a recent book-length examination and defense of this view, see Spencer R. Weart, *Never At War: Why Democracies Will Not Fight One Another* (New Haven CT: Yale University Press, 1998).

3. Quincy Wright makes this point in *A Study of War*, Vol. 2, pp. 843–48.

4. Weart's *Never at War* goes into this issue in depth while examining many difficult historical cases. He makes some valuable points while at the same time showing how difficult the issue is. He cites two reliable signs of an authoritarian (nondemocratic, nonrepublican) regime: (1) a flock of political refugees and/or (2) the threat of a violent take-over of the regime (p. 162). A difficulty is that there may be a very authoritarian regime which prevents disgruntled people from leaving and/or from even trying to organize a *coup d'état*. Consider Saddam Hussein's Iraq.

5. On the side that democracies are in fact more peaceful, see Bruce Russett, *Grasping the Democratic Peace* (Princeton NJ: Princeton University Press, 1993), and Max Singer & Aaron Wildavsky, *The Real World Order: Zones of Peace/Zones of Turmoil* (Chatham NJ: Chatham House, 1993). On the negative side, see Samuel P. Huntington, *The Clash of Civilizations* (New York: Simon & Schuster, 1996) and Miriam Fendius Elman (ed.), *Paths to Peace: Is Democracy the Answer?* (Cambridge MA: The MIT Press, 1997).

6. For support of this statement on the basis of public reactions in the United States during the Vietnamese War, see Robert W. Tucker, *A New Isolationism: Threat or Promise* (New York: Universe Books, 1972), pp. 99–101.

7. A paper by Timothy J. Lomperis of St. Louis University presented at the meeting of the American Political Science Association in Washington DC on September 2, 2000, titled "IR Theory and the Wreckage of Kosovo: Intervention, Precision-Guided Munitions, and the 'Democratic Peace'" discusses this point at length in relation to current U.S. policy in Kosovo. The address for contacting Professor Lomperis is: Department of Political Science, St. Louis University, 221 No. Grand, St. Louis MO 63103.

8. Schuman, *International Politics*, pp. 220–21.

9. R.J. Rummel, "As Though a Nuclear War: The Death Toll of Absolutism," *International Journal on World Peace*, Vol. 5, No. 3 (July–Sept. 1988), pp. 27–43. The quotation is from p. 40.

10. Rummel, "As Though a Nuclear War," *International Journal on World Peace*, p. 28.

11. Rummel, "As Though a Nuclear War," *International Journal on World Peace*, p. 39.

12. Rummel, "As Though a Nuclear War," *International Journal on World Peace*, p. 39. See also Rummel's later books on the topic: *Death by Government: Genocide and Mass Murder Since 1900* (New Brunswick NJ: Transaction Publishers, 1994) and *Power Kills: Democracy as a Method of Nonviolence* (New Brunswick NJ, Transaction Publishers, 1997).

13. One good orientation to this alternative approach is Robert L. Holmes (ed.), *Nonviolence in Theory and Practice* (Belmont CA: Wadsworth Publishing Co., 1990). For contemporary discussion of nonviolence, one can turn to *The Acorn*, journal of the Gandhi-King Society, Box 13, St. Bonaventure University, St. Bonaventure NY 14778. The web address for *The Acorn* is <http://web.sbu.edu/nonviolence/acorn.htm>.

14. Gene Sharp in *Exploring Nonviolent Alternatives* (Boston: Porter Sargent, 1970) lists 85 cases of nonviolent action (pp. 115–23) and indicates that slightly more than 60 percent occurred under dictatorships. With regard to success, Sharp says only that "in some of these cases the nonviolent actionists partly or fully succeeded in achieving the desired objectives" (p. 122).

15. For a collection of articles on nonviolent resistance, see Severyn T. Bruyn and Paula M. Rayman (eds.), *Nonviolent Action and Social Change* (New York: Irvington, 1979). A classic on all phases of nonviolent resistance is Gene Sharp, *The Politics of Nonviolent Action* (3 vols.) (Boston: Porter Sargent, 1973).

16. See Thomas Weber, "The Marchers Simply Walked Forward Until Struck Down," *Peace and Change*, Vol. 18, No. 3 (July 1988), pp. 267–89, especially pp. 276–79.

17. See Fred Halliday, "The Iranian Revolution: Uneven Development and Religious Populism," *Journal of International Affairs*, Vol. 36, No. 2 (Fall/Winter 1982/83), pp. 187–207, especially p. 190, and Ralph Summy, "The Efficacy of Nonviolence: Examining 'The Worst Case Scenario,'" *Peace Research*, Vol. 25, No. 2 (May 1993), pp. 1–19, especially pp. 8–9.

18. Richard Deats, "The Philippines: The Nonviolent Revolution That Surprised the World" in Robert L. Holmes (ed.), *Nonviolence in Theory and Practice* (Belmont CA: Wadsworth, 1990), pp. 203–06. For a detailed popular account of the events leading to the ouster of Marcos, see Harry Anderson and others, "The Showdown," *Newsweek*, March 3, 1986, pp. 30–41.

19. See Adam Roberts, *Civil Resistance in the East European and Soviet Revolutions* (Monograph #4 published by the Albert Einstein Institution, 1430 Massachusetts Ave., Cambridge MA 02138, 1992).

20. See Peter Frier, "Soft Revolutions of Homegrown Rage," *The Christian Science Monitor*, October 11, 2000, pp. 1 and 7.

Chapter Fifteen. Reforming the Policies of National Governments

1. For a carefully worked out and well-documented defense of this proposition see Bueno de Mesquita, *The War Trap* (New Haven CT: Yale Univ. Press, 1981).

2. World Bank, *Entering the 21st Century, World Development Report 1999/2000*, pp. 230–31.

3. World Bank, *Entering the 21st Century, World Development Report 1999/2000*, p. 231. These figures for 1998 show that the U.S. Gross National Product is $7,921.3 billion while the world total is $28,862.2 billion. Thus the United States accounts for over 27 percent of the total.

4. Since the term "transarmament" has been used to refer to both of these approaches, it will be less confusing if we do not use it for either. "Transarmament" is used to describe the shift from offensive to defensive weaponry by Dietrich Fischer, *Preventing War in the Nuclear Age* (Totawa NJ: Rowman and Allanheld, 1984), pp. 7–8, 26, 106, 108–11, 199, 221–22, while that term is also used for the shift from military to nonmilitary efforts by Gene Sharp, whose views are advanced by the Association for Transarmament Studies.

5. Johann Galtung, *There Are Alternatives: Four Roads to Peace and Security* (Nottingham, England: Russell, 1984, distributed in the U.S. by Dufour Editions, Chester PA 19425), p. 173.

6. Gene Sharp's view is available in *National Security Through Civilian-Based Defense* published by the Association for Transarmament Studies, 3636 Lafayette Avenue, Omaha NE 68131 in 1985.

7. For a restrained but cogent response to Sharp's proposal, see Michael Walzer, *Just and Unjust Wars: A Moral Argument with Historical Illustrations*, pp. 329–35.

8. Schuman, *International Politics*, p. 248.

9. Schuman, *International Politics*, p. 248.

10. U.N. Department of Public Information, *Everyone's United Nations*, p. 430.

11. U. S. Arms Control and Disarmament Agency, *Arms Control and Disarmament Agreements, 1996 Edition*, p. 129.

12. U. S. Arms Control and Disarmament Agency, *Arms Control and Disarmament Agreements, 1996 Edition*, p. 129.

13. *New York Times*, Sept. 21, 1961, p. 10.

14. Charles Osgood, *An Alternative to War or Surrender* (Urbana IL: University of Illinois, 1962).

15. The latter formulation is used by Osgood in his preface to the 1970 edition of *An Alternative to War or Surrender*.

16. Amatai Etzioni, "The Kennedy Experiment," *The Western Political Quarterly*, Vol. 20 (1967), pp. 361–80.

17. Etzioni, "The Kennedy Experiment," *Western Political Quarterly*, pp. 368–69.

18. Etzioni, "The Kennedy Experiment," *Western Political Quarterly*, pp. 367–68.

19. For a succinct statement of the issues and various views related to this question, see Stanley Hoffmann, *Duties Beyond Borders: On the Limits and Possibilities of Ethical International Politics* (Syracuse NY: Syracuse University, 1981), pp. 10–27.

20. Muzafer Sherif's *In Common Predicament* (Boston: Houghton Mifflin, 1966) describes the classical experiments with boys on the value of cooperative projects in overcoming group antagonism.

21. See Joseph V. Montville, "Transnationalism and the Role of Track-Two Diplomacy" in Thompson and Jensen, *Approaches to Peace*, pp. 255–69, especially p. 262.

22. Robert L. Butterworth, *Managing Interstate Conflict, 1945–74: Data with Synopses* (Pittsburgh: University Center for International Studies, 1976), pp. 131–32.

23. Butterworth, *Managing Interstate Conflict*, pp. 94–96.

24. Butterworth, *Managing Interstate Conflict*, pp. 392–93.

25. Butterworth, *Managing Interstate Conflict*, pp. 235–37.

26. *New York Times*, Dec. 6, 1977, p. 8, and Jan. 26, 1978, p. 6.

27. *The Interdependent*, Vol. 10, No. 5 (Sept./Oct. 1984), p. 5.

28. Butterworth, *Managing Interstate Conflict*, pp. 341–44.

29. See *Time*, Vol. 114, No. 22 (Nov. 26, 1979), pp. 62–64.

30. Butterworth, *Moderation from Management*, p. 66.

31. This 53-page booklet is available from the Department of Public Information, United Nations, New York NY 10017.

32. See Michael Renner, "Preparing for Peace" in Brown and others, *State of the World, 1993*, p. 154. For information on efforts to implement this proposal for a U.N. Surveillance System, contact War Control Planners, Inc., Box 19127, Washington DC 20036.

33. See Michael Ignatieff, "The High Price of Gunboat Diplomacy," originally in the weekly *Observer* of London and reprinted in *World Press Review*, Vol. 40, No. 3 (March 1993), p. 13.

34. According to IISS, *The Military Balance, 1999–2000*, page 305, the total world military spending for 1998 was $785.269 billion. If that number is divided by 365, the figure is $2.1514219 billion per day.

35. According to IISS, *The Military Balance, 1999–2000*, pages 300 and 305, U.S. military spending for 1998 was $265.89 billion while the world total was $785.269 billion. The division indicates that the U.S. portion of the total is 33.84 percent.

36. The address is U.S. Institute of Peace, 1550 M Street, N.W., Washington DC 20005.

37. Kenneth Boulding, *The Meaning of the Twentieth Century* (New York: Harper and Row, 1964), p. 103. Information about current efforts is available from the International Peace Research Association, Bjoern Moeller, COPRI, University of Copenhagen, Fredericiagade 18, DK-1310 Copenhagen K, Denmark <bmoeller@copri.dk>.

38. Two good sources of information about peace education are Betty A. Reardon, *Comprehensive Peace Education: Educating for Global Responsibility* (Wolfeboro NH 03894-0939: Teachers College Press, 1988), and Ian M. Harris, *Peace Education* (Jefferson NC: McFarland, 1988).

39. Dyer, *War*, p. 159.

Chapter Sixteen. Reforming the International System

1. Francis Anthony Boyle, *World Politics and International Law* (Durham NC: Duke University Press, 1985), p. 70.

2. Boyle, *World Politics and International Law*, p. 72.

3. U.N. Association of U.S.A., *A Global Agenda: Issues Before the 53rd General Assembly of the United Nations*, p. 151.

4. Information acquired on 14 July 2000 from the website for oceans law at <http://www.un.org/Depts/los/ITLOS/Hdqrts>.

5. In Dec. 1979 the U.N. General Assembly accepted the draft of an agreement covering the Activities of States on the Moon and Other Celestial Bodies and asked the Secretary-General to open the Agreement for signature and ratification. Article 11 of the Agreement declares that "the moon and its natural resources are the common heritage of mankind" and calls for the establishment of "an international regime … to govern the exploitation of the natural resources of the moon as such exploitation is about to become feasible." For more details see *Keesing's Contemporary Archives*, May 2, 1980, pp. 30226–28 and *The United Nations Treaties on Outer Space* (New York: United Nations Publications, 1984), pp. 27–37.

6. Joseph E. Schwartzberg, "Needed: A Revitalized United Nations," *Global Dialogue*, Vol. 2, No. 2 (Spring 2000), p. 24.

7. Greenville Clark and Louis Sohn, *World Peace Through World Law*, 3rd ed. enlarged (Cambridge MA: Harvard University, 1966), pp. 513–15.

8. Hudson, "Time for Mutations in the United Nations," *Bulletin of the Atomic Scientists*, Vol. 32, No. 9 (Nov. 1976), pp. 39–43. The latest version of this proposal is given in *Global Report*, No. 53 (Summer 1998), published by the Center for War-Peace Studies, 180 W. 80th St., New York NY 10024.

9. Joseph E. Schwartzberg, "Needed: A Revitalized United Nations," *Global Dialogue*, Vol. 2, No. 2 (Spring 2000), pp. 19–31, especially pp. 25–26. For a longer presentation (including maps) about how the EQ system can be developed in the Security Council, see Joseph E. Schwartzberg, "Towards a More Representative and Effective Security Council," *Political Geography*, Vol. 13, No. 6 (Nov. 1994), pp. 483–91.

10. See Joseph E. Schwartzberg, "A New Perspective on Peacekeeping: Lessons from Bosnia and Elsewhere," *Global Governance*, Vol. 3, No. 1 (1997), pp. 1–15, and Joseph E. Schwartzberg, "Needed: A Revitalized United Nations," *Global Dialogue*, Vol. 2, No. 2 (Spring 2000), pp. 27–28, and Georgios Kostakos, "A Rapid Reaction Capability for the United Nations?," *Global Dialogue*, Vol. 2, No. 2 (Spring 2000), pp. 32–39.

11. For a detailed discussion of this idea, see Dieter Heinrich, *The Case for a United Nations Parliamentary Assembly*, published in 1992 by the World Federalist Movement (777 U.N. Plaza, New York NY 10017). For updated information contact Dieter Heinrich, 199 Pearson Avenue, Toronto, Ontario M6R 1G6 Canada or Jeffrey Segall, 308 Cricklewood Lane, London NW2 2PX, United Kingdom.

12. Norman Alcock and others, *1982* (Oakville, Ontario: Canadian Peace Research Institute Press, 1978), pp. 141, 146–60.

13. Alan Newcombe, "A World Peace-Makers Association of Nations," and Norman Alcock and Arnold Simoni, "Peacemakers Association of Nations." Copies of both these articles are available from Peace Research Institute–Dundas, 25 Dundana Ave., Dundas, Ontario L9H 4E5.

14. See Beverly Woodward, "Nonviolent Struggle, Nonviolent Defense, and Nonviolent Peacemaking," *Peace and Change*, Vol. 7, No. 4 (Fall 1981), pp. 62–63, and Carolyn Stephenson, "Alternative Methods for International Security: A Review of the Literature" in the same volume. Johansen's proposal is described in Robert C. Johansen and Saul H. Mendlovitz, "The Role of Enforcement of Law in the Establishment of a New International Order: A Proposal for a Transnational Police Force," *Alternatives*, VI (1980), pp. 307–37, especially pp. 335–37. Those interested in learning more about present efforts involving nonviolent peacemaking can contact Peace Brigades International/USA, 1904 Franklin St. #505, Oakland CA 94612, phone (510) 663–2362. The website is <http://www.igc.apc.org/pbi/usa.html>.

15. For a book length narrative account of PBI activities see Liam Mahony and Luis Enrique Eguren, *Unarmed Bodyguards: International Accompaniment for the Protection of Human Rights* (West Hartford CT: Kumarian Press, 1997).

16. For a view of American history in the 1780s as a model for the formation of a federal world government, see Carl Van Doren, *The Great Rehearsal* (New York: Viking, 1949; republished by Viking-Penguin, 1986).

17. Clarence Streit, *Union Now* (printed privately in 1938; then published by Harper Brothers in New York in 1939 with an enlarged postwar edition by the same publisher in 1949). A study which is somewhat related to Streit's proposal is *Political Community and the North Atlantic Area* by Karl W. Deutsch and others (Princeton NJ: Princeton University, 1957; and New York: Greenwood, 1969). Other relevant books are James R. Huntley, *Uniting the Democracies*, and James R. Huntley, *Pax Democratica*.

18. Tyler Marshall and Norman Kempster, "Albright Announces Final Goals of Tenure — 4 More Democracies," *San Francisco Chronicle*, Jan. 18, 1999.

19. On the long-term increasing size of political communities see Hornell Hart and Donald Taylor, "Was There a Prehistoric Trend from Smaller to Larger Political Units?" *The American Journal of Sociology*, Vol. 49, No. 4 (Jan. 1944), 289–301; Hornell Hart, *Can World Government Be Predicted by Mathematics? A Preliminary Report* (Ann Arbor MI: Edwards Brothers, Inc. lithoprinted in 1944, 16 pp.); and Hornell Hart, "The Logistic Growth of Political Areas," *Social Forces*, Vol. 26, No. 4 (May 1948), 396–408.

20. The idea of a world government brought about through the agreement of the leaders of all nations rather than by conquest seems to have been first advanced in 1623 by Parisian monk Eméric Crucé in a book entitled *The New Cineas* (trans. by C. Frederick Farrell, Jr., and Edith R. Farrell, New York and London: Garland, 1972). The idea of a world government was also espoused in China by K'ang Yu-wei (1858–1927) in *Ta T'ung Shu [The One-World Philosophy]*, tr. by Laurence G. Thompson (London: George Allen & Unwin, 1958). The idea of a world government brought about by consent has also been espoused by Western philosophers such as Rousseau, Kant, Bentham, and Russell and noted scientists such as Einstein. For a recent history of the world federalist movement since the end of World War II, see Joseph P. Baratta, "The International Federalist Movement: Toward Global Governance," *Peace and Change*, Vol. 24, No. 3 (July 1999), pp. 340–77. Two of the more influential works about world federalism published during World War II were Mortimer J. Adler, *How to Think About War and Peace* (New York: Simon and Schuster, 1944; republished by Fordham University Press, New York, 1995), and Emery Reves, *The Anatomy of Peace* (New York and London: Harper and Brothers, 1945; republished by Peter Smith, Publisher, Gloucester MA, 1969, and Robert Betchov, Geneva, Switzerland, 1995). The world federalist view is promoted in the United States by the World Federalist Association, 420 7th St. SE, Washington DC 20003. At the global level it is promoted by the World Federalist Movement, 777 U.N. Plaza, New York NY 10017.

21. Lewis Richardson, in his groundbreaking statistical and historical study of wars from 1820 to 1945, concluded that once a single government is established over previously sovereign groups, the longer these groups are under a common government the less likely they are to go to war with each other. See *Statistics of Deadly Quarrels*, pp. xi, 189–90, 295–96, 311–13.

22. A recent statement of this argument can be found in Hidemi Suganami, *The Domestic Analogy and World Order Proposals* (Cambridge: Cambridge University Press, 1989), p. 190. This argument along with the world federalist response to it is discussed in Ronald J. Glossop, *World Federation? A Critical Analysis of Federal World Government* (Jefferson NC: McFarland, 1993), pp. 18–19, 108–11, and 156–61.

23. James A. Yunker, "Rethinking World Government: A New Approach," *International Journal of World Peace*, Vol. 17, No. 1 (March 2000), pp. 3–33, and James A. Yunker, *Common Progress: The Case for a World Economic Equalization Program* (Westport CT: Praeger, 2000).

24. See Robert Wright, *Nonzero: The Logic of Human Destiny* (New York: Pantheon, 2000.) For Wright's own application of his general observation to the specific issue of world governance, see Robert Wright, "World Government Is Coming. Deal With It. Continental Drift," *The New Republic*, Jan. 17, 2000, pp. 18–23.

25. The Report of the Commission on Global Governance, *Our Global Neighborhood* (Oxford: Oxford University Press, 1995).

26. Ingvar Carlsson and Shridath Ramphal, "Co-Chairmen's Foreword," The Report of the Commission on Global Governance, *Our Global Neighborhood*, p. xvi. For a collection of essays arguing that global governance does in fact require global government, see Harris and Yunker, *Toward Genuine Global Governance: Critical Reactions to "Our Global Neighborhood."*

27. The Report of the Commission on Global Governance, *Our Global Neighborhood*, p. 337.

28. The Report of the Commission on Global Governance, *Our Global Neighborhood*, p. 347.

29. Robert C. Johansen, "A Turning Point in International Relations? Establishing a Permanent International Criminal Court," *Report* of the Joan B. Kroc Institute for International Peace Studies, University of Notre Dame, Notre Dame IN, for Fall 1997 (No. 13), and David Fromkin, "International Law at the Frontiers," *World Policy Journal*, Vol. 15, No. 4 (Winter 1998–99), pp. 59–72.

30. U.N. Association of the U.S.A., *A Global Agenda: Issues Before the 53rd General Assembly of the United Nations*, pp. 147–53, and U.N. Association of the U.S.A., *A Global Agenda: Issues Before the 54th General Assembly of the United Nations*, pp. 144–49.

31. U.N. Secretary-General Kofi Annan said in his Millenium Report that "national sovereignty must not be used as a shield for those who wantonly violate the rights and lives of their fellow human beings." The text of the report is available at <http://www.un.org/millenium/sg/report/summ.htm>.

32. See U.N. Association of U.S.A., *A Global Agenda: Issues Before the 55th General Assembly of the United Nations*, pp. 4–5.

33. See Ethan B. Kapstein, "A Global Third Way: Social Justice and the World Economy," *World Policy Journal*, Vol. 15, No. 4 (Winter 1998–99), pp. 23–35.

34. David Mitrany, *A Working Peace System* (London: Royal Institute of International Affairs, 1943).

35. Ernst B. Haas, *Beyond the Nation-State: Functionalism and International Organization* (Stanford CA: Stanford University, 1964).

36. See James P. Speer, *World Polity: Conflict and War: History, Causes, Consequences, Cures* (Q.E.D. Press, 155 Cypress St., Ft. Bragg CA 95437, 1985), pp. 170–76, for a detailed statement of the federalist view concerning the futility of the functionalist approach.

37. The creation of such an agency was proposed by Sri Lanka at the 1978 U.N. Special Session on Disarmament, and France proposed an international satellite agency to help monitor arms control agreements. See *Keesing's Contemporary Archives*, Oct. 20, 1978, p. 29263.

38. John C. de V. Roberts, *World Citizenship and Mundialism: A Guide to the Building of a World Community* (Westport CT: Praeger, 1999).

39. The address of the World Citizen Foundation is P.O. Box 2304, South Burlington VT 05403. A website is maintained at <http://worldservice.org>. His e-mail address is <worldlaw@globalnetisp.net>. A recent book about his life and ideas is Garry Davis, *Dear World: A Global Odyssey* (South Burlington VT: World Government House, 2000).

40. The address of the World Service Authority is 1012 14th Street NW, Suite 1106, Washington DC 20005.

41. The address of the International Registry of World Citizens in Paris is 66 Bd. Vincent Auriol, 75013 Paris, France. There is also an office at Les Nids, 49190 St. Aubin de Luigne, France. The website is <http://perso.wanadoo.fr/dan.cdm/irmc/citizen.html#organization>.

42. The address of the Association of World Citizens is 55 New Montgomery Street, Suite 224, San Francisco CA 94105 and its website is <www.worldcitizens.org>.

43. See Alan Newcombe and Hanna Newcombe, "Mundialization: World Community at the Doorstep" in Israel W. Charny (ed.), *Strategies Against Violence: Design for Nonviolent Change* (Boulder CO: Westview, 1978), pp. 314–30.

44. For the whole list of mundialized cities, see the website for "Tutmondintaj Urboj kaj Komunumoj" (Esperanto for "Mundialized Cities and Communities") at <http://perso.wanadoo.fr/dan.cmd/dem/monduboj.htm>.

45. The address of World Citizen, Inc., is 2145 Ford Parkway, Suite 300, St. Paul MN 55116 and the website is <http://www.peacesites.org>.

46. Jacques Maritain, *Man and the State* (Chicago: University of Chicago, 1951), pp. 212–16.

47 The Bertrand Russell Peace Foundation is located in Bertrand Russell House, Gamble St., Nottingham NG7 4ET, England. A website with information about its past activities is <http://www.homeusers.prestel.co.uk/littleton/br_brpf.htm>.

48. This endeavor has been coordinated by the World Constitution and Parliament Association, 8800 West 14th Avenue, Lakewood CO 80215. The website is <http://www.scruz.net/~tgilman>. A book promoting this effort and containing a copy of the proposed world constitution is Errol E. Harris, *One World or None: Prescription for Survival* (Atlantic Highlands NJ: Humanities Press, 1993).

49. The address of *World Peace News* is U.N. Secretariat, 4th Floor Press Slots, United Nations, New York NY 10017 and the phone number is 212/686–1069.

50. The address of *United World* is 401 So. Dixon, Carbondale IL 62901.

51. The mailing address for EarthAction Network in the United States is 30 Cottage Street, Amherst MA 01002-9971. The website is <http://www.oneworld.org/earthaction>.

52. The website for Global Action to Prevent War is <http:www.globalactionpw.org>.

53. See Hanna Newcombe, "Alternative Approaches to World Government — II" in *Peace Research Reviews*, Vol. 5, No. 2 (Feb. 1974). For a compilation of abstracts which deal with many books and articles addressed to the development of a just and peaceful world society, see Hanna Newcombe (comp.), *World Unification Plans and Analyses* (Peace Research Institute — Dundas, 25 Dundana Ave., Dundas, Ontario L9H 4E5, Canada, 1980).

54. Two well-known spokespersons for the "world order" approach are Saul H. Mendlovitz of Rutgers University and Richard A. Falk of Princeton University. This approach is also promoted by the World Policy Institute (formerly the Institute for World Order), 777 U.N. Plaza, New York NY 10017, which publishes the quarterly *World Policy Journal.*

Selected Bibliography

Ackerman, Peter, and Jack DuVall. *A Force More Powerful: A Century of Nonviolent Conflict.* New York: St. Martin's Press, 2000.

Adler, Mortimer J. *Haves Without Have-Nots: Essays for the 21st Century on Democracy and Socialism.* New York: Macmillan, 1991.

_____. *How to Think About War and Peace.* New York: Simon & Schuster, 1944. Republished (with Introduction by John Logue) by Fordham University Press, New York, 1995.

Alexander, Yonah (ed.). *International Terrorism: National, Regional, and Global Perspectives.* New York: Praeger, 1976.

Andregg, Michael. *On the Causes of War.* Minneapolis MN: Ground Zero Minnesota, 2nd printing, 1999.

Barash, David P. *Introduction to Peace Studies.* Belmont CA: Wadsworth, 1991.

_____ (ed.). *Approaches to Peace: A Reader in Peace Studies.* New York and Oxford: Oxford University Press, 2000.

Baratta, Joseph P. *Strengthening the United Nations: A Bibliography on U.N. Reform and World Federalism.* New York: Greenwood, 1987.

Beitz, Charles R., and Theodore Herman (eds.). *Peace and War.* San Francisco: W.H. Freeman, 1973.

Berkowitz, Leonard. *Aggression: Its Causes, Consequences, and Control.* Philadelphia: Temple University Press, 1993.

Boulding, Kenneth E. *The Meaning of the Twentieth Century: The Great Transition.* New York: Harper & Row, 1964.

_____. *Stable Peace.* Austin: University of Texas Press, 1978.

Boutros-Ghali, Boutros. *Unvanquished: A U.S.-U.N. Saga.* New York: Random House, 1999.

Boyle, Francis A. *World Politics and International Law.* Durham: Duke University Press, 1985.

Bramson, Leon, and George W. Goethals (eds.). *War: Studies from Psychology, Sociology, Anthropology,* rev. ed. New York: Basic Books, 1968.

Brodie, Bernard. *The Absolute Weapon.* New York: Harcourt, Brace, 1946.

_____. *War and Politics.* New York: Macmillan, 1973.

Brown, Lester R., Christopher Flavin, and Hilary French (eds.). *State of the World, 1999.* New York: W. W. Norton, 1999.

Bueno de Mesquita, Bruce. *The War Trap.* New Haven: Yale University Press, 1981.

Butterworth, Robert L. *Managing Interstate Conflict, 1945–74: Data with Synopses.* Pittsburgh: University Center for International Studies, 1976.

_____. *Moderation from Management: International Organization and Peace.* Pittsburgh: University Center for International Studies, 1978.

Charny, Israel W. (ed.). *Strategies Against Violence: Design for Nonviolent Change.* Boulder CO: Westview, 1978.

Clark, Grenville, and Louis Sohn. *World Peace Through World Law,* 3rd ed. enlarged. Cambridge MA: Harvard University Press, 1966.

Claude, Inis L., Jr. *Swords into Plowshares: The Problems and Progress of International Organization,* 4th ed. New York: Random House, 1971.

Clausewitz, Carl von. *On War* (edited with an introduction by Anatol Rapoport, tr. by J.J. Graham). New York: Penguin Books, 1968.

Cleveland, Harlan. *Birth of a New World: An Open Moment for International Leadership.* San Francisco: Jossey-Bass, 1993.

_____. *The Third Try at World Order.* New York: Aspen Institute for Humanistic Studies, 1977.

Commission on Global Governance. *Our Global Neighborhood: The Report of the Commission on Global Governance.* Oxford and New York: Oxford University Press, 1995.

Cooling, Benjamin F. (ed.). *War, Business, and American Society: Historical Perspectives on the Military-Industrial Complex.* Port Washington NY: Kennikat, 1977.

Deitchman, Seymour J. *New Technology and Military Power: General Purpose Military Forces for the 1980s and Beyond.* Boulder CO: Westview, 1979.

Dyer, Gwynne. *War.* Homewood IL: Dorsey, 1985.

Eckhardt, William. *Civilizations, Empires, and Wars: A Quantitative History of War.* Jefferson NC: McFarland, 1992.

Eibl-Eibesfeldt, Irenaus. *The Biology of Peace and War: Man, Animals, and Aggression.* Tr. by Eric Mosbacher. New York: Viking Press, 1979.

Elman, Miriam Fendius (ed.). *Paths to Peace: Is Democracy the Answer?* Cambridge MA: The MIT Press, 1997.

Falk, Richard A., and Samuel S. Kim (eds.). *The War System: An Interdisciplinary Approach.* Boulder CO: Westview, 1980.

_____, _____, and Saul H. Mendlovitz (eds.). *Toward a Just World Order.* Boulder CO: Westview, 1982.

Ferencz, Benjamin. *A Common Sense Guide to World Peace.* New York: Oceana, 1985.

_____. *New Legal Foundations for Global Survival: Security Through the Security Council.* New York: Oceana, 1994.

Fischer, Dietrich. *Preventing War in the Nuclear Age.* Totawa NJ: Rowman & Allanheld, 1984.

Freedman, Lawrence (ed.). *War.* Oxford and New York: Oxford University Press, 1994.

Fried, Morton, Marvin Harris, and Robert Murphy (eds.). *War: The Anthropology of Armed Conflict and Aggression.* Garden City NY: Natural History Press, 1967.

Galtung, Johann. *There Are Alternatives: Four Roads to Peace and Security.* Nottingham, England: Russell, 1984. (Distributed in the U.S. by Dufour Editions, Chester PA 19425.)

Geller, Daniel S., and J. David Singer. *Nations at War: A Scientific Study of International Conflict.* Cambridge: Cambridge University Press, 1998.

Ginsberg, Robert (ed.). *The Critique of War: Contemporary Philosophical Explorations.* Chicago: Henry Regnery, 1969.

Glossop, Ronald J. *World Federation? A Critical Analysis*

of Federal World Government. Jefferson NC: McFarland, 1993.

Groebel, Jo, and Robert A. Hinde (eds.). *Aggression and War: Their Biological and Social Bases.* Cambridge: Cambridge University Press, 1989.

Grossman, David. *On Killing: The Psychological Cost of Learning to Kill in War and Society.* Boston: Little, Brown & Co., 1996.

Guibernau, Montserrat. *Nations Without States: Political Communities in a Global Age.* Cambridge: Polity Press, 1999.

Gutman, Roy, and David Rieff. *Crimes of War: What the Public Should Know.* New York: W. W. Norton, 1999.

Haas, Ernst B. *Beyond the Nation-State: Functionalism and International Organization.* Stanford CA: Stanford University Press, 1964.

Harris, Errol E. *One World or None: Prescription for Survival.* Atlantic Highlands NJ: Humanities Press, 1993.

_____, and James A. Yunker (eds.). *Toward Genuine Global Governance: Critical Reactions to "Our Global Neighborhood."* Westport CT: Praeger, 1999.

Harris, Ian. *Peace Education.* Jefferson NC: McFarland, 1988.

Heater, Derek. *World Citizenship and Government: Cosmopolitan Ideas in the History of Western Political Thought.* New York: St. Martin's Press, 1996.

Heilbroner, Robert L. *Visions of the Future: The Distant Past, Yesterday, Tomorrow.* New York: Oxford University Press, 1995.

Held, David. *Democracy and the Global Order: From the Modern State to Cosmopolitan Governance.* Stanford CA: Stanford University Press, 1995.

Hoffmann, Stanley. *Studies Beyond Borders: On the Limits and Possibilities of Ethical International Politics.* Syracuse NY: Syracuse University Press, 1981.

Holmes, Robert L. (ed.). *Nonviolence in Theory and Practice.* Belmont CA: Wadsworth, 1990.

Holsti, Kalevi J. *Peace and War: Armed Conflicts and International Order 1648-1989.* Cambridge: Cambridge University Press, 1991.

_____. *The State, War, and the State of War.* Cambridge: Cambridge University Press, 1996.

Huntington, Samuel P. *The Clash of Civilizations and the Remaking of World Order.* New York: Simon & Schuster, 1996.

Huntley, James R. *Pax Democratica: A Strategy for the 21st Century.* New York: St. Martin's Press, 1998.

International Institute of Security Studies, *The Military Balance, 1999-2000.* London: Oxford University Press, 1999. (This annual report is an excellent source of information about global military developments.)

Johnson, James Turner. *Can Modern War Be Just?* New Haven: Yale University Press, 1984.

_____. *Just War Tradition and the Restraint of War.* Princeton: Princeton University Press, 1991.

Jones, Walter S. *The Logic of International Relations,* 6th ed. Boston: Scott, Foresman, 1988.

Kaku, Michio, and Daniel Axelrod. *To Win a Nuclear War: The Pentagon's Secret War Plans.* Boston: South End Press, 1986.

K'ang Yu-wei. *Ta T'ung Shu [The One-World Philosophy].* Tr. by Laurence G. Thompson. London: George Allen & Unwin, 1958.

Keegan, John. *A History of Warfare.* New York: Alfred A. Knopf, 1993.

Kiang, John. *One World: The Approach to Permanent Peace on Earth and the General Happiness of Mankind.* Notre Dame IN: One World Movement, 1984.

Lorenz, Konrad. *On Aggression.* New York: Harcourt Brace Jovanovich, 1966.

Mahony, Liam, and Luis Enrique Eguren. *Unarmed Bodyguards: International Accompaniment for the Protection of Human Rights.* West Hartford CT: Kumarian Press, 1997.

Mayer, Peter (ed.). *The Pacifist Conscience.* Chicago: Henry Regnery Company's Gateway Edition, 1966.

Mitrany, David. *A Working Peace System.* London: Royal Institute of International Affairs, 1943.

Newcombe, Hanna. *Design for a Better World.* Lanham MD: University Press of America, 1983.

Nussbaum, Martha C., and others, Joshua Cohen (ed.). *For Love of Country: Debating the Limits of Patriotism.* Boston: Beacon Press, 1996.

Osgood, Charles E. *An Alternative to War or Surrender.* Urbana: University of Illinois Press, 1962.

Otterbein, Keith. *The Evolution of War: A Cross-Cultural Study.* New Haven CT: Yale University-HRAF, 1970.

Rapoport, Anatol. *Fights, Games, and Debates.* Ann Arbor: University of Michigan Press, 1960.

_____. *The Origins of Violence: Approaches to the Study of Conflict.* New York: Paragon House, 1989.

Reardon, Betty A. *Comprehensive Peace Education: Educating for Global Responsibility.* Wolfeboro NH: Teachers College Press, 1988.

Reisman, W. Michael and Chris T. Antoniou (eds.). *The Laws of War: A Comprehensive Collection of Primary Documents on International Laws Governing Armed Conflict.* New York: Vintage Books, Random House, 1994.

Renner, Michael. *Ending Violent Conflict.* Washington: Report #146 of Worldwatch Institute, 1999.

Reves, Emery. *The Anatomy of Peace.* New York: Harper & Brothers, 1945. Republished in 1969 by Peter Smith, Publisher, Gloucester MA, and in 1995 by Robert Betchov, 53 Avenue du Lignon, 1219, Geneva, Switzerland.

Richardson, Lewis F. *Arms and Insecurity.* Pittsburgh: Boxwood, 1960.

_____. *Statistics of Deadly Quarrels.* Pittsburgh: Boxwood, 1960.

Ringler, Dick (ed.). *Dilemmas of War and Peace: A Sourcebook.* Madison WI: Board of Regents of University of Wisconsin System and the Corporation for Public Broadcasting, 1993.

Roberts, Adam (ed.). *Civilian Resistance as a National Defense.* Harrisburg PA: Stackpole, 1968.

Roberts, John C. de V. *World Citizenship and Mundialism: A Guide to the Building of a World Community.* Westport CT: Praeger, 1999.

Rousseau, Jean-Jacques. *On the Social Contract with Geneva Manuscript and Political Economy.* Roger D. Masters (ed.), Judith R. Masters (tr.). New York: St. Martin's Press, 1978.

Rummel, R. J. *Death by Government: Genocide and Mass Murder Since 1900.* New Brunswick NJ and London: Transaction Publishers, 1994.

_____. *Power Kills: Democracy as a Method of Nonviolence.* New Brunswick NJ and London: Transaction Publishers, 1997.

_____. *Understanding Conflict and War,* 5 vols. Beverly Hills: Sage, 1975-1981.

Russett, Bruce. *Grasping the Democratic Peace.* Princeton NJ: Princeton University Press, 1993.

Schuman, Frederick L. *International Politics,* 7th ed. New York: McGraw-Hill, 1969.

Sharp, Gene. *Civilian-Based Defense: A Post-Military Weapons System.* Princeton: Princeton University Press, 1990.

_____. *Exploring Nonviolent Alternatives.* Boston: Porter Sargent, 1970.

_____. *The Politics of Nonviolent Action,* 3 vols. Boston: Porter Sargent, 1973.

Singer, J. David, and associates, *Explaining War: Selected Papers from the Correlates of War Project.* Beverly Hills: Sage Publications, 1979.

Singer, Max, and Aaron Wildavsky. *The Real World Order: Zones of Peace/Zones of Turmoil.* Chatham NJ: Chatham House, 1993.

Sivard, Ruth Leger. *World Military and Social Expenditures.* Washington: World Priorities, 1987–88, 1991, 1993, and 1996 editions.

Small, Melvin, and J. David Singer (eds.). *International War: An Anthology and Study Guide,* 2nd ed. Chicago: Dorsey Press, 1989,

_____. *Resort to Arms: International and Civil Wars, 1816–1980.* Beverly Hills: Sage, 1982.

Smith, Anthony D. *Theories of Nationalism,* 2nd ed. New York: Holmes & Meier, 1983.

Stephenson, Carolyn M. (ed.). *Alternative Methods for International Security.* Lanham MD: University Press of America, 1982.

Stoessinger, John G. *Why Nations Go to War,* 7th ed. New York: St. Martin's, 1998.

Streit, Clarence. *Union Now,* enlarged ed. New York: Harper, 1949.

Suganami, Hidemi. *The Domestic Analogy and World Order Proposals.* Cambridge: Cambridge University Press, 1989.

_____. *On the Causes of War.* Oxford: Clarendon Press, 1996.

Thompson, W. Scott, and Kenneth M. Jensen (eds.). *Approaches to Peace: An Intellectual Map.* Washington DC: U.S. Institute of Peace, 1991.

United Nations Association of the U.S.A. *A Global Agenda: Issues Before the 55th General Assembly of the United Nations.* Lanham MD; Rowman & Littlefield, 2000. (This annual publication is a very valuable source of contemporary information about various global problems.)

Vasquez, John A. *The War Puzzle.* Cambridge: Cambridge University Press, 1993.

Waltz, Kenneth. *Man, the State, and War.* New York: Columbia University Press, 1959.

Walzer, Michael. *Just and Unjust Wars: A Moral Argument with Historical Illustrations.* New York: Basic Books, 1977.

Weart, Spencer R. *Never at War: Why Democracies Will Not Fight One Another.* New Haven CT: Yale University Press, 1998.

Wells, Donald A. *The War Myth.* New York: Pegasus, 1967.

World Bank. *Entering the 21st Century: World Development Report 1999/2000.* New York: Oxford University Press, 1999.

Wright, Quincy. *A Study of War.* Chicago: University of Chicago Press, 1942; abridged ed. by Louise Wright, 1964.

Wright, Robert. *Nonzero: The Logic of Human Destiny.* New York: Pantheon, 2000.

Yunker, James A. *Common Progress: The Case for a World Economic Equalization Program.* Westport CT: Praeger, 2000.

_____. *World Union on the Horizon: The Case for Supernational Federation.* Lanham MD: University Press of America, 1993.

Ziegler, David W. *War, Peace, and International Politics,* 7th ed. New York: Addison Wesley Longman, 1997.

Index